MOON



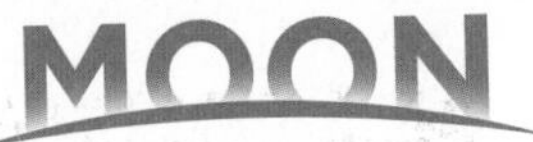

# CHARLESTON & SAVANNAH

JIM MOREKIS

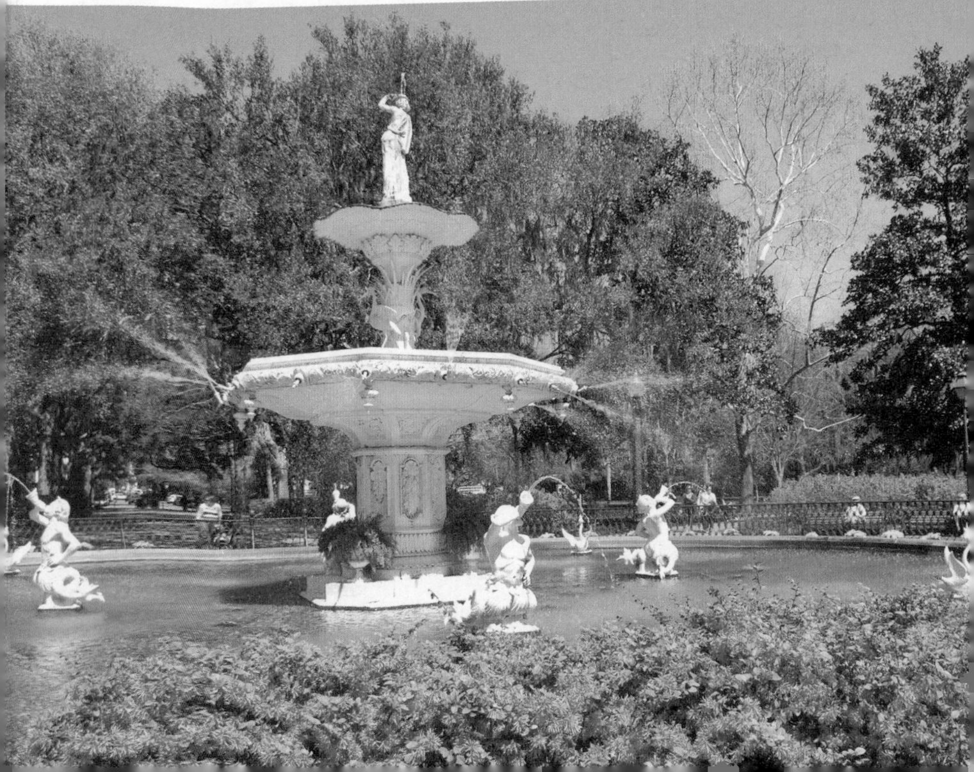

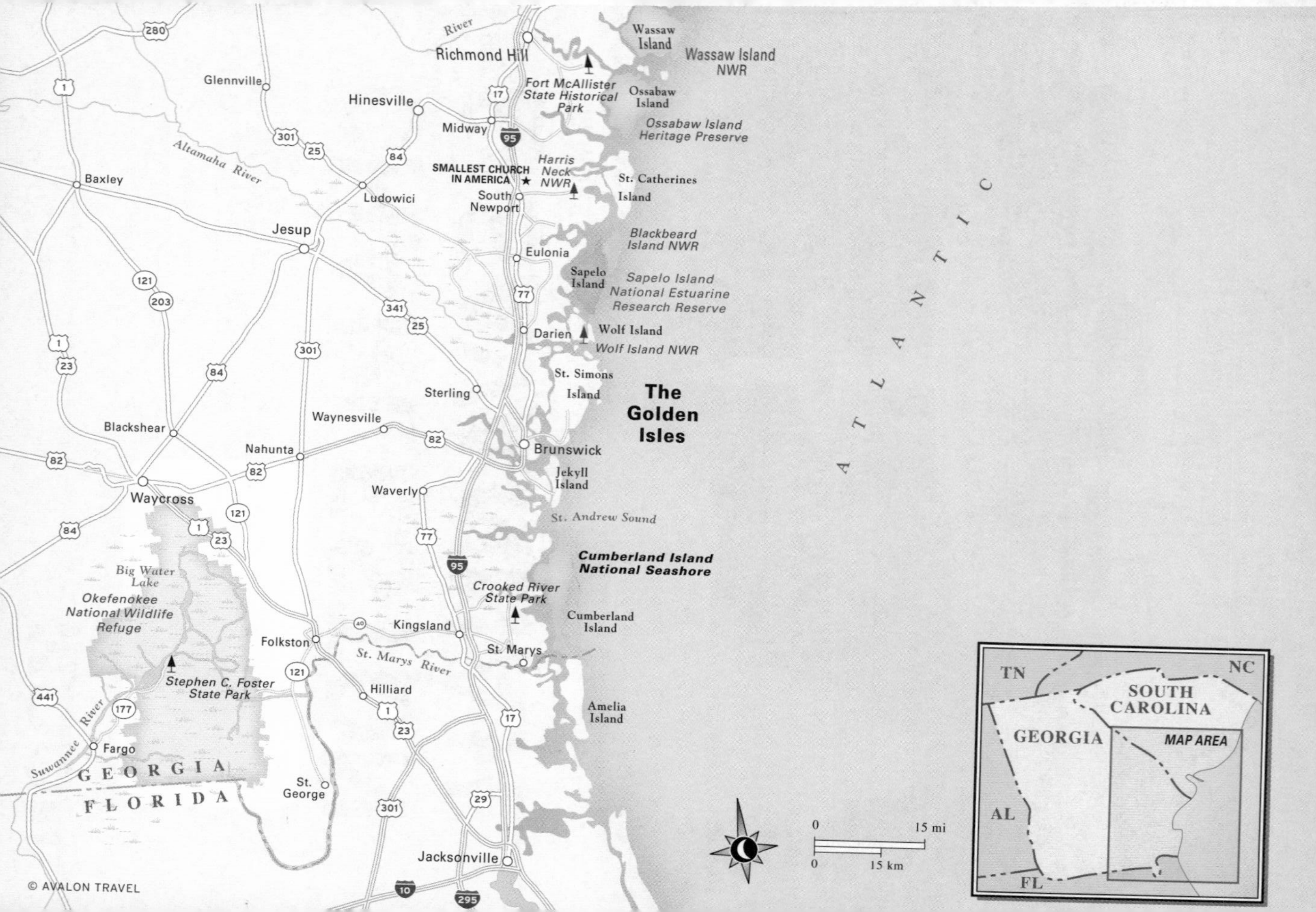

Richmond Hill
Wassaw Island
Wassaw Island NWR
Glennville
Hinesville
Fort McAllister State Historical Park
Ossabaw Island
Midway
Ossabaw Island Heritage Preserve
Altamaha River
Baxley
SMALLEST CHURCH IN AMERICA
Harris Neck NWR
St. Catherines Island
Ludowici
South Newport
Jesup
Blackbeard Island NWR
Eulonia
Sapelo Island
Sapelo Island National Estuarine Research Reserve
Darien
Wolf Island
Wolf Island NWR
St. Simons Island
Sterling
The Golden Isles
Blackshear
Waynesville
Nahunta
Brunswick
Jekyll Island
Waycross
Waverly
St. Andrew Sound
Cumberland Island National Seashore
Big Water Lake
Okefenokee National Wildlife Refuge
Crooked River State Park
Kingsland
Cumberland Island
Folkston
St. Marys
St. Marys River
Stephen C. Foster State Park
Hilliard
Amelia Island
Suwannee River
Fargo
GEORGIA
FLORIDA
St. George
Jacksonville
ATLANTIC
0 15 mi
0 15 km
TN
NC
SOUTH CAROLINA
GEORGIA
MAP AREA
AL
FL
River

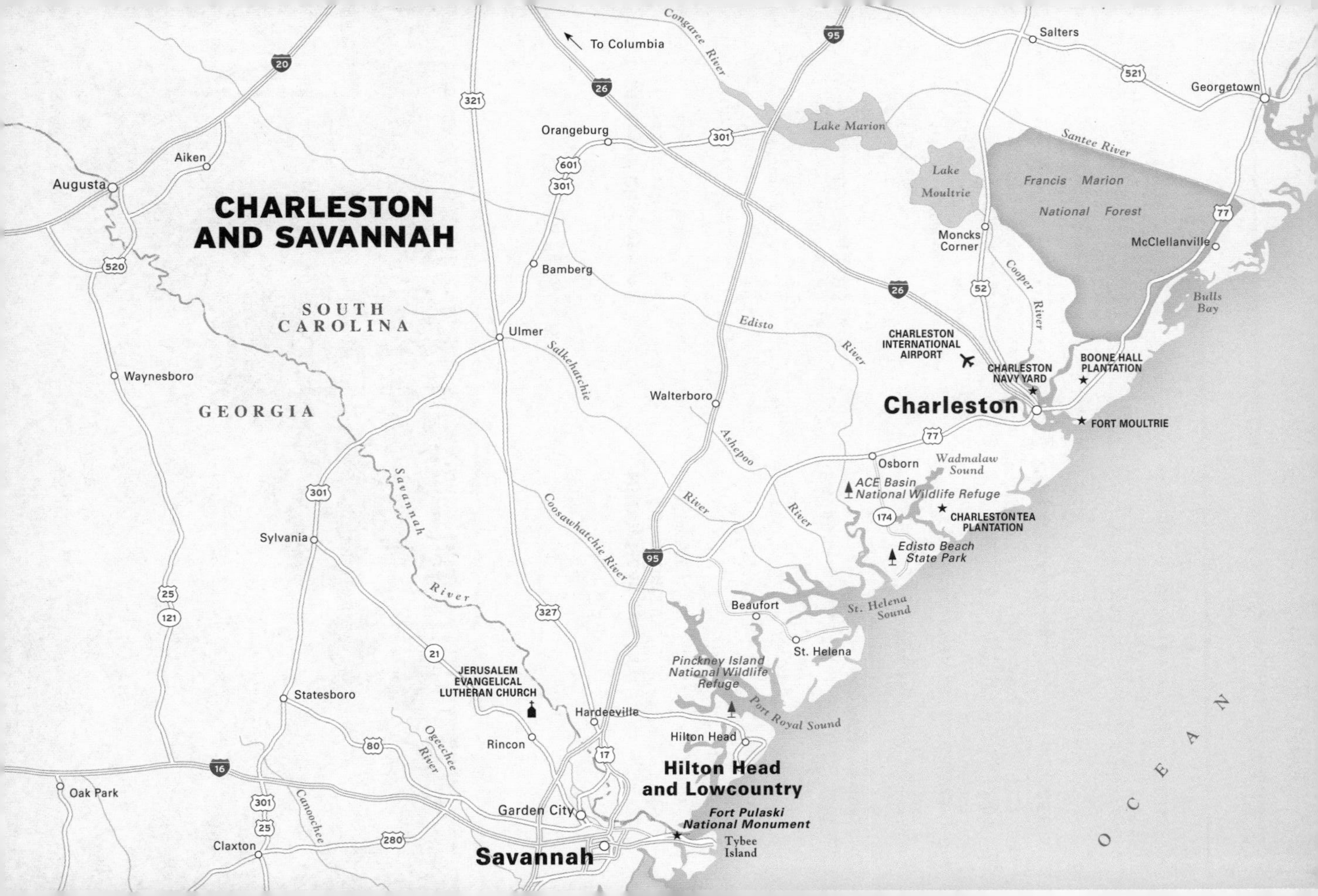

CHARLESTON AND SAVANNAH
To Columbia
Congaree River
Salters
Georgetown
Lake Marion
Santee River
Orangeburg
Aiken
Augusta
Lake Moultrie
Francis Marion National Forest
Moncks Corner
McClellanville
Bamberg
Cooper River
Bulls Bay
SOUTH CAROLINA
Ulmer
Edisto River
CHARLESTON INTERNATIONAL AIRPORT
CHARLESTON NAVY YARD
BOONE HALL PLANTATION
Waynesboro
Salkehatchie
Walterboro
GEORGIA
Charleston
FORT MOULTRIE
Ashepoo River
Osborn
Wadmalaw Sound
Savannah River
ACE Basin National Wildlife Refuge
CHARLESTON TEA PLANTATION
Coosawhatchie River
Sylvania
Edisto Beach State Park
Beaufort
St. Helena Sound
St. Helena
JERUSALEM EVANGELICAL LUTHERAN CHURCH
Pinckney Island National Wildlife Refuge
Statesboro
Hardeeville
Port Royal Sound
Ogeechee River
Rincon
Hilton Head
Hilton Head and Lowcountry
Oak Park
Canoochee
Garden City
Fort Pulaski National Monument
Tybee Island
Claxton
Savannah
OCEAN
20
26
95
321
521
301
601
77
520
52
174
25
121
327
21
80
17
16
280

# Contents

DISCOVER

# Charleston & Savannah

No doubt about it: The travel spotlight is shifting South. Taking their place alongside old favorites like Paris, New York, and San Francisco are the smaller but just as delectable destinations of Charleston and Savannah, each now enjoying an unprecedented boom in visitor interest.

As more and more people discover the subtle, compelling charms of these two Southern gems, the inevitable comparisons begin. Stereotypes abound, such as the famous adage "In Charleston they ask what your mother's maiden name is, and in Savannah they ask what you're drinking." But the truth is that Savannah can be just as obsessed with arcane genealogy, and anyone who's ever spent a weekend night in downtown Charleston knows that city is no stranger to a carousing good time.

The key difference between the two is mostly physical. Charleston's charms are more serendipitous, its architecture more Caribbean. The compact, winding downtown means a new surprise awaits you around every corner. That's the magic of Charleston.

Savannah, with its more spacious downtown, has more room to breathe, to walk, and to stretch out. And there are those matchless, tidy squares, still studied

**Clockwise from top left:** the Telfair Academy of Arts and Sciences in Savannah; wild horses on Cumberland Island; Bonaventure Cemetery in Savannah; the ruins of the Old Sheldon Church near Beaufort; a headstone in Magnolia Cemetery; the Mills House Hotel in Charleston.

as marvels of urban design. Savannah's classically Anglophilic architecture tends more toward the stately. While both cities love a good time, Charleston—with its vast selection of nationally renowned restaurants—is definitely more of a foodie's paradise. Savannah, on the other hand, loves nothing more than a boisterous party.

Perhaps we should be talking instead about the things that tie the two together. Charleston and Savannah share a parallel history; stubborn individuality and defiance against the norm have been constants, as evidenced by their key roles in the American Revolution and the Civil War. The entire area has in common a rare natural beauty, with the South Carolina Lowcountry and the Georgia coast together composing the largest contiguous salt marsh in the world and one of the planet's unique ecosystems. Kayakers are at home paddling in the blackwater of the ACE Basin or the vast Okefenokee Swamp. Beachgoers are amazed at the underrated quality of the area's serene strands.

Most of all, however, the greatest treasure of this region is its people. The folks down here love a good story, a good conversation, and a good laugh. It's not just the fabled Southern hospitality; it's a joie de vivre born of great weather and proximity to the ever-invigorating rivers, marshes, and ocean.

---

**Clockwise from top left:** Savannah's River Street; the Jekyll Island Club; a carriage in Charleston; Hunting Island Light.

# 10 TOP EXPERIENCES

**1 Historic Tours:** Learn about the historic downtown areas of Charleston and Savannah in a number of unique ways (page 24).

**2 Southern Cooking:** Some of America's finest award-winning chefs ply their trade in these southern cities, serving up dishes both homestyle and high style (page 23).

**3 Festival Fever:** From St. Patrick's Day in Savannah to Spoleto in Charleston, these cities love their cultural events—and know how to have a good time at them (pages 81 and 221).

**4** **Cemetery Scenery:** For both intriguing American history and scenic beauty, check out **Bonaventure Cemetery** (page 207), **Laurel Grove Cemetery** (page 204), and **Colonial Cemetery** (page 195) in Savannah, as well as **Magnolia Cemetery** (page 70) and **Unitarian Church Cemetery** (page 63) in Charleston.

**5** **African American Heritage:** Charleston's history is black history, from the somber remembrances of the Old Slave Mart Museum to the vivid legacies of *Porgy and Bess* and Cabbage Row (page 25).

**6** **Touring Great Houses:** Some of the nation's finest house museums are here, including the Regency-era **Owens-Thomas House** (page 193) in Savannah and the expertly preserved **Drayton Hall** (page 67) in Charleston.

**7** **Garden Delights:** Home to the near-royal gardens of **Middleton Place** (page 68) and **Magnolia Plantation and Gardens** (page 68), Charleston is truly a city of flowers.

**8** **To-Go Cup Revelry:** Savannah is one of the few cities in the United States where you can stroll the streets enjoying an adult beverage—legally (page 220)!

**9** **Golfing on Hilton Head Island:** Experience one of the world's greatest golf centers by attending the annual RBC Heritage—or by teeing up yourself at one of over 20 courses on the island (page 151).

**10** **A Day at the Beach:** From family-friendly beaches on Hilton Head Island to romantic solitude on Cumberland Island, there's a beach here for everyone (page 30).

# Planning Your Trip

## Where to Go

### Charleston

One of America's oldest cities and an early national center of **arts and culture,** Charleston's legendary taste for the high life is matched by its forward-thinking outlook. The **birthplace of the Civil War** is not just a city of museums resting on its historic laurels. Situated on a hallowed spit of land known as "the peninsula," the Holy City is now a **vibrant, creative hub** of the New South.

### Savannah

Surprisingly **cosmopolitan** for a Deep South city, Savannah's quirky hedonism permeates any visit. The brainchild of General James Oglethorpe, the city's layout is studied even today as a **masterpiece of urban design.** Whether you're admiring an **antebellum home** from the cotton era or enjoying the sea breeze and a cocktail out on **Tybee Island,** a sense of fun imbues all parts of life here.

### Hilton Head and the Lowcountry

The Lowcountry's **mossy, laid-back pace** belies its former status as the heart of American plantation culture and the original cradle of secession. Today it is a mix of **history** (Beaufort and Bluffton), **natural beauty** (the ACE Basin), **resort development** (Hilton Head), **military bases** (Parris Island), and **relaxed beaches** (Edisto and Hunting Islands).

### The Golden Isles

Georgia's Golden Isles are home to one-third of the East Coast's **salt marsh,** and their **natural beauty** is a testament to the Gilded Age millionaires who kept the area largely undeveloped over the years. Even today, this region evokes a **timeless mystique** redolent of Spanish missions, Native American shell ring ceremonies, insular but friendly shrimping communities, and lonely colonial English outposts.

blooming azaleas and live oaks at Magnolia Plantation and Gardens in Charleston

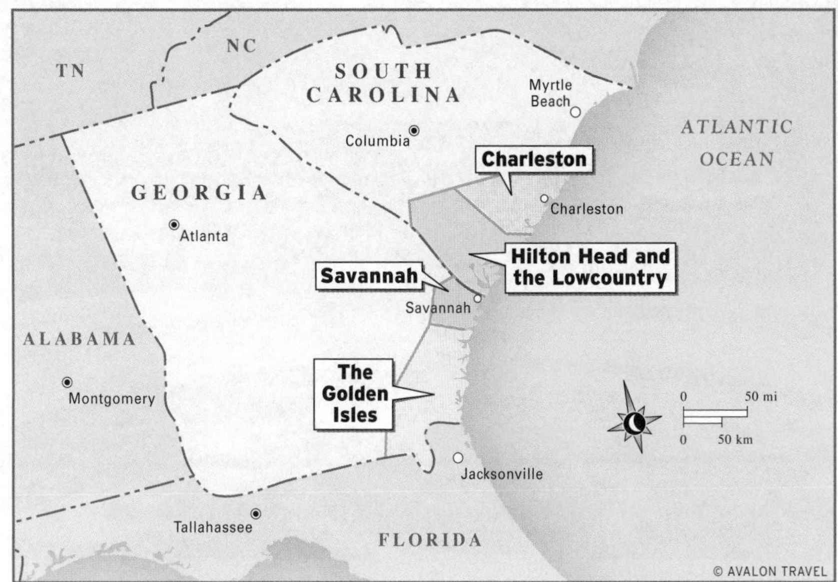


# Know Before You Go

## High and Low Seasons

Springtime is for lovers, and it's no coincidence that spring is when most love affairs with the region begin. Unless you have severe pollen allergies—not a trivial concern given the explosion of plant life at this time—you should try to experience this area at its peak of natural beauty during the magical period from **mid-March to mid-May.** Not surprisingly, lodging is the most expensive and most difficult to secure at that time.

The **hardest time to get a room** in Charleston is during Spoleto from **Memorial Day through mid-June.** Hilton Head's busiest time is during the **RBC Heritage golf tournament** in mid-April. Savannah's tricky time of year is the **St. Patrick's Day** celebration, a multiday event clustering around March 17. While last-minute cancellations are always possible, the only real guarantee is to secure reservations as far in advance as possible (a full year in advance is not unusual for these peak times).

Activity here slows down noticeably in **July and August.** But overall, summertime in the South gets a bad rap and is often not appreciably worse than summers north of the Mason-Dixon Line—though it's certainly more humid.

My favorite time of year on the southeastern coast is the **middle of November,** when the tourist crush noticeably subsides. Not only are the days delightful and the nights crisp (but not frigid), you can get a room at a good price.

## What to Pack

Unless you're coming in the winter to take advantage of lower rates or to enjoy the copious seasonal cheer, there's not much need for a heavy jacket. A **sweater or windbreaker** will do fine for chillier days. Also note that the ocean and the larger rivers can generate some surprisingly crisp breezes, even on what otherwise might be a warm day.

Because of the area's temperate climate, perspiration is likely to be a constant travel companion;

St. Patrick's Day in Savannah

pack accordingly. Whatever you wear, stay with **natural fabrics** such as cotton. The humidity and generally warm weather combine for a miserable experience with polyester and other synthetic fabrics.

Biting insects, such as mosquitos and sand gnats, are frequent unwelcome companions in this part of the country. Plan a trip to the drugstore or supermarket to buy some **bug spray** or Skin So Soft, an Avon product that keeps away the gnats.

# The Best of Charleston and Savannah

Both cities share an abiding respect for social manners and mores, for history, for making money, and for good food and strong drink. They differ in outlook: Charleston has one well-shod foot firmly in the global future, whereas Savannah tends to be more insular. The difference is also one of scale: Savannah's downtown is bigger and has more room to breathe and stretch out, whereas Charleston's charms are more compact and serendipitous. This "Best of" tour will allow you to come to your own conclusions.

## Day 1

### CHARLESTON

Begin your journey in Charleston, the Holy City, named not for its piety but for the steeples in its skyline. First, feel the pulse of the city by going to its bustling heart, **Marion Square.** Maybe do a little shopping on **King Street** and at **Old City Market** afterward. Take a sunset stroll around **The Battery** and admire **Rainbow Row** before diving right into a great meal at one of the city's fine restaurants.

## Day 2

Today you put your historian's hat on and visit one of Charleston's great house museums, such as the **Aiken-Rhett House** or the **Edmondston-Alston House.** Have a hearty Southern-style lunch, and then take an afternoon trip to **Fort Sumter.** After another fantastic Charleston dinner, take a stroll or carriage ride through the French Quarter to close the evening.

## Day 3

### BEAUFORT

After a hearty breakfast, make the 20-minute drive over the Ashley River to gorgeous **Middleton Place,** where you'll tour the gardens. Then stop at adjacent **Drayton Hall** and see

Charleston's Old City Market

Rainbow Row in Charleston

one of the oldest and best-preserved plantation homes in the nation. Make the hour-long drive into Beaufort and spend the afternoon walking around the beautifully preserved historic district. If you have time, go over the bridge to St. Helena Island and visit historic **Penn Center.**

## Day 4

### HILTON HEAD TO SAVANNAH

From Beaufort, drive to **Hilton Head Island,** where you can spend a few hours sunning or biking on the family-friendly beach, shop, or visit the free and informative **Coastal Discovery Museum at Honey Horn**. A half hour away, make a late-afternoon stop in **Old Town Bluffton** to shop for art, see the beautiful **Church of the Cross** on the May River, and have a light dinner. Another half hour's drive puts you into a cute B&B in Savannah to relax for the night, maybe stopping in a pub for a pint or two.

## Day 5

### SAVANNAH

Hit downtown Savannah hard today, starting with a walk down **River Street.** Then enjoy the aesthetic charms of the two adjacent museums, one traditional and one modern, composing the **Telfair Museums.** Tour the exquisite **Owens-Thomas House Museum** and then take a walk through the squares, visiting the **Cathedral of St. John the Baptist** in Lafayette Square and the **Mercer-Williams House** on Monterey Square.

## Day 6

On your way out to Tybee Island, stop for a walk through amazing **Bonaventure Cemetery**—about 15 minutes outside downtown—and pay your respects to native son Johnny Mercer. A half-hour drive takes you to scenic and historically important **Fort Pulaski National Monument.** Scoot on into Tybee another 10 minutes and climb to the top of the **Tybee Lighthouse** before dinner.

## Day 7

### THE GOLDEN ISLES

Drive down scenic U.S. 17 through the Altamaha River estuary, about an hour and a half south of Savannah, and stop by historic **Hofwyl-Broadfield Plantation,** near Brunswick, for

# Southern Cooking: High Style and Homestyle

## FRESH SEAFOOD

The best seafood places put a premium on freshly harvested fish and shellfish.

- **Bowens Island Restaurant,** Charleston (page 110): Gloriously unpretentious.
- **39 Rue de Jean,** Charleston (page 105): Amazing mussels and fish.
- **Desposito's,** Savannah (page 243): Shrimp and oysters dockside.
- **Red Fish,** Hilton Head Island (page 153): Stylish but always fresh.
- **Saltus River Grill,** Beaufort (page 132): Meeting and eating place.
- **Speed's Kitchen,** Shellman Bluff (page 281): Delicacies right off the boat.

## NEW SOUTHERN

The area is home to some adventurous chefs offering an updated take on Lowcountry classics.

- **The Grey,** Savannah (page 239): Savannah's new world-class restaurant, competitive with the best in the nation.
- **FIG,** Charleston (page 101): Three words: tomato *tarte tatin.*
- **The Glass Onion,** Charleston (page 106): Farm-to-table goodness in an informal setting.
- **McCrady's,** Charleston (page 99): A tasting-menu experience from one of the great minds in Southern regional cuisine, Sean Brock.

## CLASSIC SOUTHERN

Your best bets for fine old-school Southern cooking:

- **Hominy Grill,** Charleston (page 106): Comfort-food hit with locals and visitors alike.
- **See Wee Restaurant,** Charleston (page 108): Possibly the best she-crab soup on the planet.
- **Mrs. Wilkes' Dining Room,** Savannah (page 242): Old-school "pass the plate" community seating in a historic home.
- **17Hundred90,** Savannah (page 240): Enjoy dinner and soothing piano music in one of Savannah's most historic buildings.

the peel 'n' eat shrimp at The Glass Onion in Charleston

## BARBECUE

The pleasures of the pig are never far away in this region. Here are a pair of the best coastal 'cue joints:

- **Fiery Ron's Home Team BBQ,** Charleston (page 107): My favorite barbecue spot in the world, believe it or not.
- **Sandfly BBQ,** Savannah (page 243): Excellent Memphis-style barbecue on the south side of Savannah.

## Historic Tours

There's so much to learn about these historically significant cities, and so many different perspectives to get on them. Here are some picks for the best tours in each city.

### CHARLESTON

- One of the best walking tours in the city is from **Ed Grimball's Walking Tours** (page 47), led by a longtime local expert with a vast amount of knowledge. Advance reservations are a must.
- For a unique perspective of Charleston, check out **Bulldog Tours** (page 47), which has exclusive access to the Old City Jail through the Haunted Jail Tour.
- **Carriage tours** (page 49) are particularly conducive to Charleston, with its winding, narrow avenues and cozy neighborhoods. All the companies are equally good and humanely regulated by the city of Charleston.

### SAVANNAH

- **Old City Walks** (page 169) offers a great range of personally guided tours by engaging local experts.
- For a culinary adventure that includes food and drink, look no further than **Savannah Taste Experience** (page 180).
- **Carriage tours** (page 180) are also fun and romantic in Savannah.
- **Savannah Bike Tours** (page 181) will take you on a fun and informative ride though the historic district.

a glimpse at an authentic old rice plantation. Make the five-minute trip over the causeway and enjoy the afternoon at **The Village** on St. Simons Island, with a visit to historic **Fort Frederica National Monument.**

### Day 8

This morning, a 20-minute drive takes you into the **Jekyll Island Historic District.** Tour the grounds and have lunch at any of the great restaurants on-site. Rent a bike and pedal up to the **Clam Creek Picnic Area,** checking out the **Horton House Tabby Ruins** along the way. Ride on the sand to **Driftwood Beach** and relax awhile.

### Day 9

This morning, drive an hour south to St. Marys and have a walk around the cute little downtown area before heading out on the ferry to **Cumberland Island National Seashore.** The 45-minute ferry ride takes you to a full day of biking or hiking the many trails among the ruins and dunes.

### Day 10

Make the half-hour drive into Folkston and the Suwanee Canal Recreation Area at **Okefenokee National Wildlife Refuge.** Take a guided tour up and down the blackwater canal, or walk the trails out to the swamp's prairie vistas and drink in this unique natural beauty.

# African American Heritage

TOP EXPERIENCE

The cities and Sea Islands of the Lowcountry and Georgia coast are integral to a full understanding of the experience of African Americans in the South. More than that, they are living legacies, with a thriving culture—called Gullah in South Carolina and Geechee in Georgia—whose roots can be traced directly back to West Africa.

## Charleston

Charleston is planning to build the $75 million International African American Museum, probably at Calhoun and Concord Streets not far from Museum Row. While building has yet to begin, there are plenty of other spots to enjoy in the meantime. Pay your respects to the victims of the 2015 mass shooting at **Emanuel AME Church** on Calhoun Street. Shop in **City Market;** it never hosted a slave auction, but during its heyday, it was home to a number of African American entrepreneurs and vendors. Don't forget to walk by **Cabbage Row,** inspiration for Catfish Row of the African American-themed George Gershwin opera *Porgy and Bess.* Visit the **Old Slave Mart** and learn more about the Middle Passage and how Charleston's black population overcame the legacy of slavery. Browse the research library at the **Avery Research Center,** one of the main repositories of Gullah culture and history. Take the ferry out to **Fort Sumter,** where the Civil War began. From the fort you can see nearby undeveloped Morris Island, scene of the 1863 Battle of Battery Wagner. That battle included the first all-black regiment in the U.S. Army, the 54th Massachusetts, whose tale was recounted in the film *Glory.* Visit the wrought-iron garden of the noted black Charleston artisan **Philip Simmons.** Take a guided African American history tour of downtown Charleston or tour the **Aiken-Rhett House,** with its excellently and respectfully preserved artifacts of the enslaved African American servants who made the historic property run. Visit **Drayton Hall;** take the guided tour and pay respects at the African American cemetery.

Emanuel AME Church in Charleston

# Coastal Cruising on U.S. 17

Fans of retro Americana and roadside kitsch will find a treasure trove of down-home sites along the old Coastal Highway, now known as U.S. 17. Before the arrival of the interstate highway system, U.S. 17 was by far the most traveled route in the region. While now just a shadow of its former self, it is still a vital roadway and contains a lot of interesting, little-known history. Here's a look at some of the highlights, beginning just north of Charleston and ending at Brunswick, Georgia. This is a fun road trip you could easily accomplish in a day, just checking out the sights along the way.

- **Sweetgrass Baskets:** A stretch of U.S. 17 in Mt. Pleasant north of Charleston has been dubbed the "Sweetgrass Basket Makers Highway" in honor of the many wooden stalls along its length hosting local African American artisans selling their homemade sweetgrass baskets, a centuries-old tradition with African roots.
- **Arthur Ravenel Jr. Bridge:** The longest cable-stayed bridge in the western hemisphere joins Mt. Pleasant with Charleston proper. It has a pedestrian and bike lane too.
- **The Coburg Cow:** This nearly century-old dairy advertisement—a slowly rotating milk cow—was once amid pastureland outside the Charleston city limits. Find it in West Ashley on the portion of U.S. 17 known as the "Savannah Highway," just west of Charleston, about 15 minutes from the Ravenel Bridge.
- **Old Sheldon Church:** A very short drive off U.S. 17, the ruins of the Old Sheldon Church—burned by both the British during the Revolution and the Yankees during the Civil War—are huge, stark, and poignant. After going south on U.S. 17 for about an hour out of Charleston, take a right onto Old Sheldon Church Road.
- **Firework Stands:** About half an hour from the Old Sheldon Church, at the intersection of U.S. 17 and I-95 at Hardeeville, South Carolina, you'll find many garish, colorful stores selling enough fireworks to blow you to the moon and back.
- **Midway Church:** Forty-five minutes south of Savannah in the Liberty County town of Midway is this beautiful 1792 church, whose congregation once boasted two of Georgia's signers of the Declaration of Independence. Don't miss the historic cemetery across the street.

weaving a sweetgrass basket

- **Smallest Church in North America**: About 15 minutes south of Midway on the side of the road near South Newport is the miniscule and charming Memory Park Christ Chapel. The current building was rebuilt after arson sadly destroyed the original in 2015.
- **Butler Island:** In another 15 minutes or so, just south of Darien, Georgia, on the west side of U.S. 17, you'll find this tall chimney—the only remnant of the Butler plantation. English actress Fanny Kemble, who married a Butler heir, wrote the influential abolitionist work *Journal of a Residence on a Georgian Plantation* after witnessing the miserable life of the enslaved people who worked here. (Strangely, the nearby historical marker makes no mention of this.)
- **Brunswick Stew:** Allegedly the container in which the first batch of Brunswick stew was cooked up, you can find this cast-iron pot in Mary Ross Waterfront Park in downtown Brunswick, Georgia.

## Hilton Head and the Lowcountry

While walking around the scenic historic district, visit the **Robert Smalls House,** home of the African American Civil War hero Robert Smalls, as well as his burial site at the **Tabernacle Baptist Church.** Drive by the **Berners Barnwell Sams House** to see where Harriet Tubman worked as a nurse and helped ferry slaves to freedom on the Underground Railroad. Visit **Beaufort National Cemetery** and see the memorial to the African American troops of the 54th and 55th Massachusetts Regiments of the U.S. Army in the Civil War. Make the short drive to St. Helena Island and visit the campus of the **Penn Center,** a key clearinghouse for the study and celebration of Gullah culture and the site of activism by Martin Luther King Jr. in the 1960s. Head on into Hilton Head, stop by the **Coastal Discovery Museum at Honey Horn,** and take an African American heritage tour, visiting the site of Mitchelville, the first community of freed slaves in the United States. An alternate plan is to make the trip inland to Walterboro to visit the **Tuskegee Airmen Memorial** at the regional airport.

## Savannah and the Golden Isles

Check out the **African American Monument** at Rousakis Plaza on River Street. Head over to the former center of black life in Savannah, Martin Luther King Jr. Boulevard (once West Broad St.), and see the **Ralph Mark Gilbert Civil Rights Museum,** and then tour the **First African Baptist Church** in City Market, the oldest black congregation in North America. Nearby is the **Haitian Monument,** a nod to the volunteers who helped the cause of independence in the Revolutionary War. Visit the **Second African Baptist Church,** where Sherman announced the famous "40 acres and a mule" field order. Close by is the **Beach Institute,** a repository of African American art, culture, and history. Check out the restored schoolroom at **Massie Heritage Center,** Savannah's first African American school, and the **Carnegie Branch Library,** Savannah's first black library, where future Supreme Court Justice Clarence Thomas once studied. Pay your respects at **Laurel Grove Cemetery South,** a historic African American cemetery with stirring memorials to some of Savannah's most notable black figures.

the Haitian Monument in Savannah

a bike on Hilton Head Island

Head down to **Harris Neck National Wildlife Refuge,** once the site of an African American community displaced for a World War II airfield. Be sure to visit the vernacular **Gould Cemetery** near the landing within the refuge. An alternate plan is to drive all the way down to little Meridian near Darien and ride the ferry out to **Sapelo Island,** taking a guided day tour of the island and its rich Gullah-Geechee history, including the community of Hog Hammock.

# Best Recreation

While Charleston and Savannah are globally renowned for their history and architecture, a short drive outside their historic districts will take you to a unique natural wonderland. The Lowcountry and Georgia coast is framed by the largest contiguous salt marsh in the world. It's not only a kayaker's paradise but also an amazing natural habitat for indigenous and migratory birds. Here are some highlights for an active outdoor journey.

## Biking

Ride 12 miles across the expansive hard-packed sand all around **Hilton Head Island,** which also offers a number of more strenuous adventures. **Sullivan's Island** offers a long stretch of easy beach bicycling just outside Charleston.

## Bird-Watching

October-March is the perfect time for bird-watchers to visit the 22-acre **Crab Bank Seabird Sanctuary** in Charleston Harbor. Serious bird-watchers can visit the **Bear Island** and **Donnelly Wildlife Management Areas** within the ACE Basin, as well as the impounded rice paddies at the **Ernest F. Hollings ACE Basin National Wildlife Refuge.** The **Savannah National Wildlife Refuge,** with parts in both South Carolina and Georgia, also has an excellent bird-watching (and gator-watching!) area.

## Camping

Head down to Tybee Island outside Savannah for a day trip across the Back River to undeveloped

# Family Fun

A steady diet of house museums and long-ago history will bore anyone to tears, not just the young folks in your traveling party. Fortunately, there's a range of options here to please children of all ages.

## CHARLESTON

- **Children's Museum of the Lowcountry:** Conveniently located on "Museum Row," this indoor playground offers a variety of hands-on activities for kids 3 months-12 years.
- **Old Exchange and Provost Dungeon:** For a real-life Pirates of the Caribbean experience, take a guided tour of this spooky spot from colonial times, complete with animatronic-style figures of pirates and scoundrels.
- **Sewee Visitor and Environmental Education Center:** Visit a pack of red wolves (indigenous to the coastal area) at this center devoted to preserving the species and educating people about these magnificent little animals.
- **South Carolina Aquarium:** This very informative installation features aspects of every habitat in the ecologically diverse Palmetto State—from Lowcountry marshland to Upstate mountain rivers—anchored by an enormous three-floor central observation tank filled with marinelife.
- **Waterfront Park:** The park's outdoor fountain sculptures are sure to please any carefree spirit in your group.

## SAVANNAH

- **Ellis Square:** This square's modernist renovation includes a large wading fountain—a great spot to cool off when it gets hot.
- **Georgia State Railroad Museum:** Climb aboard and take a short train ride complete with old-fashioned steam whistle. As a bonus, also located within the complex is the small but growing **Savannah Children's Museum.**
- **Jepson Center for the Arts:** You'll find a neat children's section, the **Artzeum,** inside this shiny new arts center.
- **Oatland Island Educational Center:** To view wildlife up close and personal, head a few minutes east of town to this facility, which houses cougars and an entire wolf pack along its winding marsh-side nature trail.
- **Fort Pulaski National Monument:** Kids can climb on the parapets, earthworks, and cannons, and explore the great nature trail nearby. They'll no doubt learn a few things as well.

## HILTON HEAD, BEAUFORT, AND THE LOWCOUNTRY

- **Coastal Discovery Museum at Honey Horn:** This museum comes with acres of peaceful green space containing a plethora of artifacts, livestock, and historic re-creations and outbuildings.
- **Henry C. Chambers Waterfront Park:** This verdant green space along the beautiful Beaufort River is a great place to play or relax in bench swings.
- **Highway 21 Drive-In:** Yep, an actual old-fashioned drive-in movie theater, just like in the old days.
- **Hunting Island Light:** Head to the top of this historic lighthouse for a gorgeous 360 degree view.
- **Edisto Island Serpentarium:** Let's face it, kids love snakes, even if you might not. Enjoy them up close and personal here.

## GEORGIA'S GOLDEN ISLES

- **Summer Waves:** This water park on the south end of Jekyll Island offers a great respite from the summer heat.
- **Georgia Sea Turtle Center:** This rescue and research facility is also a high quality, hands-on museum. Don't miss the tour of the area where the turtles are kept while they rehabilitate.
- **Driftwood Beach:** Kids can climb for hours on the driftwood found on this Jekyll Island beach.
- **Neptune Park:** A kid-friendly play area is a key feature of this beachfront area next to the St. Simons Island Pier.

# A Day at the Beach

There are plenty of beaches to enjoy on the Georgia and South Carolina coast, many of them made even more enjoyable by the fact that they tend to get much less traffic than more touristy areas. Here's a quick guide to match the beach to the trip:

## FAMILY FRIENDLY

- **Hilton Head Island**'s beaches are roomy and spotlessly maintained. And because no alcohol is allowed on them, they're geared to families with children.
- **Isle of Palms** outside Charleston is home to the Wild Dunes Resort, which caters to beach-loving families.
- Quiet **Edisto Island** has absolutely none of the flash that young people tend to gravitate to, but it is extraordinarily safe and friendly.
- Popular state park **Hunting Island State Park** is a great place to enjoy family time on the beach. Don't miss the hike to the top of the lighthouse!
- A playground for the people of Georgia by order of the state legislature, **Jekyll Island** is a safe, roomy, and friendly getaway.

## PEACE AND QUIET

- Romantic and isolated, **Cumberland Island** is virtually the mossy picture of the old Sea Island South.
- The total lack of chain hotels and high-rises on **Edisto Island** means a laid-back and thoroughly noncommercial beach experience.
- Low-traffic **Sapelo Island** offers friendly folks and a really beautiful beach.
- Even lower-traffic **Daufuskie Island** is where you want to go when only the most laid-back will do.

a dog on one of Hilton Head's beaches

## DOG FRIENDLY

- Easily the two most dog-friendly beaches in the area covered by this book are **Hunting Island State Park,** South Carolina, and **Jekyll Island,** Georgia. Just keep 'em on a leash and you're fine year-round.
- For a Charleston-area dog beach, go straight to **Isle of Palms.**
- **Hilton Head** doesn't allow canines 10am-5pm Memorial Day-Labor Day, but you can take them on a leash 10am-5pm April 1 until the day before Memorial Day.
- On **Edisto Island,** your pup must be on a leash May 1-October 31 and under voice command or on a leash at all other times.

Wormsloe State Historical Site

**Little Tybee Island,** where wilderness camping is allowed. **Skidaway State Park** also offers great camping.

## Fishing

Inshore **fishing charters** abound in these coastal waters and are a great way to pass a day or half day. Some standouts are Telecaster Charters in Savannah and Barrier Island Eco Tours out of Charleston.

## Kayaking

**Cape Romain National Wildlife Refuge** is a delightful oasis of nearly pristine marsh habitat north of Charleston. Bull Island and Capers Island are highlights of this largely maritime preserve, which comprises 66,000 acres of kayaking opportunities. You can easily kayak for a full day or two in the **ACE Basin,** comprising the estuaries of the Ashepoo, Combahee, and Edisto Rivers (the latter being the largest and most traveled). Public landings and guided tours abound for trips on these nearly pristine blackwater runs.

## Surfing

Believe it or not, Charleston's **Folly Beach** offers some of the East Coast's best surfing. McKevlin's Surf Shop is your go-to source for gear and info.

## Scenic Walks

While the coast's particularly flat nature—not to mention the heat and humidity—doesn't lend itself to strenuous hiking, there are plenty of enjoyable outdoor strolls. In the Savannah area, the entire area surrounding **Fort Pulaski National Monument** features extensive maritime forest walking trails, including a converted rail bed. **Skidaway State Park** and nearby **Wormsloe State Historic Site** both offer walking trails along the marsh and river. For hiking in the Charleston area, try the **Awendaw Passage** in the Francis Marion National Forest north of town.

# Seaside Romance

Bonaventure Cemetery

Spanish moss, friendly beaches, sunsets over the water, sultry weather, moonlit carriage rides—what more could you ask for? The Lowcountry and Georgia coast pretty much wrote the book on romantic getaways. Here's a starter list of the most romantic spots.

## CHARLESTON

- Romantic B&Bs include the **John Rutledge House Inn** and **Two Meeting Street Inn.**
- Enjoy an Italian dinner at **Fulton Five** or a fantastic Southern dinner at **Circa 1886.**
- Don't forget a carriage ride or art gallery stroll through the **French Quarter.**
- Shopping can be sexy! Visit the great stores on **King Street.**

## HILTON HEAD AND THE LOWCOUNTRY

- Take a walkable, picturesque stroll of historic **Beaufort Homes.**
- Visit the driftwood beach on nearby **Hunting Island State Park** and enjoy the stunning views from the top of the lighthouse.
- **Edisto Island** is a wonderful place for a relaxing, quiet, no-hassle beach getaway.

## SAVANNAH

- Relax on the grass at vast, scenic **Forsyth Park,** surrounded by Victorian architecture.
- Yes, cemeteries can be romantic, especially gorgeous **Bonaventure Cemetery.**
- Avoid the lines at The Lady & Sons and instead have a delightful dinner at **The Grey** or **Elizabeth on 37th.** Share a coffee, sweet treat, or perhaps a signature martini at **Lulu's Chocolate Bar.**
- Have a nightcap at **Rocks on the Roof** on top of the Bohemian Hotel Savannah and watch the big cargo ships roll in and out on the river.
- Up for a crazy night of dancing? **Club One Jefferson** is the ticket.

## THE GOLDEN ISLES

- Stay at the **Jekyll Island Club,** former stomping ground of the world's richest people. Rent a bike and crisscross the whole island in the late afternoon, coming back to the club to enjoy a romantic dinner by the fireplace at the **Courtyard at Crane.**
- Take the ferry to **Cumberland Island National Seashore,** surely one of the most romantic locations on earth. Rent a bike on arrival and take your time pedaling among the ruins of the old mansions, making sure to visit the chapel at the **First African Baptist Church,** site of the wedding of John F. Kennedy Jr. and Carolyn Bessette. Before you board the ferry to conclude your journey, maybe you'll get lucky and encounter some of the island's famous wild horses, fitting symbols of passion and romance.

# Charleston

Look for ★ to find recommended sights, activities, dining, and lodging.

# Highlights

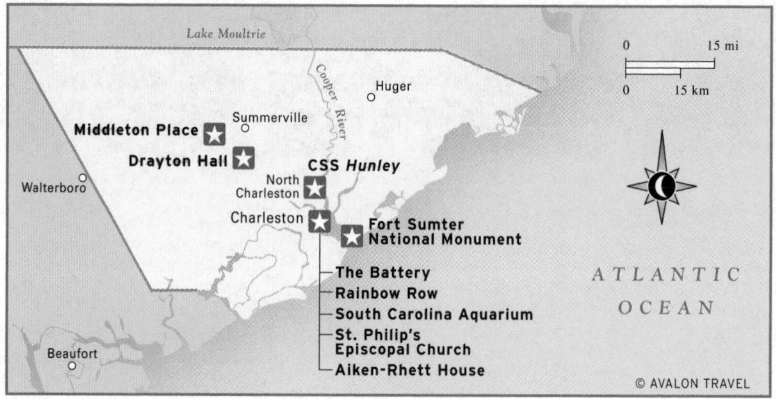


★ **The Battery:** Tranquil surroundings combine with beautiful views of Charleston Harbor, historical points key to the Civil War, and amazing mansions (page 49).

★ **Rainbow Row:** Painted in warm pastels, these old merchant homes near the cobblestoned waterfront take you on a journey to Charleston's antebellum heyday (page 51).

★ **South Carolina Aquarium:** Experience the state's surprising breadth of underwater habitat (page 54).

★ **Fort Sumter National Monument:** Take a ferry to see where the Civil War began, with gorgeous views along the way (page 56).

★ **St. Philip's Episcopal Church:** A sublimely beautiful sanctuary and two historic graveyards await you in the heart of the evocative French Quarter (page 58).

★ **Aiken-Rhett House:** There are certainly more ostentatious house museums in Charleston, but none that provide such a virtually intact glimpse into real antebellum life (page 65).

★ **Drayton Hall:** Don't miss Charleston's oldest surviving plantation home and one of the country's best examples of professional historic preservation (page 67).

★ **Middleton Place:** Wander around one of the world's most beautifully landscaped gardens—and the first in North America (page 68).

★ **CSS *Hunley*:** The first submarine to sink a ship in battle is a moving example of bravery and sacrifice (page 70).

Everyone who spends time in Charleston comes away with a story about the locals' courtesy and hospitality.

Mine came while walking through the French Quarter and admiring a handsome old single house on Church Street, one of the few that survived the fire of 1775. To my surprise, the woman chatting with a friend nearby turned out to be the homeowner. Noticing my interest, she invited me, a total stranger, inside to check out the progress of her renovation. This is a city that takes civic harmony seriously—it even boasts the country's only "Livability Court," a legally binding board that meets regularly to enforce local quality-of-life ordinances.

In 2015, however, Charleston gained national prominence when a white gunman murdered nine worshippers in the historically black Emanuel AME Church on Calhoun Street downtown. The nation was transfixed not only by the horror of the incident, but also by Charleston's community response, which was wholly in keeping with its character: hopeful, forgiving, resilient, and compassionate. Charleston's nickname, the "Holy City," derives from the skyline's abundance of church steeples rather than any excess of piety among its citizens, but its response to the Mother Emanuel tragedy seemed to lend a new meaning.

While many visitors come to see the historical south of Charleston—finding it and then some, of course—they leave impressed by the diversity of Charlestonian life. It's a surprisingly cosmopolitan mix of students, professionals, and longtime inhabitants—who discuss the finer points of Civil War history as if it were last year, party on Saturday night like there's no tomorrow, and go to church on Sunday morning dressed in their finest.

This city, so known for its history, is also quietly booming as one of the nation's key centers of tech and digital development. Highly educated and motivated millennials from all over the country are flocking to Charleston for its blend of start-up friendliness, great nightlife, eco-friendly sensibilities, and vibrant arts and cultural scene.

**Previous:** the French Quarter; Pineapple Fountain. **Above:** a decorative iron horse hitch in Charleston.

## Greater Charleston

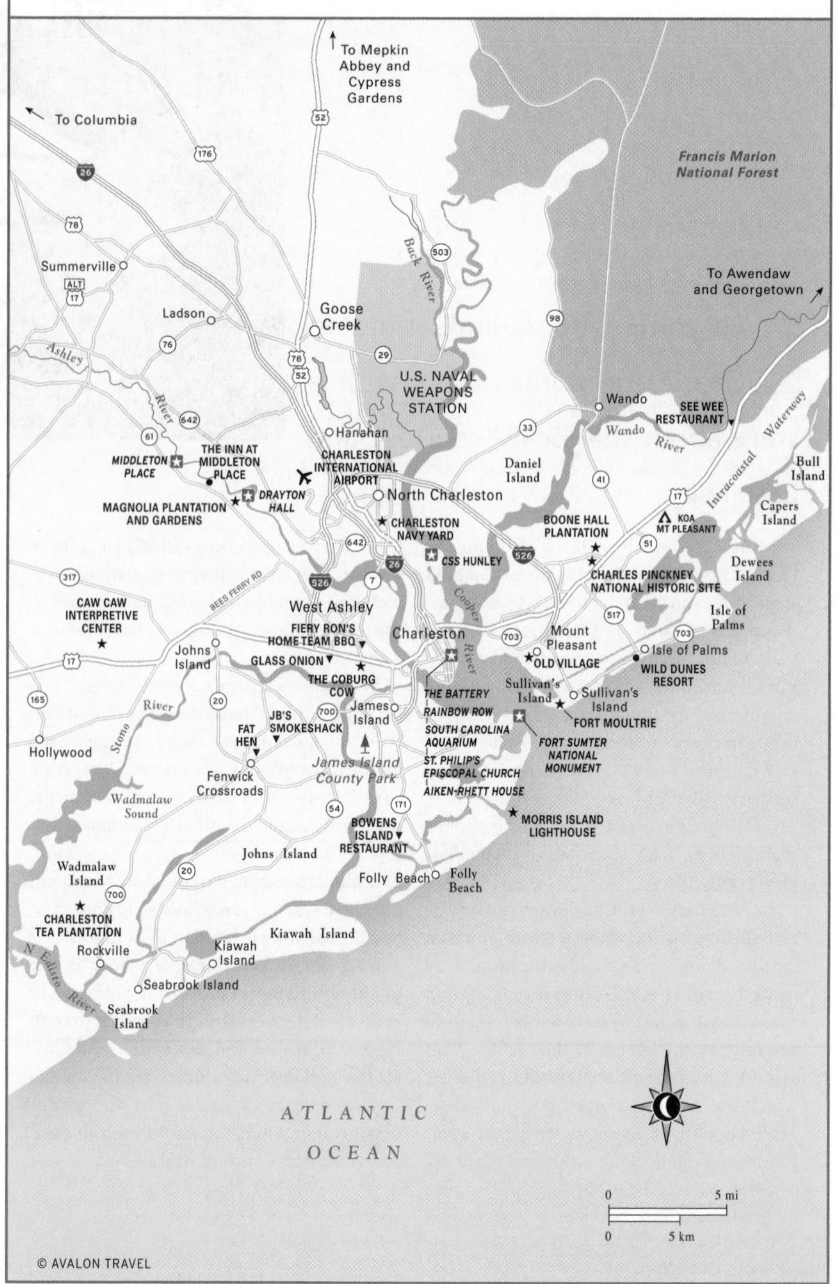

## HISTORY

Unlike the many English colonies in America that were based on freedom from religious persecution, Carolina was strictly a commercial venture from the beginning. The tenure of the Lords Proprietors—the eight English aristocrats who literally owned the colony—began in 1670 when the *Carolina* finished its journey from Barbados at Albemarle Creek on the west bank of the Ashley River.

Those first colonists set up a small fortification called Charles Towne, named for Charles II, the first monarch of the Restoration. A year later they were joined by settlers from the prosperous but overcrowded British colony of Barbados, who brought a Caribbean sensibility that exists in Charleston to this day.

Finding the first Charles Towne not very fertile and vulnerable to attack from Native Americans and the Spanish, they moved to the peninsula and down to "Oyster Point," what Charlestonians now call White Point Gardens. Just above Oyster Point they set up a walled town, bounded by modern-day Water Street to the south (then a marshy creek, as the name indicates), Meeting Street to the west, Cumberland Street to the north, and the Cooper River on the east.

Growing prosperous as a trading center for deerskin from the great American interior, Charles Towne came into its own after two nearly concurrent events in the early 1700s: the decisive victory of a combined force of Carolinians and Native American allies against the fierce Yamasee people, and the final eradication of the pirate threat with the deaths of Blackbeard and Stede Bonnet.

Flush with a new spirit of independence, Charles Towne threw off the control of the anemic, disengaged Lords Proprietors, tore down the old defensive walls, and was reborn as an outward-looking, expansive, and increasingly cosmopolitan city that came to be called Charleston. With safety from hostile incursions came the time of the great rice and indigo plantations. Springing up all along the Ashley River soon after the introduction of the crops, they turned the labor and expertise of enslaved Africans into enormous profit for their owners. However, the planters preferred the pleasures and sea breezes of Charleston, and gradually summer homes became year-round residences.

It was during this colonial era that the indelible Charlestonian character was stamped: a hedonistic aristocracy that combined a love of carousing with a love of the arts; a code of chivalry meant to both reflect a genteel spirit and reinforce the social order; and, ominously, an ever-increasing reliance on slave labor.

As the storm clouds of civil war gathered in the early 1800s, the majority of Charleston's population was of African descent, and the city had long been America's main importation point for the transatlantic slave trade. The worst fears of white Charlestonians seemed confirmed during the alleged plot by slave leader Denmark Vesey in the early 1820s to start a rebellion. The Lowcountry's reliance on slave labor put it front and center in the coming national confrontation over abolition, which came to a head with the bombardment of Fort Sumter in Charleston Harbor in April 1861.

By war's end, not only did the city lay in ruins—mostly from a disastrous fire in 1861, as well as from a 545-day Union siege—so did its way of life. Pillaged by Northern troops and formerly enslaved people, the great plantations along the Ashley became the sites of the first strip mining in the United States as poverty-stricken owners scraped away the layer of phosphate under the topsoil to sell—perhaps with a certain poetic justice—as fertilizer.

The Holy City didn't really wake up until the great "Charleston Renaissance" of the 1920s and 1930s, when the city rediscovered art, literature, and music in the form of jazz and the world-famous Charleston dance. This was also the time that the world rediscovered Charleston. In the 1920s, George Gershwin read local author DuBose Heyward's novel *Porgy* and decided to write a score around the story. Along with lyrics written by Ira Gershwin, the three men's collaboration became the first American opera, *Porgy and Bess,* which debuted in New York in 1935. It

# Map 1: Downtown Charleston

## SIGHTS

- **2** South Carolina Aquarium
- **3** Fort Sumter National Monument
- **5** Philip Simmons Garden
- **19** Kahal Kadosh Beth Elohim Reform Temple
- **20** William Rhett House
- **32** Old City Market
- **37** Old City Jail
- **39** Unitarian Church
- **48** Confederate Museum
- **58** Gibbes Museum of Art
- **59** Circular Congregational Church
- **60** Old Powder Magazine
- **63** St. Philip's Episcopal Church
- **76** Dock Street Theatre
- **78** French Huguenot Church
- **80** Old Slave Mart Museum
- **84** Waterfront Park
- **90** Four Corners of Law
- **91** St. Michael's Episcopal Church
- **95** Rainbow Row
- **96** The Old Exchange and Provost Dungeon
- **97** Cabbage Row
- **98** Heyward-Washington House
- **99** Nathaniel Russell House
- **100** Miles Brewton House
- **101** The Battery
- **102** Calhoun Mansion
- **103** Edmondston-Alston House

**Tours**

- **1** Spiritline Cruises
- **4** Sandlapper Water Tours
- **35** Bulldog Tours
- **36** Ed Grimball's Walking Tours
- **66** Charleston Culinary Tours
- **72** Charleston Strolls
- **74** Charleston Footprints

## RESTAURANTS

- **17** Jestine's Kitchen
- **21** Circa 1886
- **22** Black Tap Coffee
- **25** Charleston Grill
- **26** Hyman's Seafood
- **27** FIG
- **29** Cru Café
- **33** Peninsula Grill
- **34** Kaminsky's
- **38** Queen Street Grocery
- **40** Fulton Five
- **47** City Lights Coffeehouse
- **56** Husk
- **57** Poogan's Porch
- **65** Magnolias
- **67** Slightly North of Broad
- **81** McCrady's
- **89** Gaulart & Maliclet

## NIGHTLIFE

- **23** Vickery's Bar and Grill
- **52** Tommy Condon's Irish Pub
- **68** The Gin Joint
- **82** Rooftop Bar

## ARTS AND CULTURE

- **15** The Have Nots!
- **42** Sylvan Gallery
- **43** The Audubon Gallery
- **49** Gallery Chuma
- **61** Corrigan Gallery
- **64** The Footlight Players
- **69** Robert Lange Studios
- **77** Charleston Stage
- **79** Pink House Gallery
- **85** City Gallery at Waterfront
- **92** Ann Long Fine Art
- **93** Charleston Renaissance Gallery
- **94** Helena Fox Fine Art

## SHOPS

- **7** The Skinny Dip
- **6** Simply J Boutique
- **8** Bob Ellis Shoe Store
- **9** Copper Penny Shooz
- **10** Art Jewelry by Mikhail Smolkin
- **11** Croghan's Jewel Box
- **12** Spartina 449
- **13** M. Dumas & Sons
- **14** The Trunk Show
- **16** Half Moon Outfitters
- **18** Rangoni of Florence
- **24** Pauline Books and Media
- **30** Belmond Charleston Place
- **41** George C. Birlant & Co.
- **46** Golden & Associates
- **50** City Market
- **53** Preservation Society of Charleston Book and Gift Shop
- **54** Jacques' Antiques
- **55** Alexandra AD
- **62** Curiosity
- **70** Indigo
- **75** Shops of Historic Charleston Foundation
- **88** Berlins Men's and Women's

0 250 yds
0 250 m

**DISTANCE ACROSS MAP**
**Approximate: 1.7 mi or 2.8 km**

COMING ST
WENTWORTH ST
21
PITT ST
22
BEAUFAIN ST
NORTH OF BROAD
MAGAZINE ST
37
Old City Jail
Unitarian Church
QUEEN ST
38
LOGAN ST
BROAD ST
86
87
TRADD ST
LENWOOD ST
LEGARE ST
GIBBES ST
Miles Brewton House
100
KING ST
LAMBOLL ST
The Battery
101
MURRAY BLVD
S BATTERY ST
White Point Gardens

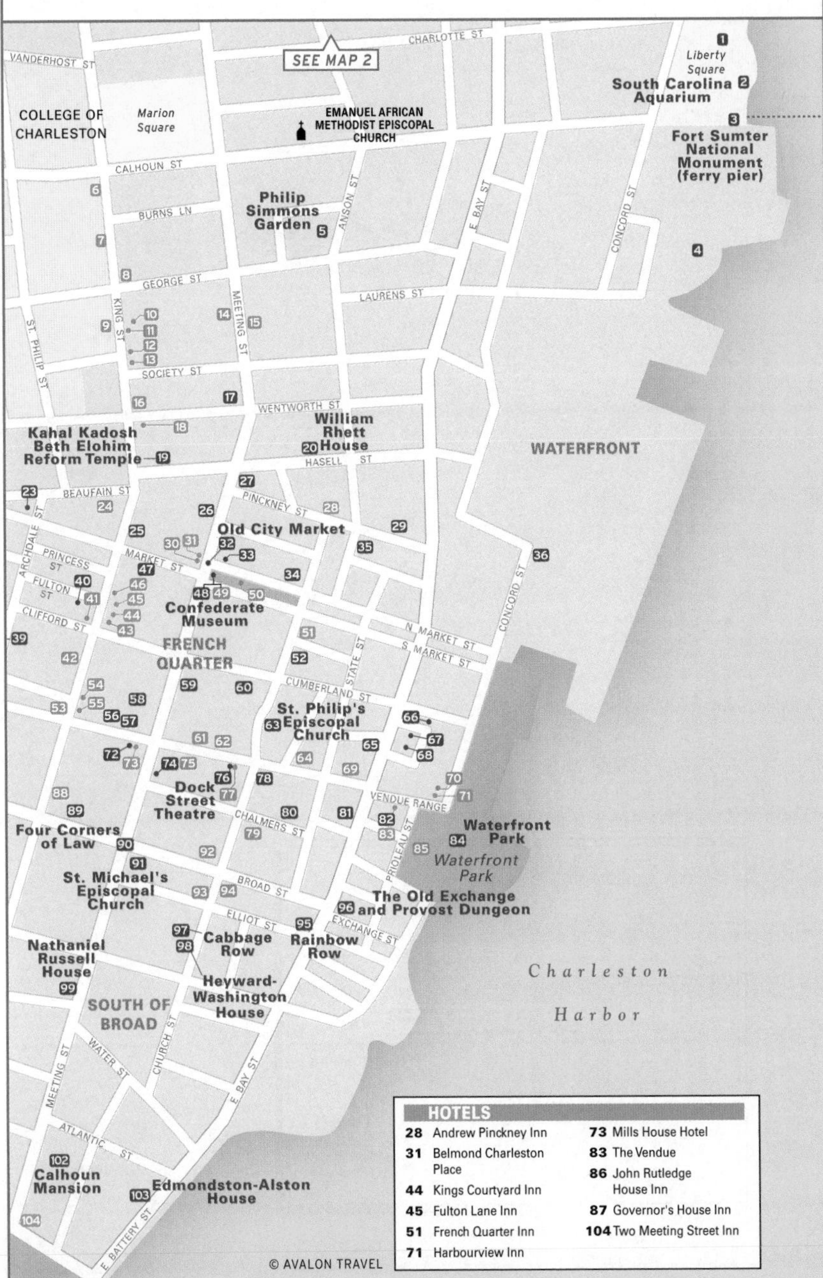

SEE MAP 2
CHARLOTTE ST
VANDERHOST ST
Liberty Square
South Carolina Aquarium
COLLEGE OF CHARLESTON
Marion Square
EMANUEL AFRICAN METHODIST EPISCOPAL CHURCH
Fort Sumter National Monument (ferry pier)
CALHOUN ST
Philip Simmons Garden
BURNS LN
ANSON ST
E BAY ST
CONCORD ST
GEORGE ST
LAURENS ST
KING ST
MEETING ST
ST. PHILIP ST
SOCIETY ST
WENTWORTH ST
William Rhett House
Kahal Kadosh Beth Elohim Reform Temple
HASELL ST
WATERFRONT
BEAUFAIN ST
PINCKNEY ST
Old City Market
ARCHDALE ST
PRINCESS ST
MARKET ST
FULTON ST
Confederate Museum
CLIFFORD ST
N MARKET ST
S MARKET ST
FRENCH QUARTER
CUMBERLAND ST
STATE ST
St. Philip's Episcopal Church
Dock Street Theatre
VENDUE RANGE
CHALMERS ST
Waterfront Park
Four Corners of Law
PRIOLEAU ST
Waterfront Park
St. Michael's Episcopal Church
BROAD ST
The Old Exchange and Provost Dungeon
ELLIOT ST
EXCHANGE ST
Cabbage Row
Rainbow Row
Nathaniel Russell House
Heyward-Washington House
Charleston Harbor
SOUTH OF BROAD
WATER ST
CHURCH ST
MEETING ST
E BAY ST
ATLANTIC ST
Calhoun Mansion
Edmondston-Alston House
E BATTERY ST
© AVALON TRAVEL
HOTELS
28 Andrew Pinckney Inn
31 Belmond Charleston Place
44 Kings Courtyard Inn
45 Fulton Lane Inn
51 French Quarter Inn
71 Harbourview Inn
73 Mills House Hotel
83 The Vendue
86 John Rutledge House Inn
87 Governor's House Inn
104 Two Meeting Street Inn

# Map 2: Upper King and Hampton Park

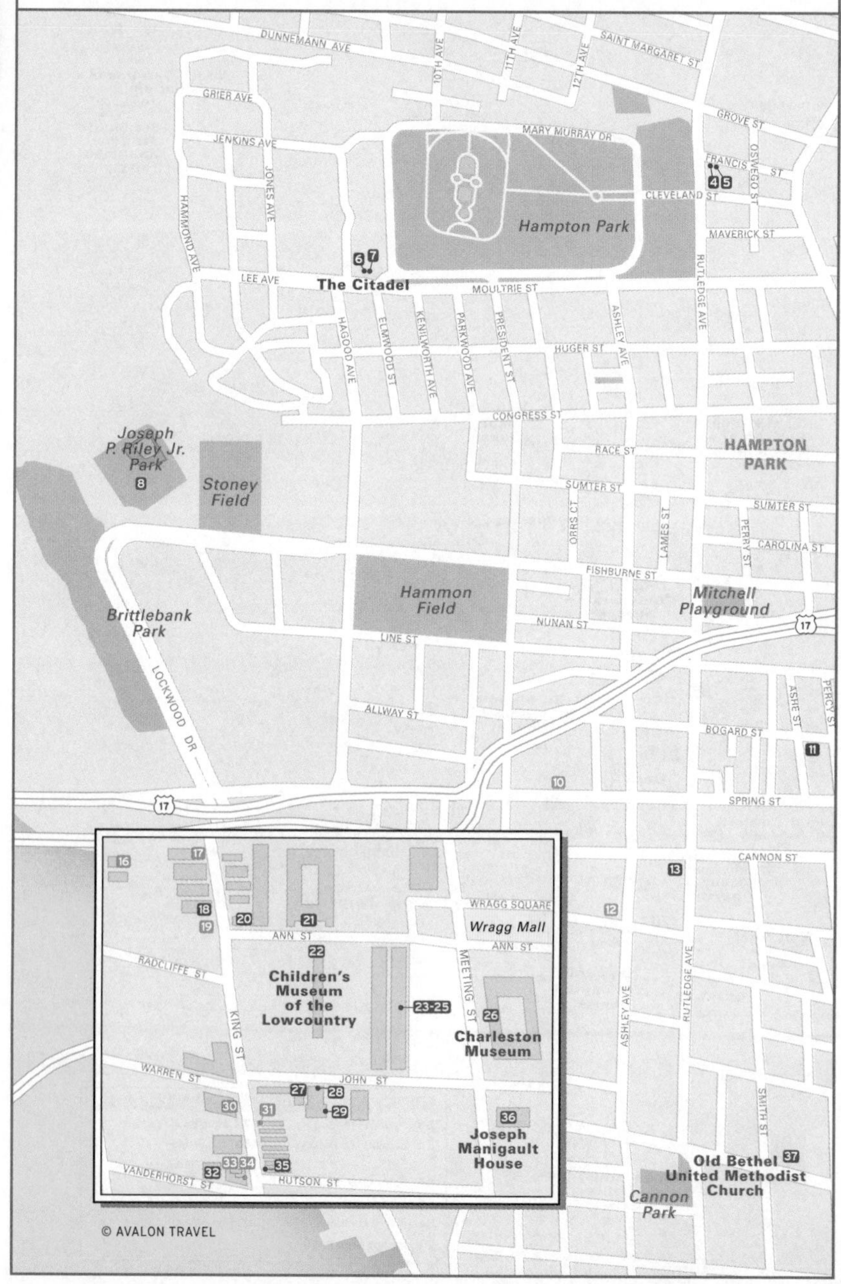

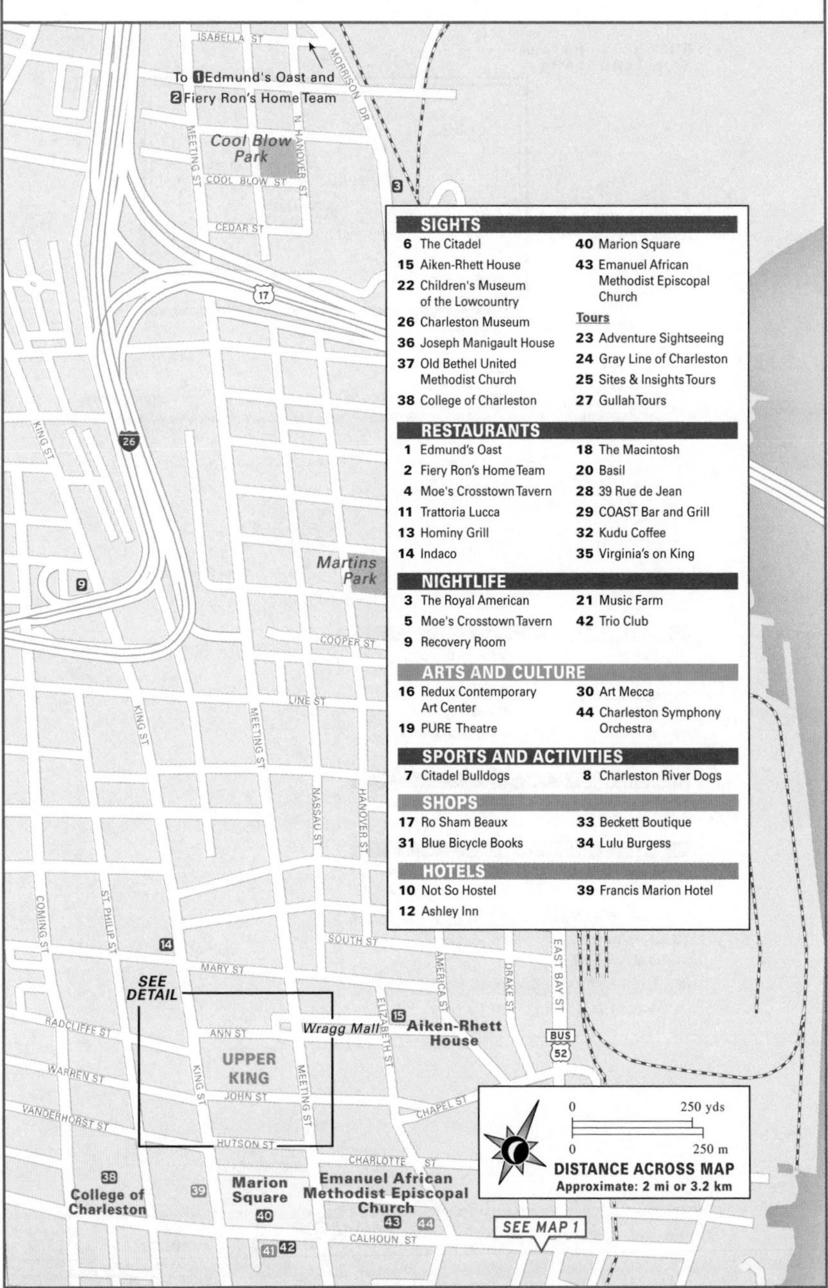

ISABELLA ST
To 1 Edmund's Oast and
2 Fiery Ron's Home Team
MORRISON DR
Cool Blow Park
MEETING ST
N HANOVER ST
COOL BLOW ST
CEDAR ST
17
26
KING ST
Martins Park
COOPER ST
LINE ST
MEETING ST
KING ST
NASSAU ST
HANOVER ST
COMING ST
ST. PHILIP ST
SOUTH ST
MARY ST
AMERICA ST
DRAKE ST
EAST BAY ST
SEE DETAIL
RADCLIFFE ST
ANN ST
Wragg Mall
ELIZABETH ST
Aiken-Rhett House
UPPER KING
WARREN ST
KING ST
MEETING ST
JOHN ST
VANDERHORST ST
CHAPEL ST
BUS 52
HUTSON ST
CHARLOTTE ST
College of Charleston
Marion Square
Emanuel African Methodist Episcopal Church
CALHOUN ST
SEE MAP 1
0
250 yds
0
250 m
DISTANCE ACROSS MAP
Approximate: 2 mi or 3.2 km
SIGHTS
6 The Citadel
15 Aiken-Rhett House
22 Children's Museum of the Lowcountry
26 Charleston Museum
36 Joseph Manigault House
37 Old Bethel United Methodist Church
38 College of Charleston
40 Marion Square
43 Emanuel African Methodist Episcopal Church
Tours
23 Adventure Sightseeing
24 Gray Line of Charleston
25 Sites & Insights Tours
27 Gullah Tours
RESTAURANTS
1 Edmund's Oast
2 Fiery Ron's Home Team
4 Moe's Crosstown Tavern
11 Trattoria Lucca
13 Hominy Grill
14 Indaco
18 The Macintosh
20 Basil
28 39 Rue de Jean
29 COAST Bar and Grill
32 Kudu Coffee
35 Virginia's on King
NIGHTLIFE
3 The Royal American
5 Moe's Crosstown Tavern
9 Recovery Room
21 Music Farm
42 Trio Club
ARTS AND CULTURE
16 Redux Contemporary Art Center
19 PURE Theatre
30 Art Mecca
44 Charleston Symphony Orchestra
SPORTS AND ACTIVITIES
7 Citadel Bulldogs
8 Charleston River Dogs
SHOPS
17 Ro Sham Beaux
31 Blue Bicycle Books
33 Beckett Boutique
34 Lulu Burgess
HOTELS
10 Not So Hostel
12 Ashley Inn
39 Francis Marion Hotel

## Map 3: West Ashley and North Charleston

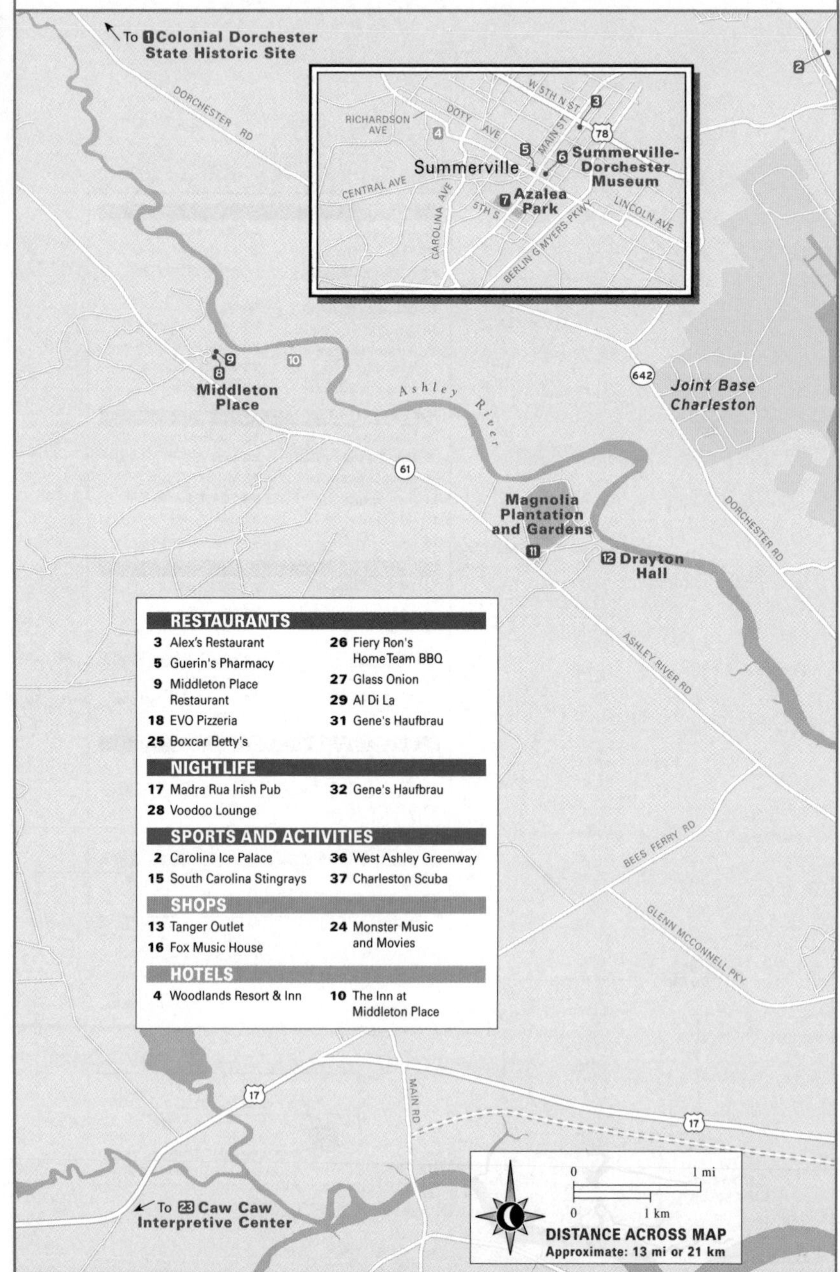

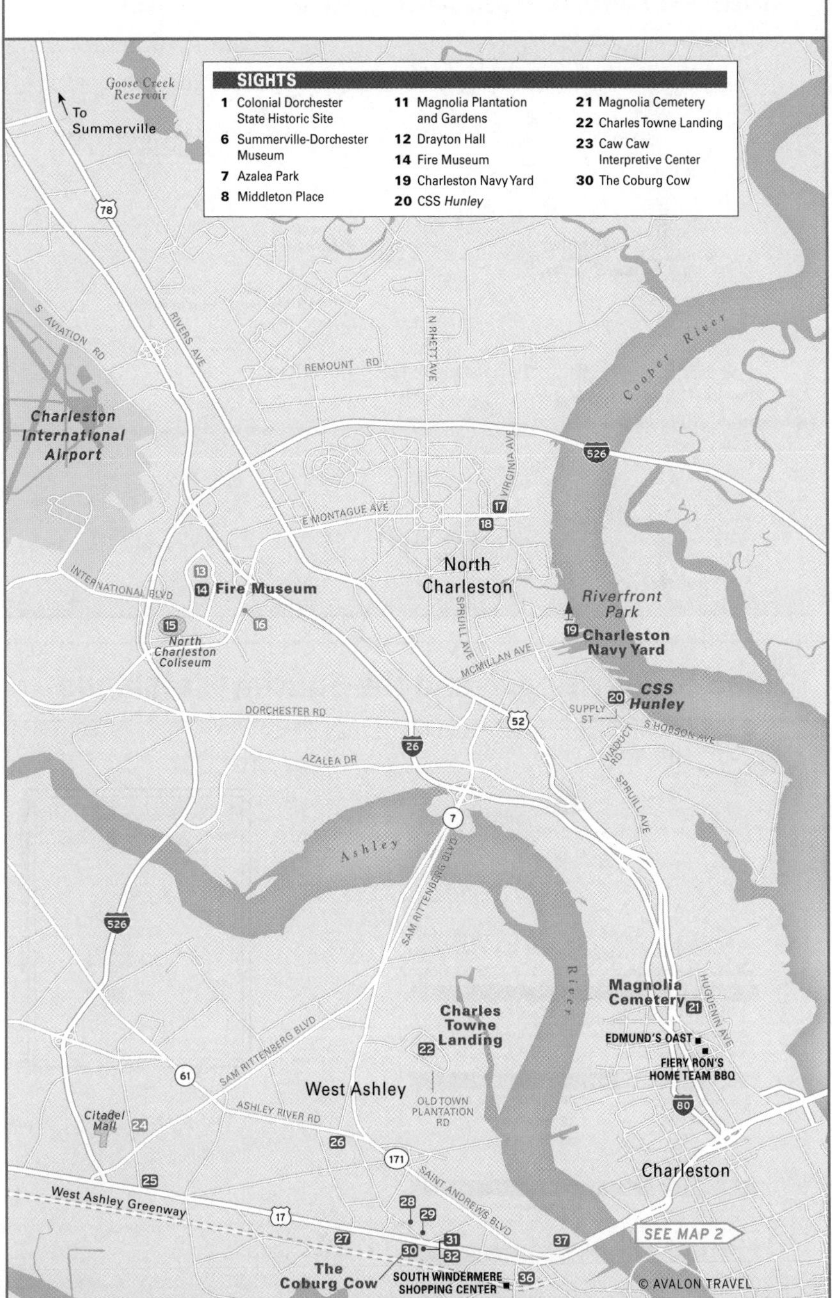

SIGHTS
1 Colonial Dorchester State Historic Site
6 Summerville-Dorchester Museum
7 Azalea Park
8 Middleton Place
11 Magnolia Plantation and Gardens
12 Drayton Hall
14 Fire Museum
19 Charleston Navy Yard
20 CSS Hunley
21 Magnolia Cemetery
22 Charles Towne Landing
23 Caw Caw Interpretive Center
30 The Coburg Cow
Goose Creek Reservoir
To Summerville
Charleston International Airport
S AVIATION RD
RIVERS AVE
REMOUNT RD
N RHETT AVE
Cooper River
VIRGINIA AVE
E MONTAGUE AVE
INTERNATIONAL BLVD
Fire Museum
North Charleston Coliseum
North Charleston
SPRUILL AVE
MCMILLAN AVE
Riverfront Park
Charleston Navy Yard
CSS Hunley
SUPPLY ST
S HOBSON AVE
VIADUCT RD
DORCHESTER RD
AZALEA DR
Ashley River
SAM RITTENBERG BLVD
Magnolia Cemetery
HUGUENIN AVE
EDMUND'S OAST
FIERY RON'S HOME TEAM BBQ
Charles Towne Landing
West Ashley
OLD TOWN PLANTATION RD
Citadel Mall
ASHLEY RIVER RD
SAINT ANDREWS BLVD
Charleston
West Ashley Greenway
SEE MAP 2
The Coburg Cow
SOUTH WINDERMERE SHOPPING CENTER
© AVALON TRAVEL

## Map 4: Mount Pleasant and East Cooper

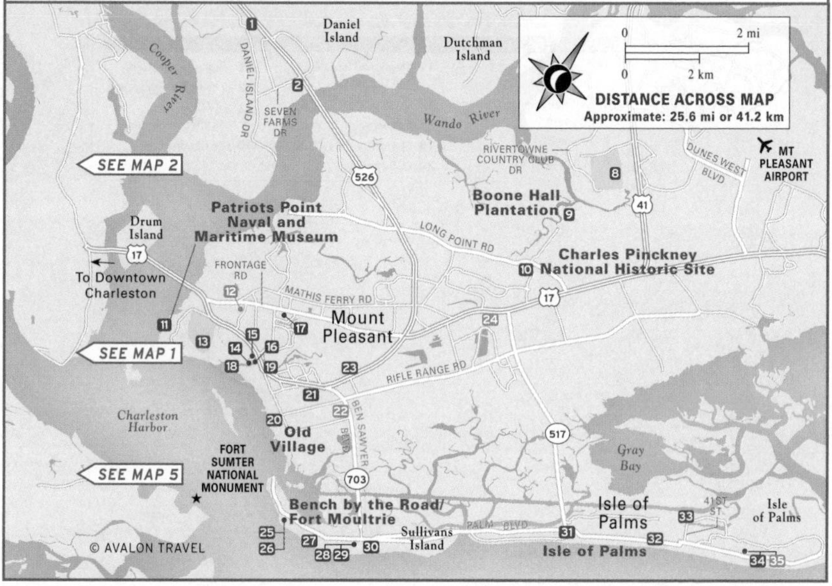

Daniel Island
Dutchman Island
Cooper River
Wando River
DANIEL ISLAND DR
SEVEN FARMS DR
DISTANCE ACROSS MAP
Approximate: 25.6 mi or 41.2 km
0 2 mi
0 2 km
RIVERTOWNE COUNTRY CLUB DR
DUNES WEST BLVD
MT PLEASANT AIRPORT
SEE MAP 2
526
Boone Hall Plantation
41
Patriots Point Naval and Maritime Museum
Drum Island
LONG POINT RD
17
To Downtown Charleston
FRONTAGE RD
Charles Pinckney National Historic Site
MATHIS FERRY RD
Mount Pleasant
SEE MAP 1
RIFLE RANGE RD
Charleston Harbor
Old Village
BEN SAWYER BLVD
517
Gray Bay
FORT SUMTER NATIONAL MONUMENT
SEE MAP 5
703
Bench by the Road/ Fort Moultrie
Isle of Palms
41ST ST
Isle of Palms
PALM BLVD
Sullivans Island
Isle of Palms
© AVALON TRAVEL

## Map 5: Folly Beach and the Southwest Islands

BEARS BLUFF RD
Deep Water Vineyards
0 2 mi
0 2 km
DISTANCE ACROSS MAP
Approximate: 25 mi or 40 km
700
N Edisto River
MAYBANK HWY
Charleston Tea Plantation
Bohicket Creek
BETSY KERRISON PKY
Folly Beach
E INDIAN AVE
W HURON AVE
HUDSON AVE
CENTER ST
ERIE AVE
COOPER AVE
ASHLEY AVE
ARTIC AVE
Kiawah River
KIAWAH ISLAND PKY
GOVERNORS DR

**SIGHTS**

1 Deep Water Vineyards
2 Charleston Tea Plantation
4 Angel Oak Park
10 Legare Farms
17 Folly Beach

**RESTAURANTS**

3 Sunrise Bistro
5 Tattooed Moose
6 Fat Hen
15 Bowens Island Restaurant
18 Lost Dog Café
20 Taco Boy
24 Blu Restaurant

**NIGHTLIFE**

9 The Pour House
22 Sand Dollar Social Club
25 Blu Bar

**ARTS AND CULTURE**

8 Terrace Theatre

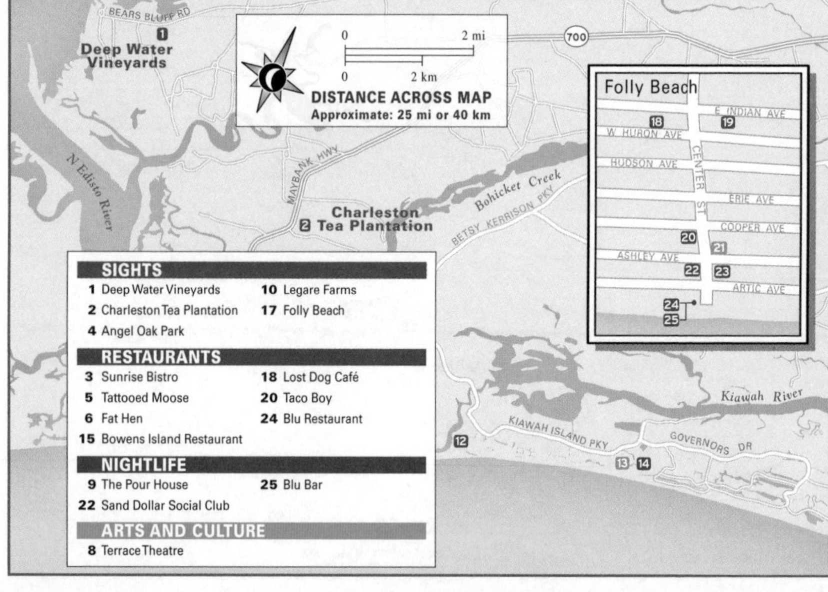

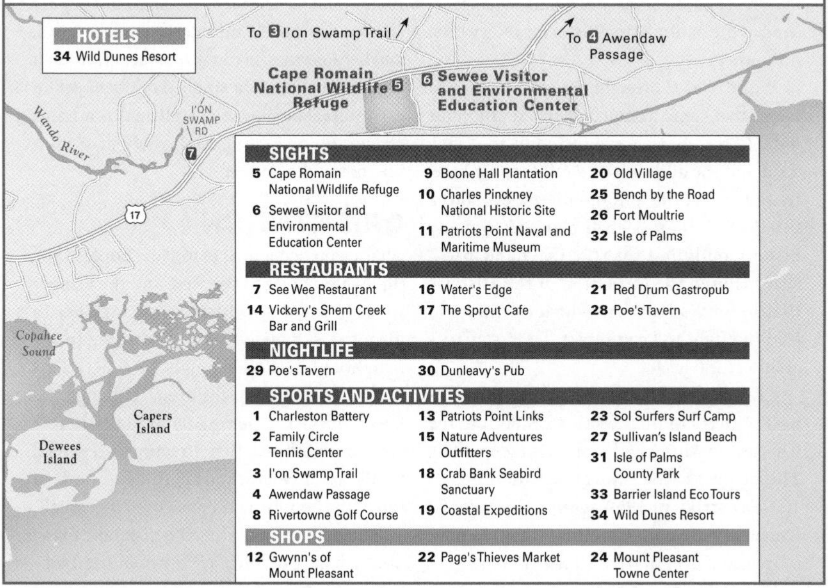
HOTELS
34 Wild Dunes Resort
To 3 I'on Swamp Trail
To 4 Awendaw Passage
Cape Romain National Wildlife Refuge 5
6 Sewee Visitor and Environmental Education Center
I'ON SWAMP RD
7
Wando River
17
Copahee Sound
Capers Island
Dewees Island
SIGHTS
5 Cape Romain National Wildlife Refuge
6 Sewee Visitor and Environmental Education Center
9 Boone Hall Plantation
10 Charles Pinckney National Historic Site
11 Patriots Point Naval and Maritime Museum
20 Old Village
25 Bench by the Road
26 Fort Moultrie
32 Isle of Palms
RESTAURANTS
7 See Wee Restaurant
14 Vickery's Shem Creek Bar and Grill
16 Water's Edge
17 The Sprout Cafe
21 Red Drum Gastropub
28 Poe's Tavern
NIGHTLIFE
29 Poe's Tavern
30 Dunleavy's Pub
SPORTS AND ACTIVITES
1 Charleston Battery
2 Family Circle Tennis Center
3 I'on Swamp Trail
4 Awendaw Passage
8 Rivertowne Golf Course
13 Patriots Point Links
15 Nature Adventures Outfitters
18 Crab Bank Seabird Sanctuary
19 Coastal Expeditions
23 Sol Surfers Surf Camp
27 Sullivan's Island Beach
31 Isle of Palms County Park
33 Barrier Island Eco Tours
34 Wild Dunes Resort
SHOPS
12 Gwynn's of Mount Pleasant
22 Page's Thieves Market
24 Mount Pleasant Towne Center

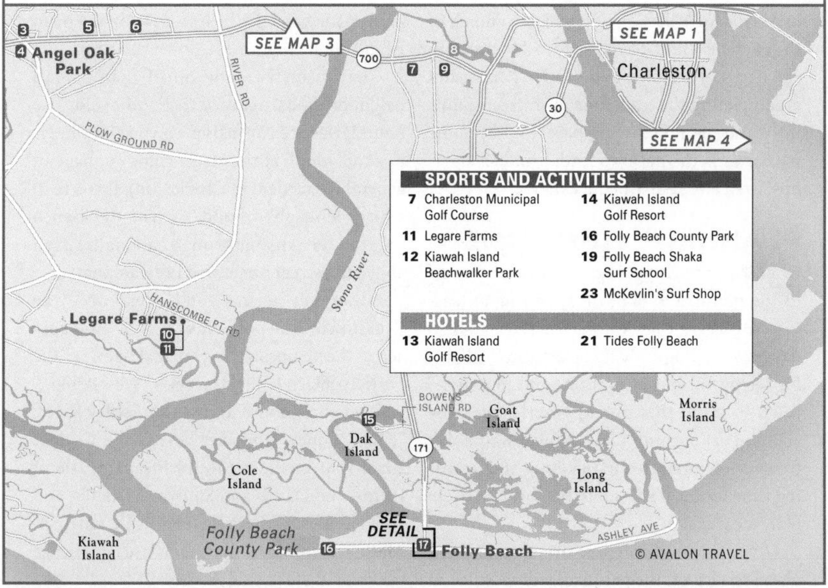
3 5 6
4 Angel Oak Park
SEE MAP 3
700
8
7 9
SEE MAP 1
Charleston
RIVER RD
30
PLOW GROUND RD
SEE MAP 4
SPORTS AND ACTIVITIES
7 Charleston Municipal Golf Course
11 Legare Farms
12 Kiawah Island Beachwalker Park
14 Kiawah Island Golf Resort
16 Folly Beach County Park
19 Folly Beach Shaka Surf School
23 McKevlin's Surf Shop
HOTELS
13 Kiawah Island Golf Resort
21 Tides Folly Beach
Stono River
HANSCOMBE PT RD
Legare Farms
10
11
BOWENS ISLAND RD
Goat Island
Morris Island
15
Dak Island
171
Cole Island
Long Island
SEE DETAIL
Folly Beach County Park
16
17
Folly Beach
ASHLEY AVE
Kiawah Island
© AVALON TRAVEL

was also during this time that a new appreciation for Charleston's history sprang up, as the Preservation Society of Charleston spearheaded the nation's first historic preservation ordinance.

World War II brought the same economic boom that came to much of the South, most notably through an expansion of the Navy Yard and the addition of a military air base. By the 1950s, the automobile suburb and a thirst for "progress" had claimed so many historic buildings that the inevitable backlash inspired the formation of the Historic Charleston Foundation, which continues to lead the fight to keep intact the Holy City's architectural legacy.

Civil rights came to Charleston in earnest with a landmark suit to integrate the Charleston Municipal Golf Course in 1960. The biggest battle, however, would be the 100-day strike in 1969 against the Medical University of South Carolina—then, as now, a large employer of African Americans.

Charleston's next great renaissance—still ongoing today—came with the redevelopment of its downtown and the fostering of the tourism industry under the nearly 40-year tenure of Mayor Joe Riley, during which so much of the current visitor-friendly infrastructure became part of daily life here. Today, Charleston is completing the transition away from a military and manufacturing base, and by some measures is the nation's leader in tech startups, even ahead of Silicon Valley.

## PLANNING YOUR TIME

Even if you're just going to confine yourself to the peninsula, plan on spending at least **two nights** in Charleston. You'll want half a day for shopping on King Street and a full day for seeing various attractions and museums. Keep in mind that one of Charleston's key sights, Fort Sumter, takes almost half a day to see once you factor in ticketing and boarding time for the ferry out to the fort and back; plan accordingly.

If you have a car, there are several great places to visit off the peninsula, especially the three plantations along the Ashley—Drayton Hall, Magnolia Plantation, and Middleton Place—and Charles Towne Landing. They are all no more than 30 minutes from downtown, and because they're roughly adjacent, you can visit all of them in a single day if you get an early start. The sites and excellent down-home restaurants on Johns Island are about 45 minutes out of downtown.

## ORIENTATION

Charleston occupies a peninsula bordered by the Ashley River to the west and the Cooper River to the east, which "come together to form the Atlantic Ocean," according to the haughty phrase once taught to generations of Charleston schoolchildren. Although the lower tip of the peninsula actually points closer to southeast, that direction is regarded locally as due south, and anything toward the top of the peninsula is considered due north.

The peninsula is ringed by islands, many of which have become heavily populated suburbs. Clockwise from the top of the peninsula, they are: Daniel Island, Mount Pleasant, Isle of Palms, Sullivan's Island, Morris Island, Folly Island, and James Island. The resort island of Kiawah and the less-developed Edisto Island are farther south, down the coast.

Charleston is made up of many small neighborhoods, many of them quite old. The boundaries are confusing, so your best bet is to simply look at the street signs (signage in general is excellent in Charleston). If you're in a historic neighborhood, such as the French Quarter or Ansonborough, a smaller sign above the street name will indicate that.

Other key terms you'll hear are "the Crosstown," the portion of U.S. 17 that goes across the peninsula; "Savannah Highway," the portion of U.S. 17 that traverses "West Ashley," which is the suburb across the Ashley River; "East Cooper," the area across the Cooper River that includes Mount Pleasant, Isle of Palms, and Daniel and Sullivan's Islands; and "the Neck," up where the peninsula narrows. These are the terms that locals use, and hence what you'll see in this guide.

North Charleston is not only a separate municipality, it's also a different state of mind. A sprawling combination of malls, light industry, and low-income housing, it also boasts some of the more cutting-edge urban redesign activity in the area.

While Charlestonians would scoff, the truth is that Charleston proper has a surprising amount in common with Manhattan. Both are on long spits of land situated roughly north-south. Both were settled originally at the peninsula's lower end behind walled fortifications—Charleston's walls came down in 1718, while Manhattan still has its Wall Street as a reminder. Both cityscapes rely on age-old north-south streets that run nearly the whole length—Charleston's King and Meeting Streets, with only a block between them, and Manhattan's Broadway and Fifth Avenue. And like Manhattan, Charleston also has its own "Museum Mile" just off of a major green space, in Charleston's case up near Marion Square—though certainly its offerings are not as expansive as those a short walk from New York's Central Park.

Unfortunately, also like Manhattan, parking is at a premium in downtown Charleston. Luckily the city has many reasonably priced parking garages, which I recommend that you use. But cars should be used only when necessary. Charleston is best enjoyed on foot, both because of its small size and the cozy, meandering nature of its old streets, designed not for cars and tour buses but for boots, horseshoes, and carriage wheels.

# Sights

[illegible] tralized [illegible] leston [illegible] ves.

## TOURS

For more tour information in Charleston, visit the **Charleston Visitor Reception and Transportation Center** (375 Meeting St., 800/774-0006, www.charlestoncvb.com, Mon.-Fri. 8:30am-5:30pm), where they have entire walls of brochures for all the latest tours and an on-site staff of local tourism experts.

### Walking Tours

#### ED GRIMBALL'S WALKING TOURS

Since 1996, Ed Grimball's Walking Tours has run twice-weekly historical tours that take you through the heart of Charleston, courtesy of the knowledgeable and sprightly Ed himself, a native Charlestonian. All of Ed's popular walks start from the big Pineapple Fountain in Waterfront Park, and reservations are a must.

**MAP 1:** Waterfront Park, Concord St., 843/813-4447, www.edgrimballtours.com; $22 adults, $8 children

#### BULLDOG TOURS

Ghost tours are very popular in Charleston. Bulldog Tours has exclusive access to the Old City Jail, which features prominently in most of its tours. The most popular tour, the Haunted Jail Tour, leaves daily at 7pm, 8pm, 9pm, and 10pm; meet at the jail (21 Magazine St.) if you've purchased tickets online. Another option is the Ghosts and Dungeons tour (Mar.-Nov. Tues.-Sat. 7pm and 9pm). This company provides a wide variety of tours, so check the website for other options.

**MAP 1:** 18 Anson St., 843/722-8687, www.bulldogtours.com; $25 adults, $15 children

#### CHARLESTON STROLLS

Charleston Strolls is a popular tour featuring historical overview and tidbits. The two-hour tours leave twice daily from the Mills House Hotel. Advance reservations are strongly advised.

**MAP 1:** Mills House Hotel, 115 Meeting St., 843/722-8687, www.charlestonstrolls.com; daily 10am and 2pm; $25 adults, $15 children

### CHARLESTON FOOTPRINTS

Seventh-generation Charlestonian Michael Trouche leads these entertaining and popular two-hour tours. They leave every day at 10:30am and 2pm from the Historic Charleston Foundation Gift Shop across the street from the Mills House Hotel. These are a hot ticket and reservations are required; no walk-ups.

**MAP 1:** 108 Meeting St., 843/478-4718, www.charlestonfootprints.com; $20 pp

## Water Tours

### SANDLAPPER WATER TOURS

Sandlapper Water Tours offers many types of evening and dolphin cruises on a 45-foot catamaran. The company also offers Charleston's only waterborne ghost tour. Most of the tours leave from the Maritime Center near East Bay and Calhoun Streets.

**MAP 1:** Charleston Maritime Center, 10 Wharfside St., 843/849-8687, www.sandlappertours.com; Mar.-Aug.; $20-27

### SPIRITLINE CRUISES

The best all-around tour of Charleston Harbor is the 90-minute ride offered by Spiritline Cruises, which leaves from either Aquarium Wharf or Patriots Point. Allow about 30 minutes for ticketing and boarding. Spiritline also has a three-hour dinner cruise in the evening leaving from Patriots Point (about $50 pp) and a cruise to Fort Sumter. These are usually seasonal and begin in March each year and take a break for the winter.

**MAP 1:** Charleston Harbor, 800/789-3678, www.spiritlinecruises.com; $24 adults, $12 ages 4-11

## Foodie Tours

### CHARLESTON CULINARY TOURS

Charleston Culinary Tours offers a huge range of foodie-friendly tours, from their signature Downtown Charleston tour to an Oyster Tour to a Mixology tour, and more. These are walking tours that go rain or shine. Alcohol isn't included. Advance reservations are required; no walk-ups.

**MAP 1:** 5 Cumberland St., 843/259-2966, www.charlestonculinarytours.com; from $40 pp

## African American History Tours

### GULLAH TOURS

Alphonso Brown's Gullah Tours features stories told in the Gullah dialect. Tours run Monday-Saturday and leave from the bus shed at the Charleston Visitors Center.

**MAP 2:** Charleston Visitor Reception and Transportation Center, 375 Meeting St., 843/763-7551, www.gullahtours.com; Mon.-Sat. 11am and 1pm, $20

### SITES & INSIGHTS TOURS

Al Miller's Sites & Insights Tours has several packages, including a Black History and Porgy & Bess Tour as well as a good combo city and island tour, all departing from the visitors center.

**MAP 2:** Charleston Visitor Reception and Transportation Center, 375 Meeting St., 843/552-9995, www.sitesandinsightstours.com; tour times vary; $15-20

## Motorized Tours

### ADVENTURE SIGHTSEEING

Adventure Sightseeing offers several comfortable 1.5- to 2-hour rides, including the only motorized tour to the Citadel area, leaving at various times throughout the day.

**MAP 2:** Charleston Visitor Reception and Transportation Center, 375 Meeting St., 843/762-0088, www.adventuresightseeing.com; daily tour times vary; from $25 adults

### GRAY LINE OF CHARLESTON

The old faithful Gray Line of Charleston offers a good basic 90-minute Historic Charleston Tour. Tours depart from the visitors center every 30 minutes. Build combo tours as you like; consult their website. Hotel pickup is available by reservation. During the off-season, the last tour leaves at 2pm.

**MAP 2:** Charleston Visitor Reception and Transportation Center, 375 Meeting St., 843/722-4444, www.graylineofcharleston.com; Mar.-Nov. daily

## Carriage Tours

Tours leave from the Palmetto Carriage Barn in Charleston.

The city of Charleston strictly regulates the treatment and upkeep of carriage horses and mules as well as the allowed amount of carriage traffic. Only 20 carriages are allowed out on the streets at any one time, so occasionally yours will have to wait until another one returns.

There's not a lot of difference in service or price among the carriage companies, and that's chiefly by design. The city divides the tours into three routes, or "zones." Which zone your driver explores is determined by lottery at the embarkation point—you don't get to decide the zone and neither does your driver. Typically, rides take 1-1.5 hours and hover around $25 pp adults, about half that for children. The tours are, however, of uniformly high quality.

Tours sometimes book up early, so call ahead. The oldest and in my opinion best service in town is **Palmetto Carriage Works** (40 N. Market St., 843/723-8145, www.palmettocarriage.com), which offers free parking at its "red barn" base near City Market. Another popular tour is **Old South Carriage Company** (14 Anson St., 843/723-9712, www.oldsouthcarriage.com) with its Confederate-clad drivers. **Carolina Polo & Carriage Company** (16 Hayne St., 843/577-6767, www.cpcc.com) leaves from several spots, including the Doubletree Hotel and the company's Hayne Street stables.

9:30am-3pm, Dec.-Feb daily 9:30am-2pm; from $23 adults

## SOUTH OF BROAD

Wander among these narrow streets and marvel at the lovingly restored old homes, but keep in mind that almost everything down here is in private hands. Don't wander into a garden or take photos inside a window unless you're invited to do so.

### ★ THE BATTERY

For many, The Battery is the single most iconic Charleston spot, drenched in history and boasting dramatic views. South is the Cooper River, with views of Fort Sumter, Castle Pinckney, and Sullivan's Island; north is the old carrier *Yorktown* moored at Mount Pleasant; and landward is the adjoining peaceful **White Point Gardens,** the sumptuous mansions of the Battery.

If you had been one of the first European visitors to this tip of the peninsula about 400 years ago, you'd have seen how it got its first name, Oyster Point: This entire area was once home to an enormous outcropping of oysters. Their shells glistened bright white in the harsh Southern sun as a ship approached from sea, hence its subsequent name, White Point. Although the oysters are long gone and much of the area you're walking on is actually reclaimed marsh, the Battery and White Point Gardens are still a balm for the soul.

Once the bustling (and sometimes seedy) heart of Charleston's maritime activity, the Battery was where "the gentleman pirate" Stede Bonnet and 21 of his men were hanged in 1718. The area got its name for hosting cannons during the War of 1812, with the current distinctive seawall structure built in the 1850s.

Contrary to popular belief, no guns fired from here on Fort Sumter, as they would have been out of range. However, many inoperable cannons, mortars, and piles of shot still reside here, much to the delight of kids. This is where Charlestonians gathered in a giddy, party-like atmosphere to watch the shelling of Fort Sumter in 1861, blissfully ignorant of the horrors to come. A short time later, the North would return the favor as the Battery and all of Charleston up to Broad Street would bear the brunt of shelling during the long siege of the city (the rest was out of reach of Union guns).

Today, the Battery is a place to relax, not fight. There's usually plenty of free parking all along Battery Street. A promenade all around the periphery is a great place to stroll or jog. Add the calming, almost constant sea breeze and the meditative influence of the wide, blue Cooper River and you'll see why this land's end—once so martial in nature—is now a favorite place for after-church family gatherings, travelers, love-struck couples, and weddings (about 200 a year at the gazebo in White Point Gardens).

Still, military history is never far away in Charleston, and one of the chief landmarks

historic remnants at The Battery

at the Battery is the USS *Hobson* Memorial, which remembers the sacrifice of the men of that vessel when it sank after a collision with the carrier USS *Wasp* in 1952.

Look for the three-story private residence where East Battery curves northward. You won't be taking any tours of it, but you should be aware that it's the **DeSaussure House** (1 E. Battery St.), best known in Charleston history for hosting rowdy celebratory crowds on the roof and the piazzas to watch the 34-hour shelling of Fort Sumter in 1861.

**MAP 1:** S. Battery St. and Murray Blvd., 843/724-7321; daily 24 hours; free

## EDMONDSTON-ALSTON HOUSE

The most noteworthy attraction on the Battery is the 1825 Edmondston-Alston House, the only Battery home open to the public for tours. This is one of the most unique and well-preserved historic homes in the United States, thanks to the ongoing efforts of the Alston family, who acquired the house from shipping merchant Charles Edmondston

## One Day in Charleston

Enjoying the full breadth of Charleston's offerings is difficult to do in one day—but it is possible, thanks to the city's walkability and the relatively small scale of its historic downtown.

Start your morning in the bracing ocean breeze of **The Battery** overlooking Ft. Sumter and Charleston Harbor. Continue north on East Bay Street and enjoy the view of the quaint and colorful houses on **Rainbow Row.**

When you get to Broad Street, take the informative and fun tour of the **Old Exchange and Provost Dungeon,** which has hosted pirates and presidents alike, and which is usually considered South Carolina's most historic single building.

Head west a couple of blocks to enjoy brunch or an early lunch at **Poogan's Porch.** Work it off with some shopping on bustling **King Street,** or head straight for scenic **Marion Square** and arrive at Charleston's **"Museum Mile."** I suggest a tour of either the **Aiken-Rhett House** (my favorite) or the **Charleston Museum** for a more generally informative experience.

Now's the time to head west by car (either your own or via rideshare) to visit one of the historic plantation sites along the Ashley River. I suggest **Drayton Hall,** which is expertly curated by the National Trust for Historic Preservation.

If you're hungry, nearby you'll find the best barbecue in Charleston at **Fiery Ron's Home Team.** Be sure to order the brisket and a craft brew. Or you can head back over the river into downtown proper for a classic dinner at **FIG** or **McCrady's.**

after the Panic of 1837 and still live on the 3rd floor (tours only visit the first two stories).

Over 90 percent of the home's furnishings are original items from the Alston era. Originally built in the Federal style, second owner Charles Alston added several Greek Revival elements, notably the parapet, balcony, and piazza, from which General P. G. T. Beauregard watched the attack on Fort Sumter. Today, the house is owned and administered by the Middleton Place Foundation, best known for its stewardship of Middleton Place along the Ashley River.

**MAP 1:** 21 E. Battery St., 843/722-7171, www.middletonplace.org; Sun.-Mon. 1pm-4:30pm, Tues.-Sat. 10am-4:30pm; $12 adults, $8 students

### ★ RAINBOW ROW

One of the most photographed sights in the United States, Rainbow Row is nine pastel-colored mansions facing the Cooper River. The bright, historically accurate colors are one of the vestiges of Charleston's Caribbean heritage, a legacy of the English settlers from the colony of Barbados who were among the city's first citizens.

The homes are unusually old for this fire-, hurricane-, and earthquake-ravaged city, with most dating from 1730 to 1750. These houses were originally right on the Cooper River, their lower stories serving as storefronts on the wharf. The street was created later on top of landfill, or "made land" as it's called locally.

Rainbow Row is also of vital importance to American historic preservation. These were the first Charleston homes to be renovated and brought back from early-20th-century seediness. The restoration projects on Rainbow Row directly inspired the creation of the Preservation Society of Charleston, the first such group in the United States.

Continue walking up the High Battery past Rainbow Row and find Water Street. This aptly named little avenue was in fact a creek in the early days, acting as the southern border of the original walled city. The large brick building on the seaward side housing the Historic Charleston Foundation sits on the site of the old Granville bastion, a key defensive point in the wall.

**MAP 1:** 79-107 E. Bay St.

### NATHANIEL RUSSELL HOUSE

Considered one of Charleston's grandest homes despite being built by an outsider from Rhode

## Know Your Charleston Houses

Charleston's homes boast not only a long pedigree, but an interesting and unique one as well. Here are the basics of local architecture.

- **Single House:** Thus named for its single-room width. With full-length piazzas, or long verandas, on the south side to take advantage of breezes, the single house is perhaps the nation's first sustainable house design. The house is lengthwise on the lot, with the entrance on the side. This means the "backyard" is actually the side yard. Church Street has great examples, including 90, 92, and 94 Church Street, and the oldest single house in town, the 1730 Robert Brewton House (71 Church St.).
- **Double House:** This layout is two rooms wide with a central hallway and a porched facade facing the street. Double houses often had separate carriage houses. The Aiken-Rhett and Heyward-Washington Houses are good examples.
- **Charleston Green:** This uniquely Charlestonian color—extremely dark green that looks pitch black in low light—has its roots in the aftermath of the Civil War. The government distributed surplus black paint to contribute to the reconstruction of the ravaged peninsula, but Charlestonians were too proud to use it as-is. So they added a tiny bit of yellow, producing Charleston green.
- **Earthquake Bolt:** Due to structural damage after the 1886 earthquake, many buildings were retrofitted with one or more wall-to-wall iron rods to keep them stable. The rod was capped at both ends by a "gib plate," often disguised with a decorative element such as a lion's head, an S or X shape, or some other design. Notable examples are at 235 Meeting Street, 198 East Bay Street, 407 King Street, and 51 East Battery (a rare star design); 190 East Bay Street is unusual for having both an X and an S plate on the same building.
- **Joggling Board:** This long (10- to 15-foot) flexible plank of cypress, palm, or pine with a handle at each end served various recreational purposes. Babies were bounced to sleep, small children used it as a trampoline, and it was also a method of courtship. A couple would start out at opposite ends and bounce until they met in the middle.
- **Carolopolis Award:** The Preservation Society of Charleston hands out these badges, to be mounted near the doorway, to local homeowners who have renovated historic properties downtown. On the award is "Carolopolis," the Latinized name of the city; "Condita AD 1670," the Latin word for "founding" with the date of Charleston's inception; and the date the award was given.
- **Ironwork:** Wrought iron was a widely used ornament before the mid-1800s. Charleston's best-known blacksmith, Philip Simmons, worked in wrought iron. His masterpieces are visible most notably at the Philip Simmons Garden (91 Anson St.), a gate for the visitors center (375 Meeting St.), and the Philip Simmons Children's Garden at Josiah Smith Tennent House (Blake St. and E. Bay St.). Chevaux-de-frise are iron bars on top of a wall that project menacing spikes. They became popular after the Denmark Vesey slave revolt conspiracy of 1822. The best example is at the Miles Brewton House (27 King St.).

Island, the Nathaniel Russell House is now a National Historic Landmark and one of the country's best examples of neoclassicism. Built in 1808 by Nathaniel Russell, a.k.a. "King of the Yankees," the home is furnished as accurately as possible to represent not only the lifestyle of the Russell family, but also the 18 enslaved African Americans who shared the premises.

When you visit, keep in mind that you're in the epicenter of not only Charleston's historic preservation movement but perhaps the nation's as well. In 1955 the Nathaniel Russell House was the first major project of the Historic Charleston Foundation, which raised $65,000 to purchase it. For an extra $6, you can gain admission to the Aiken-Rhett

House farther uptown, also administered by the Historic Charleston Foundation.

**MAP 1:** 51 Meeting St., 843/724-8481, www.historiccharleston.org; daily 10am-5pm, last tour begins 4:30pm; $12 adults, $5 children

### CALHOUN MANSION

The single largest of Charleston's surviving grand homes, the 1876 Calhoun Mansion boasts 35 opulent rooms (with 23 fireplaces!) in a striking Italianate design taking up a whopping 24,000 square feet. The grounds feature some charming garden spaces. A 90-minute "grand tour" is available for $75 pp; call for an appointment. Though the interiors at this privately run house are packed with antiques and furnishings, not all of them are accurate for the period.

**MAP 1:** 16 Meeting St., 843/722-8205, www.calhounmansion.net; tours daily 11am-5pm; $17

### MILES BREWTON HOUSE

A short distance from the Nathaniel Russell House but much less viewed by visitors, the circa-1769 Miles Brewton House, now a private residence, is maybe the best example of Georgian-Palladian architecture in the world. The almost medieval wrought-iron fencing, or chevaux-de-frise, was added in 1822 after rumors of a slave uprising spread through town. This imposing double house was the site of not one but two headquarters of occupying armies, that of British general Henry Clinton in the Revolution and the federal garrison after the end of the Civil War. The great Susan Pringle Frost, principal founder of the Preservation Society of Charleston and a Brewton descendant, grew up here.

**MAP 1:** 27 King St.

### HEYWARD-WASHINGTON HOUSE

The Heyward-Washington House takes the regional practice of naming a historic home for the two most significant names in its pedigree to its logical extreme. Built in 1772 by the father of Declaration of Independence signer Thomas Heyward Jr., the house also hosted George Washington during the president's visit to Charleston in 1791. It's now owned and operated by the Charleston Museum. The main attraction at the Heyward-Washington House is its masterful woodwork, exemplified by the cabinetry of legendary Charleston carpenter Thomas Elfe.

**MAP 1:** 87 Church St., 843/722-0354, www.charlestonmuseum.org; Mon.-Sat. 9am-5pm, Sun. noon-5pm; $12 adults, $5 children, combo tickets to Charleston Museum and Manigault House available

### CABBAGE ROW

You'll recognize the addresses that make up Cabbage Row as "Catfish Row" from Gershwin's opera *Porgy and Bess* (based on the book *Porgy* by the Charleston author DuBose Heyward, who lived at 76 Church St.). Today this complex—which once housed 10 families—is certainly upgraded from years past, but the row still has the humble appeal of the tenement housing it once was, primarily for formerly enslaved African Americans after the Civil War. The house nearby at 94 Church Street was where John C. Calhoun and others drew up the infamous Nullification Acts that eventually led to the South's secession.

**MAP 1:** 89-91 Church St.

### ST. MICHAEL'S EPISCOPAL CHURCH

The oldest church in South Carolina, St. Michael's Episcopal Church is actually the second sanctuary built on this spot, the first being St. Philip's, which was rebuilt on Church Street. As a response to the overflowing congregation at the new St. Philip's, St. Michael's was built from 1752 to 1761, in the style of Christopher Wren. Other than a small addition on the southeast corner in 1883, the St. Michael's you see today is unchanged, including the massive pulpit, outsized in the style of the time.

Services here over the years hosted such luminaries as the Marquis de Lafayette, George Washington, and Robert E. Lee, the latter two of whom are known to have sat in the "governor's pew." Two signers of the U.S. Constitution, John Rutledge and Charles

Cotesworth Pinckney, are buried in the sanctuary.

St. Michael's offers free, informal tours after Sunday services; contact the greeter for more information.

**MAP 1:** 71 Broad St., 843/723-0603; services Sun. 8am and 10:30am, tours available after services

### FOUR CORNERS OF LAW

The famous intersection of Broad and Meeting Streets, named the Four Corners of Law for its confluence of federal law (the post office building), state law (the state courthouse), municipal law (city hall), and God's law (St. Michael's Episcopal Church), has been key to Charleston from the beginning. Meeting Street was laid out around 1672 and takes its name from the White Meeting House of early Dissenters, meaning non-Anglicans. Broad Street was also referred to as Cooper Street in the early days. Right in the middle of the street once stood the very first statue in the United States, a figure of William Pitt erected in 1766.

**MAP 1:** Broad St. and Meeting St.

## WATERFRONT

### THE OLD EXCHANGE AND PROVOST DUNGEON

The Old Exchange and Provost Dungeon is brimming with history. The last building erected by the British before the American Revolution, it's also one of the three most historically significant colonial buildings in the United States, along with Philadelphia's Independence Hall and Boston's Faneuil Hall.

This is actually the former Royal Exchange and Custom House, the cellar of which served as a British prison. The complex was built in 1771 over a portion of the original 1698 seawall, some of which you can see today during the short but fascinating tour of the "dungeon" (actually built as a warehouse). Three of Charleston's four signers of the Declaration of Independence did time downstairs for sedition against the crown. Later, happier times were experienced in the ballroom upstairs, as it was here that the state selected its delegates to the Continental Congress and ratified the U.S. Constitution; it's also where George Washington took a spin on the dance floor during his raucous "Farewell Tour" in 1791.

While the highlight for most is the basement dungeon, or provost, where the infamous "gentleman pirate" Stede Bonnet was imprisoned in 1718 before being hanged, visitors shouldn't miss the sunny upstairs ballroom and its selection of Washington-oriented history.

**MAP 1:** 122 E. Bay St., 843/727-2165, www.oldexchange.com; daily 9am-5pm; $10 adults, $5 children and students

### WATERFRONT PARK

Dubbing it "this generation's gift to the future," Mayor Joe Riley made this eight-acre project another part of his downtown renovation. Situated on Concord Street roughly between Exchange Street and Vendue Range, Waterfront Park was, like many waterfront locales in Charleston, built on what used to be marsh and water. This particularly massive chunk of "made land" juts about a football field's length farther out than the old waterline. Children will enjoy the large "Vendue" wading fountain at the park's entrance off Vendue Range, while a bit farther south is the large and quite artful Pineapple Fountain with its surrounding wading pool. Contemporary art lovers of all ages will appreciate the nearby **Waterfront Park City Gallery** (34 Prioleau St., www.citygalleryatwaterfrontpark.com, Tues.-Fri. 10am-6pm, Sat.-Sun. noon-5pm, free).

**MAP 1:** Concord St., 843/724-7327; daily dawn-dusk; free

### ★ SOUTH CAROLINA AQUARIUM

The South Carolina Aquarium is a great place for the whole family to have some fun while getting educated about the rich aquatic life off the coast and throughout this small but ecologically diverse state.

When you enter you're greeted with the 15,000-gallon Carolina Seas tank, with placid

## The Great Charleston Earthquake

earthquake bolts on a building in Charleston

The Charleston peninsula is bordered by three faults: the Woodstock Fault above North Charleston, the Charleston Fault running along the east bank of the Cooper River, and the Ashley Fault to the west of the Ashley River. On August 31, 1886, one of them buckled, causing one of the most damaging earthquakes ever to hit the United States.

The earthquake of 1886 was signaled by foreshocks earlier that week, but Charlestonians remained unconcerned. Then, that Tuesday at 9:50pm, came the big one. With an epicenter somewhere near the Middleton Place Plantation, the Charleston earthquake is estimated to have measured about 7 on the Richter scale. Tremors were felt across half the country, with the ground shaking in Chicago and a church damaged in Indianapolis. A dam 120 miles away in Aiken gave way, washing a train off the tracks. Cracks opened up parallel to the Ashley River, with part of the riverbank falling into the water. Thousands of chimneys all over the state fell or were rendered useless. The quake brought a series of "sand blows," a phenomenon where craters open and spew sand and water into the air. In Charleston's case, some of the craters were 20 feet wide, shooting debris another 20 feet into the air. The whole event lasted less than a minute.

In crowded Charleston, the damage was horrific: over 2,000 buildings destroyed, a quarter of the city's value gone, 27 killed immediately and almost 100 more to die from injuries and disease. Because of the large numbers of newly homeless, tent cities sprang up in every available park and green space. The American Red Cross's first field mission soon brought some relief, but the scarcity of food and especially freshwater made life difficult.

Almost every surviving building had experienced structural damage, in some cases severe. This led to the widespread use of the "earthquake bolt" now seen throughout older Charleston homes. Essentially acting as a very long screw with a washer on each end, the idea of the earthquake bolt is simple: Poke a long iron rod through two walls that need stabilizing, and cap the ends. Charleston being Charleston, the caps were often decorated with a pattern or symbol.

The seismic activity of Charleston's earthquake was so intense that more than 300 aftershocks occurred in the 35 years after the event. Geologists think that most seismic events measured in the region today are probably also aftershocks.

## Mayor Joe's Legacy

Few cities anywhere have been as greatly influenced by one mayor as Charleston has by Joseph P. "Joe" Riley, who finally declined to run for reelection in 2015 after his 10th four-year term. "Mayor Joe," or just "Joe," as he's usually called, is not only responsible for the majority of redevelopment in the city; he also set the bar for its award-winning tourism industry.

Riley won his first mayoral race at the age of 32, the second Irish American mayor of the city. The lawyer, Citadel grad, and former member of the state legislature had a clear vision for his administration: to bring unprecedented numbers of women and minorities into city government, rejuvenate then-seedy King Street, and enlarge the city's tax base by annexing surrounding areas (during Riley's tenure the city grew from 16.7 square miles to over 100).

Here's only a partial list of the major projects and events Mayor Joe has made happen in Charleston:

- Charleston Maritime Center
- Charleston Place
- Children's Museum of the Lowcountry
- Hampton Park rehabilitation
- King Street-Market Street retail district
- Joseph P. Riley Jr. Park (named after the mayor at the insistence of city council)
- MOJA Arts Festival
- Piccolo Spoleto
- South Carolina Aquarium
- Spoleto USA
- Waterfront Park
- West Ashley Bikeway & Greenway

nurse sharks and vicious-looking moray eels. Other exhibits highlight the five key South Carolina ecosystems: beach, salt marsh, coastal plain, piedmont, and mountain forest. Another neat display is the Touch Tank, a hands-on collection of invertebrates found along the coast, such as sea urchins and horseshoe crabs. The pièce de résistance, however, is the three-story Great Ocean Tank with its hundreds of deeper-water marine creatures, including sharks, puffer fish, and sea turtles.

A key part of the aquarium's research and outreach efforts is the Turtle Hospital, which, in partnership with the state of South Carolina, attempts to rehabilitate and save sick and injured specimens. The hospital has saved many sea turtles, the first one being a 270-pound female affectionately known as "Edisto Mama." Tour the hospital or visit the interactive Sea Turtle Recovery exhibit to learn more about these efforts.

**MAP 1:** 100 Aquarium Wharf, 843/720-1990, www.scaquarium.org; Mar.-Aug. daily 9am-5pm, Sept.-Feb. daily 9am-4pm; $30 adults, $23 children, 4-D film extra, combo tickets with Fort Sumter tour available

### ★ FORT SUMTER NATIONAL MONUMENT

This is the place that brought about the beginning of the Civil War, a Troy for modern times. Though many historians insist the war would have happened regardless of President Lincoln's decision to keep Fort Sumter in federal hands, the stated casus belli was Major Robert Anderson's refusal to surrender the fort when requested to do so in the early-morning hours of April 12, 1861. A few hours later came the first shot of the war, fired from Fort Johnson by Confederate captain George James. That 10-inch mortar shell, a signal for the general bombardment to begin, exploded above Fort Sumter. The first return shot from Fort Sumter was fired by none other than Captain Abner Doubleday, the man once credited as the father of baseball. Today the battered but still-standing Fort Sumter remains astride the entrance to Charleston Harbor on an artificial 70,000-ton sandbar, being part of the Third System of fortifications ordered after the War of 1812.

You can only visit by boats run by the approved concessionaire **Fort Sumter Tours** (843/881-7337, www.fortsumtertours.com, $21 adults, $13 ages 6-11, $18.50 seniors). Once at the fort, there's no charge for admission. Ferries leave from Liberty Square at Aquarium Wharf on the peninsula three times a day during the high season (Apr.-Oct.); call or check the website for times. Make sure to arrive about 30 minutes before the ferry departs. You can also get to Fort Sumter by ferry from Patriots Point at Mount Pleasant through the same concessionaire.

Budget at least 2.5 hours for the whole trip, including an hour at Fort Sumter. At Liberty Square on the peninsula is the **Fort Sumter Visitor Education Center** (340 Concord St., www.nps.gov/fosu, daily 8:30am-5pm, free), so you can learn more about where you're about to go. Once at the fort, you can be enlightened by the regular ranger talks on the fort's history and construction (generally at 11am and 2:30pm), take in the interpretive exhibits throughout the site, and enjoy the view of the spires of the Holy City from afar. For many, the highlight is the boat trip itself, with beautiful views of Charleston Harbor and the islands of the Cooper River estuary.

Some visitors are disappointed to find many of the fort's gun embrasures bricked over. This was done during the Spanish-American War, when the old fort was turned into an earthwork and the newer Battery Huger (huge-EE) was built on top of it.

**MAP 1:** 843/883-3123, www.nps.gov/fosu; hours seasonal; fort admission free, ferry transportation extra

Catch the ferry at Fort Sumter Visitor Education Center.

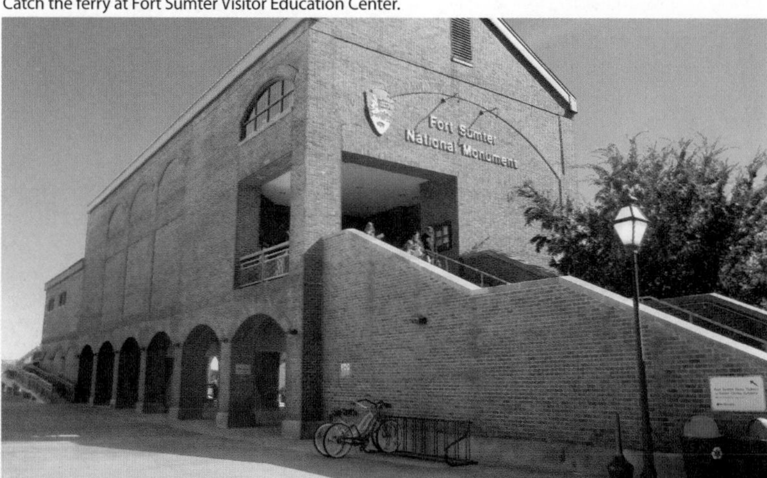

# FRENCH QUARTER

## ★ ST. PHILIP'S EPISCOPAL CHURCH

With a pedigree dating back to the colony's fledgling years, St. Philip's Episcopal Church is the oldest Anglican congregation south of Virginia. The first St. Philip's was built in 1680 at the corner of Meeting Street and Broad Street, the present site of St. Michael's Episcopal Church. It was badly damaged by a hurricane in 1710, so the city fathers approved the building of a new sanctuary dedicated to the saint on Church Street. Alas, the second St. Philip's burned to the ground in 1835. Construction immediately began on a replacement, and it's that building you see today. Heavily damaged by Hurricane Hugo in 1989, a $4.5 million renovation kept the church usable.

South Carolina's great statesman John C. Calhoun—who ironically despised Charlestonians for what he saw as their loose morals—was originally buried across Church Street in the former "stranger's churchyard," or West Cemetery, after his death in 1850. (Charles Pinckney and Edward Rutledge are two other notable South Carolinians buried here.) But near the end of the Civil War, Calhoun's body was moved to an unmarked grave closer to the sanctuary in an attempt to hide its location from Union troops.

**MAP 1:** 142 Church St., 843/722-7734, www.stphilipschurchsc.org; sanctuary Mon.-Fri. 10am-noon and 2pm-4pm, services Sun. 8:15am

## CIRCULAR CONGREGATIONAL CHURCH

The historic Circular Congregational Church has one of the most interesting pedigrees of any house of worship in Charleston. Services were originally held on the site of the "White Meeting House," for which Meeting Street is named; they were moved here beginning in 1681 and catered to a polyglot mix of Congregationalists, Presbyterians, and Huguenots. For that reason it was often called the Church of Dissenters ("dissenter" being the common term at the time for anyone not an Anglican). As with many structures in town, the 1886 earthquake necessitated a rebuild, and the current edifice dates from 1891.

**MAP 1:** 150 Meeting St., 843/577-6400, www.circularchurch.org; tours Mon.-Fri. 10:30am, services fall-spring Sun. 11am, summer Sun. 10:15am

## FRENCH HUGUENOT CHURCH

One of the oldest congregations in town, the French Huguenot Church also has the

St. Philip's Episcopal Church

distinction of being the only remaining independent Huguenot church in the country. Founded around 1681 by French Calvinists, the church had about 450 congregants by 1700. The original sanctuary was built in 1687, but was deliberately destroyed as a firebreak during the great conflagration of 1796. The church was replaced in 1800, but that building was in turn demolished in favor of the picturesque stucco-coated Gothic Revival sanctuary you see today, which was completed in 1845. Sunday services are conducted in English now, but a single annual service in French is still celebrated in April.

**MAP 1:** 44 Queen St., 843/722-4385, www.frenchhuguenotchurch.org; liturgy Sun. 10:30am

### DOCK STREET THEATRE

Any thespian or lover of the stage must pay homage to the first theater built in North America, the Dock Street Theatre. The original 1736 Dock Street Theatre burned down, but a second theater opened on the same site in 1754. That building was in turn demolished for a grander edifice in 1773, which, you guessed it, also burned down. The current building dates from 1809, when the Planter's Hotel was built near the site of the original Dock Street Theatre. To mark the theater's centennial, the hotel added a stage facility in 1835, and it's that building you see now.

In addition to a very active and well-regarded annual season from the resident Charleston Stage Company, the 464-seat venue has hosted umpteen events of the Spoleto Festival over the past three decades and continues to do so. The wonderfully restored interior is worth checking out whether or not you come see a show; just go into the lobby during daytime hours and ask to have a look around.

**MAP 1:** 135 Church St., 843/720-3968, www.charlestonstage.com; box office Mon.-Fri. 1pm-5pm, tickets $63-67

### OLD POWDER MAGAZINE

The Old Powder Magazine may be small, but the building is quite historically significant. The 1713 edifice is the oldest public building in South Carolina and the only one remaining from the days of the Lords Proprietors. As the name indicates, this was where the city's gunpowder was stored during the Revolution. The magazine is designed to implode rather than explode in the event of a direct hit. This is another labor of love of the Historic Charleston Foundation, which has leased the building from The Colonial Dames since 1993. It was opened to the public as an attraction in 1997. Next door is the privately owned, circa-1709 **Trott's Cottage,** the first brick dwelling in Charleston.

**MAP 1:** 79 Cumberland St., 843/722-9350, www.powdermag.org; Mon.-Sat. 10am-4pm, Sun. 1pm-4pm; $6 adults, $3 children

### OLD SLAVE MART MUSEUM

Slave auctions became big business in the South after 1808, when the United States banned the importation of enslaved people, thus increasing both price and demand. The auctions generally took place in public buildings where everyone could watch the wrenching spectacle. In the 1850s, public auctions in Charleston were put to a stop when city leaders discovered that visitors from European nations—all of which had banned slavery years before—were horrified at the practice. The slave trade was moved indoors to "marts" near the waterfront, where sales could be conducted out of the public eye. The last remaining such structure is the Old Slave Mart Museum. Built in 1859, its last auction was held in November 1863. There are two main areas: the orientation area, where visitors learn about the transatlantic slave trade and the architectural history of the building itself, and the main exhibit area, where visitors can see documents, tools, and displays recreating what happened inside during this sordid chapter in local history and celebrating the resilience of the area's African American population.

**MAP 1:** 6 Chalmers St., 843/958-6467, www.oldslavemart.org; Mon.-Sat. 9am-5pm; $8 adults, $5 children, free under age 6

## French Huguenots

the French Huguenot Church

A visitor can't spend a few hours in Charleston without coming across many French-sounding names. Some are common surnames, such as Ravenel, Manigault (MAN-i-go), Gaillard, Laurens, or Huger (huge-EE). Some are street or place names, such as Mazyck or Legare (le-GREE). The Gallic influence in Charleston was of the Calvinist Protestant variety. Known as Huguenots, these French immigrants—refugees from an increasingly intolerant Catholic regime in France—were numerous enough in the settlement by the 1690s that they were granted full citizenship and property rights if they swore allegiance to the British crown.

Unlike other colonies, Carolina never put much of a premium on religious conformity, a trait that exists to this day despite the area's overall conservatism. And unlike many who fled European monarchies to come to the New World, the French Huguenots were far from poverty-stricken. Most arrived already well educated and skilled in one or more useful trades. In Charleston's early days, they were mostly farmers or tar burners (makers of tar and pitch for maritime use). Their pragmatism and work ethic would lead them to higher positions in local society, such as lawyers, judges, and politicians. One of the wealthiest Charlestonians, the merchant Gabriel Manigault, was by some accounts the richest person in the American colonies during the early 1700s. South Carolina's most famous French Huguenot was Francis Marion, the "Swamp Fox" of Revolutionary War fame. Born on the Santee River, Marion grew up in Georgetown and is now interred near Moncks Corner.

The library of the **Huguenot Society of Carolina** (138 Logan St., 843/723-3235, www.huguenotsociety.org, Mon.-Fri. 9am-2pm) is a great research tool for anyone interested in French Protestant history and genealogy.

To this day, the spiritual home of Charleston's Huguenots is the same as always: the French Huguenot Church on Church Street, one of the earliest congregations in the city. The church still holds a liturgy in French every April.

## NORTH OF BROAD

### CONFEDERATE MUSEUM

Located on the 2nd floor of City Market's iconic main building, Market Hall on Meeting Street, the small Confederate Museum hosts an interesting collection of Civil War memorabilia, with an emphasis on the military side, and is the local headquarters of the United Daughters of the Confederacy. Perhaps its best contribution, however, is its research library.

**MAP 1:** 188 Meeting St., 843/723-1541, www.confederatemuseumcharlestonsc.com; Tues.-Sat. 11am-3:30pm; $5 adults, $3 children, cash only

### GIBBES MUSEUM OF ART

The Gibbes Museum of Art is one of those rare Southern museums that manages a good blend of the modern and the traditional, the local and the international. Their permanent collection spans a wide range of Southern art from the colonial era on, and they arguably have the most distinctive collection of portrait miniatures in the nation. Begun in 1905 as the Gibbes Art Gallery—the final wish of James Shoolbred Gibbes, who willed $100,000 for its construction—the complex has grown through the years in size and influence. The Gibbes Art School in the early 20th century formed a close association with the Woodstock School in New York, bringing important ties and prestige to the fledgling institution. Georgia O'Keeffe brought an exhibit here in 1955.

**MAP 1:** 135 Meeting St., 843/722-2706, www.gibbesmuseum.org; Tues. and Thurs.-Sat. 10am-5pm, Wed. 10am-8pm, Sun. 1pm-5pm, $15 adults, $10 students, $6 ages 4-17

### KAHAL KADOSH BETH ELOHIM REFORM TEMPLE

The birthplace of Reform Judaism in the United States and the oldest continuously active synagogue in the nation is Kahal Kadosh Beth Elohim Reform Temple. The congregation—*Kahal Kadosh* means "holy community" in Hebrew—was founded in 1749, with the current temple dating from 1840 and built in the Greek Revival style. The temple's Reform roots came about indirectly because of the great fire of 1838. In rebuilding, some congregants wanted to bring an organ into the temple, and the Orthodox contingent lost the debate. So the new building became the first home of Reform Judaism in the country, a fitting testament to Charleston's long-standing ecumenical spirit of religious tolerance and inclusiveness.

**MAP 1:** 90 Hasell St., 843/723-1090, www.kkbe.org; services Sat. 11am, tours Mon.-Fri. 10am-noon, Sun. 10am-4pm

### OLD CITY JAIL

If you were to make a movie called *Dracula Meets the Lord of the Rings*, the imposing Old City Jail might make a great set. Its history is also the stuff from which movies are made. Built in 1802 on a lot set aside for public use since 1680, the edifice was the Charleston County lockup until 1939. Some of the last pirates were jailed here in 1822 while awaiting hanging, as was slave rebellion leader Denmark Vesey. During the Civil War, prisoners of both armies were held here at various times.

The only way to tour the Old Jail is through **Bulldog Tours** (18 Anson St., 843/722-8687, www.bulldogtours.com). Their Haunted Jail Tour ($20 adults, $10 children) starts daily at 7pm, 8pm, 9pm, and 10pm.

**MAP 1:** 21 Magazine St., 843/577-5245

### OLD CITY MARKET

Part kitschy tourist trap, part glimpse into the Old South, part community gathering place, Old City Market remains Charleston's most reliable attraction. It is certainly the practical center of the city's tourist trade, not least because so many tours originate nearby. No matter what anyone tries to tell you, Charleston's City Market never hosted a single slave auction. When the Pinckney family donated this land to the city for a "Publick Market," one stipulation was that no enslaved people were ever to be sold here—or else the property would immediately revert to the family's descendants. A recent multimillion-dollar

## The New Charleston Green

Most people know "Charleston green" as a unique local color, the result of adding a few drops of yellow to post-Civil War surplus black paint. But these days the phrase also refers to environmentally friendly development in Charleston.

The most obvious example is the ambitious Navy Yard redevelopment, which seeks to repurpose the closed-down facility. From its inception in 1902 at the command of President Theodore Roosevelt through the end of the Cold War, the Charleston Navy Yard was one of the city's biggest employers. Though the yard was closed in 1995, a 340-acre section now hosts an intriguing mix of green-friendly design firms, small nonprofits, and commercial maritime companies. Clemson University—with the help of a massive federal grant, the largest in the school's history—will oversee one of the world's largest wind turbine research facilities, centered on Building 69.

Also in North Charleston, local retail chain Half Moon Outfitters has a green-friendly warehouse facility in an old grocery store. The first LEED (Leadership in Energy and Environmental Design) Platinum-certified building in South Carolina, the warehouse features solar panels, rainwater reservoirs, and locally harvested or salvaged interiors. There's also the LEED-certified North Charleston Elementary School as well as North Charleston's adoption of a "dark skies" ordinance to cut down on light pollution. On the peninsula, the historic meetinghouse of the Circular Congregational Church has a green addition with geothermal heating and cooling, rainwater cisterns, and Charleston's first vegetative roof.

For many Charlestonians, the green movement manifests in simpler things: the pedestrian and bike lanes on the Ravenel Bridge, the thriving city recycling program, and the Sustainable Seafood Initiative, a partnership of local restaurants, universities, and conservation groups that brings the freshest, most environmentally responsible dishes to your table when you dine out in Charleston.

This forward-thinking mode doesn't just mean enhanced quality of life for Charleston residents. It also pays off in attracting tech businesses and other cutting-edge employers, and the well-educated millennial knowledge workers who founded and staff them.

Charleston's tech economy is among the fastest growing in the nation, 26 percent faster than the national average, faster even than Austin, Texas, and Raleigh-Durham, North Carolina. Nearly 100 firms are part of the public-private **Charleston Digital Corridor** (www.charlestondigitalcorridor.com). The growth has garnered so much attention that some are using the nickname "Silicon Harbor" for the Charleston region.

renovation has prettified the bulk of City Market into more of a big-city air-conditioned pedestrian shopping mall. It's not as shabbily charming as it once was, but it certainly offers a more comfortable stroll during the warmer months.

**MAP 1:** Meeting St. and Market St., 843/973-7236; daily 6am-11:30pm

### PHILIP SIMMONS GARDEN

Charleston's most beloved artisan is the late Philip Simmons. Born on nearby Daniel Island in 1912, Simmons became one of the most sought-after decorative ironworkers in the United States. In 1982 the National Endowment for the Arts awarded him its National Heritage Fellowship. His work is on display at the Smithsonian Institution and the Museum of International Folk Art in Santa Fe, New Mexico, among many other places. In 1989, the congregation at Simmons's St. John's Reformed Episcopal Church voted to make the church garden a commemoration of the life and work of this legendary African American artisan, who died in 2009 at age 97. Completed in two phases, the Bell Garden and the Heart Garden, the project is a delightful blend of Simmons's signature graceful, sinuous style and fragrant flowers.

**MAP 1:** 91 Anson St., 843/722-4241, http://philipsimmons.us

the deliberately overgrown Unitarian Church cemetery

TOP EXPERIENCE

### UNITARIAN CHURCH

In a town filled with cool old church cemeteries, the coolest belongs to the Unitarian Church. As a nod to the beauty and power of nature, vegetation and shrubbery in the cemetery have been allowed to take their natural course (walkways excepted).

The church itself—the second-oldest such edifice in Charleston and the oldest Unitarian sanctuary in the South—was built in 1776 because of overcrowding at the Circular Congregational Church, but the building saw rough usage by British troops during the Revolution. Repairs were made in 1787 and an extensive modernization took place in 1852. Sadly, the 1886 earthquake toppled the original tower, and the version you see today is a subsequent and less grand design.

To see the sanctuary at times other than weekend mornings, go by the office next door Monday-Friday 9am-2pm and they'll let you take a walk through the interior.

**MAP 1:** 4 Archdale St., 843/723-4617, www.charlestonuu.org; services Sun. 11am, free tours Sat. 10am-1pm

### WILLIAM RHETT HOUSE

The oldest standing residence in Charleston is the circa-1713 William Rhett House, which once belonged to the colonel who captured the pirate Stede Bonnet. It's now a private residence, but you can admire this excellent prototypical example of a Charleston single house easily from the street and read the nearby historical marker.

**MAP 1:** 54 Hasell St.

## UPPER KING

### MARION SQUARE

While the Citadel moved lock, stock, and barrel almost a century ago, the college's old home, the South Carolina State Arsenal, still overlooks 6.5-acre **Marion Square** (between King St. and Meeting St. at Calhoun St., 843/965-4104, daily dawn-dusk), a reminder of the days when this was the institute's parade ground, the "Citadel Green" (the old Citadel is now a hotel). Marion Square is named for the "Swamp Fox" himself, Revolutionary War hero and father of modern guerrilla warfare Francis Marion. Marion Square hosts many events, including a farmers market every Saturday early April-late November.

**MAP 2:** between King St. and Meeting St. at Calhoun St., 843/965-4104; daily dawn-dusk

### COLLEGE OF CHARLESTON

The oldest college in South Carolina and the first municipal college in the country, the College of Charleston represents a chunk of the city's history, but its 12,000-plus students bring a modern, youthful touch to many of the city's public activities. Though the college has its share of modernistic buildings, a stroll around the gorgeous campus will uncover some historic gems. The oldest building on campus, the Bishop Robert Smith House, dates from the year of the college's founding, 1770, and is now the president's house; find it on Glebe Street between Wentworth and

George. Movies that have had scenes shot on campus include *Cold Mountain, The Patriot,* and *The Notebook*. If you have an iPhone, you can download a neat self-guided tour, complete with video, from the iTunes App Store (www.apple.com, search "College of Charleston Tour," free).

**MAP 2:** 66 George St., 843/805-5507, www.cofc.edu

### EMANUEL AFRICAN METHODIST EPISCOPAL CHURCH

Known simply as "Mother Emanuel," Emanuel African Methodist Episcopal Church has a distinguished history as one of the South's oldest African American congregations. Prior to the Civil War, one of the church's founders, Denmark Vesey, was implicated in planning a slave uprising. The edifice was burned as retaliation for Vesey's involvement (and the founding of the Citadel as a military academy nearby was directly related to white unrest over the plot). In the wake of the Nat Turner revolt in 1834, open worship by African Americans was outlawed in Charleston and went underground until after the Civil War. The congregation adopted the "Emanuel" name with the building of a new church in 1872, a wooden structure that unfortunately didn't survive the great earthquake of 1886. The simple, elegant, and deceptively large church you see today dates from 1891, and has hosted luminaries such as Booker T. Washington, Martin Luther King Jr., and Coretta Scott King. In 2015, the historically black church was the site of the horrific murders of nine worshippers—including its pastor, Clementa Pinckney—by a white racist. At Pinckney's memorial service, President Barack Obama spoke and led the congregation in singing *Amazing Grace*.

**MAP 2:** 110 Calhoun St., www.emanuelamechurch.org; services Sun. 9:30am

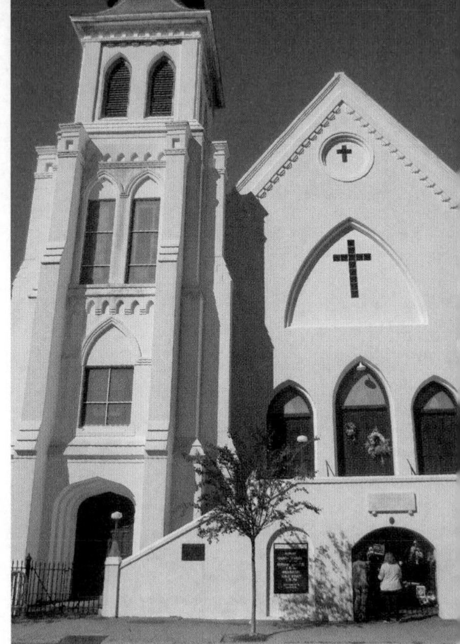

the Emanuel AME Church

### CHARLESTON MUSEUM

During its long history, the Charleston Museum has moved literally all over town. It's currently housed in a noticeably modern building, but make no mistake: This is the nation's oldest museum, founded in 1773. It strives to stay as fresh and relevant as any new museum, with a rotating schedule of special exhibits in addition to its very eclectic permanent collection. For a long time this was the only place to get a glimpse of the CSS *Hunley,* albeit just a fanciful replica in front of the main entrance. (Now you can see the real thing at its conservation site in North Charleston, and it's even smaller than the replica would indicate.)

Much of the museum's collection focuses on aspects of everyday life of Charlestonians, from the aristocracy to enslaved people, including items such as utensils, clothing, and furniture. There are quirks as well, such as the Egyptian mummy and the fine fan made out of turkey feathers. A particular and possibly surprising specialty includes work and research by noted regional naturalists like John James Audubon, André Michaux, and Mark Catesby. There are also numerous exhibits chronicling the local history of Native Americans and African Americans.

**MAP 2:** 360 Meeting St., 843/722-2996, www.charlestonmuseum.org; Mon.-Sat. 9am-5pm, Sun. noon-5pm; $12 adults, $5 children, combo tickets to Heyward-Washington and Manigault Houses available

## JOSEPH MANIGAULT HOUSE

Owned and operated by the nearby Charleston Museum, the Joseph Manigault House is sometimes called the "Huguenot House." This grand circa-1803 National Historic Landmark was designed by wealthy merchant Gabriel Manigault for his brother, Joseph, a rice planter of local repute. The three-story brick town house is a great example of Adams, or Federal, architecture. Each December, the Manigault House offers visitors a special treat, as the Garden Club of Charleston decorates it in period seasonal fashion, using only flowers that would have been used in the 19th century.

**MAP 2:** 350 Meeting St., 843/723-2926, www.charlestonmuseum.org; Mon.-Sat. 10am-5pm, Sun. noon-5pm, last tour 4:30pm; $12 adults, $5 children, combo tickets to Charleston Museum and Heyward-Washington House available

## ★ AIKEN-RHETT HOUSE

An acquisition of the Historic Charleston Foundation, the Aiken-Rhett House shows another side of the organization's mission. Whereas the Historic Charleston-run Nathaniel Russell House seeks to recreate a specific point in time, work at the Aiken-Rhett House emphasizes conservation and research. Built in 1818 and expanded by South Carolina governor William Aiken Jr., after whom we know the house today, parts of this rambling, almost Dickensian house remained sealed from 1918 until 1975, when the family relinquished the property to the Charleston Museum. While the docents are friendly and helpful, the main way to enjoy the Aiken-Rhett House is by way of a self-guided MP3 player audio tour, which is unique in Charleston.

**MAP 2:** 48 Elizabeth St., 843/723-1159, www.historiccharleston.org; daily 10am-5pm, last tour 4:15pm; $12 adults, $5 children

## CHILDREN'S MUSEUM OF THE LOWCOUNTRY

Another example of Charleston's savvy regarding the tourist industry is the Children's Museum of the Lowcountry. Recognizing that historic homes and Civil War memorabilia aren't enough to keep a family with young children in town for long, the city established this museum in 2005 specifically to give families with kids ages 3 months to

the Aiken-Rhett House

12 years a reason to spend more time (and money) downtown.

**MAP 2:** 25 Ann St., 843/853-8962, www.explorecml.org; Tues.-Sat. 9am-5pm, Sun. noon-5pm; $12 non-SC residents, $10 SC residents

### OLD BETHEL UNITED METHODIST CHURCH

The history of the Old Bethel United Methodist Church, the third-oldest church building in Charleston, is a little confusing. Completed in 1807, the church once stood across Calhoun Street until a schism formed in the church community over whether black parishioners should be limited to sitting in the galleries (in those days in the South, all races attended church together far more frequently than during the Jim Crow era). The entire African American congregation wanted out, so in 1852 the original building was moved aside for the construction of a new church for whites, and then entirely across the street in 1880. Look across the street and sure enough you'll see the circa-1853 **Bethel Methodist Church** (57 Pitt St., 843/723-4587, services Sun. 9am and 11:15am).

**MAP 2:** 222 Calhoun St., 843/722-3470

## HAMPTON PARK

### THE CITADEL

The Citadel was originally sited at the Old State Arsenal at Marion Square, born out of panic over the threat of a slave rebellion organized in 1822 by Denmark Vesey. The school moved to its current 300-acre site farther up the peninsula along the Ashley River in 1922. The Citadel (technically named The Citadel, The Military College of South Carolina) has entered popular consciousness through the works of graduate Pat Conroy, especially his novel *Lords of Discipline*, starring a thinly disguised "Carolina Military Institute."

There's a lot for visitors to see, including **The Citadel Museum** (843/953-6779, daily noon-5pm, free), on the right just as you enter campus, inside the Daniel Library; the "Citadel Murals" in the Daniel Library; "Indian Hill," the highest point in Charleston and former site of an Indian trader's home; and the grave of U.S. general Mark Clark of World War II fame, who was Citadel president from 1954 to 1966. Ringing vast Summerall Field—the huge open space where you enter campus—are the many castle-like cadet barracks.

The most interesting single experience for visitors to the Citadel is the Friday afternoon dress parade on Summerall Field, in which cadets pass for review in full dress uniform (the fabled "long gray line") accompanied by a marching band and pipers. Often called "the best free show in Charleston," the parade happens almost every Friday at 3:45pm during the school year; consult the website before your visit to confirm. Arrive well in advance to avoid parking problems.

**MAP 2:** 171 Moultrie St., 843/953-3294, www.citadel.edu; grounds daily 8am-6pm

## WEST ASHLEY

### CHARLES TOWNE LANDING

Any look at West Ashley must start where everything began, with the 600-acre state historic site Charles Towne Landing. This is where Charleston's original settlers first arrived and camped in 1670, remaining only a few years before eventually moving to the more defensible peninsula where the Holy City now resides. A beautiful and fully seaworthy replica of a settlers' ship is the main highlight, docked in the creek on the far side of the long and well-done exploration trail through the site. You can get on board, and a ranger will explain aspects of both the ship and the original settlement. Another highlight is the remnant of the original palisade wall (there's a reconstructed palisade to show what it looked like). Ranger-guided programs are available Wednesday-Friday at 10am; call ahead for reservations.

This is also a great place to bring the family; it has Charleston's only zoo, the Animal Forest, featuring otters, bears, cougars, and buffalo, and 80 acres of beautiful gardens to relax in, many featuring fabulously ancient live oaks and other indigenous flora. Don't miss the fantastic exhibits inside the visitors center as well, which are particularly well done and give a comprehensive and informative look back at the time of the original settlers.

**MAP 3:** 1500 Old Town Plantation Rd., 843/852-4200, www.southcarolinaparks.com/ctl; daily 9am-5pm; $10 adults, $6 students, free under age 6

**TOP** EXPERIENCE

## ★ DRAYTON HALL

A mecca for historic preservationists from all over the country, Drayton Hall is remarkable not only for its pedigree, but also for the way in which it has been preserved. This stately redbrick Georgian-Palladian building, the oldest plantation home in the country open to the public, is literally historically preserved—as in no electricity, heat, or running water. There's no furniture to speak of; only bare rooms decorated with original paint, no matter how little remains.

Since its construction in 1738 by John Drayton, son of Magnolia Plantation founder Thomas, Drayton Hall has survived almost completely intact through the ups and downs of Lowcountry history. In its heyday before the American Revolution, Drayton Hall was widely considered the finest home in all the colonies, the very symbol of the extraordinary wealth of the South Carolina aristocracy. John Drayton died while fleeing the British in 1779; subsequently his house served as the headquarters of British generals Henry Clinton and Charles Cornwallis. During the Civil War, Drayton Hall escaped the depredations of the conquering Union army, one of only three area plantation homes to survive.

The guides hold degrees in the field, and a tour of the house, which starts on the half hour, takes every bit of 50 minutes. A separate 45-minute program called "Connections: From Africa to America" chronicles the diaspora of the enslaved people who originally worked this plantation, from their capture to their eventual freedom. "Connections" is presented at 11:15am, 1:15pm, and 3:15pm.

The site comprises not only the main house but two self-guided walking trails, one along the peaceful Ashley River and another along the marsh. Also on-site is an African American cemetery with at least 33 known graves. It's kept deliberately untended and unlandscaped to honor the final wish of Richmond Bowens (1908-1998), the seventh-generation descendant of some of Drayton Hall's original enslaved laborers.

Drayton Hall

**MAP 3:** 3380 Ashley River Rd., 843/769-2600, www.draytonhall.org; Mon.-Sat. 9am-5pm, Sun. 11am-5pm, tours on the half hour; $22 adults, $10 ages 12-18, $6 ages 6-11, grounds only $10

TOP EXPERIENCE

## MAGNOLIA PLANTATION AND GARDENS

A different legacy of the Drayton family is Magnolia Plantation and Gardens. It claims not only the first garden in the United States, dating back to the 1680s, but also the first public garden, dating to 1872. Thomas Drayton Jr.—scion of Norman aristocracy, son of a wealthy Barbadian planter—came from the Caribbean to build his own fortune; he immediately married the daughter of Stephen Fox, who began this plantation in 1676. Magnolia has stayed in the possession of an unbroken line of Drayton descendants to this day.

As a privately run attraction, Magnolia has little of the academic veneer of other plantation sites in the area, and there's a slightly kitschy feel here, the opposite of the quiet dignity of Drayton Hall. And unlike Middleton Place a few miles down the road, the gardens here are anything but manicured, with a wild, almost playful feel. That said, Magnolia can claim fame to being one of the earliest bona fide tourist attractions in the United States and the beginning of Charleston's now-booming tourist industry.

While spring remains the best—and the most crowded—time to come, a huge variety of camellias bloom in early winter, a time marked by a yearly Winter Camellia Festival. Children will enjoy finding their way through "the Maze" of manicured camellia and holly bushes, complete with a viewing stand to look within the giant puzzle. Plant lovers will enjoy the themed gardens such as the Biblical Garden, the Barbados Tropical Garden, and the Audubon Swamp Garden, complete with alligators and named after John James Audubon, who visited here in 1851. House tours, the 45-minute Nature Train tour, the 45-minute Nature Boat tour, and a visit to the Audubon Swamp Garden run about $8 pp extra for each offering.

**MAP 3:** 3550 Ashley River Rd., 843/571-1266, www.magnoliaplantation.com; daily 8:30am-4:30pm; $20 adults, $10 children, free under age 6

TOP EXPERIENCE

## ★ MIDDLETON PLACE

With the first landscaped garden in North America and still one of the most magnificent in the world, Middleton Place is a sublime, unforgettable combination of history and sheer natural beauty. Nestled along a quiet bend in the Ashley River, the grounds contain a historic restored home, working stables, 60 acres of breathtaking gardens, and the Inn at Middleton Place, a stunning piece of modern architecture.

First granted in 1675, Middleton Place is the culmination of the Lowcountry rice plantation aesthetic. In 1741 the plantation became the family seat of the Middletons, one of the most notable surnames in U.S. history. As the Civil War wound down, on February 22, 1865, the 56th New York Volunteers burned the main house and destroyed the gardens, leaving only the circa-1755 guest wing, which today is the excellently restored **Middleton Place House Museum** (4300 Ashley River Rd., 843/556-6020, www.middletonplace.org, guided tours Mon. 1:30pm-4:30pm, Tues.-Sun. 10am-4:30pm, $15). The 1886 earthquake added its mark, and it wasn't until 1916 that renovation of the property began. In 1971 Middleton Place was named a National Historic Landmark.

A short walk takes you to the **Plantation Stableyards,** where costumed craftspeople work using historically authentic tools and methods, all while surrounded by a happy family of domestic animals. The Stableyards is also home to a pair of magnificent male water buffalo. Henry Middleton originally imported a pair to work the rice fields—the first in North America—but these guys are just there to relax and add atmosphere. Meet them daily 9am-5pm.

The 53-room **Inn at Middleton Place** (www.theinnatmiddletonplace.com) has a bold Frank Lloyd Wright-influenced design, comprising four units joined by walkways. But both inside and outside it manages to blend quite well with the surrounding fields, trees, and riverbanks. The inn also offers kayak tours and instruction—a particularly nice way to enjoy the grounds from the waters of the Ashley—and features its own organic garden and labyrinth, intriguing modern counterpoints to the formal gardens of the plantation itself.

They still grow the exquisite Carolina Gold rice in a field at Middleton Place, harvested in the old style each September. You can sample some of it in many dishes at the **Middleton Place Restaurant** (843/556-6020, www.middletonplace.org, lunch daily 11am-3pm, dinner Tues.-Thurs. 6pm-8pm, Fri.-Sat. 6pm-9pm, Sun. 6pm-8pm, $15-25). You can tour the gardens for free if you arrive for a dinner reservation at 5:30pm or later.

**MAP 3:** 4300 Ashley River Rd., 843/556-6020, www.middletonplace.org; daily 9am-5pm; $28 adults, $15 students, $10 children, guided house tour $15 extra

## THE COBURG COW

The entire stretch of U.S. 17 (Savannah Hwy.) heading into Charleston from the west is redolent of a particularly Southern brand of retro Americana. The chief example is the famous Coburg Cow, a large, rotating dairy cow accompanied by a bottle of chocolate milk. The current installation dates from 1959, though a version of it was on this site as far back as the early 1930s, when this area was open countryside. During Hurricane Hugo the Coburg Cow was moved to a safe location. In 2001 the attached dairy closed down, and the city threatened to have the cow moved or demolished. But community outcry preserved the delightful landmark, which is visible today on the south side of U.S. 17 in the 900 block. You can't miss it—it's a big cow on the side of the road.

**MAP 3:** 900 block of U.S. 17

## CAW CAW INTERPRETIVE CENTER

About 10 minutes west of Charleston on U.S. 17 you'll find the unique Caw Caw Interpretive Center, a treasure trove for history buffs and naturalists wanting to learn more about the old rice culture of the South. Most Wednesday and Saturday mornings, guided bird walks are held at 8:30am ($10 pp). You can put in your

the scenic gardens at Middleton Place

own canoe ($10) Saturday-Sunday October-April. Bikes and dogs aren't allowed on the grounds.

**MAP 3:** 5200 Savannah Hwy., Ravenel, 843/889-8898, www.ccprc.com; Tues.-Sun. 9am-5pm; $2

# NORTH CHARLESTON

TOP EXPERIENCE

## MAGNOLIA CEMETERY

Although not technically in North Charleston, historic Magnolia Cemetery is well north of the downtown tourist district in the area called "the Neck." This historic burial ground, while not quite the aesthetic equal of Savannah's famed Bonaventure Cemetery, is still a stirring site for its natural beauty and ornate memorials as well as for its historical aspects. Here are buried the crewmen who died aboard the CSS *Hunley,* reinterred after their retrieval from Charleston Harbor. In all, over 2,000 Civil War dead are buried here, including 5 Confederate generals and 84 rebels who fell at Gettysburg and were moved here.

**MAP 3:** Cunnington Ave. at Huguenin Ave., 843/722-8638; Sept.-May daily 8am-5pm, June-Aug. daily 8am-6pm

## ★ CSS *HUNLEY*

In 1864, the Confederate submarine CSS *Hunley* mysteriously sank right after successfully destroying the USS *Housatonic* with the torpedo attached to its bow, marking the first time a sub ever sank a ship in battle. For the longest time, the only glimpse of the ill-fated Confederate submarine afforded to visitors was a not-quite-accurate replica outside the Charleston Museum. But in 1995, after a 15-year search, maritime novelist and adventurer Clive Cussler and his team finally found the submarine off Sullivan's Island. In 2000, a team comprising the nonprofit **Friends of the Hunley**, the federal government, and private partners successfully implemented a plan to safely raise the vessel.

Today you can view the sub, see the life-size model from the TNT movie *The Hunley,* and look at artifacts such as the "lucky" gold piece of the commander at the Warren Lasch Conservation Center. You can even see facial reconstructions of some of the eight sailors who died on board. The remains of the crew lie in Magnolia Cemetery, where they were buried in 2004 with full military honors.

The Lasch Center is only open to visitors on weekends so that research and conservation can be performed during the week. Because of this limited window of opportunity and the popularity of the site, reserve tickets ahead of time.

To get to the Warren Lasch Conservation Center from Charleston, take I-26 north to exit 216B. Take a left onto Spruill Avenue and a right onto McMillan Avenue. Once in the Navy Yard, take a right on Hobson Avenue, and after about one mile take a left onto Supply Street. The Lasch Center is the low white building on the left.

**MAP 3:** Warren Lasch Conservation Center, 1250 Supply St., Bldg. 255, 866/866-9938, www.hunley.org; Sat. 10am-5pm, Sun. noon-5pm; $16 adults, $8 students, free under age 5

## CHARLESTON NAVY YARD

A vast postindustrial wasteland to some and a fascinating outdoor museum to others, the Charleston Navy Yard is in the baby steps of rehabilitation from one of the Cold War era's major military centers to the largest single urban redevelopment project in the United States. The U.S. Navy's gone now, forced off the site during a phase of base realignment in the mid-1990s. But a 340-acre section, the **Navy Yard at Noisette** (1360 Truxtun Ave., 843/302-2100, daily 24 hours), now hosts an intriguing mix of homes, green design firms, nonprofits, and commercial maritime companies and was named the country's sixth-greenest neighborhood by *Natural Home* magazine in 2008. It has even played host to some scenes of the Lifetime TV series *Army Wives.*

Enter on Spruill Avenue and you'll find yourself on wide streets lined with huge, boarded-up warehouse facilities, old machine shops, and dormant power stations. A notable project is the restoration of **10 Storehouse Row** (2120 Noisette Blvd., 843/302-2100, Mon.-Fri. 9am-5pm), which now hosts design firms, galleries, and a small café. Nearby, Clemson University will soon be administering one of the world's largest wind turbine research facilities. At the north end lies the new **Riverfront Park** (843/745-1087, daily dawn-dusk) in the old Chicora Gardens military residential area. There's a nifty little fishing pier on the Cooper River, an excellent naval-themed band shell, and many sleekly designed modernist sculptures paying tribute to the sailors and ships that made history here. From Charleston you get to the Navy Yard by taking I-26 north to exit 216B (you can reach the I-26 junction by just going north on Meeting Street). After exiting, take a left onto Spruill Avenue and a right onto McMillan Avenue, which takes you straight in.

**MAP 3:** west bank of Cooper River, south of Riverfront Park

### FIRE MUSEUM

The North Charleston and American LaFrance Fire Museum and Education Center, which shares a huge 25,000-square-foot space with the North Charleston Visitors Center, is primarily dedicated to maintaining and increasing its collection of antique American LaFrance firefighting vehicles and equipment. The 18 fire engines here date from 1857 to 1969. The museum's exhibits have taken on greater poignancy in the wake of the tragic loss of nine Charleston firefighters killed trying to extinguish a warehouse blaze on U.S. 17 in summer 2007—second only to the 9/11 attacks as the largest single loss of life for a U.S. firefighting department.

**MAP 3:** 4975 Centre Pointe Dr., North Charleston, 843/740-5550, www.northcharlestonfiremuseum.org; Mon.-Sat. 10am-5pm, Sun. 1pm-5pm, last ticket 4pm; $6 adults, free under age 12

## SUMMERVILLE

Founded as Pineland Village in 1785, Summerville made its reputation as a place for plantation owners and their families to escape the insects and heat of the swampier areas of the Lowcountry. Summerville boasts a whopping 700 buildings in the National Register of Historic Places. For a walking tour of the historic district, download the map at www.visitsummerville.com or pick up a hard copy at the **Summerville Visitors Center** (402 N. Main St., 843/873-8535, Mon.-Fri. 9am-5pm, Sat. 10am-3pm, Sun. 1pm-4pm).

### AZALEA PARK

Much visitor activity in Summerville centers on Azalea Park, named for its most scenic inhabitants. Several fun yearly events take place here, most notably the **Flowertown Festival** (www.flowertownfestival.com, free) each April, a three-day affair heralding the coming of spring and the blooming of the flowers. One of the biggest festivals in South Carolina, 250,000 people usually attend. Another event, **Sculpture in the South** (www.sculptureinthesouth.com) in May, takes advantage of the extensive public sculpture in the park.

**MAP 3:** S. Main St. and W. 5th St. S.; daily dusk-dawn; free

### COLONIAL DORCHESTER STATE HISTORIC SITE

Just south of Summerville on the way back to Charleston is the interesting Colonial Dorchester State Historic Site, chronicling a virtually unknown segment of Carolina history. A contingent of Massachusetts Puritans ("Congregationalists" in the parlance of the time) were given special dispensation in 1697 to form a settlement of their own specifically to enhance commercial activity on the Ashley River. Today little is left of old Dorchester but the tabby walls of the 1757 fort overlooking the Ashley. Don't miss the unspectacular but still historically vital remains of the wooden wharf on the walking trail along the river, once the epicenter of a thriving port. The most-photographed thing on-site is the bell tower of the Anglican church of St. George—which actually wasn't where the original settlers worshipped, and was in fact quite resented by them, since they were forced to pay for its construction.

**MAP 3:** 300 County Rd. S-18-373, 843/873-1740, www.southcarolinaparks.com; daily 9am-6pm; $2 adults, free under age 16

### SUMMERVILLE-DORCHESTER MUSEUM

To learn more about Summerville's interesting history, go just off Main Street to the Summerville-Dorchester Museum. Located in the former town police station, the museum has a wealth of good exhibits. The museum opened in 1992 thanks to a group of Summerville citizens who wanted to preserve the region's history.

**MAP 3:** 100 E. Doty Ave., 843/875-9666, www.summervilledorchestermuseum.org; Tues.-Sat. 9am-2pm; donation

## MOUNT PLEASANT AND EAST COOPER

The main destination in this area on the east bank of the Cooper River is the island of Mount Pleasant, primarily known as a peaceful, fairly affluent suburb of Charleston—a role it has played for 300 years. Through Mount Pleasant is also the only land route to access Sullivan's Island, Isle of Palms, and historic Fort Moultrie.

### PATRIOTS POINT NAVAL AND MARITIME MUSEUM

Directly across Charleston Harbor from the old city lies the Patriots Point Naval and Maritime Museum, one of the first chapters in Charleston's tourism renaissance. The project began in 1975 with what is still its main attraction, the World War II aircraft carrier USS *Yorktown*, named in honor of the carrier lost at the Battle of Midway. Much of "The Fighting Lady" is open to the public, and kids and nautical buffs will thrill to walk the decks and explore the many stations below deck on this massive 900-foot vessel, a veritable floating city.

Other ships moored beside the *Yorktown* and open for tours are the Coast Guard cutter USCGC *Ingham*, the submarine USS *Clamagore*, and the destroyer USS *Laffey*, which survived being hit by three Japanese bombs and five kamikaze attacks—all within an hour.

A big plus is the free 90-minute guided tour. If you want to make a family history day out of it, you can hop on the ferry from Patriots Point to Fort Sumter and back.

**MAP 4:** 40 Patriots Point Rd., 843/884-2727, www.patriotspoint.org; daily 9am-6:30pm; $22 adults, $14 ages 6-11, free for active-duty military

### OLD VILLAGE

Mount Pleasant's history is almost as old as Charleston's, encapsulated by the Old Village. First settled for farming in 1680, it soon acquired cachet as a great place for planters to spend the hot summers away from the mosquitoes inland. The main drag is Pitt Street, where you can shop and meander among plenty of stores and restaurants (try an ice cream soda at the historic Pitt Street Pharmacy). The huge meeting hall on the waterfront, Alhambra Hall, was the old ferry terminal.

**MAP 4:** West of Royall Ave. to the waterfront, Mount Pleasant

### BOONE HALL PLANTATION

Unusual for this area, where fortunes were originally made mostly on rice, Boone Hall Plantation's main claim to fame was as a cotton plantation as well as a noted brickmaking plant. Boone Hall takes the phrase "living history" to its extreme: It's not only an active agricultural facility, it also lets visitors go on "u-pick" walks through its fields, which boast succulent strawberries, peaches, tomatoes, and even pumpkins in October—as well as free hayrides. Keep in mind that the plantation's "big house" is not original; it's a 1935 reconstruction. The most poignant and educational structures by far are the nine humble brick slave cabins from the 1790s, expertly restored and most fitted with interpretive displays. Summers see some serious Civil War reenacting going on. In all, three different tours are available: a 30-minute house tour, a tour of Slave Street, and a garden tour.

**MAP 4**: 1235 Long Point Rd., 843/884-4371, www.boonehallplantation.com; mid-Mar.-Labor Day Mon.-Sat. 8:30am-6:30pm, Sun. noon-5pm, Labor Day.-mid-Mar. Mon.-Sat. 9am-5pm, Sun. noon-5pm; $24 adults, $12 children

### CHARLES PINCKNEY NATIONAL HISTORIC SITE

The Charles Pinckney National Historic Site is one of my favorite sights in Charleston, for its uplifting, well-explored subject matter as well as its tastefully maintained house and grounds. Sometimes called "the forgotten founder," Charles Pinckney was not only a hero of the American Revolution and a notable early abolitionist, but also one of the main authors of the U.S. Constitution. His great-aunt Eliza Lucas Pinckney was the first woman agriculturalist in the United States, responsible for opening up the indigo trade. The current main house, doubling as the visitors center, dates from 1828, built 11 years after Pinckney sold Snee Farm to pay off debts. That said, it's still a great example of Lowcountry architecture. It replaces Pinckney's original home, where President George Washington slept and had breakfast under a nearby oak tree in 1791 while touring the South.

**MAP 4**: 1240 Long Point Rd., 843/881-5516, www.nps.gov/chpi; daily 9am-5pm; free

### ISLE OF PALMS

This primarily residential area of about 5,000 people received the state's first "Blue Wave" designation from the Clean Beaches Council for its well-managed and preserved beaches. Like adjacent Sullivan's Island, there are pockets of great wealth here, but also a laid-back, windswept beach-town vibe. Aside from the whole scene, the main attraction here is the **Isle of Palms County Park** (14th Ave., 843/886-3863, www.ccprc.com, May-Labor Day daily 9am-7pm, Mar.-Apr. and Sept.-Oct. daily 10am-6pm, Nov.-Feb. daily 10am-5pm, $7 per vehicle, free for pedestrians and cyclists), with its oceanfront beach, complete with an umbrella rental front, volleyball court, playground, and lifeguards. The island's other claim to fame is the excellent (and surprisingly affordable) **Wild Dunes Resort** (5757 Palm Blvd., 888/778-1876, www.wilddunes.com), with its two Fazio golf courses and 17 clay tennis courts. Breach Inlet, between Isle of Palms and Sullivan's Island, is where the Confederate sub *Hunley* sortied to do battle with the USS *Housatonic*.

To get here from Mount Pleasant, take the Isle of Palms Connector (Hwy. 517) off U.S. 17 (Johnnie Dodds/Chuck Dawley Blvd.). To get to the county park, go through the light at Palm Boulevard and take the next left at the gate.

**MAP 4**: off U.S. 17, via Hwy. 517

## Sullivan's Island

Part funky beach town, part ritzy getaway, Sullivan's Island has a certain timeless quality. While much of it was rebuilt after Hurricane Hugo's devastation, plenty of local character remains, as evidenced by some cool little bars in its tiny "business district" on the main drag of Middle Street. There's a ton of history on Sullivan's, but you can also just while the day away on the quiet, windswept beach on the Atlantic or ride a bike all over the island and back. Unless you have a boat, you can only get here from Mount Pleasant. From U.S. 17, follow the signs for Highway 703 and Sullivan's Island. Cross the Ben Sawyer Bridge, and then turn right onto Middle Street; continue for about 1.5 miles.

### FORT MOULTRIE

While Fort Sumter gets the bulk of the attention, the older Fort Moultrie on Sullivan's Island has a much more sweeping history. Furthering the irony, Major Robert Anderson's detachment at Fort Sumter at the opening of the Civil War was actually the Fort Moultrie garrison, reassigned to Sumter because Moultrie was thought too vulnerable from the landward side. Moultrie's first incarnation, a perimeter of felled palm trees, didn't even have a name when it was unsuccessfully attacked by the British in the summer of 1776, the first victory by the colonists in the Revolution. The redcoat cannonballs bounced off those flexible trunks, and thus was born South Carolina's nickname, "the Palmetto State."

In 1809 a brick fort was built here; it soon gained notoriety as the place where the great chief Osceola was detained after his capture. The chief died at the fort in 1838, and his modest grave site is still here, in front of the fort on the landward side. Other famous people to have trod on Sullivan's Island include Edgar Allan Poe, who was inspired by Sullivan's lonely, evocative environment to write *The Gold Bug* and other works. There's a Gold Bug Avenue and a Poe Avenue here today, and the local library is named after him as well. A young Lieutenant William Tecumseh Sherman was also stationed here during his Charleston stint in the 1830s, well before his encounter with history in the Civil War.

Moultrie's main Civil War role was as a target for Union shot during the long siege of Charleston. It was pounded so hard and for so long that its walls fell below a nearby sand hill and were finally unable to be hit anymore. A full military upgrade happened in the late 1800s, extending over most of Sullivan's Island (some private owners have even bought some of the old batteries and converted them into homes). It's the series of later forts that you'll visit on your trip to the Moultrie site, which is technically part of the Fort Sumter National Monument and administered by the National Park Service.

Most of the outdoor tours are self-guided, but ranger programs typically happen Memorial Day-Labor Day daily at 11am and 2:30pm. There's a bookstore and visitors center across the street offering a 20-minute video on the hour and half hour 9am-4:30pm. Keep in mind there's no regular ferry to Fort Sumter from Fort Moultrie; the closest ferry to Sumter leaves from Patriots Point on Mount Pleasant.

**MAP 4**: 1214 Middle St., 843/883-3123, www.nps.gov/fosu; daily 9am-5pm; $3, free under age 16

### BENCH BY THE ROAD

Scholars say that about half of all African Americans alive today had an ancestor who once set foot on Sullivan's Island. As the first point of entry for at least half of all the enslaved people imported to the United States, the island's "pest houses" acted as quarantine areas so enslaved people could be checked for communicable diseases before going to auction in Charleston proper. But few people seem to know this. In a 1989 magazine interview, African American author and Nobel laureate Toni Morrison said about historic sites concerning slavery, "There is no suitable memorial, or plaque, or wreath or wall, or park or skyscraper lobby. There's no 300-foot tower, there's no small bench by the road." In 2008, that last item became a reality, as the first of several planned "benches by the road" was installed on Sullivan's Island to mark the sacrifice of enslaved African Americans. It's a simple black steel bench with an attached marker and a nearby plaque.

**MAP 4**: Fort Moultrie visitors center, 1214 Middle St.

## Awendaw and Points North

This area just north of Charleston along U.S. 17—named for the Sewee Native American village originally located here and known to the world chiefly as the place where Hurricane Hugo made landfall in 1989—is seeing some new growth but still hews to its primarily rural, nature-loving roots.

### CAPE ROMAIN NATIONAL WILDLIFE REFUGE

One of the best natural experiences in the area is about a 30-minute drive north of Charleston at Cape Romain National Wildlife Refuge. Essentially comprising four barrier islands, the 66,000-acre refuge—almost all of which is marsh—provides a lot of great paddling opportunities, chief among them **Bulls Island** (no overnight camping). A fairly lengthy trek from where you put in is famous Boneyard Beach, where hundreds of downed trees lie on the sand, bleached by sun and salt. Slightly to the south within the refuge, **Capers Island**

**Heritage Preserve** (843/953-9300, www.dnr.sc.gov, daily dawn-dusk, free) is a popular camping locale. Get permits in advance by calling the South Carolina Department of Natural Resources. You can kayak to the refuge yourself or take the only approved ferry service from **Coastal Expeditions** (514-B Mill St., Mount Pleasant, 843/881-4582, www.coastalexpeditions.com, 30 minutes, $40 adults, $20 children). **Barrier Island Eco Tours** (50 41st Ave., Isle of Palms, 843/886-5000, www.nature-tours.com, 3.5-hour boat excursions $38 adults, $28 children) on Isle of Palms also runs trips to the area.

**MAP 4:** 5801 U.S. 17 N., 843/928-3264, www.fws.gov/caperomain; daily dawn-dusk; free

### SEWEE VISITOR AND ENVIRONMENTAL EDUCATION CENTER

Twenty miles north of Charleston is the Sewee Visitor and Environmental Education Center. Besides being a gateway of sorts for the almost entirely aquatic Cape Romain National Wildlife Refuge, Sewee is primarily known for housing several rare red wolves, which were part of a unique release program on nearby Bull Island begun in the late 1970s. They're kept at the center to maintain the genetic integrity of the species.

**MAP 4:** 5821 U.S. 17, 843/928-3368, www.fws.gov/seweecenter; Wed.-Sat. 9am-5pm; free

## FOLLY BEACH AND THE SOUTHWEST ISLANDS

### FOLLY BEACH

A large percentage of the town of Folly Beach was destroyed by Hurricane Hugo in 1989, and erosion since then has increased and hit the beach itself pretty hard. All that said, enough of Folly's funky charm is left to make it worth visiting. Called "the Edge of America" during its heyday as a swinging resort getaway from the 1930s through the 1950s, Folly Beach is now a slightly beaten but still enjoyable little getaway on this barrier island. Folly's main claim to larger historical fame is playing host to George Gershwin, who stayed at a cottage on West Arctic Avenue to write the score for *Porgy and Bess*, set across the harbor in downtown Charleston. (Ironically, Gershwin's opera couldn't be performed in its original setting until 1970 because of segregationist Jim Crow laws.) Original *Porgy* author DuBose Heyward stayed around the corner at a summer cottage on West Ashley Avenue that he dubbed "Follywood."

Called Folly Road until it gets to the beach, Center Street is the main drag here, dividing the beach into east and west. In this area you'll find the **Folly Beach Fishing Pier** (101 E. Arctic Ave., 843/588-3474, Apr.-Oct. daily 6am-11pm, Nov. and Mar. daily 7am-7pm, Dec.-Feb. daily 8am-5pm, $5-7 parking, $8 fishing fee), which replaced the grand old wooden pier-and-pavilion structure that burned down in 1960.

To get to Folly Beach from Charleston, go west on Calhoun Street and take the James Island Connector. Take a left on Folly Road (Hwy. 171), which becomes Center Street once in Folly Beach.

At the far east end of Folly Island, about 300 yards offshore, you'll see the **Morris Island Lighthouse,** an 1876 beacon that was once surrounded by lush green landscape, but is now completely surrounded by water after the land eroded around it. Now privately owned, there's an extensive effort to save and preserve the lighthouse (www.savethelight.org). There's also an effort to keep high-dollar condo development off beautiful bird-friendly Morris Island (www.morrisisland.org). To get here while there's still something left to enjoy, take East Ashley Street until it dead-ends. Park in the lot and take a 0.25-mile walk to the beach.

**MAP 5:** south of Charleston via Hwy. 30 and Hwy. 171

## Kiawah Island

The beautiful island of Kiawah—about 45 minutes from downtown Charleston—has as its main attraction the sumptuous **Kiawah Island Golf Resort** (12 Kiawah Beach Dr., 800/654-2924, www.kiawahgolf.com, $600-800), a key location for PGA tournaments.

But even if you don't play golf, the resort is an amazing stay. The main component is **The Sanctuary,** an upscale hotel featuring an opulent lobby complete with grand staircases, a large pool area overlooking the beach, tasteful Spanish Colonial-style architecture, and 255 smallish but excellently appointed guest rooms. Several smaller, private, family-friendly resorts also exist on Kiawah, with fully furnished homes and villas and every amenity you could ask for. Go to www.explorekiawah.com for a full range of options or call 800/877-0837.

Through the efforts of the **Kiawah Island Conservancy** (23 Beachwalker Dr., 843/768-2029, www.kiawahconservancy.org), over 300 acres of the island have been kept as an undeveloped nature preserve. The island's famous bobcat population has made quite a comeback; the bobcats are vital to the island ecosystem, since as top predator they help cull what would otherwise become untenably large populations of deer and rabbit.

The beach at Kiawah is a particular delight, set as it is on such a comparatively undeveloped island. No matter where you stay on Kiawah, a great thing about the island is the notable lack of light pollution—don't forget to look up at night and enjoy the stars!

## Seabrook Island

Like its neighbor Kiawah, **Seabrook Island** is a private resort-dominated island. In addition to offering miles of beautiful beaches, on its 2,200 acres are a wide variety of golfing, tennis, equestrian, and swimming facilities as well as extensive dining and shopping options. There are a lot of kids' activities as well. For information on lodging options and packages, go to www.seabrook.com or call 866/249-9934. Seabrook Island is about 45 minutes from Charleston. From downtown, take Highway 30 West to Maybank Highway, then take a left onto Cherry Point Road.

## Johns Island

### ANGEL OAK PARK

The outlying community of Johns Island is where you'll find the inspiring Angel Oak Park, home of a massive live oak, 65 feet in circumference, that's over 1,000 years old and commonly considered the oldest tree east of the Mississippi River. As is the case with all live oaks, don't expect impressive height—when oaks age they spread *out*, not up. The sprawling, picturesque tree and the park containing it are owned by the city of Charleston, and the scenic grounds are often used for weddings and special events. Angel Oak Park is

Kiawah Island Golf Resort

about 30 minutes from Charleston. Take U.S. 17 over the Ashley River, then Highway 171 to Maybank Highway. Take a left onto Bohicket Road, and then look for signs on the right.

**MAP 5:** 3688 Angel Oak Rd.; Mon.-Sat. 9am-5pm, Sun. 1pm-5pm; free

#### LEGARE FARMS

Legare Farms is open to the public for various activities, including its annual pumpkin patch in October, its "sweet corn" festival in June, and bird walks (Sat. 8:30am, $6 adults, $3 children) in fall. To make the 20-minute drive from downtown Charleston, take Highway 30 West to Maybank Highway, then make a left onto River Road and a right onto Jenkins Farm Road.

**MAP 5:** 2620 Hanscombe Point Rd., 843/559-0763, www.legarefarms.com; hours vary

### Wadmalaw Island

#### CHARLESTON TEA PLANTATION

Currently owned by the R. C. Bigelow Tea corporation, the Charleston Tea Plantation is no cute living-history exhibit; it's a big working tea plantation—the only one in the United States—with acre after acre of *Camellia sinensis* being worked by modern farm machinery. Visitors get to see how the tea is brought "from the field to the cup." Factory tours are free, and a trolley tour of the "Back 40" is $10. And, of course, there's a gift shop where you can sample and buy all types of teas and tea-related products. Growing season is April-October. The tea bushes, direct descendants of plants brought over in the 1800s from India and China, "flush up" 2-3 inches every few weeks during growing season. Charleston Tea Plantation is about 30 minutes from Charleston. Take the Ashley River Bridge, stay left to Folly Road (Hwy. 171), turn right onto Maybank Highway and follow it 18 miles, and look for the sign on the left.

**MAP 5:** 6617 Maybank Hwy., 843/559-0383, www.charlestonteaplantation.com; Mon.-Sat. 10am-4pm, Sun. noon-4pm; free

#### DEEP WATER VINEYARDS

South Carolina has several good wineries, among them Wadmalaw's own Deep Water Vineyards, formerly Irvin House Vineyards, the Charleston area's only vineyard. They make several varieties of muscadine wine here, with tastings ($5) and a gift shop. Every Saturday they host a "Wine-Down" party (noon-4pm). Also on the grounds you'll find **Firefly Distillery** (6775 Bears Bluff Rd., 843/559-6867, www.fireflyvodka.com, Tues.-Sat. 10am-5pm), home of their signature Firefly Sweet Tea Vodka. To get here from Charleston, go west on Maybank Highway about 10 miles to Bears Bluff Road, veering right on the latter. The vineyard entrance is on the left after about eight miles.

**MAP 5:** 6775 Bears Bluff Rd., 843/559-6867, www.deepwatervineyard.com; Tues.-Sat. 10am-5pm

## Entertainment and Nightlife

Unlike the locals-versus-tourists divide you find so often in other destination cities, in Charleston it's nothing for a couple of visitors to find themselves at a table next to four or five college students enjoying themselves in true Charlestonian fashion: loudly and with lots of good food and strong drink nearby. Indeed, the Holy City is downright ecumenical in its partying. The smokiest dives also have some of the best brunches. Tourist hot spots written up in all the guidebooks also have their share of local regulars. But through it all, one constant remains: Charleston's finely honed ability to seek out and enjoy the good life.

Bars close in Charleston at 2am, though there is a movement afoot to make the closing time earlier in some areas of town, mostly the Upper King neighborhood, the youngest and most vibrant nightlife area in Charleston. All hard-liquor sales stop at 7pm, with none at all on Sunday. You can buy beer and wine in grocery stores 24-7.

Charleston's live music scene is on the upswing after a long period of relative dormancy. With the long-ago passing of the heyday of Hootie & the Blowfish, there had been no distinct "Charleston sound" to speak of (though Hootie front man-turned-country star Darius Rucker still plays frequently in the area).

Now a new breed of local indie artists, such as Shovels and Rope, Susto, and Heyrocco, are staples not only in local venues but very popular on the Southeast touring and festival circuit. The best place to find up-to-date music listings is the local free weekly *Charleston City Paper* (www.charlestoncitypaper.com).

## WATERFRONT

### Lounges

#### ROOFTOP BAR

Located atop the Vendue hotel, the aptly named Rooftop Bar is a very popular happy hour spot from which to enjoy the sunset over the Charleston skyline.

**MAP 1:** 23 Vendue Range, 843/723-0485; Tues.-Sat. 6pm-2am

#### THE GIN JOINT

If artisan cocktails are your thing, head straight to The Gin Joint, where you can get drinks with names like Thieve's Tonic (rum, turmeric, lime, coconut, ginger honey) and Studmuffin (madeira, chicory liqueur, coffee liqueur, and bay leaf ice cubes). With most cocktails running about $12, they're actually bargains when you consider the curated ingredients going into each one. Got a big party? Order one of four signature punches to share, prepared tableside (about $40). Fair warning: These aren't your typical office party punches and pack a commensurately large, well, punch. Thankfully, there is a good little menu of tapas to soak up all the alcohol.

**MAP 1:** 182 E. Bay St., 843/577-6111, www.theginjoint.com; Thurs.-Fri. 5pm-2am, Sat. 3pm-2am, Sun.-Wed. 5pm-midnight

## FRENCH QUARTER

### Bars and Pubs

#### TOMMY CONDON'S IRISH PUB

The Guinness flows freely at touristy Tommy Condon's Irish Pub—after the obligatory and traditional slow-pour, that is—as do the patriotic Irish songs performed live most nights.

**MAP 1:** 160 Church St., 843/577-3818, www.tommycondons.com; Sun.-Thurs. 11am-2am, dinner until 10pm, Fri.-Sat. 11am-2am, dinner until 11pm

## NORTH OF BROAD

### Bars and Pubs

#### VICKERY'S BAR AND GRILL

If it's a nice day out, a good place to relax and enjoy happy hour outside is Vickery's Bar and Grill, actually part of a small regional chain based in Atlanta. Start with the oyster bisque and maybe try the turkey and brie sandwich or crab cakes for your entrée.

Vickery's Bar and Grill has become quite popular with gay and lesbian clientele—not least because of the good reputation its parent tavern in Atlanta has with that city's large and influential gay community.

**MAP 1:** 15 Beaufain St., 843/577-5300, www.vickerysbarandgrill.com; Mon.-Sat. 11:30am-2am, Sun. 11am-1am, kitchen closes 1am

## UPPER KING

### Bars and Pubs

#### RECOVERY ROOM

The hottest hipster dive bar is the Recovery Room on bustling Upper King. Proof of their hipster credentials? They claim to be the nation's number-two overall retail seller of Pabst Blue Ribbon. Otherwise, the drinks are cheap and stiff, and the bar food is addictively tasty (two words: Tater Tots!).

**MAP 2:** 685 King St., 843/727-0999; Mon.-Fri. 4pm-2am, Sat. 3pm-2am, Sun. noon-2am

### Dance Clubs

#### TRIO CLUB

The Trio Club, right off Marion Square, is a favorite place to make the scene. There's a relaxing outdoor area with piped-in music, an intimate sofa-filled upstairs bar for dancing

## Doin' the Charleston

It has been called the biggest song-and-dance craze of the 20th century. It first entered the American public consciousness via New York City in a 1923 Harlem musical called *Runnin' Wild,* but the roots of the dance soon to be known as the Charleston were indeed in the Holy City. No one is quite sure of the day and date, but local lore assures us that members of Charleston's legendary Jenkins Orphanage Band were the first to start dancing that crazy "Geechie step," a development that soon became part of the band's act.

The Jenkins Orphanage was started in 1891 by the African American Baptist minister Reverend D. J. Jenkins and was originally housed in the Old Marine Hospital at 20 Franklin Street (which you can see today, although it's not open to the public). To raise money, Reverend Jenkins acquired donated instruments and started a band comprising talented orphans from the house. The orphans traveled as far away as London, where they were a hit with the locals but not with the constabulary, who unceremoniously fined them for stopping traffic. A Charleston attorney who happened to be in London at the time, Augustine Smyth, paid their way back home, becoming a lifelong supporter of the orphanage in the process.

From then on, playing in donated old Citadel uniforms, the Jenkins Orphanage Band frequently took their act on the road. They played at the St. Louis and Buffalo expositions and even at President Taft's inauguration. They also frequently played in New York, and it was there that African American pianist and composer James P. Johnson heard the Charlestonians play and dance to their Gullah rhythms, considered exotic at the time. Johnson would incorporate what he heard into the tune "Charleston," one of many songs in the revue *Runnin' Wild.* The catchy song and its accompanying loose-limbed dance seemed tailor-made for the Roaring '20s and its liberated, hedonistic spirit. Before long the Charleston had swept the nation, becoming a staple of jazz clubs and speakeasies across the country and, indeed, the world.

and chilling, and the dark candlelit downstairs with frequent live music leaning toward hip-hop sounds.

**MAP 2:** 139 Calhoun St., 843/965-5333; Thurs.-Sat. 9pm-2am

### Live Music

#### MUSIC FARM

The venerable Music Farm on Upper King isn't much to look at from the outside, but inside the cavernous space has played host to all sorts of bands over the past two decades. Recent concerts have included Neko Case, Matisyahu, and the Drive-By Truckers.

**MAP 2:** 32 Ann St., 843/722-8904, www.musicfarm.com

#### THE ROYAL AMERICAN

Keep heading a bit north of the Upper King area to find The Royal American, which though a bit off the beaten path is a go-to for a relaxed local music-oriented hangout. Set in a restored railroad depot, it has the suitably downscale vibe you'd expect from a repurposed industrial facility. This is the kind of place to rideshare to and from, since there's not much else worth visiting around it. As a plus, the bar-food menu is top-notch.

**MAP 2:** 970 Morrison Dr., 843/817-6925; Mon.-Fri. 4pm-2am, Sat. 4pm-2am, Sun. noon-2am

## HAMPTON PARK

### Bars and Pubs

#### MOE'S CROSSTOWN TAVERN

One of Charleston's favorite neighborhood spots is Moe's Crosstown Tavern at Rutledge and Francis in the Wagener Terrace-Hampton Square area. A newer location, **Moe's Downtown Tavern** (5 Cumberland St., 843/577-8500, daily 11am-2am) offers a similar vibe and menu, but the original, and best, Moe's experience is at the Crosstown.

**MAP 2:** 714 Rutledge Ave., 843/722-3287; daily 11am-2am

## Craft Breweries

The craft beer revolution has hit Charleston hard. Here are a few notable places to try:

- **Palmetto Brewing** (289 Huger St., 843/937-0903, www.palmettobrewery.com, tasting room Tues.-Wed. 3pm-7pm, Thurs. 3pm-9pm, Fri. 1pm-10pm, Sat. 1pm-7pm) has roots in Charleston going back before the Civil War and was the city's first post-Prohibition brewery. Known for their nitro beers and their Espresso Porter, among many others, they have an extensive outdoor seating area and often feature live music on weekends.
- **COAST Brewing** (1250 2nd St. N., 843/343-4727, www.coastbrewing.com, Thurs.-Fri. 4pm-7pm, Sat. 11am-4pm) in North Charleston focuses on sustainable and organic ingredients. Try the Blackbeerd Stout if it's available, and any Kölsch. This is more of a casual, all-outdoor tasting experience, so keep weather in mind.
- **Holy City Brewing** (4155C Dorchester Rd., www.holycitybrewing.com, Mon.-Thurs. 11am-8pm, Fri.-Sat. 11am-9pm, Sun. 11am-5pm), also in North Charleston, is known for its porters and stouts. This is also a great choice if you're hungry, as they have a full menu. Try the namesake Holy City Burger.
- **The Frothy Beard** (1401 Sam Rittenburg Blvd., 843/872-4201, www.frothybeard.com, Mon.-Sat. 11am-11pm, Sun. 11am-10pm), in West Ashley, is a new micropub with a diverse selection of beers brewed on premises. The attached Zombie Pizza inside the building makes an incredible pie to accompany the beer selection.

## WEST ASHLEY

### Bars and Pubs

#### GENE'S HAUFBRAU

Located not too far over the Ashley River on U.S. 17, Charleston institution Gene's Haufbrau is worth making a special trip into West Ashley and its burgeoning nightlife district. Boasting the largest beer selection in Charleston, Gene's also claims to be the oldest bar in town, established in 1952. The Sunday brunch is outstanding as well.

**MAP 3**: 17 Savannah Hwy., 843/225-4363, www.geneshaufbrau.com; daily 11:30am-2am

### Lounges

#### VOODOO LOUNGE

Across the street from Gene's Haufbrau, the retro-chic Voodoo Lounge is another very popular hangout. It has a wide selection of trendy cocktails and killer gourmet tacos.

**MAP 3**: 15 Magnolia Rd., 843/769-0228; Mon.-Fri. 4pm-2am, Sat.-Sun. 5:30pm-2am, kitchen until 1am

## NORTH CHARLESTON

### Bars and Pubs

#### MADRA RUA IRISH PUB

If you find yourself up in North Charleston, stop by Madra Rua Irish Pub, an authentic watering hole with a better-than-average pub-food menu that's also a great place to watch a soccer game.

**MAP 3**: 1034 E. Montague Ave., 843/554-2522; daily 11am-1am

## MOUNT PLEASANT AND EAST COPPER

### Bars and Pubs

#### DUNLEAVY'S PUB

Though Sullivan's Island has a lot of high-dollar homes, it still has friendly watering holes like Dunleavy's Pub. Inside is a great old-school bar festooned with memorabilia, or you can enjoy a patio table.

**MAP 4**: 2213-B Middle St., 843/883-9646; Sun.-Thurs. 11:30am-1am, Fri.-Sat. 11:30am-2am

Poe's Tavern on Sullivan's Island

### POE'S TAVERN

The other Sullivan's watering hole of note is Poe's Tavern, across the street, a nod to Edgar Allan Poe and his service on the island as a clerk in the U.S. Army. It's a lively, mostly local scene, set within a fun but suitably dark interior (though you might opt for one of the outdoor tables on the raised patio). No trip to Sullivan's is complete without a stop at one (or possibly both) of these two local landmarks.

**MAP 4:** 2210 Middle St., 843/883-0083, www.poestavern.com; daily 11am-2am, kitchen closes 10pm

## FOLLY BEACH AND THE SOUTHWEST ISLANDS

### Bars and Pubs

### BLU RESTAURANT AND BAR

If you're in Folly Beach, enjoy the great views and the great cocktails at Blu Restaurant and Bar inside the Tides Folly Beach hotel. There's nothing like a Spiked Lemonade on a hot Charleston day at the beach.

**MAP 5:** 1 Center St., 843/588-6658, www.blufollybeach.com; daily 7am-10pm

### SAND DOLLAR SOCIAL CLUB

A notable Folly Beach watering hole is the Sand Dollar Social Club, the kind of cash-only, mostly local dive you often find in little beach towns. You have to pony up for a "membership" to this private club, but it's only a buck. There's a catch, though: You can't get in until your 24-hour "waiting period" is over.

**MAP 5:** 7 Center St., 843/588-9498; Sun.-Fri. noon-1am, Sat. noon-2am

### Live Music

### THE POUR HOUSE

The hippest music spot in town is out on James Island at The Pour House, where the local characters are sometimes just as entertaining as the acts onstage. There is music schedule almost every night, in a wide range from Americana to funk.

**MAP 5:** 1977 Maybank Hwy., 843/571-4343, www.charlestonpourhouse.com; 9pm-2am on nights with music scheduled

TOP EXPERIENCE

## FESTIVALS AND EVENTS

Charleston is a festival-mad city, especially in the spring and early fall. And new festivals are being added every year, further enhancing the hedonistic flavor of this city that has also mastered the art of hospitality.

### January

Held on a Sunday in late January at historic Boone Hall Plantation in Mount Pleasant, the **Lowcountry Oyster Festival** (Sun. 11am-5pm, $8, food additional) features literal truckloads of the sweet shellfish for your enjoyment, and claims to be the world's largest such event. Gates open at 10:30am, and there's plenty of parking. Oysters are sold by the bucket and served with crackers and cocktail sauce. Bring your own shucking knife or glove, or buy them on-site.

### February

One of the unique events in town is the

**Southeastern Wildlife Exposition** (various venues, 843/723-1748, www.sewe.com, $12.50 per day, $30 for 3 days, free under age 13). For the last quarter century, the Wildlife Expo has brought together hundreds of artists and exhibitors to showcase just about any kind of naturally themed art you can think of in over a dozen galleries and venues all over downtown. Kids will enjoy the live animals on hand as well.

## March

Generally straddling late February and the first days of March, the four-day **Charleston Food & Wine Festival** (www.charlestonfoodandwine.com, various venues and admission) is a glorious celebration of one of the Holy City's premier draws: its amazing culinary community. While the emphasis is on Lowcountry chefs, guest chefs from New York, New Orleans, and Los Angeles routinely come to show off their skills. Oenophiles, especially of domestic wines, will be in heaven as well. This event has boomed in recent years and downtown gets quite crowded. Tickets aren't cheap—an all-event pass is over $500 pp—but then again, this is one of the nation's great food cities.

Immediately before the Festival of Houses and Gardens is the **Charleston Antiques Show** (40 E. Bay St., 843/722-3405, www.historiccharleston.org, admission varies), held at the Gaillhyard Center. It features over 30 of the nation's best-regarded dealers and offers lectures and tours.

Mid-March to April, the perennial favorite **Festival of Houses and Gardens** (843/722-3405, www.historiccharleston.org, admission varies) is sponsored by the Historic Charleston Foundation and held at the very peak of the spring blooming season for maximum effect. In all, the festival goes into a dozen historic neighborhoods to view about 150 homes. Each day sees a different three-hour tour of a different area, at about $50 pp. This is a fantastic opportunity to peek inside some amazing old privately owned properties that are inaccessible to visitors at other times. A highlight is a big oyster roast and picnic at Drayton Hall.

Not to be confused with the above festival, the **Garden Club of Charleston House and Garden Tours** (843/530-5164, www.thegardenclubofcharleston.com, $35) are held over a weekend in late March. Highlights include the Heyward-Washington House and the private garden of the late great Charleston horticulturalist Emily Whaley.

One of Charleston's newest and most fun events, the five-night **Charleston Fashion Week** (www.charlestonfashionweek.com, admission varies) benefits local women's and children's charities. Mimicking New York's Fashion Week events under tenting in Bryant Park, Charleston's version features runway action under big tents in Marion Square—and, yes, past guests have included former contestants on *Project Runway.*

## April

The annual **Cooper River Bridge Run** (www.bridgerun.com) happens the first Saturday in April (unless that's Easter weekend, in which case it runs the week before) and features a six-mile jaunt across the massive Arthur Ravenel Bridge over the Cooper River, the longest cable span in the western hemisphere. It's not for those with a fear of heights, but it's still one of Charleston's best-attended events—there are well over 30,000 participants.

One of the newest and most buzzworthy new events in town is the **High Water Music Festival** (843/308-4746, www.highwaterfest.com, admission varies), a weekend-long celebration of indie music with a lineup curated by local faves Shovels and Rope. Held in North Charleston's Riverfront Park, there is plenty of craft brew and great food available for purchase as well. The 2018 edition featured Band of Horses, St. Paul and the Broken Bones, and Jeff Tweedy.

Previously known as the Family Circle Cup, the **Volvo Car Open** (161 Seven Farms Dr., Daniel Island, 843/856-7900, www.volvocaropen.com, admission varies) is held at

Daniel Island's Family Circle Tennis Center, specifically built for the event. Almost 100,000 people attend the multiple-week event. Individual session tickets go on sale the preceding January.

Mount Pleasant is the home of Charleston's shrimping fleet, and each April sees all the boats parade by the Alhambra Hall and Park for the **Blessing of the Fleet** (843/884-8517, www.townofmountpleasant.com). Family events and lots and lots of seafood are also on tap.

## May

Free admission and free parking are not the only draws at the outdoor **North Charleston Arts Festival** (5000 Coliseum Dr., www.northcharleston.org), but let's face it, they are important. Held beside North Charleston's Performing Arts Center and Convention Center, the festival features music, dance, theater, multicultural performers, and storytellers. There are a lot of kids' events as well.

Held over three days at the Holy Trinity Greek Orthodox Church up toward the Neck, the **Charleston Greek Festival** (30 Race St., 843/577-2063, www.charlestongreekfestival.com, $5 admission, food extra) offers a plethora of live entertainment, dancing, Greek wares, and, of course, fantastic Greek cuisine cooked by the congregation. Parking is not a problem, and there's even a shuttle to the church from the lot.

Indisputably Charleston's single biggest and most important event, **Spoleto Festival USA** (843/579-3100, www.spoletousa.org, admission varies) has come a long way since it was a sparkle in the eye of the late Gian Carlo Menotti three decades ago. Though Spoleto long ago broke ties with its founder, his vision remains indelibly stamped on the event from start to finish. There's plenty of music, to be sure, in genres that include orchestral, opera, jazz, and avant-garde, but you'll find something in every other performing art, such as dance, drama, and spoken word, in traditions from Western to African to Southeast Asian. For 17 days from Memorial Day weekend through early June, Charleston hops and hums nearly 24 hours a day to the energy of this vibrant, cutting-edge (yet accessible) artistic celebration.

As if all the hubbub around Spoleto didn't give you enough to do, there's also **Piccolo Spoleto** (843/724-7305, www.piccolospoleto.com, various venues and admission), literally "little Spoleto," running concurrently. The intent of Piccolo Spoleto—begun just a couple of years after the larger festival came to town and run by the city's Office of Cultural Affairs—is to give local and regional performers a time to shine, sharing some of that larger spotlight on the national and international performers at the main event. Of particular interest to visiting families will be Piccolo's children's events, a good counter to some of the decidedly more adult fare at Spoleto USA.

## June

Technically part of Piccolo Spoleto but gathering its own following, the **Sweetgrass Cultural Arts Festival** (www.sweetgrassfestival.org) is held the first week in June in Mount Pleasant at the Laing Middle School (2213 U.S. 17 N.). The event celebrates the traditional sweetgrass basket-making skills of African Americans in the historic Christ Church Parish area of Mount Pleasant. If you want to buy some sweetgrass baskets made by the world's foremost experts in the field, this would be the time.

## July

Each year over 30,000 people come to see the **Patriots Point Fourth of July Blast** (866/831-1720), featuring a hefty barrage of fireworks shot off the deck of the USS *Yorktown* moored on the Cooper River in the Patriots Point complex. Food, live entertainment, and kids' activities are also featured.

## September

From late September into the first week of October, the city-sponsored **MOJA Arts Festival** (843/724-7305, www.mojafestival.com, various venues and admission)

## A Man, a Plan: Spoleto!

Sadly, Gian Carlo Menotti is no longer with us, having died in 2007 at the age of 95. But the overwhelming success of the composer's brainchild and labor of love, **Spoleto Festival USA,** lives on, enriching the cultural and social life of Charleston and serving as the city's chief calling card to the world at large.

Menotti began writing music at age seven in his native Italy. As a young man he moved to Philadelphia to study music, where he shared classes—and lifelong connections—with Leonard Bernstein and Samuel Barber. His first full-length opera, *The Consul,* would garner him the Pulitzer Prize, as would 1955's *The Saint of Bleecker Street.* But by far Menotti's best-known work is the beloved Christmas opera *Amahl and the Night Visitors,* composed specially for NBC television in 1951. At the height of his fame in 1958, the charismatic and mercurial genius—fluent and witty in five languages—founded the "Festival of Two Worlds" in Spoleto, Italy, specifically as a forum for young American artists in Europe. But it wasn't until nearly two decades later, in 1977, that Menotti was able to make his long-imagined dream of an American counterpart a reality.

Attracted to Charleston because of its long-standing support of the arts, its undeniable good taste, and its small size—ensuring that his festival would always be the number-one activity in town while it was going on—Menotti worked closely with the man who was to become the other key part of the equation: Charleston mayor Joe Riley, then in his first term in office. Since then, the city has built on Spoleto's success by founding its own local version, **Piccolo Spoleto**—literally, "little Spoleto"—which focuses exclusively on local and regional talent.

Things haven't always gone smoothly. Menotti and the stateside festival parted ways in 1993, when he took over the Rome Opera. Making matters more uneasy, the Italian festival—run by Menotti's longtime partner (and later adopted son), Chip—also became estranged from what was intended to be its soul mate in South Carolina. (Chip was later replaced by the Italian Culture Ministry.) But perhaps this kind of creative tension is what Menotti intended all along. Indeed, each spring brings a Spoleto USA that seems to thrive on the inherent conflict between the festival's often cutting-edge offerings and the very traditional city that hosts it. Spoleto still challenges its audiences, just as Menotti intended it to. Depending on the critic and the audience member, that modern opera debut you see may be groundbreaking or gratuitous. The drama you check out may be exhilarating or tiresome.

Each year, a total of about 500,000 people attend both Spoleto and Piccolo Spoleto. Nearly one-third of the attendees are Charleston residents—the final proof that when it comes to supporting the arts, Charleston puts its money where its mouth is.

highlights the cultural contributions of African Americans and people from the Caribbean with dance, visual art, poetry, cuisine, crafts, and music in genres that include gospel, jazz, reggae, and classical. In existence since 1984, MOJA's name comes from the Swahili word for "one," and its diverse range of offerings in so many media have made it one of the Southeast's premier events. Some events are ticketed, while others, such as the kids' activities and many of the dance and film events, are free.

For five weeks from the last week of September into October, the Preservation Society of Charleston hosts the much anticipated **Fall Tours of Homes & Gardens** (843/722-4630, www.preservationsociety.org, $45). The tour takes you into more than a dozen local residences and is the nearly 90-year-old organization's biggest fund-raiser. Tickets typically go on sale the previous June, and they tend to sell out very quickly.

Another great food event in this great food city, the **Taste of Charleston** (1235 Long Point Rd., 843/577-4030, www.charlestonrestaurantassociation.com, 11am-5pm, $12) is held on a weekend in October at Boone Hall Plantation in Mount Pleasant and sponsored by the Greater Charleston Restaurant Association. Over 50 area chefs and restaurants come together so you can sample their wares, including a wine and food pairing, with proceeds going to charity.

### October

Local company Half Moon Outfitters (843/853-0990, 843/881-9472, www.halfmoonoutfitters.com) sponsors an annual six-mile **Giant Kayak Race** at Isle of Palms Marina in late October benefiting the Coastal Conservation League.

### November

**Plantation Days at Middleton Place** (4300 Ashley River Rd., 843/556-6020, www.middletonplace.org, daily 9am-5pm, last tour 4:30pm, guided tour $10) happen each Saturday in November, giving visitors a chance to wander the grounds and see artisans at work practicing authentic crafts, as they would have done in antebellum days, with a special emphasis on the contributions of African Americans. A special treat comes on Thanksgiving, when a full meal is offered on the grounds at the Middleton Place Restaurant (843/556-6020, www.middletonplace.org, reservations strongly advised).

One of Charleston's newest annual events is the **Charleston International Film Festival** (843/817-1617, www.charlestoniff.com, various venues and prices). Despite being a relative latecomer to the film-festival circuit, the event is pulled off with Charleston's usual aplomb, and generally centers on the Charleston Music Hall (37 John St.) near Upper King.

### December

A yuletide in the Holy City is an experience you'll never forget, as the **Christmas in Charleston** (843/724-3705) events clustered around the first week of the month prove. For some reason—whether it's the old architecture, the friendly people, the churches, the carriages, or all of the above—Charleston feels right at home during Christmas. The festivities begin with the mayor lighting the city's 60-foot Tree of Lights in Marion Square, followed by a parade of brightly lit boats from Mount Pleasant all the way around Charleston up the Ashley River. The key event is the Sunday Christmas Parade through downtown, featuring bands, floats, and performers in the holiday spirit. The Saturday farmers market in the square continues through the middle of the month with a focus on holiday items.

## Arts and Culture

Unlike the more (literally) puritanical colonies farther up the North American coast, Charleston was an arts-friendly settlement from the beginning. The first theatrical production on the continent happened in Charleston in January 1735, when a nomadic troupe rented a space at Church and Broad Streets to perform Thomas Otway's *The Orphan*. The play's success led to the building of the Dock Street Theatre on what is now Queen Street. Notable thespians performing in town included Edwin Booth, Junius Booth Jr. (brothers of Lincoln's assassin, John Wilkes), and Edgar Allan Poe's mother, Eliza.

While not considered a visual arts mecca, the Holy City has been fertile ground for visual artists since native son Joseph Allen Smith began one of the country's first art collections in Charleston in the late 1700s. For most visitors, the center of gallery activity is in the French Quarter between South Market and Tradd Streets.

## Art Walks

The best way to experience visual art galleries in Charleston is to go on one of the popular and free **Charleston Gallery Association ArtWalks** (843/724-3424, www.charlestongalleryassociation.com, 1st Fri. of Mar., May, Oct., and Dec. 5pm-8pm), which feature lots of wine, food, and, of course, art. Over 40 galleries throughout downtown, with a special focus on the French Quarter, are featured. You can download a map at the website and visit them all yourself, whether or not you're here for the ArtWalk.

# SOUTH OF BROAD

## Art Galleries

### CHARLESTON RENAISSANCE GALLERY

Charleston Renaissance Gallery specializes in 19th- and 20th-century oils and sculpture and features artists from the American South, including some splendid pieces from the Charleston Renaissance.

**MAP 1:** 103 Church St., 843/723-0025, www.fineartsouth.com; Mon.-Sat. 10am-5pm

### HELENA FOX FINE ART

Helena Fox Fine Art deals in 20th-century representational art, realist oil paintings, and one-of-a-kind designer jewelry.

**MAP 1:** 106-A Church St., 843/723-0073, www.helenafoxfineart.com; Mon.-Sat. 10am-5pm

# WATERFRONT

## Art Galleries

### CITY GALLERY AT WATERFRONT

The City Gallery at Waterfront is funded by the city, with exhibits focusing on local and regional culture and folkways.

**MAP 1:** 34 Prioleau St., 843/958-6484, www.citygalleryatwaterfrontpark.com; Tues.-Fri. 10am-6pm, Sat.-Sun. noon-5pm

# FRENCH QUARTER

## Art Galleries

### ANN LONG FINE ART

Incorporating works from the estate of Charleston legend Elizabeth O'Neill Verner is Ann Long Fine Art, which seeks to combine the painterly aesthetic of the Old World with the edgy vision of the New.

**MAP 1:** 54 Broad St., 843/577-0447, www.annlongfineart.com; Mon.-Sat. 11am-5pm

### CORRIGAN GALLERY

One of the French Quarter's most beloved galleries, the Corrigan deals in some of the best current local artists, along with a focus on the Charleston Renaissance and the Charleston printmaking tradition.

**MAP 1:** 62 Queen St., 843/722-9868, www.corrigangallery.com; daily 10am-5pm

### PINK HOUSE GALLERY

The Pink House Gallery is housed in the oldest tavern building in the South, built circa 1694. The exhibits here offer a glimpse into old Charleston, including exclusive antique prints.

**MAP 1:** 17 Chalmers St., 843/723-3608, http://pinkhousegallery.tripod.com; Mon.-Sat. 10am-5pm

### ROBERT LANGE STUDIOS

Robert Lange Studios is oriented toward modern art. It hosts not only the work of its owners, Robert and Megan Lange, but also a slate of up-and-coming regional artists. This is a great place to be on the regular first Friday monthly art walks and events.

**MAP 1:** 2 Queen St., 843/805-8052, www.robertlangestudios.com; daily 11am-5pm

## Performing Arts

### CHARLESTON STAGE

Several high-quality troupes continue to keep Charleston's proud theater tradition alive, chief among them being Charleston Stage, the resident company of the Dock Street Theatre. In addition to its well-received regular season of classics and modern staples,

## Chamber Music in Charleston

The excellent music department at the College of Charleston sponsors the annual **Charleston Music Fest** (Simons Center for the Arts, 54 St. Philip St., $25), a series of chamber music concerts at various venues around the beautiful campus, featuring many faculty members of the college as well as visiting guest artists. Other college musical offerings include the **College of Charleston Concert Choir** (www.cofc.edu/music), which performs at various venues, usually churches, around town during the fall; the **College of Charleston Opera,** which performs at least one full-length production during the school year and often takes the stage at Piccolo Spoleto; and the popular **Yuletide Madrigal Singers,** who sing in early December at a series of concerts in historic Randolph Hall.

**Chamber Music Charleston** (various locations, 843/763-4941, www.chambermusiccharleston.org), which relies on many core Charleston Symphony Orchestra musicians, continues to perform around town, including at Piccolo Spoleto. They play a wide variety of picturesque venues, including the **Sottile Theatre** (44 George St.) and Kiawah Island. They can also be found at private house concerts, which sell out quickly.

Charleston Stage has debuted more than 30 original scripts over the years, a recent example being *Gershwin at Folly,* recounting the composer's time at Folly Beach working on *Porgy and Bess.*

**MAP 1:** Dock Street Theatre, 135 Church St., 843/577-7183, www.charlestonstage.com

#### THE FOOTLIGHT PLAYERS

The Footlight Players is the oldest continuously active company in town, founded in 1931. This community-based amateur company performs a mix of crowd-pleasers (*Who's Afraid of Virginia Woolf?*) and creative adaptations (*Miracle in Bedford Falls,* a musical based on *It's a Wonderful Life*) at its space at 20 Queen Street.

**MAP 1:** Footlight Players Theatre, 20 Queen St., 843/722-4487, www.footlightplayers.net

## NORTH OF BROAD

### Art Galleries

#### SYLVAN GALLERY

For a more modern take from local artists, check out the Sylvan Gallery, which specializes in 20th- and 21st-century art and sculpture.

**MAP 1:** 171 King St., 843/722-2172, www.thesylvangallery.com; Mon.-Fri. 9am-5pm, Sat. 10am-5pm, Sun. 11am-4pm

#### THE AUDUBON GALLERY

Specializing in original Audubon prints and antique botanical prints is The Audubon Gallery, the sister store of the Joel Oppenheimer Gallery in Chicago.

**MAP 1:** 190 King St., 843/853-1100, www.audubonart.com; Mon.-Sat. 10am-5pm

#### GALLERY CHUMA

Within City Market is Gallery Chuma, which specializes in the art of the Gullah people of the South Carolina coast. They put on lots of cultural and educational events about Gullah culture as well as display art on the subject.

**MAP 1:** 188 Meeting St., 843/722-1702, www.gallerychuma.com; daily 9:30am-6pm

### Performing Arts

#### THE HAVE NOTS!

The city's most unusual players are The Have Nots!, with a rotating ensemble of dozens of comedians who perform their brand of edgy adults-only improv at Theatre 99. Friday is the most reliable improve night, while Wednesday and Saturday may feature more sketch comedy.

**MAP 1:** Theatre 99, 280 Meeting St., 843/853-6687, www.theatre99.com; Wed. 8pm, Fri.-Sat. 8pm and 10pm; $5-13

# UPPER KING

## Art Galleries

### ART MECCA

This inviting modernist space specializes in local and regional contemporary artists. It's a great place to get a flavor of what Charleston's younger up-and-coming artists are doing, in a friendly and relaxed setting.

**MAP 2:** 427 King St., 843/577-0603, www.artmeccaofcharleston.com; Mon.-Fri. 10am-6pm, Sat. 10am-7pm, Sun. 11am-5pm

### PURE THEATRE

Recently celebrating their 15th season, the players of PURE Theatre perform in a black-box space in the heart of the Upper King entertainment and nightlife district. Their shows emphasize compelling mature drama, beautifully performed. This is where to catch less glitzy, grittier productions like *If I Forget, The Royale,* and *American Buffalo.*

**MAP 2:** 477 King St., 843/723-4444, www.puretheatre.org

### REDUX CONTEMPORARY ART CENTER

One of the most important single venues for art, the nonprofit Redux Contemporary Art Center features modernistic work in a variety of media, including illustration, video installation, blueprints, performance art, and graffiti. Outreach is hugely important to this venture and includes lecture series, classes, workshops, and internships.

**MAP 2:** 136 St. Philip St., 843/722-0697, www.reduxstudios.org; Tues.-Fri. 10am-6pm, Sat. noon-5pm

## Performing Arts

### CHARLESTON SYMPHONY ORCHESTRA

The Charleston Symphony Orchestra (CSO) performed for the first time on December 28, 1936, at the Hibernian Hall on Meeting Street. During that first season the CSO accompanied *The Recruiting Officer,* the inaugural show at the renovated Dock Street Theatre. For seven decades, the CSO continued to provide world-class orchestral music, gaining

PURE Theatre

"Metropolitan" status in the 1970s, when they accompanied the first-ever local performance of *Porgy and Bess,* which despite its Charleston setting couldn't be performed locally before then due to segregation laws. Now under the direction of conductor Ken Lam, the CSO performs at the Gaillard Center, modeled on European concert halls. Check the website for upcoming concerts.

**MAP 2:** Gaillard Center, 95 Calhoun St., 843/554-6060, www.charlestonsymphony.com

# FOLLY BEACH AND THE SOUTHWEST ISLANDS

## Cinema

### TERRACE THEATRE

The most interesting art-house and indie venue in town is The Terrace, and not only because they offer beer and wine that you can enjoy at your seat. It's west of Charleston on James Island; get there by taking U.S. 17 west from Charleston and go south on Highway 171, then take a right on Maybank Highway (Hwy. 700).

**MAP 5:** 1956D Maybank Hwy., 843/762-4247, www.terracetheater.com

# Shops

Shopping in Charleston centers on King Street, unique not only for the fact that so many national-name stores are lined up so close to each other, but also because there are so many great restaurants of so many different types scattered in and among the retail outlets, ideally positioned for when you need to take a break to rest and refuel. **Lower King** is primarily top-of-the-line antiques stores (most are closed Sunday, so plan your trip accordingly); **Middle King** is where you'll find upscale and name-brand outlets such as Banana Republic and American Apparel as well as some excellent shoe stores; and **Upper King,** north of Calhoun Street, is where you'll find more cutting-edge boutiques and housewares shops, often locally owned with a personal touch.

## WATERFRONT

### Home Goods

#### INDIGO

Indigo, a favorite home accessories store, has plenty of one-of-a-kind pieces, many of them by regional artists and rustic in flavor, almost like outsider art.

**MAP 1:** 4 Vendue Range, 800/549-2513; www.indigohome.com, Sun.-Thurs. 10am-6pm, Fri.-Sat. 10am-7pm

## FRENCH QUARTER

### Antiques and Vintage

#### CURIOSITY

A cute little shop tucked away in an alley, Curiosity is a find even by the standards of antiques- and vintage-crazy Charleston. A nice plus is the prices here are a bit lower than in the premier antiques shops on Lower King Street, which would never be accused of being bargain-priced.

**MAP 1:** 56½ Queen St., 843/647-7763, www.curiositycharleston.com

### Books and Music

#### SHOPS OF HISTORIC CHARLESTON FOUNDATION

The great Shops of Historic Charleston Foundation is housed in a beautiful building

Most shops on King Street are located in restored historic storefronts.

and has plenty of tasteful Charleston-themed gift ideas, from books to kitchenware.
**MAP 1:** 108 Meeting St., 843/724-8484, www.historiccharleston.org

# NORTH OF BROAD

## Antiques

### ALEXANDRA AD

Alexandra AD features great chandeliers, lamps, and fabrics, and specialized in rare finds of vintage household goods and furnishings.
**MAP 1:** 156 King St., 843/722-4897; Mon.-Sat. 10am-5pm

### GEORGE C. BIRLANT & CO.

Since 1929, George C. Birlant & Co. has been importing 18th- and 19th-century furniture, silver, china, and crystal, and it deals in the famous "Charleston Battery Bench," replicas of the signature public seats a bit farther south along the Battery overlooking Charleston harbor.
**MAP 1:** 191 King St., 843/722-3842; Mon.-Sat. 9am-5:30pm

### GOLDEN & ASSOCIATES

One of King Street's most fun antiquing experiences is at Golden & Associates, where you can wander the showroom for hours and still feel like you need to come back and browse some more. You'll find a bit of everything here, from high-end estate items to retro kitsch, from European fixtures to Caribbean furniture.
**MAP 1:** 204-206 King St., 843/723-8886, www.goldenassociatesantiques.com

### JACQUES' ANTIQUES

Jacques' Antiques is a headquarters for spectacular European pieces, from objets d'art to furniture and lighting, with a particular emphasis on French items.
**MAP 1:** 160 King St., 843/577-0104; Mon.-Sat. 10am-5pm

## Books and Music

### PAULINE BOOKS AND MEDIA

The charming Pauline Books and Media is run by the Daughters of Saint Paul and carries Christian books, Bibles, rosaries, and images from a Roman Catholic perspective.
**MAP 1:** 243 King St., 843/577-0175; Mon.-Sat. 10am-6pm

### PRESERVATION SOCIETY OF CHARLESTON BOOK AND GIFT SHOP

It's easy to overlook at the far southern end of the retail development on King, but the excellent Preservation Society of Charleston Book and Gift Shop is perhaps the best place in town to pick up books on Charleston lore and history as well as locally themed gift items.
**MAP 1:** 147 King St., 843/722-4630; Mon.-Sat. 10am-5pm

## Clothes

### M. DUMAS & SONS

Now beginning its second century in business, M. Dumas & Sons is perhaps the iconic King Street retail name. It's a classic men's shop, with upscale business and formal wear, backed up by an old-school emphasis on meticulous tailoring. While it's steeped in tradition—Mendel Dumas opened it in 1917 as a uniform shop for service workers—Dumas stays on top of recent trends as well. A 2015 renovation has made it an even more expansive and delightful experience.
**MAP 1:** 294 King St., 843/723-8603, www.mdumasandsons.com; Mon.-Sat. 9am-7pm, Sun. 11:30am-5:30pm

### BERLINS MEN'S AND WOMEN'S

A charmingly old-school and notable locally owned clothing store on King Street is the classy Berlins Men's and Women's, dating from 1883. Despite the name, Berlins focuses on men's clothing, offering designs from Canali, Coppley, Jack Victor, and more.
**MAP 1:** 114-120 King St., 843/722-1665; Mon.-Sat. 9:30am-6pm

### THE TRUNK SHOW

The incredible consignment store The Trunk Show offers one-of-a-kind vintage and designer wear and accessories. Some finds are bargains, some not so much, but there's no denying the quality and breadth of the offerings.

**MAP 1:** 281 Meeting St., 843/722-0442; Mon.-Sat. 10am-6pm

### SIMPLY J BOUTIQUE

Simply J Boutique focuses on hip, casual wear for women at realistic price points, with an assortment of unique designs not to be found elsewhere. They are known for personalized and friendly customer service in the true Charleston tradition of hospitality.

**MAP 2:** 377 King St., 843/641-0224, www.simplyjboutique.com; Mon.-Thurs. 10am-6pm, Fri.-Sat. 9:30am-6pm, Sun. 10:30am-5pm

### THE SKINNY DIP

For a wide assortment of designers brands, The Skinny Dip is a well-curated collection with a strong regional presence and a solid national selection of boutique designs. They also have a men's and children's selection. The upstairs space hosts frequent community events—seminars, trunk shows, yoga, and wine tastings.

**MAP 2:** 345 King St., 843/872-5610, www.skinnydipcharleston.com; Thurs.-Sat. 10am-8pm, Mon.-Wed. 10am-6pm, Sun. 11am-6pm

### SPARTINA 449

A small regional chain based in nearby Bluffton, South Carolina, Spartina 449 offers a distinctive design take on women's clothes and accessories, with a branded color and design palette.

**MAP 2:** 300 King St., 843/974-4684, www.spartina449.com; Mon.-Sat. 10am-6pm, Sun. noon-5pm

## Jewelry

### ART JEWELRY BY MIKHAIL SMOLKIN

Art Jewelry by Mikhail Smolkin features one-of-a-kind pieces by this St. Petersburg, Russia, native.

**MAP 1:** 312 King St., 843/722-3634, www.fineartjewelry.com; Mon.-Sat. 10am-5pm

### CROGHAN'S JEWEL BOX

Since 1919, Croghan's Jewel Box has offered amazing locally crafted diamonds, silver, and designer pieces to generations of Charlestonians. An expansion in the late 1990s tripled the size of the historic location. From estate jewelry to bridal wear, they offer an incredible browsing experience.

**MAP 1:** 308 King St., 843/723-3594, www.croghansjewelbox.com; Mon.-Fri. 9:30am-5:30pm, Sat. 10am-5pm

## Shoes

### BOB ELLIS SHOE STORE

A famous locally owned place for footwear is Bob Ellis Shoe Store, which has served Charleston's elite with high-end shoes since 1950.

**MAP 1:** 332 King St., 843/722-2515, www.bobellisshoes.com; Mon.-Sat. 10am-6pm

### COPPER PENNY SHOOZ

Copper Penny Shooz combines hip and upscale footwear for women, "curated with a Southern eye," as this Charleston-based regional chain's motto goes.

**MAP 1:** 317 King St., 843/723-3838; Mon.-Sat. 10am-7pm, Sun. noon-6pm

### RANGONI OF FLORENCE

Rangoni of Florence imports the best women's shoes from Italy, with a few men's designs as well. Brands include Rangoni of Florence, Valentine Rangoni, Petra, d'Rossana, Via Spiga and others. Men's designs include Cole-Haan and Bruno Magli.

**MAP 1:** 237 King St., 843/577-9554; Mon.-Thurs. 10am-6pm, Fri.-Sat. 10am-7pm, Sun. 12:30pm-5:30pm

## Shopping Centers and Malls

### BELMOND CHARLESTON PLACE

Belmond Charleston Place, usually just called "Charleston Place," is a combined retail-hotel development with highlights such as

Gucci, Talbots, Louis Vuitton, Yves Delorme, Everything But Water, and Godiva.

**MAP 1:** 205 Meeting St., 843/722-4900, www.charlestonplaceshops.com; Mon.-Wed. 10am-6pm, Thurs.-Sat. 10am-8pm, Sun. noon-5pm

### CITY MARKET

For years dominated by a flea-market vibe, City Market was recently upgraded and is now chockablock with boutique retail all along its lengthy interior. The humbler crafts tables are toward the back. If you must have one of the handcrafted sweetgrass baskets, try out your haggling skills—the prices have wiggle room built in. In addition to the myriad tourist-oriented shops in the City Market itself, there are a few gems in the surrounding area that also appeal to locals.

**MAP 1:** Meeting St. and Market St., 843/973-7236; daily 9:30am-10:30pm

## Sporting Goods

### HALF MOON OUTFITTERS

With retail locations in Charleston and throughout South Carolina and Georgia and a new cutting-edge eco-friendly warehouse in North Charleston, Half Moon Outfitters is something of a local legend. Here you can find not only top-of-the-line camping and outdoor gear and tips on local recreation, but also some really stylish outdoorsy apparel as well.

**MAP 1:** 280 King St., 843/853-0990, www.halfmoonoutfitters.com; Mon.-Sat. 10am-7pm, Sun. noon-6pm

# UPPER KING

## Books and Music

### BLUE BICYCLE BOOKS

Housed in an extremely long and narrow storefront, Jonathan Sanchez's funky and friendly Blue Bicycle Books deals primarily in used books and has a particularly nice stock of local and regional titles, art books, and fiction.

**MAP 2:** 420 King St., 843/722-2666, www.bluebicyclebooks.com; Mon.-Sat. 10am-7:30pm, Sun. 1pm-6pm

## Home Goods and Gifts

### RO SHAM BEAUX

For cutting-edge sustainable home goods and lighting with a very high level of taste, visit Ro Sham Beaux. They can help design custom fixtures to your taste. The bead selection alone is mind-blowing.

**MAP 2:** 493 King St., 843/641-7087, www.ro-sham-beaux.com; Mon.-Sat. 10am-7:30pm, Sun. 1pm-6pm

Blue Bicycle Books

#### LULU BURGESS

Probably the best single gift shop-stop in Charleston is Lulu Burgess, actually an expansion of a Beaufort, South Carolina-based regional chain. Their eclectic mix of gifts and whimsical home goods ranges from humorous to more unique locally-themed items, and the staff tries hard to keep everyone happy.

**MAP 2:** 409 King St., 843/641-7087, www.luluburgess.com; Mon.-Thurs. 10am-7pm, Fri.-Sat. 10am-8pm, Sun. 11am-6pm

### Clothing

#### BECKETT BOUTIQUE

Adjacent to Lulu Burgess, Beckett Boutique combines fashion-forward designs for women with great wearability. Regular clients give it strong word-of-mouth.

**MAP 2:** 409 King St., 843/405-1105, www.beckettboutique.com; Mon.-Fri. 10am-6:30pm, Sat. 11am-6:30pm, Sun. noon-6pm

## WEST ASHLEY

### Music

#### MONSTER MUSIC AND MOVIES

In an age when it's harder and harder to find brick-and-mortar music and movie stores, Monster Music and Movies is a great discovery. They have new and used vinyl and CDs and feature great sales and in-store performances for the annual Record Store Day in April.

**MAP 3:** 946 Orleans Rd., 843/571-4657; Mon.-Sat. 10am-9pm, Sun. noon-7pm

## NORTH CHARLESTON

### Music

#### FOX MUSIC HOUSE

Fox Music House is a neighborhood favorite, and has been locally owned since 1928. They specialize in pianos and keyboards.

**MAP 3:** 3005 W. Montague Ave., 843/740-7200; Mon.-Fri. 10am-6pm, Sat. 10am-5pm

### Shopping Centers

#### TANGER OUTLET

The Tanger Outlet has factory-priced bargains from stores such as Adidas, Banana Republic, Brooks Brothers, CorningWare, Old Navy, Timberland, and more.

**MAP 3:** 4840 Tanger Outlet Blvd., 843/529-3095, www.tangeroutlet.com; Mon.-Sat. 10am-9pm, Sun. 11am-6pm

## MOUNT PLEASANT AND EAST COOPER

### Antiques

#### PAGE'S THIEVES MARKET

Mount Pleasant boasts a fun antiques and auction spot, Page's Thieves Market. Its rambling interior has hosted bargain and vintage shoppers for 50 years, and it's routinely voted Charleston's best antiques store.

**MAP 4:** 1460 Ben Sawyer Blvd., 843/884-9672, www.pagesthievesmarket.com; Mon.-Fri. 9am-5:30pm, Sat. 9am-5pm

### Shopping Centers

#### MOUNT PLEASANT TOWNE CENTER

The most pleasant mall in the area is the retro-themed, pedestrian-friendly Mount Pleasant Towne Center. In addition to national chains you'll find a few cool local stores in here, like Stella Nova spa and day salon and Copper Penny Shooz.

**MAP 4:** 1600 Palmetto Grande Dr., 843/216-9900, www.mtpleasanttownecentre.com; Mon.-Sat. 10am-9pm, Sun. noon-6pm

#### GWYNN'S OF MOUNT PLEASANT

In a Harris Teeter grocery shopping center, Gwynn's is an old-fashioned department store specializing in women's clothing and shoes, with a distinct local and Southern sensibility.

**MAP 4:** 916 Houston Northcutt Blvd., 843/884-9518; Mon.-Sat. 10am-7pm

# Sports and Activities

Because of the generally great weather in Charleston, encouraged by the steady, soft sea breeze, outdoor activities are always popular and available. Though it's not much of a spectator sports town, there are plenty of things to do on your own, such as play golf and tennis, walk, hike, boat, and fish.

The country's first golf course was constructed in Charleston in 1786, so as you'd expect there's great golfing in the area, generally on the outlying islands. The folks at the nonprofit **Charleston Golf** (423 King St., 843/958-3629, www.charlestongolfguide.com) are your best one-stop resource for tee times and packages.

Charleston-area beaches are perfect for a leisurely bike ride on the sand. Sullivan's Island is a particular favorite, and you might be surprised at how long you can ride in one direction on these beaches. Those desiring a more demanding use of their legs can walk or ride their bike in the dedicated pedestrian and bike lane on the massive **Arthur Ravenel Jr. Bridge** over the Cooper River, the longest cable-stayed bridge in the western hemisphere.

For casual fishing off a pier, try the well-equipped **Folly Beach Fishing Pier** (101 E. Arctic Ave., Folly Beach, 843/588-3474, daily dawn-dusk, $5-7 parking, $8 fishing fee, rod rentals available) on Folly Beach or the **North Charleston Riverfront Park** (843/745-1087, www.northcharleston.org, daily dawn-dusk) along the Cooper River on the grounds of the old Navy Yard. Get onto the Navy Yard grounds by taking I-26 north to exit 216B. Take a left onto Spruill Avenue and a right onto McMillan Avenue.

Key local marinas include **Shem Creek Marina** (526 Mill St., 843/884-3211, www.shemcreekmarina.com), **Charleston Harbor Marina** (24 Patriots Point Rd., 843/284-7062, www.charlestonharbormarina.com), **Charleston City Marina** (17 Lockwood Dr., 843/722-4968), **Charleston Maritime Center** (10 Wharfside St., 843/853-3625, www.cmcevents.com), and the **Cooper River Marina** (1010 Juneau Ave., 843/554-0790, www.ccprc.com).

The best fishing charter outfit in the area is Barrier Island Eco Tours (see listing below) out of Isle of Palms. Other good outfits include **Bohicket Boat Adventure & Tour Co.** (2789 Cherry Point Rd., 843/559-3525, www.bohicketboat.com, half-day $375 for 1-2 passengers) out of the Edisto River and **Reel Fish Finder Charters** (315 Yellow Jasmine Court, Moncks Corner, 843/697-2081, www.reelfishfinder.com, half-day $400 for 1-3 passengers). Captain James picks up clients at many different marinas in the area. For a list of all public landings in Charleston County, go to www.ccprc.com.

Offshore diving centers on a network of **artificial reefs** (see www.dnr.sc.gov for a list and locations), particularly the "Charleston 60" sunken barge and the popular "Train Wreck," comprising 50 deliberately sunk New York City subway cars. In addition to the highly regarded **Charleston Scuba** (335 Savannah Hwy., 843/763-3483, www.charlestonscuba.com), you also might want to check out **Cooper River Scuba** (843/572-0459, www.cooperriverdiving.com) and **Atlantic Coast Dive Center** (209 Scott St., 843/884-1500).

Many kayakers put in at the Shem Creek Marina or the public Shem Creek Landing in Mount Pleasant. From here it's a safe easy paddle—sometimes with appearances by dolphins or manatees—to the Intracoastal Waterway. Some kayakers like to go from Shem Creek straight out into Charleston Harbor to Crab Bank Heritage Preserve, a prime birding island. Another good place to put in is at **Isle of Palms Marina** (50 41st Ave., 843/886-0209) behind the Wild Dunes Resort on Morgan Creek, which empties into the Intracoastal Waterway. Behind Folly Beach is an extensive

## Water Parks

During the summer months, Charleston County operates three water parks: **Splash Island Waterpark** (444 Needlerush Pkwy., Mount Pleasant, 843/884-0832); **Whirlin' Waters Adventure Waterpark** (University Blvd., North Charleston, 843/572-7275); and **Splash Zone Waterpark at James Island County Park** (871 Riverland Dr., 843/795-7275), on James Island west of town. Admission runs about $10 pp. Go to www.ccprc.com for more information.

network of waterways, including lots of areas that are great for camping and fishing. The Folly River Landing is just over the bridge to the island.

# HAMPTON PARK

## Spectator Sports

### CHARLESTON RIVER DOGS

A New York Yankees Class A affiliate in the South Atlantic League, the Charleston River Dogs play April-August at **Joseph P. Riley Jr. Park**, a.k.a. "The Joe." This fantastic park was inspired by the retro design of Baltimore's Oriole Park at Camden Yards. There are no bad seats, so you might as well save a few bucks and go for the general admission ticket. There are a lot of fun promotions to keep things interesting should the play on the field be less than stimulating. Expect to pay $5 for parking.

**MAP 2:** Joseph P. Riley Jr. Park, 360 Fishburne St., 843/577-3647, www.riverdogs.com; $8-11 general admission

### CITADEL BULLDOGS

The Citadel plays Southern Conference football home games at **Johnson Hagood Stadium,** next to the campus on the Ashley River near Hampton Park. The basketball team plays home games at **McAlister Field House** on campus. The school's hockey team skates home games at the **Carolina Ice Palace** (7665 Northwoods Blvd., North Charleston).

**MAP 2:** The Citadel, 171 Moultrie St., 843/953-3294, www.citadelsports.com; ticket prices vary

# WEST ASHLEY

## Diving

### CHARLESTON SCUBA

Charleston's best-regarded outfitter and charter operator is Charleston Scuba. They offer training classes, charters, and offshore diving trips.

**MAP 3:** 335 Savannah Hwy., 843/763-3483, www.charlestonscuba.com

## Hiking and Biking

### WEST ASHLEY GREENWAY

The West Ashley Greenway is an urban walking and biking trail built on a former rail bed. The 10-mile trail runs parallel to U.S. 17 and passes parks, schools, and the Clemson Experimental Farm, ending near Johns Island. To get to the trailhead from downtown, drive west on U.S. 17. About 0.5 miles after you cross the bridge, turn left onto Folly Road (Hwy. 171). At the second light, turn right into South Windermere Shopping Center; the trail is behind the center on the right.

**MAP 3:** South Windermere Shopping Center (80 Folly Rd.) to Johns Island, paralleling U.S. 17; daily dawn-dusk

# NORTH CHARLESTON

## Ice-Skating

### CAROLINA ICE PALACE

Ice-skating in South Carolina? Yep, 100,000 square feet of it, year-round, at the two NHL-size rinks of the Carolina Ice Palace. This is also the practice facility for the local hockey team, the Stingrays, as well as where the Citadel's hockey team plays.

**MAP 3:** 7665 Northwoods Blvd., 843/572-2717, www.carolinaicepalace.com; daily public sessions; $7 adults, $6 children

# SPECTATOR SPORTS

### SOUTH CAROLINA STINGRAYS

An ECHL professional hockey team, the South Carolina Stingrays get a good crowd out to their rink at the North Charleston Coliseum, playing October-April.

**MAP 3:** North Charleston Coliseum, 5001 Coliseum Dr., 843/744-2248, www.stingrayshockey.com; $15

## MOUNT PLEASANT AND EAST COOPER

### Beaches

#### ISLE OF PALMS COUNTY PARK

On Isle of Palms you'll find Isle of Palms County Park, which has restrooms, showers, a picnic area, a beach volleyball area, and beach chair and umbrella rentals. Get there by taking the Isle of Palms Connector (Hwy. 517) to the island, go through the light at Palm Boulevard, and take the next left at the park gate. There's good public beach access near the Pavilion Shoppes on Ocean Boulevard, accessed via J. C. Long Boulevard.

**MAP 4:** 14th Ave., Isle of Palms, 843/886-3863, www.ccprc.com; fall-spring daily 10am-dark, summer daily 9am-dark; $5 per vehicle, free for pedestrians and cyclists

#### SULLIVAN'S ISLAND BEACH

For a totally go-it-alone type of beach day, go to the three-mile-long beach on the Atlantic Ocean at Sullivan's Island. There are no facilities, no lifeguards, strong offshore currents, and no parking lots on this residential island (park on the side of the street). Get there from downtown by crossing the Ravenel Bridge over the Cooper River and bearing right onto Coleman Boulevard, which turns into Ben Sawyer Boulevard. Take the Ben Sawyer Bridge onto Sullivan's Island. Beach access is plentiful and marked.

**MAP 4:** Station 18 St., 843/883-3198, www.sullivansisland-sc.com; free

### Bird-Watching

#### CRAB BANK SEABIRD SANCTUARY

Right in Charleston Harbor is the little Crab Bank Seabird Sanctuary, where thousands of migratory birds can be seen, depending on the season. The sanctuary has been designated an Important Bird Area by Audubon. Mid-October to mid-March you can either kayak there yourself or take a charter with **Nature Adventures Outfitters** (1900 Iron Swamp Rd., Awendaw Island, 800/673-0679). During nesting season, mid-March to mid-October, the sanctuary is closed to the public.

**MAP 4:** Charleston Harbor, 803/734-3886, www.dnr.sc.gov; Oct. 16-Mar. 14 daily dawn-dusk

#### I'ON SWAMP TRAIL

Once part of a rice plantation, the I'on Swamp Trail is one of the premier bird-watching sites in South Carolina, particularly during spring and fall migrations. The rare Bachman's warbler, commonly considered one of the most elusive birds in North America, has been seen here. To get here, make the 10-minute drive to Mount Pleasant, then head north on U.S. 17 and take a left onto I'on Swamp Road (Forest Rd. 228). The parking area is 2.5 miles ahead on the left.

**MAP 4:** 15 miles northeast of Charleston, via U.S. 17, 843/928-3368, www.fs.fed.us; daily dawn-dusk; free

### Boating

#### BARRIER ISLAND ECO TOURS

Barrier Island Eco Tours can take you on a passenger boat ride up to the Cape Romain National Wildlife Refuge out of Isle of Palms, with a focus on undeveloped Capers Island. Plan on seeing plenty of dolphins!

**MAP 4:** 50 41st Ave., 843/886-5000, www.nature-tours.com; $38 adults, $28 children

### Golf

#### PATRIOTS POINT LINKS

The 18-hole Patriots Point Links on the Charleston Harbor, right over the Ravenel Bridge, is one of the most convenient courses in the area, and it boasts some phenomenal views.

**MAP 4:** 1 Patriots Point Rd., Mount Pleasant, 843/881-0042, www.patriotspointlinks.com; $100 for 18 holes

#### RIVERTOWNE GOLF COURSE

In Mount Pleasant you will find perhaps the best course in the area for the money, the award-winning Rivertowne Golf Course at the

## Free Tennis, Anyone?

There are four free, public, city-funded facilities on the peninsula:

- **Moultrie Playground:** Broad St. and Ashley Ave., 843/769-8258, www.charlestoncity.info; six lighted hard courts
- **Jack Adams Tennis Center:** 290 Congress St.; six lighted hard courts
- **Hazel Parker Playground:** 70 E. Bay St., on the Cooper River; one hard court
- **Corrine Jones Playground:** Marlowe St. and Peachtree St.; two hard courts

Rivertowne Country Club. Opened in 2002, the course was designed by Arnold Palmer.

**MAP 4:** 1700 Rivertowne Country Club Dr., Mount Pleasant, 843/856-9808, www.rivertownecountryclub.com; $150 for 18 holes

### WILD DUNES RESORT

Two excellent resort-style public courses are at Wild Dunes Resort on Isle of Palms. The resort has been named one of the state's best by *Golf Digest.*

**MAP 4:** 5757 Palm Blvd., Isle of Palms, 888/845-8932, www.wilddunes.com; $165 for 18 holes

## Hiking and Biking

### AWENDAW PASSAGE

The most ambitious trail in South Carolina is the **Palmetto Trail,** begun in 1997 and eventually covering 425 miles from the Atlantic to the Appalachians. The coastal terminus of the Palmetto Trail, the seven-mile Awendaw Passage, winds through the Francis Marion National Forest. It begins at the trailhead at the Buck Hall Recreational Area, which has parking and restroom facilities. Get here by taking U.S. 17 north from Charleston about 20 miles and through the Francis Marion National Forest and then Awendaw. Take a right onto Buck Hall Landing Road.

**MAP 4:** Buck Hall Recreational Area, McClellanville, 843/887-3257, www.palmettoconservation.org; $5 vehicle fee

## Spectator Sports

### CHARLESTON BATTERY

The professional United Soccer League team Charleston Battery plays April-July at **MUSC Health Stadium** on Daniel Island, north of Charleston.

**MAP 4:** MUSC Health Stadium, 1990 Daniel Island Dr., 843/971-4625, www.charlestonbattery.com; about $10

## Surfing

### SOL SURFERS SURF CAMP

Mount Pleasant is home to Sol Surfers Surf Camp, which offers surf camps during the summer and private and group lessons throughout the year. The surf camp shuttle picks up students at the Parrot Surf Shop (811 Coleman Blvd.). Surf camps take place on the eastern end of Folly Beach.

**MAP 4:** 1170 Lazy Lane, Mount Pleasant, 843/881-6700, www.solsurfers.net

## Tennis

### FAMILY CIRCLE TENNIS CENTER

Tennis fans are in for a treat at the Family Circle Tennis Center on Daniel Island. This multimillion-dollar facility is owned by the city of Charleston and was built in 2001 specifically to host the annual Family Circle Cup women's competition, which is now known as the Volvo Car Open. But it's also open to the public year-round (except when the Volvo Car Open is on) with 17 courts.

**MAP 4:** 161 Seven Farms Dr., 800/677-2293, www.volvocaropen.com; Mon.-Thurs. 8am-8pm, Fri. 8am-7pm, Sat. 8am-5pm, Sun. 9am-5pm; $15 per hour

## Kayaking Tours

### COASTAL EXPEDITIONS

An excellent outfit for guided kayak tours is Coastal Expeditions, which also runs the only approved ferry service to the Cape Romain National Wildlife Refuge. They'll rent you a kayak for roughly $50 per day. Coastal Expeditions also sells an outstanding kayaking, boating, and fishing map of the area (about $12).

**MAP 4:** 654 Serotina Court, 843/881-4582, www.coastalexpeditions.com

### NATURE ADVENTURES OUTFITTERS

The best tour operator close to downtown is Nature Adventures Outfitters, which puts in on Shem Creek in Mount Pleasant for most of its 2-, 2.5-, 3-, and 3.5-hour and full-day guided trips, with prices ranging $40-85. They also offer blackwater tours out of landings at other locations; see the website for specific directions for those tours.

**MAP 4:** Shrimp Boat Lane, 843/568-3222, www.kayakcharlestonsc.com

# FOLLY BEACH AND THE SOUTHWEST ISLANDS

Behind Folly Beach is an extensive network of waterways, including lots of areas that are great for camping and fishing. The Folly River Landing is just over the bridge to the island.

## Beaches

### FOLLY BEACH COUNTY PARK

In addition to the charming town of Folly Beach itself, there's the modest county-run Folly Beach County Park at the far west end of Folly Island. It has a picnic area, restrooms, outdoor showers, and beach chair and umbrella rentals. Get there by taking Highway 171 (Folly Rd.) until it turns into Center Street, and then take a right on West Ashley Avenue.

**MAP 5:** 1100 W. Ashley Ave., Folly Beach, 843/588-2426, www.ccprc.com; May-Feb. daily 10am-dark, Mar.-Apr. daily 9am-dark; $7 per vehicle, free for pedestrians and cyclists

### KIAWAH ISLAND BEACHWALKER PARK

On the west end of Kiawah Island to the south of Charleston is Kiawah Island Beachwalker Park, the only public facility on this mostly private resort island. It has restrooms, showers, a picnic area with grills, and beach chair and umbrella rentals. Get there from downtown Charleston by taking Lockwood Avenue onto the Highway 30 Connector bridge over the Ashley River. Turn right onto Folly Road, then take a left onto Maybank Highway. After about 20 minutes you'll take another left onto Bohicket Road, which leads you to Kiawah in 14 miles. Turn left from Bohicket Road onto the Kiawah Island Parkway. Just before the security gate, turn right on Beachwalker Drive and follow the signs to the park.

**MAP 5:** Kiawah Island, 843/768-2395, www.ccprc.com; Mar.-Apr. and Oct. Sat.-Sun. 10am-6pm, May-Aug. daily 9am-7pm, Sept. daily 10am-6pm; $7 per vehicle, free for pedestrians and cyclists

## Bird-Watching

### LEGARE FARMS

On Johns Island southwest of Charleston is Legare Farms, which holds migratory bird walks ($6 adults, $3 children) in the fall each Saturday at 8:30am.

**MAP 5:** 2620 Hanscombe Point Rd., Johns Island, 843/559-0788, www.legarefarms.com; hours vary

## Golf

### CHARLESTON MUNICIPAL GOLF COURSE

The main public course is the 18-hole City of Charleston Golf Course, affectionately referred to as The Muni. To get there from the peninsula, take U.S. 17 south over the Ashley River, take Highway 171 (Folly Rd.) south, and then take a right onto Maybank Highway.

**MAP 5:** 2110 Maybank Hwy., 843/795-6517, www.charleston-sc.gov/golf; $22-24 for 18 holes

### KIAWAH ISLAND GOLF RESORT

Probably the most renowned area facilities are at the acclaimed Kiawah Island Golf Resort, about 20 miles from Charleston. The resort has five courses in all, the best known of which is the **Kiawah Island Ocean Course,** site of the famous "War by the Shore" 1991 Ryder Cup. This 2.5-mile course, which is walking-only until noon each day, hosted the Senior PGA Championship in 2007 and the PGA Championship in 2012. The resort offers a golf academy and private lessons galore. These are public courses, but be aware that tee times are limited for golfers who aren't guests at the resort.

**MAP 5:** 12 Kiawah Beach Dr., Kiawah Island, 800/654-2924, www.kiawahresort.com/golf; $150-350 for 18 holes, 25 percent discount for resort guests

## Surfing and Kiteboarding

The surfing at the famous Washout area on the east side of Folly Beach isn't what it used to be due to storm activity and beach erosion. But diehards still gather at this area when the swell hits. Check out the conditions yourself from the three views of the **Folly Surfcam** (www.follysurfcam.com).

### FOLLY BEACH SHAKA SURF SCHOOL

Folly Beach Shaka Surf School offers private and group surf lessons, including youth surf camps throughout summer, women-only weekend outings, and yoga classes geared toward surfers. Surf camps are located on the east end of Folly Beach.

**MAP 5:** 107 E. Indian Ave., Folly Beach, 843/607-9911, www.shakasurfschool.com

### MCKEVLIN'S SURF SHOP

The best local surf shop is undoubtedly the historic McKevlin's Surf Shop on Folly Beach, one of the first surf shops on the East Coast, dating to 1965.

**MAP 5:** 8 Center St., Folly Beach, 843/588-2247, www.mckevlins.com; spring-summer daily 10am-6pm, fall-winter daily 10am-5:30pm

## Tennis

### KIAWAH ISLAND GOLF RESORT

The best resort tennis activity is at the Kiawah Island Golf Resort. The resort's Roy Barth Tennis Center has nine clay and three hard courts, while the West Beach Tennis Club has 10 Har-Tru courts and 2 lighted hard courts.

**MAP 5:** 12 Kiawah Beach Dr., Kiawah Island, 800/654-2924, www.kiawahresort.com; $44 per hour nonguests

# Restaurants

Charleston's long history of good taste and livability combines with an affluent and sophisticated population to attract some of the brightest chefs and restaurateurs in the country. A long list of James Beard Award nominees each year confirms the city's role as perhaps the preeminent hub of culinary excellence in the American South.

Kitchens here eschew fickle trends, instead emphasizing quality, professionalism, and, most of all, freshness of ingredients. The farm-to-table movement is as strong here as anywhere in the country and drives the menus of most of the premier establishments.

If you come here in the first week or two of the New Year, keep in mind that is usually the time when Charleston's more popular restaurants might close briefly for renovations.

## WATERFRONT

### New Southern

#### ★ MCCRADY'S $$$

Few restaurants in Charleston have inspired such impassioned advocates as legendary chef Sean Brock's flagship restaurant, McCrady's. In the restaurant's early days, Brock's then-groundbreaking sous vide (or vacuum cooking technique) was spoken of in reverent tones by his clientele. In an expansion and reimagining, Brock moved the original McCrady's to a spot right next door, where it continues to offer the sophisticated, almost frighteningly delicious tasting-menu experience for which it is renowned ($125 pp, $85 pp wine pairing). Brock repurposed the former McCrady's space as **McCrady's Tavern,** a return to the original 1770s use of the building as a watering hole and community gathering spot. In a nod to a

## Best Restaurants

★ **Greatest Food Adventure:** Sean Brock's flagship restaurant, **McCrady's** combines old-school attention to service and detail with a daring approach to cuisine.

★ **Most Delightful Date Night:** The award-winning **FIG** offers incredible fine dining with friendly service in a classy but relaxed atmosphere.

★ **Most Muscular Mussels:** The best bowl of mussels you'll have outside France is at the bistro **39 Rue de Jean.**

★ **Greatest Grits:** Enjoy spirited takes on the classic Southern brunch at **Hominy Grill.**

★ **Freshest Comfort Food:** Charleston is full of great farm-to-table spots, but **The Glass Onion** offers the most accessible Southern classics made from local produce.

★ **Best Bar for Burgers:** In West Ashley, **Gene's Haufbrau** combines an awesome beer selection with some of the best burgers in town.

★ **Most Ridiculous Ribs:** The smoky slabs at **Fiery Ron's Home Team BBQ** are so good you'll hardly be able to stand it, but try anyway.

★ **Best She-Crab Soup:** Just north of town on U.S. 17 you'll find **See Wee Restaurant,** known for its seafood.

★ **Closest Intersection of France and South Carolina:** On Johns Island is **Fat Hen,** where the specialties are Southern in origin and French in execution.

more egalitarian dining experience, the tavern has a more casual New Southern menu. Either spot is a core stop of any Charleston foodie pilgrimage.

**MAP 1:** 2 Unity Alley and 155 Bay St., www.mccradysrestaurant.com; Wed.-Thurs. and Sun. 7pm seating, Fri.-Sat. 6:30pm and 8:45pm seatings

### MAGNOLIAS $$$

Magnolias began life as one of Charleston's first serious eating spots. While the interior has since been given a warm renovation, the menu remains as attractive as ever, with a delightful take on Southern classics like the lump crab cakes, the shellfish over grits, and the rainbow trout. The appetizers are particularly strong—start with the famous fried green tomatoes or maybe the boiled peanut hummus.

**MAP 1**: 185 E. Bay St., 843/577-7771, www.magnoliascharleston.com; Mon.-Sat. 11:30am-10pm, Sun. 3:45pm-10pm

### SLIGHTLY NORTH OF BROAD $$$

Slightly North of Broad, or "SNOB," is an ironic play on the often pejorative reference to the insular South of Broad neighborhood. This hot spot, routinely voted best restaurant in town in such contests, is anything but snobby. Hopping with happy foodies for lunch and dinner, the fun is enhanced by the long, open kitchen with its own counter area. The dynamic but comforting menu here is practically a bible of the new wave of Lowcountry cuisine, with dishes like beef tenderloin, jumbo lump crab cakes, grilled barbecue tuna—and, of course, the pan-seared flounder. An interesting twist at SNOB is the selection of "medium plates," dishes that are a little more generous than an appetizer but with the same adventurous spirit.

**MAP 1**: 192 E. Bay St., 843/723-3424, www.snobcharleston.com; daily 11:30am-2:30pm and 5pm-10pm

# NORTH OF BROAD

## Classic Southern

### HUSK $$$

Executive chef Sean Brock of McCrady's fame already had a reputation as one of the country's leading purveyors of the farm-to-table fine-dining movement, but he cemented that reputation with Husk, voted "Best New Restaurant in the U.S." by *Bon Appétit* magazine soon after its 2011 opening. Brock says of his ingredients, "If it doesn't come from the South, it's not coming through the door." The spare, focused menu is constantly changing with the seasons. On a recent lunch visit, my party enjoyed two types of catfish (a fried catfish BLT on Texas toast and a lightly cornmeal-dusted broiled catfish with local vegetables), Husk's signature cheeseburger, and—wait for it—lamb barbecue. Reservations are strongly recommended.

**MAP 1:** 76 Queen St., 843/577-2500, www.huskrestaurant.com; Mon.-Thurs. 11:30am-2pm and 5:30pm-10pm, Fri.-Sat. 11:30am-2pm and 5:30pm-11pm, Sun. 10am-2:30pm and 5:30pm-10pm

### POOGAN'S PORCH $$

In business for over 40 years now, Poogan's Porch is the prototype of a classic Charleston restaurant: lovingly restored old home, professional but unpretentious service, great fried green tomatoes, and rich, calorie-laden Lowcountry classics like crab cakes and shrimp and grits. Brunch is the big thing here, a bustling affair with ample portions, Bloody Marys, mimosas, and soft sunlight.

**MAP 1:** 72 Queen St., 843/577-2337, www.poogansporch.com; Mon.-Fri. 11:30am-2:30pm and 5pm-9:30pm, Sat.-Sun. 9am-3pm and 5pm-9:30pm

### PENINSULA GRILL $$$

Walk through the gaslit courtyard of the Planter's Inn at Market and Meeting Streets into the intimate dining room of the Peninsula Grill and begin an epicurean journey you'll not soon forget. Peninsula Grill might be Charleston's quintessential purveyor of high-style Lowcountry cuisine. You'll want to start with the sampler trio of soups and finish with the legendary coconut cake. Reservations are strongly recommended.

**MAP 1:** 112 N. Market St., 843/723-0700, www.peninsulagrill.com; daily from 5:30pm

### JESTINE'S KITCHEN $$

Follow Rachael Ray's lead and wait in the long lines outside Jestine's Kitchen to enjoy a simple Southern take on such meat-and-three comfort food classics as meat loaf, pecan-fried fish, and fried green tomatoes. Most of the recipes are handed down from the restaurant's namesake, Jestine Matthews, the African American woman who raised owner Dana Berlin.

**MAP 1:** 251 Meeting St., 843/722-7224; Tues.-Thurs. 11am-9:30pm, Fri.-Sat. 11am-10pm

## New Southern

### CRU CAFÉ $$$

Cru Café boasts an adventurous menu within a traditional-looking Charleston single house just around the corner from the main stable for the city's carriage tours, with a choice of interior or exterior seating. Sample entrées include poblano and mozzarella fried chicken and seared maple leaf duck breast.

**MAP 1:** 18 Pinckney St., 843/534-2434, www.crucafe.com; Tues.-Thurs. 11am-3pm and 5pm-10pm, Fri.-Sat. 11am-3pm and 5pm-11pm

### ★ FIG $$$

The intimate bistro and stylish bar FIG has a passion for fresh, simple ingredients. FIG—short for "Food Is Good"—attracts young professional scenesters as well as die-hard foodies. Chef Mike Lata won James Beard's Best Chef of the Southeast award in 2009. FIG is one of Charleston's great champions of the Sustainable Seafood Initiative, and the kitchen staff strives to work as closely as possible with local farmers and anglers in determining its seasonal menu.

**MAP 1:** 232 Meeting St., 843/805-5900, www.eatatfig.com; Mon.-Thurs. 6pm-11pm, Fri.-Sat. 6pm-midnight

### CHARLESTON GRILL $$$

Inside the plush Charleston Place Hotel you'll find Charleston Grill, one of the city's favorite (and priciest) fine-dining spots, popular with locals and visitors alike. The menu specializes in French-influenced Lowcountry cuisine, with dishes like the niçoise vegetable tart. There are a lot of great fusion dishes as well, such as the tuna and *hamachi* sashimi topped with pomegranate molasses and lemongrass oil. Reservations are a must.

**MAP 1:** 224 King St., 843/577-4522, www.charlestongrill.com; dinner daily from 6pm

### CIRCA 1886 $$$

Focusing on purely seasonal offerings that never stay on the menu longer than three months, Circa 1886 combines the best Old World tradition of Charleston with the vibrancy of its more adventurous kitchens. The restaurant—surprisingly little known despite its four-star Mobil rating—is located in the former carriage house of the grand Wentworth Mansion B&B just west of the main College of Charleston campus. The menu has featured such entrées as robust beef au poivre and shrimp-and-crab-stuffed flounder. Be sure to check the daily prix fixe offerings; they can be a great deal.

**MAP 1:** 149 Wentworth St., 843/853-7828, www.circa1886.com; Mon.-Sat. 5:30pm-9:30pm

## Coffee, Tea, and Sweets

### BLACK TAP COFFEE $

Considered the best coffeehouse in town, Black Tap Coffee features an array of Counter Culture beans roasted and served to perfection by skilled baristas. Cold brew and pour-over cups are specialties of the house, as is their signature Lavender Latte. It's smallish and a bit off the beaten King Street path but still well within walking distance of that shopping thoroughfare.

**MAP 1:** 70.5 Beaufain St., 843/793-4402; Mon.-Fri. 7am-7pm, Sat.-Sun. 8am-6pm

Cru Café is a popular spot in a restored historic home downtown.

### CITY LIGHTS COFFEEHOUSE $

If you find yourself needing a quick pick-me-up while shopping on King Street, avoid the lines at the two Starbucks locations on the avenue and instead turn east on Market Street and duck inside City Lights Coffeehouse. The sweet goodies are delectable in this cozy little Euro-style place, and the Counter Culture organic coffee is to die for. If you're lucky, they'll have some of their Ethiopian Sidamo brewed.

**MAP 1:** 141 Market St., 843/853-7067; Mon.-Thurs. 7am-9pm, Fri.-Sat. 7am-10pm, Sun. 8am-6pm

### KAMINSKY'S $

Routinely voted as having the best desserts in the city, the cakes alone at Kaminsky's are worth the trip to the City Market area. The fresh fruit torte, the red velvet, and the "Mountain of Chocolate" are the three best sellers.

**MAP 1:** 78 N. Market St., 843/853-8270; daily noon-2am

## French

### GAULART & MALICLET $$

On the north side of Broad Street you'll find Gaulart & Maliclet, subtitled "Fast and French." This is a gourmet bistro with a strong takeout component. Prices are especially reasonable for this area of town, with great lunch specials under $10, Thursday night Fondue for Two specials at about $20, and breakfast all day.

**MAP 1:** 98 Broad St., 843/577-9797, www.fastandfrenchcharleston.com; Mon. 8am-4pm, Tues.-Thurs. 8am-10pm, Fri.-Sat. 8am-10:30pm

### QUEEN STREET GROCERY $

Queen Street Grocery is the kind of place frequented almost exclusively by locals. At this corner store you can load up on some of the tastiest made-to-order crepes this side of France—as well as light groceries, beer, wine, and cigarettes.

**MAP 1:** 133 Queen St., 843/723-4121, www.queenstreetgrocerycafe.com; kitchen Mon.-Sat. 10am-5pm, Sun. 11am-3pm, store Mon.-Sat. 8am-8:30pm

## Italian

### FULTON FIVE $$$

The cuisine of northern Italy comes alive in the bustling, dimly lit room of Fulton Five, from the *insalata de funghi* to the sublime risotto. It's not cheap, and the portions aren't necessarily the largest, but with these tasty, non-tomato-based dishes and this romantic, gusto-filled atmosphere, you'll be satiated with life itself.

**MAP 1:** 5 Fulton St., 843/853-5555, www.fultonfive.com; Mon.-Sat. 5:30pm-close

## Seafood

### HYMAN'S SEAFOOD $$

Hyman's Seafood is thought by many locals to border on a tourist trap, and it's mostly visitors who line up for hours to get in. To keep things manageable, Hyman's offers the same menu and prices for both lunch and dinner. After asking for some complimentary fresh boiled peanuts in lieu of bread, start with the Carolina Delight, a delicious appetizer (also available as an entrée) involving a lightly fried cake of grits topped with your choice of delectable seafood, or maybe a half-dozen oysters from the Half Shell oyster bar. Definitely try the she-crab soup, one of the best you'll find anywhere. As for entrées, the ubiquitous Lowcountry crispy scored flounder is always a good bet.

**MAP 1:** 215 Meeting St., 843/723-6000, www.hymanseafood.com; Mon.-Thurs. 11am-9pm, Fri.-Sun. 11am-11pm

# UPPER KING

## Classic Southern

### VIRGINIA'S ON KING $$

One of a comparatively few great Charleston restaurants with an equally expert focus on breakfast as on the other meals, Virginia's on King is a great place to enjoy Southern classics like fried green tomatoes, tomato pie, and their signature she-crab soup. The salmon BLT lunch dish (or in their old Southern parlance, "dinner," with "supper" being the name of the last meal of the day) is one of the best seafood dishes I've had anywhere. As for breakfast, the omelets are solid and most of the lunch menu is also available.

**MAP 2:** 412 King St., 912/735-5800, www.holycityhospitality.com; Mon.-Fri. 7am-10pm, Sat. 8am-10pm, Sun. 10am-3pm

### THE MACINTOSH $$

Rapidly gaining a reputation as one of the best brunch scenes in town, The Macintosh combines the best of Charleston's classic or New South style with a gastropub sensibility, complete with an extensive craft beer menu. The chef is three-time James Beard semifinalist Jeremiah Bacon, which means you can't really go wrong. But for brunch I'd suggest the baked chorizo, and from the small but artfully curated dinner menu, any seafood dish is good. Happy hour (Mon.-Fri. 5pm-7pm) is also a big draw here, with its own special $5 small-plate bar food menu.

**MAP 2:** 479 King St., 843/789-4299, www.themacintoshcharleston.com; Mon.-Sat. 6:30am-7pm, Sun. 9am-6pm

## Lowcountry Locavores

Charleston has merged its own indigenous and abiding culinary tradition with the "new" idea that you should grow your food as naturally as possible and purchase it as close to home as you can. From bacon and snapper to sweet potatoes, the typical Charleston dish of today harks back to its soulful Southern roots, before the days of factory food.

Spurred in part by an influx of trained chefs after the establishment of the Spoleto Festival in the 1970s, the locavore movement in Charleston came from the efforts of epicureans committed to sustainability and the principles of community-supported agriculture (CSA). Spearheaded by visionaries like the James Beard Award-winning Mike Lata of the bistro FIG and Sean Brock of McCrady's, sustainable food initiatives have sprung up in Charleston and the Lowcountry, such as the South Carolina Aquarium's Sustainable Seafood Initiative (http://scaquarium.org), partnering with local restaurants to ensure a sustainable wild-caught harvest; Certified South Carolina (www.certifiedsc.com), guaranteeing that the food you eat was grown in the Palmetto State; and a local chapter of the Slow Food Movement (http://slowfoodcharleston.org).

The list of Holy City restaurants relying almost exclusively on local and sustainable sources is long, but here are a few notable examples:

- **Husk** (76 Queen St., 843/577-2500, www.huskrestaurant.com)
- **Charleston Grill** (224 King St., 843/577-4522, www.charlestongrill.com)
- **FIG** (232 Meeting St., 843/805-5900, www.eatatfig.com)
- **Al Di La** (25 Magnolia Rd., 843/571-2321, www.aldilarestaurant.com)
- **Queen Street Grocery** (133 Queen St., 843/723-4121, www.queenstreetgrocerycafe.com)
- **Middleton Place Restaurant** (4300 Ashley River Rd., 843/556-6020, www.middletonplace.org)
- **Circa 1886** (149 Wentworth St., 843/853-7828, www.circa1886.com)
- **COAST Bar and Grill** (39D John St., 843/722-8838, www.coastbarandgrill.com)
- **Cru Café** (18 Pinckney St., 843/534-2434, www.crucafe.com)
- **Hominy Grill** (207 Rutledge Ave., 912/937-0930, www.hominygrill.com)
- **Peninsula Grill** (112 N. Market St., 843/723-0700, www.peninsulagrill.com)

## American

### EDMUND'S OAST $

Charleston's fave rave is Edmund's Oast, a boisterous beer garden-brewpub on the Upper Peninsula, boasting a 40-tap array, several brews made on-site, and, perhaps surprisingly, an excellent cocktail menu. The small plates, though, might be what stay with you. Expressive, excellent charcuterie and pitch-perfect sliders are the highlights. If you sit at the bar, the $4 per plate happy hour items (4:30pm-6:30pm) are a must-try; I suggest the smoked wings.

**MAP 2:** 1081 Morrison Dr., 843/727-1145, www.edmundsoast.com; Mon.-Thurs. 5:30pm-10pm, Fri.-Sat. 5:30pm-11pm, Sun. 10am-2:30pm and 5:30pm-10pm

## Asian

### BASIL $$

There's usually a long wait to get a table at the great Thai place Basil on Upper King, since they don't take reservations. But Basil also has one of the hippest, most happening bar scenes in the area, so you won't necessarily mind. Revelers enjoy fresh succulent takes on Thai classics like cashew chicken and pad thai. The signature dish is the basil duck.

**MAP 2:** 460 King St., 843/724-3490, www.

Basil

basilthairestaurant.com; Mon.-Thurs. 11:30am-2:30pm and 5pm-10:30pm, Fri.-Sat. 5pm-11pm, Sun. 5pm-10pm

## Barbecue

### FIERY RON'S HOME TEAM $

The Downtown/Upper Peninsula outpost of Charleston's favorite barbecue chain, Fiery Ron's Home Team BBQ, boasts a bit of an upscale feel compared to the original West Ashley location and the Sullivan's Island version. But don't be deceived by the excellent artisanal cocktail menu; the barbecue here is just as good.

**MAP 2:** 126 Williman St., 843/225-7427, www.hometeambbq.com; daily 11am-10pm

## Coffee, Tea, and Sweets

### KUDU COFFEE $

One of the best java joints in Charleston is Kudu Coffee. A kudu is an African antelope, and the African theme extends to the beans, which all have an African pedigree. Poetry readings and occasional live music add to the mix. A lot of green-friendly, left-of-center community activism goes on here as well.

**MAP 2:** 4 Vanderhorst St., 843/853-7186; Mon.-Sat. 6:30am-7pm, Sun. 9am-6pm

## French

### ★ 39 RUE DE JEAN $$$

The best mussels I've ever had were at 39 Rue de Jean. But anything off the bistro-style menu is unbelievably tasty, from the foie gras to the confit to the coq au vin to the *steak frites*. There are incredible Prohibition-style cocktails to go along with the extensive wine list.

**MAP 2:** 39 John St., 843/722-8881, www.holycityhospitality.com; Mon.-Thurs. 11:30am-11pm, Fri.-Sat. 11:30am-1am, Sun. 10am-11pm

## Italian

### INDACO $$$

One of Upper King's "it" restaurants, Indaco features a small but well-curated menu of antipasti, custom wood-fired gourmet pizzas, and delicious Italian specialties like black pepper tagliatelle. Yes, there's brussels sprout pizza, and it's quite delicious! Indaco is set in a stylish, bustling restored warehouse.

**MAP 2:** 525 King St., 843/727-1218, www.indacocharleston.com; Sun.-Thurs. 5pm-10pm, Fri.-Sat. 5pm-midnight

## Seafood

### COAST BAR AND GRILL $$$

Near 39 Rue de Jean you'll find the affiliated COAST Bar and Grill, which makes the most of its loud, hip setting in a former warehouse. The raw bar is satisfying, with a particularly nice selection of ceviche. COAST is a strong local advocate of the Sustainable Seafood Initiative, in which restaurants work directly with the local fishing industry.

**MAP 2:** 39D John St., 843/722-8838, www.coastbarandgrill.com; daily 5:30pm-close

## HAMPTON PARK

### Classic Southern

#### ★ HOMINY GRILL $$

With a motto like "Grits are good for you," you know what you're in store for at Hominy Grill, set in a renovated barbershop at Rutledge Avenue and Cannon Street near the Medical University of South Carolina. Primarily revered for his Sunday brunch, chef Robert Stehling has fun—almost mischievously so—breathing new life into American and Southern classics. Because this is largely a locals' place, you can impress your friends back home by saying you had the rare pleasure of the Hominy's sautéed shad roe with bacon and mushrooms—when the shad are running, that is.

**MAP 2:** 207 Rutledge Ave., 912/937-0930, www.hominygrill.com; Mon.-Fri. 7:30am-8:30pm, Sat.-Sun. 9am-8:30pm

#### MOE'S CROSSTOWN TAVERN $$

Moe's Crosstown Tavern is not only one of the classic Southern dives, but also has one of the best kitchens on this side of town, known for hand-cut fries, great wings, and, most of all, excellent burgers. On Tuesdays, the burgers are half price at happy hour—one of Charleston's best deals.

**MAP 2:** 714 Rutledge Ave., 843/722-3287; Mon.-Sat. 11am-midnight, bar until 2am

### Italian

#### TRATTORIA LUCCA $$$

A rave of Charleston foodies is the Tuscan-inspired fare of chef Ken Vedrinski at Trattoria Lucca. The menu is simple but perfectly focused, featuring handmade pasta and signature items like the pork chop or the fresh cheese plate. You'll be surprised at how much food your money gets you here. Monday evenings see a family-style prix fixe communal dinner.

**MAP 2:** 41 Bogard St., 843/973-3323, www.luccacharleston.com; Mon.-Sat. 6pm-10pm

## WEST ASHLEY

### Classic Southern

#### MIDDLETON PLACE RESTAURANT $$

Tucked away on the grounds of the Middleton Place Plantation is the romantic Middleton Place Restaurant. Theirs is a respectful take on traditional plantation fare like hoppin' John, gumbo, she-crab soup, and collards. The special annual Thanksgiving buffet is a real treat. Reservations are required for dinner. A nice plus is being able to wander the gorgeous landscaped gardens before dusk if you arrive at 5:30pm or later with a dinner reservation.

**MAP 3:** 4300 Ashley River Rd., 843/556-6020, www.middletonplace.org; Tues.-Thurs. and Sun. 11am-3pm and 6pm-8pm, Fri.-Sat. 11am-3pm and 6pm-9pm

### New Southern

#### ★ THE GLASS ONION $$

One of the more unassuming advocates of farm-to-table dining, The Glass Onion is in an equally unassuming location on U.S. 17 (Savannah Hwy.) on the western approach to town. That said, their food is right in the thick of the sustainable food movement and is incredibly tasty to boot (not to mention that there is more parking there than there is downtown). The interior says "diner," and indeed the emphasis here is on Southern soul and comfort-food classics. The Glass Onion also boasts a good variety of specialty craft brews to wash it all down. Another plus: In this town full of Sunday brunches, Glass Onion's specialty is a Saturday brunch.

**MAP 3:** 1219 Savannah Hwy., 843/225-1717, www.ilovetheglassonion.com; Mon.-Thurs. 11am-9pm, Fri. 11am-10pm, Sat. 10am-3pm and 4pm-10pm

### American

#### ★ GENE'S HAUFBRAU $

Gene's Haufbrau is worth making a special trip into West Ashley. Claiming to be the oldest bar in continuous operation in town (since 1952), Gene's complements its fairly typical bar-food menu with some good wraps. Start with the "Drunken Trio" (beer-battered cheese sticks, mushrooms, and onion rings) and follow with a portobello wrap or a good old-fashioned crawfish po'boy. One of the best meals in town for the money is Gene's $8.50 blue plate special, a rotating comfort food entrée like country-fried steak or pot roast, offered Monday-Friday 11:30am-4pm. The late-night kitchen hours, until 1am, are a big plus.

**MAP 3:** 17 Savannah Hwy., 843/225-4363, www.genes-haufbrau.com; daily 11:30am-2am

### BOXCAR BETTY'S $

If you're any kind of fan of fried chicken, whether good old-fashioned Southern fried or the type of sandwich you might get at Chick-fil-A, you will want to check out Boxcar Betty's. Be warned, these juicy, incredibly tasty flour-breaded fried chicken sandwiches are addictive.

**MAP 3:** 1922 Savannah Hwy., 843/225-7470, www.boxcarbetty.com; daily 11am-9pm

## Barbecue

### ★ FIERY RON'S HOME TEAM BBQ $$

My favorite barbecue joint, the rowdy and always hopping Fiery Ron's Home Team BBQ has pulled pork and ribs that rank with the best I've had anywhere in the country. Even the sides are amazing here, including perfect collards and tasty mac and cheese. Pitmaster Madison Ruckel provides an array of tableside sauces, including hot sauce, indigenous South Carolina mustard sauce, and his own "Alabama white," a light and delicious mayonnaise-based sauce. As if that weren't enough, the owners' close ties to the regional jam-band community mean there's great live blues and indie rock after 10pm most nights (Thursday is bluegrass night) to spice up the bar action, which goes until 2am.

**MAP 3:** 1205 Ashley River Rd., 843/225-7427, www.hometeambbq.com; Mon.-Sat. 11am-9pm, Sun. 11:30am-9pm

## Mediterranean

### AL DI LA $$

Anything on this northern Italian-themed menu is good, but the risotto—a legacy of original chef John Marshall—is the specialty dish at Al Di La, a very popular West Ashley fine-dining spot. Reservations are recommended.

**MAP 3:** 25 Magnolia Rd., 843/571-2321, www.aldilarestaurant.com; Tues.-Sat. 6pm-10pm

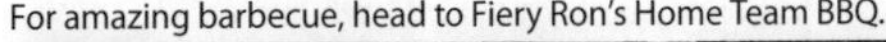

For amazing barbecue, head to Fiery Ron's Home Team BBQ.

## NORTH CHARLESTON

### Pizza

#### EVO PIZZERIA $$

If you have a hankering for pizza in North Charleston, don't miss EVO Pizzeria in the Olde North Charleston area at Park Circle. They specialize in a small but rich menu of unusual gourmet pizza toppings, like pistachio pesto.

**MAP 3:** 1075 E. Montague Ave., 843/225-1796, www.evopizza.com; Tues.-Fri. 11am-2:30pm and 5pm-10pm, Sat. 6pm-10pm

## SUMMERVILLE

### American

#### ALEX'S RESTAURANT $

For a down-home-style pancakes-and-sandwich place that's popular with the locals at all hours of the day, try Alex's Restaurant.

**MAP 3:** 120 E. 5th N. St., 843/871-3202; daily 24 hours

#### GUERIN'S PHARMACY $

A popular local landmark is Guerin's Pharmacy, which claims to be the state's oldest pharmacy. Complete with an old-fashioned soda fountain, they offer malted milk shakes and lemonade.

**MAP 3:** 140 S. Main St., 843/873-2531; Mon.-Fri. 9am-6pm, Sat. 9am-5pm

## MOUNT PLEASANT AND EAST COOPER

In Mount Pleasant, most of the restaurant action centers on the picturesque shrimping village of Shem Creek, which is dotted on both banks with bars and restaurants, most dealing in fresh local seafood. As with Murrells Inlet up the coast, some spots on Shem Creek border on tourist traps. Don't be afraid to go where the lines aren't.

### American

#### POE'S TAVERN $$

For a burger and an adult beverage or two, go straight to friendly Poe's Tavern, a nod to Edgar Allan Poe's stint at nearby Fort Moultrie.

**MAP 4:** 2210 Middle St., 843/883-0083, www.poestavern.com; daily 11am-2am, kitchen until 10pm

## To Market, to Market

A fun and favorite local fixture April-mid-December, the **Charleston Farmers Market** (843/724-7309, www.charlestoncity.info, Sat. 8am-2pm) rings beautiful Marion Square with stalls of local produce, street eats, local arts and crafts, and kids' activities.

Running April-October, East Cooper has its own version in the **Mount Pleasant Farmers Market** (843/884-8517, http://townofmountpleasant.com, Tues. 3pm-dark) at the Moultrie Middle School on Coleman Boulevard.

### Seafood

#### RED DRUM GASTROPUB $$

At the Red Drum Gastropub, the food is just as important as the drink. While you're likely to need reservations for the dining room, where you can enjoy Lowcountry-Tex-Mex fusion-style cuisine with a typically Mount Pleasant-like emphasis on seafood, the bar scene is very hopping and fun, with live music every Wednesday-Thursday night.

**MAP 4:** 803 Coleman Blvd., 843/849-0313, www.reddrumrestaurant.com; daily 5:30pm-10pm, lunch-brunch Sat.-Sun. 10:30am-2pm

#### ★ SEE WEE RESTAURANT $$

A must-stop roadside diner in the Awendaw area is See Wee Restaurant, about 20 minutes north of Charleston by car. Housed in a humble former general store on the west side of U.S. 17 (the restrooms are still outside), this diner draws folks from far and wide to enjoy signature menu items like the grouper and the unreal she-crab soup, considered by some epicures to be the best in the world. You can't miss with any of their seafood entrées. Occasionally the crowds can get thick, but rest assured it's worth the wait.

**MAP 4:** 4808 U.S. 17 N., 843/928-3609; Mon.-Thurs. 11am-8:30pm, Fri.-Sat. 11am-9:30pm, Sun. 11am-8pm

### VICKERY'S SHEM CREEK BAR AND GRILL $$

A popular spot, especially for the younger crowd, Vickery's Shem Creek Bar and Grill has a similar menu to its partner location on the peninsula, but this Vickery's has the pleasant added bonus of a beautiful view overlooking the creek. You'll get more of the Vickery's Cuban flair here, with a great black bean soup and an awesome Cuban sandwich.

**MAP 4:** 1313 Shrimp Boat Lane, 843/884-4440; daily 11:30am-1am

### WATER'S EDGE $$$

A well-regarded spot on Shem Creek is Water's Edge, which consistently takes home a *Wine Spectator* Award of Excellence for its great selection of vintages. Native Charlestonian Jimmy Purcell concentrates on fresh seafood with a slightly more upscale flair than many Shem Creek places.

**MAP 4:** 1407 Shrimp Boat Lane, 843/884-4074; daily 11am-11pm

## Vegetarian

### THE SPROUT CAFE $

For a real change of pace, try The Sprout Cafe on U.S. 17. Dealing totally in raw foods, the restaurant emphasizes healthy and fresh ingredients. You might be surprised at the inventiveness of their breakfast-through-dinner seasonal menu, which might include a tasty crepe topped with a pear-and-nut puree and maple syrup, or a raw squash and zucchini "pasta" dish topped with walnut "meatballs."

**MAP 4:** 629 Johnnie Dodds Blvd., 843/849-8554, www.thehealthysprout.com; Mon.-Fri. 6am-8pm, Sat. 9am-3pm, Sun. 11am-3pm

# FOLLY BEACH AND THE SOUTHWEST ISLANDS

## American

### TATTOOED MOOSE $

Three words: duck fat fries. The Tattooed Moose is a dive bar sensation on Johns Island, combining classic bar food with a typically Charlestonian touch of Old South culinary bravado. While the fries—served straight up with roasted garlic and blue cheese or with gravy—are the signature menu item, the sandwiches are simply fantastic. Try the duck confit sandwich or the pork belly sandwich. Brunch is becoming huge here, too, and live music is featured most nights.

**MAP 5:** 3328 Maybank Hwy., 843/277-2990, www.tattooedmoose.com; daily 11:30am-1am

## Breakfast and Brunch

### LOST DOG CAFÉ $

The closest thing to a taste of old Folly is the Lost Dog Café, so named for its bulletin board stacked with alerts about lost pets, pets for adoption, and new pups and kittens for sale or giveaway. It opens early to offer a tasty, healthy breakfast to the surfing crowd. It's a great place to pick up a quick, inexpensive, and tasty meal while you're near the beach.

**MAP 5:** 106 W. Huron Ave., 843/588-9669; daily 6:30am-3pm

### SUNRISE BISTRO $

For a hearty and delicious breakfast, go to Sunrise Bistro, one of those unassuming diners that always seems to have an eager crowd. Everything, from the omelets to the pancakes down to the simplest bagel with coffee, is spot-on, and a great value to boot. The best offerings here are during the day.

**MAP 5:** 1797 Main Rd., 843/718-1858, www.sunrise-bistro.com; Tues.-Thurs. 7am-2:30pm, Fri.-Sat. 7am-2:30pm and 5pm-9pm, Sun. 9am-1pm

## French

### ★ FAT HEN $$

Fat Hen is a self-styled "country French bistro" begun by a couple of old Charleston restaurant hands. The fried oysters are a particular specialty. There's also a bar menu (4pm-10pm).

**MAP 5:** 3140 Maybank Hwy., 843/559-9090; Tues.-Sat. 11:30am-3pm and 5:30pm-10pm, Sun. 10am-3pm

## Mexican

### TACO BOY $

Taco Boy is a fun place to get a fish taco, have a margarita, and take a walk on the nearby beach afterward. Though no one is under any

illusions that this is an authentic Mexican restaurant, the fresh guacamole is particularly rave-worthy, and there's a good selection of tequilas and beers *hecho en México*, with the bar staying open until 2am on weekends.
**MAP 5:** 15 Center St., 843/588-9761; Sun.-Thurs. 11am-10pm, Fri.-Sat. 11am-11pm

### Seafood

#### BLU $$

Set within the trendy Tides Folly Beach boutique hotel, Blu offers an equally high standard of food and decor, along with some amazing views of the ocean. The menu isn't particularly pretentious, but it does offer high-quality Sustainable Seafood Initiative options, all of which are recommended.
**MAP 5:** 1 Center St., 843/588-6658, www.blufollybeach.com; breakfast daily 7am-11am, lunch daily 11am-5pm, dinner Sun.-Thurs. 5pm-9pm, Fri.-Sat. 5pm-10pm

#### BOWENS ISLAND RESTAURANT $

Fans of the legendary Bowens Island Restaurant on James Island went into mourning when it burned to the ground in 2006. But you can't keep a good oysterman down, and owner Robert Barber rebuilt. A universe removed from the Lexus-and-khaki scene downtown, Bowens Island isn't the place for the uptight. This is the spot to go when you want shovels of oysters literally thrown onto your table, freshly steamed and delicious and all-you-can-eat.

To get to Bowens Island from the peninsula, take Calhoun Street west onto the James Island Connector (Hwy. 30). Take exit 3 onto Highway 171 south and look for Bowens Island Road on the right. The restaurant will be on the left in a short while, after passing by several ritzy McMansions that in no way resemble the restaurant you're about to experience.
**MAP 5:** 1870 Bowens Island Rd., 843/795-2757; Tues.-Sat. 5pm-10pm; cash only

# Hotels

Due to the city's long-standing tradition of hospitality and the high standards it has set for itself, hotels and bed-and-breakfasts are generally well maintained and have a high level of service.

No one can say lodging is inexpensive near the tourist areas of the city, but you almost always get what you pay for—and then some. The price differential is not that much between the peninsula and the outskirts. You'll pay more to stay in the tourist areas, but not *that* much more, with the bonus of being able to walk to most places you want to see. The farther south you go on the peninsula, the quieter and more affluent it tends to be. Folks looking for a more wild and woolly good time will be drawn to the Upper King area, farther north.

Charleston County runs a family-friendly, fairly boisterous campground at **James Island County Park** (871 Riverland Dr., 843/795-7275, www.ccprc.com, $31 tent site, $37 pull-through site). A neat feature here is the $5-pp round-trip shuttle to the visitors center downtown, Folly Beach Pier, and Folly Beach County Park. The park also has 10 furnished cottages (843/795-4386, $138) for rent, sleeping up to eight people. Reservations are recommended. For more commercial camping in Mount Pleasant, try the **KOA of Mt. Pleasant** (3157 U.S. 17 N., 843/849-5177, www.koa.com, from $30 tent sites, from $50 pull-through sites).

## SOUTH OF BROAD

#### ★ GOVERNOR'S HOUSE INN $$$

On the south side of Broad Street is a great old Charleston lodging, Governor's House Inn. This circa-1760 building, a National Historic Landmark, is associated with

## Best Hotels

★ **Closest Brush with the Declaration of Independence:** Before purchasing what is now the **Governor's House Inn** and being elected chief executive of South Carolina, Edward Rutledge was the youngest signer of the Declaration.

★ **Most Romantic Getaway:** Local legend has it that as a young naval officer, John F. Kennedy met one of his many paramours, an alleged German spy, at **Two Meeting Street Inn.**

★ **Best Rooftop Bar:** Enjoy views of the French Quarter and the Waterfront from the famous Rooftop Bar on top of **The Vendue.**

★ **Cozy in the City:** Though close to the City Market area's tourist bustle, the classy **Andrew Pinckney Inn** is quiet and calming.

★ **Most Comfortable Lap of Luxury:** The **Belmond Charleston Place** is right downtown and offers the city's premier lodging and spa facilities steps away from Charleston's prime shopping district.

★ **Closest Brush with the Constitution:** The only B&B in the United States that was once the home of a signer of the Constitution, the **John Rutledge House Inn** is one of the South's most sumptuous and highest-rated lodgings.

★ **Least Expensive Awesome Stay:** The charming **Not So Hostel** offers friendly and informal communal lodging a quick bike ride away from downtown.

★ **Most Calming Commune with Nature:** The sparsely modernist **The Inn at Middleton Place** offers a relaxing, state-of-the-art getaway in the scenic and peaceful heart of the old Middleton Place Plantation grounds.

★ **Best Outdoor Pool:** The **Kiawah Island Golf Resort** not only offers first-class golf and accommodations on a beautifully preserved barrier island, it also has a huge resort-style pool just off a windswept beach.

Edward Rutledge, signer of the Declaration of Independence. Though most of its 11 guest rooms—all with four-poster beds, period furnishings, and high ceilings—go for around $300, some of the smaller guest rooms can be had for closer to $200 in the off-season.
**MAP 1:** 117 Broad St., 843/720-2070, www.governorshouse.com

### ★ TWO MEETING STREET INN $$

The nine guest rooms of Two Meeting Street Inn down by the Battery are individually appointed, with themes like "The Music Room" and "The Spell Room." The decor in this 1892 Queen Anne bed-and-breakfast is very traditional, with lots of floral patterns and hunt club-style pieces and artwork. It's considered by many to be the most romantic lodging in town, and you won't soon forget the experience of sitting on the veranda enjoying the sights, sounds, and breezes. Three of the guest rooms—the Canton, Granite, and Roberts—can be had for not much over $200.
**MAP 1:** 2 Meeting St., 843/723-7322, www.twomeetingstreet.com

## WATERFRONT

### ★ THE VENDUE $$$

The guest rooms and the thoroughly hospitable service are the focus at nearby The Vendue.

All guest rooms are sumptuously appointed in boutique style, with lots of warm rich fabrics, unique pieces, and high-end bath amenities. That said, the public spaces are cool as well, with a focus on featuring quality art that essentially turns the property into one huge exhibition space. The inn gets a lot of traffic in the evenings because of the popular and hopping Rooftop Bar, which has amazing views.
**MAP 1:** 19 Vendue Range, 800/845-7900, www.thevendue.com

### HARBOURVIEW INN $$$

About as close to the Cooper River as a hotel gets, the Harbourview Inn comprises a "historic wing" and a larger, newer, but still tastefully done main building. For the best of those eponymous harbor views, try to get a room on the 3rd floor or you might have some obstructions. It's the little touches that keep guests happy here, with wine, cheese, coffee, tea, and cookies galore and an emphasis on smiling, personalized service. The guest rooms are quite spacious, with big baths and 14-foot ceilings. You can take your complimentary breakfast—good but not great—in your room or eat it on the nice rooftop terrace.
**MAP 1:** 2 Vendue Range, 843/853-8439, www.harbourviewcharleston.com

## FRENCH QUARTER

### FRENCH QUARTER INN $$$

A great place in this part of town is the French Quarter Inn. The decor in the 50 surprisingly spacious guest rooms is suitably high-period French, with low-style noncanopied beds and crisp fresh linens. Many guest rooms feature fireplaces, whirlpool baths, and private balconies.
**MAP 1:** 166 Church St., 843/722-1900, www.fqicharleston.com

## NORTH OF BROAD

### ★ ANDREW PINCKNEY INN $$

It calls itself a boutique hotel, perhaps because each room is unique and sumptuously appointed. But the charming Andrew Pinckney Inn is very nearly in a class by itself in Charleston, not only for its great rates but for its casual West Indies-style decor, charming courtyard, gorgeous three-story atrium, and rooftop terrace on which you can enjoy your delicious included breakfast. For the money and the amenities, it's possibly the single best lodging package in town.
**MAP 1:** 199 Church St., 843/937-8800, www.andrewpinckneyinn.com

### KINGS COURTYARD INN $$$

If you plan on some serious shopping, you might want to stay right on the city's main shopping thoroughfare at the Kings Courtyard Inn. This 1853 Greek Revival building houses a lot more guest rooms—more than 40—than meets the eye, and it can get a little crowded at times. Still, its charming courtyard and awesome location on King Street are big bonuses, as is the convenient but cramped parking lot right next door (about $12 per day, a bargain for this part of town), with free in-and-out privileges.
**MAP 1:** 198 King St., 866/720-2949, www.kingscourtyardinn.com

### FULTON LANE INN $$$

Affiliated with the Kings Courtyard—and right next door, in fact—is the smaller, cozier Fulton Lane Inn, with its lobby entrance on tiny Fulton Lane between the two inns. Small, simple guest rooms—some with fireplaces—have comfortable beds and spacious baths. This is the kind of place for active people who plan to spend most of their days out and about but want a cozy place to come back to at night. You mark down your continental breakfast order at night, leave it on your doorknob, and it shows up at the *exact* time you requested the next morning. Then when you're ready to shop and walk, just go down the stairs and take the exit right out onto busy King Street. Also nice is the $12-per-day parking with free in-and-out privileges.
**MAP 1:** 202 King St., 866/720-2940, www.fultonlaneinn.com

## MILLS HOUSE HOTEL $$$

Although it is a newer building by Charleston standards, the Mills House Hotel boasts an important pedigree. Dating to 1853, the first incarnation was a grand edifice that hosted luminaries such as Robert E. Lee. Through the years, fire and restoration wrought their changes, and the modern version basically dates from an extensive renovation in the 1970s. The hotel has a very good restaurant and lounge inside, the Barbadoes Room (breakfast, lunch, dinner, and Sunday brunch), as well as a healthy banquet and event schedule. This isn't the place to go for peace and quiet. Rather, this Wyndham-affiliated property is where you go to feel the bustle of downtown Charleston and to be conveniently close to its main sightseeing and shopping attractions. Some of the upper floors of this seven-story building offer spectacular views.

**MAP 1:** 115 Meeting St., 843/577-2400, www.millshouse.com

## ★ BELMOND CHARLESTON PLACE $$$

Considered Charleston's premier hotel, Charleston Place maintains a surprisingly high level of service and decor for its massive 440-room size. Currently owned by the London-based Orient-Express Hotels, Belmond Charleston Place is routinely rated as one of the best hotels in North America by *Condé Nast Traveler* and other publications. The guest rooms aren't especially large, but they are well appointed, featuring Italian marble baths, high-speed Internet, and voice messaging—and, of course, there's a pool available. A series of suite offerings—Junior, Junior Executive, Parlor, and the 800-square-foot Senior—feature enlarged living areas and multiple TVs and phones. The on-site **spa** (843/937-8522) offers all kinds of massages, including couples and "mommy to be" sessions. Diners and tipplers have three fine options to choose from: the famous **Charleston Grill** (843/577-4522, daily 6pm-close, $27-65) for fine dining; the breakfast, lunch, and brunch hot spot **Palmetto Cafe** (843/722-4900, daily 6:30am-3pm, $24-31); and the **Thoroughbred Club** (daily 11am-midnight) for cocktails and, for groups of 10 or more, afternoon tea.

**MAP 1:** 205 Meeting St., 843/722-4900, www.charlestonplace.com

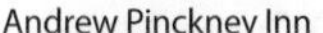

Andrew Pinckney Inn

### ★ JOHN RUTLEDGE HOUSE INN $$$

On the north side of Broad Street, the magnificent John Rutledge House Inn is very close to the old South of Broad neighborhood not only in geography but in feel. Known as "America's most historic inn," the Rutledge House boasts a fine old pedigree indeed: Built for Constitution signer John Rutledge in 1763, it's one of only 15 homes belonging to the original signers to survive. George Washington breakfasted here with Mrs. Rutledge in 1791. The interior is stunning: Italian marble fireplaces, original plaster moldings, and masterful ironwork abound in the public spaces. The inn's 19 guest rooms are divided among the original mansion and two carriage houses.

**MAP 1:** 116 Broad St., 843/723-7999, www.johnrutledgehouseinn.com

John Rutledge House Inn

## UPPER KING

### ASHLEY INN $

Stretching the bounds of the "Upper King" definition, the Ashley Inn is located well northwest of Marion Square, almost in the Citadel area. Although it's too far to walk from here to any historical attraction in Charleston, the Ashley Inn does provide free bikes to its guests as well as free off-street parking, a particularly nice touch. It also deserves a special mention not only because of the romantic well-appointed nature of its six guest rooms, suite, and carriage house but for its outstanding breakfasts. You get to pick a main dish, such as Carolina sausage pie, stuffed waffles, or cheese blintzes.

**MAP 2:** 201 Ashley Ave., 843/723-1848, www.charleston-sc-inns.com

### FRANCIS MARION HOTEL $$

In a renovated 1924 building overlooking beautiful Marion Square, the Francis Marion Hotel offers quality accommodations in the hippest, most bustling area of the peninsula—but be aware that it's quite a walk down to the Battery from here. The guest rooms are plush and big, though the baths can be cramped. The hotel's parking garage costs a reasonable $12 per day, with valet parking available until about 8pm. A Starbucks in the lobby pleases many guests on their way out or in. Most rooms hover around $300, but some are a real steal.

**MAP 2:** 387 King St., 843/722-0600, www.francismarionhotel.com

## HAMPTON PARK

### ★ NOT SO HOSTEL $

Downtown Charleston's least-expensive lodging is also its most unique: the Not So Hostel. The already reasonable prices also include a make-your-own bagel breakfast, off-street parking, bikes, high-speed Internet access in the common room, and even an airport, train, and bus shuttle. The inn actually comprises three 1840s Charleston single houses, all with the obligatory piazzas. (However, unlike some hostels, there's air-conditioning in all the rooms.) Because the free bike usage makes up for its off-the-beaten-path location, a stay at the Not So Hostel is a fantastic way to enjoy the Holy City on a budget. They now have an annex at 33 Cannon Street with all-private rooms ($75-85).

**MAP 2:** 156 Spring St., 843/722-8383, www.notsohostel.com

## WEST ASHLEY

### ★ THE INN AT MIDDLETON PLACE $$

Looking like Frank Lloyd Wright parachuted into a 300-year-old plantation and got to work, The Inn at Middleton Place is one of Charleston's unique lodgings—and not only because it's on the grounds of the historic and beautiful Middleton Place Plantation. The four connected buildings, comprising over 50 guest rooms, are modern yet deliberately blend in with the forested, neutral-colored surroundings. The spacious guest rooms have that same woodsy minimalism, with excellent fireplaces, spacious Euro-style baths, and huge floor-to-ceiling windows overlooking the grounds and the river. Guests also have full access to the rest of the gorgeous Middleton grounds. The only downside is that you're a lengthy drive from the peninsula and all its attractions, restaurants, and nightlife. But don't worry about food—the excellent Middleton Place Restaurant is open for lunch and dinner. There are nightly happy hours at the lodge, a great way to meet some of your fellow lodging mates and relax.

**MAP 3:** 4290 Ashley River Rd., 843/556-0500, www.theinnatmiddletonplace.com

## SUMMERVILLE

### WOODLANDS RESORT & INN $$$

The renowned Woodlands Resort & Inn is one of a handful of inns in the United States with a five-star rating both for lodging and dining. Its 18 guest rooms within the 1906 great house are decorated in a mix of old-fashioned plantation high style and contemporary designer aesthetics, with modern luxurious baths. There's also a freestanding guest cottage ($950) that seeks to replicate a hunting lodge vibe. There's a full day spa on the premises; the most basic offering, a one-hour massage, will run about $120. Within Woodlands is its award-winning world-class restaurant, simply called **The Dining Room** (Mon.-Sat. 11am-2pm and 6pm-9pm, brunch Sun. 11:30am-2pm, $40-50). The 900-entry wine list and sommelier are collectively fantastic, as are the desserts. Jackets are required, and reservations are strongly advised.

**MAP 3:** 125 Parsons Rd., 843/875-2600, www.woodlandsmansion.com

## MOUNT PLEASANT AND EAST COOPER

### WILD DUNES RESORT $$$

One of the more accessible and enjoyable resort-type stays in the Charleston area is on the Isle of Palms at Wild Dunes Resort. This is the place to go for relaxing, beach-oriented vacation fun in your choice of a traditional hotel room, a house, or a villa. Bustling Mount Pleasant is only a couple of minutes away, and Charleston proper not much farther.

**MAP 4:** 5757 Palm Blvd., 888/778-1876, www.wilddunes.com

## FOLLY BEACH AND THE SOUTHWEST ISLANDS

### TIDES FOLLY BEACH $$$

The upbeat but still cozy Tides Folly Beach boutique hotel has a combination of attentive staff, great oceanfront views, and an excellent on-site restaurant, Blu.

**MAP 5:** 1 Center St., 843/588-6464, www.tidesfollybeach.com

### ★ KIAWAH ISLAND GOLF RESORT $$$

The beautiful island of Kiawah—about 45 minutes from downtown Charleston—has as its main attraction the sumptuous Kiawah Island Golf Resort, a frequent venue for PGA tournaments. But even if you don't play golf, the resort is an amazing stay. The main component is The Sanctuary, an upscale hotel featuring an opulent lobby complete with grand staircases, a large pool area overlooking the beach, tasteful Spanish Colonial-style architecture, and 255 smallish but excellently appointed guest rooms.

**MAP 5:** 1 Sanctuary Beach Dr., 800/654-2924, www.kiawahgolf.com

# Transportation and Services

## AIR

Way up in North Charleston is **Charleston International Airport** (CHS, 5500 International Blvd., 843/767-1100, www.chs-airport.com), served by American (www.aa.com), Delta (www.delta.com), JetBlue (www.jetblue.com), and Southwest (www.southwest.com).

It'll take about 20 minutes to make the 12-mile drive from the airport to downtown, and vice versa. The airport is conveniently located just off the I-526/Mark Clark Expressway perimeter highway off I-26. As in most cities, taxi service from the airport is regulated. This translates to about $30 for two people from the airport to Charleston Place downtown.

## CAR

There are two main routes into Charleston: I-26 from the west-northwest (which dead-ends downtown) and U.S. 17 from the west (called Savannah Highway when it gets close to Charleston proper), which continues east over the Ravenel Bridge into Mount Pleasant and beyond. There's a fairly new perimeter highway, I-526 (Mark Clark Expressway), which loops around the city from West Ashley to North Charleston to Daniel Island and into Mount Pleasant. It's accessible both from I-26 and U.S. 17.

Keep in mind that I-95, while certainly a gateway to the region, is actually about 30 miles west of Charleston. Charleston is almost exactly two hours from Savannah by car, and about an hour's drive from Beaufort and Hilton Head.

### Car Rentals

Charleston International Airport has rental kiosks for **Avis** (843/767-7031), **Budget** (843/767-7051), **Dollar** (843/767-1130), **Enterprise** (843/767-1109), **Hertz** (843/767-4550), **National** (843/767-3078), and **Thrifty** (843/647-4389). There are a couple of rental locations downtown: **Budget** (390 Meeting St., 843/577-5195) and **Enterprise** (398 Meeting St., 843/723-6215). **Hertz** has a location in West Ashley (3025 Ashley Town Center Dr., 843/573-2147), as does **Enterprise** (2004 Savannah Hwy., 843/556-7889).

## BUS

Public transportation by **Charleston Area Regional Transit Authority** (CARTA, 843/724-7420, www.ridecarta.com) is a convenient and inexpensive way to enjoy Charleston without the more structured nature of an organized tour. There's a wide variety of routes, but most visitors will limit their acquaintance to the tidy, trolley-like **DASH** (Downtown Area Shuttle, free) buses run by CARTA primarily for visitors. It's a free hop-on, hop-off service that helps you avoid having to find a place to park in more congested downtown areas.

## TAXI

The South is generally not big on taxis, and Charleston is no exception. The best bet is simply to call rather than try to flag one down. Charleston's most fun service is **Charleston Black Cabs** (843/216-2627, www.charlestonblackcabcompany.com), using Americanized versions of the classic British taxi. A one-way ride anywhere on the peninsula below the bridges is about $10 pp, and rates go up from there. They're very popular, so call as far ahead as you can or try to get one at their stand at Charleston Place. Two other good services are **Safety Cab** (843/722-4066) and **Yellow Cab** (843/577-6565).

You can also try a human-powered taxi service from **Charleston Rickshaw** (843/723-5685). A cheerful (and energetic) young cyclist will pull you and a friend to most points on the Lower Peninsula for about $10-15. Call 'em or find one by City Market. They work late on Friday and Saturday nights too.

# PARKING

As you'll quickly see, parking is at a premium in downtown Charleston. An exception seems to be the large number of free spaces all along the Battery, but unless you're an exceptionally strong walker, that's too far south to use as a reliable base from which to explore the whole peninsula.

Metered spaces run two dollars an hour and are enforced 9am-10pm Monday-Saturday. Most metered parking is on and around Calhoun Street, Meeting Street, King Street, Market Street, and East Bay Street.

The city has a dozen conveniently located and comparatively inexpensive parking garages which generally charge a dollar an hour, which is very reasonable. I strongly suggest that you make use of them. They're located at the aquarium, Camden and Exchange Streets, Charleston Place, Concord and Cumberland Streets, East Bay and Prioleau Streets, Marion Square, Gaillard Auditorium, Liberty and St. Philip Streets, Majestic Square, the Charleston Visitor Reception and Transportation Center, and Wentworth Street.

A great option is to park in the garage of the main visitors center on 375 Meeting Street and take the free hop-on, hop-off DASH Trolley, which runs all over the peninsula making very frequent stops.

The city's website (www.charleston-sc.gov) has a good interactive map of parking.

# VISITOR INFORMATION

## Visitors Centers

I highly recommend a stop at the **Charleston Visitor Reception and Transportation Center** (375 Meeting St., 800/774-0006, www.charlestoncvb.com, Mon.-Fri. 8:30am-5:30pm). The center has several high-tech interactive exhibits, including an amazing model of the city under glass; well-stocked, well-organized brochures that will keep you informed on everything a visitor would ever want to know about or see in the city; and an incredibly friendly and knowledgeable staff, who will help you book tours or accommodations. I also recommend using the attached parking garage not only for your stop at the center but also anytime you want to see the many sights this part of town has to offer, such as the Charleston Museum, the Manigault and Aiken-Rhett Houses, and the Children's Museum. Go to the center to take advantage of the great deal offered by the **Charleston Heritage Passport** (www.heritagefederation.org), which gives you 40 percent off admission to all of Charleston's key historic homes, the Charleston Museum, and the two awesome plantation sites on the Ashley River: Drayton Hall and Middleton Place. You can get the Heritage Passport *only* at the Charleston Visitor Reception and Transportation Center on Meeting Street.

Other area visitors centers include the **Mount Pleasant-Isle of Palms Visitors Center** (99 Harry M. Hallman Jr. Blvd., 800/774-0006, daily 9am-5pm) and the **North Charleston Visitors Center** (4975B Centre Pointe Dr., 843/853-8000, Mon.-Sat. 10am-5pm).

## Hospitals

If there's a silver lining in getting sick or injured in Charleston, it's that there are plenty of high-quality medical facilities available. The premier institution is the **Medical University of South Carolina** (171 Ashley Ave., 843/792-2300, www.muschealth.com) in the northwest part of the peninsula. Two notable facilities are near each other downtown: **Roper Hospital** (316 Calhoun St., 843/402-2273, www.roperhospital.com) and **Charleston Memorial Hospital** (326 Calhoun St., 843/792-2300). In Mount Pleasant there's **East Cooper Regional Medical Center** (1200 Johnnie Dodds Blvd., www.eastcoopermedctr.com). In West Ashley there's **Bon Secours St. Francis Hospital** (2095 Henry Tecklenburg Ave., 843/402-2273, www.ropersaintfrancis.com).

## Police

For nonemergencies in Charleston, West Ashley, and James Island, contact the **Charleston Police Department**

(843/577-7434, www.charlestoncity.info). You can also contact the police department in Mount Pleasant (843/884-4176). North Charleston is a separate municipality with its own police department (843/308-4718, www.northcharleston.org). Of course, for emergencies always call **911.**

## Media

The daily newspaper of record is the ***Post and Courier*** (www.charleston.net). Its entertainment insert, ***Preview,*** comes out on Thursday. The free alternative weekly is the ***Charleston City Paper*** (www.charlestoncity-paper.com), which comes out on Wednesday and is the best place to find local music and arts listings. A particularly well-done and lively metro glossy is ***Charleston*** magazine (www.charlestonmag.com), which comes out once a month.

The National Public Radio affiliate is the South Carolina ETV radio station WSCI at 89.3 FM. South Carolina ETV is on television at WITV. The local NBC affiliate is WCBD, the CBS affiliate is WCSC, the ABC affiliate is WCIV, and the Fox affiliate is WTAT.

## Libraries

The main branch of the **Charleston County Public Library** (68 Calhoun St., 843/805-6801, www.ccpl.org, Mon.-Thurs. 9am-9pm, Fri.-Sat. 9am-6pm, Sun. 2pm-5pm) has been at its current site since 1998. Named for Sullivan's Island's most famous visitor, the **Edgar Allan Poe Library** (1921 I'on Ave., 843/883-3914, www.ccpl.org, Mon. and Fri. 2pm-6pm, Tues., Thurs., and Sat. 10am-2pm) has been housed in Battery Gadsden, a former Spanish-American War gun emplacement, since 1977.

The College of Charleston's main library is the **Marlene and Nathan Addlestone Library** (205 Calhoun St., 843/953-5530, www.cofc.edu), home to special collections, the Center for Student Learning, the main computer lab, the media collection, and even a café. The college's **Avery Research Center for African American History and Culture** (125 Bull St., 843/953-7609, www.cofc.edu/avery, Mon.-Fri. 10am-5pm, Sat. noon-5pm) houses documents relating to the history and culture of African Americans in the Lowcountry.

For other historical research on the area, check out the collections of the **South Carolina Historical Society** (100 Meeting St., 843/723-3225, www.southcarolinahistoricalsociety.org, Mon.-Fri. 9am-4pm, Sat. 9am-2pm). There's a $5 research fee for nonmembers.

## LGBTQ Resources

Contrary to many media portrayals of the region, Charleston is quite open to the LGBTQ community, which plays a major role in arts, culture, and business. As with any other place in the South, however, it's generally expected that people—straights as well—will keep personal matters and politics to themselves in public settings. A key local advocacy group is the **Alliance for Full Acceptance** (29 Leinbach Dr., Suite D-3, 843/883-0343, www.affa-sc.org). The **Lowcountry Gay and Lesbian Alliance** (843/720-8088) holds a potluck the last Sunday of each month. For the most up-to-date happenings, try the *Charleston City Paper.*

# Hilton Head and the Lowcountry

Look for ★ to find recommended sights, activities, dining, and lodging.

# Highlights

★ **Henry C. Chambers Waterfront Park:** While away the time on a porch swing at this clean and inviting gathering place on the serene Beaufort River (page 123).

★ **St. Helena's Episcopal Church:** To walk through this Beaufort sanctuary and its walled graveyard is to walk through history (page 125).

★ **Penn Center:** Visit the center of modern Gullah culture and education—and a key site in the history of the civil rights movement (page 134).

★ **Hunting Island State Park:** One of the most peaceful natural getaways on the East Coast is only minutes away from the civilized temptations of Beaufort (page 137).

★ **ACE Basin:** You can take a lifetime to learn your way around this massive, marshy estuary—or just a few hours to soak in its lush beauty (page 138).

★ **Edisto Beach State Park:** Relax at this quiet, friendly, and relatively undeveloped park on Sea Island, a mecca for shell collectors (page 141).

★ **Pinckney Island National Wildlife Refuge:** This well-maintained sanctuary is a major birding location and a great getaway from nearby Hilton Head (page 144).

★ **Coastal Discovery Museum at Honey Horn:** This beautifully repurposed plantation house with spacious grounds is a great place to learn about Hilton Head history, both human and natural (page 144).

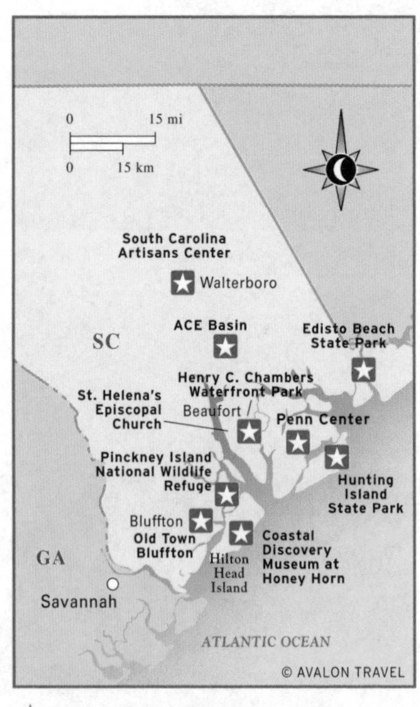


★ **Old Town Bluffton:** By turns gossipy and gorgeous, the charming "Old Town" on the May River centers on a thriving artists colony (page 156).

★ **South Carolina Artisans Center:** Visual artists and fine craftspeople from all over the state contribute work to this high-quality collective in Walterboro (page 161).

For many people around the world, the Lowcountry is the first image that comes to mind when they think of the American South.

History hangs in the humid air here, starting with the ancient roots of Native Americans, then the interruption of Spanish and French colonizers, followed by the English. Although traces of all of these occupants are mostly gone now, you can almost hear their ghosts in the rustle of the branches in a sudden sea breeze or in the piercing call of a heron over the marsh.

The defining characteristic of the Lowcountry is its liquid nature—not only literally, in the creeks and waterways that dominate every vista and the seafood cooked in all manner of ways, but figuratively too, in the slow but deep quality of life here. Not so very long ago, before the influx of resort development, retirement subdivisions, and tourism, much of the Lowcountry was like a flatter, more humid Appalachia—poverty-stricken and desperately underserved. While the archetypal South has been marketed in any number of ways to the rest of the world, here you get a sense that this is the real thing—timeless, endlessly alluring, but somehow very familiar.

South of Beaufort is the historically significant Port Royal area and the East Coast Marine Corps Recruit Depot of Parris Island. East of Beaufort is the center of Gullah culture, St. Helena Island, and the scenic gem of Hunting Island. To the south is the scenic but entirely developed golf and tennis mecca, Hilton Head Island, and Hilton Head's close neighbor but diametrical opposite in every other way, Daufuskie Island, another important Gullah center. Nestled between is the close-knit and gossipy little village of Bluffton on the gossamer May River.

## PLANNING YOUR TIME

A commonsense game plan is to use centrally located Beaufort as a home base and spend **three days** exploring the region. Take at least half a day of leisure to walk all over Beaufort, a delightfully walkable place. If you're in the mood for a road trip, dedicate a full day to tour the area to the north and northeast, with

**Previous:** sunset on St. Helena Island; the Grove Plantation House in the ACE Basin. **Above:** Edisto Island.

## Hilton Head and the Lowcountry

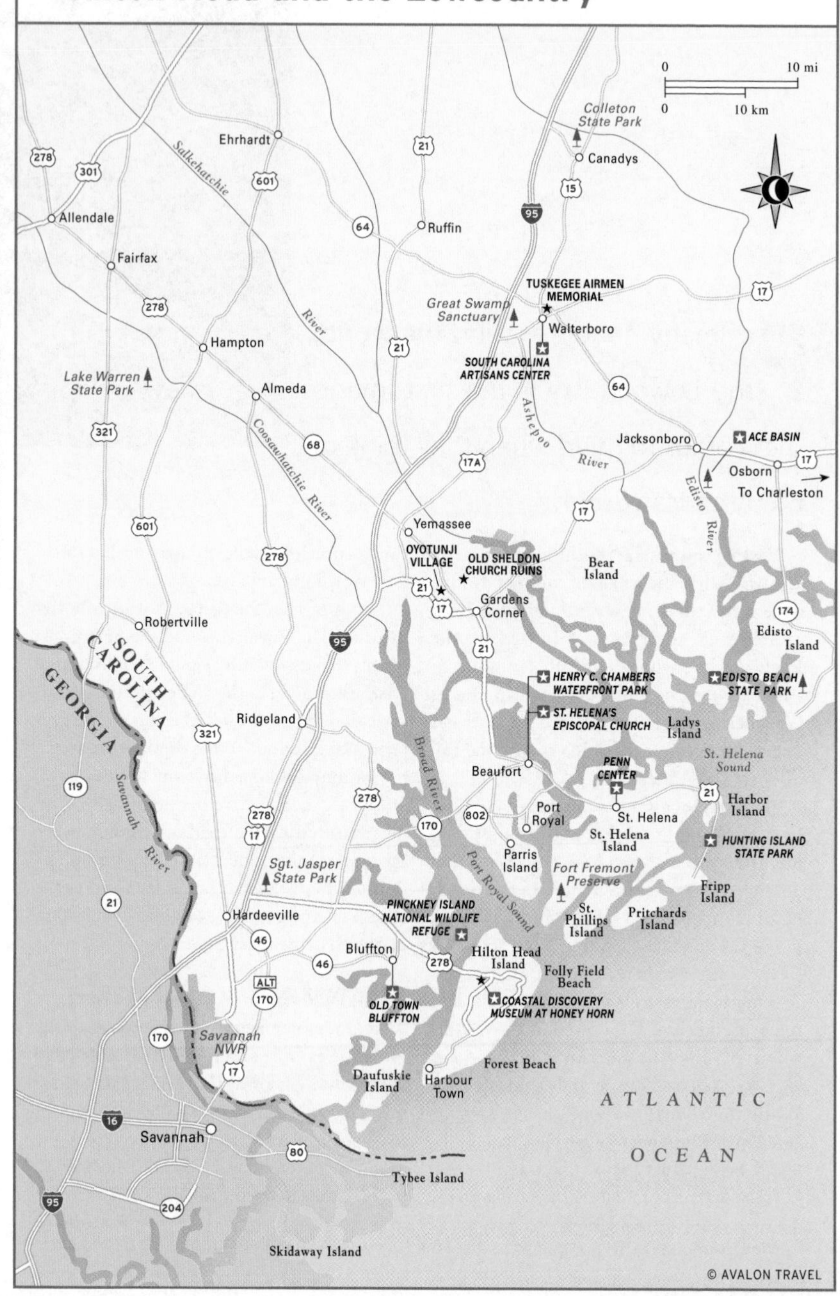

a jaunt to the ACE Basin National Wildlife Refuge. While the New York accents fly fast and furious on Hilton Head Island, that's no reason for you to rush. Plan on at least half a day just to enjoy the fine broad beaches alone. I recommend another half day to tour the island itself, maybe including a stop in Sea Pines for a late lunch or dinner.

# Beaufort



Sandwiched halfway between the prouder, louder cities of Charleston and Savannah, Beaufort is in many ways a more authentic slice of life from the past than either of those two. If you want to party, stay in those two cities. If you want to relax in a similar environment, Beaufort's your ticket.

Long a staple of movie crews seeking to portray some archetypal aspect of the Old South (*The Prince of Tides, The Great Santini, Forrest Gump*) or just to film beautiful scenery for its own sake (*Jungle Book, Last Dance*), Beaufort—pronounced "BYOO-fert," by the way, not "BO-fort"—features many well preserved examples of Southern architecture, most all of them in idyllic, family-friendly neighborhoods.

While you'll run into plenty of charming and gracious locals during your time here, you might be surprised at the number of transplanted Northerners. That's due not only to the high volume of retirees who've moved to the area, but also to the active presence of three major U.S. Navy facilities: the Marine Corps Air Station Beaufort, the Marine Corps Recruit Depot on nearby Parris Island, and the Beaufort Naval Hospital.

The two main avenues to remember are Bay Street, along the Beaufort River and the real center of downtown; and Boundary Street, which becomes Carteret Street as you arrive into downtown proper.

## HISTORY

This was the site of the second landing by the Spanish on the North American continent, the expedition of Captain Pedro de Salazar in 1514 (Ponce de León's more famous landing at St. Augustine was but a year earlier). A Spanish slaver made a brief stop in 1521, long enough to name the area Santa Elena. Port Royal Sound didn't get its modern name until the first serious European attempt at a permanent settlement, Jean Ribault's exploration in 1562. Though ultimately disastrous, Ribault's base of Charlesfort was the first French settlement in America.

In 1776, Beaufort planter Thomas Heyward Jr. was a signer of the Declaration of Independence. After independence, Lowcountry planters turned to cotton as the main cash crop, since England had been their prime customer for indigo. The gambit paid off, and Beaufort soon became one of the wealthiest towns in the new nation. In 1861, only seven months after secessionists fired on Fort Sumter in nearby Charleston, a Union fleet sailed into Port Royal and occupied the Lowcountry for the duration of the war.

Gradually developing their own distinct dialect and culture, much of it linked to their West African roots, isolated Lowcountry African Americans became known as the Gullah. Evolving from an effort by abolitionist missionaries early in the Civil War, in 1864 the Penn School was formed on St. Helena Island specifically to teach the children of the Gullah communities. Now known as the Penn Center, the facility has been a beacon for the study of this aspect of African American culture ever since.

## SIGHTS

### ★ Henry C. Chambers Waterfront Park

A tastefully designed, well-maintained, and user-friendly mix of walkways, bandstands, and patios, **Henry C. Chambers**

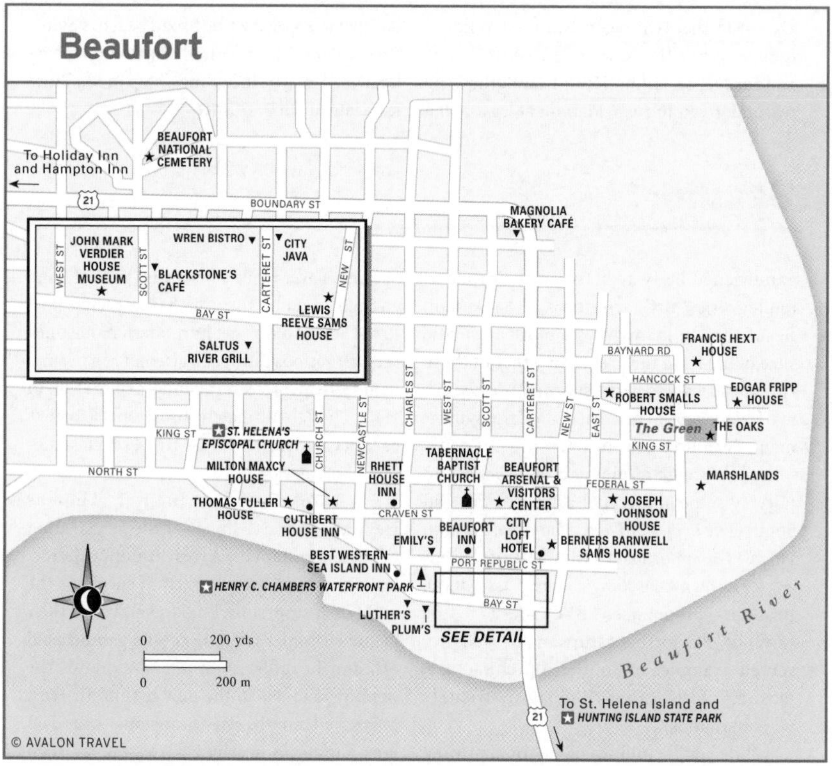

## Beaufort

**Waterfront Park** (843/525-7054, www.cityofbeaufort.org, daily 24 hours) is a favorite gathering place for locals and visitors alike, beckoning one and all with its open green space and wonderful marsh-front views.

### John Mark Verdier House Museum

A smallish but stately Federalist building on the busiest downtown corner, the **John Mark Verdier House Museum** (801 Bay St., 843/379-6335, www.historicbeaufort.org, tours on the half hour Mon.-Sat. 10:30am-3:30pm, $5) is the only historic Beaufort planter's home open to regular tours. Built in 1805 for John Mark Verdier, its main claims to fame are acting as the Union headquarters during the long occupation of Beaufort during the Civil War and hosting Revolutionary War hero the Marquis de Lafayette, who stayed at the Verdier House on his 1825 U.S. tour. In 2011 the Verdier House was extensively and professionally restored, with exterior paint reflecting the home's authentic 1863 look.

### Beaufort Arsenal Visitors Center and History Museum

The imposing yellow-gray tabby facade of the 1852 **Beaufort Arsenal** (713 Craven St.) houses the **Beaufort Visitors Center** (843/986-5400, www.beaufortsc.org, Mon.-Sat. 9am-5pm, Sun. noon-5pm) and **Beaufort History Museum** (www.beauforthistorymuseum.com, Mon.-Sat. 10am-4pm, $7). The visitors center is a great place to purchase various tour tickets, and the adjacent museum is a small but informative stop to learn more about the area's long and important history. There are also public restrooms.

## ★ St. Helena's Episcopal Church

Nestled within a low brick wall surrounding this historic church and cemetery, **St. Helena's Episcopal Church** (505 Church St., 843/522-1712, Tues.-Fri. 10am-4pm, Sat. 10am-1pm) has witnessed some of Beaufort's most compelling tales. Built in 1724, this was the parish church of Thomas Heyward, one of South Carolina's signers of the Declaration of Independence. John "Tuscarora Jack" Barnwell, one of Beaufort's founders, is buried on the grounds.

While the cemetery and sanctuary interior are likely to be your focus, take a close look at the church exterior—many of the bricks are actually ships' ballast stones. Also be aware that you're not looking at the church's original footprint; the building has been expanded several times since its construction (a hurricane in 1896 destroyed the entire east end). A nearly $3 million restoration, mostly for structural repairs, was completed in 2000.

## Reconstruction Era National Monument

One of Barack Obama's last acts as president was the creation of the **Reconstruction Era National Monument** (www.nps.gov/reer, hours vary, free). Encompassing several sites in the Beaufort area, this isn't a single park you visit but rather a collection of locations that were important in the years immediately following the Civil War. Currently the monument is very much a work in progress, so keep in mind most of the locations aren't open yet on a regular basis. The National Park Service plans to open them in turn as soon as feasible.

The easiest site to visit is the **Beaufort Firehouse** (706 Craven St.) downtown across from the Beaufort Arsenal and Museum. Once home to private businesses and now deeded to the National Park Service, the firehouse marks the site of community gatherings in the post-Civil War occupation era. As the national monument takes shape, it will serve as the visitors center.

Two key sites on St. Helena Island are **Darrah Hall** on the Penn Center campus (for which there's a separate listing in this chapter) and the **Brick Baptist Church,** just across the street from the Penn Center. Darrah Hall is the epicenter of one of the nation's first schools for emancipated enslaved people. The Brick Baptist Church was built by enslaved people in 1855 and is the oldest church on St. Helena Island.

The **Camp Saxton-Emancipation Oak**

St. Helena's Episcopal Church

site is on the grounds of the Beaufort Naval Hospital. While currently not open to the public, that will likely change at some point in the future.

## Tabernacle Baptist Church

Built in 1845, the handsome **Tabernacle Baptist Church** (911 Craven St., 843/524-0376) had a congregation of over 3,000 before the Civil War. Enslaved people made up most of the congregation, and during the war newly freed people purchased the church. A congregant was the war hero Robert Smalls, who seized the Confederate steamer he was forced to serve on and delivered it to Union forces. He is buried in the church cemetery and has a nice memorial dedicated to him facing the street.



## Beaufort National Cemetery

Begun by order of Abraham Lincoln in 1863, **Beaufort National Cemetery** (1601 Boundary St., daily 8am-sunset) is one of the few cemeteries containing the graves of both Union and Confederate troops. This national cemetery is where 19 soldiers of the all-black 54th and 55th Massachusetts Infantries were reinterred after being found on Folly Island near Charleston. Also buried here is "the Great Santini" himself, novelist Pat Conroy's father, Donald.

## Santa Elena History Center

The actual historic site is on nearby Parris Island, but in downtown Beaufort you'll find the **Santa Elena History Center** (1501 Bay St., 843/379-1550, www.santa-elena.org, Tues.-Sat. 10am-4pm, $10 adults, $5 ages 5-12), detailing the Spanish occupation of the area beginning 450 years ago, long before English-speaking settlers arrived. This is a new and growing venture, and exhibits and resources will be added as funds become available.

## A Walking Tour of Beaufort Homes

Here's a walking tour of some of Beaufort's fine historic homes in private hands. You can't tour any of the interiors, but these homes are part of the legacy of the area and are locally valued as such. Be sure to respect the privacy of the inhabitants by keeping the noise level down and not trespassing on private property to take photos.

- **Thomas Fuller House:** Begin at the corner of Harrington and Bay Streets and view the 1796 Thomas Fuller House (1211 Bay St.), one of the oldest in Beaufort and unique in that much of the building material is tabby (hence the home's other name, the Tabby Manse).
- **Milton Maxcy House:** Walk east on Bay Street one block and take a left on Church Street; walk up to the corner of Church and Craven Streets. Otherwise known as the Secession House (113 Craven St.), this 1813 home was built on a tabby foundation dating from 1743. In 1860, when it was the residence of attorney Edmund Rhett, the first Ordinance of Secession was signed here, and the rest, as they say, is history.
- **Lewis Reeve Sams House:** Resume the walking tour on the other side of the historic district at the foot of the bridge in the old neighborhood simply called "The Point." The beautiful Lewis Reeve Sams House (601 Bay St.) at the corner of Bay and New Streets, with its double-decker veranda, dates from 1852, and like many Beaufort mansions served as a Union hospital during the Civil War.
- **Berners Barnwell Sams House:** Continue up New Street, where shortly ahead on the left you'll find the 1818 Berners Barnwell Sams House (310 New St.), which served as the African American hospital during the Union occupation. Harriet Tubman of Underground Railroad fame worked here for a time as a nurse.
- **Joseph Johnson House:** Continue up New Street and take a right on Craven Street. Cross East Street to find the 1850 Joseph Johnson House (411 Craven St.),

with the massive live oak in the front yard. Legend has it that when the Yankees occupied Hilton Head, Johnson buried his valuables under an outhouse. After the war he returned to find his home for sale due to unpaid back taxes. He dug up his valuables, paid the taxes, and resumed living in the home. You might recognize the home from the film *Forces of Nature*.

- **Marshlands:** Backtrack to East Street, walk north to Federal Street, and go to its end. Built by James R. Verdier, Marshlands (501 Pinckney St.) was used as a hospital during the Civil War, as many Beaufort homes were, and is now a National Historic Landmark. It was the setting of Francis Griswold's 1931 novel *A Sea Island Lady.*
- **The Oaks:** Walk up to King Street and take a right. Soon after you pass a large open park on the left, King Street dead-ends at Short Street. The Oaks (100 Laurens St.) at this corner was owned by the Hamilton family, who lost a son who served with General Wade Hampton's cavalry in the Civil War. After the conflict, the family couldn't afford the back taxes; neighbors paid the debts and returned the deed to the Hamiltons.
- **Edgar Fripp House:** Continue east on Laurens Street toward the water to find this handsome Lowcountry mansion, sometimes called Tidalholm (1 Laurens St.). Built in 1856 by the wealthy planter for whom nearby Fripp Island is named, this house was a key setting in *The Big Chill* and *The Great Santini.*
- **Francis Hext House:** Go back to Short Street, walk north to Hancock Street, and take a left. A short way ahead on the right, the handsome red-roofed estate known as Riverview (207 Hancock St.) is one of the oldest structures in Beaufort; it was built in 1720.
- **Robert Smalls House:** Continue west on Hancock Street, take a short left on East Street, and then a quick right on Prince Street. The 1834 Robert Smalls House (511 Prince St.) was the birthplace of Robert Smalls, a formerly enslaved Beaufort native who stole the Confederate ship *Planter* from Charleston Harbor while serving as helmsman and delivered it to Union troops in Hilton Head. Smalls and a few compatriots commandeered the ship while the officers were at a party at Fort Sumter. Smalls used the bounty he earned for the act of bravery to buy his boyhood home. After the war, Smalls was a longtime U.S. congressman.

## ENTERTAINMENT AND NIGHTLIFE

### Performing Arts

Beaufort's fine arts scene is small but professional in outlook. Most performances are based in the nice Performing Arts Center on the oak-lined campus of the **University of South Carolina Beaufort** (USCB, 801 Carteret St., 843/521-4100, www.uscb.edu). A prime mover of the local performing arts scene is **Beaufort Performing Arts,** formed by a mayoral task force in 2003 specifically to encourage arts and cultural development within the area. Ticket prices typically range $12-40.

Perhaps surprising for such a small place, Beaufort boasts its own full orchestra, the **Beaufort Orchestra** (1106 Carteret St., 843/986-5400, www.beaufortorchestra.org), which plays in the Performing Arts Center.

### Cinema

One of only two functional drive-ins in the state, the **Highway 21 Drive In** (55 Parker Dr., 843/846-4500, www.hwy21drivein.com) has two screens, great sound, movies Friday-Sunday, and awesome concessions that include Angus beef hamburgers. All you need to provide is the car and the company.

### Festivals and Events

Surprising for a town so prominent in so many films, Beaufort didn't have its own film festival until 2007. The **Beaufort Film Festival** (843/986-5400, www.beaufortfilmfestival.com) is held in February. It's small

## Pat Conroy's Lowcountry

Pat Conroy

No person was as closely associated with the South Carolina Lowcountry as beloved author Pat Conroy, who died in 2016. After moving around as a child in a military family, he began high school in Beaufort. His painful teen years there formed the basis of his first novel, a brutal portrait of his domineering Marine pilot father, Colonel Donald Conroy, a.k.a. Colonel Bull Meecham of *The Great Santini* (1976). Many scenes from the 1979 film adaptation were filmed at the famous Tidalholm, the Edgar Fripp House (1 Laurens St.) in Beaufort. (The house was also front and center in *The Big Chill.*)

Conroy's pattern of thinly veiled autobiography actually began with his first book, the self-published *The Boo,* a tribute to a teacher at the Citadel in Charleston while Conroy was still a student there. His second work, *The Water is Wide* (1972), is a chronicle of his experiences teaching in a one-room African American school on Daufuskie Island. Though ostensibly a straightforward first-person journalistic effort, Conroy changed the location to the fictional Yamacraw Island, supposedly to protect Daufuskie's fragile culture from curious outsiders. The 1974 film adaptation starring Jon Voight was titled *Conrack* after the way his students mispronounced his name. You can visit that same one-room school today on Daufuskie. Known as the Mary Field School, the building is now a local community center.

Conroy would go on to publish in 1980 *The Lords of Discipline,* a reading of his real-life experience with the often-savage environment faced by cadets at the Citadel—though Conroy would change the name, calling it the Carolina Military Institute. Still, when it came time to make a film adaptation in 1983, the Citadel refused to allow it to be shot there, so the "Carolina Military Institute" was filmed in England instead. Conroy also wrote the foreword to the cookbook *Gullah Home Cooking the Daufuskie Way: Smokin' Joe Butter Beans, Ol' 'Fuskie Fried Crab Rice, Sticky-Bush Blackberry Dumpling, and Other Sea Island Favorites* by Daufuskie native and current Savannah resident Sallie Ann Robinson.

For many of his fans, Conroy's *The Prince of Tides* is his ultimate homage to the Lowcountry. Surely, the 1991 film version starring Barbra Streisand and Nick Nolte—shot on location and awash in gorgeous shots of the Beaufort River marsh—did much to implant an idyllic image of the area with audiences around the world. According to local legend, Streisand originally didn't intend to make the film in Beaufort, but a behind-the-scenes lobbying effort allegedly coordinated by Conroy himself, and including a stay at the Rhett House Inn, convinced her.

The Bay Street Inn (601 Bay St.) in Beaufort was seen in the film, as was the football field at the old Beaufort High School. The beach scenes were shot on nearby Fripp Island. Interestingly, some scenes set in a Manhattan apartment were actually shot within the old Beaufort Arsenal (713 Craven St.), now a visitors center. Similarly, the Beaufort Naval Hospital doubled as New York's Bellevue.

Despite the many personal tribulations he faced in the area, to the end Conroy never gave up on the Lowcountry. He is interred in the old Gullah Cemetery on St. Helena Island, near the historic Penn Center, beside civil rights heroine Agnes Sherman. As for the "Great Santini" himself, you can visit the final resting place of Colonel Conroy in the Beaufort National Cemetery—Section 62, Grave 182.

in scale but growing steadily each year and boasts a diverse range of high-quality, cutting-edge entries, including shorts and animation. Most events are held at the University of South Carolina Beaufort campus (805 Carteret St.).

Now over 20 years old, the **Gullah Festival of South Carolina** (www.theoriginalgullahfestival.org) celebrates Gullah history and culture on Memorial Day weekend in May at various locations throughout town, mostly focusing on Waterfront Park.

By far the biggest single event on the local festival calendar is the over 50-year-old **Beaufort Water Festival** (www.bftwaterfestival.com), held over two weeks in July each year, centering on the Waterfront Park area. There are arts and crafts, live music, various tournaments, a waterski show, a Grand Parade the closing Saturday, and the annual Blessing of the Fleet the closing Sunday.

Fall in the Lowcountry means shrimping season, and early October brings the **Beaufort Shrimp Festival** (www.beaufortsc.org). Various cooking competitions are held, obviously centering on the versatile crustaceans that are the raison d'être of the shrimp fleet.

St. Helena Island hosts the three-day **Penn Center Heritage Days** (www.penncenter.com) each November, the Beaufort area's second-biggest celebration after the Water Festival. Focusing on Gullah culture, history, and delicious food, Heritage Days does a great job of combining fun with education.

## SHOPS

The recently renovated Old Bay Marketplace, with a facade so bright red you can't miss it, hosts a few cute shops, most notably the stylish **Lulu Burgess** (917 Bay St., 843/524-5858, Mon.-Sat. 10am-6pm, Sun. noon-5pm), an eclectic store that brings a rich, quirky sense of humor to its otherwise tasteful assortment of gift items for the whole family.

A great women's clothing store nearby is **Go Fish** (719 Bay St., 843/379-8448, www.shopgofish.com, Mon.-Thurs. 10am-6pm, Fri.-Sat. 10am-8pm), a regional chain with particularly high-quality but affordable garments, jewelry, and shoes.

At the far end of Bay Street is **Bay Street Treasures** (1001 Bay St., 843/379-4488, Mon.-Sat. 10am-5pm), an eclectic home goods and furnishings store, strong with regional and Lowcountry appeal.

My favorite shop in Beaufort is **Nevermore Books** (702 Craven St., 843/812-9460, www.nevermorebooks.com, Tues.-Fri. 10am-5pm, Sat. 11am-4pm). While Edgar Allan Poe is the ostensible theme of this locally owned shop—check out the awesome window display—they specialize in fiction of all types and have a range of regional books as well.

### Art Galleries

A complete art experience blending the traditional with the cutting edge is at the **I. Pinckney Simons Art Gallery** (711 Bay St., 843/379-4774, www.ipinckneysimonsgallery.com, Tues.-Fri. 11am-5pm, Sat. 11am-3pm). The name is pronounced "Simmons" despite the spelling.

For a taste of Gullah-themed art, head to **LyBenson's Gallery & Studio** (211 Charles St., 843/525-9006, www.lybensons.com). Not just a place to enjoy and purchase art, they have some small exhibits on local history and culture, including a room dedicated to local African American hero Robert Smalls.

Right on the water is a fun local favorite, the **Longo Gallery** (103 Charles St., 843/522-8933, Mon.-Sat. 11am-5pm). Owners Suzanne and Eric Longo provide a whimsical assortment of less traditional art than you might find in the more touristy waterfront area. Take Charles Street as it works its way toward the waterfront; the gallery is right behind a storefront on the corner of Charles and Bay Streets.

You'll find perhaps the area's best-known gallery over the bridge on St. Helena Island. Known regionally as one of the best places to find Gullah folk art, **Red Piano Too** (870 Sea Island Pkwy., 843/838-2241, www.redpianotoo.com, Mon.-Sat. 10am-5pm) is on the corner before you turn onto the road to the historic Penn Center. Over 150 artists from a diverse range of traditions and styles are represented in this charming little 1940 building with a red tin awning.

## SPORTS AND ACTIVITIES

Beaufort County comprises over 60 islands, so it's no surprise that nearly all recreation in the area revolves around the water, which dominates so many aspects of life in the Lowcountry. The closer to the ocean you get, the more it's a salt marsh environment. But as you explore more inland, including the sprawling ACE Basin, you'll encounter primarily blackwater.

### Kayaking

The Lowcountry is tailor-made for kayaking. Most kayakers put in at the public landings in nearby **Port Royal** (1 Port Royal Landing Dr., 843/525-6664) or **Lady's Island** (73 Sea Island Pkwy., 843/522-0430), across the river from downtown Beaufort. If you don't feel comfortable with your navigation skills, it's a good idea to contact Kim and David at **Beaufort Kayak Tours** (843/525-0810, www.beaufortkayaktours.com), who rent kayaks and can guide you on a number of excellent tours. They charge about $40 adults, $30 children for a two-hour trip. A tour with Beaufort Kayak Tours is also the best (and nearly the only) way to access the historically significant ruins of the early British tabby Fort Frederick, now located on the grounds of the Beaufort Naval Hospital and inaccessible by car.

### Fishing and Boating

Key marinas in the area are the **Downtown Marina** (1006 Bay St., 843/524-4422) in Beaufort, the **Lady's Island Marina** (73 Sea Island Pkwy., 843/522-0430), and the **Port Royal Landing Marina** (1 Port Royal Landing Dr., 843/525-6664). Hunting Island has a popular 1,000-foot fishing pier at its south end. A good local fishing charter service is Captain Josh Utsey's **Lowcountry Guide Service** (843/812-4919, www.beaufortscfishing.com). Captain Ed Hardee (843/441-6880) offers good inshore charters.

### Biking

Despite the Lowcountry's, well, lowness, biking opportunities abound. It might not get your heart rate up like a ride in the Rockies, but the area lends itself to laid-back two-wheeled enjoyment. Many local B&Bs provide bikes free for guests, and you can rent your own just across the river from Beaufort in Lady's Island at **Lowcountry Bikes** (102 Sea Island Pkwy., 843/524-9585, Mon.-Tues. and Thurs.-Fri. 10am-6pm, Wed. 10am-1pm, Sat. 10am-3pm, about $5 per hour). They can also hook you up with some good routes around the area.

### Tours

Colorful character Jon Sharp has retired from his popular walking tours, but filling his shoes is Janet Matlock, who took over the venture and now runs the equally popular **Janet's Walking History Tour** (843/226-4412, www.janetswalkinghistory.com, $25). This highly recommended two-hour jaunt begins and ends at the Downtown Marina (1006 Bay St.) and takes you all through the downtown area. Tours leave at 12:30pm Monday and 11am Tuesday-Saturday; during the hot months of June-September they leave at 10am Monday-Saturday.

**The Spirit of Old Beaufort** (103 West St. Extension, 843/525-0459, www.thespiritofoldbeaufort.com, Mon.-Sat. 10:30am, 2pm, and 7pm, $18) runs a good year-round series of themed walking tours, roughly two hours long, with guides usually in period dress. If you don't want to walk, you can hire one of their guides to join you in your own vehicle (from $50).

As you might expect, few things could be more Lowcountry than an easygoing carriage ride through the historic neighborhoods. **Southurn Rose Buggy Tours** (843/524-2900, www.southurnrose.com, daily 10am-5pm, $18 adults, $7 children)—yes, that's how

## Lowcountry Boil or Frogmore Stew?

Near Beaufort it's called Frogmore stew after the township (now named St. Helena) just over the river. Closer to Savannah it's simply called Lowcountry boil. Supposedly the first pot of this delectable, hearty concoction was made by Richard Gay of the Gay Fish Company. As with any vernacular dish, dozens of local and family variants abound. The key ingredient that makes Lowcountry boil-Frogmore stew what it is—a well-blended mélange with a character all its own rather than just a bunch of stuff thrown together in a pot of boiling water—is some type of crab-boil seasoning. You'll find Zatarain's seasoning suggested on a lot of websites, but Old Bay is far more common in the eponymous Lowcountry where the dish originated.

In any case, here's a simple six-serving recipe to get you started. The only downside is that it's pretty much impossible to make it for just a few people. The dish is intended for large gatherings, whether a football tailgate party on a Saturday or a family afternoon on Sunday. Note the typical ratio of one ear of corn and ½ pound each of meat and shrimp per person.

- 6 ears fresh corn on the cob, cut into 3-inch sections
- 3 pounds smoked pork sausage, cut into 3-inch sections
- 3 pounds fresh shrimp, shells on
- 5 pounds new potatoes, halved or quartered
- 3 ounces Old Bay Seasoning

Put the sausage and potato pieces, along with the Old Bay, in two gallons of boiling water. When the potatoes are about halfway done, about 15 minutes in, add the corn and boil for about half that time, 7 minutes. Add the shrimp and boil for another 3 minutes, until they just turn pink. Do not overcook the shrimp. Take the pot off the heat and drain; serve immediately. If you cook the shrimp just right, the oil from the sausage will cause those shells to slip right off.

This is but one of dozens of recipes. Some cooks add some lemon juice and beer in the water as it's coming to a boil; others add onion, garlic, or green peppers.

they spell it—offers 50-minute narrated carriage rides of the Point, including movie locations, embarking and disembarking near the Downtown Marina about every 40 minutes.

## FOOD

Because of Beaufort's small size and insular nature, many of its restaurants double as nightlife hot spots, with hopping bar scenes—or as hopping as it gets here, anyway—at dinner hours and beyond, often with a crowd of regulars. That said, those looking for a rowdy late-night time will be happier seeking it in the notorious party towns of Charleston and Savannah.

### New Southern

The stylishly appointed **Wren Bistro, Bar and Market** (210 Carteret St., 843/524-9463, www.wrenbeaufort.com, Mon.-Sat. 11am-11pm, $15-25) is known for its chicken dishes. While the food is great, the interior is particularly well done, simultaneously warm and classy. As seems to be typical of Beaufort, the lunches are as good as the dinners, and the bar scene is quite active.

### Breakfast and Brunch

One of the best breakfasts I've had anywhere was a humble two-egg plate for five bucks at Beaufort's most popular morning hangout, ★ **Blackstone's Café** (205 Scott St., 843/524-4330, Mon.-Sat. 7:30am-2:30pm, Sun. 7:30am-2pm, under $10). The dish is complete with tasty hash browns, a comparative rarity in this part of the country, where grits rule as the breakfast starch of choice.

## Burgers and Sandwiches

A lunch favorite is **Magnolia Bakery Café** (703 Congress St., 843/524-1961, www.magnoliacafebeaufort.com, breakfast Tues.-Fri. 8am-11am, brunch Sat.-Sun. 8am-3pm, Mon.-Sat. 9am-5pm, lunch Tues.-Fri. 9am-3pm, $10). Shrimp and grits are a specialty item, but you can't go wrong with any of the sandwiches. Vegetarian diners are particularly well taken care of with a large selection of black bean burger plates. As the name indicates, the range of desserts here is tantalizing, with the added bonus of a serious espresso bar.

## Coffee, Tea, and Sweets

The closest thing to a hip coffeehouse in Beaufort is **City Java and News** (301 Carteret St., 843/379-5282, www.cityofthotel.com, Mon.-Sat. 6am-6:30pm, Sun. 7am-6:30pm), a sunny and well-kept little modernist space within the similarly modernist City Loft Hotel. Their espresso is big-city quality, their periodicals are timely, and their pastries and sandwiches are good for tiding you over when you need some quick energy for more walking around town.

A few blocks across downtown is a great coffee place, **Common Ground Coffeehouse and Market Cafe** (102 West St., 843/524-2326, daily 7:30am-10pm). Located in a historic building facing the river, this is not just a serenely pleasant and convenient place to enjoy your coffee, but the cakes, cookies, light sandwiches, and fresh Italian gelato are all delightfully delicious. Get here by strolling down Bay Street; it's at the end of an alley between two blocks, and is right on the Waterfront Park. There's an open mike every Friday night.

## Seafood

The hottest dinner table in town is at the ★ **Saltus River Grill** (802 Bay St., 843/379-3474, www.saltusrivergrill.com, Sun.-Thurs. 5pm-9pm, Fri.-Sat. 5pm-10pm, $10-39), famous throughout the state for its raw bar. Other specialties include she-crab bisque, lump crab cakes, and the ubiquitous

Common Ground Coffeehouse and Market Cafe

shrimp and grits. The Saltus River Grill is more upscale in feel and in price than most Lowcountry places, with a very see-and-be-seen attitude and a hopping bar. Reservations are recommended.

The short and focused menu at **Plum's** (904½ Bay St., 843/525-1946, www.plumsrestaurant.com, lunch daily 11am-4pm, dinner daily 5pm-10pm, $15-25) keys in on entrées highlighting local ingredients, such as the shrimp penne *all'amatriciana* and fresh black mussel pasta. An outstanding microbrew selection makes Plum's a big nightlife hangout as well.

## Steaks

★ **Luther's Rare & Well Done** (910 Bay St., 843/521-1888, daily 10am-midnight, from $8) on the waterfront is the kind of meat-lover's place where even the French onion soup has a morsel of rib eye in it. While the patented succulent rubbed steaks are a no-brainer here, the handcrafted specialty pizzas are also quite popular. Housed in a historic pharmacy building, Luther's is also a great place for late eats and beer or cocktails after many other places in this quiet town have rolled up the sidewalk. A limited menu of appetizers and bar food to nosh on at the inviting and popular bar is available after 10pm. Karaoke is every Tuesday night.

### Tapas

**Emily's** (906 Port Republic St., 843/522-1866, www.beaufortrestaurant.com, dinner daily 4pm-10pm, bar until 2am, $10-20) is a very popular fine-dining spot that specializes in a more traditional brand of rich, tasty tapas and is known for its active bar scene.

## ACCOMMODATIONS

Beaufort's historic district is blessed with an abundance of high-quality accommodations that blend well with their surroundings.

### Under $150

The **Best Western Sea Island Inn** (1015 Bay St., 843/522-2090, www.bestwestern.com, $135-170) is a good value for those for whom the B&B experience is not paramount. Anchoring the southern end of the historic district in a tasteful low brick building, the Best Western offers decent service, basic amenities, and surprisingly attractive rates for the location on Beaufort's busiest street.

### $150-300

Any list of upscale Beaufort lodging must highlight the ★ **Beaufort Inn** (809 Port Republic St., 843/379-4667, www.beaufortinn.com, $152-425), consistently voted one of the best B&Bs in the nation. It's sort of a hybrid in that it comprises not only the 1897 historic central home, but also a cluster of freestanding historic cottages, each with a charming little porch and rocking chairs.

The 18-room circa-1820 **Rhett House Inn** (1009 Craven St., 843/524-9030, www.rhetthouseinn.com, $175-320) is the local vacation getaway for the stars. Such arts and entertainment luminaries as Robert Redford, Julia Roberts, Ben Affleck, Barbra Streisand, Dennis Quaid, and Demi Moore have all stayed here at one time or another.

There's nothing like enjoying the view of the Beaufort River from the expansive porches of the ★ **Cuthbert House Inn** (1203 Bay St., 843/521-1315, www.cuthberthouseinn.com, $205-250). This grand old circa-1790 Federal mansion was once the home of the wealthy Cuthbert family of rice and indigo planters. Some of the king rooms have fireplaces



the Beaufort Inn

and claw-foot tubs. Of course you get a full Southern breakfast in addition to sunset hors d'oeuvres on the veranda.

While a stay at a B&B is the classic way to enjoy Beaufort, many travelers swear by the **City Loft Hotel** (301 Carteret St., 843/379-5638, www.cityloftthotel.com, $200). Housed in a former motel, City Loft represents a total modernist makeover, gleaming from stem to stern with chrome and various art deco touches.

## TRANSPORTATION AND SERVICES

The **Beaufort Visitors Information Center** (713 Craven St., 843/986-5400, www.beaufortsc.org, Mon.-Sat. 9am-5pm, Sun. noon-5pm), the headquarters of the Beaufort Chamber of Commerce and Convention and Visitors Bureau, has relocated from its old Carteret Street location and can now be found within the Beaufort Arsenal.

### Air

While the Marines can fly their F-18s directly into Beaufort Naval Air Station, you won't have that luxury. The closest major airport to Beaufort is the **Savannah/Hilton Head International Airport** (SAV, 400 Airways Ave., 912/964-0514, www.savannahairport.com) off I-95 outside Savannah. From there it's about an hour to Beaufort. If you're not going into Savannah for any reason, the easiest route to the Beaufort area from the airport is to take I-95's exit 8, and from there take U.S. 278 east to Highway 170.

Alternatively, you could fly into **Charleston International Airport** (CHS, 5500 International Blvd., www.chs-airport.com), but because that facility is on the far north side of Charleston, it will take a bit longer (about an hour and 20 minutes) to get to Beaufort. From the Charleston Airport the best route south to Beaufort is U.S. 17 south, exiting onto U.S. 21 at Gardens Corner and then into Beaufort.

### Car

If you're coming into the region by car, I-95 will be your likely primary route, with your main point of entry being exit 8 off I-95 connecting to U.S. 278 east to Highway 170. Beaufort is a little over an hour from Charleston.

Don't be discouraged by the big-box sprawl that assaults you on the approaches to Beaufort on Boundary Street, lined with the usual discount megastores, fast-food outlets, and budget motels. After you make the big 90-degree bend where Boundary turns into Carteret Street—known locally as the "Bellamy Curve"—it's like entering a whole new world of slow-paced, Spanish moss-lined avenues, friendly people, gentle breezes, and inviting storefronts.

# Outside Beaufort

The areas outside tourist-traveled Beaufort can take you even farther back into sepia-toned Americana, into a time of sharecropper homesteads, sturdy oystermen, and an altogether variable and subjective sense of time.

About 15 minutes east of Beaufort is the center of Gullah culture, St. Helena Island, and the scenic gem of Hunting Island. Just a few minutes south of Beaufort is the East Coast Marine Corps Recruit Depot of Parris Island. About 10 minutes away is the little community of Port Royal.

## SIGHTS

### ★ Penn Center

By going across the Richard V. Woods Memorial Bridge over the Beaufort River on the Sea Island Parkway (which turns into U.S. 21), you'll pass through Lady's Island and reach St. Helena Island. Known to old-timers as Frogmore, the area took back its old Spanish-derived place name in the 1980s. Today St. Helena Island is most famous for the **Penn Center** (Penn Center Circle W., 843/838-2474, www.penncenter.com, Tues.-Sat. 9am-4pm, $7 adults, $3 seniors and children), the spiritual home of Gullah culture and history. When you visit here among the live oaks and humble but well-preserved buildings, you'll instantly see why Martin Luther King Jr. chose this as one of his major retreat and planning sites during the civil rights era. The Penn Center continues to serve an important civil rights role by providing legal counsel to African American homeowners in St. Helena. Because clear title is difficult to acquire in the area due to the fact that so much of the land has stayed in the families of formerly enslaved people, developers are constantly making shady offers so that ancestral land can be opened to upscale development.

The 50-acre campus is part of the Penn School Historic District, a National Historic Landmark comprising 19 buildings, most of historical significance. The Retreat House was intended for King to continue his strategy meetings, but he was assassinated before being able to stay here. The welcome center, museum, and bookshop are housed in the Cope Building, now called the York W. Bailey Museum.

To get to the Penn Center from Beaufort (about 10 miles), proceed over the bridge until you get to St. Helena Island. Take a right onto MLK Jr. Drive when you see the Red Piano Too Art Gallery. The Penn Center is a few hundred yards down on the right. If you drive past the Penn Center and continue a few hundred yards down MLK Jr. Drive, look for the ancient tabby ruins on the left side of the road. This is the **Chapel of Ease,** the remnant of a 1740 church destroyed by a forest fire in the late 1800s.

## Fort Fremont Preserve

Military historians and sightseers of a particularly adventurous type will want to drive several miles past the Penn Center on St. Helena Island to visit **Fort Fremont Preserve** (Lands End Rd., www.fortfremont.org, daily 9am-dusk, free). Two artillery batteries remain of this Spanish-American War-era coastal defense fort (an adjacent private residence is actually the old army hospital). The fort was active until 1921, but now the big guns are long gone. Their heavy concrete emplacements, however—along with many dark

Penn Center on St. Helena's Island

tunnels and small rooms—are still here and make for a very interesting visit. Guided docent tours happen the fourth Saturday of the month starting at 10:30am at the St. Helena Branch of the Beaufort County Library (6355 Jonathan Francis Senior Rd.). The two-hour tours are free, and reservations aren't required.

## Old Sheldon Church

About 20 minutes north of Beaufort are the poignantly desolate ruins of the once-magnificent **Old Sheldon Church** (Old Sheldon Church Rd., off U.S. 17 just past Gardens Corner, daily dawn-dusk, free). One of the first Greek Revival structures in the United States, the house of worship held its first service in 1757. The sanctuary was first burned by the British in 1779. After being rebuilt in 1826, the sanctuary survived until General Sherman's arrival in 1865, whereupon Union troops razed it once more. Nothing remains now but these towering walls and columns made of red brick instead of the tabby often seen in similar ruins on the coast. It's now owned by the nearby St. Helena's Episcopal Church in Beaufort, which holds outdoor services here the second Sunday after Easter.

## Port Royal

This sleepy hamlet between Beaufort and Parris Island touts itself as a leader in "small-town New Urbanism," with an emphasis on livability, retro-themed shopping areas, and relaxing walking trails. However, **Port Royal** is still pretty sleepy—but not without very real charms, not the least of which is the fact that everything is within easy walking distance of everything else. The highlight of the year is the annual Softshell Crab Festival, held each April to mark the short-lived harvesting season for that favorite crustacean.

While much of the tiny historic district has a scrubbed, tidy feel, the main historic structure is the charming little **Union Church** (11th St., 843/524-4333, Mon.-Fri. 10am-4pm, donation), one of the oldest buildings in town, with guided docent tours.

Don't miss the boardwalk and observation tower at **The Sands** municipal beach and boat ramp. The 50-foot-tall structure provides a commanding view of Battery Creek. The little beach is artificial (made from dredged material) but still somewhat unusual in this area. To get to The Sands, head east onto 7th Street off the main drag of Parris Avenue. Seventh Street turns into Sands Beach Road for a brief

the ruins of Old Sheldon Church

Hunting Island Light

stretch and then merges with 6th Street, taking you directly to The Sands.

A must-stop for families is the **Port Royal Maritime Center** (310 Okatie Hwy., 843/645-7774, www.portroyalsoundfoundation.org, Tues.-Sat. 10am-5pm, free), a venture that is a great resource for learning about the area's ecological history.

## Parris Island

Though more commonly known as the home of the legendary **Marine Corps Recruit Depot Parris Island** (283 Blvd. de France, 843/228-3650, www.mcrdpi.marines.mil, free), the island is also of historical significance as the site of some of the earliest European presence in the New World. Today it's where all female U.S. Marine recruits and most male recruits east of the Mississippi River go through the Corps' grueling 13-week boot camp. Almost every Friday during the year marks the graduation of a company of newly minted Marines. That's why you might notice an influx of visitors to the area each Thursday, a.k.a. "Family Day," with the requisite amount of celebration on Friday after that morning's ceremony.

Unlike many military facilities in the post-9/11 era, Parris Island still hosts plenty of visitors. Just check in with the sentry at the gate and show your valid driver's license, registration, and proof of insurance. Rental car drivers should be prepared to show a copy of the rental agreement. On your way to the depot proper, there are a couple of beautiful picnic areas. Once inside, stop first at the **Douglas Visitor Center** (Bldg. 283, Blvd. de France, 843/228-3650, Mon.-Fri. 7:30am-4pm), a great place to find maps and information. As you go by the big parade ground, or "deck," be sure to check out the beautiful sculpture recreating the famous photo of Marines raising the flag on Iwo Jima. A short way ahead is the **Parris Island Museum** (Bldg. 111, 111 Panama St., 843/228-2951, www.parrisislandmuseum.com, daily 10am-4:30pm, free), detailing the proud history of the Corps with a particular focus on this Recruit Depot.

The Spanish built Santa Elena near the original French settlement, Charlesfort. They then built two other settlements, San Felipe and San Marcos. The Santa Elena site, now on the circa-1950s Parris Island Depot golf course, is a National Historic Landmark. So far, archaeologists have found the residence of a wealthy family in the town and have identified two of Santa Elena's five forts. Many artifacts are viewable at the nearby **Clubhouse-Interpretive Center** (daily 7am-5pm, free). You can take a self-guided tour; to get to the site from the museum, continue on Panama Street and take a right on Cuba Street. Follow the signs to the golf course and continue through the main parking lot of the course.

## ★ Hunting Island State Park

Rumored to be a hideaway for Blackbeard himself, the aptly named Hunting Island was indeed for many years a notable hunting preserve, and its abundance of wildlife remains to this day. The island is one of the

## The Lost Art of Tabby

Tabby is a unique construction technique combining oyster shells, lime, water, and sand found along the South Carolina and Georgia coasts.

Contrary to popular belief, it did not originate with Native Americans. The confusion is due to the fact that the native population left behind many middens, or trash heaps, of oyster shells. While these middens indeed provided the bulk of the shells for tabby buildings to come, Native Americans had little else to do with it. Also contrary to lore, although the Spanish were responsible for the first use of tabby in the Americas, almost all remaining tabby in the area dates from later English settlement. The British first fell in love with tabby after the siege of Spanish-held St. Augustine, Florida, and quickly began building with it in their colonies to the north.

Scholars are divided as to whether tabby was invented by West Africans or its use spread to Africa from Spain and Portugal, circuitously coming to the United States through the knowledge of imported enslaved Africans. The origin of the word itself is also unclear, as similar words exist in Spanish, Portuguese, Gullah, and Arabic to describe various types of wall.

We do know for sure how tabby is made: The primary technique was to burn alternating layers of oyster shells and logs in a deep hole in the ground, thus creating lime. The lime was then mixed with oyster shells, sand, and freshwater and poured into wooden molds, or "forms," to dry and then be used as building blocks, much like large bricks. Tabby walls were usually plastered with stucco. Tabby is remarkably strong and resilient, able to survive the hurricanes that often batter the area. It also stays cool in the summer and is insect-resistant, two enormous advantages down here.

Following are some great examples of true tabby you can see today on the South Carolina and Georgia coasts, from north to south:

- **Dorchester State Historic Site** in Summerville, north of Charleston, contains a well-preserved tabby fort.
- Several younger tabby buildings still exist in downtown Beaufort: the **Barnwell-Gough House** (705 Washington St.); the Thomas Fuller House, or **"Tabby Manse"** (1211 Bay St.); and the **Saltus House** (800 block of Bay St.), perhaps the tallest surviving tabby structure.
- The **Chapel of Ease** on St. Helena Island dates from the 1740s. If someone tells you General Sherman burned it down, don't believe it; the culprit was a forest fire.

East Coast's best birding spots and also hosts dolphins, loggerheads, alligators, and deer. A true family-friendly outdoor adventure spot, **Hunting Island State Park** (2555 Sea Island Pkwy., 866/345-7275, www.huntingisland.com, winter daily 6am-6pm, during daylight saving time daily 6am-9pm, $5 adults, $3 children) has something for everyone—kids, parents, and newlyweds. Yet it still retains a certain sense of lush wildness—so much so that it doubled as Vietnam in the movie *Forrest Gump.*

At the north end past the campground is the island's main landmark, the historic **Hunting Island Light,** which dates from 1875. Although the lighthouse ceased operations in 1933, a rotating light—not strong enough to serve as an actual navigational aid—is turned on at night. While the 167-step trek to the top (donation $2 pp) is strenuous, the view is stunning.

### ★ ACE Basin

Occupying pretty much the entire area between Beaufort and Charleston, the **ACE Basin**—the acronym signifies its role as the collective estuary of the Ashepoo, Combahee, and Edisto Rivers—is one of the most enriching natural experiences the country has to offer. The ACE Basin's three core rivers, the Edisto being the largest, are the framework for a matrix of waterways crisscrossing its

the Chapel of Ease on St. Helena Island

- The **Stoney-Baynard Ruins** in Sea Pines Plantation on Hilton Head are all that's left of the home of the old Braddock's Point Plantation. Foundations of a slave quarters are nearby.
- **Wormsloe Plantation** near Savannah has the remains of Noble Jones's fortification on the Skidaway Narrows.
- **St. Cyprian's Episcopal Church** in Darien is one of the largest tabby structures still in use.
- **Fort Frederica** on St. Simons Island has not only the remains of a tabby fort but many foundations of tabby houses in the surrounding settlement.
- The remarkably intact walls of the **Horton-DuBignon House** on Jekyll Island, Georgia, date from 1738, and the house was occupied into the 1850s.

approximately 350,000 acres of salt marsh. While the ACE Basin can in no way be called "pristine," it's a testament to the power of nature that after 6,000 years of human presence and often intense cultivation, the basin manages to retain much of its untamed feel.

About 12,000 acres of the ACE Basin Project make up the **Ernest F. Hollings ACE Basin National Wildlife Refuge** (8675 Willtown Rd., 843/889-3084, www.fws.gov/acebasin, grounds year-round daily dawn-dusk, office Mon.-Fri. 7:30am-4pm, free), run by the U.S. Fish and Wildlife Service. The historic 1828 **Grove Plantation House** is in this portion of the basin and houses the refuge's headquarters. Sometimes featured on local tours of homes, it's one of only three antebellum homes left in the ACE Basin. Surrounded by lush, ancient oak trees, it's really a sight in and of itself.

This section of the refuge, the **Edisto Unit,** is about an hour's drive from Beaufort. To get to the Edisto Unit of the Hollings ACE Basin National Wildlife Refuge, take U.S. 17 to Highway 174 (going all the way down this route takes you to Edisto Island) and turn right onto Willtown Road. The unpaved entrance road is about two miles ahead on the left. There are restrooms and a few picnic tables.

You can also visit the two parts of the **Combahee Unit** of the refuge, which offers a similar scene of trails among impounded wetlands along the Combahee River, with parking; it's farther west, near Yemassee. The Combahee Unit is about 30 minutes from Beaufort. Get here by taking a left off U.S. 17 onto Highway 33. The larger portion of the Combahee Unit is soon after the turnoff, and the smaller, more northerly portion is about five miles up the road.

## Recreation

### KAYAKING

A premier local outfitter for ACE Basin tours is **Carolina Heritage Outfitters** (U.S. 15 in Canadys, 843/563-5051, www.canoesc.com), which focuses on the Edisto River trail. In addition to guided tours ($30) and rentals, you can camp overnight in their cute tree houses ($125) along the kayak routes. They load you up with your gear and drive you 22 miles upriver, then you paddle downriver to the tree house for the evening. The next day, you paddle yourself the rest of the way downriver back to home base.

To have a drier experience of the ACE Basin from the deck of a larger vessel, try **ACE Basin Tours** (1 Coosaw River Dr., Beaufort, 843/521-3099, Mar.-Nov. Wed. and Sat. 10am, $35 adults, $15 children), which will take you on a three-hour tour in the 40-passenger *Dixie Lady.* To get to their dock from Beaufort, take Carteret Street over the bridge to St. Helena Island, and then take a left on Highway 802 east (Sam's Point Rd.). Continue until you cross Lucy Point Creek; the ACE Basin Tours marina is on your immediate left after you cross the bridge.

### GOLF

Golf is much bigger in Hilton Head than in the Beaufort area, but there are some local highlights. The best-regarded public course in the area, and indeed one of the best military courses in the world, is **Legends at Parris Island** (Bldg. 299, Parris Island, 843/228-2240, www.mccssc.com, $30). Call in advance for a tee time.

Another popular public course is **South Carolina National Golf Club** (8 Waveland Ave., Cat Island, 843/524-0300, www.scnational.com, $70). Get to secluded Cat Island by taking the Sea Island Parkway onto Lady's Island and continuing south as it turns into Lady's Island Drive. Turn onto Island Causeway and continue for about three miles.

### CAMPING

**Hunting Island State Park** (2555 Sea Island Pkwy., 866/345-7275, www.huntingisland.com, winter daily 6am-6pm, during daylight saving time daily 6am-9pm, $5 adults, $3 children, $25 RV sites, $19 tent sites, $87-172 cabin) has 200 campsites with individual water and electric hookups on the north end of the island. There used to be plenty of cabins for rent, but beach erosion has sadly made the ones near the water uninhabitable. One cabin near the lighthouse is still available for rent, and it is in such high demand that the park encourages you to camp instead.

Another neat place to camp is **Tuck in the Wood** (22 Tuc in de Wood Lane, St. Helena, 843/838-2267, $25), a very well-maintained 74-site private campground just past the Penn Center on St. Helena Island.

# Edisto Island

One of the last truly unspoiled places in the Lowcountry, Edisto Island has been highly regarded as a getaway spot since the Edisto people first started coming here for shellfish. In fact, locals swear that the island was settled by English-speaking colonists even before Charleston was settled in 1670.

There are rental homes galore on Edisto Island. Because of the lack of hotels, this is the most popular option for most vacationers—indeed, it's just about the only option. Contact **Edisto Sales and Rentals Realty** (1405 Palmetto Blvd., 800/868-5398, www.edistorealty.com).

## SIGHTS

The **Edisto Museum** (8123 Chisolm Plantation Rd., 843/869-1954, www.edistomuseum.org, Tues.-Sat. noon-5pm, $5 adults, $2 children, free under age 10), a project of the Edisto Island Historic Preservation Society, has recently expanded and incorporated a nearby slave cabin. Its well-done exhibits of local lore and history are complemented by a gift shop. The Edisto Museum is before you get to the main part of the island, off Highway 174.

Opened in 1999 by local snake hunters the Clamp brothers, the **Edisto Island Serpentarium** (1374 Hwy. 174, 843/869-1171, www.edistoserpentarium.com, May-Labor Day, hours vary, $15 adults, $11 ages 4-12, free under age 4) is educational and fun, taking you up close to a variety of reptilian creatures native to the area.

The **Botany Bay Wildlife Management Area** (www.preserveedisto.org, Wed.-Mon. dawn-dusk, free) is a great way to enjoy the unspoiled nature of Edisto Island. On the grounds of two former rice and indigo plantations and comprising 4,000 acres, Botany Bay features several remains of the old plantations and a wonderful small beach. There are no facilities to speak of, so pack and plan accordingly. Botany Bay is closed on hunt days, which vary depending on the hunting season but are fairly rare. Check the website to find out when they will take place.

## SPORTS AND ACTIVITIES

As the largest river of the ACE (Ashepoo, Combahee, Edisto) Basin complex, the Edisto River figures large in the lifestyle of residents and visitors. A good public landing is at Steamboat Creek off Highway 174 on the way down to the island. Take Steamboat Landing Road (Hwy. 968) from Highway 174 near the James Edwards School. Live Oak Landing is farther up Big Bay Creek near the interpretive center at the state park. The **Edisto Marina** (3702 Docksite Rd., 843/869-3504) is on the far west side of the island.

Riding a bike on Edisto Beach and all around the island is a great and relaxing way to get some exercise and enjoy its scenic, laid-back beauty. The best place to rent a bike—or a kayak or canoe, for that matter—is **Island Bikes and Outfitters** (140 Jungle Rd., 843/869-4444, Mon.-Sat. 9am-4pm). Bike rentals run about $16 per day; single kayaks are about $60 per day.

### ★ Edisto Beach State Park

**Edisto Beach State Park** (8377 State Cabin Rd., 843/869-2156, www.southcarolinaparks.com, Nov.-mid-Mar. daily 8am-6pm, mid-Mar.-Oct. daily 6am-10pm, $5 adults, $3 children, free under age 6) is one of the world's foremost destinations for shell collectors. Largely because of fresh loads of silt from the adjacent ACE Basin, there are always new specimens, many of them fossils, washing ashore. The park stretches almost three miles and features the state's longest system of fully accessible hiking and biking trails, including one leading to a 4,000-year-old shell midden, now much eroded from past millennia. The particularly well-done **Interpretive Center** (Tues.-Sat. 9am-4pm) has plenty of interesting exhibits about the nature and history of the park as well as the surrounding ACE Basin.

### CAMPING

A great thing about Edisto Island is the total absence of ugly chain lodging or beachfront condo development. My recommended option is staying at **Edisto Beach State Park** (843/869-2156, www.southcarolinaparks.com, $25 tent sites, $75-100 cabins) itself, either at a campsite on the Atlantic side or in a marshfront cabin on the northern edge. During high season (Apr.-Nov.), there's a minimum weeklong stay in the cabins; during the off-season, the minimum stay is two days. You can book cabins up to 11 months in advance.

## FOOD

A popular joint on the island is **Whaley's** (2801 Myrtle St., 843/869-2161, www.whaleyseb.com, Tues.-Sat. 11:30am-2pm and 5pm-9pm, bar daily 5pm-2am, $5-15), a down-home place in an old gas station a few blocks off the beach. This is a good place for casual seafood like boiled shrimp, washed down with a lot of beer. The bar is open seven days a week.

The legendary ★ **Old Post Office** (1442 Hwy. 174, 843/869-2339, www.theoldpostofficerestaurant.com, Tues.-Sun. 5:30pm-10pm, $20), a Lowcountry-style fine-dining spot, served a devoted clientele for 20 years. It recently reopened with a bang and thankfully kept its old-school mystique intact. Specialties include fine crab cakes drizzled with mousseline sauce, the pecan-encrusted Veal Edistonian, and a Carolina rib eye topped with a pimiento cheese sauce.

## TRANSPORTATION

Edisto Island is basically halfway between Beaufort and Charleston. There's one main land route here, south on Highway 174 off U.S. 17. It's a long way down from U.S. 17 to Edisto, but the 20- to 30-minute drive is scenic and enjoyable. Most activity on the island centers on the township of Edisto Beach, which voted to align itself with Colleton County for its lower taxes (the rest of Edisto Island is part of Charleston County).

### Tours

Edisto has many beautiful plantation homes, relics of the island's longtime role as host to cotton plantations. While all are in private hands and therefore off-limits to the public, an exception is offered through **Edisto Island Tours & T'ings** (843/869-9092, $20 adults, $10 under age 13). You'll take a van tour around Edisto's beautiful churches and old plantations.

# Hilton Head Island

Literally the prototype of the modern planned resort community, Hilton Head Island is also a case study in how a landscape can change when money is introduced. From Reconstruction until the post-World War II era, the island consisted almost entirely of African Americans with deep roots in the area. In the mid-1950s Hilton Head began its transformation into an almost all-white, upscale golf, tennis, and shopping mecca populated largely by Northern and Midwestern transplants and retirees. As you can imagine, the flavor here is now quite different from surrounding areas of the Lowcountry, to say the least, with an emphasis on material excellence, top prices, get-it-done-yesterday punctuality, and the attendant aggressive traffic.

These days, Hilton Head gets the most national media attention for the RBC Heritage golf tournament each April, when the entire island is packed with golf fans for this extremely popular PGA event.

# Hilton Head Island

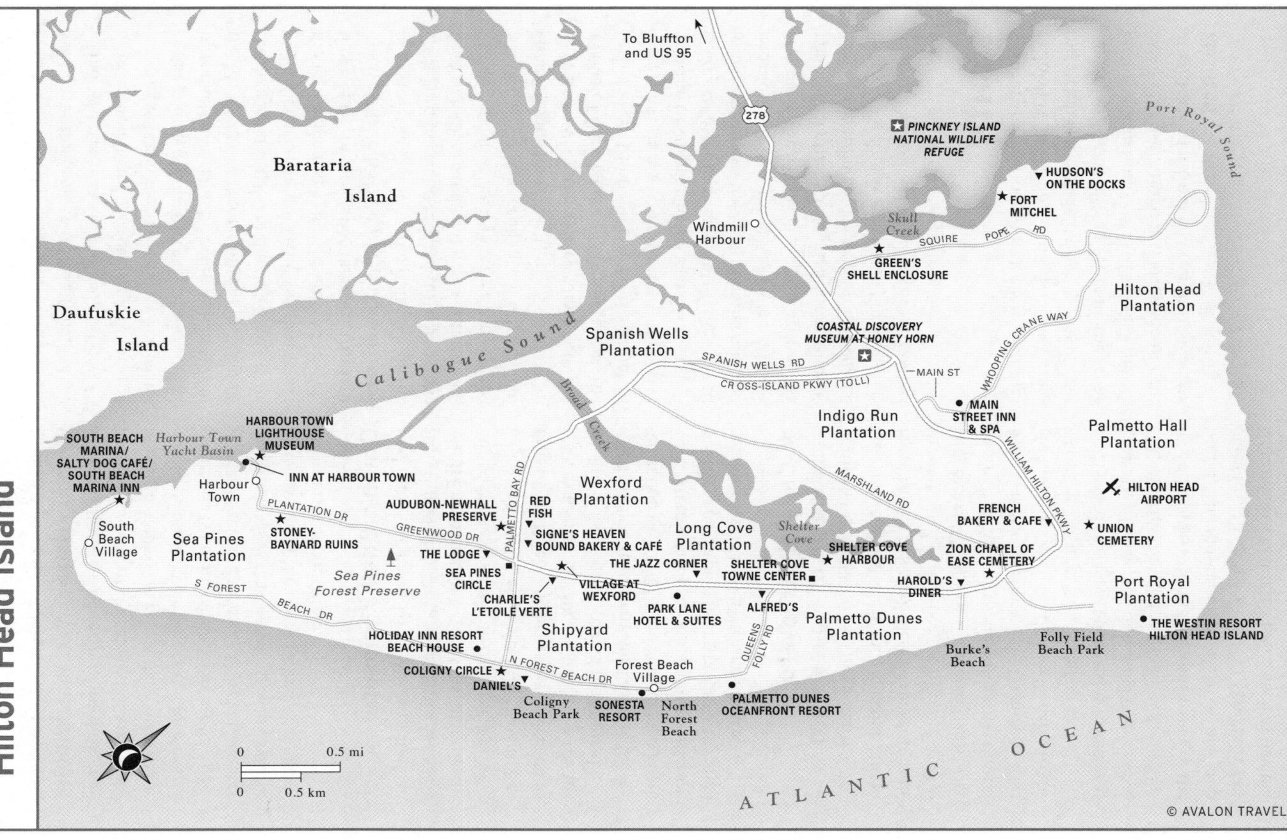

## HISTORY

The second-largest barrier island on the East Coast was named in 1663 by adventurer Sir William Hilton, who thoughtfully named the island—with its notable headland or "Head"—after himself. Later it gained fame as the first growing location of the legendary Sea Island cotton, a long-grain variety that, following its introduction in 1790 by William Elliott II of the Myrtle Bank Plantation, would soon be the dominant version of the cash crop.

Though it seems unlikely given the island's modern demographics, Hilton Head was almost entirely African American through much of the 20th century. When Union troops occupied the island at the outbreak of the Civil War, freed and escaped enslaved people flocked to the island, and many of the dwindling number of African Americans on the island today are descendants of this original Gullah population.

In the 1950s the Fraser family bought 19,000 of the island's 25,000 acres with the intent to continue forestry on them. But in 1956—not at all coincidentally the same year the first bridge to the island was built—Charles Fraser convinced his father to sell him the southern tip. Fraser's brainchild and decades-long labor of love—some said his obsession—Sea Pines Plantation became the prototype for the golf-oriented resort communities so common today on both U.S. coasts. Fraser himself was killed in a boating accident in 2002 and is buried under the famous Liberty Oak in Harbour Town.

## SIGHTS

Contrary to what many think, there are things to do on Hilton Head that don't involve swinging a club at a little ball or shopping for designer labels, but instead celebrate the area's history and natural setting. The following are some of those attractions, arranged in geographical order from where you first access the island.

### ★ Pinckney Island National Wildlife Refuge

Consisting of many islands and hammocks, **Pinckney Island National Wildlife Refuge** (912/652-4415, daily dawn-dusk, free) is the only part of this small but very well-managed 4,000-acre refuge that's open to the public. Almost 70 percent of the former rice plantation is salt marsh and tidal creeks, making it a perfect microcosm for the Lowcountry as a whole, as well as a great place to kayak or canoe. Some of the state's richest birding opportunities abound here.

### Green's Shell Enclosure

Less known than the larger Native American shell ring farther south at Sea Pines, **Green's Shell Enclosure** (803/734-3886, daily dawn-dusk) is certainly easier to find, and you don't have to pay $6 to enter the area, as with Sea Pines. This three-acre heritage preserve dates back to at least the 1300s. The heart of the site is a low embankment, part of the original fortified village. To get here, take a left at the intersection of U.S. 278 and Squire Pope Road. Turn left into Green's Park, pass the office on the left, and park. The entrance to the shell enclosure is on the left behind a fence.

### ★ Coastal Discovery Museum at Honey Horn

With the acquisition of Honey Horn's 70-acre spread of historic plantation land, Hilton Head finally has a full-fledged museum worthy of the name, and the magnificent **Coastal Discovery Museum** (70 Honey Horn Dr., 843/689-6767, www.coastaldiscovery.org, Mon.-Sat. 9am-4:30pm, Sun. 11am-3pm, free) is a must-see, even for those who came to the island mostly to golf and soak up sun.

The facility centers on the expertly restored Discovery House, the only antebellum house still existing on Hilton Head, with exhibits and displays devoted to the history of the island. The museum is also a great one-stop place to sign up for a variety of specialty on-site and off-site guided tours, such as birding and Gullah history tours. The cost for most on-site tours is a reasonable $10 adults, $5 children.

But the real draw is the 0.5-mile trail through the Honey Horn grounds, including several boardwalk viewpoints over the marsh, a neat little butterfly habitat, a replica Native American shell ring, a wonderful heirloom camellia garden, and a stable and pasture that host Darling and Comet, the museum's two Marsh Tackies—short, tough little ponies descended from Spanish horses and used to great effect by Francis "Swamp Fox" Marion and his freedom fighters in the American Revolution.

While a glance at a map and area signage might convince you that you must pay the $1.25 toll on the Cross Island Parkway to get to Honey Horn, that isn't so. The exit to Honey Horn on the parkway is actually before you get to the toll plaza; therefore access is free. You can exit back onto U.S. 278 without needing to pay the toll.

## Union Cemetery

A modest but key aspect of African American history on Hilton Head is at **Union Cemetery** (Union Cemetery Rd.), a small burial ground featuring several graves of black Union Army troops (you can tell by the designation "USCI" on the tombstone, for "United States Colored Infantry"). Also of interest are the charming hand-carved cement tombstones of nonveterans. To get here, turn north off William Hilton Parkway onto Union Cemetery Road. The cemetery is a short way ahead on the left. There is no signage or site interpretation.

## Zion Chapel of Ease Cemetery

More like one of the gloriously desolate scenes common to the rest of the Lowcountry, this little cemetery in full view of the William Hilton Parkway at Folly Field Road is all that remains of one of the "Chapels of Ease," a string of chapels set up in the 1700s. The **Zion Chapel of Ease Cemetery** (daily dawn-dusk, free) is said to be haunted by the ghost of William Baynard, whose final resting place is in a mausoleum on the site (the remains of his ancestral home are farther south at Sea Pines Plantation).

## Audubon-Newhall Preserve

Plant lovers shouldn't miss this small but very well-maintained 50-acre wooded tract in the south-central part of the island on Palmetto Bay Road between the Cross Island Parkway and the Sea Pines Circle. Almost all plantlife, even that in the water, is helpfully marked

Coastal Discovery Museum at Honey Horn

and identified. The **Audubon-Newhall Preserve** (year-round dawn-dusk, free) is open to the public, but you can't camp here. For more information, call the **Hilton Head Audubon Society** (843/842-9246).

## Sea Pines Plantation

This private residential resort development at the extreme west end of the island—the first on Hilton Head and the prototype for every other such development in the country—hosts several attractions that collectively are worth the $6 per vehicle "road use" fee, which you pay at the main entrance gate.

### HARBOUR TOWN

It's not particularly historic and not all that natural, but **Harbour Town** is still pretty cool. The dominant element is the squat, colorful **Harbour Town Lighthouse Museum** (149 Lighthouse Rd., 843/671-2810, www.harbourtownlighthouse.com, daily 10am-dusk, $4.25, free under age 5), which has never really helped a ship navigate. The 90-foot structure was built in 1970 purely to give visitors a little atmosphere, and that it does, as kids especially love climbing the stairs to the top and looking out over the island's expanse.

### STONEY-BAYNARD RUINS

The **Stoney-Baynard ruins** (Plantation Dr., dawn-dusk, free), tabby ruins in a residential neighborhood, are what remains of the circa-1790 central building of the old Braddock's Point Plantation, first owned by patriot and raconteur Captain "Saucy Jack" Stoney and later by the Baynard family. Active during the island's heyday as a cotton center, the plantation was destroyed after the Civil War.

### SEA PINES FOREST PRESERVE

The **Sea Pines Forest Preserve** (175 Greenwood Dr., 843/363-4530, free) is set amid the Sea Pines Plantation golf resort development, but you don't need a bag of clubs to enjoy this 600-acre preserve, which is built on the site of an old rice plantation (dikes and logging trails are still visible). Here you can ride a horse, fish, or just take a walk on the eight miles of trails (dawn-dusk) and enjoy the natural beauty around you. No bike riding is allowed on the trails, however.

In addition to the Native American shell ring farther north off Squire Pope Road, the Sea Pines Forest Preserve also boasts a shell ring set within a canopy of tall pines.

## Tours and Cruises

Most guided tours on Hilton Head focus on the water. **Harbour Town Cruises** (843/363-9023, www.vagabondcruise.com, $30-60) offers several sightseeing tours as well as excursions to Daufuskie and Savannah. They also offer a tour on a former America's Cup racing yacht.

Dolphin tours are extremely popular on Hilton Head, and there is no shortage of operators. **Dolphin Watch Nature Cruises** (843/785-4558, $25 adults, $10 children) departs from Shelter Cove, as does **Lowcountry Nature Tours** (843/683-0187, www.lowcountrynaturetours.com, $40 adults, $35 children, free under age 3). **Outside Hilton Head** (843/686-6996, www.outsidehiltonhead.com) runs a variety of water ecotours and dolphin tours as well as a guided day-trip excursion to Daufuskie, complete with golf cart rental.

There is a notable land-based tour by **Gullah Heritage Trail Tours** (leaves from Coastal Discovery Museum at Honey Horn, 843/681-7066, www.gullahheritage.com, $32 adults, $15 children) delving into the island's rich, if poorly preserved, African American history from slavery through the time of the freedmen.

# ENTERTAINMENT AND NIGHTLIFE

## Nightlife

The highest-quality live entertainment on the island is at **The Jazz Corner** (1000 William Hilton Pkwy., 843/842-8620, www.thejazzcorner.com, dinner daily 6pm-9pm, late-night menu after 9pm, dinner $15-20, cover varies), which brings in big names in the genre to perform in this space in the unlikely setting of

The Jazz Corner is a great place for live music.

a boutique mall, the Village at Wexford. The dinners are actually quite good, but the attraction is definitely the music. Reservations are recommended. Live music starts around 7pm.

For years islanders jokingly referred to the "Barmuda Triangle," an area named for the preponderance of bars within vague walking distance of Sea Pines Circle. While some of the names have changed over the years, the long-time anchor of the Barmuda Triangle is the **Tiki Hut** (1 S. Forest Beach Dr., 843/785-5126, Sun.-Thurs. 11am-8pm, Fri.-Sat. 11am-10pm, bar until 2am), actually part of The Beach House hotel at the entrance to Sea Pines. This popular watering hole is the only beachfront bar on the island, which technically makes it the only place you can legally drink alcohol on a Hilton Head beach. Another Triangle fave is **The Lodge** (7 Greenwood Dr., 843/842-8966, www.hiltonheadlodge.com, daily 11:30am-midnight). After the martini-and-cigar craze waned, this popular spot successfully remade itself into a beer-centric place with 36 rotating taps.

Despite its location in the upscale strip mall of the Village at Wexford, the **British Open Pub** (1000 William Hilton Pkwy./U.S. 278, 843/686-6736, daily 11am-10pm) offers a fairly convincing English vibe with, as the name suggests, a heavy golf theme. The fish-and-chips and shepherd's pie are both magnificent.

Inside Sea Pines is the **Quarterdeck Lounge and Patio** (843/842-1999, www.seapines.com, Sun.-Thurs. 5:30pm-10pm, Fri.-Sat. 5:30pm-midnight) at the base of the Harbour Town Lighthouse. This is where the party's at after a long day on the fairways during the Heritage golf tournament. Within Sea Pines at the South Beach Marina is also where you'll find **The Salty Dog Cafe** (232 S. Sea Pines Dr., 843/671-2233, www.saltydog.com, lunch daily 11am-3pm, dinner daily 5pm-10pm, bar daily until 2am), one of the area's most popular institutions (some might even call it a tourist trap) and something akin to an island empire, with popular T-shirts, a gift shop, books, and an ice cream shop, all overlooking the marina. My suggestion, however, is to make the short walk to the affiliated **Wreck of the Salty Dog** (843/671-7327, daily until 2am), where the marsh views are better and the atmosphere not quite so tacky.

A gay-friendly bar on Hilton Head is **Cool Cats Lounge** (32 Palmetto Bay Rd., Mon.-Fri. 8pm-3am, Sat. 8pm-2am), with a welcoming dive-bar atmosphere and a small but lively dance floor.

## Performing Arts

The range of offerings won't rival New York City, but because so many residents migrated here from art-savvy metropolitan areas in the Northeast, Hilton Head maintains a high standard of entertainment. Much of the activity centers on the multimillion-dollar **Arts Center of Coastal Carolina** (14 Shelter Cove Lane, 843/842-2787, www.artshhi.com), which hosts touring shows, resident companies, musical concerts, dance performances, and visual arts exhibits.

Under the direction of maestro John

Morris Russell, the acclaimed **Hilton Head Symphony Orchestra** (843/842-2055, www.hhso.org) performs a year-round season of masterworks and pops programs at the First Presbyterian Church (540 William Hilton Pkwy./U.S. 278).

### Cinema

There's an art house on Hilton Head, the charming **Coligny Theatre** (843/686-3500, www.colignytheatre.com) tucked away in the Coligny Plaza shopping center before you get to Sea Pines. For years this was the only movie theater for miles around, opening in 1972 and shuttering briefly in 1997. But since reopening in 2002 it has reincarnated as a primarily indie film venue. Look for the entertaining murals on the outside walls by local artist Ralph Sutton.

### Festivals and Events

Late February-early March brings the **Hilton Head Wine and Food Festival** (www.hiltonheadhospitality.org), culminating in what they call "the East Coast's Largest Outdoor Public Tasting and Auction," which is generally held at the Coastal Discovery Museum at Honey Horn. Some events charge admission.

Without question, Hilton Head's premier event is the **RBC Heritage Golf Tournament** (843/671-2248, http://theheritagegolfsc.com), held each April, usually the week after the Masters, at the Harbour Town Golf Links on Sea Pines Plantation. Formerly known as the Verizon Heritage Classic, the event is South Carolina's only PGA Tour event and brings thousands of visitors to town. The entire island gets quite crowded during this time, so be aware.

A fun and fondly anticipated yearly event is the **Kiwanis Club Chili Cookoff** (www.hiltonheadkiwanis.org), held each October at Honey Horn on the south end. A low admission price gets you all the chili you can eat plus free antacids. All funds go to charity, and all excess chili goes to a local food bank.

Every November brings Hilton Head's second-largest event, the **Hilton Head Concours d'Elegance & Motoring Festival** (www.hhiconcours.com), a multi-day affair bringing together vintage car clubs from throughout the nation and culminating in a prestigious "Best of Show" competition. It started as a fund-raiser for the Hilton Head Symphony, but now people come from all over the country to see these fine vintage cars in a beautiful setting.

## SHOPS

As you'd expect, Hilton Head is a shopper's delight, with an emphasis on upscale stores and prices to match. Keep in mind that hours may be shortened in the off-season (Nov.-Mar.). Here's a rundown of the main island shopping areas in the order you'll encounter them as you enter the island.

### Shelter Cove

**Shelter Cove Towne Centre** (40 Shelter Cove Lane, www.sheltercovetownecentre.com), a wonderfully repurposed former mall space, centers on a Belk anchor store and a Kroger but also offers a growing array of shops and new restaurants and watering holes in this brand new, attractive construction. Shelter Cove Community Park is adjacent, and features a safe playground space for young children and multiuse greenway. Retail highlights include **ArtWare** (23 Shelter Cove Lane, 843/682-3400, www.artwaredesigns.com), a whimsical boutique featuring clothing, home and garden goods, and pet goods, and **Spartina 449** (28 Shelter Cove Lane, 843/342-7722, www.spartina449.com), a women's clothing and accessory store with a distinctive Lowcountry flavor and color palette.

The nearby **Plaza at Shelter Cove** (50 Shelter Cove Lane, www.theplazaatsheltercove.com) features many shops, including a Whole Foods and the flagship location of **Outside Hilton Head** (843/686-6996, www.outsidehiltonhead.com, Mon.-Sat. 10am-5:30pm, Sun. 11am-5:30pm), a complete outdoor outfitter with a knowledgeable staff.

## Village at Wexford

This well-shaded shopping center on William Hilton Parkway (U.S. 278), one of the older on the island, hosts plenty of well-tended shops, including the foodie equipment store **Le Cookery** (843/785-7171, Mon.-Sat. 10am-6pm), the Lily Pulitzer signature women's store **S. M. Bradford Co.** (843/686-6161, Mon.-Sat. 10am-6pm), and the aromatic **Scents of Hilton Head** (843/842-7866, Mon.-Fri. 10am-6pm, Sat. 10am-5pm).

My favorite shop at Wexford is **The Oilerie** (843/681-2722, www.oilerie.com, Mon.-Sat. 10am-7pm, Sun. noon-5pm). This franchise provides free samples of all its high-quality Italian olive oils and vinegars. After you taste around awhile, you pick what you want and the friendly staff bottles it for you in souvenir-quality glassware. They also have a selection of spices, soaps, and other goodies.

## Coligny Circle

Often called "Hilton Head's downtown" because it was the first shopping area of note on the island, dating back to the 1950s, Coligny is the closest Hilton Head comes to funkier beach towns like Tybee Island or Folly Beach, although it doesn't really come that close. You'll find plenty somewhat quirky stores here, many keeping long hours in the summer, like the self-explanatory **Coligny Kite & Flag Co.** (843/785-5483, Mon.-Sat. 10am-9pm, Sun. 11am-6pm), the comprehensive and stylish **Quiet Storm Surf Shop** (843/671-2551, daily 10am-9pm), and **Fresh Produce** (843/842-3410, www.freshproduceclothes.com, Mon.-Sat. 10am-10pm, Sun. 10am-9pm), actually a very cute women's clothing store. Kids will love both **The Shell Shop** (843/785-4900, Mon.-Sat. 10am-9pm, Sun. noon-9pm) and **Black Market Minerals** (843/785-7090, Mon.-Sat. 10am-10pm, Sun. 11am-8pm). **The Bird's Nest** (843/785-3737) has a great selection of jewelry and fashionable handbags.

## Harbour Town

The **Shoppes at Harbour Town** (www.seapines.com) are a collection of about 20 mostly boutique stores along Lighthouse Road in Sea Pines Plantation. At **Planet Hilton Head** (843/363-5177, www.planethiltonhead.com, daily 10am-9pm) you'll find some cute eclectic gifts and home goods. Other clothing highlights include **Knickers Men's Store** (843/671-2291, daily 10am-9pm) and **Radiance** (843/363-5176, Mon.-Tues. 10am-5pm, Wed.-Sat. 10am-9pm, Sun. 11am-9pm), a very cute and fashion-forward women's store.

The **Top of the Lighthouse Shoppe** (843/671-2810, www.harbourtownlighthouse.com, daily 10am-9pm) is where many a climbing visitor has been coaxed to part with some of their disposable income. And, of course, as you'd expect being near the legendary Harbour Town links, there's the **Harbour Town Pro Shop** (843/671-4485, daily 7am-5pm), routinely voted one of the best pro shops in the nation.

## South Beach Marina

On South Sea Pines Drive at the marina you'll find several worthwhile shops, including a good marine store and all-around grocery dealer **South Beach General Store** (843/671-6784, daily 8am-10pm). I like to stop in **Blue Water Bait and Tackle** (843/671-3060, daily 7am-8pm) and check out the cool nautical stuff. They can also hook you up with a variety of kayak trips and fishing charters. And, of course, right on the water there's the ever-popular **Salty Dog Cafe** (843/671-2233, www.saltydog.com, lunch daily 11am-3pm, dinner daily 5pm-10pm), whose ubiquitous T-shirts seem to adorn every other person on the island.

## Art Galleries

Despite the abundant wealth apparent in some quarters here, there's no freestanding art museum in the area, that role being filled by independent galleries. A good representative example is **Morris & Whiteside Galleries** (220 Cordillo Pkwy., 843/842-4433, www.morris-whiteside.com, Mon.-Fri. 9am-5pm, Sat. 10am-4pm), located in the historic

Red Piano Too Art Gallery building, which features a variety of paintings and sculpture, heavy on landscapes but also showing some fine figurative work. The nonprofit **Art League of Hilton Head** (14 Shelter Cove Lane, 843/681-5060, Mon.-Sat. 10am-6pm) is located in the Walter Greer Art Gallery within the Arts Center of Coastal Carolina and displays work by member artists in all media. The **Nash Gallery** (13 Harbourside Lane, 843/785-6424, Mon.-Fri. 10am-9pm, Sat. 10am-8pm, Sun. 11am-5pm) in Shelter Cove Harbour deals more in North American craft styles. Hilton Head art isn't exactly known for its avant-garde nature, but you can find some whimsical stuff at **Picture This** (78D Arrow Rd., 843/842-5299, Mon.-Fri. 9:30am-5:30pm, Sat. 9:30am-12:30pm), including a selection of Gullah craft items.

## SPORTS AND ACTIVITIES

### Beaches

First, the good news: Hilton Head Island has 12 miles of some of the most beautiful, safe beaches you'll find anywhere. The bad news is that there are only a few ways to gain access, generally at locations referred to as "beach parks." Don't just drive into a residential neighborhood and think you'll be able to park and find your way to the beach; the vast majority of beach access on the island is in private hands, where trespassing and illegal parking is frowned upon.

Driessen Beach Park has 207 long-term parking spaces, costing $0.25 for 30 minutes. There's free parking but fewer spaces at the Coligny Beach Park entrance and at Fish Haul Creek Park. Also, there are 22 metered spaces at Alder Lane Beach Access, 51 at Folly Field Beach Park, and 13 at Burkes Beach Road. Most other beach parks have permit parking only. Clean, well-maintained public restrooms are available at all the beach parks. You can find **beach information** at 843/342-4580 and www.hiltonheadislandsc.gov. Beach park hours vary: Coligny Beach Park is open daily 24 hours; all other beach parks are open March-September daily 6am-8pm and October-February daily 6am-5pm. Alcohol is strictly prohibited on Hilton Head's beaches.

### Kayaking

Kayakers will enjoy Hilton Head Island, which offers several gorgeous routes, including Calibogue Sound to the south and west and Port Royal Sound to the north. For particularly good views of life on the salt marsh,

There are a lot of activities on Hilton Head's beaches.

try Broad Creek, which nearly bisects Hilton Head Island, and Skull Creek, which separates Hilton Head from the natural beauty of Pinckney Island. Broad Creek Marina is a good place to put in.

If you want a guided tour, there are plenty of great kayak tour outfits to choose from in the area. Chief among them is **Outside Hilton Head** (32 Shelter Cove Lane, 800/686-6996, www.outsidehiltonhead.com).

## Biking

Although the very flat terrain is not challenging, Hilton Head provides some scenic and relaxing cycling opportunities. Thanks to wise planning and foresight, the island has an extensive and award-winning 50-mile network of biking trails that does a great job of keeping cyclists out of traffic. A big plus is the long bike path paralleling the William Hilton Parkway, enabling cyclists to use that key artery without braving its traffic. There is even an underground bike path beneath the parkway to facilitate crossing that busy road. In addition, there are also routes along Pope Avenue as well as North and South Forest Beach Drive. Go to www.hiltonheadisland.org/biking to download a map of the island's entire bike path network.

**Palmetto Dunes Oceanfront Resort** (4 Queens Folly Rd., 800/827-3006, www.palmettodunes.com) has a particularly nice 25-mile network of bike paths that all link up to the island's larger framework. Within the resort is **Palmetto Dunes Outfitters** (843/785-2449, www.pdoutfitters.com, daily 9am-5pm), which will rent you any type of bike you might need. Sea Pines Plantation also has an extensive 17-mile network of bike trails; you can pick up a map at most information kiosks within the plantation.

There's a plethora of bike rental facilities on Hilton Head with competitive rates. Be sure to ask if they offer free pickup and delivery. Try **Hilton Head Bicycle Company** (112 Arrow Rd., 843/686-6888, daily 9am-5pm, $16 per day).

## Horseback Riding

Within the Sea Pines Forest Preserve is **Lawton Stables** (190 Greenwood Dr., 843/671-2586, www.lawtonstableshhi.com), which features pony rides, a small-animal farm, and guided horseback rides through the preserve. You don't need any riding experience, but you do need reservations.

## Bird-Watching

The premier birding locale in the area is the **Pinckney Island National Wildlife Refuge** (U.S. 278 east, just before Hilton Head, 912/652-4415, www.fws.gov, free). You can see bald eagles, ibis, wood storks, painted buntings, and many more species. Birding is best in spring and fall. The refuge has several freshwater ponds that serve as wading bird rookeries. During migration season, so many beautiful birds make such a ruckus that you'll think you've wandered onto an Animal Planet shoot.

TOP EXPERIENCE

## Golf

Hilton Head is one of the world's great golf centers, with no fewer than 23 courses, and one could easily write a book about nothing but that. This, however, is not that book. Perhaps contrary to what you might expect, most courses on the island are public, and some are downright affordable. All courses are 18 holes unless otherwise described; greens fees are averages and vary with season and tee time.

The best-regarded course, with prices to match, is **Harbour Town Golf Links** (Sea Pines Plantation, 843/363-4485, www.seapines.com, $239). It's on the island's south end at Sea Pines and is the home of the annual RBC Heritage Classic, far and away the island's number-one tourist draw.

There are two Arthur Hills-designed courses on the island, **Arthur Hills at Palmetto Dunes Resort** (843/785-1140, www.palmettodunes.com, $125) and **Arthur Hills at Palmetto Hall** (Palmetto Hall

Plantation, 843/689-4100, www.palmetto-hallgolf.com, $130), both of which now offer the use of Segway vehicles on the fairways. The reasonably priced **Barony Course** at Port Royal Plantation (843/686-8801, www.portroyalgolfclub.com, $98) also boasts some of the toughest greens on the island. Another challenging and affordable course is the **George Fazio at Palmetto Dunes** Resort (843/785-1130, www.palmettodunes.com, $105).

It's wise to book tee times through the **Golf Island Call Center** (888/465-3475, www.golfisland.com), which can also hook you up with good packages.

### Tennis

One of the top tennis destinations in the country, Hilton Head has over 20 tennis clubs, some of which offer court time to the public (walk-on rates vary; call for information). They are: **Palmetto Dunes Tennis Center** (Palmetto Dunes Resort, 843/785-1152, www.palmettodunes.com, $30 per hour), **Port Royal Racquet Club** (Port Royal Plantation, 843/686-8803, www.portroyalgolfclub.com, $25 per hour), **Sea Pines Racquet Club** (Sea Pines Plantation, 843/363-4495, www.seapines.com, $25 per hour), **South Beach Racquet Club** (Sea Pines Plantation, 843/671-2215, www.seapines.com, $25 per hour), and **Shipyard Racquet Club** (Shipyard Plantation, 843/686-8804, $25 per hour).

Free, first-come, first-served play is available at the following public courts, maintained by the Island Recreation Association (www.islandreccenter.org): **Chaplin Community Park** (Singleton Beach Rd., 4 courts, lighted), **Cordillo Courts** (Cordillo Pkwy., 4 courts, lighted), **Fairfield Square** (Adrianna Lane, 2 courts), **Hilton Head High School** (School Rd., 6 courts), and **Hilton Head Middle School** (Wilborn Rd., 4 courts).

### Zip Line

Billing itself as the only zip line experience within 250 miles, the **Zip Line Hilton Head** (33 Broad Creek Marina Way, 843/682-6000, www.ziplinehiltonhead.com) offers an extensive canopy tour making great use of the area's natural scenery and features. You generally "fly" in groups of about eight. Reservations are strongly advised. The latest offering is "Aerial Adventure" ($50), a challenging two-hour trip with about 50 obstacles.

## FOOD

Because of the cosmopolitan nature of the population, with so many transplants from the northeastern United States and Europe, there is uniformly high quality in Hilton Head restaurants. Hilton Head has shed its reputation as a somewhat stodgy food town and does offer some fun, cutting-edge, big city-style spots to enjoy.

### Bistro

Combining rib-sticking comfort food with hearty European-style cuisine is ★ **Lucky Rooster** (841 William Hilton Pkwy., 843/681-3474, www.luckyroosterhhi.com, daily 5pm-10pm, $15). This really is one of the most vibrant and satisfying menus on the island, from the fried green tomatoes to the pan-fried sweetbread starters, to the short rib and shrimp and grits and mushroom lasagna entrées. A lively full bar complements the bistro-style scene.

An upgrade of a longtime island favorite called simply Daniel's, **Crave by Daniel's** (2 N. Forest Beach Dr., 843/341-9379, http://danielshhi.com, daily 4pm-2am, $25) is now an upscale steak house with a twist. In addition to offering gorgeous cuts of meat like a center-cut filet mignon, they specialize in what they call "big small plates." Try a sizzling cinnamon steak kebab or a gyro pizzetta.

### Breakfast and Brunch

There are a couple of great diner-style places on the island. Though known more for its hamburgers and Philly cheesesteaks, **Harold's Diner** (641 William Hilton Pkwy., 843/842-9292, Mon.-Sat. 7am-3pm, $4-6) has great pancakes as well as its trademark brand of sarcastic service. The place is small, popular, and does not take reservations.

**The French Bakery** (28 Shelter Cove Lane, 843/342-5420, Mon.-Sat. 7am-4pm, Sun. 8am-3pm, frenchbakeryhiltonhead.com, $12) in the attractive new Shelter Cove Towne Centre is a great breakfast-brunch type spot, with an emphasis on rustic and hearty Euro-inspired breakfast sandwiches (breakfast is served through 11:30am) and various sweet and savory crepes. The lunch salads are outstanding.

If you need a bite in the Coligny Plaza area, go to **Skillets** (1 N. Forest Beach Dr., 843/785-3131, www.skilletscafe.com, breakfast daily 7am-5pm, dinner daily 5pm-9pm, $5-23) in Coligny Plaza. Their eponymous stock-in-trade is a layered breakfast dish of sautéed ingredients served in a porcelain skillet, like the "Kitchen Sink": pancakes ringed with potatoes, sausage, and bacon, topped with two poached eggs.

A great all-day breakfast place with a twist is ★ **Signe's Heaven Bound Bakery & Café** (93 Arrow Rd., 843/785-9118, www.signesbakery.com, Mon.-Fri. 8am-4pm, Sat. 9am-2pm, $5-10). Breakfast is tasty dishes like frittatas and breakfast polenta, while the twist is the extensive artisanal bakery, with delicious specialties like the signature key lime pound cake. Expect a wait during peak periods.

## German

I'm pretty sure you didn't come all the way to South Carolina to eat traditional German food, but while you're here, check out ★ **Alfred's** (807 William Hilton Pkwy./U.S. 278, 843/341-3117, wwww.alfredshiltonhead.com, Mon.-Sat. 5pm-11pm, $20-30), one of the more unique spots on Hilton Head and a big favorite with the locals. Expect a wait. Bratwurst, veal cordon bleu, and of course Wiener schnitzel are all standouts. I recommend the German Mix Platter ($25), which features a brat, some sauerbraten, and a schnitzel.

## Seafood and Southern

Honest-to-goodness Southern cookin' isn't always that easy to come by on this island full of transplants from outside the South. But a great place to find it is **A Lowcountry Backyard** (32 Palmetto Bay Rd., Suite 4A, www.hhbackyard.com, Mon.-Sat. 11am-3pm and 4:30pm-9pm, Sat. brunch 9am-noon, Sun. brunch 9am-3pm, $15). As the name implies, this is regional cuisine served in a relaxed and casual atmosphere fitting for island life. As with many Hilton Head establishments, it's located within a strip mall setting, the Village Exchange.

Not to be confused with Charley's Crab House next door to Hudson's, seafood lovers will enjoy the experience down near Sea Pines at ★ **Charlie's L'Etoile Verte** (8 New Orleans Rd., 843/785-9277, http://charliesgreenstar.com, lunch Tues.-Sat. 11:30am-2pm, dinner Mon.-Sat. 5:30pm-10pm, $25-40), which is considered by many connoisseurs to be Hilton Head's single best restaurant. The emphasis here is on "French country kitchen" cuisine—think Provence, not Paris. In keeping with that theme, each day's menu is concocted from scratch and handwritten. Reservations are essential.

A longtime Hilton Head favorite is **Red Fish** (8 Archer Rd., 843/686-3388, www.redfishofhiltonhead.com, lunch Mon.-Sat. 11:30am-2pm, dinner daily beginning with early-bird specials at 5pm, $20-37). Strongly Caribbean in decor as well as menu, with romanticism and panache to match, this is a great place for couples. Reservations are essential.

Fresh seafood lovers will enjoy one of Hilton Head's staples, the huge **Hudson's on the Docks** (1 Hudson Rd., 843/681-2772, www.hudsonsonthedocks.com, lunch daily 11am-4pm, dinner daily from 5pm, $14-23) on Skull Creek just off Squire Pope Road on the less-developed north side. Much of the catch—though not all of it, by any means—comes directly off the boats you'll see dockside. Try the stuffed shrimp filled with crabmeat. Leave room for one of the homemade desserts crafted by Ms. Bessie, a 30-year veteran employee of Hudson's.

## ACCOMMODATIONS

Generally speaking, accommodations on Hilton Head are often surprisingly affordable given their overall high quality and the breadth of their amenities.

### Under $150

You can't beat the rates at **Park Lane Hotel and Suites** (12 Park Lane, 843/686-5700, www.hiltonheadparklanehotel.com, $130). This is your basic suite-type hotel (formerly a Residence Inn) with kitchens, laundry, a pool, and a tennis court. The allure here is the rates, hard to find anywhere these days at a resort location. For a nonrefundable fee, you can bring your pet. The one drawback is that the beach is a good distance away. The hotel does offer a free shuttle, however, so it would be wise to take advantage of that and avoid the usual beach-parking hassles. As you'd expect given the rates, rooms here tend to go quickly; reserve early.

### $150-300

A great place for the price is the **South Beach Inn** (232 S. Sea Pines Dr., 843/671-6498, www.sbinn.com, $186) in Sea Pines. Located near the famous Salty Dog Cafe and outfitted in a similar nautical theme, the inn not only has some pretty large guest rooms for the rates, it offers a lovely view of the marina and has a very friendly feel. As with all Sea Pines accommodations, staying on the plantation means you don't have to wait in line with other visitors to pay the $5-per-day "road fee." Sea Pines also offers a free trolley to get around the plantation.

One of Hilton Head's favorite hotels for beach lovers is **The Beach House** (1 S. Forest Beach Dr., 855/474-2882, www.beachhousehhi.com, $200), formerly the Holiday Inn Oceanfront and home of the famed Tiki Hut bar on the beach. Staff turnover is less frequent here than at other local accommodations, and while it's no Ritz-Carlton and occasionally shows signs of wear, it's a good value in a bustling area of the island.

One of the better resort-type places for those who prefer the putter and the racquet to the Frisbee and the surfboard is the **Inn and Club at Harbour Town** (7 Lighthouse Lane, 843/363-8100, www.seapines.com, $199) in Sea Pines. The big draw here is the impeccable service, delivered by a staff of "butlers" in kilts, mostly Europeans who take the venerable trade quite seriously. While it's not on the beach, you can take advantage of the free Sea Pines Trolley every 20 minutes.

Recently rated the number one family resort in the United States by *Travel + Leisure* magazine, the well-run ★ **Palmetto Dunes Oceanfront Resort** (4 Queens Folly Rd., 800/827-3006, www.palmettodunes.com, $150-300) offers something for everybody in terms of lodging. There are small, cozy condos by the beach or larger villas overlooking the golf course, and pretty much everything in between. The prices are perhaps disarmingly affordable considering the relative luxury and copious recreational amenities, which include 25 miles of very well-done bike trails, 11 miles of kayak and canoe trails, and, of course, three signature links. As with most developments of this type on Hilton Head, the majority of the condos are privately owned, and therefore each has its own particular set of guidelines and cleaning schedules.

A little farther down the island you'll find the **Sonesta Resort** (130 Shipyard Dr., 843/842-2400, www.sonesta.com/hiltonheadisland, $160-200), which styles itself as Hilton Head's only green-certified accommodations. The guest rooms are indeed state-of-the-art, and the expansive, shaded grounds near the beach are great for relaxation. No on-site golf here, but immediately adjacent is a well-regarded tennis facility with 20 courts.

Another good resort-style experience heavy on the golf is on the grounds of the Port Royal Plantation on the island's north side, **The Westin Resort Hilton Head Island** (2 Grasslawn Ave., 843/681-4000, www.westin.com/hiltonhead, from $200), which hosts three PGA-caliber links. The beach is also but a short walk away. This AAA four diamond-winning Westin offers a mix of suites and larger villas.

### Vacation Rentals

Many visitors to Hilton Head choose to rent a home or villa for an extended stay, and there is no scarcity of availability. Try **Resort Rentals of Hilton Head** (www.hhivacations.com) or **Destination Vacation** (www.destinationvacationhhi.com).

## TRANSPORTATION AND SERVICES

The best place to get information on Hilton Head, book a room, or secure a tee time is just as you come onto the island at the **Hilton Head Island Chamber of Commerce Welcome Center** (100 William Hilton Pkwy., 843/785-3673, www.hiltonheadisland.org, daily 9am-6pm).

### Air

A few years back, the **Savannah/Hilton Head International Airport** (SAV, 400 Airways Ave., Savannah, 912/964-0514, www.savannahairport.com) added Hilton Head to its name specifically to identify itself with that lucrative market. Keep in mind that when your plane touches down in Savannah, you're still about a 45-minute drive to Hilton Head. From the airport, go north on I-95 into South Carolina, and take exit 8 onto U.S. 278 east.

There is a local regional airport as well, the **Hilton Head Island Airport** (HXD, 120 Beach City Rd., 843/689-5400, www.bcgov.net). While attractive and convenient, keep in mind that it only hosts propeller-driven commuter planes because of the runway length and concerns about noise.

### Getting Around

Hilton Head Islanders have long referred to their island as the "shoe" and speak of driving to the toe or going to the heel. If you take a look at a map, you'll see why: Hilton Head bears an uncanny resemblance to a running shoe pointed toward the southwest, with the aptly named Broad Creek forming a near facsimile of the Nike "swoosh" symbol.

Running the length and circumference of the shoe is the main drag, U.S. 278 Business (William Hilton Parkway), which crosses onto Hilton Head right at the "tongue" of the shoe, a relatively undeveloped area. The Cross Island Parkway toll route (U.S. 278), beginning up toward the ankle as you first get on the island, is a quicker route straight to the toe near Sea Pines.

Sonesta Resort

While making your way around the island, always keep in mind that the bulk of it consists of private developments, and local law enforcement frowns on people who aimlessly wander among the condos and villas.

Other than taxi services, there is no public transportation in Hilton Head, unless you want to count the free shuttle around Sea Pines Plantation. Taxi services include **Yellow Cab** (843/686-6666), **Island Taxi** (843/683-6363), and **Ferguson Transportation** (843/842-8088).

# Bluffton and Daufuskie Island

Just outside Hilton Head are two of the Lowcountry's true gems, Bluffton and Daufuskie Island. While Bluffton's outskirts have been taken over by the same gated community and upscale strip mall sprawl spreading throughout the coast, at its core it is a delightfully charming little community on the quiet May River, now called Old Bluffton, where you'd swear you just entered a time warp.

Daufuskie Island still maintains much of its age-old isolated, timeless personality, and the island—still accessible only by boat—is one of the spiritual centers of the Gullah culture and lifestyle.

## ★ OLD TOWN BLUFFTON

Similar to Beaufort, but even quieter and smaller, historic Bluffton is an idyllic village on the banks of the serene May River. Bluffton was the original hotbed of secession, with Charleston diarist Mary Chesnut famously referring to the town as "the center spot of the fire eaters." During their Civil War occupation, Union troops repaid the favor of those original Bluffton secessionists, which is why only nine homes in Bluffton are of antebellum vintage; the rest were torched in a search for Confederate guerrillas.

The center of tourist activity is "Old Town," the **Old Bluffton Historic District,** several blocks of 1800s-vintage buildings clustered between the parallel Boundary and Calhoun Streets (old-timers sometimes call this "the original square mile"). Many of the buildings are private residences, but most have been converted into art studios and antiques stores.

### Heyward House Historic Center

The **Heyward House Historic Center** (70 Boundary St., 843/757-6293, www.heyward-house.org, Mon.-Fri. 10am-5pm, Sat. 10am-4pm, tours $5 adults, $2 students) is not only open to tours but also serves as Bluffton's visitors center. Built in 1840 as a summer home for the owner of Moreland Plantation, John Cole, the house was later owned by George Cuthbert Heyward, grandson of Declaration of Independence signer Thomas Heyward. (Remarkably, it stayed in the family until the 1990s.) The Heyward House also sponsors walking tours of the historic district (843/757-6293, by appointment only, $15). Download your own walking tour map at www.heyward-house.org.

### Church of the Cross

Don't fail to go all the way to the end of Calhoun Street, as it dead-ends on a high bluff on the May River at the Bluffton Public Dock. Overlooking this peaceful marsh-front vista is the photogenic **Church of the Cross** (110 Calhoun St., 843/757-2661, www.thechurchofthecross.net, free tours Mon.-Sat. 10am-2pm). The current sanctuary was built in 1854 and is one of only two local churches not burned in the Civil War. The parish itself began in 1767, with the first services on this spot held in the late 1830s. While the church looks as if it were made of cypress, it's actually constructed of heart pine.

### Bluffton Oyster Company

You might want to get a gander at the state's

last remaining working oyster house, the **Bluffton Oyster Company** (63 Wharf St., 843/757-4010, www.blufftonoyster.com, Mon.-Sat. 9am-5:30pm), and possibly purchase some of their maritime bounty. Larry and Tina Toomer continue to oversee the oyster-harvesting-and-shucking family enterprise, which has its roots in the early 1900s.

## SHOPS

Bluffton's eccentric little art studios, most clustered in a two-block stretch on Calhoun Street, are by far its main shopping draw. Named for the Lowcountry phenomenon you find in the marsh at low tide among the fiddler crabs, Bluffton's **Pluff Mudd Art** (27 Calhoun St., 843/757-5551, Mon.-Sat. 10am-5:30pm) is a cooperative of 16 talented young painters and photographers from throughout the area. The **Guild of Bluffton Artists** (20 Calhoun St., 843/757-5590, Mon.-Sat. 10am-4:30pm) features works from many local artists, as does the outstanding **Society of Bluffton Artists** (48 Boundary St., 843/757-6586, Mon.-Sat. 10am-5pm, Sun. 11:30am-3pm). For cool, custom handcrafted pottery, try **Preston Pottery and Gallery** (10 Church St., 843/757-3084, Tues.-Sat. 10am-5pm). Another great Bluffton place is the hard-to-define **Eggs'n'tricities** (71 Calhoun St., 843/757-3446, Mon.-Sat. 10am-5pm). The name pretty much says it all for this fun and eclectic vintage, junk, jewelry, and folk art store.

If you want to score some fresh local seafood for your own culinary adventure, the no-brainer choice is the **Bluffton Oyster Company** (63 Wharf St., 843/757-4010, Mon.-Sat. 9am-5:30pm), the state's only active oyster facility. They also have shrimp, crab, clams, and fish, nearly all of it from the nearly pristine May River on whose banks the facility sits.

For a much more commercially intense experience, head just outside of town on U.S. 278 on the way to Hilton Head to find the dual **Tanger Outlet Centers** (1414 Fording Island Rd., 843/837-4339, Mon.-Sat. 10am-9pm, Sun. 11am-6pm), an outlet-shopper's paradise with virtually every major brand represented.

## FOOD

### American

Probably the single most popular place in Bluffton is the friendly **Old Town Dispensary** (15 Captains Cove, 843/837-1893, daily 11am-2am, $15-25), just off the Calhoun Street center of activity. This is an

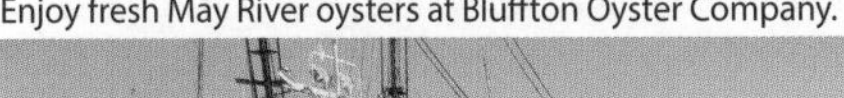

Enjoy fresh May River oysters at Bluffton Oyster Company.

outstanding place to go for some cut-above pub and bar food or casual drinks, with plenty of outdoor seating and usually some live music going on.

Another very popular casual spot in Old Town, and frequented by many locals, is **Captain Woody's Bar & Grill** (17 State of Mind St., 843/757-6222, $10-15). Unpretentious and friendly, this is a good place to enjoy a burger and a beer in a relaxed, patio-style environment with plenty going on around you.

### Breakfast and Brunch

No discussion of Bluffton cuisine is complete without the famous **Squat 'n' Gobble** (1231 May River Rd., 843/757-4242, daily 24 hours). Long a site of gossiping and politicking as well as, um, squatting and gobbling, this humble diner on May River Road is an indelible part of the local consciousness.

### Coffee

If you're looking for a coffeehouse in Old Town, go no farther than ★ **Corner Perk** (1297 May River Rd., Fording Island Rd., 843/816-5674, Tues.-Thurs. 7am-4pm., Fri.-Sat. 7am-11pm, Sun. brunch 7am-4pm, $10-20) in The Promenade, just off the main drag. Their coffee is truly wonderful, and the sandwich-heavy lunch menu compares with anything else in town. Upstairs is The Roasting Room, a more upscale, full-service bourbon bar.

### French

Most dining in Bluffton is pretty casual, but you'll get the white-tablecloth treatment at **Claude & Uli's Signature Bistro** (1533 Fording Island Rd., 843/837-3336, lunch Mon.-Fri. 11:30am-2:30pm, dinner Mon.-Sat. from 5pm, $18-25) just outside of town in Moss Village. Chef Claude does a great veal cordon bleu as well as a number of fine seafood entrées, such as an almond-crusted tilapia and an excellent seafood pasta.

### Mexican

My favorite restaurant in Bluffton is ★ **Mi Tierra** (101 Mellichamp Center, 843/757-7200, lunch daily 11am-4pm, dinner Mon.-Fri. 4pm-9pm, Sat.-Sun. 4pm-10pm, $3-15). They serve very high-quality but unpretentious Tex-Mex-style food in a fun atmosphere at affordable prices.

### New Southern

The hottest new table in Old Town Bluffton is ★ **Farm** (1301 May River Rd., 843/707-2341, www.farmbluffton.com, Tues.-Thurs. lunch 11am-2pm and dinner 5pm-9pm, Fri.-Sat. lunch 11am-2pm and dinner 5pm-10pm, Sun. noon-5pm, $30), which utilizes mostly local and regional meat and produce to deliver an amazing experience on par with the Charleston food scene. The menu changes seasonally and frequently, but a sample dinner might start with the May River Blue Crab Rice, go on to an entree of Buttermilk Fried Chicken Breast with Hoppin' John, and finish with Fried Honey Nut Crunch Hand Pie.

## ACCOMMODATIONS

### Under $150

A quality bargain stay right between Bluffton and Hilton Head is the **Holiday Inn Express Bluffton** (35 Bluffton Rd., 843/757-2002, www.ichotelsgroup.com, $120), on U.S. 278 as you make the run onto Hilton Head proper. It's not close to the beach or to Old Town Bluffton, so you'll definitely be using your car, but its central location will appeal to those who want to keep their options open.

### Over $300

For an ultra-upscale spa and golf resort environment near Bluffton, the clear pick is the **Inn at Palmetto Bluff** (19 Village Park Square, 843/706-6500, www.palmettobluffresort.com, $650-900) just across the May River. This property was picked recently as the number two U.S. resort by *Condé Nast Traveler* magazine. There are three top-flight dining options on the grounds: the fine-dining **River House Restaurant** (843/706-6542,

## Who Are the Gullah?

A language, a culture, and a people with a shared history, Gullah is more than that—it's also a state of mind. Simply put, the Gullah are African Americans of the Sea Islands of South Carolina and Georgia. (In Georgia, the term *Geechee,* from the nearby Ogeechee River, is more or less interchangeable.) Protected from outside influence by the isolation of this coastal region after the Civil War, Gullah culture is the closest living cousin to the West African traditions of those brought to this country as slaves.

While you might hear that *Gullah* is a corruption of "Angola," some linguists think it simply means "people" in a West African language. In any case, the Gullah speak what is known as a creole language, meaning one derived from several sources. Gullah combines elements of Elizabethan English, Jamaican patois, and several West African dialects; for example, "goober" (peanut) comes from the Congo *n'guba.* Another creole element is a word with multiple uses; for example, Gullah's *shum* could mean "see them," "see him," "see her," or "see it" in either past or present tense, depending on context. Several white writers in the 1900s published collections of Gullah folk tales, but it wasn't until later linguistic research was done that the Gullah tongue was recognized as something more than just broken English. Lorenzo Dow Turner's groundbreaking *Africanisms in the Gullah Dialect,* published in 1949, traced elements of the language to Sierra Leone in West Africa and more than 300 Gullah words directly to Africa.

Gullah is typically spoken very rapidly, which of course only adds to its impenetrability to the outsider. Gullah also relies on colorful turns of phrase. *"E tru mout"* ("He true mouth") means the speaker is referring to someone who doesn't lie. *"Le een crack muh teet"* ("I didn't even crack my teeth") means "I kept quiet." A forgetful Gullah speaker might say, *"Mah head leab me"* ("My head left me").

Gullah music, as practiced by the world-famous Hallelujah Singers of St. Helena Island, also uses many distinctly African techniques, such as call-and-response (the folk hymn "Michael Row the Boat Ashore" is a good example). The most famous Americans with Gullah roots are late boxer Joe Frazier (Beaufort), hip-hop star Jazzy Jay (Beaufort), NFL great Jim Brown (St. Simons Island, Georgia), and Supreme Court justice Clarence Thomas (Pin Point, Georgia, near Savannah).

Upscale development continues to claim more and more traditional Gullah areas, generally by pricing the Gullah out through rapidly increasing property values. Today, the major pockets of living Gullah culture in South Carolina are in Beaufort, St. Helena Island, Daufuskie Island, Edisto Island, and a northern section of Hilton Head Island.

The old ways are not as prevalent as they were, but several key institutions are keeping alive the spirit of Gullah: the **Penn Center** (16 Martin Luther King Dr., St. Helena, 843/838-2474, www.penncenter.com, Mon.-Sat. 11am-4pm, $4 adults, $2 seniors and children) on St. Helena Island near Beaufort; the **Avery Research Center** (66 George St., Charleston, 843/953-7609, www.cofc.edu/avery, Mon.-Fri. 10am-5pm, Sat. noon-5pm) at the College of Charleston; and **Geechee Kunda** (622 Ways Temple Rd., Riceboro, Georgia, 912/884-4440, www.geecheekunda.com) near Midway off U.S. 17.

breakfast daily 7am-11am, lunch or "porch" menu daily 11am-10pm, dinner daily 6pm-10pm, $30-40); the **May River Grill** (Tues.-Sat. 11am-4pm, $9-13) at the golf clubhouse; and the casual **Buffalo's** (843/706-6630, Sun.-Tues. 11:30am-5pm, Wed.-Sat. 11:30am-9pm, $10-15).

## DAUFUSKIE ISLAND

Sitting between Savannah and Hilton Head Island and accessible only by water, Daufuskie Island—pronounced "da-FUSK-ee"—has about 500 full-time residents, most of whom ride around on golf carts or bikes (there's only one paved road, Haig Point Road). Once the home of rice and indigo plantations and rich oyster beds—the latter destroyed by pollution and overharvesting—the two upscale residential resort communities on the island, begun in the 1980s, give a clue as to where the future might lie, although the global economic downturn in 2008 slowed development to a standstill for a few years.

The area of prime interest to visitors is the unincorporated western portion, or **Historic District,** the old stomping grounds of Pat Conroy during his stint as a teacher of resident African American children. His old one-room schoolhouse of *The Water Is Wide* fame, the **Mary Field School,** is still here, as is the adjacent 140-year-old **Union Baptist Church,** but Daufuskie students now have a surprisingly modern new facility (middle school students are still ferried to mainland schools every day). Farther north on Haig Point Road is the new **Billie Burn Museum,** housed in the old Mount Carmel Church and named after the island's resident historian. On the southern end you'll find the **Bloody Point Lighthouse,** named for the vicious battle fought nearby during the Yamasee War of 1815 (the light was actually moved inland in the early 1900s). Other areas of interest throughout the island include Native American sites, tabby ruins, the old Baptist church, and a couple of cemeteries.

Download a very well-done, free self-guided tour of Daufuskie's historic sites at www.hiltonheadisland.org; look for the "Robert Kennedy Historic Trail Guide" (not a nod to the former attorney general and U.S. senator, but a longtime island resident and historian).

For overnight stays, you can rent a humble but cozy cabin at **Freeport Marina** (843/785-8242, $100-150, golf cart $60 extra per day), near the ferry dock and overlooking the water. There are vacation rental options island-wide as well; go to www.daufuskieislandrentals.com for info on a wide variety of offerings. Sorry, no camping is available!

There are no grocery stores as commonly understood on Daufuskie, only a couple of general store-type places. So if you've booked a vacation rental, most grocery items need to be brought in with you.

For the freshest island seafood, check out the **Old Daufuskie Crab Company** (Freeport Marina, 843/785-6652, daily 11:30am-9pm, $8-22). The deviled crab is the house specialty.

For hand-crafted island art, go to **Iron Fish Gallery** (168 Benjies Point Rd., 843/842-9448, call for hours), featuring the work of Chase Allen. His "coastal sculptures" include fanciful depictions of fish, stingrays, and even mermaids.

## Transportation and Services

The main public ferry between Daufuskie and Hilton Head is operated by **Calibogue Cruises** (18 Simmons Rd., 843/342-8687, www.daufuskiefreeport.com). Taking off from Broad Creek Marina on Hilton Head, the pleasant short ride—30 minutes each way—brings you in on the landward side of the island. Cost is $33 pp round-trip, or $64 pp round-trip including a meal at the Old Daufuskie Crab Company and a golf cart rental. Ferries run three times a day Monday, Wednesday, and Friday, and twice a day Tuesday, Thursday, Saturday, and Sunday. Ferry reservations are essential.

While the ferry trip and many vacation rentals include the rental of a golf cart, for *à la carte* service—get it?—rent one near Freeport Marina by calling 843/342-8687 (rates vary but hover around $30 pp per day). As the number of golf carts is limited, I strongly recommend reserving yours in advance. All standard rules of the road apply, including needing a valid driver's license.

# Points Inland



It's likely that at some point you'll find yourself traveling inland from Beaufort, given that region's proximity to I-95. While this area is generally more known for offering interstate drivers a bite to eat and a place to rest their heads, there are several spots worth checking out in their own right, especially Walterboro and the Savannah National Wildlife Refuge.

## WALTERBORO

Walterboro is chiefly known to the world at large for being one of the best antiquing locales on the East Coast. Indeed, many of the high-dollar antiques shops on Charleston's King Street actually do their picking right here in the local stores, selling their finds at a significant markup in Charleston! (Another advantage Walterboro antiques shopping has over Charleston: plenty of free parking.)

Convenient and walkable, the two-block **Arts and Antiques District** on Washington Street features more than a dozen antiques and collectible stores, interspersed with a few gift shops and eateries. The best shop, though by no means the only one you should check out, is **Bachelor Hill Antiques** (255 E. Washington St., 843/549-1300, Mon.-Sat. 9am-6pm, Sun. 9am-4pm), which has several rooms packed with interesting and unique items, from collectibles to furniture to most everything in between.

### Sights

#### ★ SOUTH CAROLINA ARTISANS CENTER

Don't miss the **South Carolina Artisans Center** (334 Wichman St., 843/549-0011, www.scartisanscenter.com, Mon.-Sat. 9am-5pm, Sun. 1pm-5pm, free), an expansive and vibrant collection of the best work of local and regional painters, sculptors, jewelers, and other craftspeople, for sale and for enjoyment. The Artisans Center hosts numerous receptions, and every third Saturday of the month they hold live artist demonstrations 11am-3pm.

#### MUSEUMS

Walterboro boasts three small museums. The relocated and upgraded **Colleton Museum**

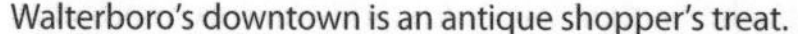
Walterboro's downtown is an antique shopper's treat.

## Tuskegee Airmen in Walterboro

In a state where all too often African American history is studied in the context of slavery, a refreshing change is the tale of the Tuskegee Airmen, one of the most lauded American military units of World War II. Though named for their origins at Alabama's Tuskegee Institute, the pilots of the famed 332nd Fighter Group actually completed their final training in South Carolina at Walterboro Army Airfield, where the regional airport now sits.

The U.S. military was segregated during World War II, with African Americans mostly relegated to support roles. An interesting exception was the case of the 332nd, formed in 1941 as the 99th Pursuit Squadron by an act of Congress and the only all-black flying unit in the American military at the time. Mostly flying P-47 Thunderbolts and P-51 Mustangs, the pilots of the 332nd had one of the toughest missions of the war: escorting bombers over the skies of Germany and protecting them from Luftwaffe fighters. Though initially viewed with skepticism, the Tuskegee Airmen wasted no time in proving their mettle.

In fact, it wasn't long before U.S. bomber crews—who were, needless to say, all white—specifically requested that they be escorted by the airmen, who were given the nickname "Red-tail Angels" because of the distinctive markings of their aircraft. While legend has it that the 332nd never lost a bomber, this claim has been debunked. But as Tuskegee Airman Bill Holloman said, "The Tuskegee story is about pilots who rose above adversity and discrimination and opened a door once closed to black America, not about whether their record is perfect." The 332nd's reputation for aggressiveness in air combat was so widely known that the Germans also had a nickname for them—*Schwartze Vogelmenschen,* or "Black Birdmen."

Today Walterboro honors the airmen with a monument on the grounds of the Lowcountry Regional Airport, on U.S. 17 just northeast of town. In an easily accessible part of the airport grounds, the monument features a bronze statue and several interpretive exhibits. Another place to catch up on Tuskegee Airmen history is at the **Colleton Museum** (506 E. Washington St., 843/549-2303, www.colletonmuseum.org, Tues. noon-6pm, Wed.-Fri. 10am-5pm, Sat. 10am-2pm, free), which has a permanent exhibit on the pilots and their history in the Walterboro area.

Walterboro Army Airfield's contribution to the war effort was not limited to the Tuskegee Airmen. Seven of the famed Doolittle Raiders were trained here, there was a compound for holding German prisoners of war, and it was also the site of the U.S. military's largest camouflage school.

(506 E. Washington St., 843/549-2303, www.colletonmuseum.org, Tues. noon-6pm, Wed.-Fri. 10am-5pm, Sat. 10am-2pm, free) is one of the best examples of a small-town museum you're likely to find. Adjacent is the **farmers market** (May-Oct. Tues. 2pm-6pm, Sat. 10am-2pm).

The **Bedon-Lucas House Museum** (205 Church St., 843/549-9633, Thurs.-Sat. 1pm-4pm, $3 adults, free under age 8) was built by a local planter in 1820. An example of the local style of "high house," built off the ground to escape mosquitoes and catch the breeze, the house today is a nice mix of period furnishings and unadorned simplicity.

The **Slave Relic Museum** (208 Carn St., 843/549-9130, www.slaverelics.org, by appointment, $6 adults, $5 children) houses the Center for Research and Preservation of the African American Culture. It features artifacts, photos, and documents detailing the Atlantic passage, slave life, and the Underground Railroad.

### TUSKEGEE AIRMEN MEMORIAL

Yes, the Tuskegee Airmen of World War II fame were from Alabama, not South Carolina. But a contingent trained in Walterboro, at the site of the present-day **Lowcountry Regional Airport** (537 Aviation Way, 843/549-2549), a little north of downtown on U.S. 17. A publicly accessible, low-security area of the airport hosts the **Tuskegee Airmen Memorial,** an outdoor monument to these brave flyers. There's a bronze statue and several interpretive exhibits.

### GREAT SWAMP SANCTUARY

Just south of town is the **Great Swamp Sanctuary** (www.thegreatswamp.org, daily dawn-dusk, free), a still-developing ecotourism project focusing on the Lowcountry environment. Located in one of the region's few braided-creek habitats accessible to the public, the 842-acre sanctuary has three miles of walking and biking trails, some along the path of the old Charleston-Savannah stagecoach route. Kayakers and canoeists can paddle more than two miles of winding creeks. There are three entry points to the Great Swamp Sanctuary, all off Jefferies Boulevard. In west-to-east order from I-95: north onto Beach Road, north onto Detreville Street (this is considered the main entrance), and west onto Washington Street.

## Festivals and Events

In keeping with South Carolina's tradition of towns hosting annual events to celebrate signature crops and products, Walterboro's **Colleton County Rice Festival** (http://thericefestival.org, free) happens every April. There's a parade, live music, a 5K run, and the crowning of the year's "Rice Queen."

## Food

The story of food in Walterboro revolves around ★ **Duke's Barbecue** (949 Robertson Blvd., 843/549-1446, Wed. 11am-8pm, Thurs.-Sat. 11am-9pm, Sun. 11am-2pm, $7), one of the best-regarded barbecue spots in the Lowcountry and one of the top two joints named "Duke's" in the state (the other, by common consensus, is in Orangeburg). The pulled pork is delectable, cooked with the indigenous South Carolina mustard-based sauce.

## Accommodations

If you're looking for big-box lodging, the section of Walterboro close to I-95 is chockablock with it. The quality is surprisingly good, perhaps because they tend to cater to Northerners on their way to and from Florida. A good choice is **Holiday Inn Express & Suites** (1834 Sniders Hwy., 843/538-2700, www.hiexpress.com, $85), or try the **Comfort Inn & Suites** (97 Downs Lane, 843/538-5911, www.choicehotels.com, $95).

If you'd like something with a bit more character, there are two B&Bs on Hampton Street downtown. **Old Academy Bed & Breakfast** (904 Hampton St., 843/549-3232, www.oldacademybandb.com, $80-115, no credit cards) has four guest rooms housed in Walterboro's first school building. They offer a full continental breakfast. Although built recently (by local standards), the 1912 **Hampton House Bed and Breakfast** (500 Hampton St., 843/542-9498, www.hamptonhousebandb.com, $125-145) has three well-appointed guest rooms and offers a full country breakfast. By appointment only, you can see its Forde Doll and Dollhouse Collection, with over 50 dollhouses and oodles of antique dolls.

# SAVANNAH NATIONAL WILDLIFE REFUGE

Roughly equally divided between Georgia and South Carolina, the sprawling, 30,000-acre **Savannah National Wildlife Refuge** (912/652-4415, www.fws.gov/savannah, daily dawn-dusk, free) is one of the premier bird-watching and nature-observing locales in the Southeast. The system of dikes and paddy fields once used to grow rice now helps make this an attractive stopover for migrating birds. Bird-watching is best October to April. While you can kayak on your own on miles of creeks, you can also call **Swamp Girls Kayak Tours** (843/784-2249, www.swampgirls.com), who work out of nearby Hardeeville, for a guided tour. The wildlife refuge is about 20 minutes from Savannah, two hours from Charleston, and an hour from Beaufort. To get here, take exit 5 off I-95 onto U.S. 17. Go south to U.S. 170 and look for Laurel Hill Wildlife Drive. Be sure to stop by the **visitors center** (Laurel Hill Wildlife Dr., off U.S. 170, Mon.-Sat. 9am-4:30pm).

# Savannah

In an increasingly homogenized society, Savannah is one of the last places where eccentricity is celebrated and even encouraged. This outspoken, often stubborn determination to make one's own way in the world is personified by the old Georgia joke about Savannah being the capital of "the state of Chatham," a reference to the county in which it resides. In typical contrarian fashion, Savannahians take this nickname as a compliment.

Savannah was built as a series of rectangular "wards," each constructed around a central square. As the city grew, each square took on its own characteristics, depending on who lived on the square and how they made their livelihood. Sounds simple—and it is. That's why its effectiveness has lasted so long.

It is this individuality that is so well documented in John Berendt's *Midnight in the Garden of Good and Evil.* The squares of Savannah's downtown—since 1965 a National Landmark Historic District—are also responsible for the city's walkability, another defining characteristic. Just as cars entering a square must yield to traffic already within, pedestrians are obliged to slow down and interact with the surrounding environment, both constructed and natural. You become participant and audience simultaneously, a feat made easier by the local penchant for easy conversation.

This spirit of independence extends to Savannah's growing hipster culture, helped along by the steady expansion of the Savannah College of Art and Design (SCAD), which boasts much of downtown Savannah as its campus.

Savannah is also known for being able to show you a rowdy good time, and not only during its massive world-famous St. Patrick's Day celebration. Savannahians will use any excuse for a party, exemplified by the city's very liberal open-container law—adults can walk with alcoholic beverages around downtown—which adds to the generally merry atmosphere.

**Previous:** Bonaventure Cemetery; River Street. **Above:** azaleas in downtown Savannah.

Look for ★ to find recommended sights, activities, dining, and lodging.

## Highlights

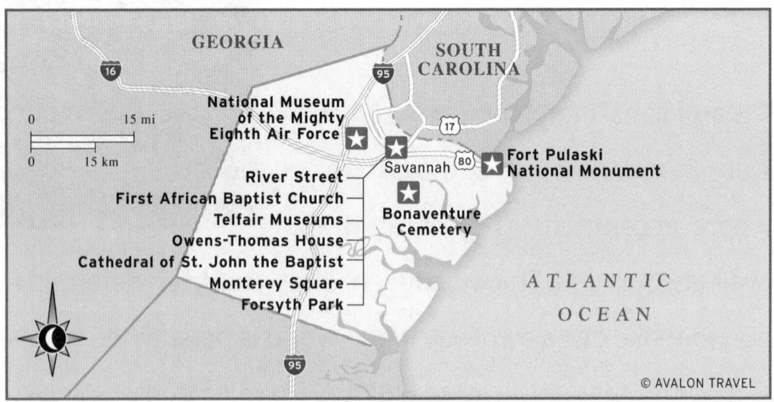


★ **River Street:** Despite River Street's tourist tackiness, there's nothing like strolling the cobblestones amid the old cotton warehouses, enjoying the cool breeze off the river, and watching the huge ships on their way to the bustling port (page 182).

★ **First African Baptist Church:** The oldest black congregation in the United States still meets in this historic sanctuary, a key stop on the Underground Railroad (page 186).

★ **Telfair Museums:** Old school meets new school in this museum complex that comprises the ultramodern **Jepson Center for the Arts** (page 192) and the traditional **Telfair Academy of Arts and Sciences** (page 193).

★ **Owens-Thomas House:** Savannah's single greatest historic home is one of the country's best examples of Regency architecture and a fine example of state-of-the-art historical preservation (page 193).

★ **Cathedral of St. John the Baptist:** This soaring Gothic Revival edifice is complemented by its ornate interior and its matchless location on verdant Lafayette Square, stomping ground of the young Flannery O'Connor (page 197).

★ **Monterey Square:** Savannah's quintessential square has some of the best examples of local architecture and world-class ironwork all around its periphery (page 199).

★ **Forsyth Park:** This verdant expanse ringed by old live oaks is the true center of downtown life; it's Savannah's backyard (page 202).

★ **Bonaventure Cemetery:** This historic burial ground is the final resting place for some of Savannah's favorite citizens, including the great Johnny Mercer (page 207).

★ **Fort Pulaski National Monument:** This well-run site, built with the help of a young Robert E. Lee, is not only historically significant, its beautiful setting makes it a great place for the entire family (page 209).

★ **National Museum of the Mighty Eighth Air Force:** This museum tells the story of the U.S. Eighth Air Force, which executed bombing missions over Nazi Germany, and includes restored World War II and Cold War-era aircraft (page 216).

## HISTORY

To understand the inferiority complex that Savannah occasionally feels with regards to Charleston, you have to remember that from day one Savannah was intended to play second fiddle to its older, richer neighbor to the north. By the early 1700s, the land south of Charleston had become a staging area for attacks on the settlement by the Spanish and Native Americans. So in 1732, King George II granted a charter to the Trustees of Georgia, a proprietary venture that was the brainchild of a 36-year-old general and member of parliament, General James Edward Oglethorpe. Though the mission was to found a colony to buffer Charleston from the Spanish, Oglethorpe had a far more sweeping vision in mind.

On February 12, 1733, the *Anne* landed with 114 passengers along the high bluff on the south bank of the Savannah River. Oglethorpe laid out his settlement in a deceptively simple plan that is still studied the world over as a model of nearly perfect urban design. He bonded with Tomochichi, chief of the local Creek people, and the colony prospered. Ever the idealist, Oglethorpe had a plan for the new "classless society" in Savannah that prohibited slavery, rum, and—wait for it—lawyers! But as the settlers enviously eyed the dominance of Charleston's slavery-based rice economy, the Trustees bowed to public pressure and relaxed restrictions on slavery and rum.

By 1753, the crown reclaimed the charter, making Georgia England's 13th American colony. Though part of the new United States in 1776, Savannah was captured by British forces in 1778, who held the city against a combined assault a year later. After the Revolution, Savannah became the first capital of Georgia, a role it had until 1786.

Despite hurricanes and yellow fever epidemics, Savannah's heyday was the antebellum period from 1800 to 1860, when for a time it outstripped Charleston as a center of commerce. Savannah's population boomed after an influx of European immigrants, chief among them Irish workers coming to lay track on the new Central of Georgia line.

Blockaded for most of the Civil War, Savannah didn't see much action other than the fall of Fort Pulaski in April 1862, when a Union force successfully laid siege using rifled artillery, a revolutionary technology that instantly rendered the world's masonry forts obsolete. War came to Savannah's doorstep when General William T. Sherman's March to the Sea concluded with his capture of the town in December 1864. On December 22, Sherman sent a now-legendary telegram to President Lincoln bearing these words: "I beg to present you as a Christmas gift, the City of Savannah with 150 heavy guns and plenty of ammunition and also about 25,000 bales of cotton."

After a lengthy Reconstruction period, Savannah began reaching out to the outside world. From 1908 to 1911 it was a national center of road racing. In the Roaring '20s, native son Johnny Mercer rose to prominence, and the great Flannery O'Connor was born in downtown Savannah. World War II provided an economic lift, but the city was still known as the "pretty woman with a dirty face," as Britain's Lady Astor famously described it in 1946.

Almost in answer to Astor's quip, city leaders in the 1950s began a misguided program to retrofit the city's infrastructure for the automobile era. Savannah's preservation movement had its seed in the fight by seven Savannah women to save the Davenport House and other buildings from demolition.

Savannah played a pioneering, though largely unsung, role in the civil rights movement. Ralph Mark Gilbert, pastor of the historic First African Baptist Church, launched one of the first black voter registration drives in the South. Gilbert's efforts were kept alive in the 1950s and 1960s by the beloved W. W. Law, a letter carrier who was head of the local chapter of the NAACP for many years.

The opening of the Savannah College of Art and Design in 1979 ushered another important chapter in Savannah's renaissance, which is ongoing to this day.

# Savannah Area

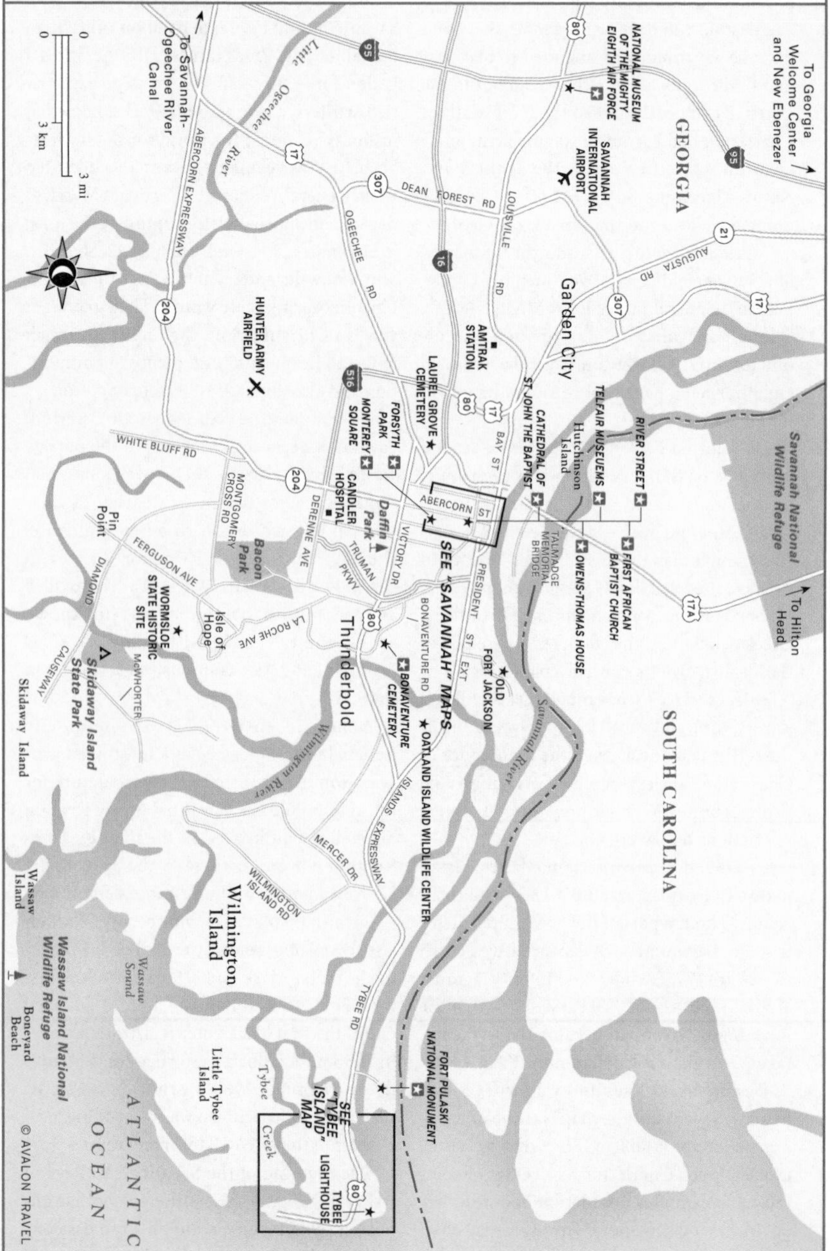

To Georgia Welcome Center and New Ebenezer
GEORGIA
NATIONAL MUSEUM OF THE MIGHTY EIGHTH AIR FORCE
SAVANNAH INTERNATIONAL AIRPORT
To Savannah-Ogeechee River Canal
0 3 mi
0 3 km
Little Ogeechee River
ABERCORN EXPRESSWAY
DEAN FOREST RD
LOUISVILLE RD
AUGUSTA RD
OGEECHEE RD
Garden City
AMTRAK STATION
HUNTER ARMY AIRFIELD
LAUREL GROVE CEMETERY
ST JOHN THE BAPTIST
CATHEDRAL OF
TELFAIR MUSEUMS
RIVER STREET
Hutchinson Island
Savannah National Wildlife Refuge
BAY ST
FORSYTH PARK
MONTEREY SQUARE
WHITE BLUFF RD
ABERCORN ST
CANDLER HOSPITAL
Daffin Park
TALMADGE MEMORIAL BRIDGE
OWENS-THOMAS HOUSE
FIRST AFRICAN BAPTIST CHURCH
To Hilton Head
MONTGOMERY CROSS RD
DERENNE AVE
Bacon Park
TRUMAN PKWY
VICTORY DR
SEE "SAVANNAH" MAPS
PRESIDENT ST
PRESIDENT ST EXT
Pin Point
FERGUSON AVE
DIAMOND CAUSEWAY
WORMSLOE STATE HISTORIC SITE
Isle of Hope
LA ROCHE AVE
Thunderbold
BONAVENTURE RD
OLD FORT JACKSON
SOUTH CAROLINA
Skidaway Island State Park
McWHORTER
Skidaway Island
BONAVENTURE CEMETERY
OATLAND ISLAND WILDLIFE CENTER
Savannah River
Wilmington River
ISLANDS EXPRESSWAY
MERCER DR
WILMINGTON ISLAND RD
Wilmington Island
Wassaw Island
Wassaw Sound
Wassaw Island National Wildlife Refuge
Boneyard Beach
TYBEE RD
FORT PULASKI NATIONAL MONUMENT
Little Tybee Island
Tybee Creek
SEE "TYBEE ISLAND" MAP
TYBEE LIGHTHOUSE
ATLANTIC OCEAN

After the publication of John Berendt's *Midnight in the Garden of Good and Evil* in 1994, nothing would ever be the same in Savannah. Old-money families cringed as idiosyncrasies and hypocrisies were laid bare in "The Book." Local merchants and politicians, however, delighted in the influx of tourists which continues unabated—and growing—to this day.

## PLANNING YOUR TIME

Plan on **two nights** at an absolute minimum—not only to enjoy all the sights, but to fully soak in the local color and attitude. You don't need a car to have a great time and see most sights worth enjoying. A strong walker can easily traverse the length and breadth of downtown in a day, although less energetic travelers should consider a central location or make use of the free downtown shuttle. To fully enjoy Savannah, however, you'll need access to a vehicle so you can go east to Tybee Island and south to various historic sites with spottier public transportation. You'll appreciate downtown all the more when you can get away and smell the salt air.

Much more than just a parade, St. Patrick's Day in Savannah—an event generally expanded to include several days before and after the holiday itself—is also a time of immense crowds, with the city's usual population of about 150,000 doubling with the influx of partying visitors. Be aware that lodging on and around March 17 fills up well in advance.

## ORIENTATION

The downtown area is bounded on the east by East Broad Street and on the west by Martin Luther King Jr. Boulevard (formerly West Broad St.). Technically, Gwinnett Street is the southern boundary of the National Historic Landmark District, though in practice locals extend the boundary several blocks southward. The Eastside includes many areas that are technically islands, but their boundaries are so blurred by infill of the marsh and by well-constructed roads that you'll sense little difference from the mainland. To most locals, "Southside" refers to the generic strip mall sprawl below DeRenne Avenue, but for our purposes here the term also includes some outlying islands. I include them in the southern part of town because of the general direction and length of travel.



# Sights

If you're not planning on taking a tour, it's best to introduce yourself to the sights of Savannah by traveling from the river southward. It's no small task to navigate the nation's largest contiguous historic district, but when in doubt it's best to follow James Oglethorpe's original plan of using the five "monumental" squares on Bull Street (Johnson, Wright, Chippewa, Madison, and Monterey) as focal points.

## TOURS

Savannah's tourism boom has resulted in an explosion of well over 50 separate tour services, ranging from simple guided trolley journeys to horse-drawn carriage rides to specialty tours to ecotourism adventures. Fair warning: Although local tour guides technically must pass a competency test demonstrating their knowledge of Savannah history, in practice facts are often thrown out the window in favor of whatever sounds good at the time. Keep in mind that not everything you hear from a tour guide may be true.

### Walking Tours

#### OLD CITY WALKS

The premium tour option is Old City Walks, explorations of well-known and of little-known Savannah attractions, guided by longtime local experts. These aren't budget tours, but they are the state of the art locally. There

# Map 1: Downtown Savannah

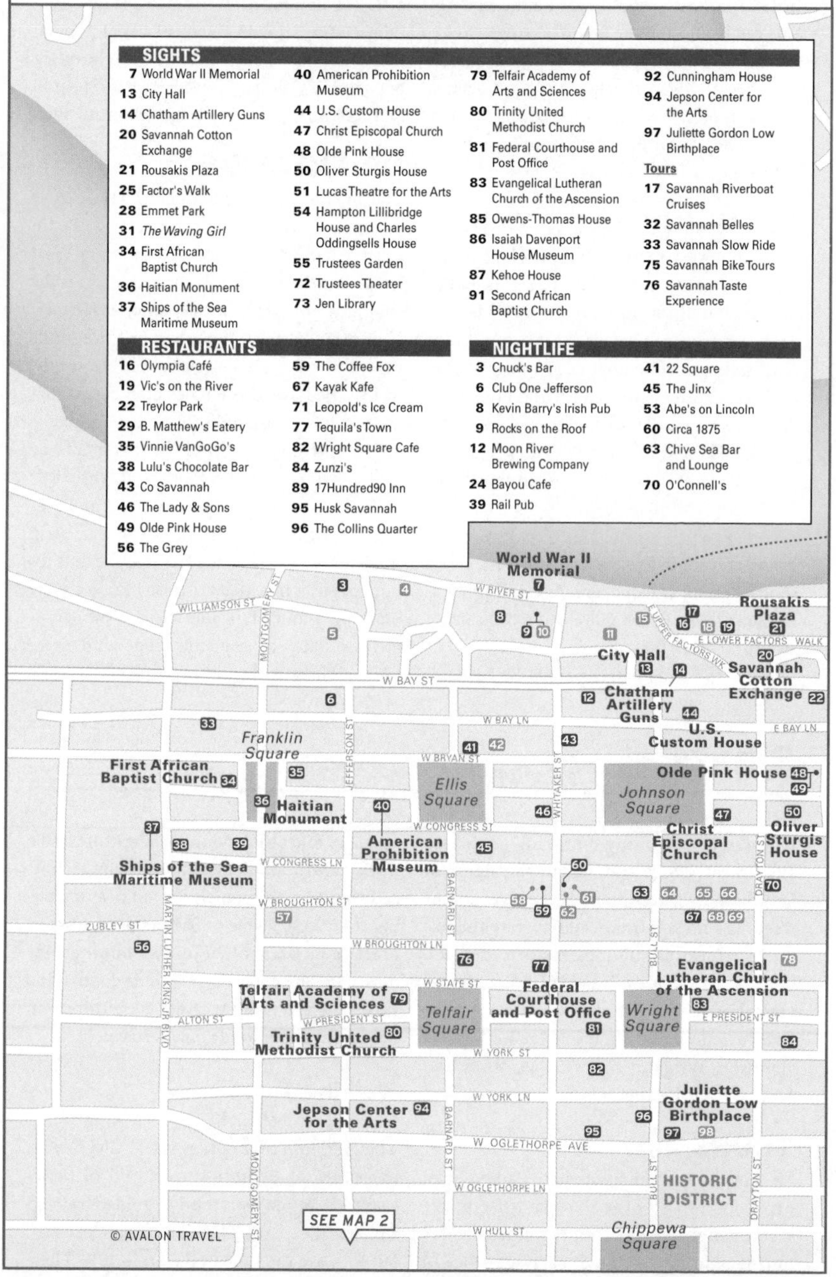

SIGHTS
7 World War II Memorial
13 City Hall
14 Chatham Artillery Guns
20 Savannah Cotton Exchange
21 Rousakis Plaza
25 Factor's Walk
28 Emmet Park
31 The Waving Girl
34 First African Baptist Church
36 Haitian Monument
37 Ships of the Sea Maritime Museum
40 American Prohibition Museum
44 U.S. Custom House
47 Christ Episcopal Church
48 Olde Pink House
50 Oliver Sturgis House
51 Lucas Theatre for the Arts
54 Hampton Lillibridge House and Charles Oddingsells House
55 Trustees Garden
72 Trustees Theater
73 Jen Library
79 Telfair Academy of Arts and Sciences
80 Trinity United Methodist Church
81 Federal Courthouse and Post Office
83 Evangelical Lutheran Church of the Ascension
85 Owens-Thomas House
86 Isaiah Davenport House Museum
87 Kehoe House
91 Second African Baptist Church
92 Cunningham House
94 Jepson Center for the Arts
97 Juliette Gordon Low Birthplace
Tours
17 Savannah Riverboat Cruises
32 Savannah Belles
33 Savannah Slow Ride
75 Savannah Bike Tours
76 Savannah Taste Experience
RESTAURANTS
16 Olympia Café
19 Vic's on the River
22 Treylor Park
29 B. Matthew's Eatery
35 Vinnie VanGoGo's
38 Lulu's Chocolate Bar
43 Co Savannah
46 The Lady & Sons
49 Olde Pink House
56 The Grey
59 The Coffee Fox
67 Kayak Kafe
71 Leopold's Ice Cream
77 Tequila's Town
82 Wright Square Cafe
84 Zunzi's
89 17Hundred90 Inn
95 Husk Savannah
96 The Collins Quarter
NIGHTLIFE
3 Chuck's Bar
6 Club One Jefferson
8 Kevin Barry's Irish Pub
9 Rocks on the Roof
12 Moon River Brewing Company
24 Bayou Cafe
39 Rail Pub
41 22 Square
45 The Jinx
53 Abe's on Lincoln
60 Circa 1875
63 Chive Sea Bar and Lounge
70 O'Connell's
World War II Memorial
W RIVER ST
WILLIAMSON ST
MONTGOMERY ST
Rousakis Plaza
E LOWER FACTORS WALK
E UPPER FACTORS WK
City Hall
Savannah Cotton Exchange
W BAY ST
Chatham Artillery Guns
W BAY LN
E BAY LN
U.S. Custom House
Franklin Square
JEFFERSON ST
W BRYAN ST
First African Baptist Church
Ellis Square
WHITAKER ST
Olde Pink House
Johnson Square
Haitian Monument
American Prohibition Museum
W CONGRESS ST
Christ Episcopal Church
Oliver Sturgis House
DRAYTON ST
Ships of the Sea Maritime Museum
W CONGRESS LN
BARNARD ST
W BROUGHTON ST
ZUBLEY ST
MARTIN LUTHER KING JR BLVD
W BROUGHTON LN
BULL ST
Evangelical Lutheran Church of the Ascension
Telfair Academy of Arts and Sciences
W STATE ST
Federal Courthouse and Post Office
Telfair Square
Wright Square
ALTON ST
W PRESIDENT ST
E PRESIDENT ST
Trinity United Methodist Church
W YORK ST
W YORK LN
Juliette Gordon Low Birthplace
Jepson Center for the Arts
W OGLETHORPE AVE
W OGLETHORPE LN
HISTORIC DISTRICT
SEE MAP 2
W HULL ST
Chippewa Square
© AVALON TRAVEL

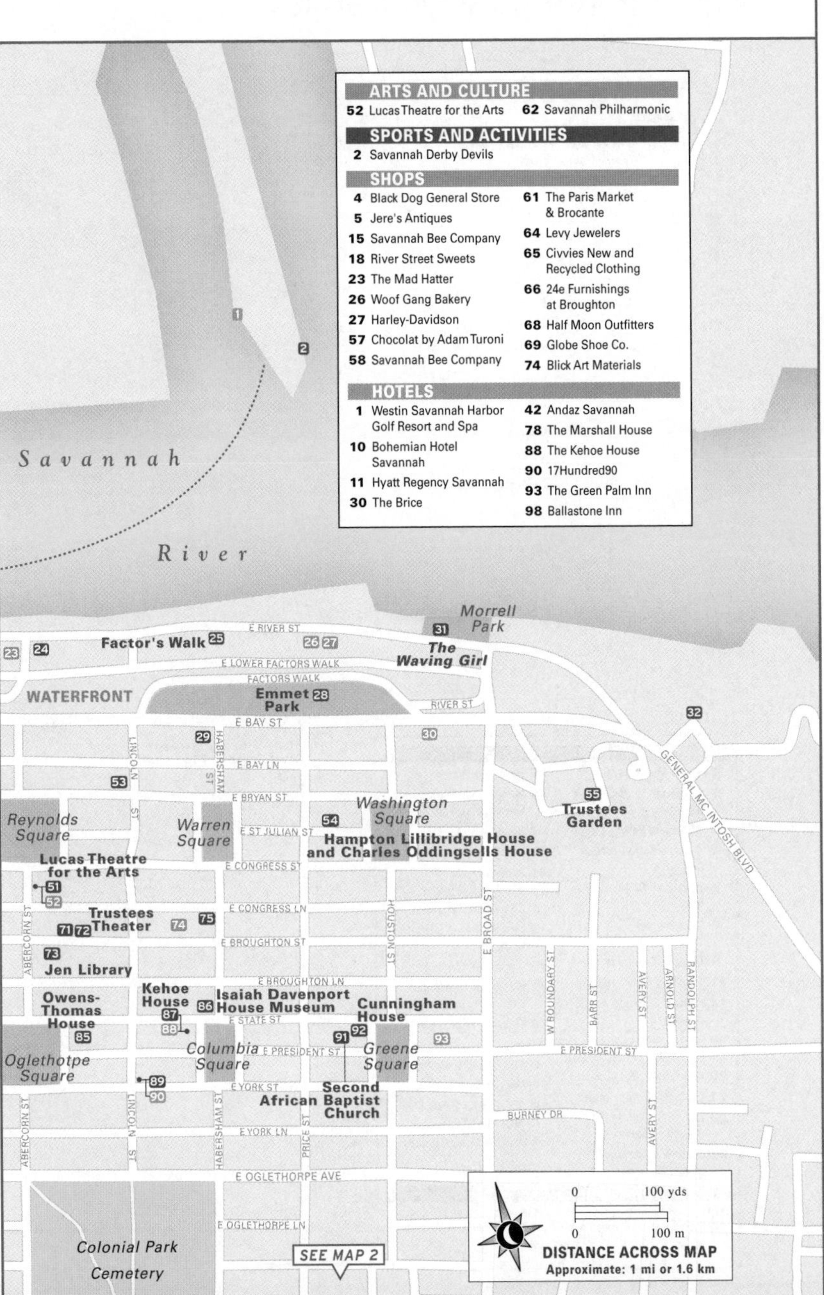
ARTS AND CULTURE
52 Lucas Theatre for the Arts
62 Savannah Philharmonic
SPORTS AND ACTIVITIES
2 Savannah Derby Devils
SHOPS
4 Black Dog General Store
5 Jere's Antiques
15 Savannah Bee Company
18 River Street Sweets
23 The Mad Hatter
26 Woof Gang Bakery
27 Harley-Davidson
57 Chocolat by Adam Turoni
58 Savannah Bee Company
61 The Paris Market & Brocante
64 Levy Jewelers
65 Civvies New and Recycled Clothing
66 24e Furnishings at Broughton
68 Half Moon Outfitters
69 Globe Shoe Co.
74 Blick Art Materials
HOTELS
1 Westin Savannah Harbor Golf Resort and Spa
10 Bohemian Hotel Savannah
11 Hyatt Regency Savannah
30 The Brice
42 Andaz Savannah
78 The Marshall House
88 The Kehoe House
90 17Hundred90
93 The Green Palm Inn
98 Ballastone Inn
Savannah
River
Morrell Park
The Waving Girl
Factor's Walk
E RIVER ST
E LOWER FACTORS WALK
FACTORS WALK
WATERFRONT
Emmet Park
RIVER ST
E BAY ST
E BAY LN
E BRYAN ST
LINCOLN ST
HABERSHAM ST
GENERAL MC INTOSH BLVD
Trustees Garden
Washington Square
Reynolds Square
Warren Square
E ST JULIAN ST
Hampton Lillibridge House and Charles Oddingsells House
Lucas Theatre for the Arts
E CONGRESS ST
E CONGRESS LN
Trustees Theater
E BROUGHTON ST
HOUSTON ST
E BROAD ST
ABERCORN ST
Jen Library
E BROUGHTON LN
Owens-Thomas House
Kehoe House
Isaiah Davenport House Museum
Cunningham House
E STATE ST
W BOUNDARY ST
BARR ST
AVERY ST
ARNOLD ST
RANDOLPH ST
Oglethotpe Square
Columbia Square
E PRESIDENT ST
Greene Square
E YORK ST
Second African Baptist Church
BURNEY DR
E YORK LN
PRICE ST
E OGLETHORPE AVE
E OGLETHORPE LN
Colonial Park Cemetery
SEE MAP 2
0
100 yds
0
100 m
DISTANCE ACROSS MAP
Approximate: 1 mi or 1.6 km

# Map 2: Historic District South

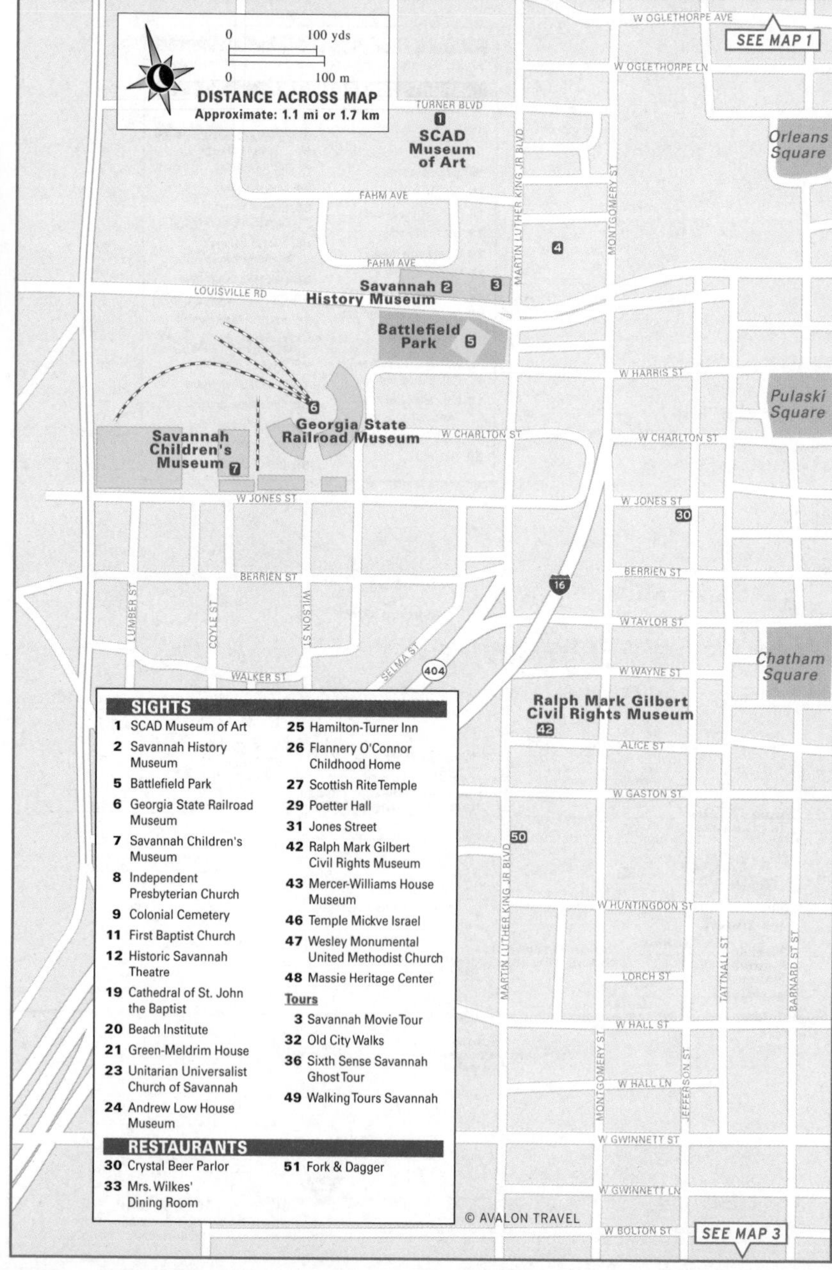


**SIGHTS**

1 SCAD Museum of Art
2 Savannah History Museum
5 Battlefield Park
6 Georgia State Railroad Museum
7 Savannah Children's Museum
8 Independent Presbyterian Church
9 Colonial Cemetery
11 First Baptist Church
12 Historic Savannah Theatre
19 Cathedral of St. John the Baptist
20 Beach Institute
21 Green-Meldrim House
23 Unitarian Universalist Church of Savannah
24 Andrew Low House Museum
25 Hamilton-Turner Inn
26 Flannery O'Connor Childhood Home
27 Scottish Rite Temple
29 Poetter Hall
31 Jones Street
42 Ralph Mark Gilbert Civil Rights Museum
43 Mercer-Williams House Museum
46 Temple Mickve Israel
47 Wesley Monumental United Methodist Church
48 Massie Heritage Center

Tours

3 Savannah Movie Tour
32 Old City Walks
36 Sixth Sense Savannah Ghost Tour
49 Walking Tours Savannah

**RESTAURANTS**

30 Crystal Beer Parlor
33 Mrs. Wilkes' Dining Room
51 Fork & Dagger

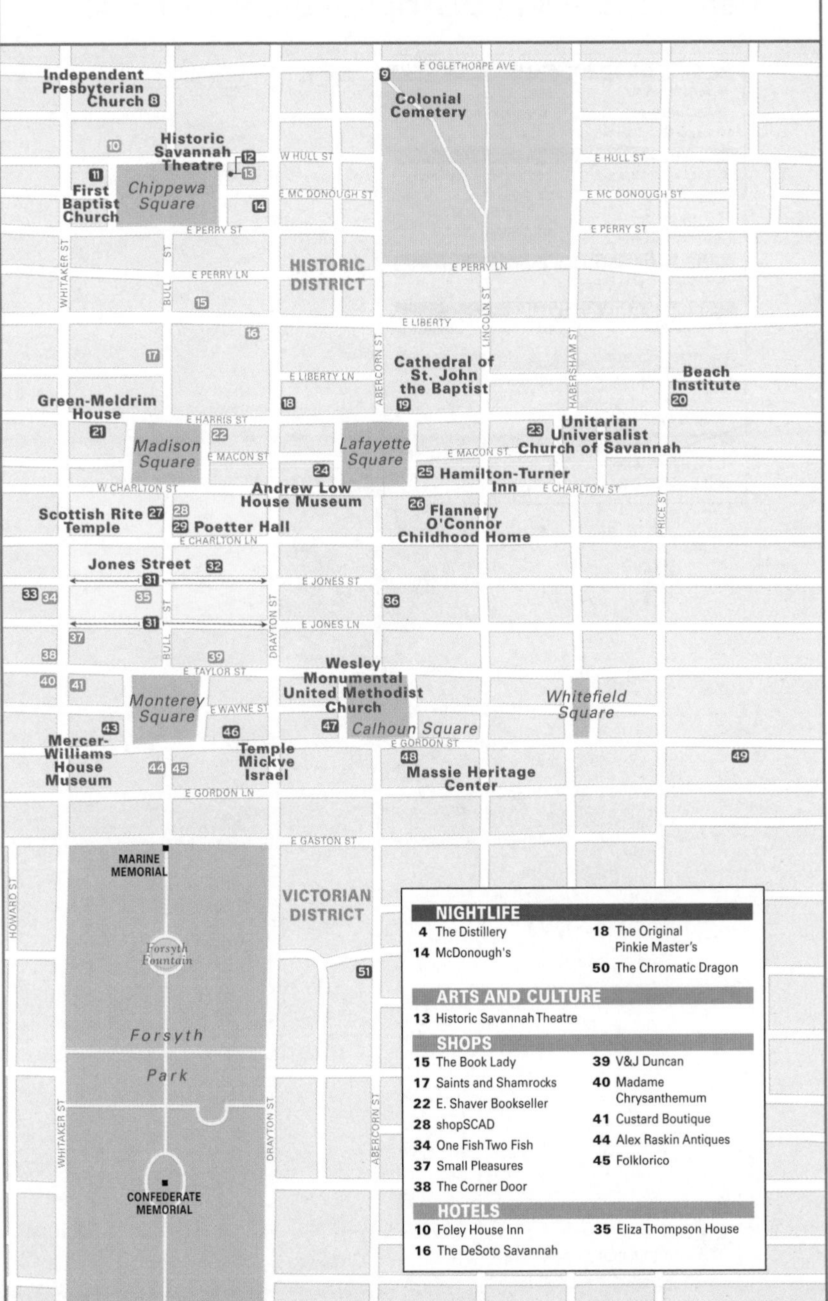

Independent Presbyterian Church
Colonial Cemetery
Historic Savannah Theatre
First Baptist Church
Chippewa Square
HISTORIC DISTRICT
Cathedral of St. John the Baptist
Beach Institute
Green-Meldrim House
Unitarian Universalist Church of Savannah
Madison Square
Lafayette Square
Hamilton-Turner Inn
Andrew Low House Museum
Scottish Rite Temple
Poetter Hall
Flannery O'Connor Childhood Home
Jones Street
Wesley Monumental United Methodist Church
Whitefield Square
Monterey Square
Calhoun Square
Mercer-Williams House Museum
Temple Mickve Israel
Massie Heritage Center
MARINE MEMORIAL
VICTORIAN DISTRICT
Forsyth Fountain
Forsyth Park
CONFEDERATE MEMORIAL
E OGLETHORPE AVE
W HULL ST
E HULL ST
E MC DONOUGH ST
E PERRY ST
E PERRY LN
E LIBERTY
E LIBERTY LN
E HARRIS ST
E MACON ST
W CHARLTON ST
E CHARLTON ST
E CHARLTON LN
E JONES ST
E JONES LN
E TAYLOR ST
E WAYNE ST
E GORDON ST
E GORDON LN
E GASTON ST
WHITAKER ST
BULL ST
ABERCORN ST
LINCOLN ST
HABERSHAM ST
PRICE ST
DRAYTON ST
HOWARD ST
NIGHTLIFE
4 The Distillery
14 McDonough's
18 The Original Pinkie Master's
50 The Chromatic Dragon
ARTS AND CULTURE
13 Historic Savannah Theatre
SHOPS
15 The Book Lady
17 Saints and Shamrocks
22 E. Shaver Bookseller
28 shopSCAD
34 One Fish Two Fish
37 Small Pleasures
38 The Corner Door
39 V&J Duncan
40 Madame Chrysanthemum
41 Custard Boutique
44 Alex Raskin Antiques
45 Folklorico
HOTELS
10 Foley House Inn
16 The DeSoto Savannah
35 Eliza Thompson House

# Map 3: Victorian District and SoFo District

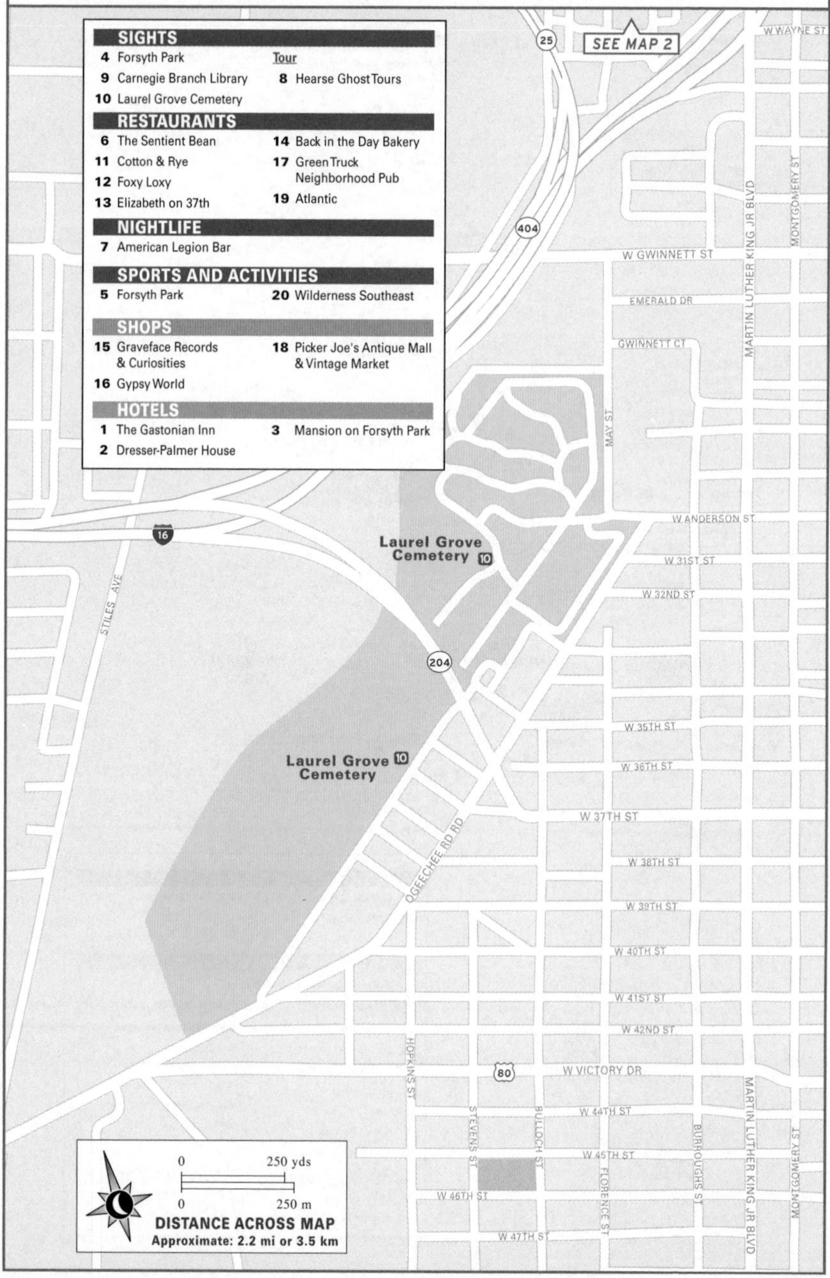

Chatham Square
Monterey Square
Calhoun Square
SEE MAP 2
Mother Matilda Beasley Park
E GORDON LN
W GASTON ST
MARINE MEMORIAL
E GASTON LN
E HUNTINGDON ST
E HUNTINGDON LN
BARNARD ST
Forsyth Fountain
E HALL ST
E HALL LN
PRICE ST
VICTORIAN DISTRICT
WHITAKER ST
CONFEDERATE MEMORIAL
E GWINNETT ST
Forsyth Park
DRAYTON ST
ABERCORN ST
LINCOLN ST
HABERSHAM ST
E BOLTON ST
EAST BROAD ST
E WALDBURG ST
THE HIKER
E PARK AVENUE LN
E DUFFY ST
E HENRY ST
Carnegie Branch Library
E ANDERSON ST
E 31ST ST
W 32ND ST
W 33RD ST
W 34TH ST
E 35TH ST
SOFO
E 36TH ST
E 37TH ST
W 38TH ST
E 38TH ST
W 39TH ST
E 39TH ST
E 40TH ST
W 40TH ST
REYNOLDS ST
ATLANTIC AVE
PAULSEN ST
W 41ST ST
E 41ST ST
E 41ST LN
W 42ND ST
E VICTORY DR
E 44TH ST
E 45TH ST
BULL ST
E 46TH ST
CHATHAM CRES
WASHINGTON AVE
© AVALON TRAVEL

## Map 4: Southside and Eastside

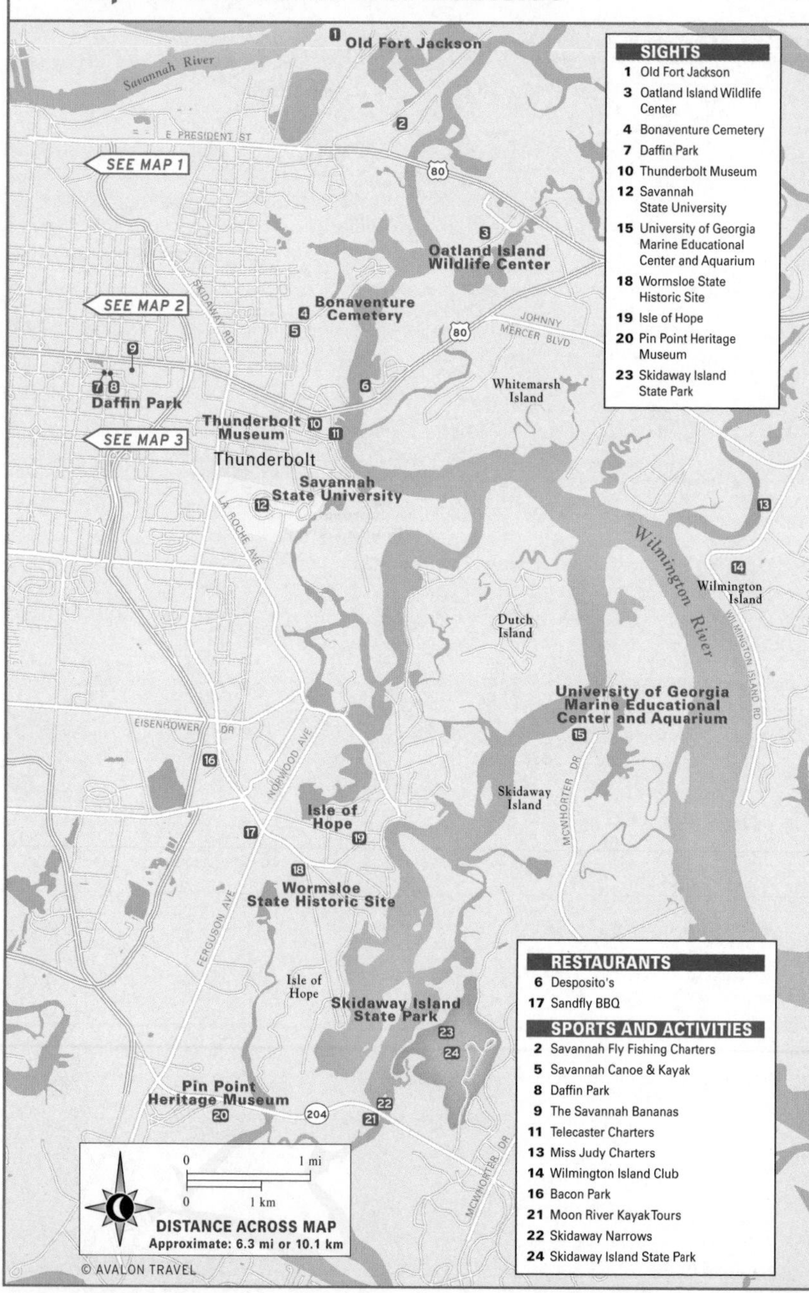

# Map 5: Tybee Island

# Map 6: Greater Savannah

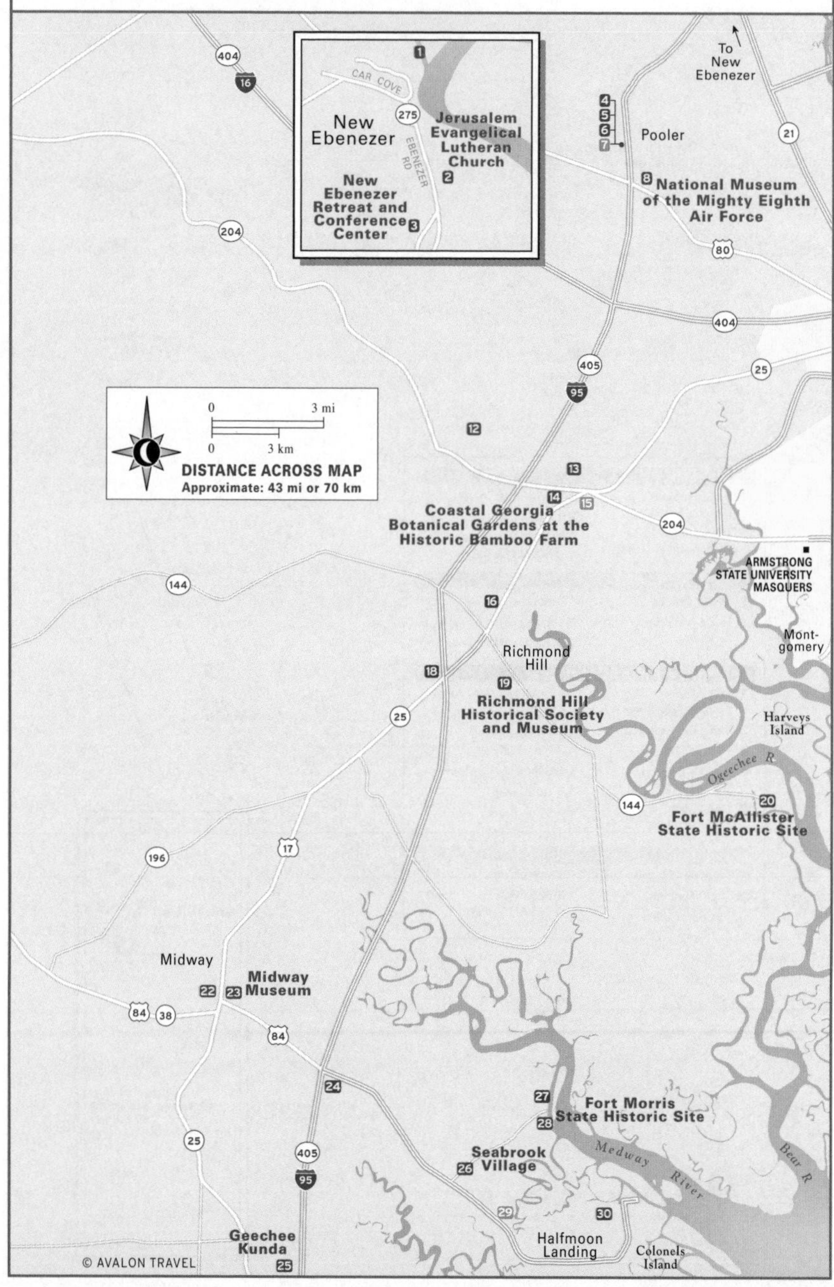


SAVANNAH

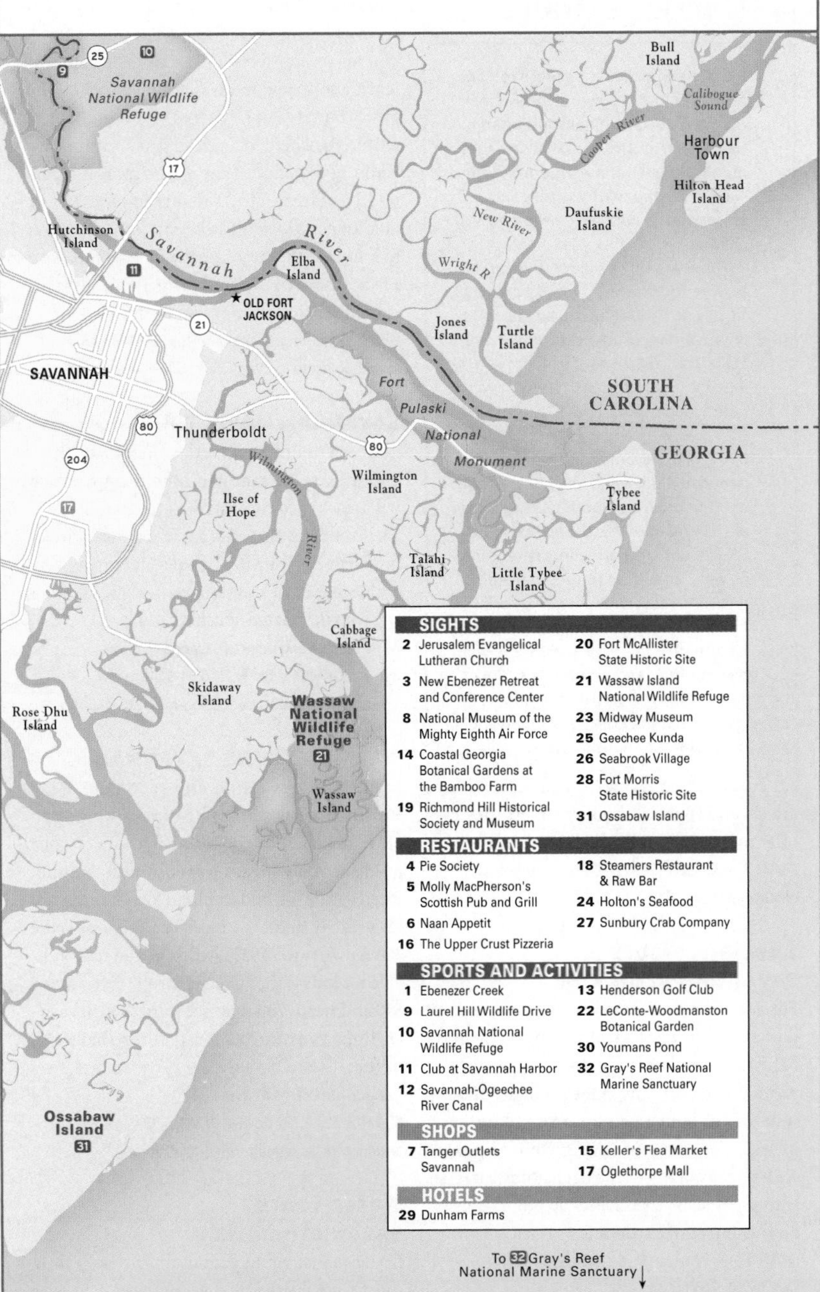
Savannah National Wildlife Refuge
Hutchinson Island
Savannah River
Elba Island
OLD FORT JACKSON
SAVANNAH
Thunderboldt
Wilmington River
Isle of Hope
Wilmington Island
Fort Pulaski National Monument
Jones Island
Turtle Island
New River
Wright R
Daufuskie Island
Cooper River
Bull Island
Calibogue Sound
Harbour Town
Hilton Head Island
SOUTH CAROLINA
GEORGIA
Tybee Island
Talahi Island
Little Tybee Island
Cabbage Island
Skidaway Island
Rose Dhu Island
Wassaw National Wildlife Refuge
Wassaw Island
Ossabaw Island
To 32 Gray's Reef National Marine Sanctuary
SIGHTS
2 Jerusalem Evangelical Lutheran Church
3 New Ebenezer Retreat and Conference Center
8 National Museum of the Mighty Eighth Air Force
14 Coastal Georgia Botanical Gardens at the Bamboo Farm
19 Richmond Hill Historical Society and Museum
20 Fort McAllister State Historic Site
21 Wassaw Island National Wildlife Refuge
23 Midway Museum
25 Geechee Kunda
26 Seabrook Village
28 Fort Morris State Historic Site
31 Ossabaw Island
RESTAURANTS
4 Pie Society
5 Molly MacPherson's Scottish Pub and Grill
6 Naan Appetit
16 The Upper Crust Pizzeria
18 Steamers Restaurant & Raw Bar
24 Holton's Seafood
27 Sunbury Crab Company
SPORTS AND ACTIVITIES
1 Ebenezer Creek
9 Laurel Hill Wildlife Drive
10 Savannah National Wildlife Refuge
11 Club at Savannah Harbor
12 Savannah-Ogeechee River Canal
13 Henderson Golf Club
22 LeConte-Woodmanston Botanical Garden
30 Youmans Pond
32 Gray's Reef National Marine Sanctuary
SHOPS
7 Tanger Outlets Savannah
15 Keller's Flea Market
17 Oglethorpe Mall
HOTELS
29 Dunham Farms

## Carriage Tours

Ah, yes—what could be more romantic than enjoying downtown Savannah the way it was originally intended to be traveled, by horse-drawn carriage? Indeed, this is one of the most fun ways to see the city, for couples as well as for those with horse-enamored children.

There are three main purveyors of equine tourism in town: **Carriage Tours of Savannah** (912/236-6756, www.carriagetoursofsavannah.com), **Historic Savannah Carriage Tours** (888/837-1011, www.savannahcarriage.com), and **Plantation Carriage Company** (912/201-0001, http://plantationcarriagecompany.com). The length of the basic tour and the price are about the same for all—45-60 minutes, about $25 adults, $15 children. All offer specialty tours as well, from ghost tours to evening romantic rides with champagne. Embarkation points vary; check company websites for pickup points. Some will pick you up at your hotel. The City of Savannah does regulate these tours in times of extreme heat or icy road conditions for the animals' safety.

are several tours and many times; they also offer privately scheduled tours.

**MAP 2:** E. Jones Lane, 912/358-0700, www.oldcitywalks.com; $48

## Specialty Tours

### SAVANNAH SLOW RIDE

For a unique tour experience, take a seat on the Savannah Slow Ride, a sort of combination bar, bicycle, and carriage ride. You get on with a group and everyone helps pedal around the squares on about a two-hour ride at five mph or less. You can even bring your to-go cup with you, as many of the bachelorette parties who use the service do. Pickup points depend on the tour; call for details.

**MAP 1:** 420 W. Bryan St., 912/414-5634, www.savannahslowride.com; $30

### SAVANNAH TASTE EXPERIENCE

Consistently one of the highest-quality tours in town, Savannah Taste Experience takes you on several foodie stops to taste, sip, and learn about Savannah's culinary scene. The basic tour is "First Squares" ($49 adults, $37 children), which focuses on spots within easy walking distance of the waterfront; it meets on River Street. The "Famous and Secret East Side Tour" ($57 adults, $47 children) takes you to more off-the-beaten-path spots; it meets on Liberty Street. Food and drink is of course included, so come hungry and thirsty!

**MAP 1:** meeting points vary, 912/221-4439, www.savannahtasteexperience.com; prices vary

### SAVANNAH MOVIE TOUR

To learn about Savannah's history of filmmaking, try a Savannah Movie Tour, which will take you to various film locations in town. The company also offers an enormous, three-hour Foody Tour ($62 adults) featuring several local eateries, and they offer several other non-movie-related specialty tours.

**MAP 2:** meeting point at Savannah Visitors Center, 301 MLK Jr. Blvd., 912/234-3440, www.savannahmovietours.com; $30 adults, $18 children

### WALKING TOURS SAVANNAH

Longtime tour guide and raconteur Greg Proffit and his staff offer fun walking "pub crawls," wherein the point is to meet your guide at some local tavern, ramble around, learn a little bit, and imbibe a lot—though not necessarily in that order. The adult tour is the "Creepy Crawl" ($25), whereas the tour suitable for kids is the "Creepy Stroll" ($16 adults, $10 children). You may not want to believe everything you hear, but you're sure to have a lot of fun. The tours book up early, so make arrangements in advance.

**MAP 2:** 527 E. Gordon St., 912/238-3843, www.walkingtourssavannah.com; $10-18 adults

## Water Tours

### SAVANNAH BELLES

If you've just *got* to get out on the river for a short time, by far the best bargain is to take

## Trolley Tours

Old Town Trolley Tours

The vehicles of choice for the bulk of the masses visiting Savannah, trolleys allow you to sit back and enjoy the views in reasonable comfort. As in other cities, the guides provide commentary while attempting, with various degrees of success, to navigate the cramped downtown traffic environment. The main trolley companies in town are **Old Savannah Tours** (912/234-8128, www.oldsavannahtours.com, basic on-off tour $28 adults, $12 children) and **Old Town Trolley Tours** (800/213-2474, www.trolleytours.com, basic on-off tour $30 adults, $11 children). Both embark from the Savannah Visitors Center on Martin Luther King Jr. Boulevard about every 15-30 minutes on the same schedule, daily 9am-4:30pm.

Frankly there's not much difference between them, as they all offer a very similar range of services for similar prices. While the common "on-off privileges" allow trolley riders to disembark for a while and pick up another of the same company's trolleys at marked stops, be aware there's no guarantee the next trolley—or the one after that—will have enough room to take you on board.

one of the nifty water ferries of the Savannah Belles, named after famous women in Savannah history, which shuttle passengers from River Street to Hutchinson Island and back every 15-20 minutes. Pick one up on River Street in front of City Hall or at the Waving Girl Landing a few blocks east. The watercraft are ADA accessible.

**MAP 1:** River St. at City Hall and Waving Girl Landing, www.catchacat.org; daily 7am-midnight; free

### SAVANNAH RIVERBOAT CRUISES

The heavy industrial buildup on the Savannah River means that the main river tours, all departing from the docks in front of the Hyatt Regency Savannah, tend to be disappointing in their unrelenting views of cranes, docks, and smokestacks. Still, for those into that kind of thing, narrated trips up and down the river on the *Georgia Queen* and the *Savannah River Queen* are offered by Savannah Riverboat Cruises. You can opt for just sightseeing, or an added dinner cruise.

**MAP 1:** 9 E. River St., 912/232-6404, www.savannahriverboat.com; from $25 adults, $16 ages 4-12

## Biking Tours

### SAVANNAH BIKE TOURS

To see downtown Savannah by bicycle—quite a refreshing experience—let Savannah Bike

Tours take you on a two-hour trip through 19 squares and Forsyth Park. Pedaling around the squares and stopping to explore certain sights is a unique pleasure. Tours leave at 9am, 12:30pm, and 4pm daily, plus 6pm in summer. Rent bikes or ride your own.

**MAP 1:** 41 Habersham St., 912/704-4043, www.savannahbiketours.com; $25 adults, $10 under age 12



## Ghost Tours

### SIXTH SENSE SAVANNAH GHOST TOUR

For those who take their paranormal activity *very* seriously, there's Shannon Scott's Sixth Sense Savannah Ghost Tour, an uncensored, straightforward look at Savannah's poltergeist population.

**MAP 2:** Meeting point Clary's Cafe, 404 Abercorn St., 866/666-3323, www.sixthsensesavannah.com; $20, midnight tour $39

### HEARSE GHOST TOURS

The many ghost tours, offered by all the companies, can be fun for the casual visitor who wants entertainment rather than actual history. Students of the paranormal are likely to be disappointed by the cartoonish, Halloween aspect of some of the tours. A standout in the ghost field is Hearse Ghost Tours, a unique company that also operates tours in New Orleans and St. Augustine, Florida. Up to eight guests at a time ride around in the open top of a converted hearse—painted all black, of course—and get a 75-minute, suitably over-the-top narration from the driver-guide. It's still pretty cheesy, but a hip kind of cheesy.

**MAP 3:** 412 E. Duffy St., 912/695-1578, www.hearseghosttours.com; $17

# WATERFRONT

## ★ River Street

It's much tamer than it was 30 years ago—when muscle cars cruised its cobblestones and a volatile mix of local teenagers, sailors on shore leave, and soldiers on liberty made things less than family-friendly after dark—but River Street still has more than enough edginess to keep things interesting. Families are safe and welcome here, but energetic pub crawling remains a favorite pastime for locals and visitors alike.

If you have a car, park it somewhere else and walk. The cobblestones—actually old ballast stones from some of the innumerable ships that docked here over the years—are tough on the suspension, and much of River Street is dedicated to pedestrian traffic anyway.

### FACTOR'S WALK

One level up from River Street, Factor's Walk has nothing to do with math, though a lot of money has been counted here. In arcane usage, a "factor" was a broker, i.e. a middleman for the sale of cotton, Savannah's chief export during most of the 1800s. Factors mostly worked in Factor's Row, the traditional phrase for the actual buildings on River Street, most all of which were used in various import-export activities before their current transformation into a mélange of shops, hotels, restaurants, and taverns. Factor's Walk is divided into Lower Factor's Walk, comprising the alleys and back entrances behind Factor's Row, and Upper Factor's Walk, the system of crosswalks at the upper levels of Factor's Row that lead directly to Bay Street.

**MAP 1:** E. River St. between Bull St. and Lincoln St.

### ROUSAKIS PLAZA

Rousakis Plaza is a focal point for local festivals. It's a great place to sit, feed the pigeons, and watch the huge container ships go back and forth from the Georgia Ports Authority's sprawling complex farther upriver (you can see the huge Panamax cranes in the distance). The **African American Monument** at the edge of Rousakis Plaza was erected in 2002 to controversy for its stark tableau of a dazed-looking African American family with broken shackles around their feet. Adding to the controversy was the graphic content of the inscription at the base of the 12-foot statue, written especially for the monument by famed poet Maya Angelou. It reads:

*The Waving Girl* statue on the waterfront

> We were stolen, sold and bought together from the African continent. We got on the slave ships together. We lay back to belly in the holds of the slave ships in each other's excrement and urine together, sometimes died together, and our lifeless bodies thrown overboard together. Today, we are standing up together, with faith and even some joy.

Nearby you can't miss the huge, vaguely cubist Hyatt Regency Savannah, another controversial local landmark. The modern architecture of the Hyatt caused quite a stir when it was first built in 1981, not only because it's so contrary to the area's historic architecture but because its superstructure effectively cuts off one end of River Street from the other. "Underneath" the Hyatt—actually still River Street—you'll find elevators to the hotel lobby, the best way to get up off the waterfront if you're not up for a walk up the cobblestones. Immediately outside the west side of the Hyatt up toward Bay Street is another exit and entry point, a steep and solid set of antebellum stairs that, despite its decidedly pre-Americans with Disabilities Act aspect, is nonetheless one of the quicker ways to leave River Street for those with strong legs and good knees.

**MAP 1:** E. River St., behind City Hall

### THE WAVING GIRL

At the east end of River Street is the statue of Florence Martus, a.k.a. *The Waving Girl,* set in the emerald-green expanse of little Morrell Park. Beginning in 1887 at the age of 19, Martus—who actually lived several miles downriver on Elba Island—took to greeting every passing ship with a wave of a handkerchief by day and a lantern at night, without fail for the next 40 years. Ship captains returned the greeting with a salute of their own on the ship's whistle, and word spread all over the world of the beguiling woman who waited on the balcony of that lonely house. Martus was a lifelong spinster who lived with her brother, the lighthouse keeper, and was by most accounts an eccentric, delightful person. After her brother died, Martus moved into a house on the Wilmington River, whiling away the hours by—you guessed it—waving at passing cars. Martus became such an enduring symbol of the personality and spirit of Savannah that a U.S. Liberty ship was named for her in 1943. She died at the age of 75, a few months after the ship's christening.

**MAP 1:** Morrell Park, E. River St. and E. Broad St.

### WORLD WAR II MEMORIAL

Near the foot of the Bohemian Hotel Savannah Riverfront on River Street is a 21st-century addition to Savannah's public monuments. Installed in 2010, the World War II Memorial—fairly modernist by local standards—features a copper-and-bronze globe torn in half to represent the European and Pacific theaters of the war. The more than 500 local people who gave their lives in that conflict are memorialized by name.

**MAP 1:** W. River St., near Bohemian Hotel Savannah Riverfront, 102 W. Bay St.

## Bay Street

Because so few downtown streets can accommodate 18-wheelers, Bay Street unfortunately has become the default route for industrial traffic in the area on its way to and from the industrial west side of town. In front of the Hyatt Regency Savannah is a concrete bench marking the spot on which Oglethorpe pitched his first tent.



### CITY HALL

Dominating Bay Street is City Hall, with its gold-leaf dome. The 1907 building was designed by acclaimed architect Hyman Witcover and erected on the site of Savannah's first town hall.

**MAP 1:** 2 E. Bay St.

### CHATHAM ARTILLERY GUNS

Directly adjacent to City Hall on the east is a small canopy sheltering two cannons, which together compose the oldest monument in Savannah. These are the Chatham Artillery Guns, presented to the local militia group of the same name by President George Washington during his one and only visit to town in 1791. Today, locals use the phrase "Chatham Artillery" differently, to refer to a particularly potent local punch recipe that mixes several hard liquors.

**MAP 1:** Adjacent to City Hall, 2 E. Bay St.

### SAVANNAH COTTON EXCHANGE

Directly behind the Chatham Artillery Guns is the ornate Savannah Cotton Exchange, built in 1886 to facilitate the city's huge cotton export business. Once nicknamed "King Cotton's Palace" but now a Masonic lodge, this delightful building by William Gibbons Preston is one of Savannah's many great examples of the Romanesque style.

**MAP 1:** 100 E. Bay St.

### U.S. CUSTOM HOUSE

The large gray Greek Revival building directly across from City Hall is the U.S. Custom House (not "customs," regardless of what the tour guides may say). Built on the spot of Georgia's first public building in 1852, the Custom House was also Georgia's first federal building and was the first local commission for renowned New York architect John Norris, who went on to design 22 other buildings in Savannah. Within its walls was held the trial of the captain and crew of the notorious slave ship *Wanderer*, which illegally plied its trade after a national ban on the importation of slaves. Local newspaper publisher and educator John H. DeVeaux worked here after his appointment as the first African American U.S. Collector of Customs.

**MAP 1:** 1 E. Bay St.

# CITY MARKET

## Ellis Square

Ellis Square's history as Savannah's main open-air marketplace goes back to 1755, when there was a single City Market building in the square itself. The fourth City Market was built in 1872, an ornate Romanesque affair with a 50-foot roofline. In 1954, the city decided to build a parking garage in the square. So the magnificent City Market building—and Ellis Square—simply ceased to exist.

Several large warehouses surrounding City Market survived. Now a hub of tourism, City Market encompasses working art studios, hip bars, cute cafés, live music in the east end of the courtyard, cutting-edge art galleries, gift shops, and restaurants.

The eyesore that was the Ellis Square parking garage is gone, and the square has been rebuilt as a pedestrian hangout, complete with a fountain, all atop a huge underground parking garage. Be sure to check out the smallish bronze of native Savannahian and Oscar-winning lyricist Johnny Mercer on the square's western edge.

There is a small staffed visitors center (Aug.-Oct. daily 10am-9pm, Mar.-July daily 10am-10pm, Feb. and Nov. daily 10am-8pm, Dec.-Jan. daily 10am-6pm) with public restrooms on the northwest corner of the square.

## American Prohibition Museum

During the Prohibition era, Savannah was

## A Visionary Aristocrat

statue of Oglethorpe in Chippewa Square

One of the greatest products of the Enlightenment, **James Edward Oglethorpe** was a study in contrasts, embodying all the vitality, contradiction, and ambiguity of that turbulent age. A stern moralist yet an avowed liberal, an aristocrat with a populist streak, an abolitionist and an anti-Roman Catholic, a man of war who sought peace—the founder of Georgia would put his own inimitable stamp on the new nation to follow, a legacy personified to this day in the city he designed.

After making a name for himself fighting the Turks, the young London native and Oxford graduate would return home only to serve a two-year prison sentence for killing a man in a brawl. The experience was a formative one for Oglethorpe, scion of a large and upwardly mobile family, as he was now forced to see how England's underbelly really lived. Upon his release, the 25-year-old Oglethorpe ran for the "family" House of Commons seat once occupied by his father and two brothers, and won. He distinguished himself as a campaigner for human rights and an opponent of slavery. Another jail-related epiphany came when Oglethorpe saw a friend die of smallpox in debtors prison. More than ever, Oglethorpe was determined to right what he saw as a colossal wrong in the draconian English justice system. His crusade took the form of establishing a sanctuary for debtors in North America.

To that end, he and his friend Lord Perceval established the Trustees, a 21-member group who lobbied King George for permission to establish such a colony. The grant from the king—who was more interested in containing the Spanish than in any humanitarian concerns—would include all land between the Altamaha and Savannah Rivers and from the headwaters of these rivers to the "south seas." Ironically, there were no debtors among Savannah's original colonists. Nonetheless, the new settlement was indeed a reflection of its founder's core values, banning rum as a bad influence (though beer and wine were allowed), prohibiting slavery, and eschewing lawyers on the theory that a gentleman should always be able to defend himself.

Nearing 40 and distracted by war with the Spanish, Oglethorpe's agenda gradually eroded in the face of opposition from settlers, who craved not only the more hedonistic lifestyle of their neighbors to the north in Charleston but the economic advantage that city enjoyed through the use of slave labor. In nearly the same hour as his greatest military victory, crushing the Spanish at the Battle of Bloody Marsh on St. Simons Island, Oglethorpe also suffered an ignominious defeat: being replaced as head of the 13th colony, which he had founded.

He went back to England, never to see the New World again. But his heart was always with the colonists. After successfully fending off a political attack and a court-martial, Oglethorpe married and commenced a healthy retirement. He supported independence for the American colonies, making a point to enthusiastically receive the new ambassador from the United States, one John Adams. The old general died on June 30, 1785, at age 88. Fittingly for this lifelong philanthropist and humanitarian, his childhood home in Godalming, Surrey, is now a nursing home.

a major rum-running point on the bootlegging circuit. That scofflaw history is commemorated in the new American Prohibition Museum, a collection of artifacts and fun living history from costumed docents. The museum is organized and run by a local trolley tour company, so don't expect Smithsonian-level standards of scholarship, though it is fun. Of course there is a "speakeasy" on-site where those 21 and over can enjoy adult beverages.
**MAP 1:** City Market, 209 W. St. Julian St., 855/245-8892, www.trolleytours.com; daily 10am-5 pm.; $12 adults, $9 students and seniors



## Franklin Square

Until recently, Franklin Square was, like Ellis Square, a victim of "progress," this time in the form of a highway going right through the middle of it. But as part of the city's effort to reclaim its history, Franklin Square was returned to its original state in the mid-1980s.

The First African Baptist Church is home to the oldest black congregation in America.

### ★ FIRST AFRICAN BAPTIST CHURCH

The premier historical attraction on Franklin Square is the First African Baptist Church, the oldest black congregation in North America, dating from 1777. The church also hosted the first African American Sunday school, begun in 1826. The church's founding pastor, George Liele, was the first black Baptist in Georgia and perhaps the first black missionary in the country. The present building dates from 1859 and was built almost entirely by members of the congregation themselves, some of whom redirected savings intended to purchase their freedom toward the building of the church. A key staging area for the Underground Railroad, First African Baptist still bears the scars of that turbulent time. In the floor of the fellowship hall—where many civil rights meetings were held, because it was safer for white citizens to go there instead of black activists going outside the church—you'll see breathing holes, drilled for use by escaped enslaved people hiding in a cramped crawlspace.
**MAP 1:** 23 Montgomery St., 912/233-2244, http://firstafricanbc.com; tours Tues.-Sat. 11am, 2pm, and 4pm, Sun. 1pm; $10 adults, $9 students and seniors

### HAITIAN MONUMENT

The Haitian Monument in the center of the square commemorates the sacrifice and service of "Les Chasseurs Volontaires de Saint-Domingue," the 750 Haitian volunteers who fought for American independence and lost many of their number during the unsuccessful attempt to wrest Savannah back from the British in 1779.
**MAP 1:** Franklin Square

# HISTORIC DISTRICT NORTH

## Johnson Square

Due east of City Market, Johnson Square, Oglethorpe's very first square, is named for Robert Johnson, governor of South Carolina at the time of Georgia's founding. The roomy, shaded square, ringed with major bank branches and insurance firms, is dominated by the **Nathanael Greene Monument** in honor of George Washington's

## How to Pronounce Savannah Names

With so many visitors to town also comes plenty of opportunities to mispronounce local place names. Don't sound like a tourist—here's how to say it the way locals do:

- **Broughton Street:** BRAW-ton. What's now Savannah's main shopping thoroughfare is named for Thomas Broughton, a colonial governor of South Carolina.
- **Tybee Island:** TIE-bee. The name supposedly means "salt" in a Native American language.
- **Chatham County:** CHAT-um. The second "h" is silent, in the British fashion.
- **Houston Street:** HOUSE-ton. You're not in Texas! Houston Street in New York City is pronounced the same as Savannah's. Both streets are actually named for the same person, William Houstoun of Georgia, a member of the Continental Congress and an original Trustee of the University of Georgia.
- **Abercorn Street:** No, it's not "Abercrombie." That's a clothing brand. It's pronounced "Abber-corn."
- **Habersham Street:** HAB-er-shum, again clipped short in the British fashion.
- **Barnard Street:** BAR-nerd. Not barnyard, nor Bernard.
- **DeRenne Avenue:** duh-REN. The traditional, if somewhat inaccurate, dividing line between "old" Savannah and suburban Savannah.

second-in-command, who was granted nearby Mulberry Grove plantation for his efforts. The Marquis de Lafayette himself laid the cornerstone for the monument during his famous Southern tour in 1825. In typically maddening Savannah fashion, there is a separate square named for Greene, which has no monument to him at all.

#### CHRIST EPISCOPAL CHURCH

The southeast corner of Johnson Square is dominated by Christ Episcopal Church, a.k.a. Christ Church, a historic house of worship also known as the "Mother Church of Georgia" because its congregation traces its roots to that first Anglican service in Savannah, held the same day Oglethorpe landed. While this spot on Johnson Square was reserved for the congregation from the very beginning, this is actually the third building on the site, dating from 1838. Much of the interior is more recent than that, however, since a fire gutted the inside of the church in 1895. In the northeast bell tower is a bell forged in 1919 by Revere and Sons of Boston.

**MAP 1:** 28 Bull St., 912/236-2500, www.christchurchsavannah.org

### Reynolds Square

Walk directly east of Johnson Square to find yourself at Reynolds Square, named for John Reynolds, the first (and exceedingly unpopular) royal governor of Georgia. First called "Lower New Square," Reynolds Square originally served as site of the filature, or cocoon storage warehouse, during the fledgling colony's ill-fated flirtation with the silk industry (a federal building now occupies the site). As with Johnson Square, the monument in Reynolds Square has nothing to do with its namesake, but is instead a likeness of John Wesley dedicated in 1969 near the spot believed to have been his home.

#### OLDE PINK HOUSE

A Reynolds Square landmark, the Olde Pink House is not only one of Savannah's most romantic restaurants but quite a historic site as well. It's the oldest Savannah mansion from the 18th century still standing as

## One Day in Savannah

Savannah's beautiful, walkable historic district makes for a relatively easy way to spend a day.

Begin with a morning stroll through big, scenic **Forsyth Park** and enjoy this jewel of Victorian green-space design. Don't forget the no-brainer selfie stop at the Forsyth Park Fountain!

Next, walk a block northeast to Calhoun Square for a stop at the **Massie Heritage Center,** probably the best one-stop place for a full but digestible Savannah history lesson, via its state-of-the-art displays.

Walk a few blocks north to check out the stunning **Cathedral of St. John the Baptist** on Lafayette Square, the old stomping grounds of Southern author Flannery O'Connor. Another block north is **Colonial Cemetery,** the city's oldest, which you can walk through on your way to **Kayak Kafe** on Broughton Street for a quick and tasty lunch.

After lunch, walk a few blocks to the **Owens-Thomas House** and enjoy a tour of America's best single example of Regency architecture. After your tour, head around the corner and take a stroll on **Broughton Street,** Savannah's main shopping thoroughfare, and maybe enjoy a cone at **Leopold's Ice Cream Shop.**

Either via your own car or a rideshare, spend the rest of the afternoon on a side trip to beautiful and historic **Bonaventure Cemetery** on the city's eastside.

End with an early evening stroll on the ballast stones of **River Street before** heading to **17Hundred90** to dine in a historic building with a great menu. Consider following up with a nightcap on top of the Bohemian Hotel at **Rocks on the Roof,** with great drinks and a gorgeous view of the entire waterfront.

well as the first place in Savannah where the Declaration of Independence was read aloud. The Georgian mansion was built in 1771 for rice planter James Habersham Jr., one of America's richest men at the time and a member of the notorious "Liberty Boys" who plotted revolution. The building's pink exterior was a matter of serendipity, resulting from its core redbrick seeping through the formerly white stucco outer covering.

**MAP 1:** 23 Abercorn St.

### LUCAS THEATRE FOR THE ARTS

Built in 1921 as part of Arthur Lucas's regional chain of movie houses, the wonderfully ornate Lucas Theatre for the Arts also featured a stage for road shows. In 1976, the Lucas closed after a screening of *The Exorcist.* When the building faced demolition in 1986, a group of citizens created a nonprofit to save it and its expert craftsmanship. Despite numerous starts and stops, the 14-year campaign finally paid off in a grand reopening in 2000, an event helped by timely donations from the cast and crew of the locally shot *Midnight in the Garden of Good and Evil* and *Forrest Gump.* The theater's schedule stays pretty busy, so it should be easy to check out a show while you're in town.

**MAP 1:** 32 Abercorn St., 912/525-5040, www.lucastheatre.com

### OLIVER STURGIS HOUSE

At the southwest corner of Reynolds Square is the understated Oliver Sturgis House, former home of the partner with William Scarbrough in the launching of the SS *Savannah.* This is one of the few Savannah buildings to feature the stabilizing earthquake rods that are much more common in Charleston. Don't miss the dolphin downpour spouts at ground level.

**MAP 1:** 27 Abercorn St.

## Columbia Square

Named for the mythical patroness of America, Columbia Square features at its center not an expected portrait of that female warrior figure but the original fountain from Noble Jones's Wormsloe Plantation, placed there in 1970.

### ISAIAH DAVENPORT HOUSE MUSEUM

Columbia Square is primarily known as the home of the Isaiah Davenport House Museum. The house museum is a delightful stop in and of itself because of its elegant simplicity, sweeping double staircase, and near-perfect representation of the Federalist style. But the Davenport House occupies an exalted place in Savannah history as well, because the fight to save it began the preservation movement in the city. In 1955 the Davenport House, then a tenement, was to be demolished for a parking lot. But Emma Adler and six other Savannah women, angered by the recent destruction of Ellis Square, refused to let it go down quietly. Together they formed the Historic Savannah Foundation in order to raise the $22,500 needed to purchase the Davenport House.

Most Octobers, the Davenport House hosts living history dramatizations based on Savannah's yellow fever plague of the 1820s. Despite the grim subject matter, the little playlets are usually quite entertaining. Other special seasonal tours include a madeira wine tour and "Tea with Mrs. Davenport."

**MAP 1:** 324 E. State St., 912/236-8097, www.davenporthousemuseum.org; Mon.-Sat. 10am-4pm, Sun. 1pm-4pm; $9 adults, $5 children

### KEHOE HOUSE

Across the corner from the Davenport House is the Classical Revival masterpiece Kehoe House, designed for local ironworks owner William Kehoe in 1892 by DeWitt Bruyn. Sadly, the proof of Kehoe's self-described "weakness for cupolas" no longer exists, the cupola having rotted away. Once a funeral home, the Kehoe House is now one of Savannah's premier bed-and-breakfasts. It's unique not only in its exuberantly Victorian architecture but in its twin fireplaces and ubiquitous rococo ironwork, courtesy of the irrepressible Kehoe himself.

**MAP 1:** 123 Habersham St.

## Warren and Washington Squares

Warren Square and its neighbor Washington Square formed the first extension of Oglethorpe's original four squares, and they boast some of the oldest houses in the historic district. Both squares are lovely little garden spots, ideal for a picnic in the shade.

### HAMPTON LILLIBRIDGE HOUSE AND CHARLES ODDINGSELLS HOUSE

Two houses near Washington Square were restored by the late Jim Williams of *Midnight* fame: the Hampton Lillibridge House, which once hosted an Episcopal exorcism, and the Charles Oddingsells House.

**MAP 1:** 507 E. St. Julian St. and 510 E. St. Julian St.

## Greene Square

Named for Revolutionary War hero Nathanael Greene, but bearing no monument to him whatsoever, Greene Square is of particular importance to local African American history. In 1818, the residence at 542 East State Street was constructed for free blacks Charlotte and William Wall. The property at 513 East York Street was built for Catherine DeVeaux, part of a prominent African American family.

### CUNNINGHAM HOUSE

At the corner of Houston (pronounced "HOUSE-ton") and East State Streets is the 1810 Cunningham House, built for Henry Cunningham, the formerly enslaved founding pastor of the Second African Baptist Church.

**MAP 1:** Houston St. and State St.

### SECOND AFRICAN BAPTIST CHURCH

The Second African Baptist Church, on the west side of the square, is where General Sherman made his famous promise of "40 acres and a mule." The founding pastor of the church was Henry Cunningham, whose home is also on Green Square.

**MAP 1:** 124 Houston St., 912/233-6163, www.secondafrican.org

## Old Fort

One of the lesser-known aspects of Savannah history is this well-trod neighborhood at the east end of Bay Street, once the site of groundbreaking experiments and piratical intrigue, and then a diverse melting pot of Savannah citizenry.

### EMMET PARK

Just north of Reynolds Square on the north side of Bay Street you'll come to Emmet Park, first a Native American burial ground and then known as "the Strand" or "Irish Green" because of its proximity to the Irish slums of the Old Fort. In 1902 the park was named for Robert Emmet, an Irish patriot of the early 1800s, who was executed by the British for treason. Within it is the eight-foot **Celtic Cross,** erected in 1983 and carved of Irish limestone. The Celtic Cross is at the center of a key ceremony for local Irish Catholics during the week prior to St. Patrick's Day.

Close by is one of Savannah's more recent monuments, the **Vietnam War Memorial** at East Bay Street and Rossiter Lane. The reflecting pool is in the shape of Vietnam itself, and the names of all 106 Savannahians killed in the conflict are carved into an adjacent marble tablet.

Walk a little farther east and you'll find my favorite little chapter of Bay Street history, the **Beacon Range Light,** tucked into a shady corner. Few visitors bother to check out this masterfully crafted 1858 navigation aid, intended to warn approaching ships of the old wrecks sunk in the river as a defense during the Revolutionary War.

**MAP 1:** E. Bay St. west of E. Broad St.

### TRUSTEES' GARDEN

At the east end of Bay Street where it meets East Broad Street rises a bluff behind a masonry wall—at 40 feet off the river, still the highest point in Chatham County. This is Trustees' Garden, the nation's first experimental garden. Trustees' Garden became the site of Fort Wayne, named after General "Mad Anthony" Wayne of Revolutionary War fame, who retired to a plantation near Savannah. The Fort Wayne area—still called the "Old Fort" neighborhood by old-timers—fell from grace and became associated with the "lowest elements" of Savannah society, which in the 19th and early 20th centuries were Irish and African Americans. It also became known for its illegal activity and as the haunt of sea salts such as the ones who frequented what is now the delightfully schlocky **Pirates' House** restaurant. That building began life in 1753 as a seamen's inn and was later chronicled by Robert Louis Stevenson in *Treasure Island* as a rogue's gallery of pirates and nautical ne'er-do-wells.

Find the **Herb House** on East Broad Street, the older-looking clapboard structure next to the Pirates' House entrance. You're looking at what is considered the single oldest building in Georgia and one of the oldest in the United States. Constructed in 1734, it was originally the home of Trustees' Garden's chief gardener.

To the rear of Trustees' Garden is the 1881 Hillyer building, now the **Charles H. Morris Center,** a mixed-use performing arts and meeting space that is heavily used during the springtime Savannah Music Festival. Adjacent to this space is the newly renovated Kehoe Iron Works, including an outdoor event space and a restored historic ironworks building, also a multiuse space.

**MAP 1:** 10 E. Broad St., 912/443-3277, http://trusteesgarden.com

## Broughton Street

Downtown's main shopping district for most of the 20th century was Broughton Street. Postwar suburbs and white flight brought neglect to the area by the 1960s, and many thought Broughton was gone for good. But with the downtown renaissance brought about largely by the Savannah College of Art and Design (SCAD), Broughton was able not only to get back on its feet, but also to thrive as a commercial center once again.

## A Southern St. Paddy's Day

Savannah hosts the second-largest St. Patrick's Day celebration in the world, second only to New York City's. With its fine spring weather and walkability—not to mention its liberal rules allowing you to carry an adult beverage on the street—Savannah is tailor-made for a boisterous outdoor celebration.

Ironically, given St. Patrick's Day's current close association with the Roman Catholic faith, the first parade in Savannah was organized by Irish Protestants. Thirteen members of the local Hibernian Society—the country's oldest Irish society—took part in a private procession to Independent Presbyterian Church in 1813. The first public procession was in 1824, when the Hibernians invited all local Irishmen to parade through the streets. The first recognizably modern parade, with bands and a "grand marshal," happened in 1870.

Organized by a "committee" of about 700 local Irish residents, today's three-hour procession includes marchers from all the local Irish organizations, in addition to marching bands and floats representing many local groups. The assembled clans wear kelly-green blazers, brandishing their walking canes and to-go cups, some pushing future committee members in strollers.



#### JEN LIBRARY

The Savannah College of Art and Design's Jen Library is a state-of-the-art facility set in the circa-1890 Levy and Maas Brothers department stores.

**MAP 1:** 201 E. Broughton St.

#### TRUSTEES THEATER

Around the corner from the Lucas Theatre on Reynolds Square is the art moderne Trustees Theater, a Savannah College of Art and Design (SCAD) operation that seats 1,200 and hosts concerts, film screenings, and the school's much-anticipated spring fashion show. It began life in the postwar boom of 1946 as the Weis Theatre, another one of those ornate Southern movie houses that took full commercial advantage of being the only buildings at the time to have air-conditioning. But by the end of the 1970s it had followed the fate of Broughton Street, lying dormant and neglected until its purchase and renovation by SCAD in 1989.

This block of Broughton in front of Trustees Theater is usually blocked off to mark the gala opening of the SCAD Savannah Film Festival each fall. Searchlights crisscross the sky, limos idle in wait, and Hollywood guests strike poses for the photographers.

**MAP 1:** 216 E. Broughton St., 912/525-5051, www.trusteestheater.com

### Wright Square

The big monument in Wright Square, Oglethorpe's second square, has nothing to do with James Wright, royal governor of Georgia before the Revolution, for whom it's named. Instead the monument honors William Gordon, former mayor and founder of the Central of Georgia Railway. More importantly, Wright Square is the final resting place for the great Yamacraw chief Tomochichi, buried in 1737 in an elaborate state funeral at James Oglethorpe's insistence. A huge boulder of North Georgia granite honoring the chief was placed in a corner of the square in 1899 under the auspices of William Gordon's daughter-in-law. Tomochichi is not buried under the boulder but somewhere underneath the Gordon monument.

#### EVANGELICAL LUTHERAN CHURCH OF THE ASCENSION

Next to the old courthouse is the historic Evangelical Lutheran Church of the Ascension, built in the 1870s for a congregation that traced its roots to some of the first Austrian Salzburgers to come to Savannah in 1734.

**MAP 1:** 120 Bull St., 912/232-4151, www.elcota.org

### FEDERAL COURTHOUSE AND POST OFFICE

On the west side of Wright Square is the Federal Courthouse and Post Office, built in 1898 out of Georgia marble. The building's stately facade makes an appearance in several films, including the original *Cape Fear* and *Midnight in the Garden of Good and Evil*. **MAP 1:** 125-127 Bull St.

## Telfair Square

Telfair Square was named for Mary Telfair, last heir of a family that was one of the most important in Savannah history. Mary bequeathed the family mansion to the Georgia Historical Society upon her death in 1875 to serve as a museum. Originally called St. James Square after a similar square in London, Telfair was the last of Oglethorpe's original four squares.

Telfair Square hosts two of the three buildings operated by **Telfair Museums,** an umbrella organization that relies on a combination of private and public funding and has driven much of the arts agenda in Savannah for the last 125 years. The third building operated by Telfair Museums is the Owens-Thomas House on Oglethorpe Square.

Get a triple-site pass to the Jepson Center, the Telfair Academy, and the Owens-Thomas House for $20 pp.

### ★ JEPSON CENTER FOR THE ARTS

The proudest addition to the Telfair Museums group is the striking, 64,000-square-foot Jepson Center for the Arts, whose ultramodern exterior sits catty-corner from the Telfair Academy of Arts and Sciences. Promoting a massive, daringly designed new facility devoted to nothing but modern art was a hard sell in this traditional town, especially when renowned architect Moshe Safdie insisted on building a glassed-in flyover across a lane between two buildings. After a few delays in construction, the Jepson opened its doors in 2006 and has since wowed locals and visitors alike with its cutting-edge traveling exhibits and rotating assortment of late 20th-century and 21st-century modern art. If you get hungry, you can enjoy lunch in the expansive atrium café, and, of course, there's a nice gift shop.

Each late January-early February, the Jepson Center hosts most events of the unique Pulse Art + Technology Festival, a celebration of the intersection of cutting-edge technology and performing and visual arts.

the Jepson Center for the Arts

MAP 1: 207 W. York Lane, 912/790-8800, www.telfair.org; Sun.-Mon. noon-5pm, Tues.-Sat. 10am-5pm; $12 adults, $5 students

### ★ TELFAIR ACADEMY OF ARTS AND SCIENCES

The oldest public art museum in the South, the Telfair Academy of Arts and Sciences was built in 1821 by the great William Jay for Alexander Telfair, scion of that famous Georgia family. The five statues in front are of Phidias, Raphael, Rubens, Michelangelo, and Rembrandt. As well as displaying Sylvia Judson Shaw's now-famous *Bird Girl* sculpture, which originally stood in Bonaventure Cemetery (actually the third of four casts by the sculptor), the Telfair Academy features an outstanding collection of primarily 18th- and 20th-century works, most notably the largest public collection of visual art by Khalil Gibran. Major paintings include works by Childe Hassam, Frederick Frieseke, Gari Melchers, and the massive *Black Prince of Crécy* by Julian Story.

MAP 1: 121 Barnard St., 912/790-8800, www.telfair.org; Sun.-Mon. noon-5pm, Tues.-Sat. 10am-5pm; $12 adults, $5 students

### TRINITY UNITED METHODIST CHURCH

Directly between the Telfair and the Jepson stands Trinity United Methodist Church, Savannah's first Methodist church. Built in 1848 on the site of the Telfair family garden, its masonry walls are of famous "Savannah Gray" bricks—a lighter, more porous, and elegant variety—under stucco. Virgin longleaf pine was used for most of the interior, fully restored in 1969. The sanctuary occasionally hosts secular concerts, which are well-attended. Call ahead for a tour.

MAP 1: 225 W. President St., 912/233-4766, www.trinitychurch1848.org; sanctuary daily 9am-5pm, services Sun. 8:45am and 11am

## Oglethorpe Square

Don't look for a monument to Georgia's founder in the square named for him. His monument is in Chippewa Square. Originally called "Upper New Square," Oglethorpe Square was created in 1742.

### JULIETTE GORDON LOW BIRTHPLACE

Around the corner from Wright Square at Oglethorpe and Bull is the Juliette Gordon Low Birthplace, declared the city's very first National Historic Landmark in 1965, and fresh off a significant restoration effort. The founder of the Girl Scouts of the USA lived here from her birth in 1860 until her marriage. The house was completed in 1821 for Mayor James Moore Wayne, future Supreme Court justice, but the current furnishings, many original, are intended to reflect the home during the 1880s.

Also called the Girl Scout National Center, the Low birthplace is probably Savannah's most festive historic site because of the heavy traffic of Girl Scout troops from across the United States. They flock here year-round to take part in programs and learn more about their organization's founder, whose family sold the house to the Girl Scouts in 1953. You don't have to be affiliated with the Girl Scouts to tour the home. Tours are given every 15 minutes, and tickets are available at the Oglethorpe Avenue entrance.

MAP 1: 10 E. Oglethorpe Ave., 912/233-4501, www.juliettegordonlowbirthplace.org; Mar.-Oct. Mon.-Sat. 10am-4pm; $15 adults, $12 children, $10 Girl Scouts

TOP EXPERIENCE

### ★ OWENS-THOMAS HOUSE

The square's main claim to fame, the Owens-Thomas House, lies on the northeast corner. Widely known as the finest example of Regency architecture in the United States, the Owens-Thomas House was designed by brilliant young English architect William Jay. One of the first professionally trained architects in the United States, Jay was only 24 when he designed the home for cotton merchant or "factor" Richard Richardson, who lost the house in the depression of 1820 (all that remains of Richardson's tenure are three marble-top tables). The house's current name is derived from Savannah mayor George Owens, who bought the house in 1830.

Perhaps most interestingly, a complex plumbing system features rain-fed cisterns, flushing toilets, sinks, bathtubs, and a shower. When built, the Owens-Thomas House in fact had the first indoor plumbing in Savannah. On the south facade is a beautiful cast-iron veranda from which Revolutionary War hero Marquis de Lafayette addressed a crowd of starstruck Savannahians during his visit in 1825. The associated slave quarters are in a surprisingly intact state, including the original "haint blue" paint. The carriage house, where all tours begin, is now the home's gift shop.

The Owens-Thomas House is owned and operated by the Telfair Museums. Get a combination pass to all Telfair sites—the Jepson Center for the Arts, the Telfair Academy of Arts and Sciences, and the Owens-Thomas House—for $20 pp.

**MAP 1:** 124 Abercorn St., 912/233-9743, www.telfair.org; Sun.-Mon. noon-5pm, Tues.-Sat. 10am-5pm, last tour 4:30pm; $20 adults, $15 students, ticket includes Jepson Center and Telfair Academy

## Martin Luther King Jr. Boulevard

### SHIPS OF THE SEA MARITIME MUSEUM

One of Savannah's more unique museums is the quirky Ships of the Sea Maritime Museum. The stunning Greek Revival building in which it resides is known as the Scarbrough House because it was initially built in 1819 by the great William Jay for local shipping merchant William Scarbrough, co-owner of the SS *Savannah,* the first steamship to cross the Atlantic. After the Scarbroughs sold the property, it became the West Broad School for African Americans from Reconstruction through integration.

Inside, children, maritime buffs, and crafts connoisseurs can find intricate and detailed scale models of various historic vessels, such as Oglethorpe's *Anne,* the SS *Savannah,* and the NS *Savannah,* the world's first nuclear-powered surface vessel. There's even a model of the *Titanic.*

**MAP 1:** 41 MLK Jr. Blvd., 912/232-1511, http://shipsofthesea.org; Tues.-Sun. 10am-5pm; $9 adults, $7 students

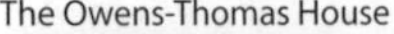
The Owens-Thomas House

## Scout's Honor

Known as "Daisy" to family and friends, **Juliette Magill Kinzie Gordon** was born to be a pioneer. Her father's family took part in the original settlement of Georgia, and her mother's kin were among the founders of Chicago. Mostly known as the founder of the **Girl Scouts of the USA,** Daisy was also an artist, adventurer, and healer. Born and raised in the house on Oglethorpe Avenue in Savannah known to Girl Scouts across the nation as simply "the Birthplace," she was an animal lover with an early penchant for theater, drawing, and poetry.

In 1911 while in England, Daisy met Robert Baden-Powell, founder of the Boy Scouts and Girl Guides in Britain. Struck by the simplicity and usefulness of his project, she carried the seeds of a similar idea back with her to the United States. "I've got something for the girls of Savannah, and all of America, and all the world, and we're going to start it tonight," were her famous words in a phone call to a cousin after meeting Baden-Powell. So on March 12, 1912, Daisy gathered 18 girls to register the first troop of American Girl Guides, later the Girl Scouts of the USA.

Juliette "Daisy" Gordon Low died of breast cancer in her bed in the Andrew Low House on January 17, 1927. She was buried in Laurel Grove Cemetery. Girl Scout troops from all over the United States visit her birthplace, the Andrew Low House, and her gravesite to this day, often leaving flowers and small personal objects near her tombstone as tokens of respect and gratitude.

# HISTORIC DISTRICT SOUTH

## Chippewa Square

Named for a battle in the War of 1812, Chippewa Square has a large monument not to the battle, natch, but to James Oglethorpe, clad in full soldier's regalia. Notice the general is still facing south, toward the Spanish.

Yes, the bench on the square's north side is in the same location as the one Tom Hanks occupied in *Forrest Gump,* but it's not the same bench that hosted the two-time Oscar winner's backside—that one was donated by Paramount Pictures to be displayed in the Savannah History Museum on MLK Jr. Boulevard.

**TOP** EXPERIENCE

### COLONIAL CEMETERY

Just north of Chippewa Square is Oglethorpe Avenue, originally called South Broad and the southern boundary of the original colony. At Oglethorpe and Abercorn Streets is Colonial Cemetery, first active in 1750. You'd be forgiven for assuming it's the "DAR" cemetery; the Daughters of the American Revolution contributed the ornate iron entranceway in 1913, thoughtfully dedicating it to themselves instead of the cemetery itself.

Unlike the picturesque beauty of Bonaventure and Laurel Grove Cemeteries, Colonial Cemetery has a morbid feel. The fact that burials stopped here in 1853 plays into that desolation, but maybe another reason is because it's the final resting ground of many of Savannah's yellow fever victims. Famous people buried here include Button Gwinnett, one of Georgia's three signers of the Declaration of Independence. The man who reluctantly killed Gwinnett in a duel, General Lachlan McIntosh, is also buried here. The original burial vault of Nathanael Greene is in the cemetery, although the Revolutionary War hero's remains were moved to Johnson Square over a century ago.

**MAP 2:** Oglethorpe St. and Abercorn St., www.savannahga.gov; daily 8am-dusk; free

### FIRST BAPTIST CHURCH

The nearby First Baptist Church—not to be confused with the more famous First African Baptist Church on Franklin Square—claims to be the oldest original church building in Savannah, with a cornerstone dating from 1830. Services were held here throughout the Civil War, with Union troops attending during the occupation. The church was renovated by renowned local architect Henrik Wallin in 1922. Call ahead for a tour.

**MAP 2:** 223 Bull St., 912/234-2671; service Sun. 11am

### HISTORIC SAVANNAH THEATRE

At the square's northeast corner is the Historic Savannah Theatre, which claims to be the oldest continuously operating theater in the United States. Designed by William Jay, it opened in 1818 with a production of *The Soldier's Daughter.* In the glory days of gaslight theater in the 1800s, some of the nation's best actors, including Edwin Booth, brother to Lincoln's assassin, regularly trod the boards of its stage. Due to a fire in 1948, little remains of Jay's original design except a small section of exterior wall. The building is currently home to a semiprofessional revue company specializing in oldies shows.

**MAP 2:** 222 Bull St., 912/233-7764, www.savannahtheatre.com

### INDEPENDENT PRESBYTERIAN CHURCH

Built in 1818, possibly by William Jay—scholars are unsure of the scope of his involvement—Independent Presbyterian Church is called the "mother of Georgia Presbyterianism." A fire destroyed most of Independent Presbyterian's original structure in 1889, but the subsequent rebuilding was a very faithful rendering of the original design, based on London's St. Martin-in-the-Fields. The church's steeple made a cameo appearance in *Forrest Gump* as a white feather floated by. Lowell Mason, composer of the hymn "Nearer My God to Thee," was organist at Independent Presbyterian. In 1885 Woodrow Wilson married local parishioner Ellen Louise Axson in the manse to the rear of the church. During the Great Awakening in 1896, almost 3,000 people jammed the sanctuary to hear famous evangelist D. L. Moody preach. Call ahead for a tour.

**MAP 2:** 207 Bull St., 912/236-3346, www.ipcsav.org; services Sun. 11am, Wed. noon

## Madison Square

Named for the nation's fourth president, Madison Square memorializes a local hero who gave his life for his city during the American Revolution. Irish immigrant Sergeant William Jasper, hero of the Battle of Fort Moultrie in Charleston three years earlier, was killed leading the American charge during the 1779 Siege of Savannah, when an allied army failed to retake the city from the British. The monument in the square honors Jasper, but he isn't buried here; his body was interred in a mass grave near the battlefield along with other colonists and soldier-immigrants killed in the one-sided battle.

The two small, suitably warlike cannons in the square have nothing to do with the Siege of Savannah. They commemorate the first two highways in Georgia, today known as Augusta Road and Ogeechee Road.

### GREEN-MELDRIM HOUSE

Given the house's beauty and history, visitors will be forgiven for not immediately realizing that the Green-Meldrim House is also the rectory of the adjacent St. John's Episcopal Church, which acquired it in 1892. This is the place where Sherman formulated his ill-fated "40 acres and a mule" Field Order No. 15, giving most of the Sea Islands of Georgia and South Carolina to freed blacks. A tasteful example of Gothic Revival architecture, this 1850 design by John Norris features a beautiful external gallery of filigree ironwork.

**MAP 2:** 1 W. Macon St., 912/232-1251, www.stjohnssav.org; tours every 30 minutes Tues. and Thurs.-Fri. 10am-4pm, Sat. 10am-1pm; $10 adults, $5 students and children

### POETTER HALL

The Savannah College of Art and Design's first building, Poetter Hall, known to old-timers as the Savannah Volunteer Guards Armory, is directly across from the Scottish Rite Temple. With its imposing but somewhat whimsical facade right out of a Harry Potter movie, this brick and terra-cotta gem of a Romanesque Revival building was built in

the Cathedral of St. John the Baptist

1893 by William Gibbons Preston. It housed National Guard units (as well as a high school) until World War II, when the USO occupied the building during its tenant unit's service in Europe.

**MAP 2:** 342 Bull St., www.scad.edu

### SCOTTISH RITE TEMPLE

The old Scottish Rite Temple at Charlton and Bull Streets was designed by Hyman Witcover, who also designed City Hall. A popular drugstore with a soda fountain for many years, it currently houses the **Gryphon Tea Room,** run by the Savannah College of Art and Design.

**MAP 2:** Charlton St. and Bull St., 912/525-5880; Mon.-Sat. 11am-6pm, Sun. 11am-3pm

## Lafayette Square

One of Savannah's favorite squares, especially on St. Patrick's Day, verdant Lafayette Square boasts a number of important sights and attractions.

### ANDREW LOW HOUSE MUSEUM

A major landmark on Lafayette Square is the Andrew Low House Museum, once the home of Juliette "Daisy" Gordon Low, the founder of the Girl Scouts of the USA, who was married to cotton heir William "Billow" Low, Andrew Low's son. Despite their happy-go-lucky nicknames, the union of Daisy and Billow was a notably unhappy one. Still, divorce was out of the question, so the couple lived separate lives until William's death in 1905. The one good thing that came out of the marriage was the germ for the idea for the Girl Scouts, which Juliette got from England's Girl Guides while living there with her husband, Savannah being the couple's winter residence. Designed by the great New York architect John Norris, the Low House is a magnificent example of the Italianate style. Check out the cast-iron balconies on the long porch, a fairly rare feature in historic Savannah homes. Antiques junkies will go nuts over the furnishings, especially the massive secretary in the parlor, one of only four of this type in existence (a sibling is in New York's Metropolitan Museum of Art). Author William Makepeace Thackeray ate in the dining room, now sporting full French porcelain service, and slept in an upstairs room; he also wrote at the desk by the bed. Also on the 2nd floor you'll see the room where Robert E. Lee stayed during his visit and the bed where Juliette Gordon Low died.

**MAP 2:** 329 Abercorn St., 912/233-6854, www.andrewlowhouse.com; Mon.-Sat. 10am-4pm, Sun. noon-4pm; $10 adults, $9 children

### ★ CATHEDRAL OF ST. JOHN THE BAPTIST

Spiritual home to Savannah's Irish community and the oldest Roman Catholic church in Georgia, the Cathedral of St. John the Baptist was initially known as Our Lady of Perpetual Help. It's the place to be for mass the morning of March 17 at 8am, as the clans gather in their green jackets and white dresses to take a sip of communion wine before moving on to harder stuff in honor of St. Patrick.

Despite its overt Celtic character today,

the parish was originally founded by French émigrés from Haiti who arrived after the successful overthrow of the colonial government by a slave uprising on the island in the late 1700s. The first sanctuary on the site was built in 1873. Fire swept through the edifice in 1898, leaving only two spires and the external walls, but the cathedral was completely rebuilt within a year and a half. In the years since, many renovations have been undertaken. The most recent, from 1998 to 2000, involved the intricate removal, cleaning, and releading of more than 50 of the cathedral's stained-glass windows, a roof replacement, and an interior makeover, introducing a 9,000-pound altar and an 8,000-pound baptismal font, both made of Italian marble.

**MAP 2:** 222 E. Harris St., 912/233-4709, www.savannahcathedral.org; daily 9am-noon and 12:30pm-5pm, mass Sun. 8am, 10am, 11:30am, Mon.-Sat. noon, Latin mass Sun. 1pm

### FLANNERY O'CONNOR CHILDHOOD HOME

On a corner of Lafayette Square stands the rather Spartan facade of the Flannery O'Connor Childhood Home. The Savannah-born novelist lived in this three-story townhome from her birth in 1925 until 1938 and attended church at the cathedral across the square. Once a fairly nondescript attraction for so favorite a native daughter, a recent round of renovations has returned the two main floors to the state Flannery would have known, including an extensive library. A nonprofit association sponsors O'Connor-related readings and signings. While the current backyard garden dates to 1993, it's the place where five-year-old Flannery is said to have taught a chicken to walk backward, foreshadowing the eccentric, Gothic flavor of her writing.

**MAP 2:** 207 E. Charlton St., 912/233-6014, www.flanneryoconnorhome.org; Fri.-Wed. 1pm-4pm; $6 adults, $5 students, free under age 15

### HAMILTON-TURNER INN

Across from the O'Connor house is the Hamilton-Turner Inn. Now a privately owned bed-and-breakfast, this 1873 Second Empire mansion is best known for the showmanship of its over-the-top Victorian appointments and its role in *Midnight in the Garden of Good and Evil* as the home of Joe Odom's girlfriend, "Mandy Nichols" (real name Nancy Hillis). In 1883 it was reportedly the first house in Savannah to have electricity.

**MAP 2:** 330 Abercorn St., 912/233-1833, www.hamilton-turnerinn.com

## Troup Square

Low-key Troup Square boasts the most modern-looking monument downtown, the **Armillary Sphere.** Essentially an elaborate sundial, the sphere is a series of astrologically themed rings with an arrow that marks the time by shadow. It is supported by six tortoises.

### BEACH INSTITUTE

Just east of Troup Square, near the intersection of Harris and Price Streets, is the Beach Institute. Built as a school by the Freedmen's Bureau soon after the Civil War, it was named after its prime benefactor, Alfred Beach, editor of *Scientific American*. It served as an African American school through 1919. Restored by SCAD and given back to the city to serve as a museum, the Beach Institute houses the permanent Ulysses Davis collection and a rotating calendar of art events with a connection to black history.

**MAP 2:** 502 E. Harris St., 912/234-8000; Tues.-Sun. noon-5pm; $4

### JONES STREET

There aren't a lot of individual attractions on Jones Street, the east-west avenue between Taylor and Charlton Streets just north of Monterey Square. Rather, it's the small-scale, throwback feel of the place and its tasteful, dignified homes, including the former home of **Joe Odom** (16 E. Jones St.), that are the attraction. The **Eliza Thompson House** (5 W.

## The Story of "Jingle Bells"

Boston and Savannah vie over bragging rights as to where the classic Christmas song "Jingle Bells" was written. The song's composer, James L. Pierpont, led a life at times as carefree as the song itself. Born in Boston, Pierpont ventured from his wife and young children in 1849 to follow the gold rush to San Francisco. When his brother John was named minister of the new Unitarian congregation in Savannah in 1853, Pierpont followed him, becoming music director and organist, again leaving behind his wife and children in Boston. During this time Pierpont became a prolific composer of secular tunes, including polkas, ballads, and minstrel songs.

In August 1857, a Boston-based publisher, Oliver Ditson and Co., published Pierpont's song "One Horse Open Sleigh." Two years later it was rereleased with the current title, "Jingle Bells." At neither time, however, was the song a popular hit. It took action by his son Juriah in 1880 to renew the copyright to what would become one of the most famous songs of all time.

In Massachusetts, they swear Pierpont wrote the song while at the home of one Mrs. Otis Waterman. In Georgia, scholars assure us a homesick Pierpont wrote the tune during a winter at a house at Oglethorpe and Whitaker Streets, long since demolished. The Savannah contingent's ace in the hole is the fact that "Jingle Bells" was first performed in public at a Thanksgiving program at the local Unitarian Universalist Church in 1857. And despite persistent claims in Massachusetts that he wrote the song there in 1850, Southern scholars point out that Pierpont was actually in California in 1850.



Jones St.), now a bed-and-breakfast, was the first home on Jones Street.

**MAP 2:** Jones St. between Taylor St. and Charlton St.

### UNITARIAN UNIVERSALIST CHURCH OF SAVANNAH

Troup Square is the home of the historic Unitarian Universalist Church of Savannah. This original home of Savannah's Unitarians, who sold the church when the Civil War came, was recently reacquired by the congregation. It is where James L. Pierpont first performed his immortal tune "Jingle Bells." When he did so, however, the church was actually on Oglethorpe Square. The entire building was moved to Troup Square in the mid-1800s.

**MAP 2:** 313 E. Harris St., 912/234-0980, www.jinglebellschurch.org; service Sun. 11am

## ★ Monterey Square

Originally named "Monterrey Square" to commemorate the local Irish Jasper Greens' participation in a victorious Mexican-American War battle in 1846, the spelling morphed into its current version somewhere along the way. But Monterey Square remains one of the most visually beautiful and serene spots in all of Savannah. At the center of the square is a monument not to the victory for which it is named but to Count Casimir Pulaski, killed while attempting to retake the city from the British, and whose remains supposedly lie under the 55-foot monument. As early as 1912, people began noticing the disintegration of the monument due to substandard marble used in some key parts, but it wasn't until the 1990s that a full restoration was accomplished. The restoration company discovered that one of the monument's 34 sections had been accidentally installed upside down. In the true spirit of preservation, they dutifully put the section back—upside down. The *Goddess of Liberty* atop the monument, however, is not original; you can see her in the Savannah History Museum. Fans of ironwork will enjoy the ornate masterpieces in wrought iron featured at many houses on the periphery of the square.

### MERCER-WILLIAMS HOUSE MUSEUM

The Mercer-Williams House Museum sees a lot of visitors due to its role in the hugely popular *Midnight in the Garden of Good and*

*Evil.* While this grand John Norris building is now primarily known as a crime scene involving late antiques dealer Jim Williams and his lover, if you take a tour of the home, you might hear less about "The Book" than you may have expected. Now proudly owned by Jim Williams's sister Dorothy Kingery, an established academic in her own right, the Mercer-Williams House deliberately concentrates on the early history of the home and Jim Williams's prodigious talent as a collector and conservator of fine art and antiques. Tours are worth it for art aficionados even though the upstairs, Dr. Kingery's residence, is off-limits.

The house was built for General Hugh W. Mercer, Johnny Mercer's great-grandfather, in 1860, but the war interrupted construction. General Mercer—descendant of the Revolutionary War general and George Washington's close friend Hugh Mercer—survived the war, in which he was charged with the defense of Savannah. But he soon fell on hard times and was forced to sell the house to John Wilder, who moved in after completion in 1868. Despite what any tour guide might tell you, no member of the Mercer family—including the great Johnny Mercer himself—ever lived in the house.

**MAP 2:** 429 Bull St., 912/236-6352, www.mercerhouse.com; Mon.-Sat. 10:30am-4pm, Sun. noon-4pm; $12.50 adults, $8 students

### TEMPLE MICKVE ISRAEL

Directly across Monterey Square from the Mercer House is Temple Mickve Israel, a notable structure for many reasons: It's Georgia's first synagogue; it's the only Gothic synagogue in the country; and it's the third-oldest Jewish congregation in North America, following those in New York and Newport, Rhode Island. Notable congregants have included Dr. Samuel Nunes Ribeiro, who helped stop an epidemic in 1733, and his descendant Raphael Moses, considered the father of the peach industry in the Peach State.

Mickve Israel offers 30- to 45-minute tours of the sanctuary and museum. No reservations are necessary for tours.

**MAP 2:** 20 E. Gordon St., 912/233-1547, www.mickveisrael.org; Mon.-Fri. 10am-1pm and 2pm-4pm, closed Jewish holidays; $4 suggested donation

## Calhoun Square

The last of the 24 squares in Savannah's original grid, Calhoun Square is also the only square with all its original buildings intact.

the Mercer-Williams House Museum

### MASSIE HERITAGE CENTER

Dominating the south side of Calhoun Square is Savannah's first public elementary school and the spiritual home of Savannah educators, the Massie Heritage Center. In 1841, Peter Massie, a Scots planter with a populist streak, endowed the school to give poor children as good an education as the children of rich families (like Massie's own) received. Another of Savannah's masterpieces by John Norris—whose impressive oeuvre includes the Andrew Low House, the Mercer-Williams House, and the Green-Meldrim House—the central portion of the trifold building was completed in 1856. After the Civil War, the "Massie School," as it's known locally, was designated as the area's African American public school. Classes ceased in 1974, and it now operates as a living-history museum, centering on the period-appointed one-room "heritage classroom" but with several other exhibit spaces of note.

A million-dollar renovation in 2012 added an interactive model of Oglethorpe's urban design and several interesting exhibits on aspects of Savannah architecture and history. In all, Massie provides possibly the best one-stop tour for an all-encompassing look at Savannah history and culture. You can either do a self-guided tour or take the very informative guided tour at 11am or 2pm for the same admission price.

**MAP 2:** 207 E. Gordon St., 912/201-5070, www.massieschool.com; Mon.-Sat. 10am-4pm, Sun. noon-4pm; $9 adults, $7 youth

### WESLEY MONUMENTAL UNITED METHODIST CHURCH

The Wesley Monumental United Methodist Church, named not only for movement founder John Wesley but also for his musical younger brother Charles, is home to Savannah's first Methodist parish. Built in 1875 on the model of Queen's Kirk in Amsterdam and the fourth incarnation of the parish home, this is another great example of Savannah's Gothic churches. Its acoustically wonderful sanctuary features a magnificent Noack organ, which would no doubt please the picky ears of Charles Wesley himself, author of the lyrics to "Hark! The Herald Angels Sing."

**MAP 2:** 429 Abercorn St., 912/232-0191, www.wesleymonumental.org; sanctuary daily 9am-5pm, services Sun. 8:45am and 11am

## Martin Luther King Jr. Boulevard

### BATTLEFIELD PARK

Right off MLK Jr. Boulevard is Battlefield Park, a.k.a. the Spring Hill Redoubt, a reconstruction of the British fortifications at the Siege of Savannah, with an interpretive site. Recent archaeology discovered the actual location of the original redoubt, and it is also recreated about 100 yards west. Eight hundred granite markers signify the battle's casualties, most of whom were buried in mass graves soon afterward. Sadly, most of the remains of these brave men were simply bulldozed up and discarded without ceremony during later construction projects.

**MAP 2:** Corner of MLK Jr. Blvd. and Louisville Rd.; dawn-dusk; free

### GEORGIA STATE RAILROAD MUSEUM

The Georgia State Railroad Museum, a.k.a. "The Roundhouse," is an ongoing homage to the deep and strangely underreported influence of the railroad industry on Savannah. Constructed in 1830 for the brand-new Central of Georgia line, the Roundhouse's design was cutting-edge for the time, the first building to put all the railroad's key facilities in one place. Spared by Sherman, the site saw its heyday after the Civil War. The highlight of the Roundhouse is the thing in the middle that gave the structure its name, a huge central turntable for positioning rolling stock for repair and maintenance. Frequent demonstrations occur with an actual steam locomotive firing up and taking a spin on the turntable.

**MAP 2:** 601 W. Harris St., 912/651-6823, www.chsgeorgia.org; daily 9am-5pm; $10 adults, $6 students

### SAVANNAH CHILDREN'S MUSEUM

Next to the Railroad Museum is the Savannah Children's Museum, open since 2012. The children's museum is a work in progress that currently has an outdoor "Exploration Station" and a pending larger facility.

**MAP 2:** 655 Louisville Rd., 912/651-6823, www.savannahchildrensmuseum.org; summer Mon.-Sat. 9am-2pm, school year Wed.-Sat. 10am-4pm; $7.50

### RALPH MARK GILBERT CIVIL RIGHTS MUSEUM

One of the former black-owned bank buildings on MLK Jr. Boulevard is now home to the Ralph Mark Gilbert Civil Rights Museum. Named for a pastor of the First African Baptist Church and a key early civil rights organizer, the building was also the local NAACP headquarters for a time. Three floors of exhibits here include photos and interactive displays, the highlight for historians being a fiber-optic map of nearly 100 significant civil rights sites. The first floor features a re-creation of the Azalea Room of the local Levy's department store, an early boycott diner where blacks were not allowed to eat, though they could buy goods from the store. The second floor is more for hands-on education, with classrooms, a computer room, and a video and reading room. A film chronicles mass meetings, voter registration drives, boycotts, sit-ins, kneel-ins (the integration of churches), and wade-ins (the integration of beaches).

**MAP 2:** 460 MLK Jr. Blvd., 912/231-8900; Tues.-Sat. 10am-4pm; $10

### SAVANNAH HISTORY MUSEUM

The Savannah History Museum is the first stop for many a visitor to town because it's in the same restored Central of Georgia passenger shed as the visitors center. It contains many interesting exhibits on local history, concentrating mostly on colonial times. Toward the rear of the museum is a room for rotating exhibits, as well as one of Johnny Mercer's four Oscars, and, of course, the historic "Forrest Gump bench" that Tom Hanks sat on during his scenes in Chippewa Square.

**MAP 2:** 303 MLK Jr. Blvd., 912/651-6825, www.chsgeorgia.org; daily 9am-5:30pm; $7 adults, $4 children

### SCAD MUSEUM OF ART

In 2011, the Savannah College of Art and Design Museum of Art expanded this handsome building into an old railroad facility immediately behind it, more than doubling its exhibition space and adding the impressive Walter O. Evans Collection of African American Art. The SCAD Museum of Art now hosts a rotating series of exhibits, from standard painting to video installations, many of them commissioned by the school itself.

**MAP 2:** 601 Turner Blvd., 912/525-5220, www.scadmoa.org; Tues.-Wed. and Fri.-Sat. 10am-5pm, Thurs. 10am-8pm, Sun. noon-5pm; $10 adults, $5 students

## VICTORIAN DISTRICT

### CARNEGIE BRANCH LIBRARY

The Carnegie Branch Library is the only example of prairie architecture in town, designed by Savannah architect Julian de Bruyn Kops and built, as the name implies, with funding from tycoon-philanthropist Andrew Carnegie in 1914. But more importantly, the Carnegie Library was for decades the only public library for African Americans in Savannah. One of its patrons was a young Clarence Thomas, who would grow up to be a U.S. Supreme Court justice.

**MAP 3:** 537 E. Henry St., 912/652-3600, www.liveoakpl.org; Mon. 10am-8pm, Tues.-Thurs. 10am-6pm, Fri. 2pm-6pm, Sat. 10am-6pm

### ★ FORSYTH PARK

A favorite with locals and visitors alike, the vast, lush expanse of Forsyth Park is a center of local life. Deeply influenced by the then-trendy design of green-space areas in France, Forsyth Park's landscape design by William Bischoff dates to 1851. Named for Georgia governor John Forsyth, the park covers 30 acres, and its perimeter is about a mile.

Near the center of the park is the "fort," actually a revitalized version of an old dummy

# Walking Tour of Forsyth Park

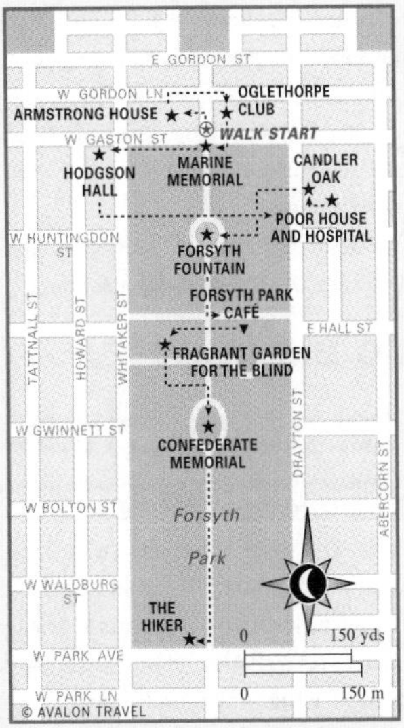

As you approach the park, don't miss the ornate ironwork on the west side of Bull Street marking the **Armstrong House,** designed by Henrik Wallin. Featured in the 1962 film *Cape Fear* as well as 1997's *Midnight in the Garden of Good and Evil,* this Italianate mansion was once home to Armstrong Junior College before its move to the city's south side. Directly across Bull Street is another site of *Midnight* fame, the **Oglethorpe Club,** one of the many brick and terra-cotta designs by local architect Alfred Eichberg.

It's easy to miss, but as you enter the park's north side, you encounter the **Marine Memorial,** erected in 1947 to honor the 24 Chatham County Marines killed in World War II. Subsequently, the names of Marines killed in Korea and Vietnam were added. Look west at the corner of Whitaker and Gaston Streets; that's **Hodgson Hall,** home of the Georgia Historical Society. This 1876 building was commissioned by Margaret Telfair to honor her late husband, William Hodgson.

Looking east at the corner of Drayton and Gaston Streets, you'll see the old **Poor House and Hospital,** in use until 1854, when it was converted to serve as the headquarters for the Medical College of Georgia. During the Civil War, General Sherman used the hospital to treat Federal soldiers. From 1930 to 1980 the building was the site of Candler Hospital. Behind the old hospital's cast-iron fence is Savannah's most famous tree, the 300-year-old **Candler Oak.** During Sherman's occupation, wounded Confederate prisoners were treated within a barricade around the oak. The tree is in the National Register of Historic Trees and was the maiden preservation project of the Savannah Tree Foundation, which secured the country's first-ever conservation easement on a single tree.

Walking south into the park proper, you can't miss the world-famous **Forsyth Fountain,** an iconic Savannah sight. Cast in iron on a French model, the fountain was dedicated in 1858. Two other versions of this fountain exist—one in Poughkeepsie, New York, and the other in, of all places, the central plaza in Cusco, Peru.

Continuing south, you'll encounter two low buildings in the center of the park. The one on the east side is the so-called "Dummy Fort," circa 1909, formerly a training ground for local militia. Now it's the **Forsyth Park Café** (daily 7am-dusk). To the west is the charming **Fragrant Garden for the Blind.** One of those precious little Savannah gems that is too often overlooked, the Fragrant Garden was initially sponsored by the local Garden Club and based on others of its type throughout the United States.

The tall monument dominating Forsyth Park's central mall is the **Confederate Memorial.** Dedicated in 1875, it wasn't finished until several years later. A New York sculptor carved the Confederate soldier atop the monument. In the wake of national controversies involving such memorials, more inclusive and descriptive signage will be added to expand the historical story told at the site.

My favorite Forsyth Park landmark is at the extreme southern end. It's the Memorial to Georgia Veterans of the Spanish-American War, more commonly known as ***The Hiker*** because of the subject's casual demeanor and confident stride. Savannah was a major staging area for the 1898 conflict, and many troops were bivouacked in the park. Sculpted in 1902 by Alice Ruggles Kitson, more than 50 replicas of *The Hiker* were made and put up all over the United States.

fort used for military drills in the early 20th century, except these days there is a public restroom.

The park is a center of activities all year long, from free festivals to concerts to Ultimate Frisbee games to the constant circuit around the periphery of walkers, joggers, dog owners, and bicyclists. The only time you shouldn't venture into the park is late at night; otherwise, enjoy.

**MAP 3:** Bordered by Drayton St., Gaston St., Whitaker St., and Park Ave., 912/351-3850; daily 8am-dusk

## SOFO DISTRICT

**TOP EXPERIENCE**

### LAUREL GROVE CEMETERY

Its natural vista isn't as alluring as Bonaventure Cemetery's, but Laurel Grove Cemetery boasts its own exquisitely carved memorials and a distinctly Victorian type of surreal beauty that not even Bonaventure can match. In keeping with the racial apartheid of Savannah's early days, there are actually two cemeteries: **Laurel Grove North** (802 W. Anderson St.) for whites, and **Laurel Grove South** (2101 Kollock St.) for blacks. Both are well worth visiting.

By far the most high-profile plot in the North Cemetery is that of Juliette Gordon Low, founder of the Girl Scouts of the USA. Other historically significant sites there include the graves of 8th Air Force founder Frank O. Hunter, Central of Georgia Railway founder William Gordon, and "Jingle Bells" composer James Pierpont. But it's the graves of the anonymous and near-anonymous that are the most poignant sights. The various sections for infants, known as "babylands," cannot fail to move. "Mr. Bones," a former Savannah police dog, is the only animal buried at Laurel Grove. There's an entire site reserved for victims of the great yellow fever epidemic. And don't blink or you'll miss the small rock pile, or cairn, near Governor James Jackson's tomb, the origin and purpose of which remains a mystery. Make sure to view the otherworldly display of Victorian statuary, originally from the grand Greenwich Plantation, which burned in the early 20th century. As with Bonaventure, throughout Laurel Grove you'll find examples of so-called "slave tiles," actually Victorian garden tiles, lining gravesites.

Laurel Grove South features the graves of Savannah's early black Baptist ministers, such as Andrew Bryan and Andrew Cox Marshall.

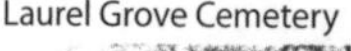

Laurel Grove Cemetery

Some of the most evocative gravesites are those of African Americans who obtained their freedom and built prosperous lives for themselves and their families. The vast majority of local firefighters in the 1800s were African Americans, and their simple graves are among the most touching, such as the headstone for one known simply as "August," who died fighting a fire.

To get to Laurel Grove North, take MLK Jr. Boulevard to Anderson Street and turn west. To get to Laurel Grove South, take Victory Drive (U.S. 80) west to Ogeechee Road. Take a right onto Ogeechee, then a right onto West 36th Street. Continue on to Kollock Street.

**MAP 3:** 802 W. Anderson St. and 2101 Kollock St.; daily 8am-5pm; free

## SOUTHSIDE

### ISLE OF HOPE

A charming, friendly seaside community and National Historic District, Isle of Hope is one of a dwindling number of places where parents still let their kids ride around all day on bikes, calling them in at dinnertime. It doesn't boast many shops or restaurants—indeed, the marina is the only real business—but the row of waterfront cottages on Bluff Drive should not be missed. You might recognize some of them from movies such as *Forrest Gump* and *Glory.* Built from 1880 to 1920, they reflect Isle of Hope's reputation as a healing area and serene Wilmington River getaway from Savannah's capitalist hustle.

To get to Isle of Hope, take Victory Drive (U.S. 80) east and take a right on Skidaway Road. Continue south on Skidaway Road and take a left on Laroche Avenue. Continue until you hit Bluff Drive.

**MAP 4:** 10 miles south of Savannah

### WORMSLOE STATE HISTORIC SITE

The one-of-a-kind Wormsloe State Historic Site was first settled by Noble Jones, who landed with Oglethorpe on the *Anne* and fought beside him in the War of Jenkins' Ear. One of the great renaissance men of history, this soldier was also an accomplished carpenter, surveyor, forester, botanist, and physician. Wormsloe became famous for its bountiful gardens, so much so that the famed naturalist William Bartram mentioned them in his diary after a visit in 1765 with father John Bartram. After his death, Noble Jones was originally buried in the family plot on the waterfront, but now his remains are at Bonaventure Cemetery. Jones's descendants donated 822 acres of Wormsloe to the Nature Conservancy, which transferred the property to the state. The house, dating from 1828, and 65.5 acres of land are still owned by his family.

The stunning entrance canopy of 400 live oaks, Spanish moss dripping down the entire length, is one of those iconic images of Savannah that will stay with you forever. A small interpretive museum, a one-mile nature walk, and occasional living-history demonstrations make this a great site for the entire family. Walk all the way to the Jones Narrows to see the ruins of the site's original 1739 fortification, one of the oldest and finest examples of tabby construction in the United States. No doubt the area's abundance of Native American shell middens, where early inhabitants discarded their oyster shells, came in handy for its construction. You can see one nearby.

To get to Wormsloe, take Victory Drive (U.S. 80) to Skidaway Road. Go south on Skidaway Road for about 10 miles and follow the signs; you'll see the grand entrance on the right.

**MAP 4:** 7601 Skidaway Rd., 912/353-3023, www.gastateparks.org/wormsloe; Tues.-Sun. 9am-5pm; $10 adults, $4.50 children

### Pin Point

Off Whitefield Avenue (Diamond Causeway) on the route to Skidaway Island is tiny Pin Point, a predominantly African American township better known as the boyhood home of Supreme Court justice Clarence Thomas. Pin Point traces its roots to a community of formerly enslaved people on Ossabaw Island. Displaced by a hurricane, they settled at this idyllic site overlooking the Moon River, itself a former plantation.

## Pin Point on the Moon River

On Ossabaw Island, formerly enslaved people had settled into freedom as subsistence farmers after the Civil War. But when a massive hurricane devastated the island in 1893, many moved to the mainland, south of Savannah along what would later be known as Moon River, to a place called Pin Point. While many continued farming, plenty gained employment at local factories, where crabs and oysters were packed and sold. The largest and longest-lived of those factories was A. S. Varn & Son, which employed nearly 100 Pin Point residents—about half of the adult population.

Because so many local people worked at the same place, Pin Point developed a strong community bond, one that was instrumental in forging the life and career of future Supreme Court justice Clarence Thomas, who was born at Pin Point in 1948. Until he was seven, Thomas lived in a tiny house there with his parents, one without plumbing and insulated with newspapers. After a house fire, Thomas moved to Savannah with his grandparents.

While times have certainly changed here—paved roads finally came in the 1970s, and most of the old shotgun shacks have been replaced with mobile homes—Pin Point remains a small, close-knit community of about 300 people, with most property still owned by descendants of the freedmen who bought it after Reconstruction. The Varn factory remained the economic heart of Pin Point until it shut down in 1985. Today, the old factory forms the heart of an ambitious new project, the **Pin Point Heritage Museum** (www.pinpointheritagemuseum.com), which conveys the spirit and history of that community, including its most famous native son, through a series of exhibits and demonstrations.

### PIN POINT HERITAGE MUSEUM

Many Pin Point residents made their living by shucking oysters at the Varn Oyster Company, the central shed of which still remains and forms the basis of the Pin Point Heritage Museum, opened in 2012. The museum tells the story of the Pin Point community through exhibits, a film, and demonstrations of some of the maritime activities at the Varn Oyster Company through the decades, such as crabbing, canning, shucking, and shrimp-net making.

**MAP 4:** 9924 Pin Point Ave., http://chsgeorgia.org/PHM; Thurs.-Sat. 9am-5pm; $8 adults, $4 children

## Skidaway Island

Skidaway Island is notable for two beautiful and educational nature-oriented sites.

### SKIDAWAY ISLAND STATE PARK

A site of interest to visitors is Skidaway Island State Park. You can camp here ($25-28), but the awesome nature trails leading out to the marsh—featuring an ancient Native American shell midden and an old whiskey still—are worth a trip on their own, especially when combined with the Marine Educational Center and Aquarium. To get here, take Victory Drive (U.S. 80) until you get to Waters Avenue and continue south as it turns into Whitefield Avenue and then the Diamond Causeway. The park is on your left after the drawbridge. An alternative route from downtown is to take the Truman Parkway all the way to its dead end at Whitefield Avenue; then take a left on Whitefield and continue as it turns into Diamond Causeway where it enters Skidaway.

**MAP 4:** 52 Diamond Causeway, 912/598-2300, www.gastateparks.org; daily 7am-10pm; parking $5

### UNIVERSITY OF GEORGIA MARINE EDUCATIONAL CENTER AND AQUARIUM

The University of Georgia Marine Educational Center and Aquarium shares a picturesque 700-acre campus on the scenic Skidaway River with the research-oriented Skidaway Institute of Oceanography, also University of Georgia (UGA) affiliated. It hosts scientists and grad students from around the nation, often for trips on its research vessel, the RV *Sea Dawg*. The main attraction of the Marine Center is the small but well-done and recently upgraded aquarium featuring 14 tanks with 200 live animals.

**MAP 4:** 30 Ocean Science Circle, 912/598-3474, http://gacoast.uga.edu; Mon.-Fri. 9am-4pm, Sat. 10am-5pm; $6 adults, $4 children, cash only

## EASTSIDE

TOP EXPERIENCE

### ★ BONAVENTURE CEMETERY

On the banks of the Wilmington River just east of town lies one of Savannah's most distinctive sights, Bonaventure Cemetery. John Muir wrote of Bonaventure's Spanish moss-bedecked beauty in his 1867 book *A Thousand-mile Walk to the Gulf.* While its pedigree as Savannah's premier public cemetery goes back 100 years, it was used as a burial ground as early as 1794. In the years since, this achingly poignant vista of live oaks and azaleas has been the final resting place of such local and national luminaries as Johnny Mercer, Conrad Aiken, Noble Jones, and, of course, the Trosdal plot, former home of the famous *Bird Girl* statue (the original is now in the Telfair Academy of Arts and Sciences). Fittingly, the late great Jack Leigh, who took the *Bird Girl* photo for the cover of *Midnight in the Garden of Good and Evil,* is interred here as well.

If you're doing a self-guided tour, go by the small visitors center at the entrance and pick up one of the free guides to the cemetery, assembled by the Bonaventure Historical Society. By all means, do the tourist thing and pay your respects at Johnny Mercer's final resting place, and go visit beautiful little "Gracie" in Section E, Lot 99. But I also suggest doing as the locals do: Bring a picnic lunch and a blanket and set yourself beside the breezy banks of the Wilmington River, taking in all the lazy beauty and evocative bygone history surrounding you.

To get here from downtown, take the President Street Extension east and take a right on Pennsylvania Avenue, then a left on Bonaventure Road. Alternatively, go east on Victory Drive (U.S. 80) and take a left on Whatley Road in the town of Thunderbolt. Veer left onto Bonaventure Road. The cemetery is one mile ahead on the right.

**MAP 4:** 330 Bonaventure Rd., 912/651-6843; daily 8am-5pm; free

### DAFFIN PARK

A century spent in Forsyth Park's more genteel shadow doesn't diminish the importance of Daffin Park as Savannah's second major green space. Daffin not only hosts a large variety of local athletes on its fields and courts, but the park's east end is the setting for Historic Grayson Stadium, home of the Savannah Bananas college summer league team. One of the great old ballparks of America, this venue dates from 1941 and has hosted greats such as Babe Ruth, Jackie Robinson, and Mickey Mantle.

Most picturesque for the visitor, however, is the massive fountain set in the middle of the expansive central pond on the park's west side. Originally built in the shape of the continental United States, the pond was the backdrop for a presidential visit by Franklin D. Roosevelt in 1933 that included a speech to an African American crowd. On the far west end of Daffin Park along Waters Avenue is a marker commemorating the site of the grandstand for the Great Savannah Races of 1911.

**MAP 4:** 1500 E. Victory Dr.; daily dawn-dusk

### OATLAND ISLAND WILDLIFE CENTER

The closest thing to a zoo in Savannah is the vast, multipurpose Oatland Island Wildlife Center. Set on a former Centers for Disease Control site, it has undergone an extensive environmental cleanup and is now owned by the local school system, although supported purely by donations. Families by the hundreds come here for a number of special Saturdays throughout the year, including an

## Johnny Mercer's Black Magic

The great Johnny Mercer is not only without a doubt Savannah's most noteworthy progeny, he is also one of the greatest lyricists music has ever known. Born in 1909, he grew up in Southside Savannah on a small river then called the Back River but since renamed Moon River in honor of his best-known song.

Armed with an innate talent for rhythm and a curious ear for dialogue—both qualities honed by his frequent boyhood contact with Savannah African American culture and musicians during the Jazz Age—Mercer wrote what is arguably his greatest song, "Moon River," in 1961. The song, debuted by Audrey Hepburn in the film *Breakfast at Tiffany's,* won an Academy Award for Best Original Song. In addition to "Moon River," Mercer won three other Oscars, for "On the Atchison, Topeka and the Santa Fe" (1946), "In the Cool, Cool, Cool of the Evening" (1951), and "Days of Wine and Roses" (1962).

Today you can pay your respects to Mercer in three places: his boyhood home (509 E. Gwinnett St., look for the historical marker in front of this private residence); the bronze sculpture of Mercer in the revitalized Ellis Square near City Market; and at his gravesite in beautiful Bonaventure Cemetery. And regardless of what anyone tells you, neither Johnny Mercer nor any member of his family ever lived in the Mercer-Williams House on Monterey Square, of *Midnight in the Garden of Good and Evil* fame. Although it was built for his great-grandfather, the home was sold to someone else before it was completed.

old-fashioned cane grinding in November and a day of sheep shearing in April.

The main attractions here are the critters, located at various points along a meandering two-mile nature trail through the woods and along the marsh. All animals at Oatland are there because they're somehow unable to return to the wild. Highlights include a tight-knit pack of eastern wolves, a pair of bison, cougars (once indigenous to the region), some really cute foxes, and an extensive raptor aviary. Kids will love the petting zoo of farm animals, some of which are free to roam the grounds at will.

**MAP 4:** 711 Sandtown Rd., 912/898-3980, www.oatlandisland.org; daily 10am-5pm; $5 adults, $3 children

### OLD FORT JACKSON

The oldest standing brick fort in Georgia, Old Fort Jackson, named for Georgia governor James Jackson (1798-1801), is also one of eight remaining examples of the so-called Second System of American forts built prior to the War of 1812. Its main claim to fame is its supporting role in the saga of the CSS *Georgia,* a Confederate ironclad now resting under 40 feet of water directly in front of the fort. The *Georgia*, wrapped in an armor girdle of rails, proved too heavy for its engine, so it was simply anchored in the channel opposite Fort Jackson as a floating battery. With General Sherman's arrival in 1864, Confederate forces evacuating to South Carolina scuttled the vessel where it lay to keep it out of Yankee hands.

Operated by the nonprofit Coastal Heritage Society, Fort Jackson is in an excellent state of preservation and provides loads of information for history buffs as well as for kids, who will enjoy climbing the parapets and running on the large parade ground (this area was once a rice field). Inside the fort's casemates underneath the ramparts you'll find well-organized exhibits on the fort's construction and history. Most visitors especially love the daily cannon firings during the summer. If you're really lucky, you'll be around when Fort Jackson fires a salute to passing military vessels on the river—the only historic fort in the United States that does so.

To get to Fort Jackson, take the President Street Extension (Islands Expressway) east out of downtown. The entrance is several miles down on the left.

**MAP 4:** Fort Jackson Rd., 912/232-3945, http://chsgeorgia.org; daily 9am-5pm; $8 adults, $4 children

### Thunderbolt

Near the Bonaventure Cemetery is the little fishing village of Thunderbolt, almost as old as Savannah itself. According to Oglethorpe, the town was named after "a rock which was here shattered by a thunderbolt, causing a spring to gush from the ground, which continued ever afterward to emit the odor of brimstone."

#### SAVANNAH STATE UNIVERSITY

Continue on River Road and you'll soon be at the entrance to Savannah State University. This historically black university began life in 1890 as the Georgia State Industrial College for Colored Youth. Famous graduates include NFL great Shannon Sharpe. The main landmark is the newly restored Hill Hall, a 1901 building featured in the film *The General's Daughter.*

**MAP 4:** 3219 College St., 912/356-2186, www.savstate.edu

#### THUNDERBOLT MUSEUM

Just off Victory Drive is the Thunderbolt Museum, housed in the humble former town hall. Cross Victory Drive onto River Road and notice how the road is built around the live oak tree in the middle of it. Most of the nice views of the river have been obscured by high-rise condos, but there's a cute public fishing pier.

**MAP 4:** Victory Dr. and Mechanics Ave., 912/351-0836, http://thunderboltmuseum.org; Wed.-Thurs. 9am-4pm, Sat. 1pm-5pm; free

## TYBEE ISLAND

Its name means "salt" in the old Euchee tongue, indicative of the island's chief export in those days. Eighteen miles and about a half-hour drive from Savannah, in truth Tybee is part and parcel of the city's social and cultural fabric. Many of the island's 3,000 full-time residents, known for their boozy bonhomie and quirky personal style, commute to work in the city.

Its wide, beautiful beaches are lined with rare sea oats waving in the Atlantic breeze. The entire island has become a focal point of Georgia's booming film industry. The 2017 reboot of *Baywatch* with Dwayne "the Rock" Johnson was filmed on Tybee's beach, as was the Miley Cyrus film *The Last Song.*

#### ★ FORT PULASKI NATIONAL MONUMENT

There's one must-see before you get to Tybee Island proper. On Cockspur Island you'll find Fort Pulaski National Monument, a delight for any history buff. The pleasure starts when you cross the drawbridge over the moat and see a cannon pointed at you from a narrow gun port. Enter the inside of the fort and take in just how big it is—Union occupiers regularly played baseball on the huge, grassy parade ground. Take a walk around the perimeter, underneath the ramparts. This is where the soldiers lived and worked, and you'll see recreations of officers' quarters, meeting areas, sick rooms, and prisoners' bunks among the cannons, where Confederate prisoners of war were held after the fort's surrender. Cannon firings happen most Saturdays.

And now for the pièce de résistance: Take the steep corkscrew staircase up to the ramparts themselves and take in the jaw-dropping view of the lush marsh, with the Savannah River and Tybee Island spreading out in the distance. (Warning: There's no railing of any kind on the inboard side of the ramparts. Keep the kids well back from the edge.) Afterward, take a stroll all the way around the walls and see the power of those Yankee guns. Though much of the devastation was soon repaired, some sections of the wall remain in their damaged state. You can even pick out a few cannonballs still stuck in the masonry.

Save some time and energy for the extensive palmetto-lined nature trail through the sandy upland of Cockspur Island on which the fort is located. There are informative markers, a picnic area, and, as a bonus, a coastal defense facility from the Spanish-American War, Battery Hambright.

## The Siege of Fort Pulaski

Fort Pulaski

Fort Pulaski's construction was part of a broader initiative by President James Madison in the wake of the War of 1812, which dramatically revealed the shortcomings of U.S. coastal defense. Based on state-of-the-art European design forged in the cauldron of the Napoleonic Wars, Fort Pulaski's thick masonry construction used 25 million bricks, many of them of the famous "Savannah Gray" variety handmade at the nearby Hermitage Plantation.

When Georgia seceded from the Union in January 1861, a small force of Confederates immediately took control of Fort Pulaski and Fort Jackson. In early 1862 a Union sea-land force came to covertly lay the groundwork for a siege of Fort Pulaski. The siege would rely on several batteries secretly set up across the Savannah River. Some of the Union guns utilized new rifled-chamber technology, which dramatically increased the accuracy, muzzle velocity, and penetrating power of their shells. The Union barrage began at 8:15am on April 10, 1862, and Fort Pulaski's walls crumbled under the withering fire. At least one shell struck a powder magazine, igniting an enormous explosion. After 30 hours, Confederate general Charles Olmstead surrendered the fortress.

It was not only Fort Pulaski that was rendered obsolete—it was the whole concept of masonry fortification. From that point forward, military forts would rely on earthwork rather than brick. The section of earthwork you see as you enter Fort Pulaski, the "demilune," was added after the Civil War.

Continue east on U.S. 80, passing over Lazaretto Creek, named for the quarantine, or "lazaretto," built in the late 1700s to make sure newcomers, mostly enslaved people, were free of disease. As you cross, look to your left over the river's wide south channel. On a tiny oyster shell islet, find the little **Cockspur Beacon** lighthouse, in use from 1848 to 1909, when major shipping was routed through the deeper north channel of the river. The site is now preserved by the National Park Service and is accessible only by boat or kayak. You have to time your arrival with the right tide; check with a local rental place for advice.

**MAP 5:** U.S. 80 E., 912/786-5787, www.nps.gov/fopu; daily 9am-5pm; $7, free under age 16

### SOUTH END

Butler Avenue is Tybee's main drag, the beach fully public and accessible from any of the numbered side streets on the left. Go all the way down to **Tybrisa Street** (formerly 16th St.) to get a flavor of old Tybee. Here's where you'll find the old five-and-dimes like T. S. Chu's, still a staple of local life, and little diners, ice cream spots, and taverns. The new pride of the island is the large, long pier structure called the **Tybrisa Pavilion II,** built in 1996 in an attempt to recreate the lost glory of the Tybrisa Pavilion, social and spiritual center of the island's gregarious resort days. Built in 1891 by the Central of Georgia Railway, the Tybrisa hosted name entertainers and big bands on its expansive dance floor. Sadly, fire destroyed it in 1967, an enormous blow to area morale.

**MAP 5:** Butler Ave.

### TYBEE ISLAND MARINE SCIENCE CENTER

At the foot of the Tybrisa Pavilion is the little Tybee Island Marine Science Center, with nine aquariums and a touch tank featuring native species. Here is the nerve center for the Tybee Island Sea Turtle Project, an ongoing effort to document and preserve the local comings and goings of the island's most beloved inhabitant and unofficial mascot, the endangered sea turtle.

**MAP 5:** 1510 Strand Ave., 912/786-5917, www.tybeemarinescience.org; daily 10am-5pm; $4 adults, $3 children

### TYBEE ISLAND LIGHT STATION AND MUSEUM

At North Campbell Avenue is the entrance to the less-populated, more historically significant north end of Tybee Island, once almost entirely taken up by Fort Screven, a coastal defense fortification of the early 1900s. Rebuilt several times in its history, the Tybee Island Light Station traces its construction to the first year of the colony, based on a design by the multitalented Noble Jones. At its completion in 1736, it was the tallest structure in the United States. One of a handful of working 18th-century lighthouses today, the facility has been restored to its 1916-1964 incarnation, featuring a nine-foot-tall first-order Fresnel lens installed in 1867.

All the outbuildings on the lighthouse grounds are original, including the residence

## The Tybee Bomb

On a dark night in 1958, at the height of the Cold War, a USAF B-47 Stratojet bomber made a simulated nuclear bombing run over southeast Georgia. A Charleston-based F-86 fighter on a mock intercept came too close, clipping the bomber's wing. Before bringing down the wounded B-47 at Savannah's Hunter Airfield, Commander Howard Richardson decided to jettison his lethal cargo: a 7,000-pound Mark 15 hydrogen bomb, serial number 47782. Richardson, who won the Distinguished Flying Cross for his efforts that night, jettisoned the bomb over water. What no one knows is exactly where. And thus began the legend of "the Tybee Bomb." Speculation ran wild, with some locals fearing a nuclear explosion, radioactive contamination, or even that a team of scuba-diving terrorists would secretly retrieve the weapon.

Commander Richardson, now retired, says the bomb wasn't armed when he jettisoned it. Environmentalists say that doesn't matter, because the enriched uranium the Air Force admits was in the bomb is toxic whether or not there's the risk of a nuclear detonation. People who work in the fishing industry on Tybee say the fact that the bomb also had 400 pounds of high explosive "nuclear trigger" is reason enough to get it out of the waterways.

The Air Force has made several attempts to locate the weapon. In 2000 it sent a team to Savannah to find the bomb, concluding it was buried somewhere off the coast in 5 to 15 feet of mud. In 2005, in another attempt to find the weapon, it sent another team of experts down to look one last time. Their verdict: The bomb's still lost.

of the lighthouse keeper, also the oldest building on the island. If you've got the legs and the lungs, definitely take all 178 steps up to the top of the lighthouse for a stunning view of Tybee, the Atlantic, and Hilton Head Island.

All around the area of the north end around the lighthouse complex you'll see low-lying concrete bunkers. These are remains of Fort Screven's coastal defense batteries, and many are in private hands. Battery Garland is open to tours, and also houses the Tybee Island Museum, a charming, almost whimsical little collection of exhibits from various eras of local history.

One entrance fee gives you admission to the lighthouse, the lighthouse museum, and the Tybee Island Museum.

**MAP 5:** 30 Meddin Ave., 912/786-5801, www.tybeelighthouse.org; Wed.-Mon. 9am-5:30pm, last ticket sold 4:30pm; $9 adults, $7 children

### TYBEE POST THEATER

The new pride of the north end is the Tybee Post Theater, a fully restored performing arts venue that was once, as the name implies, the theater for the Fort Screven military facility. The small but cozy 200-seat space now offers a range of programming from live music to live theater to film screenings, the latter its original purpose when built in 1930. Indeed, the theater was one of the first in Georgia to host the new "talkie" films.

**MAP 5:** 10 Van Horne Ave., 912/472-4790, www.tybeeposttheater.org; prices vary

## GREATER SAVANNAH

### Midway and Liberty County

Locals will tell you that Midway is named because it's equidistant from the Savannah and Altamaha Rivers on Oglethorpe's old "river road," which it certainly is, but others say the small but very historic town is actually named after the Medway River in England. In seeking to pacify the local Creek people, the Council of Georgia in 1752 granted a group of Massachusetts Puritans then residing in Dorchester, South Carolina, a 32,000-acre land grant as incentive to move south. After moving into Georgia and establishing New Dorchester, they soon founded a nearby settlement that would later take on the modern spelling of Midway. Midway's citizens were very aggressive early on in the cause for American independence, which is why the area's three original parishes were combined and named Liberty County in 1777—the only Georgia county named for a concept rather than a person. Two of Georgia's three signers

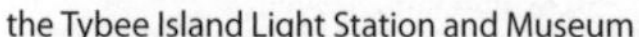
the Tybee Island Light Station and Museum

of the Declaration of Independence, Lyman Hall and Button Gwinnett, resided primarily in Midway, and both attended the historic Midway Church. A key part of Liberty County history is no more: The once-thriving seaport of Sunbury, which formerly challenged Savannah for economic supremacy in the region, no longer exists.

Tourism in this area has been made much more user-friendly by the liberal addition of signage for the "Liberty Trail," a collection of key attractions. When in doubt, follow the signs. The main highways in Midway are I-95, U.S. 17, and U.S. 84, also called Oglethorpe Highway, which becomes Highway 38 (Islands Hwy.) east of I-95.

### FORT MORRIS STATE HISTORIC SITE

Built to defend the once-proud port of Sunbury, Fort Morris State Historic Site was reconstructed during the War of 1812 and was an encampment during the Civil War. It was here that Colonel John McIntosh gave his famous reply to the British demand for his surrender: "Come and take it." The museum has displays of military and everyday life of the era. Reenactments and cannon firings are highlights. There's a visitors center and a nature trail. The site is about 50 minutes from Savannah. To get here, take exit 76 off I-95 south. Go east on Islands Highway and take a left on Fort Morris Road; the site is two miles down.

**MAP 6:** 2559 Ft. Morris Rd., 912/884-5999, www.gastateparks.org/fortmorris; Thurs.-Sat. 9am-5pm; $4.50 adults, $3 children

### GEECHEE KUNDA

A little way south of Midway on the Liberty Trail in tiny Riceboro is Geechee Kunda, a combination museum-outreach center on the site of the former Retreat rice and indigo plantation. It's now dedicated to explaining and exploring the culture of Sea Island African Americans on the Georgia coast. (Don't be confused: *Geechee* is the Georgia word for the Gullah people. Both groups share similar folkways and history, and the terms are virtually interchangeable.) There are artifacts from slavery and Reconstruction, including authentic Geechee relics. Geechee Kunda is about 40 minutes from Savannah. Take exit 67 off I-95 and head north about two miles on U.S. 17.

**MAP 6:** 622 Ways Temple Rd., Riceboro, 912/884-4440, www.geecheekunda.com; Tues.-Sat. 11am-5pm; free

the restored Tybee Post Theater

### MIDWAY MUSEUM

In Midway proper is the charming Midway Museum and the adjacent **Midway Church,** sometimes called the Midway Meetinghouse. The museum contains a variety of artifacts, most from the 18th and 19th centuries, and an extensive genealogy collection. The Midway Church, built in 1756, was burned during the Revolution but rebuilt in 1792. Both Button Gwinnett and Lyman Hall attended services here, and during the Civil War some of Sherman's cavalry set up camp on the grounds. The cemetery across the street is wonderfully poignant and is the final resting place of two Revolutionary War generals; Union cavalry kept horses within its walls. The museum, church, and cemetery are 30 miles from Savannah and easy to find: take exit 76 from I-95 south, and take a right on U.S. 84 (Oglethorpe Hwy.). Turn right on U.S. 17, and they're just ahead on the right.

**MAP 6:** 491 N. Coastal Hwy., 912/884-5837, www.themidwaymuseum.org; Tues.-Sat. 10am-4pm; adults $10, students $5

### SEABROOK VILLAGE

West off Islands Highway is Seabrook Village, a unique living-history museum chronicling the everyday life of Liberty County's African Americans, with a direct link to Sherman's famous "40 acres and a mule" Field Order No. 15. There are eight restored buildings on the 100-acre site, including the simple but sublime one-room Seabrook School. From Savannah, take exit 76 off I-95, and then a left onto U.S. 84. After about two miles, take a left onto Trade Hill Road.

**MAP 6:** 660 Trade Hill Rd., 912/884-7008; Tues. and Thurs. 10:30am-1:30pm; $3

## Ossabaw Island

### OSSABAW ISLAND

Owned and operated by Georgia as a heritage and wildlife preserve, the island was a gift to the state in 1978 from Eleanor Torrey-West and family, who still retain some property on the island. All public use of the island is managed by the **Ossabaw Island Foundation** (www.ossabawisland.org).

The 12,000-acre island is much older than Wassaw Island to its north and so has traces of human habitation back to 2000 BC. The island's name comes from an old Muskogean word referring to yaupon holly, found in abundance on the island and used by Native Americans in purification rituals to induce vomiting. There are several tabby ruins on the island, along with many miles of walking trails. Unlike the much-younger Wassaw, Ossabaw Island was not only timbered extensively but hosted several rice and cotton plantations.

Descendants of the island's enslaved workers moved to the Savannah area after the Civil War, founding the community of Pin Point. Similarly to Jekyll Island to the south, Ossabaw was a hunting preserve for wealthy families in the Roaring '20s. Even today, hunting is an important activity on the island, with lotteries choosing who gets a chance to pursue its overly large populations of deer and wild hogs, the latter of which are descended from pigs brought by the Spanish.

Now reserved exclusively for educational and scientific purposes, the island is accessible only by boat. Georgia law ensures public access to all beaches up to the high-tide mark—which simply means that the public can ride out to Ossabaw and go on the beach for day use, but any travel to the interior is restricted and you must have permission first. Contact the Ossabaw Island Foundation for information. Boat trips take about 1.5 hours and vary in price. Day trips can be arranged with charter operators at the marinas in Savannah.

**MAP 6:** Ossabaw Island, www.ossabawisland.org

## Wassaw Island

### WASSAW ISLAND NATIONAL WILDLIFE REFUGE

Unique in that it's the only Georgia barrier island never cleared for agriculture or development, the 10,000-acre Wassaw Island National Wildlife Refuge is accessible only by boat.

## Sunbury: Gone but Not Forgotten

If you spend much time in Liberty County, you'll probably hear someone mention that a certain place or person is "over near Sunbury." Such is the legacy of this long-gone piece of Georgia history that locals still refer to it in the present tense, though the old town itself is no more.

Founded soon after Midway in 1758, Sunbury rivaled Savannah as Georgia's main commercial port by 1761, with a thriving trade in lumber, rice, indigo, corn, and, unfortunately, enslaved people. At one time, seven square-rigged vessels called on the port in a single day.

At various times, all three of Georgia's signers of the Declaration of Independence—Button Gwinnett, Lyman Hall, and George Walton—had connections to Sunbury. The beginning of the end came with those heady days of revolution, however, when Sunbury was the scene of much fighting between colonists and the British army. A British siege in 1778 culminated in this immortal reply from the colonial commander, Colonel John McIntosh, to a redcoat demand for surrender: "Come and take it." By the beginning of 1779, a separate British assault did so.

After U.S. independence, Sunbury remained the Liberty County seat until 1797, but it was never the same, beset by decay, hurricanes, and yellow fever outbreaks. By 1848, nothing of the town remained but the old cemetery, which you can find a short drive from the Fort Morris State Historic Site; ask a park employee for directions.



There are striking driftwood-strewn beaches, and the interior of the island has some beautiful old-growth stands of longleaf pine and live oak. Wassaw is a veritable paradise for nature lovers and bird-watchers, with migratory activity in the spring and fall, waterfowl in abundance in the summer, and manatee and loggerhead turtle activity (about 10 percent of Georgia's transient loggerhead population makes use of Wassaw for nesting). There are also about 20 miles of trails and a decaying Spanish-American War-era battery, Fort Morgan, on the north end. National Wildlife Refuge Week is celebrated in October.

Because of its comparatively young status—it was formed only about 1,600 years ago—Wassaw Island also has some unique geographical features. You can still make out the parallel ridge features, vestiges of successive ancient shorelines. A central ridge forms the backbone of the island, reaching an amazing (for this area) elevation of 45 feet above sea level at the south end. Native Americans first settled the island, whose name comes from an ancient word for sassafras, which was found in abundance here. During the Civil War, both Confederate and Union troops occupied the island successively. In 1866 the wealthy New England businessman George Parsons bought the island, which stayed in that family's hands until it was sold to the Nature Conservancy in 1969 for $1 million. The Conservancy in turn sold Wassaw to the U.S. government for $1 to be managed as a wildlife refuge.

It's easiest to get to Wassaw Island from Savannah. Boat rides take roughly 30 minutes and cost around $50 round-trip. Charters and scheduled trips are available from **Captain Walt's Charters** (Thunderbolt Marina, 3124 River Dr., 912/507-3811, www.waltsadventure.com/charters), the **Bull River Marina** (8005 E. U.S. 80, 912/897-7300), **Delegal Marina** (1 Marina Dr., 912/598-0023), **Captain Joe Dobbs** (Delegal Marina, 1 Marina Dr., 912/598-0090, www.captjdobbs.com), and **Isle of Hope Marina** (50 Bluff Dr., 912/354-8187, www.isleofhopemarina.com). Most docking is either at the beaches on the north and south ends or in Wassaw Creek, where the U.S. Fish and Wildlife Service dock is also located (temporary mooring only). There's no camping allowed on Wassaw Island; it's for day use only.

**MAP 6:** Wassaw Island, www.fws.gov/wassaw; daily dawn-dusk

## The Salzburgers of New Ebenezer

Perhaps the most unsung chapter in Europe's great spiritual diaspora of the 1700s, the Salzburgers of New Ebenezer—a thrifty, peaceful, and hard-working people—were Georgia's first religious refugees and perhaps the most progressive as well. The year after Oglethorpe's arrival, a contingent of devout Lutherans from Salzburg in present-day Austria arrived after being expelled from their home country for their beliefs. Oglethorpe, mindful of Georgia's mission to provide sanctuary for persecuted Protestants and wishing for a military buffer to the west, eagerly welcomed them. Given land about 25 miles west of Savannah, the Salzburgers named their first settlement Ebenezer ("stone of help" in Hebrew). They later moved the site to better land nearer to the river and called it New Ebenezer, and so it remains to this day.

Because the settlers spoke German instead of English, the upriver colony maintained its isolation. Still, the Salzburgers were among Oglethorpe's most ardent and loyal supporters. Their pastor and de facto political leader, Johann Martin Boltzius, seeking to build an enlightened agrarian utopia, was an outspoken foe of slavery and the exploitative plantation system. The fragile silk industry thrived in New Ebenezer while it had failed miserably in Savannah, and the nation's first rice mill was built here.

The Trustees' turnover of Georgia to the crown in 1750 signaled the final victory of pro-slavery forces—even Pastor Boltzius acquired a couple of enslaved people as domestic servants. New Ebenezer's influence began a decline that accelerated when British forces pillaged much of the town in the Revolution. Fifty years later, nothing at all remained except the old Jerusalem Church, now the **Jerusalem Evangelical Lutheran Church.**

Although New Ebenezer is often called a "ghost town," this is a misnomer. Extensive archaeological work continues in the area, and the Georgia Salzburger Society works hard to maintain several historic buildings and keep the legacy alive through special events.

## West Chatham

### COASTAL GEORGIA BOTANICAL GARDENS AT THE HISTORIC BAMBOO FARM

A joint project of the University of Georgia and Chatham County, this farm is an education and demonstration center featuring a wide array of native species in addition to the garden's eponymous Asian "wonder weed," which has its roots in a private collection dating from the late 1800s. Many of the mature trees were planted in the 1930s. The garden also periodically holds you-pick-'em harvest days for berries. To get here, take exit 94 off of I-95 and take Highway 204 east toward Savannah. Turn right on East Gateway Boulevard, then left on Canebrake Road. Enter at the Canebrake gate. No pets are allowed on-site, even on a leash.

**MAP 6:** 2 Canebrake Rd., 912/921-5460, www.coastalgeorgiabg.org; Mon.-Fri. 8am-5pm, Sat. 10am-5pm, Sun. noon-5pm; $5 adults, $3 children

## Pooler

### ★ NATIONAL MUSEUM OF THE MIGHTY EIGHTH AIR FORCE

Military and aviation buffs should not miss the **National Museum of the Mighty Eighth Air Force** (175 Bourne Ave., Pooler, 912/748-8888, www.mightyeighth.org, daily 9am-5pm, $10 adults, $6 children and active-duty military) in Pooler, Georgia, right off I-95. The 8th Air Force was born at Hunter Field in Savannah as the 8th Bomber Command in 1942, becoming the 8th Air Force in 1944; it is now based in Louisiana.

A moving testament to the men and machines that conducted those strategic bombing campaigns over Europe in World War II, the museum also features later 8th Air Force history such as the Korean War, the Linebacker II bombing campaigns over North Vietnam, and the Persian Gulf. Inside you'll find airplanes like the P-51 Mustang and the German ME-109. The centerpiece, however, is the restored B-17 bomber *City of Savannah*, the newest jewel of the collection, acquired from the National Air and Space Museum in Washington DC.

**MAP 6:** 175 Bourne Ave., Pooler, 912/748-8888, www.mightyeighth.org; daily 9am-5pm; $12 adults, $8 children and active-duty military

## Richmond Hill and Bryan County

Known as the "town that Henry Ford built," Richmond Hill is a growing bedroom community of Savannah in adjacent Bryan County. Sherman's March to the Sea ended here with much destruction, so little history before that time is left. Most of what remains is due to Ford's philanthropic influence, still felt in many place-names around the area, including the main drag, Highway 144, known as Ford Avenue. After the auto magnate and his wife Clara made the area, then called Ways Station, a summer home, they were struck by the area's incredible poverty and determined to help improve living conditions, building hospitals, schools, churches, and homes. The Fords eventually acquired over 85,000 acres in Bryan County, including the former Richmond plantation. What is now known as Ford Plantation—currently a private luxury resort—was built in the 1930s and centered on the main house, once the central building of the famous Hermitage Plantation on the Savannah River, purchased and moved by Ford south to Bryan County.

### FORT MCALLISTER STATE HISTORIC SITE

Perhaps the main attraction in Richmond Hill, especially for Civil War buffs, is Fort McAllister State Historic Site. Unlike the masonry forts of Savannah, Fort McAllister is an all-earthwork fortification on the Ogeechee River, the site of a short but savage assault by Sherman's troops in December 1864 in which 5,000 Union soldiers quickly overwhelmed the skeleton garrison of 230 Confederate defenders. After the war, the site fell into disrepair until Henry Ford funded and spearheaded restoration in the 1930s, as he did with so many historic sites in Bryan County. The fort, which features many reenactments throughout the year, has a **Civil War Museum** (Mon.-Sat. 9am-5pm, Sun. 2pm-5pm, $5). An adjacent recreational site features a beautiful oak-lined picnic ground, a nature trail, and the nearby 65-site Savage Island Campground. Bryan County is just 15 minutes from Savannah. Take I-95 south and then exit 90. From there, head east about six miles on Highway 144 (Ford Dr.).

**MAP 6:** 3894 Ft. McAllister Rd., Richmond Hill, 912/727-2339, www.gastateparks.org; daily 7am-10pm; $7.50 adults, $4.50 children

### RICHMOND HILL HISTORICAL SOCIETY AND MUSEUM

The little Richmond Hill Historical Society and Museum is housed in a former kindergarten built by Henry Ford.

**MAP 6:** Ford Ave. and Timber Trail Rd., Richmond Hill, 912/756-3697; daily 10am-4pm; donation

## New Ebenezer

### JERUSALEM EVANGELICAL LUTHERAN CHURCH

Few people visit New Ebenezer today, west of Savannah in Effingham County. Truth is there's not much there anymore except for one old church, but, oh, what a church. The Jerusalem Evangelical Lutheran Church hosts the oldest continuous congregation in the United States. Built of local clay brick in 1769, its walls are 21 inches thick. Some original panes of glass remain, and its European bells are still rung before each service. Several surrounding structures are also heirs to New Ebenezer's Salzburg legacy.

**MAP 6:** 2966 Ebenezer Rd., Rincon, 912/754-3915, http://jerusalematebenezer.org; service Sun. 11am

### NEW EBENEZER RETREAT AND CONFERENCE CENTER

Around the corner from the Jerusalem Evangelical Lutheran Church is a much newer spiritually themed site, the New Ebenezer Retreat and Conference Center. Built in 1977, the retreat provides acres of calm surroundings, lodging, and meals in an ecumenical Christian setting.

The New Ebenezer Retreat and Conference Center offers a range of very reasonably priced lodgings, most including meals, in a beautiful setting. The extremely fast-growing town of Rincon, through which you will most likely drive on your way to New Ebenezer, offers an assortment of the usual chain food and lodging establishments.

While most facilities are for guests of the retreat, you can tour the grounds on your own. It's scenic and peaceful, and the cottages are charming.

**MAP 6:** 2887 Ebenezer Rd., Rincon, 912/754-9242, www.newebenezer.org



# Entertainment and Nightlife

Savannah is a hard-drinking town, and not just on St. Patrick's Day. The ability to legally walk downtown streets with beer, wine, or a cocktail in hand definitely contributes to the overall joie de vivre. Bars close in Savannah at 3am, a full hour later than in Charleston. A citywide indoor smoking ban is in effect, and you may not smoke cigarettes in any bar in Savannah.

## WATERFRONT

### Bars and Pubs

#### BAYOU CAFE

One of Savannah's favorite and most raucous historic taverns is possibly the River Street bar most visited by locals. The Bayou Cafe, overlooking River Street but situated on one of the cobblestone "ramps" going down from Bay Street to the waterfront, offers a convivial dive-bar type atmosphere and a solid Cajun-style pub food menu. The main floor is the traditional tavern, where the best local blues musicians play frequent gigs. The second floor is more of a game room and general younger folks' party area.

**MAP 1:** 4 N. Abercorn Ramp, 912/233-6411, daily 11am-3am

#### KEVIN BARRY'S IRISH PUB

The main landmark on the west end of River Street is the famous (or infamous, depending on which side of "The Troubles" you're on) Kevin Barry's Irish Pub, one of Savannah's most beloved establishments. KB's is open seven days a week, with evenings seeing performances by a number of Irish troubadours, all veterans of the East Coast trad circuit.

**MAP 1:** 117 W. River St., 912/233-9626, www.kevinbarrys.com; daily 11am-3am

#### ROCKS ON THE ROOF

One of the best hotel bars in the city is Rocks on the Roof, atop the Bohemian Hotel Savannah Riverfront on the waterfront. In good weather the exterior walls are opened up to reveal a large wraparound seating area with stunning views of downtown on one side and of the Savannah River on the other.

**MAP 1:** 102 W. Bay St., 912/721-3800; Fri.-Sat. 11am-1am, Sun.-Thurs. 11am-midnight

### Gay and Lesbian

#### CHUCK'S BAR

A friendly, kitschy little tavern at the far west end of River Street near the Jefferson Street ramp, Chuck's Bar is a great place to relax and see some interesting local characters. Karaoke at Chuck's is especially a hoot, and they keep the Christmas lights up all year.

**MAP 1:** 301 W. River St., 912/232-1005; Mon.-Wed. 8pm-3am, Thurs.-Sat. 7pm-3am

#### CLUB ONE JEFFERSON

Any examination of gay and lesbian nightlife in Savannah must, of course, begin with Club One Jefferson of *Midnight in the Garden of Good and Evil* fame. Come for the famous drag shows upstairs in the cabaret, or the

Abe's on Lincoln is the oldest bar in town.

rockin' 1,000-square-foot dance floor downstairs. Cabaret showtimes are Thursday-Saturday 10:30pm and 12:30am, Sunday 10:30pm, and Monday 11:30pm.

**MAP 1:** 1 Jefferson St., 912/232-0200, www.clubone-online.com; Mon.-Sat. 5pm-3am, Sun. 5pm-2am

# CITY MARKET

## Bars and Pubs

### MOON RIVER BREWING COMPANY

Moon River Brewing Company offers half a dozen handcrafted beers in a rambling old space that housed Savannah's first hotel back in antebellum days. The particular highlight these days, however, is the dog-friendly enclosed beer garden, with frequent live music and a congenial alfresco atmosphere, as well as access to the full menu.

**MAP 1:** 21 W. Bay St., 912/447-0943, www.moonriverbrewing.com; Mon.-Thurs. 11am-11pm, Fri.-Sat. 11am-midnight, Sun. 11am-10pm

### THE RAIL PUB

In the City Market area, your best bet is the Rail Pub, one of Savannah's oldest and most beloved taverns. This multifloor spot is a great place to get a pint or a shot or do karaoke in a quite boisterous but still cozy environment. You'll receive roasted peanuts with your drink; just let the shells fall on the floor like everyone else does.

**MAP 1:** 405 W. Congress St., 912/238-1311, www.therailpub.com; Mon.-Sat. 3pm-3am

### 22 SQUARE

In the modernist Andaz Savannah hotel overlooking bustling Ellis Square, 22 Square is a great place for an upscale cocktail and for meeting interesting people from all over. Try the refreshing Savannah Fizz or one of their mean Sazeracs.

**MAP 1:** 14 Barnard St., 912/233-2116, www.savannah.andaz.hyatt.com; Mon.-Thurs. 4pm-10pm, Fri.-Sat. 2pm-midnight, Sun. 4pm-10pm

## Live Music and Karaoke

### THE JINX

Despite its high-volume offerings, The Jinx is a friendly watering hole and the closest thing Savannah has to a full-on music club, with a very active calendar of rock and metal shows. Shows start late here, never before 11pm and often later than that. If you're here for the music and have sensitive ears, bring earplugs. The beer offerings are okay, but this is the kind of place where many regular patrons opt for tallboy PBRs.

**MAP 1:** 127 W. Congress St., 912/236-2281, www.thejinx.net; Mon.-Sat. 4pm-3am

# HISTORIC DISTRICT NORTH

## Bars and Pubs

### ABE'S ON LINCOLN

No, Lincoln Street in Savannah isn't named for Abraham Lincoln. But dark, fun little Abe's is on Lincoln Street, and it's also the oldest bar in town, with a very eclectic clientele.

**MAP 1:** 17 Lincoln St., 912/349-0525, http://abesonlincoln.com; Mon.-Sat. 4pm-3am

TOP EXPERIENCE

## To-Go Cup Revelry

Arguably the single most civilized trait of Savannah, and certainly one of the things that most sets it apart, is the glorious old tradition of the "to-go cup." True to its history of hard partying and general open-mindedness, Savannah, like New Orleans, legally allows you to walk the streets downtown with an open container of your favorite adult beverage. Of course, you have to be 21 or over, and the cup must be Styrofoam or plastic, never glass or metal, and no more than 16 ounces. While there are boundaries to where to-go cups are legal, in practice this includes almost all areas of the historic district frequented by visitors. The quick and easy rule of thumb is to keep your to-go cups north of Jones Street.

Every downtown watering hole has stacks of cups at the bar for patrons to use. You can either ask the bartender for a to-go cup—a.k.a. a "go cup"—or just reach out and grab one yourself. Don't be shy; it's the Savannah way.

Have fun making up your own itinerary or sample **this to-go cup crawl:** Start with a beverage at legendary dive bar Pinkie Master's. Walk with your to-go cups north to 17Hundred90's classic historic bar. Then cut over to O'Connell's Pub for a taste of Ireland. Walk west to Congress Street for a stop at The Rail Pub, or perhaps to catch a late-night rock 'n' roll show at The Jinx, both near the City Market area.

#### CHIVE SEA BAR AND LOUNGE

For swank partying on Broughton Street, head to Chive Sea Bar and Lounge, which backs up its tasty menu with a high-end bar in a wonderful, modernist space.

**MAP 1:** 4 W. Broughton St., 912/233-1748, www.chivelounge.com; Mon.-Fri. 11am-10pm, Sat. noon-midnight, Sun. 5pm-10pm

#### CIRCA 1875

Circa 1875 is a hip hangout with an excellent menu—the burgers are as good as the martinis. The vintage vibe takes you back to the days of the Parisian salons.

**MAP 1:** 48 Whitaker St., 912/443-1875, www.circa1875.com; Mon.-Thurs. 6pm-10pm, Fri.-Sat. 6pm-11pm

#### O'CONNELL'S

Without question, the place in Savannah that comes closest to replicating an authentic Irish pub environment is tiny, cozy O'Connell's, where they know how to pour a Guinness, feature Magners cider on tap, and the house specialty is the "pickleback"—a shot of Jameson's followed by a shot of, yes, pickle brine. In classic Emerald Isle tradition, most seating is bench-style, to encourage conversation.

**MAP 1:** 42 Drayton St., 912/231-2298; daily 3pm-3am

## HISTORIC DISTRICT SOUTH

### Bars and Pubs

#### THE DISTILLERY

Yes, The Distillery is located in a former distillery. As such, the atmosphere isn't exactly dark and romantic—it's sort of one big open room—but the excellent location at the corner of MLK Jr. Boulevard and Liberty Street, the long vintage bar, and the great selection of beers on tap combine to make this a happening spot. The fish-and-chips are also great.

**MAP 2:** 416 W. Liberty St., 912/236-1772, www.distillerysavannah.com; Mon.-Sat. 11am-close, Sun. noon-close

#### THE CHROMATIC DRAGON

Gamers and geeks alike will enjoy video and board game action—as well as the food and drink—at this unique spot. While you can get a meal and a brew here, the focus is on the gaming, so much so that you are asked "analog or digital?" (translation: board games or video consoles) as you walk in. They offer a vast array of both, or you can bring your own.

MAP 3: 514 MLK Jr. Blvd., 912/289-0350, www.chromaticdragon.com; Thurs.-Sat. 11am-2am, Sun.-Wed. 11am-11pm

#### THE ORIGINAL PINKIE MASTER'S

For 65 years, perhaps Savannah's most beloved dive bar has been the Original Pinkie Master's. For decades this has been a gathering place for local politicos; according to local lore, this is where President Jimmy Carter stopped during his visit for St. Patrick's Day (even though he's a teetotaler). A recent change of ownership has managed that rarest of accomplishments: They've lovingly retained the kitschy dive bar motif, complete with historic memorabilia, while expanding the drink menu and making things a bit more palatable for the general public.

MAP 2: 318 Drayton St., 912/999-7106, www.theoriginalsavannah.com; Mon.-Thurs. 3pm-3am, Fri.-Sat. noon-3am

### Live Music and Karaoke

#### MCDONOUGH'S

Savannah's undisputed karaoke champion is McDonough's, an advantage compounded by the fact that a lot more goes on here than karaoke. The kitchen at McDonough's is quite capable, and many locals swear you can get the best burger in town here. Despite the sports-bar atmosphere, the emphasis is on the karaoke, which ramps up every night at 9:30pm.

MAP 2: 21 E. McDonough St., 912/233-6136, www.mcdonoughsofsavannah.com; Mon.-Sat. 8pm-3am, Sun. 8pm-2am

## SOFO DISTRICT

### Bars and Pubs

#### AMERICAN LEGION BAR

The real hipsters hang out in ironic fashion drinking PBRs at the American Legion Bar, located in, yes, an actual American Legion post. While the Legionnaires themselves are a straitlaced patriotic bunch, the patrons of "the Legion," as the bar is colloquially known, tend toward the counterculture. That said, in a clear nod to tradition, no profanity or public displays of affection are allowed. Here is where you'll find Savannah's movers and shakers in the grassroots arts and cultural community.

Fun historical fact: The building housing the Legion was the birthplace of the U.S. 8th Air Force during World War II.

MAP 3: 1108 Bull St., 912/233-9277, http://alpost135.com; Mon.-Sat. 4pm-2am

TOP EXPERIENCE

## FESTIVALS AND EVENTS

Savannah's calendar fairly bursts with festivals, many outdoors. Dates shift from year to year, so it's best to consult the listed websites for details.

### January

Floats and bands take part in the **Martin Luther King Jr. Day Parade** downtown to commemorate the civil rights leader and Georgia native. The bulk of the route is on historic MLK Jr. Boulevard, formerly West Broad Street.

Straddling January and February is the weeklong **PULSE Art + Technology Festival** (www.telfair.org), an adventurous event that brings video artists and offbeat electronic performance art into the modern Jepson Center for the Arts.

### February

Definitely not to be confused with St. Patrick's Day, the **Savannah Irish Festival** (912/232-3448, www.savannahirish.org) focuses on Celtic music.

Hosted by the historically black Savannah State University at various venues around town, the monthlong **Black Heritage Festival** (912/691-6847) is tied into Black History Month and boasts name entertainers like the Alvin Ailey Dance Theatre (performing free!). This event also usually features plenty of historical lectures devoted to the very interesting and rich history of African Americans in Savannah.

Also in February is the quickly growing **Savannah Book Festival** (www.

## Craft Breweries

Savannah is finally catching up to the craft brewery trend, and tasting events at **Southbound Brewing Company** (107 E. Lathrop Ave., 912/335-7716, http://southboundbrewingco.com, tours 5:30pm Wed.-Fri., 2pm Sat., $15) are getting rave reviews. Tours include 36 ounces of beer served on-site and your choice of a 22-ounce bomber, a 32-ounce growler fill, a six-pack, or a pint glass. The tastings attract a large crowd, so don't dillydally. Southbound's offerings include a rotating series of special-event beers and the occasional rock concert. As is the case with many up-and-coming breweries, the large restored warehouse space isn't in the most scenic neighborhood.

Savannah's other key craft brewery is **Service Brewing** (574 Indian St., http://servicebrewing.com, tours 5:30pm-7:30pm Thurs.-Fri., 2pm-4pm Sat., $12 pp), so named because its founders are former military; they donate a portion of all profits to veterans service organizations. Basic tastings include either a 36-ounce flight of 6 ounces per pour or three 12-ounce pours. Service is a wee bit closer to downtown than is Southbound, and within walking distance of the River Street-City Market area.

The state of Georgia has finally changed the law to allow retail package sales from craft breweries, so that is a great option as well.

savannahbookfestival.org), modeled after a similar event in Washington DC and featuring many national and regional authors at various venues downtown.

### March

One of the most anticipated events for house-proud Savannahians, the **Tour of Homes and Gardens** (912/234-8054, www.savannahtourofhomes.org) offers guests the opportunity to visit six beautiful sites off the usual tourist-trod path. This is a great way to expand your understanding of local architecture and hospitality beyond the usual house museums.

One of Savannah's unique festivals is the multiday indie rock festival **Savannah Stopover** (www.savannahstopover.com) in early or mid-March. The idea is simple: Book bands that are already driving down to Austin, Texas, for the following week's South by Southwest so they can "stop over" and play at various venues in downtown Savannah. Get it? This is a great way to see up-and-coming bands before they blow up big; previous headliners have included St. Paul & The Broken Bones, Grimes, and Of Montreal. Admission is generally by ticketed wristband, and most venues are for ages 21 and over.

More than just a day, the citywide **St. Patrick's Day** (www.savannahsaintpatricksday.com) celebration generally lasts at least half a week and temporarily triples the population. The nearly three-hour parade—second biggest in the United States—always begins at 10am on St. Patrick's Day (unless that falls on a Sunday, in which case it's generally on the previous Saturday) and includes an interesting mix of marching bands, wacky floats, and sauntering local Irishmen in kelly-green jackets. The appeal comes not only from the festive atmosphere and generally beautiful spring weather, but also from Savannah's unique law allowing partiers to walk the streets with a cup filled with the adult beverage of their choice. While the parade itself is very family-friendly, afterward hard-core partiers generally head en masse to River Street—definitely not where you want to take small children. If you want to hear traditional Celtic music on St. Patrick's Day in Savannah, River Street also isn't the place to go, with the exception of Kevin Barry's on the west end. For authentic Irish music on St. Paddy's Day, wander around the pubs on the periphery of City Market.

The three-week **Savannah Music Festival** (912/234-3378, www.savannahmusicfestival.

org) is held at various historic venues around town and begins right after St. Patrick's Day. Past festivals have featured Wynton Marsalis, Dianne Reeves, and the Avett Brothers. The jazz portion is locked down tight, thanks to the efforts of festival director Rob Gibson, a Georgia native who cut his teeth as the founding director of Jazz at Lincoln Center. The classical side is helmed by one of the world's great young violinists, Daniel Hope, acting as associate director. Other genres are featured in abundance as well, including gospel, bluegrass, zydeco, world music, and the always-popular American Traditions vocal competition. The most economical way to enjoy the Savannah Music Festival is to purchase tickets online before December of the previous year at a 10 percent discount. However, if you just want to take in a few events, individual tickets are available at a tiered pricing system. You can buy tickets to individual events in town at the walk-up box office beside the Trustees Theater on Broughton Street.

## April

Short for "North of Gaston Street," the **NOGS Tour of Hidden Gardens** (912/961-4805, www.gcofsavnogstour.org, $30) is available two days in April and focuses on a selection of Savannah's amazing private gardens chosen for excellence of design, historical interest, and beauty.

Everyone loves the annual free **Sidewalk Arts Festival** (912/525-5865, www.scad.edu) presented by the Savannah College of Art and Design in Forsyth Park. Contestants claim a rectangular section of sidewalk on which to display their chalk art talent. There's a noncontest section with chalk provided.

## May

The SCAD-sponsored **Sand Arts Festival** (www.scad.edu) on Tybee Island's North Beach centers on a competition of sand castle design, sand sculpture, sand relief, and wind sculpture. You might be amazed at the level of artistry lavished on the sometimes-wondrous creations, only for them to wash away with the tide.

If you don't want to get wet, don't show up at the **Tybee Beach Bum Parade,** an uproarious event held the weekend prior to Memorial Day weekend. With a distinctly boozy overtone, this unique 20-year-old event features homemade floats filled with partiers who squirt the assembled crowds with various water pistols. The crowds, of course, pack their own heat and squirt back.

## July

Two key events happen around **Fourth of July,** primarily the large fireworks show on River Street on July 4 but also an impressive fireworks display from the Tybee pier and pavilion on July 3. A nice bonus of the Tybee event is that sometimes you can look out over the Atlantic and see a similar fireworks display on nearby Hilton Head Island, South Carolina, a few minutes away by boat (but nearly an hour by car).

## September

Around the third week in September is when the free **Savannah Jazz Festival** (savannahjazzfest.com) happens, a week-long event at multiple venues, with highlighted evening gigs usually outside on the stage in Forsyth Park. The performers feature an interesting mix of touring national artists and well-established local and regional players.

Over Labor Day weekend you can check out the **Savannah Craft Brew Festival** (International Trade & Convention Center, 1 International Dr., www.savannahcraftbrewfest.com, $50). This daylong tasting event features a healthy range of breweries from around the nation as well as Georgia's own burgeoning craft brew industry.

## October

The Savannah Philharmonic Orchestra plays a free **Picnic in the Park** concert in Forsyth Park that draws thousands of noshers. Arrive early to check out the ostentatious, whimsical picnic displays, which compete for prizes. Then set out your blanket, open a bottle of wine, and enjoy the sweet sounds.

The combined aroma of beer, sauerkraut, and sausage that you smell coming from the waterfront is the annual **Oktoberfest on the River** (www.riverstreetsavannah.com), which has evolved to be Savannah's second-largest celebration (behind only St. Patrick's Day). Live entertainment of varying quality is featured, though the attraction, of course, is the aforementioned beer and German food. A highlight is Saturday morning's "Weiner Dog Races" involving, you guessed it, competing dachshunds.

It's a fairly new festival, but the **Tybee Island Pirate Festival** (http://tybeepiratefest.com) is a fun and typically rollicking Tybee event in October featuring, well, everybody dressing up like pirates, saying "Arr" a lot, eating, drinking, and listening to cover bands. It may not sound like much, and it's really not, but it's typically very well attended.

Sponsored by St. Paul's Greek Orthodox Church, the popular **Savannah Greek Festival** (www.stpaulsgreekorthodox.org) features food, music, and Greek souvenirs. The weekend event is held across the street from the church at the parish center—in the gym, to be exact, right on the basketball court. Despite the pedestrian location, the food is authentic and delicious, and the atmosphere convivial and friendly.

Hosted by the Savannah College of Art and Design, the weeklong **SCAD Savannah Film Festival** (www.scad.edu) beginning in late October is rapidly growing not only in size but in prestige as well. Lots of older, more established Hollywood names appear as honored guests for the evening events, while buzzworthy up-and-coming actors, directors, producers, writers, and animators give excellent workshops during the day. Many of these usually jaded showbiz types really let their hair down for this festival, because, as you'll see, Savannah is the real star. The best way to enjoy this excellent event is to buy a pass, which enables you to walk from event to event. Most importantly, the passes gain you admission to what many locals consider the best part of the festival: the after-parties, where you'll often find yourself face to face with some famous star or director.

One of Savannah's most unique events is late October's **"Shalom Y'all" Jewish Food Festival** (912/233-1547, www.mickveisrael.org), held in Forsyth Park and sponsored by the historic Temple Mickve Israel. Latkes, matzo, and other nibbles are all featured along with entertainment.

# Arts and Culture

There are more art galleries per capita in Savannah than in New York City—one gallery for every 2,191 residents, to be exact. Savannah College of Art & Design (SCAD) galleries are in abundance all over town, displaying the handiwork of students, faculty, alumni, and important regional and national artists. Savannah's arts scene also shines a spotlight on theater, classical music, and cool movie houses.

## HISTORIC DISTRICT NORTH

### Cinema

#### LUCAS THEATRE FOR THE ARTS

The ornate, beautifully restored Lucas Theatre for the Arts downtown is a classic Southern movie house. The Savannah Film Society and Savannah College of Art and Design host screenings there throughout the year. Check the website for schedules.

**MAP 1:** 32 Abercorn St., 912/525-5040, www.lucastheatre.com; most screenings under $10

## A City of Art

For art lovers, the no-brainer package experience for the visitor is the combo of the **Telfair Academy of Arts and Sciences** (121 Barnard St., 912/790-8800, www.telfair.org) and the **Jepson Center for the Arts** (207 W. York St., 912/790-8800, www.telfair.org). These two arms of the Telfair Museums run the gamut of art, from old-school portraiture to cutting-edge contemporary art.

The **SCAD Museum of Art** (227 MLK Jr. Blvd., 912/525-7191, www.scad.edu) has a huge wing devoted to the Walter O. Evans Collection of African American Art.

Overlooking Ellis Square downtown is well-regarded **Kobo Gallery** (33 Barnard St., 912/201-0304, www.kobogallery.com), a local artist co-op featuring some of Savannah's best contemporary artists who frequently put on group shows.

**Roots Up Gallery** (412 Whitaker St., 912/677-2845) focuses on regional folk and outsider art with a strong emphasis on Southern roots and folkways.

**Non-Fiction Gallery** (1522 Bull St., 912/662-5152), south of Forsyth Park, exhibits work by many of Savannah's up-and-coming talents, often with exploratory themes.

Nearby is **Sulfur Studios** (2301 Bull St., sulfurstudios.org), which not only hosts rotating exhibits, but also coordinates many community forums and events of a cutting-edge nature.

Located inside the Mansion on Forsyth Park hotel, the **Grand Bohemian Gallery** (700 Drayton St., 912/721-5007) specializes in national and international artists working in a variety of media, from oils to jewelry.

### Music

#### SAVANNAH PHILHARMONIC

The Savannah Philharmonic is a professional symphony orchestra that performs concertos and sonatas at various venues around town, usually the Lucas Theatre, and is always worth checking out.

**MAP 1:** box office 216 E. Broughton St., 912/525-5050, www.savannahphilharmonic.org; Mon.-Fri. 10am-5pm

## HISTORIC DISTRICT SOUTH

### Performing Arts

#### HISTORIC SAVANNAH THEATRE

The semipro troupe at the Historic Savannah Theatre performs a busy rotating schedule of oldies revues (a typical title: *Return to the '50s*), but they make up for their lack of originality with the tightness and energy of their talented young cast of regulars.

**MAP 2:** 222 Bull St., 912/233-7764, www.savannahtheatre.com

# Shops

Savannah has also perfected the fine art of shopping, with a focus on antiques and independent home goods stores, with some unique boutiques sprinkled throughout the city. Without question, downtown Savannah's main shopping district is **Broughton Street.** There are many vibrant local shops as well as a wide variety of the usual national chain stores on the avenue, such as Michael Kors, H&M, Victoria's Secret, and Banana Republic, to name just a few.

A bit south of downtown proper, but still a short drive away, is the **Starland District**. This up-and-coming mixed-use area is home to a growing variety of more hipster-oriented shops.

Focusing on upscale art and home goods, the small but chic and friendly **Downtown**

**Design District** runs three blocks on Whitaker Street, a short walk from Forsyth Park.

## WATERFRONT

### Antiques

#### JERE'S ANTIQUES

One of the coolest antiques shops in town is Jere's Antiques. It's in a huge historic warehouse on Factor's Walk and has a concentration on fine European pieces.

**MAP 1:** 9 N. Jefferson St., 912/236-2815, www.jeresantiques.com; Mon.-Sat. 9:30am-5pm

### Clothes

#### HARLEY-DAVIDSON

You won't be buying a Softail Deluxe at this retail merchandise store, but you can certainly clothe your inner biker here. This is more a place for accessories and lifestyle items.

**MAP 1:** 503 E. River St., 912/231-8000, www.savannahhd.com; Mon.-Sat. 10am-6pm, Sun. noon-6pm

the flagship Savannah Bee Company on Broughton Street

#### THE MAD HATTER

Probably the closest thing to a unique shop on River Street proper is The Mad Hatter, which as the name suggests, offers a wide variety of headwear, from the whimsical to the practical.

**MAP 1:** 123 E. River St., 912/232-7566

### Gourmet Treats

#### SAVANNAH BEE COMPANY

This popular locally based, regional chain offers a range of honey-based goods from lip balm to lotion to, yes, honey. This store is located on the ground floor of the Hyatt Regency hotel, and the flagship location is actually just a few blocks north on Broughton Street. All locations feature an educational component as well, about the value of bees and beehives to the ecosystem.

**MAP 1:** 1 W. River St., 912/234-7088, www.savannahbee.com; Mon.-Sat. 10am-7pm, Sun. 11am-8pm

#### RIVER STREET SWEETS

Cater to your sweet tooth—and buy some goodies to bring back with you—at River Street Sweets, where you can witness Southern delicacies like pralines being made as you shop. The bright, friendly shop never fails to attract visitors strolling up and down the street. And, of course, there are free samples.

**MAP 1:** 13 E. River St., 912/234-4608, www.riverstreetsweets.com; daily 9am-11pm

### Pet Goods

#### BLACK DOG GENERAL STORE

The first Southern location of this national boutique chain offers upscale doggie treats and gear, as well as apparel and lifestyle and home items for their owners.

**MAP 1:** 211 W. River St., 912/335-7472, www.theblackdog.com; daily 10am-9pm

#### WOOF GANG BAKERY

On the opposite end of River Street from the Black Dog General store is Woof Gang Bakery, specializing in gourmet treats and food for your canine companion. Be forewarned: Some of the treats look tasty enough for you to want to sample yourself.

**MAP 1:** 425A E. River St., 912/999-6409, www.woofgangbakery.com; Fri.-Sat. 9am-9pm, Sun.-Thurs. 9am-8pm

## HISTORIC DISTRICT NORTH

### Art Supply

#### BLICK ART MATERIALS

A great art town needs a great art supply store, and in Savannah that would be Blick Art Materials, which has all the equipment and tools for the serious artist—priced to be affordable for students. But casual shoppers will enjoy it as well for its collection of offbeat gift items. The staff is very knowledgeable and helpful, and the space is cavernous but easily navigated.

**MAP 1:** 318 E. Broughton St., 912/234-0456, www.dickblick.com; Mon.-Fri. 8am-8pm, Sat. 10am-7pm, Sun. 11am-6pm

### Clothes and Fashion

#### GLOBE SHOE CO.

Broughton Street's oldest retailer still in operation, Globe Shoe Co. is a Savannah institution and a real throwback to a time of personalized retail service. They're all about simple one-to-one service, like in the old days, with a range of stylish shoes from the hip to the traditional.

**MAP 1:** 17 E. Broughton St., 912/232-8161; Mon.-Sat. 10am-6pm

#### CIVVIES NEW AND RECYCLED CLOTHING

Inhabiting a well-restored upstairs space, Civvie's is probably Savannah's best regarded vintage store, with a variety of retro clothes and shoes and a strong local following. They also have a nifty section of campy, kitschy gift items from various local vendors.

**MAP 1:** 14 E. Broughton St., 912/236-1551; Mon.-Sat. 11am-7pm, Sun. 11am-5pm

#### LEVY JEWELERS

At Bull and Broughton, Savannah's prime downtown corner, is century-old family-owned Levy Jewelers. They have a complete showcase of necklaces, watches, and rings from two dozen internationally recognized designers, in a large and attractive showroom.

**MAP 1:** 2 E. Broughton St., 912/233-1163; Mon.-Sat. 10am-9pm, Sun. noon-6pm

### Gourmet Treats

#### CHOCOLAT BY ADAM TURONI

Chocolate lovers need to head straight to this tiny space with big taste. Adam's handcrafted, high-quality chocolates are miniature works of art—and delicious ones at that. The interior design elements of the store are incredible, incorporating the chocolatier's art.

**MAP 1:** 323 W. Broughton St., 912/335-2914, www.chocolatat.com; daily 11am-6pm

#### SAVANNAH BEE COMPANY

The closest thing to a can't-miss shopping experience locally, one of the most unique Savannah retail shops is the Savannah Bee Company, which carries an extensive line of honey and honey-based merchandise, from foot lotion to lip balm. All the honey comes from area hives owned by company founder and owner Ted Dennard. This flagship location provides plenty of sampling opportunities at the little café area and even boasts a small theater space for instructional films. The staff not only knows all about the products for sale, but how they are created and collected.

**MAP 1:** 104 W. Broughton St., 912/233-7873, www.savannahbee.com; Mon.-Sat. 10am-7pm, Sun. 11am-5pm

### Home Goods

#### THE PARIS MARKET & BROCANTE

While Savannah is generally an Anglophile's dream, Francophiles will enjoy the Paris Market & Brocante, located on two floors on a beautifully restored corner of Broughton Street. Home and garden goods, bed and bath accoutrements, and a great selection

of antique and vintage items combine for a rather opulent shopping experience. Plus there's an old-school Euro café inside, where you can enjoy a coffee, tea, or hot chocolate.
**MAP 1:** 36 W. Broughton St., 912/232-1500, www.theparismarket.com; Mon.-Sat. 10am-6pm, Sun. 11am-4pm



#### 24E FURNISHINGS AT BROUGHTON

Those looking for great home decorating ideas with inspiration from both global and Southern aesthetics, traditional as well as sleekly modern, should check out 24e Furnishings at Broughton, located in an excellently restored 1921 storefront. You never know what you'll find here, from swanky style to repurposed aviation pieces. Be sure to check out the expansive second-floor showroom.
**MAP 1:** 24 E. Broughton St., 912/233-2274, www.twentyfoure.com; Mon.-Thurs. 10am-6pm, Fri.-Sat. 10am-7pm, Sun. noon-5pm

### Outdoor Outfitters

#### HALF MOON OUTFITTERS

Outdoors lovers should make themselves acquainted with Half Moon Outfitters, a full-service camping, hiking, skiing, and kayaking store. Half Moon is part of a regional chain and the staff is particularly knowledgeable about local ecotourism.
**MAP 1:** 15 E. Broughton St., 912/201-9313, www.halfmoonoutfitters.com; Mon.-Sat. 10am-7pm, Sun. noon-6pm

## HISTORIC DISTRICT SOUTH

### Antiques

#### ALEX RASKIN ANTIQUES

Possibly the most beloved antiques store in town is Alex Raskin Antiques in Monterey Square, catty-corner from the Mercer-Williams House Museum, set in the historic Hardee Mansion. A visit is worth it just to explore the home. But the goods Alex lovingly curates are among the best and most tasteful in the region.
**MAP 2:** 441 Bull St., 912/232-8205, www.alexraskinantiques.com; Mon.-Sat. 10am-5pm

#### THE CORNER DOOR

For a European take on antiques and collectibles, try the Corner Door, set in a unique building in the Downtown Design District and staffed by very friendly and knowledgeable antiques experts.
**MAP 2:** 417 Whitaker St., 912/238-5869; Tues.-Sat. 10am-5pm

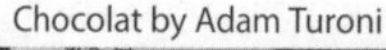

Chocolat by Adam Turoni

The Paris Market & Brocante

### SMALL PLEASURES

Small Pleasures is one of Savannah's hidden gems. They deal in a tasteful range of vintage and estate jewelry, in a suitably small but delightfully appointed space in the Downtown Design District.

**MAP 2:** 412 Whitaker St., 912/234-0277; Mon.-Sat. 10:30am-5pm

## Books and Music

### THE BOOK LADY

Specializing in "gently used" books in good condition, the Book Lady on Liberty Street features many rare first editions and lovably quirky items. Enjoy a gourmet coffee while you browse the stacks. They also host frequent author signings.

**MAP 2:** 6 E. Liberty St., 912/233-3628; Mon.-Sat. 10am-5:30pm

### E. SHAVER BOOKSELLER

Locally owned independent E. Shaver Bookseller is one of the best bookstores in town. The friendly, well-read staff can help you around the rambling old interior of their ground-level store and its generous stock of regionally themed books.

**MAP 2:** 326 Bull St., 912/234-7257; Mon.-Sat. 9am-6pm

### V&J DUNCAN

The beautiful Monterey Square location and a mention in *Midnight in the Garden of Good and Evil* combine to make V&J Duncan a Savannah "must-shop." Owner John Duncan and his wife Virginia have collected an impressive array of prints, books, and maps over the past quarter century, and are themselves a treasure trove of information.

**MAP 2:** 12 E. Taylor St., 912/232-0338, www.vjduncan.com; Mon.-Sat. 10:30am-4:30pm

## Clothes

### CUSTARD BOUTIQUE

Custard Boutique in the Downtown Design District has a cute, cutting-edge selection of women's clothes in a range of styles, and is one of the more stylistically accessible boutiques in town.

**MAP 2:** 414 Whitaker St., 912/232-4733; Mon.-Sat. 10:30am-6pm, Sun. noon-5pm

## Gifts and Souvenirs

### FOLKLORICO

Set in a stunningly restored multilevel Victorian within a block of Forsyth Park, the globally conscious Folklorico brings in a fascinating and diverse collection of sustainably made jewelry, gifts, and home goods from around the world, focusing on Central and South America and Asia, at a variety of price points.

**MAP 2:** 440 Bull St., 912/232-9300; Mon.-Sat. 10am-5pm, Sun. 1pm-5pm

### SAINTS AND SHAMROCKS

In this town so enamored of all things Irish, a great little locally owned shop is Saints and Shamrocks, across the intersection from the Book Lady. Pick up your St. Patrick's-themed gear and gifts to celebrate Savannah's highest holiday along with high-quality Irish imports.

**MAP 2:** 309 Bull St., 912/233-8858, www.saintsandshamrocks.org; Mon.-Sat. 9:30am-5:30pm, Sun. 11am-4pm

### SHOPSCAD

Not only a valuable outlet for SCAD students and faculty to sell their artistic wares, shopSCAD is also one of Savannah's most unique boutiques. You never really know what you'll find, but whatever it is, it will be one-of-a-kind. The jewelry in particular is always cutting edge in design and high quality in craftsmanship. The designer T-shirts are a hoot too.

**MAP 2:** 340 Bull St., 912/525-5180, www.shopscadonline.com; Mon.-Wed. 9am-5:30pm, Thurs.-Fri. 9am-8pm, Sat. 10am-8pm, Sun. noon-5pm

## Home Goods

### MADAME CHRYSANTHEMUM

Madame Chrysanthemum, set in a charming, cozy corner spot in the Downtown Design District, deals in fun home items and gift ideas with a hip and enjoyable Savannah style.

**MAP 2:** 101 W. Taylor St., 912/238-3355; Mon.-Sat. 10am-5pm

### ONE FISH TWO FISH

An eclectic European-style home goods store is One Fish Two Fish. Owner Jennifer Beaufait Grayson, a St. Simons Island native, came to town a decade ago to set up shop in this delightfully restored old dairy building in the Downtown Design District.

**MAP 2:** 401 Whitaker St., 912/484-4600; Mon.-Sat. 10am-5:30pm, Sun. noon-5pm

# SOFO DISTRICT

## Antiques

### PICKER JOE'S ANTIQUE MALL & VINTAGE MARKET

Probably the best single antique/vintage store in town is Picker Joe's Antique Mall & Vintage Market, housed in an old mattress factory. There is a wide variety of consignment booths with great retro stuff. This store is more along the fun, serendipitous lines of the show "American Pickers" rather than the typical stuffy antiques shop. They make frequent picking trips all over the country, and you can sometimes catch them bringing in the new finds.

**MAP 3:** 217 E. 41st St., 912/239-4657, www.pickerjoes.com, Mon.-Sat. 10am-6pm, Sun. noon-5pm

E. Shaver Bookseller

### Books and Music

#### GRAVEFACE RECORDS & CURIOSITIES

For the latest in vinyl, with new releases, vintage retro releases, locally released albums, and Record Store Day specials, check out Graveface in the Starland District. In addition to used and new vinyl, this is also a great place to get offbeat, kitschy gifts and unusual DVDs.

**MAP 3:** 5 W. 40th St., 912/335-8018; Mon.-Sat. 11am-7pm, Sun. noon-6pm

### Clothes

#### GYPSY WORLD

Easily one of the best vintage stores in town, Gypsy World in the Starland District appeals to hipster and connoisseur alike and has a remarkable range of tasteful retro styles, including vintage furs, usually well within a reasonable budget.

**MAP 3:** 2405 Bull St., 912/704-2347; Tues.-Sat. 9:30am-5pm

## GREATER SAVANNAH

### Malls

#### KELLER'S FLEA MARKET

A local tradition for 20 years, Keller's Flea Market packs in about 10,000 shoppers over the course of a typical weekend. It offers a range of bargains in antiques, home goods, produce, and general kitsch, and there are concessions on-site.

**MAP 6:** 5901 Ogeechee Rd., I-95 exit 94, Southside, 912/927-4848, www.ilovefleas.com, Sat.-Sun. 8am-6pm

#### OGLETHORPE MALL

The mall closest to downtown—though not that close, at about 10 miles south—is Oglethorpe Mall in Southside. Its anchor stores are Sears, Belk, J. C. Penney, and Macy's.

**MAP 6:** 7804 Abercorn St., Southside, 912/354-7038, www.oglethorpemall.com; Mon.-Sat. 10am-9pm, Sun. noon-6pm

#### TANGER OUTLETS SAVANNAH

This outlet mall—actually in the adjacent city of Pooler, not Savannah—is marketed as a destination in itself, and it boasts a large number of stores even by the standards of outlet malls. Brands include American Eagle, Banana Republic, Chico's, Columbia, Gap, J. Crew, Cole Haan, Crocs, Oakley, Nike, and Under Armour.

**MAP 6:** 200 Tanger Outlet Blvd., Pooler, 912/348-3125, www.tangeroutlet.com; Mon.-Sat. 9am-9pm, Sun. 10am-7pm

# Sports and Activities

Savannah offers copious outdoor options that take full advantage of the city's temperate climate and the natural beauty of its marshy environment next to the Atlantic Ocean.

Savannah is a saltwater angler's paradise, rich in trout, flounder, and king and Spanish mackerel. Offshore there's a fair amount of deep-sea action, including large grouper, white and blue marlin, wahoo, snapper, sea bass, and big amberjack near some of the many offshore wrecks.

Diving is a challenge off the Georgia coast because of the silty nature of the water and its mercurial currents. Though not particularly friendly to the novice, plenty of great offshore opportunities abound around the many artificial reefs created by the Georgia Department of Natural Resources (www.coastalgadnr.org).

Other than some action around the pier, the surfing is poor on Tybee Island, with its broad shelf, tepid wave action, and lethal rip currents. But board surfers and kiteboarders have a lot of fun on the south end of Tybee beginning at about 17th Street. The craziest surf is past the rock jetty, but be advised that the rip currents are especially treacherous there.

Hiking in Savannah and the Lowcountry is largely a 2-D experience given the flatness of the terrain, but there are plenty of good nature trails from which to observe the area's rich flora and fauna up close, in beautiful settings.

Bicycling is fun all around the Savannah area. Plenty of folks ride their bikes downtown, and it is particularly enriching and fun to pedal around the squares. Legally, however, you're not allowed to ride through the squares; you're supposed to stay on the street around them. And always yield to traffic already within the square as you enter. Other good cycling opportunities are at Fort Pulaski and Tybee Island.

Savannah was the first city in Georgia to unveil a public **bike-share program** (http://catchacat.org, $2 per half hour, daily 5:30am-11pm), and you can now be the beneficiary. Head to Ellis Square adjacent to City Market; the rack is on the south side of the square.

## WATERFRONT

### Spectator Sports

#### SAVANNAH DERBY DEVILS

For sports action that's more hard-hitting and comes with a certain hip kitsch quotient, check out the bruising bouts of the women of the Savannah Derby Devils, who bring the roller derby thunder against other regional teams. They skate across the river at the Trade Center on Hutchinson Island, and the matches are usually quite well attended.

**MAP 1:** Savannah International Trade and Convention Center, 1 International Dr., 912/651-6556, www.savannahderby.com

## SOFO DISTRICT

### Ecotours

#### WILDERNESS SOUTHEAST

The nonprofit Wilderness Southeast offers guided trips (including paddles) to historic Mulberry Grove, birding trips, and beach explorations. Regularly scheduled "Walks on the Wild Side" run the gamut from "Alligators to Anhingas" to the "Urban Forest" to "Explore the Night Sky" to the "Blackwater River Float." Custom tours are also available.

**MAP 3:** 3025 Bull St., 912/897-5108, www.naturesavannah.org; $10-35

## VICTORIAN DISTRICT

### Tennis

#### FORSYTH PARK

The closest public courts to the downtown area are at the south end of Forsyth Park, which features four free lighted courts. They are first-come, first-served and unstaffed, and as you might expect, they get serious use.

**MAP 3:** bordered by Drayton St., Gaston St., Whitaker St., and Park Ave., 912/351-3850; daily 8am-dusk; free

## SOUTHSIDE

### Bird-Watching

#### SKIDAWAY ISLAND STATE PARK

Skidaway Island State Park is part of the **Colonial Coast Birding Trail** (http://georgiawildlife.dnr.state.ga.us). Spring and fall bring a lot of the usual warbler action, while spring and summer feature nesting ospreys and painted buntings, always a delight.

**MAP 4:** 52 Diamond Causeway, 912/598-2300, www.gastateparks.org; daily 7am-10pm; parking $5 per vehicle per day

### Fishing

#### MISS JUDY CHARTERS

Perhaps the best-known local angler is Captain Judy Helmey, a.k.a. "Miss Judy." In addition to her frequent and entertaining newspaper columns, she runs a variety of well-regarded charters; four-hour trips start at $500. To get here, go west on U.S. 80, take a right onto Bryan Woods Road, a left onto Johnny Mercer Boulevard, a right onto Wilmington Island Way, and a right down the dirt lane at her sign.

**MAP 4:** 124 Palmetto Dr., 912/897-2478, www.missjudycharters.com; from $500

#### TELECASTER CHARTERS

A great inshore charter service is offered by Telecaster Charters, with 4-, 6-, and 8-hour inshore trips priced from $300 for two anglers.

**MAP 4:** 2812 River Dr., Thunderbolt, 912/308-4622, www.telecastercharters.com; from $300

## Golf

### WILMINGTON ISLAND CLUB

The Wilmington Island Club has arguably the quickest greens in town and is unarguably the most beautiful local course, set close by the Wilmington River amid lots of mature pines and live oaks.

**MAP 4:** 501 Wilmington Island Rd., 912/897-1612; greens fees about $70

## Hiking

### SKIDAWAY ISLAND STATE PARK

My favorite trails are at Skidaway Island State Park. The three-mile Big Ferry Trail is the best overall experience, taking you out to a wooden viewing tower from which you can see the vast expanse of the Skidaway Narrows. A detour takes you past a Native American shell midden, Confederate earthworks, and even a rusty old still—a nod to Skidaway Island's former notoriety as a bootlegger's sanctuary. The shorter but still fun Sandpiper Trail is wheelchair accessible.

**MAP 4:** 52 Diamond Causeway, 912/598-2300, www.gastateparks.org; daily 7am-10pm; parking $5 per vehicle per day

## Kayaking and Canoeing

### MOON RIVER KAYAK TOURS

Run by Captain Mike Neal, an experienced local boatman and conservationist, Moon River Kayak Tours focuses on 2.5-hour tours of the Skidaway Narrows and scenic Moon River, departing from the public boat ramp at the foot of the bridge to Skidaway Island. No kayaking experience is required.

**MAP 4:** 45 Diamond Causeway, 912/898-1800, www.moonriverkayak.com; $50

### SKIDAWAY NARROWS

A pleasant kayaking route is the Skidaway Narrows. Begin this paddle at the public boat ramp, which you find by taking Waters Avenue all the way until it turns to Whitefield Avenue and then Diamond Causeway. Continue all the way over the Moon River to a drawbridge; park at the foot of the bridge. Once in the water, paddle northeast. Look for the osprey nests on top of the navigational markers in the narrows as you approach Skidaway Island State Park. Continuing on, you'll find scenic Isle of Hope high on a bluff to your left, with nearly guaranteed dolphin sightings around marker 62.

**MAP 4:** intersection of Moon River and Diamond Causeway

## Tennis

### BACON PARK

On the south side, Bacon Park has 16 lighted hard courts. It's the city's best tennis facility, but it's the farthest from downtown. It's the most heavily trafficked of the city's courts, and a destination for local expert players.

**MAP 4:** 6262 Skidaway Rd., 912/351-3850; daily 8am-dusk; $3

# EASTSIDE

## Fishing

### SAVANNAH FLY FISHING CHARTERS

Shallow-water fly-fishers might want to contact Savannah Fly Fishing Charters. Captain Scott Wagner takes half- and full-day charters both day and night from Savannah all the way down to St. Simons Island. Half-day rate starts at $300. Book early.

**MAP 4:** 56 Sassafras Trail, 912/308-3700, www.savannahfly.com; from $300

## Kayaking and Canoeing

### SAVANNAH CANOE & KAYAK

The most highly regarded local canoe and kayak tour operator and rental house is Savannah Canoe & Kayak, run by the husband-wife team of Nigel and Kristin Law. They offer several kayak trips, including a short jaunt to Little Tybee Island.

**MAP 4:** 414 Bonaventure Rd., 912/341-9502, www.savannahcanoeandkayak.com; half-day tour $55

## Tennis

### DAFFIN PARK

South of Highway 80 is Daffin Park, where there are six clay courts and three lighted hard courts. This is mostly a locals-frequented spot, but the park is nice to visit.

**MAP 4:** 1001 E. Victory Dr., 912/351-3850; daily 8am-dusk; $3

## Spectator Sports

### THE SAVANNAH BANANAS

A very popular local summer pastime is going to see the college summer league team the Savannah Bananas at historic Grayson Stadium in Daffin Park, where greats such as Babe Ruth and Jackie Robinson played back in the day. This isn't NCAA ball—these young players use real wooden bats and play for the love of the game while they're out of class for the summer. The off-field entertainment is a part of the experience, and is constant, very fun, and family-friendly. Most games sell out, so get tickets early.

**MAP 4:** 1401 E. Victory Dr., 912/712-2482, http://thesavannahbananas.com; $9

# TYBEE ISLAND

## Ecotours

### SUNDIAL NATURE TOURS

The best guided water tour in the area is Captain Rene Heidt's Sundial Nature Tours. Rene is an expert in local marine life and offers a variety of tours, including dolphin watches, fossil hunts, and trips to various barrier islands.

**MAP 5:** 1615 Chatham Ave., 912/786-9470, www.sundialcharters.com; from $160 for 2 people

## Biking

### FORT PULASKI NATIONAL MONUMENT

Many locals like to load up their bikes and go to Fort Pulaski. From the grounds you can ride all over scenic and historic Cockspur Island.

**MAP 5:** 912/786-5787, www.nps.gov; daily 9am-5pm; $7, free under age 16

### MCQUEEN'S ISLAND TRAIL

Outside town, much biking activity centers on Tybee Island, with the six-mile McQueen's Island Trail being a popular and simple ride. The trail started as a rail route for Central of Georgia Railway and was converted to a multiuse trail in the 1990s.

**MAP 5:** U.S. 80 near Fort Pulaski National Monument

## Bird-Watching

### NORTH BEACH

An excellent birding spot on the **Colonial Coast Birding Trail** (http://georgiawildlife.dnr.state.ga.us) is Tybee Island's North Beach area. You'll see a wide variety of shorebirds and gulls, as well as piping plover, northern gannets, and in winter, purple sandpipers.

**MAP 5:** Savannah River to 1st St., Tybee Island; parking $5 per day, meters available

## Fishing

### AMICK'S DEEP SEA FISHING

A highly regarded local fishing charter is Tybee-based Amick's Deep Sea Fishing. Captain Steve Amick and crew run offshore charters daily. Go east on U.S. 80 and turn right just past the Lazaretto Creek Bridge.

**MAP 5:** 1 Old Hwy. 80, Tybee Island, 912/897-6759, www.amicksdeepseafishing.com; from $120 pp

## Kayaking and Canoeing

### LAZARETTO CREEK

Lazaretto Creek, on the western edge of Tybee island, is a great place to explore Tybee and environs. From here you can meander several miles through the marsh, or go the other way and head into a channel of the Savannah River. If you're into ocean kayaking, you can even head into the Atlantic from here. Put in at the Lazaretto Creek landing, at the foot of the Lazaretto Creek bridge on the south side of U.S. 80 on the way to Tybee Island. This is a peaceful, pretty paddle for novice and experienced kayakers alike. You can also put in at the nearby **Tybee Marina** (4 Old Tybee Rd., 912/786-5554, www.tybeeislandmarina.com), also on Lazaretto Creek.

**MAP 5:** intersection of U.S. 80 and Tybee Island

### LITTLE TYBEE ISLAND

Maybe the single best kayak or canoe adventure in Savannah is the run across the Back

River from Tybee to Little Tybee Island, an undeveloped state heritage site that despite its name is actually twice as big as Tybee, albeit mostly marsh. Many kayakers opt to camp on the island. You can even follow the shoreline out into the Atlantic, but be aware that wave action can get intense offshore. Begin the paddle at the public boat ramp on the Back River. To get here, take Butler Avenue all the way to 18th Street and take a right, then another quick right onto Chatham Avenue. The parking lot for the landing is a short way up Chatham Avenue on your left. Warning: Do not attempt to swim to Little Tybee, no matter how strong a swimmer you think you are. Also, do not be tempted to walk far out onto the Back River beach at low tide. The tide comes in very quickly and often strands people on the sandbar.

**MAP 5:** south of Tybee Island

#### NORTH ISLAND SURF AND KAYAK

To rent an ocean-worthy kayak on Lazaretto Creek, stop by North Island Surf and Kayak, located at Tybee Marina. Reservations are recommended.

**MAP 5:** 1C Old Hwy. 80, 912/786-4000, www.northislandkayak.com; Mon.-Fri. 10am-5pm, Sat.-Sun. 9am-6pm; $45

#### SEA KAYAK GEORGIA

On U.S. 80 just as you get on Tybee is a quality tour service, Sea Kayak Georgia. Run by locals Marsha Henson and Ronnie Kemp, Sea Kayak offers many different types of kayak tours.

**MAP 5:** 1102 U.S. 80, 888/529-2542, www.seakayakgeorgia.com; half-day tour $55

### Surfing and Boarding

#### HIGH TIDES SURF SHOP

The best—and pretty much only—surf shop in town is High Tides Surf Shop. You can get a good local surf report and forecasts at their website.

**MAP 5:** 405 U.S. 80, 912/786-6556, www.hightidesurfshop.com

### Tennis

#### TYBEE ISLAND MEMORIAL PARK

If you get the tennis jones on Tybee, there are two free hard courts at Tybee Island Memorial Park that are lighted.

**MAP 5:** Butler Ave. and 4th St., 912/786-4573, www.cityoftybee.org; daily 8am-dusk; free

## GREATER SAVANNAH

### Bird-Watching

#### LAUREL HILL WILDLIFE DRIVE

Wading birds in particular are in wide abundance at the **Savannah National Wildlife Refuge.** The views are excellent all along the Laurel Hill Wildlife Drive, which takes you through the heart of the old paddy fields that once crisscrossed the entire area. To get here, take U.S. 17 north over the big Talmadge Bridge, over the Savannah River into South Carolina. Turn left on Highway 170 south and look for the entrance to Laurel Hill Wildlife Drive on the left.

**MAP 6:** 2 miles east of Port Wentworth, 843/784-2468, www.fws.gov/savannah; daily dawn-dusk; free

#### LECONTE-WOODMANSTON BOTANICAL GARDEN

LeConte-Woodmanston Botanical Garden is a bit hard to find. Part of William Bartram's historic nature trail, this was the home of Dr. Louis LeConte, renowned 19th-century botanist, and his sons John LeConte, first president of the University of California, Berkeley, and Joseph LeConte, who founded the Sierra Club with John Muir. The highlight here is the rare tidally influenced freshwater wetland, featuring the blackwater Bulltown Swamp. This visit is best done in a 4WD vehicle. The garden is about 40 minutes from Savannah. Take I-95 south to exit 76. Turn right on U.S. 84, then left on U.S. 17. Turn right on Barrington Ferry Road until the pavement ends at Sandy Run Road. Continue until you see the historical markers. Turn left onto the dirt road, then drive another mile.

**MAP 6:** 4918 Barrington Ferry Rd., Riceboro, 912/884-6500, www.leconte-woodmanston.org; daily 9am-5pm; $5

### YOUMANS POND

Youmans Pond is a prime stop for migratory fowl. Its main claim to fame is that it was visited in 1773 by the great naturalist William Bartram on one of his treks across the Southeast. Youmans Pond has changed little since then, with its tree-studded pond and oodles of owls, ospreys, herons, egrets, wood storks, and many more. Youmans Pond is about 40 minutes from Savannah. To get here, take I-95 south to exit 76. Take a left onto Highway 38 (Islands Hwy.) and then a left onto Camp Viking Road. About one mile ahead, take a right onto Lake Pamona Drive. About 0.75 miles ahead, look for the pond on the right. It's unmarked, but there's a wooden boardwalk.

**MAP 6:** Lake Pamona Dr., Midway; daily; free

## Diving

### GRAY'S REEF NATIONAL MARINE SANCTUARY

Certainly no underwater adventure in the area would be complete without a dive at Gray's Reef National Marine Sanctuary. Administered by the National Oceanic and Atmospheric Administration, this fully protected marine sanctuary 17 miles offshore is in deep enough water to provide divers good visibility of its live-bottom habitat. Not a classic living coral reef but rather one built by sedimentary deposits, Gray's Reef provides a look at a truly unique ecosystem. Some key dive charter operators that can take you to Gray's Reef are Captain Walter Rhame's **Mako Dive Charter** (600 Priest Landing Dr., 912/604-6256), which leaves from the Landings Harbor Marina; **Georgia Offshore** (1191 Lake Dr., Midway, 912/658-3884); and **Fantasia Scuba** (3 E. Montgomery Cross Rd., 912/921-8933).

The best all-around dive shop in town is **Diving Locker and Ski Chalet** (74 W. Montgomery Cross Rd., 912/927-6603, www.divinglockerskichalet.com, Mon.-Fri. 10am-6pm, Sat. 10am-5pm) on the south side.

**MAP 6:** 16 miles east of Sapelo Island, 912/598-2345, www.graysreef.noaa.gov

## Golf

### CLUB AT SAVANNAH HARBOR

Across the Savannah River on Hutchinson Island and adjacent to the Westin Savannah Harbor Resort is the Club at Savannah Harbor, home to the Liberty Mutual Legends of Golf Tournament each spring. The club's tee times are 7:30am-3pm daily.

**MAP 6:** 2 Resort Dr., 912/201-2007, www.theclubatsavannahharbor.com; greens fees $135, twilight $70

### HENDERSON GOLF CLUB

There are a couple of strong public courses in Savannah that are also very good bargains. Chief among these has to be the Henderson Golf Club, an excellent municipal course with very reasonable greens fees that include a half cart.

**MAP 6:** 1 Al Henderson Blvd., 912/920-4653, www.hendersongolfclub.com; greens fees Mon.-Fri. $28, Sat.-Sun. $33

## Hiking

### SAVANNAH-OGEECHEE RIVER CANAL

A relic of the pre-railroad days, the Savannah-Ogeechee River Canal is a 17-mile barge route joining the two rivers. Finished in 1830, it saw three decades of prosperous trade in cotton, rice, bricks, guano, naval stores, and food crops before the coming of the railroads finished it off. You can walk some of its length today near the Ogeechee River terminus, admiring the impressive engineering of its multiple locks used to stabilize the water level. Back in the day, the canal would continue through four lift locks as it traversed 16 miles before reaching the Savannah River. Naturalists will enjoy the built-in nature trail that walking along the canal provides. Be sure to check out the unique sand hills on a nearby trail, a vestige of a bygone geological era when this area was an offshore sandbar. Kids will enjoy the impromptu menagerie of gopher turtles near the site's entrance. Bring mosquito repellent, although often there's a community spray can at the front door of the little visitors center and museum where you pay your fee.

To get here, get on I-95 south, take exit 94, and go west on Fort Argyle Road (Hwy. 204). The canal is a little over two miles from the exit.

**MAP 6:** 681 Ft. Argyle Rd., 912/748-8068, www.savannahogeecheecanal.com; daily 9am-5pm; $2 adults, $1 students

## Kayaking and Canoeing

### EBENEZER CREEK

About 18 miles north of town, but worth the trip for any kayaker, is the beautiful blackwater Ebenezer Creek, near the tiny township of New Ebenezer in Effingham County. Cypress trees lining this nationally designated Wild and Scenic River hang overhead, and wildlife abounds on this peaceful paddle. Look for old wooden sluice gates, vestiges of the area's rice plantation past. To get here, take exit 109 off I-95. Go north on Highway 21 to Rincon, Georgia, then east on Highway 275 (Ebenezer Rd.). Put in at the private Ebenezer Landing.

**MAP 6:** intersection of Ebenezer Rd. and Savannah River, New Ebenezer; $5 put-in fee

### SAVANNAH NATIONAL WILDLIFE REFUGE

One of the great overall natural experiences in the area is the massive Savannah National Wildlife Refuge. This 30,000-acre reserve—half in Georgia, half in South Carolina—is on the Atlantic flyway, so you'll be able to see birdlife in abundance, in addition to alligators and manatees. Earthen dikes crisscrossing the refuge are vestigial remnants of paddy fields from plantation days.

You can kayak on your own, but many opt to take guided tours offered by **Wilderness Southeast** (912/897-5108, www.wilderness-southeast.org, 2-hour trips from $38 for 2 people), **Sea Kayak Georgia** (888/529-2542, www.seakayakgeorgia.com, $55 pp), and **Swamp Girls Kayak Tours** (843/784-2249, www.swampgirls.com, $45). To get to the refuge, take U.S. 17 north over the big Talmadge Bridge, over the Savannah River into South Carolina. Turn left on Highway 170 south and look for the entrance to Laurel Hill Wildlife Drive on the left.

**MAP 6:** visitors center 694 Beech Hill Lane, Hardeeville, SC, 843/784-2468, www.fws.gov/refuge/savannah; daily dawn-dusk; free



# Restaurants

Savannah is a fun food town, with a selection of cuisine concocted by a cast of executive chefs who, despite their many personal idiosyncrasies, tend to go with what works rather than experiment for the sake of experimentation.

Note that there isn't a cuisine category for seafood listed below—that's because seafood is an intrinsic part of most restaurant fare in Savannah, whether through regular menu offerings or through specials. For the freshest seafood, consider a trip to Tybee Island or Thunderbolt, on the way to Tybee.

## WATERFRONT

### Classic Southern

### TREYLOR PARK $$

The bustling, friendly interior of this popular Bay Street spot plays up the shabby chic undertone of Savannah life, with tasty gourmet takes on downmarket Southern classics like the chicken biscuit, pot pie, and sloppy joe. Don't miss the signature starter dish, the PB&J Wings. A particularly tasteful cocktail menu and a well-curated craft beer list round out the experience.

**MAP 1:** 115 E. Bay St., 912/495-5557, www.treylorpark.com; Mon.-Fri. noon-1am, Sat. 10am-2am, Sun. 10am-1am

## Best Restaurants

★ **Best Breakfast Downtown:** Hands down, it's **B. Matthew's Eatery** on Bay Street, where you can't go wrong with the omelets or the pancakes.

★ **Best for Chocoholics:** From chocolate-chip cheesecake to specialty martinis, **Lulu's Chocolate Bar** can satisfy your sweet tooth.

★ **Best Repurpose:** Dine on James Beard Award-winning soul food in a former bus depot at **The Grey.**

★ **Most Luscious Lunch:** The dishes at **Kayak Kafe** are light and adventurous and make for a perfect pit stop during a day of shopping on Broughton Street.

★ **Tastiest Brush with Hollywood:** Movie producer and Savannah native Stratton Leopold is often seen behind the counter at **Leopold's Ice Cream,** helping dish out scoops of his old family recipe ice cream flavors among Hollywood memorabilia.

★ **Best South of the Border:** The best Mexican spot downtown is **Tequila's Town.**

★ **Most Authentic Southern Experience:** Eat around a communal table in a convivial atmosphere at **Mrs. Wilkes' Dining Room** and enjoy what many consider the finest fried chicken in the South, among other classic dishes.

★ **Most Romantic Date Night:** One of Savannah's original fine-dining restaurants, **Elizabeth on 37th** remains the local gold standard for a wonderful evening with wonderful food and service.

★ **Most Bodacious Burger:** The made-to-order patties at **Green Truck Neighborhood Pub** come with tasty toppings, from Greek style to pimento cheese. Wash down your burger with a selection from their great craft brew list.

★ **Best Memphis BBQ: Sandfly BBQ** serves the best Memphis-style brisket in Georgia.

### VIC'S ON THE RIVER $$$

Very few restaurants on River Street rise above tourist schlock, but a standout is Vic's on the River. With dishes like wild Georgia shrimp, stone-ground grits, and blue crab cakes with a three-pepper relish, Vic's combines a romantic old Savannah atmosphere with an adventurous take on Lowcountry cuisine. Note the entrance to the dining room is not on River Street but on the Bay Street level on Upper Factor's Walk.

**MAP 1:** 16 E. River St., 912/721-1000, www.vicsontheriver.com; Sun.-Thurs. 11am-10pm, Fri.-Sat. 11am-11pm

## Breakfast

### ★ B. MATTHEW'S EATERY $$

If you're downtown and need something more than your hotel breakfast—and you will!—go to B. Matthew's Eatery, widely considered the best breakfast in the entire Savannah historic district. The omelets—most under $10—are uniformly wonderful, and the sausage and bacon are excellent and not greasy. There are healthier selections as well, and you can actually get a decent bowl of oatmeal. Sunday brunch is incredible, but lunch and dinner here are great as well. Lunch sandwiches and salads are of similarly high quality, and dinner entrées (from $17) include killer osso buco, lamb, and seafood.

**MAP 1:** 325 E. Bay St., 912/233-1319, www.bmatthewseatery.com; Mon.-Thurs. 8am-9pm, Fri.-Sat. 8am-10pm, Sun. 9am-3pm

## Asian

### CO SAVANNAH $$

The newest and most widely regarded as best Asian fusion cuisine in town is at CO Savannah, a block off the waterfront. This regional chain has a menu particularly strong in *bánh mì* and specialty sushi rolls, with a cocktail and beer menu superior to most similar places in town. It's a fun place to get plates to share. Speaking of beverages, upstairs you'll find the affiliated **Savannah Cocktail Co.** (www.savannahcocktailco.com, daily 5pm-1am), which offers a great Sunday brunch.

**MAP 1:** 10 Whitaker St., 912/234-5375, www.eatatco.com, Sun.-Thurs. 11am-10pm, Fri.-Sat. 11am-11pm

## Greek

### OLYMPIA CAFÉ $$

A worthwhile place to stop for a relaxing and tasty meal on River Street is Olympia Café, which serves a variety of Greek dishes such as dolmas, spanakopita, seafood, and lemon chicken in a friendly atmosphere. The standard menu items aren't particularly cheap, but the daily specials often offer a surprisingly good deal for the money.

**MAP 1:** 5 E. River St., 912/233-3131, www.olympiacafe.net; daily 11am-10pm

# CITY MARKET

## Classic Southern

### THE LADY & SONS $$

Every year, thousands of visitors come to Savannah to wait for hours for a chance to sample some of local celebrity Paula Deen's "home" cooking at the Lady & Sons. There's actually a fairly typical Southern buffet with some decent fried chicken, collard greens, and mac and cheese. You must begin waiting in line as early as 9:30am for lunch and as early as 3:30pm for dinner in order to be assigned a dining time.

**MAP 1:** 102 W. Congress St., 912/233-2600, www.ladyandsons.com; Mon.-Sat. 11am-3pm and 5pm-close, Sun. 11am-5pm

## Coffee, Tea, and Sweets

### ★ LULU'S CHOCOLATE BAR $

Combine a hip bar with outrageously tasty dessert items and you get Lulu's Chocolate Bar. While the whole family is welcome before 10pm to enjoy chocolate-chip cheesecake and the like, after that it's 21-and-over. The late crowd is younger and trendier and comes mostly for the unique specialty martinis, like the pineapple upside-down martini. The prices are quite reasonable all around, and this remains one of the most fun places in town.

**MAP 1:** 42 MLK Jr. Blvd., 912/238-2012, www.luluschocolatebar.net; Sun.-Thurs. noon-midnight, Fri.-Sat. 2pm-2am

## Italian

### VINNIE VANGOGO'S $

One would never call Savannah a great pizza town, but the best pizza here is Vinnie VanGoGo's, at the west end of City Market on Franklin Square. The pizza is a thin-crust Neapolitan style—although the menu claims it to be New York style—with a delightful tangy sauce and fresh cheese. Individual slices are huge, so don't feel obliged to order a whole pie. The waiting list for a table can get pretty long.

**MAP 1:** 317 W. Bryan St., 912/233-6394, www.vinnievangogos.com; Mon.-Thurs. 4pm-11:30pm, Fri. 4pm-1am, Sat. noon-1am, Sun. noon-11:30pm; cash only

# HISTORIC DISTRICT NORTH

## Classic Southern

### ★ THE GREY $$$

Savannah's most dramatic restaurant success story is the Grey, located in a stunningly restored former bus depot. It has taken the national foodie world by storm with beloved regional vernacular and soul food cuisine classics like seafood boudin, veal sweetbreads, roasted yardbird, fisherman's stew, and more, depending on seasonal whim and sourcing availabilities. A James Beard Award finalist in 2015, the Grey features the talents of standout executive chef Mashama Bailey, who grew up in Savannah and has a close eye for what makes the South tick food-wise. At the entrance is the "Diner Bar," a smaller offset bar area offering a punchy bar-food menu strong on sandwiches.

**MAP 1:** 109 MLK Jr. Blvd., 912/662-5999, www.thegreyrestaurant.com; Sun. and Tues.-Thurs. 5:30pm-10pm, Fri.-Sat. 5:30pm-11pm, supper every 3rd Sun. of the month



### ★ KAYAK KAFE $$

The best lunch on Broughton Street is at Kayak Kafe, where you can get a killer fresh salad or a fish taco to refresh your energy level during a busy day of shopping or sightseeing. Vegetarians, vegans, and those on a gluten-free diet will be especially pleased by the available options. As one of the very few Broughton Street places with outdoor sidewalk tables, this is also a great people-watching spot.

**MAP 1:** 1 E. Broughton St., 912/233-6044, www.eatkayak.com; Mon.-Thurs. 11am-10pm, Fri.-Sat. 11am-11pm, Sun. 11am-5pm

### OLDE PINK HOUSE $$

Once the home of General James Habersham and the first place the Declaration of Independence was read aloud in Savannah, the Olde Pink House is still a hub of activity, as visitors and locals alike frequent the classic interior of the dining room and the downstairs Planter's Tavern. Olde Pink House is known for its savvy (and often sassy) service and the uniquely regional flair it adds to traditional dishes, with liberal doses of pecans, Vidalia onions, shrimp, and crab. The she-crab soup and lamb chops in particular are crowd-pleasers, and the scored crispy flounder stacks up to similar versions of this dish at several other spots in town. Reservations are recommended.

**MAP 1:** 23 Abercorn St., 912/232-4286; Sun.-Thurs. 5:30pm-10:30pm, Fri.-Sat. 5:30pm-11pm

The Grey restaurant is located in a restored bus depot.

### HUSK SAVANNAH $$$

The latest reiteration of Southern celebrity chef Sean Brock's devotion to regional food culture, Husk Savannah operates on the now tried-and-true format of all-local farm-to-table food with a rotating seasonal menu. Highlights include inspired seafood dishes with an emphasis on freshness. The restaurant occupies a historic building, with an extensive, modernist interior complete with swanky bar.

**MAP 1:** 12 W. Oglethorpe St., 912/349-2600; Sun.-Thurs. 5pm-10pm, Fri.-Sat. 5pm-11pm

### 17HUNDRED90 $$

One of Savannah's oldest continuously operating culinary institutions and lodgings, 17Hundred90 Inn and Restaurant has recently vaulted itself into the upper echelon of Savannah cuisine with the addition of a dynamic menu by executive chef Jim Deja. Expect strong showings on the usual Southern classics—the crab stew is a must-have starter—but some unique takes, which you won't find anywhere else in town, such as a mouthwatering brisket ciabatta. Even the honey butter rolls brought to each table are delectable. The dining room is nostalgically no-frills and straight out of the historic namesake era; there's live piano accompaniment in the main dining room in the evenings. The attached bar area is a popular local watering hole; you can order from the full menu at the bar if you prefer.

**MAP 1:** 307 E. President St., 912/236-7122, www.17hundred90.com; daily 5pm-9pm

## Australian

### THE COLLINS QUARTER $$

The prime location of The Collins Quarter on a central corner in downtown Savannah is a big reason for its success. Other reasons include their amazing brunches and upscale sandwich offerings. The main claim to fame, however, might be an exquisite mastery of coffee and tea. Australian owner Anthony Debreceny—the restaurant's name is inspired by a street in Melbourne—says he started his establishment because he wanted to offer a place for truly great coffee. Indeed, their coffee service opens before their kitchen in the mornings.

**MAP 1:** 151 Bull St., 912/777-4147, www.thecollinsquarter.com; coffee service from 6:30am daily, brunch Mon. 8am-3pm, Wed.-Sat. 8am-3pm, dinner Wed.-Sat. 5:30pm-10pm

## Coffee, Tea, and Sweets

### THE COFFEE FOX $

The best coffee on Broughton is at the Coffee Fox, a locally owned joint that expertly treads the fine line between hipster hangout and accessible hot spot. The freshly baked goodies are nearly as good as the freshly brewed java, which includes cold-brew and pour-over offerings.

**MAP 1:** 102 W. Broughton St., 912/401-0399, www.thecoffeefox.com; Mon.-Sat. 7am-11pm, Sun. 8am-4pm

### ★ LEOPOLD'S ICE CREAM $

He helped produce *Mission Impossible III* and other movies, but Savannah native Stratton Leopold's other claim to fame is running the 100-year-old family business at Leopold's Ice Cream. Leopold's also offers soup and sandwiches to go with its delicious sweet treats. Memorabilia from Stratton's various movies is all around the shop, which stays open after every evening performance at the Lucas Theatre around the corner. You can occasionally find Stratton himself behind the counter doling out scoops.

**MAP 1:** 212 E. Broughton St., 912/234-4442, www.leopoldsicecream.com; Sun.-Thurs. 11am-10pm, Fri.-Sat. 11am-11pm

### WRIGHT SQUARE CAFE $

For a more upscale take on sweets, check out the chocolate goodies at Wright Square Cafe. While they do offer tasty wraps and sandwiches, let's not kid ourselves; the draw here is the outrageous assortment of high-quality European-style brownies, cookies, cakes, and other sweet treats.

**MAP 1:** 21 W. York St., 912/238-1150, www.wrightsquarecafe.com; Mon.-Fri. 7:30am-5:30pm, Sat. 9am-5:30pm

## Mexican

### ★ TEQUILA'S TOWN $$

The best Mexican spot downtown is Tequila's Town, filling an oft-noted void in the Savannah foodie scene. The menu is comprehensive and authentic, a clear step above the usual gringo-oriented fat-fest. Highlights include the chiles rellenos and the seafood, not to mention the guacamole prepared table-side.

**MAP 1:** 109 Whitaker St., 912/236-3222, www.tequilastown.com; Mon.-Thurs. 11am-10pm, Fri.-Sat. 11am-11pm, Sun. noon-10pm

## South African

### ZUNZI'S $

Look for the long lunchtime line outside the tiny storefront. This takeout joint is one of Savannah's favorite lunch spots, and it's gotten a lot of national attention for its robust, rich dishes like the exquisite South African-style sausage.

**MAP 1:** 108 E. York St., 912/443-9555, http://zunzis.com; Mon.-Sat. 11am-6pm

# HISTORIC DISTRICT SOUTH

## Classic Southern

### CRYSTAL BEER PARLOR $

A very popular spot with locals and tourists alike, the Crystal Beer Parlor offers one of the best burgers downtown. With a history going back to the 1930s, this has been a friendly family tradition for generations of Savannahians. The lively bar area has a very wide range of craft brews, and there are plenty of snug booths to sit in and enjoy their solid American menu.

**MAP 2:** 301 W. Jones St., 912/349-1000, www.crystalbeerparlor.com; daily 11am-10pm

### ★ MRS. WILKES' DINING ROOM $$

The rise of Paula Deen and her Lady & Sons restaurant has only made local epicures even more exuberant in their praise for Mrs. Wilkes' Dining Room, Savannah's original comfort food mecca. The delightful Sema Wilkes herself has passed on, but nothing has changed—not the communal dining room, the cheerful service, the care taken with take-out customers, nor, most of all, the food, a succulent mélange of the South's greatest hits, including the best fried chicken in town, snap beans, black-eyed peas, and collard greens. While each day boasts a different set menu, almost all of the classics are on the table at each meal. Be prepared for a long wait, however; lines begin forming early in the morning.

**MAP 2:** 107 W. Jones St., 912/232-5997, www.mrswilkes.com; Mon.-Fri. 11am-2pm

## Fusion

### FORK & DAGGER $

A unique, folksy, and affordable place within easy walking distance of Forsyth Park, Fork & Dagger has an eclectic breakfast and lunch menu combining Southern favorites, Caribbean dishes, and New York deli staples like the hot pastrami sandwich.

**MAP 2:** 609 Abercorn St., 912/712-5115, www.forkanddaggersav.com; Mon.-Sat. 8:30am-3pm

# SOFO DISTRICT

## New Southern

### ★ ELIZABETH ON 37TH $$$

Before there was Paula Deen, there was Elizabeth Terry, Savannah's first high-profile chef and founder of Elizabeth on 37th, Savannah's most elegant restaurant. Terry has since sold the place to two of her former waiters, Greg and Gary Butch, but this restaurant has continued to maintain her high standards. Executive chef Kelly Yambor uses eclectic, seasonally shifting ingredients that blend the South with the south of France. Along with generally attentive service, it makes for a wonderfully old-school fine-dining experience. Reservations are advised.

**MAP 3:** 105 E. 37th St., 912/236-5547; daily 6pm-10pm

### COTTON & RYE $$

One of the newer and more buzzworthy eat-and-drink spots in town is Cotton & Rye, which while off the usual tourist-beaten path is certainly well worth the trip if you want to go where the locals go. Set in a smallish, restored old bank building, the atmosphere is both upscale and invitingly cozy. The menu is strong on fresh artisanal meats in the Southern style; try the hanger steak or the fried chicken. In a neat twist, the entire wine and beer menu is all-American.

**MAP 3:** 1801 Habersham St., 912/777-6286, www.cottonandrye.com, Fri.-Sat. 5pm-10:30pm, Mon.-Thurs. 5pm-10pm

### ATLANTIC $

A new darling of Savannah foodies, Atlantic provides a curated seasonal menu in a boisterous, fun space located in a completely renovated historic gas station. Owner Jason Restivo focuses on upgrades of familiar comfort food items. A nice outdoor courtyard area is also a great option. Reservations aren't taken, so there might be a short wait at this popular place.

**MAP 3:** 102 E. Victory Dr., 912/417-8887, www.atlanticsavannah.com; Fri.-Sat. 5pm-10pm, Mon.-Thurs. 5pm-9pm

### Burgers

#### ★ GREEN TRUCK NEIGHBORHOOD PUB $

The cozy Green Truck Neighborhood Pub earns rave reviews with its delicious regionally sourced meat and produce offered at reasonable prices. (The large selection of craft beers on tap is a big draw too). The marquee item is the signature five-ounce grass-fed burger. A basic burger is $7, but several other increasingly more dressed-up versions are offered, none over $12.50. Burgers are also offered with chicken or veggie patties. It's a small room that often has a big line, and they don't take reservations. But the full menu is offered at the bar, which has a well-curated craft brew selection.

**MAP 3:** 2430 Habersham St., 912/234-5885, http://greentruckpub.com; Tues.-Sat. 11am-11pm

### Coffee, Tea, and Sweets

#### BACK IN THE DAY BAKERY $$

Primarily known for its sublime sweet treats, James Beard Award-nominated Back in the Day Bakery also offers a small but delightfully tasty (and tasteful) range of lunch soups, salads, and sandwiches (11am-2pm Tues.-Sat.). Lunch highlights include the baguette with camembert, roasted red peppers, and lettuce, as well as the caprese, the classic tomato, mozzarella, and basil trifecta on a perfect ciabatta. But whatever you do, save room for dessert, which runs the full sugar spectrum: red velvet cupcakes, lemon bars, macaroons, carrot cake, and many others.

**MAP 3:** 2403 Bull St., 912/495-9292, www.backinthedaybakery.com; Tues.-Fri. 9am-5pm, Sat. 8am-3pm

#### FOXY LOXY $

Foxy Loxy is a classic coffeehouse set within a cozy multistory Victorian on Bull Street. Bonuses include the authentic Tex-Mex menu, wine and beer offerings, and freshly baked sweet treats.

**MAP 3:** 1919 Bull St., 912/401-0543, www.foxyloxycafe.com; Mon.-Sat. 7am-11pm

#### THE SENTIENT BEAN $

The coffee at the Sentient Bean is all fair trade and organic, and the all-vegetarian fare is a major upgrade above the usual coffeehouse offerings. But "The Bean" is more than a coffeehouse—it's a community. Probably the best indie film venue in town, the Bean regularly hosts screenings of cutting-edge left-of-center documentary and kitsch films, as well as rotating art exhibits.

**MAP 3:** 13 E. Park Ave., 912/232-4447, www.sentientbean.com; daily 7:30am-10pm

## EASTSIDE

### Classic Southern

#### DESPOSITO'S $$

Located just across the Wilmington River from the fishing village of Thunderbolt, Desposito's is a big hit with locals and visitors alike, although it's not in all the guidebooks. The focus here is on crab, shrimp, and oysters, and lots of them, all caught wild in local waters and served humbly on tables covered with newspapers.

**MAP 4:** 187 Old Tybee Rd., 912/897-9963, www.despositosseafood.com; Tues.-Fri. 5pm-10pm, Sat. noon-10pm

### Barbecue

#### ★ SANDFLY BBQ $

If you're out this way visiting Wormsloe or Skidaway Island State Park, or if you're just crazy about good barbecue, make a point to hit little Sandfly BBQ, unique in the area for its dedication to real Memphis-style barbecue. Anything is great—this is the best brisket in the area—but for the best overall experience try the Hog Wild platter. Service is friendly, the price is right, and everything on the menu is superb.

**MAP 4:** 8413 Ferguson Ave. 912/356-5463, www.sandflybbq.com; Mon.-Sat. 11am-8pm

## TYBEE ISLAND

### Breakfast and Brunch

#### THE BREAKFAST CLUB $

Considered the best breakfast in the Savannah area for 30 years and counting, The Breakfast

Club, with its brisk diner atmosphere and hearty Polish sausage-filled omelets, is like a little bit of Chicago in the South. Lines start early for a chance to enjoy such house specialties as Helen's Solidarity, the Athena Omelet, and the Chicago Bear Burger, but don't worry—you'll inevitably strike up a conversation with someone interesting while you wait.
**MAP 5:** 1500 Butler Ave., 912/786-5984, http://tybeeisland.com/breakfast-club; daily 6:30am-1pm

## Casual Dining

### THE CRAB SHACK $$

Set in a large former fishing camp overlooking Chimney Creek, the Crab Shack is a favorite local seafood place and something of an attraction in itself. Don't expect gourmet fare or quiet seaside dining; the emphasis is on mounds of fresh, tasty seafood, heavy on the raw-bar action. Getting there is a little tricky: Take U.S. 80 to Tybee, cross the bridge over Lazaretto Creek, and begin looking for Estill Hammock Road to Chimney Creek on the right. Take Estill Hammock Road and veer right. After that, it's hard to miss.
**MAP 5:** 40 Estill Hammock Rd., 912/786-9857, www.thecrabshack.com; Mon.-Thurs. 11:30am-10pm, Fri.-Sun. 11:30am-11pm

### HUC-A-POO'S BITES & BOOZE $

Known far and wide for its sublime pizza is Huc-a-Poo's Bites & Booze. Individual slices run about $4, can easily feed two, and are quite delicious. Out of the tourist ruckus and tucked away within a small shopping center just as you arrive onto Tybee proper, Huc-a-Poo's also has a very lively bar scene.
**MAP 5:** 1213 E. U.S. 80, 912/786-5900, http://hucapoos.com; daily 11am-11pm

### NORTH BEACH GRILL $$

One of Tybee's more cherished restaurants is on the north end in the shadow of the Tybee Light Station. Like a little slice of Jamaica near the dunes, the laid-back North Beach Grill deals in tasty Caribbean fare, such as its signature jerk chicken, fish sandwiches, and, of course, delicious fried plantains, all overseen by chef-owner "Big George" Spriggs. Frequent live music adds to the island vibe.
**MAP 5:** 33 Meddin Ave., 912/786-4442; daily 11:30am-10pm

### TYBEE ISLAND SOCIAL CLUB $$

For a leisurely and tasty dinner, try Tybee Island Social Club. Their menu is somewhat unusual for this seafood-heavy island: It's primarily an assortment of gourmet-ish tacos,

Sandfly BBQ

## To Market, to Market

Savannah's first and still premier health-food market, **Brighter Day Natural Foods** (1102 Bull St., 912/236-4703, www.brighterdayfoods.com, Mon.-Sat. 9am-7pm, Sun. noon-5:30pm) has been the labor of love of Janie and Peter Brodhead for 30 years, all of them in the same location at the southern tip of Forsyth Park. Boasting organic groceries, regional produce, a sandwich and smoothie bar with a takeout window, and an extensive vitamin, supplement, and herb section, Brighter Day is an oasis in Savannah's sea of chain supermarkets.

Opened in 2013, **Whole Foods Market** (1815 E. Victory Dr., www.wholefoodsmarket.com, daily 8am-9pm) offers the chain's usual assortment of organic produce, with a very good fresh meat and seafood selection.

The thriving **Forsyth Park Farmers Market** (www.forsythfarmersmarket.org, Sat. 9am-1pm) happens in the south end of scenic and wooded Forsyth Park. You'll find very fresh fruit and produce from a variety of fun and friendly regional farmers. If you have access to a real kitchen while you're in town, you might be glad to know there's usually a very good selection of organic, sustainably grown meat and poultry products as well—not always a given at farmers markets.

If you need some good-quality groceries downtown—especially after hours—try **Parker's Market** (222 E. Drayton St., 912/231-1001, daily 24 hours). In addition to a pretty wide array of gourmet-style grab 'n' go victuals inside, there are gas pumps outside to fuel your vehicle.

There's one 24-hour full-service supermarket in downtown Savannah: **Kroger** (311 E. Gwinnett St., 912/231-2260, daily 24 hours).



including fish, duck, and lime- and tequila-marinated steak, all under $10 each. The beer and wine list is accomplished, and the live entertainment is usually very good—which is fortunate, since the service is on the slow side.

**MAP 5:** 1311 Butler Ave., 912/472-4044, http://tybeeislandsocialclub.com; Tues. 5pm-9:30pm, Wed.-Fri. noon-9:30pm, Sat.-Sun. 11:30am-10pm

## GREATER SAVANNAH

The Pooler-West Chatham area is the fastest growing in the Savannah metro area. It is also dominated by new chain restaurants. Here are a couple of tasty departures from the mass-market trend for you to seek if you find yourself out that way.

### Pooler-West Chatham

#### PIE SOCIETY $

Get some incredibly tasty little pasties and meat pies, old English style, at this charming little family spot run by British expats. Everything is all homemade and usually fresh out of the oven. Note the early opening hours, all the better to get your piping hot, fresh breakfast baked items.

**MAP 6:** 115 Canal St., 912/856-4785, www.thebritishpiecompany.com; Mon.-Fri. 7am-6:30pm, Sat. 7am-5pm

#### MOLLY MACPHERSON'S SCOTTISH PUB AND GRILL $$

A mirror image of the one on Congress Street in Savannah, this edition of Molly's delivers the same high-quality pub items like shepherd's pie and fish-and-chips, along with an outstanding selection of beers on tap and of course, scotch.

**MAP 6:** 110 Towne Center Dr., 912/348-3200, www.macphersonspub.com; Mon.-Sat. 11am-2am, Sun. 11am-11pm

### Indian

#### NAAN APPETIT $

This is unpretentious but tasty Indian food at a good price. Try the lamb masala curry or the chili paneer.

**MAP 6:** 1024 U.S. 80, 912/348-2446, www.naanappetit.com; Tues.-Fri. 11am-3pm, 5pm-9:30pm, Sat.-Sun. noon-3pm, 5pm-10:30pm

## Midway and Liberty County

### HOLTON'S SEAFOOD $$

Many locals eat at least once a week at Holton's Seafood, an unpretentious and fairly typical family-run fried seafood place just off I-95 at the Midway exit.

**MAP 6:** 13711 E. Oglethorpe Hwy., Midway, 912/884-9151; daily lunch and dinner

### SUNBURY CRAB COMPANY $$

A restaurant of note in Midway is the Sunbury Crab Company, providing, you guessed it, great crab cakes in a casual atmosphere on the Midway River. Get here by taking Highway 38 east of Midway and then a left onto Fort Morris Road.

**MAP 6:** 541 Brigantine Dunmore Rd., Midway, 912/884-8640; Wed.-Fri. dinner, Sat.-Sun. lunch and dinner

## Richmond Hill

### STEAMERS RESTAURANT & RAW BAR $$

A popular place on U.S. 17 is Steamers Restaurant & Raw Bar, home of some good Lowcountry boil in a relaxed, homey atmosphere.

**MAP 6:** 4040 U.S. 17, Richmond Hill, 912/756-3979; daily 5pm-10pm

### THE UPPER CRUST PIZZERIA $

There's no end to the chain food offerings in Richmond Hill, but one of the better restaurants in town is the Upper Crust, a casual American place with great pizza in addition to soups, salads, and hot sandwiches.

**MAP 6:** 1702 U.S. 17, Richmond Hill, 912/756-6990; Mon.-Sat. lunch and dinner, Sun. dinner



# Hotels

The good news for visitors is that there are many comparatively new hotels of note directly in the downtown area within walking distance of most sites. Some of them are the more widely recognized chains, and others represent boutique companies and provide a commensurately higher level of service. The less-good news, especially for locals, is that the ominously rising skyline that the newer, bigger hotels represent is a change from the friendly small-scale historical footprint Savannah is known for in the first place.

Savannah's many historic bed-and-breakfasts are competitive with the hotels on price, and often outperform them on service and ambience. If you don't need a swimming pool and don't mind climbing some stairs every now and then, a B&B is usually your best bet.

The best campground in town is at the well-managed and rarely crowded **Skidaway Island State Park** (52 Diamond Causeway, 912/598-2300, www.gastateparks.org; parking $5 per vehicle per day, tent and RV sites $26-40). There are 88 sites with 30-amp electric hookups. A two-night minimum stay is required on weekends, and there's a three-night minimum for Memorial Day, Labor Day, Independence Day, and Thanksgiving.

There's one campground on Tybee Island, the **River's End Campground and RV Park** (915 Polk St., 912/786-5518, www.cityoftybee.org; water-and-electric sites $34, 50-amp full-hookup sites $45, cabins $150) on the north side. River's End offers 100 full-service sites plus some primitive tent sites. The highlight, however, are the incredibly cute little cabins; book well in advance. While During Tybee's sometimes-chilly off-season (Nov.-Mar.), you can relax and get warm inside the common River Room. River's End also offers a swimming pool and laundry facilities.

Totally wilderness camping can be done on state-owned Little Tybee, accessible across the Back River by boat only; there are no facilities. The best camping and wilderness resource locally is **Half Moon Outfitters** (15 E. Broughton St., 912/201-9393, www.halfmoonoutfitters.com).

Bohemian Hotel Savannah Riverfront

## WATERFRONT

### ★ BOHEMIAN HOTEL SAVANNAH RIVERFRONT $$$

The Bohemian Hotel Savannah Riverfront has gained a reputation as one of Savannah's premier hotels, both for the casual visitor as well as visiting celebrities. Located between busy River Street and bustling City Market, this isn't the place for peace and quiet, but its combination of boutique-style retro-hip decor and happening rooftop bar scene makes it a great place to go for a fun stay that's as much Manhattan as Savannah. Valet parking is available, which you will come to appreciate.

**MAP 1:** 102 W. Bay St., 912/721-3800, www.bohemianhotelsavannah.com

### ★ THE BRICE $$$

Housed in Savannah's first Coca-Cola bottling plant, The Brice brings a boutique-style upgrade to the historic building. With great service and 145 rooms, most complete with a modernized four-poster bed, The Brice also features **Pacci Italian Kitchen + Bar** (breakfast daily 7am-10:30am, brunch Sat.-Sun. 8am-3pm, dinner Sun.-Thurs. 5pm-10pm, Fri.-Sat. 5pm-10:30pm, $15-25), one of the better hotel restaurant/bar combos in town.

**MAP 1:** 601 E. Bay St., 912/238-1200, www.thebricehotel.com

### HYATT REGENCY SAVANNAH $$$

For years critics have called the modernist Hyatt Regency Savannah an insult to architecture and to history. Regardless, the Hyatt—a sort of exercise in cubism straddling an entire block of River Street—has avoided the neglect of many older chain properties downtown. Three sides of the hotel offer views of the bustling Savannah waterfront, with its massive ships coming in from all over the world.

**MAP 1:** 2 E. Bay St., 912/238-1234, www.savannah.hyatt.com

### WESTIN SAVANNAH HARBOR GOLF RESORT AND SPA $$

If you require a swank pool, look no farther than the Westin Savannah Harbor Golf Resort and Spa, which has a beautiful resort-style pool across the Savannah River from downtown and overlooking the old city. Accessing the hotel—located on a cross-channel island—is a bit of a process, but one made easier by charming river ferries that run regularly and free of charge. The attached golf course is a good one, and packages are available.

**MAP 1:** 1 Resort Dr., 912/201-2000, www.westinsavannah.com

## CITY MARKET

### ★ ANDAZ SAVANNAH $$$

Providing a suitably modernist decor to go with its somewhat atypical architecture for Savannah, the Andaz Savannah overlooks restored Ellis Square and abuts City Market with its shopping, restaurants, and nightlife. A boutique offering from Hyatt, the Andaz's guest rooms and suites feature top-of-the-line linens, extra-large and well-equipped baths, in-room snack bars, and technological features

## Best Hotels

★ **Best Rooftop Bar:** The boutique **Bohemian Hotel Savannah Riverfront** isn't only a swank stay on the waterfront, its Rocks on the Roof bar offers stunning wraparound alfresco views of the river and surrounding downtown area.

★ **Expertly Repurposed Coca-Cola Bottling Plant:** The historic building housing **The Brice** hasn't bottled soft drinks for decades, but it now hosts this tastefully modernist boutique hotel, complete with an upscale in-house Italian restaurant, Pacci. The Brice is in a comparatively quiet corner of downtown but still well within walking distance of most downtown attractions.

★ **Most Excellent View of Ellis Square:** A major part of the dramatic reclamation of Ellis Square was the building of the modernist **Andaz Savannah.** From its windows you get a great view of downtown, and the bar-restaurant combo is top-notch.

★ **Best Historic Hotel:** On bustling Broughton Street, **The Marshall House** probably has the rooms with the most intact historic feel.

★ **Newest Old Name:** An extensive renovation and repurposing of a veteran name in local lodging puts **The DeSoto** at the top of any list of best hotels in town.

★ **Closest B&B to the Squares:** Probably the friendliest downtown B&B, **Foley House Inn** is also among the closest in walking distance to most of the downtown action.

★ **Classiest B&B near Forsyth Park:** It's not as close to the downtown squares as other places, but **The Gastonian** inn is a world-class stay just steps away from vast, green Forsyth Park and its iconic fountain.

★ **Best Stay on The Beach:** The lodging scene on Tybee Island is hit-or-miss. If you can get a room at the delightful and charming **The Georgianne Inn,** circa 1910, you'll enjoy a peaceful stay that's still close to the entertainment on the south end of the island.

such as free Wi-Fi and, of course, the ubiquitous flat-screen TV. Customer service is a particular strong suit. Just off the lobby is a very hip lounge-wine bar that attracts locals as well as hotel guests. Keep in mind things can get a little noisy in this area at night on weekends.
**MAP 1:** 14 Barnard St., 912/233-2116, www.savannah.andaz.hyatt.com

## HISTORIC DISTRICT NORTH

### ★ THE MARSHALL HOUSE $$$

Dominating most of a block of East Broughton Street is The Marshall House, Savannah's oldest hotel and a delightful throwback in a city increasingly populated with modernist boutique hotels. The craftsmanship devoted to preservation of this circa 1851 building is impressive. While that does mean the rooms aren't huge, you're paying for prime location in the heart of Savannah's commercial district and for distinctive retro style. If you're into ghosts, it is alleged to be a haunted property as well.
**MAP 1:** 123 E. Broughton St., 912/644-7896, www.marshallhouse.com

### BALLASTONE INN $$$

Once a bordello, the 1838 mansion that is home to the 16-room Ballastone Inn is one of Savannah's favorite inns. Highlights include an afternoon tea service and one of the better full breakfasts in town. Note that some guest rooms are at what Savannah calls the "garden level," meaning sunken basement-level rooms with what amounts to a worm's-eye view.

**MAP 1:** 14 E. Oglethorpe Ave., 912/236-1484, www.ballastone.com

### THE GREEN PALM INN $$

Easily the best bed-and-breakfast for the price in Savannah is The Green Palm Inn, a folksy and romantic little Victorian number with some neat gingerbread exterior stylings and four cute guest rooms, each named after a species of palm tree. It's situated on the very easternmost edge of the Savannah Historic District—hence its reasonable rates. Delightful innkeeper Diane McCray provides a very good and generous breakfast plus a pretty much constant dessert bar.

**MAP 1:** 546 E. President St., 912/447-8901, www.greenpalminn.com

### 17HUNDRED90 INN $$

Famous for its host of resident ghosts—which many employees do swear aren't just tourist tales—17Hundred90 offers 14 cozy rooms within a historic building that dates from, yep, 1790. The addition of several nearby guest houses, booked through the inn, has expanded the footprint of this great old Savannah name. The great plus here—in addition to the ghost stories of course—is the excellent on-site restaurant and bar, popular with both locals and tourists alike.

**MAP 1:** 307 E. President St., 912/236-7122, www.17hundred90.com

### THE KEHOE HOUSE $$

One of Savannah's favorite bed-and-breakfasts, The Kehoe House is a great choice for its charm and attention to guests. Its historic location, on quiet little Columbia Square catty-corner to the Isaiah Davenport House, is within walking distance to all the downtown action, but far enough from the bustle to get some peace out on one of the rocking chairs on the veranda.

**MAP 1:** 123 Habersham St., 912/232-1020, www.kehoehouse.com

## HISTORIC DISTRICT SOUTH

### ELIZA THOMPSON HOUSE $$

One of Savannah's original historic B&Bs, the Eliza Thompson House is a bit out of the bustle on serene, beautiful Jones Street, but still close enough to get involved whenever you feel the urge. You can enjoy the various culinary offerings—breakfast, wine and cheese, nighttime munchies—either in the parlor or on the patio overlooking the house's classic Savannah garden.

**MAP 2:** 5 W. Jones St., 912/236-3620, www.elizathompsonhouse.com

### ★ THE DESOTO SAVANNAH $$

One of Savannah's key downtown landmarks is the towering edifice of The DeSoto Savannah, usually just called The DeSoto in a nod to its long history here, which includes a now-demolished high Victorian resort by the same name. While the shell of the building dates from the 1960s in its incarnation as a Hilton property, the Sotheby brand recently acquired the hotel and has unveiled an extensive modernization and renovation. The rooms are sumptuous in the modern boutique hotel tradition, and the service at the hotel stands out. The location, at arguably Savannah's most important intersection, Bull and Liberty Streets, can't be beat. The independently run restaurant downstairs, the **1540 Room** (Tues.-Thurs. 5pm-10pm, Fri.-Sat. 5pm-11pm, Sun. 10:30am-3pm), boasts local culinary heavy-hitters. A few feet away is **Edgar's Proof & Provision,** an old-school hotel bar with a separate solid menu that's offered 6:30am-midnight daily. To top it off, Savannah's favorite dive bar, Pinkie Masters, is right across the street, though unaffiliated with the hotel.

**MAP 2:** 15 E. Liberty St., 912/232-9000, www.thedesotosavannah.com

### ★ FOLEY HOUSE INN $$

The circa-1896 Foley House Inn is a four-diamond B&B with some rooms available at a three-diamond price. Its 19 individualized Victorian-decor guest rooms, in two town houses, range from the smaller Newport overlooking the "grotto courtyard" to the four-poster, bay-windowed Essex room, complete with a fireplace and a whirlpool bath. The location on Chippewa Square is pretty much perfect: well off the busy east-west thoroughfares but in the heart of Savannah's active theater district and within walking distance of anywhere.

**MAP 2:** 14 W. Hull St., 912/232-6622, www.foleyinn.com

## VICTORIAN DISTRICT

### DRESSER-PALMER HOUSE $$

A short walk from Forsyth Park, the Dresser-Palmer House features 15 guest rooms in two wings but still manages to make things feel pretty cozy. Garden-level rooms go for under $200.

**MAP 3:** 211 E. Gaston St., 912/238-3294, www.dresserpalmerhouse.com

### ★ THE GASTONIAN $$$

The Gastonian inn, circa 1868, is a favorite choice for travelers to Savannah, mostly for its 17 sumptuously decorated guest rooms and suites, all with working fireplaces, and the always outstanding full breakfast. They pile on the epicurean delights with teatime, evening nightcaps, and complimentary wine.

**MAP 3:** 220 E. Gaston St., 912/232-2869, www.gastonian.com

### MANSION ON FORSYTH PARK $$$

How ironic that a hotel built in a former mortuary would be one of the few Savannah hotels not to have a resident ghost story. But that's the case with Mansion on Forsyth Park, which dominates an entire block alongside Forsyth Park, including partially within the high-Victorian former Fox & Weeks Mortuary building. Its sumptuous guest rooms, equipped with big beds, big baths, and big-screen TVs, scream "boutique hotel," as does the swank little bar and the alfresco patio area.

**MAP 3:** 700 Drayton St., 912/238-5158, www.mansiononforsythpark.com

Mansion on Forsyth Park

## Stay the Week

For long-term stays on Tybee Island, weekly rentals are the name of the game. Though not cheap—expect to pay roughly $1,000 per week in the summer—they provide a higher level of accommodations than some hotels on the island. For weekly rentals, try **Oceanfront Cottage Rentals** (800/786-5889, www.oceanfrontcottage.com), **Tybee Island Rentals** (912/786-4034, www.tybeeislandrentals.com), or **Tybee Vacation Rentals** (866/359-0297, www.tybeevacationrentals.com).

## TYBEE ISLAND

Most of the hotels on Tybee Island see a lot of wear and tear from eager vacationers. I encourage a B&B stay. Also be aware that places on Butler Avenue, even the substandard ones, charge a premium during the high season (Mar.-Oct.).

### ATLANTIS INN $

For those looking for the offbeat, try the Atlantis Inn. Its reasonably priced, whimsically themed rooms are a hoot, and you're a short walk from the ocean and a very easy jaunt around the corner from busy Tybrisa Street. The downside, however, is no dedicated parking.

**MAP 5:** 20 Silver Ave., 912/786-8558, www.atlantisinntybee.com

### ★ THE GEORGIANNE INN $$

The best B&B-style experience on Tybee can be found at The Georgianne Inn, a short walk off the beach and close to most of the island's action, yet not so close that you can't get away when you want to. The complimentary bikes to use while you're there are a nice plus.

**MAP 5:** 1312 Butler Ave., 912/786-8710, www.georgianneinn.com

### BEACHVIEW BED & BREAKFAST $$

For a classic B&B stay very close to the Tybrisa-south end action, Beachview is where to go. The food is great and the views from the extensive wraparound porches are wonderful, especially on a breezy Tybee night.

**MAP 5:** 1701 Butler Ave., 912/348-5202, www.beachviewbbtybee.com

### LIGHTHOUSE INN $$

Tucked away on the north end near the Lighthouse, hence the name, the Lighthouse Inn offers a lot of privacy in a very cozy and lush corner lot. This is more the place for a quiet, secluded getaway.

**MAP 5:** 16 Meddin Dr., 912/786-0901, www.tybeebb.com

### RIVER'S END CAMPGROUND $

RV campers and more adventurous trekkers have a great treat in store at River's End Campground, on Tybee's somewhat less-developed north end. There are plenty of full-hookup sites ($70-90), some limited service or tent sites ($60-70), and a set of adorable little cabins that sleep six (2-night minimum, $125-160).

**MAP 5:** 5 Fort Ave., 800/786-1016, www.riversendcampground.com

## GREATER SAVANNAH

### Midway and Liberty County

### DUNHAM FARMS $$

While industry is coming quickly to Liberty County, it's still a small self-contained community with not much in the way of tourism amenities (many would say that is part of its charm). A great choice for a stay is Dunham Farms. The B&B ($165-205) is in the converted 1940s Palmyra Barn, and the self-catered circa-1840 Palmyra Cottage ($300) nearby is right on the river, with plenty of kayaking and hiking opportunities. Your hosts, Laura and Meredith Devendorf, couldn't be more charming or informed about the area, and the breakfasts are absurdly rich and filling in that hearty and deeply comforting Southern tradition.

**MAP 6:** 5836 Islands Hwy., Midway, 912/880-4500, www.dunhamfarms.com

# Transportation and Services



## AIR

Savannah is served by the fairly efficient **Savannah/Hilton Head International Airport** (SAV, 400 Airways Ave., 912/964-0514, www.savannahairport.com), directly off I-95 at exit 104. The airport is about 20 minutes from downtown Savannah and 45 minutes from Hilton Head Island. Airlines with routes to SAV include American (www.aa.com), Allegiant (www.allegiant.com), Delta (www.delta.com), JetBlue (www.jetblue.com), Sun Country (www.suncountry.com), and United (www.ual.com).

Taxis and rideshare operators provide transportation into Savannah. The maximum cab fare for destinations in the historic district is $28.

## CAR

Savannah is the eastern terminus of I-16, and that interstate is the most common entrance to the city. However, most travelers get to I-16 via I-95, taking the exit for downtown Savannah (Historic District). Once on I-16, the most common entry points into Savannah proper are via the Gwinnett Street exit, which puts you near the southern edge of the Historic District near Forsyth Park, or, more commonly, the Montgomery Street exit farther into the heart of downtown.

Paralleling I-95 is the old coastal highway, now U.S. 17, which goes through Savannah. U.S. 80 is Victory Drive for most of its length through town; after you pass through Thunderbolt on your way to the islands area, however, it reverts to U.S. 80, the only route to and from Tybee Island.

In Savannah, for quick access to the south, take the one-way streets Price (on the east side of downtown) or Whitaker (on the west side of downtown). Conversely, if you want to make a quick trip north into downtown, three one-way streets taking you there are East Broad, Lincoln, and Drayton.

When you're driving downtown and come to a square, the law says traffic within the square *always* has the right of way. In other words, if you haven't yet entered the square, you must yield to any vehicles already in the square.

### Car Rentals

The majority of rental car facilities are at the Savannah/Hilton Head International Airport, including **Avis** (800/831-2847), **Budget** (800/527-0700), **Dollar** (912/964-9001), **Enterprise** (800/736-8222), **Hertz** (800/654-3131), **National** (800/227-7368), and **Thrifty** (800/367-2277). Rental locations away from the airport are **Avis** (7810 Abercorn St., 912/354-4718), **Budget** (7070 Abercorn St., 912/355-0805), and **Enterprise** (3028 Skidaway Rd., 912/352-1424; 9505 Abercorn St., 912/925-0060; 11506-A Abercorn Expressway, 912/920-1093; 7510 White Bluff Rd., 912/355-6622).

## TRAIN

Savannah is on the New York-Miami *Silver Service* of **Amtrak** (2611 Seaboard Coastline Dr., 912/234-2611, www.amtrak.com). To get to the station on the west side of town, take I-16 west and then I-516 north. Immediately take the Gwinnett Street-Railroad Station exit and follow the Amtrak signs.

## BUS

**Chatham Area Transit** (www.catchacat.org, Mon.-Sat. 5:30am-11:30pm, Sun. 7am-9pm, $1.50, includes one transfer, free for children under 41 inches tall, exact change only), Savannah's publicly supported bus system, is quite thorough and efficient considering Savannah's relatively small size. Plenty of routes crisscross the entire area.

Of primary interest to visitors is the free and recently expanded **Dot Express Shuttle** (Mon.-Fri. 7am-7pm, Sat. 10am-7pm, Sun. 10am-6pm, www.connectonthedot.com), which travels a continuous circuit route through the historic district with 24 stops at hotels, historic sites, and the Savannah Visitors Center. It comes around roughly every 10 minutes and is wheelchair accessible. It's a great option.

## TAXI

Taxi services in Georgia tend to be less regulated than in other states, but service is plentiful in Savannah and is generally reasonable. The chief local provider is **Yellow Cab** (866/319-9646, www.savannahyellowcab.com). For wheelchair accessibility, request cab number 14. Other providers include **Adam Cab** (912/927-7466), **Magikal Taxi Service** (912/897-8294), and **Sunshine Cab** (912/272-0971).

If you're not in a big hurry, it's always fun to take a **Savannah Pedicab** (912/232-7900, www.savannahpedicab.com) for quick trips around downtown, or with the competing company **Royal Bike Taxi** (912/341-3944, www.royalbiketaxi.com). In both cases your friendly driver will pedal one or two passengers anywhere within the historic district, and you essentially pay what you think is fair (I recommend $5 pp minimum).

## PARKING

Parking is at a premium in downtown Savannah. Traditional coin-operated meter parking is available throughout the city, but more and more the city is going to self-pay kiosks, which accept debit and credit cards. There is also a free app to pay on your phone, called ParkSavannah. Bottom line: Be sure to pay for all parking weekdays and Saturday 8:30am-8pm. The rate is $2 per hour north of Liberty Street to the Savannah River, $1 per hour elsewhere.

The city operates several parking garages at various rates and hours: the **Bryan Street Garage** (100 E. Bryan St.), the **Robinson Garage** (132 Montgomery St.), the **State Street Garage** (100 E. State St.), the **Liberty Street Garage** (401 W. Liberty St.), and the new **Whitaker Street Garage,** underneath revitalized Ellis Square.

Tybee Island has paid parking year-round daily 8am-8pm.

## VISITOR INFORMATION

### Visitors Centers

The main clearinghouse for visitor information is the downtown **Savannah Visitors Center** (301 MLK Jr. Blvd., 912/944-0455, daily 9am-5:30pm). The newly revitalized Ellis Square features a small visitors kiosk (daily from 10am) at the northwest corner of the square, with public restrooms and elevators to the underground parking garage beneath the square.

Other visitors centers in the area include the **River Street Hospitality Center** (1 River St., 912/651-6662, daily 9am-8pm), the **Tybee Island Visitor Center** (S. Campbell Ave. and U.S. 80, 912/786-5444, daily 9am-5:30pm), and the **Savannah Airport Visitor Center** (464 Airways Ave., 912/964-1109, daily 8:30am-midnight).

**Visit Savannah** (101 E. Bay St., 877/728-2662, www.visitsavannah.com), the local convention and visitors bureau, maintains a list of lodgings and visitors centers on its website.

### Hospitals

Savannah has two very good hospital systems. Centrally located near midtown, **Memorial Health University Hospital** (4700 Waters Ave., 912/350-8000, www.memorialhealth.com) is the region's only Level-1 trauma center and is one of the best in the nation. The St. Joseph's-Candler Hospital System (www.sjchs.org) has two units, **St. Joseph's Hospital** (11705 Mercy Blvd., 912/819-4100) on the extreme south side and **Candler Hospital** (5401 Paulsen St., 912/819-6000), closer to midtown.

## Police

The Savannah Police Department has jurisdiction throughout the city of Savannah. For unincorporated Chatham County, the Chatham County Police Department has jurisdiction. Other municipalities, such as Tybee Island and Pooler, have their own city departments. For nonemergencies in Savannah, call 912/651-6675; for emergencies, call 911.

## Media

The daily newspaper of record is the ***Savannah Morning News*** (912/525-0796, www.savannahnow.com). It puts out an entertainment insert, called "Do," on Thursday. The free weekly newspaper in town is ***Connect Savannah*** (912/721-4350, www.connectsavannah.com), hitting stands each Wednesday. Look to it for culture and music coverage as well as an alternative take on local politics and issues.

Two glossy magazines compete: the hipper ***The South*** magazine (912/236-5501, www.thesouthmag.com) and the more establishment ***Savannah*** magazine (912/652-0293, www.savannahmagazine.com).

The National Public Radio affiliate is the Georgia Public Broadcasting station WSVH (91.1 FM). Savannah State University offers jazz, reggae, and Latin music on WHCJ (90.3 FM). Georgia Public Broadcasting is on WVAN. The local NBC affiliate is WSAV, the CBS affiliate is WTOC, the ABC affiliate is WJCL, and the Fox affiliate is WTGS.

## Libraries

The **Live Oak Public Library** (www.liveoakpl.org) is the umbrella organization for the libraries of Chatham, Effingham, and Liberty Counties. By far the largest branch is south of downtown Savannah, the **Bull Street Branch** (222 Bull St., 912/652-3600, Mon.-Tues. 9am-8pm, Wed.-Fri. 9am-6pm, Sun. 2pm-6pm). Farthest downtown and tucked away on Upper Factor's Walk is the charming little **Ola Wyeth Branch** (4 E. Bay St., 912/232-5488, Mon.-Fri. noon-3pm). In midtown Savannah is the historic **Carnegie Branch** (537 E. Henry St., 912/231-9921, Mon. 10am-8pm, Tues.-Thurs. 10am-6pm, Fri. 2pm-6pm, Sat. 10am-6am).

The **Georgia Historical Society** (501 Whitaker St., 912/651-2128, www.georgiahistory.com, Tues.-Sat. 10am-5pm) has an extensive collection of clippings, photos, maps, and other archival material at its headquarters at the corner of Forsyth Park in Hodgson Hall. Their website has been extensively revamped and is now one of the Southeast's best online resources for Georgia history information.

The **Jen Library** (201 E. Broughton St., 912/525-4700, www.scad.edu, Mon.-Fri. 7:30am-1am, Sat. 10am-1am, Sun. 11am-1am, shorter hours during school breaks), run by the Savannah College of Art and Design, has a cavernous 85,000-square-foot space. Its main claim to fame is the remarkable variety of art periodicals to which it subscribes, nearly 1,000 at last count. It was built for the school's 7,000-plus art students, but the public can enter and use it as well with photo ID (you just can't check anything out).

## Post Offices

The main post office of note for most visitors to Savannah is the **Telfair Square Station** (118 Barnard St., Mon.-Fri. 8am-5pm).

## Gay and Lesbian Resources

Visitors often find Savannah to be surprisingly cosmopolitan and diverse for a Deep South city, and nowhere is this truer than in its sizeable and influential gay and lesbian community. In line with typical Southern protocol, the community is largely apolitical and more concerned with integration than provocation. But they're still very much aware of their growing impact on the local economy and are major players in art and commerce.

The **Savannah Pride Festival** is held every autumn at various venues in town. Top-flight dance-oriented musical acts perform, restaurants show off their creativity, and activists staff information booths. The chief resource for local gay and lesbian information and concerns is the **First City Network,** whose main website (www.firstcitynetwork.net) features many useful links. Another great Internet networking resource is **Gay Savannah** (www.gaysavannah.com).

# The Golden Isles

The Georgia coast retains a timeless mystique evocative of an era before the coming of the Europeans, even before humankind itself.

Often called the Golden Isles because of the play of the afternoon sun on the vistas of marsh grass, its other nickname, "the Debatable Land," is a nod to its centuries-long role as a constantly shifting battleground of European powers.

On the map it looks relatively short, but Georgia's coastline is the longest contiguous salt marsh environment in the world—a third of the country's remaining salt marsh. Abundant with wildlife, vibrant with exotic, earthy aromas, constantly refreshed by a steady, salty sea breeze, it's a place with no real match anywhere else.

Ancient Native Americans held the area in special regard. Avaricious for gold as they were, the Spanish also admired the almost monastic enchantment of Georgia's coast, choosing it as the site of their first colony in North America. They built a subsequent chain of Roman Catholic missions, now long gone.

While the American tycoons who used these barrier islands as personal playgrounds had avarice of their own, we must give credit where it's due: Their self-interest kept these places largely untouched by the kind of development that has plagued many of South Carolina's barrier islands to the north.

## HISTORY

For over 5,000 years, the Golden Isles of what would become Georgia were an abundant food and game source for Native Americans. In those days, long before erosion and channel dredging had taken their toll, each barrier island was an easy canoe ride away from the next one—a sort of early Intracoastal Waterway—and there was bounty for everyone. But all that changed in 1526 when the Golden Isles became the site of the first European settlement in what is now the continental United States, the fabled San Miguel de Gualdape, founded nearly a century before the first English settlements in Virginia. Historians remain unsure where expedition leader Lucas de Ayllón actually set up camp with his 600 colonists and enslaved people, but recent research breakthroughs have put

**Previous:** playing croquet at the historic Jekyll Island Club; hiking to the campground at Stafford Beach on Cumberland Island. **Above:** the St. Simons Lighthouse Museum.

Look for ★ to find recommended sights, activities, dining, and lodging.

## Highlights

★ **Jekyll Island Historic District:** Relax and soak in the salty breeze at this onetime playground of the country's richest people (page 267).

★ **The Village:** The center of social life on St. Simons Island has shops, restaurants, a pier, and a beachside playground (page 273).

★ **Fort Frederica National Monument:** An excellently preserved tabby fortress dates from the first days of English settlement in Georgia (page 274).

★ **Harris Neck National Wildlife Refuge:** This former wartime airfield is now one of the East Coast's best birding locations (page 280).

★ **Cumberland Island National Seashore:** This undeveloped island paradise has wild horses, evocative abandoned ruins, and over 16 miles of gorgeous beach (page 285).

★ **Okefenokee National Wildlife Refuge:** More than just a swamp, the Okefenokee is a natural wonderland that takes you back into the mists of prehistory (page 289).

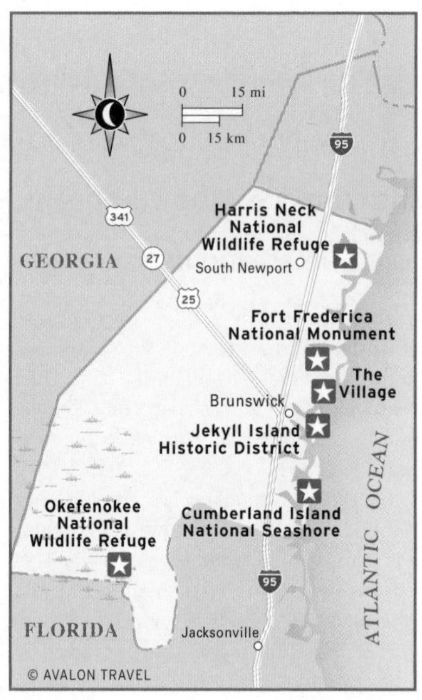

# The Golden Isles

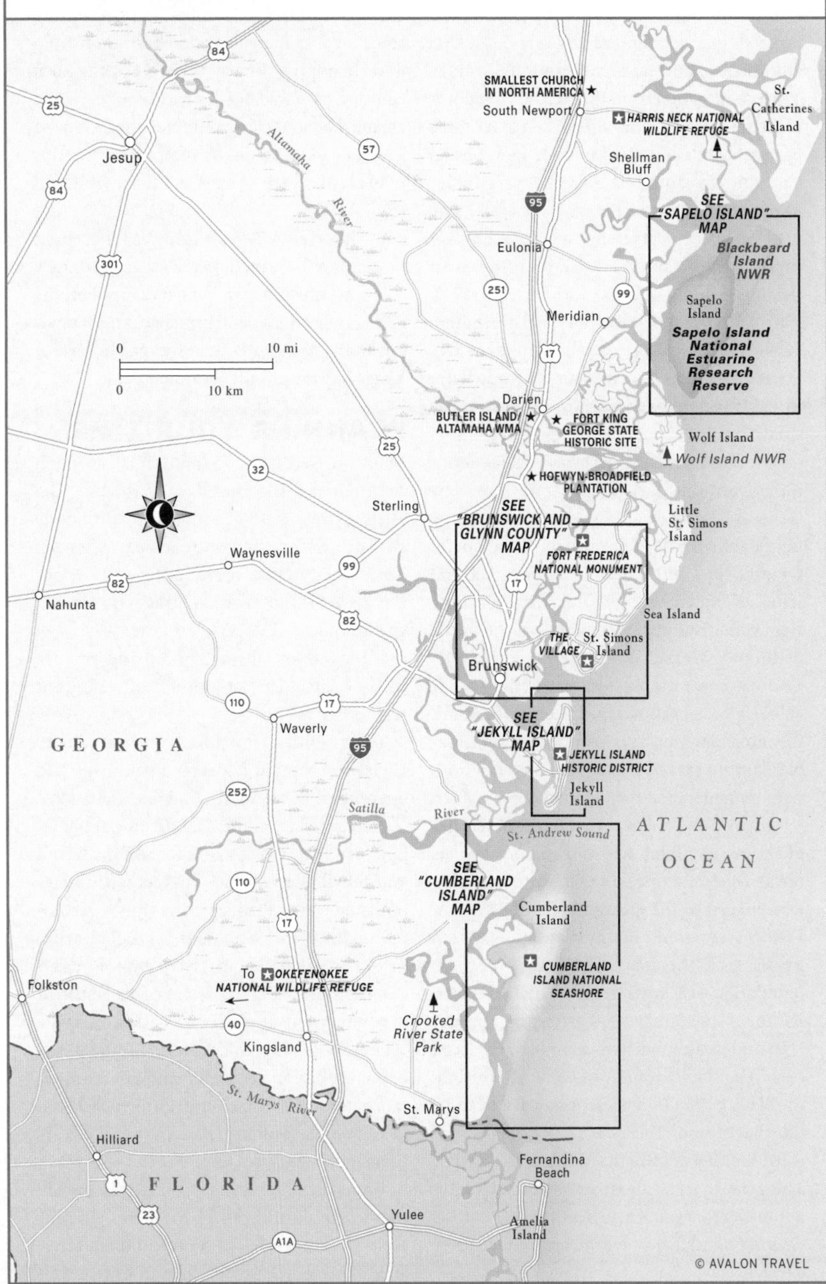

it somewhere around St. Catherine's Sound. San Miguel disintegrated within a couple of months, but it set the stage for a lengthy Spanish presence on the Georgia coast that culminated in the mission period (1580-1684). With cooperation from the coastal chiefdoms of Guale and Mocama, almost all of Georgia's barrier islands and many interior spots hosted Catholic missions, each with an accompanying contingent of Spanish regulars. The missions began retreating with the English incursion into the American Southeast in the 1600s, and the coast was largely free of European presence until an early English outpost, Fort King George near modern-day Darien, Georgia, was established decades later in 1721. Isolated and hard to provision, the small fort was abandoned seven years later.

The next English project was Fort Frederica on St. Simons Island, commissioned by General James Edward Oglethorpe following his establishment of Savannah to the north. Oglethorpe's settlement of Brunswick and Jekyll Island came soon afterward. With the final vanquishing of the Spanish at the Battle of Bloody Marsh near Fort Frederica, the Georgia coast quickly emulated the profitable rice-based plantation culture of the South Carolina Lowcountry, and indeed many notable Carolina planters expanded their holdings with marshland on the Georgia coast.

During the Civil War the southern reaches of Sherman's March to the Sea came down as far as Darien, a once vital trading port that was burned to the ground by Union troops. With slavery gone and the plantation system in disarray, the coast's African American population was largely left to its own devices. Although the famous "40 acres and a mule" land and wealth redistribution plan for freed enslaved people would not come to fruition, the black population of Georgia's Sea Islands, like that of South Carolina's, developed an inward-looking culture that persists to this day. The generic term for this culture is Gullah, but in Georgia you'll also hear it referred to as Geechee, local dialect for the nearby Ogeechee River.

As with much of the South after the Civil War, business carried on, with the area becoming a center for lumber, the turpentine trade, and an increasing emphasis on fishing and shrimping. But by the start of the 20th century, the Golden Isles had become firmly established as a playground for the rich, who hunted and dined on the sumptuous grounds of exclusive retreats such as the Jekyll Island Club.

As it did elsewhere, World War II brought new economic growth in the form of military bases, even as German U-boats ranged off the coast. Today the federal presence is most obvious in the massive Trident submarine base at Kings Bay toward the Florida border.

## PLANNING YOUR TIME

Many travelers take I-95 south from Savannah to the Golden Isles, but **U.S. 17** roughly parallels the interstate—in some cases so closely that drivers on the two roads can see each other—and is a far more scenic and enriching drive for those with a little extra time to spend. Indeed, U.S. 17 is an intrinsic part of the life and lore of the region, and you are likely to spend a fair amount of time on it regardless.

Geographically, Brunswick is similar to Charleston in that it lies on a peninsula laid out roughly north-south. And like Charleston, it's separated from the Atlantic by barrier islands, in Brunswick's case St. Simons Island and Jekyll Island. Once you get within city limits, however, Brunswick has more in common with Savannah due to its Oglethorpe-designed grid layout. **Brunswick** itself can easily be fully experienced in a **single afternoon.** But really—as its nickname "Gateway to the Golden Isles" indicates—Brunswick is an economic and governmental center for Glynn County, to which Jekyll Island and St. Simons Island, the real attractions in this area, belong.

Both Jekyll Island and St. Simons Island are well worth visiting, and have their own separate pleasures—Jekyll more contemplative, St. Simons more upscale. Give an **entire day**

**to Jekyll** so you can take full advantage of its relaxing, open feel. A **half day** can suffice for **St. Simons** because most of its attractions are clustered in the Village area near the pier, and there's little beach recreation to speak of.

Getting to the undeveloped barrier islands, Sapelo and Cumberland, takes planning because there is no bridge to either. Both require a ferry booking and hence a more substantial commitment of time. There are no real stores and few facilities on these islands, so pack along whatever you think you'll need, including food, water, medicine, suntan lotion, insect repellent, and so on. **Sapelo Island** is limited to **day use** unless you have prior reservations, with the town of Darien in McIntosh County as the gateway. The same is true for Cumberland Island National Seashore, with the town of St. Marys in Camden County as the gateway.

# Brunswick and Glynn County

Consider Brunswick sort of a junior Savannah, sharing with that larger city to the north a heavily English flavor, great manners, a city plan with squares courtesy of General James Oglethorpe, a thriving but environmentally intrusive seaport, and a busy shrimping fleet. Despite an admirable effort at downtown revitalization, most visitors to the area seem content to employ Brunswick, as its nickname implies, as a "Gateway to the Golden Isles" rather than as a destination in itself.

## SIGHTS

### Brunswick Historic District

Most of the visitor-friendly activity centers on **Newcastle Street,** where you'll find the bulk of the galleries, shops, and restored buildings. Adjacent in the historic areas are some nice residential homes.

The new pride of downtown is **Old City Hall** (1212 Newcastle St., 912/265-4032, www.brunswickgeorgia.net), an amazing circa-1889 Richardsonian Romanesque edifice designed by noted regional architect Alfred Eichberg, who also planned many similarly imposing buildings in Savannah. Today it

Mary Ross Waterfront Park

# Brunswick and Glynn County

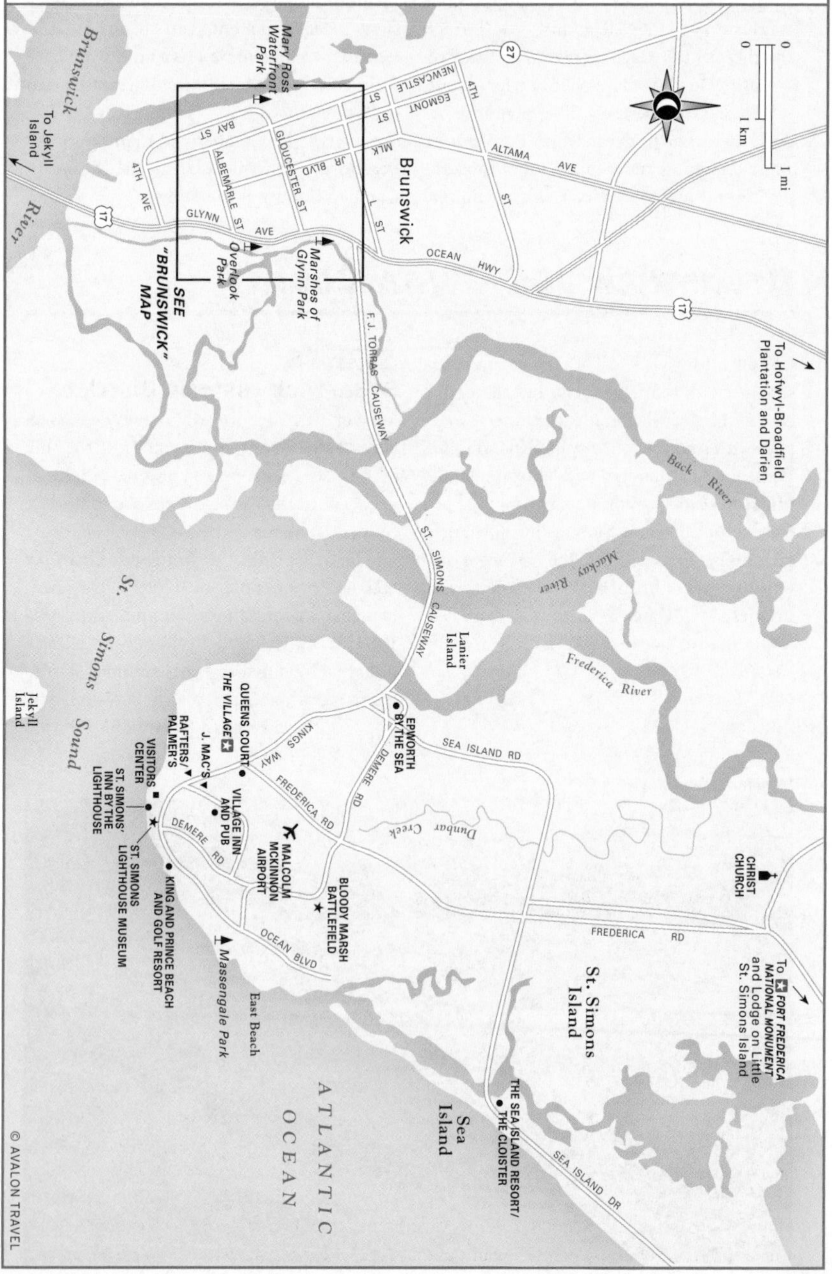

## Brunswick

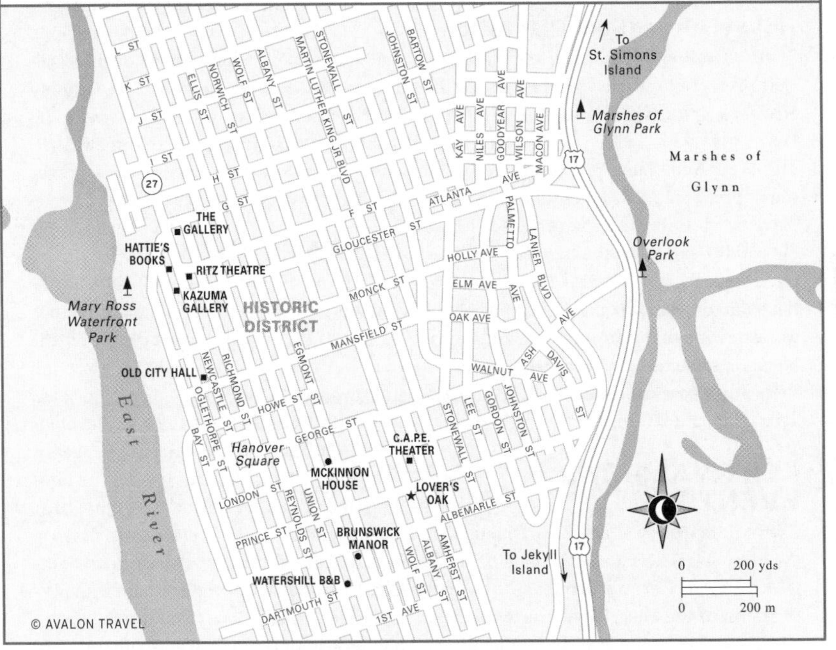


doubles as a rental event facility as well as a part-time courthouse; call ahead to look inside.

Another active restored building is the charming **Ritz Theatre** (1530 Newcastle St., 912/262-6934, www.goldenislearts.org), built in 1898 to house the Grand Opera House and the offices of the Brunswick and Birmingham Railroad. This ornate three-story Victorian transitioned with the times, becoming a vaudeville venue, then a movie house.

### Mary Ross Waterfront Park

**Mary Ross Waterfront Park,** a downtown gathering place at Bay and Gloucester Streets, also has economic importance as a center of local industry—it's here where Brunswick's shrimp fleet is often moored and the town's large port facilities begin. In 1989 the park was dedicated to Mary Ross, member of a longtime Brunswick shrimping family and author of the popular Georgia history book *The Debatable Land.* At the entrance is a nice replica of a World War II Liberty Ship, a cargo vessel of the type which was manufactured in Brunswick for the war effort.

### Lover's Oak

At the intersection of Prince and Albany Streets is the **Lover's Oak,** a nearly 1,000-year-old tree. Local lore says it has been a secret meeting place for young lovers for centuries, though one does wonder how much of a secret it actually could have been. It's about 13 feet in diameter and has 10 sprawling limbs.

Amid the light industrial sprawl of this area of the Golden Isles Parkway is the interesting little **Overlook Park,** just south of the visitors center on U.S. 17—a good, if loud, place for a picnic. From the park's picnic grounds or overlook you can see the fabled **Marshes of Glynn,** which inspired Georgia poet Sidney Lanier to write his famous poem of the same title under the **Lanier Oak,** located a little farther up the road in the median.

### Hofwyl-Broadfield Plantation

South Carolina doesn't own the patent on well-preserved old rice plantations, as the **Hofwyl-Broadfield Plantation** (5556 U.S. 17, 912/264-7333, www.gastateparks.org, Wed.-Sun. 9am-5pm, last main house tour 4pm, $8 adults, $5 children), a short drive north of Brunswick, proves. With its old paddy fields along the gorgeous and relatively undeveloped Altamaha River estuary, the plantation's main home is an antebellum wonder, with an expansive porch and a nice house museum that includes silver, a model of a rice plantation, and a slide show. There's also a pleasant nature trail.



## FESTIVALS AND EVENTS

Each Mother's Day at noon, parishioners of the local St. Francis Xavier Church hold the **Our Lady of Fatima Processional and Blessing of the Fleet** (www.brunswick.net), begun in 1938 by the local Portuguese fishing community. After the procession, at about 3pm at Mary Ross Waterfront Park, comes the actual blessing of the shrimping fleet.

Foodies will enjoy the **Brunswick Stewbilee** ($9 adults, $4 children), held on the second Saturday in October 11:30am-3pm. Pro and amateur chefs showcase their skills in creating the local signature dish and vying for the title of "Brunswick Stewmaster." There are also car shows, contests, displays, and much live music.

## SHOPS

Right in the heart of the bustle on Newcastle is a good indie bookstore, **Hattie's Books** (1531 Newcastle St., 912/554-8677, www.hattiesbooks.com, Mon.-Fri. 10am-5:30pm, Sat. 10am-4pm). Not only do they have a good selection of local and regional authors, you can also get a good cup of coffee.

Like Beaufort, South Carolina, Brunswick has made the art gallery a central component of its downtown revitalization, with nearly all of them on Newcastle Street. Near Hattie's you'll find the **Ritz Theatre** (1530 Newcastle St., 912/262-6934, Tues.-Fri. 9am-5pm, Sat. 10am-2pm), which has its own art gallery inside. Farther down is **The Gallery on Newcastle Street** (1626 Newcastle St., 912/554-0056, www.thegalleryonnewcastle.com, Thurs.-Sat. 11am-5pm), showcasing the original oils of owner Janet Powers.

## RESTAURANTS

Brunswick isn't known for its breadth of cuisine options, and, frankly, most discriminating diners make the short drive over the causeway to St. Simons Island. One exception in Brunswick that really stands out, however, is **Indigo Coastal Shanty** (1402 Reynolds St., 912/265-2007, www.indigocoastalshanty.com, Tues.-Thurs. 11am-3pm, Fri. 11am-3pm and 5pm-10pm, Sat. 5pm-10pm, $12). This friendly, smallish place specializes in creative coastal themes, with dishes like the Charleston Sauté (shrimp and ham with peppers), Fisherman's Bowl (shrimp and fish in a nice broth), and even that old Southern favorite, a pimento cheeseburger.

## HOTELS

In addition to the usual variety of chain hotels—most of which you should stay far away from—there are some nice places to stay in Brunswick at very reasonable prices if you want to make the city a base of operations. In the heart of Old Town in a gorgeous Victorian is the ★ **McKinnon House** (1001 Egmont St., 912/261-9100, www.mckinnonhouse-bandb.com, $125), which had a cameo role in the 1974 film *Conrack*. Today, this bed-and-breakfast is Jo Miller's labor of love, a three-suite affair with some plush interiors and an exterior that is one of Brunswick's most photographed spots. Surprisingly affordable for its elegance, the **WatersHill Bed & Breakfast** (728 Union St., 912/264-4262, www.watershill.com, $100) serves a full breakfast and offers a choice of five themed suites, such as the French country Elliot Wynell Room or

# Brunswick Stew

Virginians insist that the distinctive Southern dish known as Brunswick stew was named for Brunswick County, Virginia, in 1828, where a political rally featured stew made from squirrel meat. But all real Southern foodies know the dish is named for Brunswick, Georgia. Hey, there's a plaque to prove it in downtown Brunswick—although it says the first pot was cooked on July 2, 1898, on St. Simons Island, not in Brunswick at all. However, I think we can all agree that "Brunswick stew" rolls off the tongue much more easily than "St. Simons stew." You can find the famous pot in which the first batch was cooked on F Street near Mary Ross Waterfront Park.

It seems likely that what we now know as Brunswick stew is based on an old colonial recipe, adapted from Native Americans, that relied on the meat of small game—originally squirrel or rabbit but nowadays mostly chicken or pork—along with vegetables like corn, onions, and okra simmered over an open fire. Today, this tangy, thick, tomato-based delight is a typical accompaniment to barbecue throughout the Lowcountry and the Georgia coast, as well as a freestanding entrée on its own. Here's a typical recipe from Glynn County, home of the famous Brunswick Stewbilee festival held the second Saturday of October:

## SAUCE

Melt ¼ cup butter over low heat, then add:
1¾ cups ketchup
¼ cup yellow mustard
¼ cup white vinegar
Blend until smooth, then add:
½ tablespoon chopped garlic
1 teaspoon ground black pepper
½ teaspoon crushed red pepper
½ ounce Liquid Smoke
1 ounce Worcestershire sauce
1 ounce hot sauce
½ tablespoon fresh lemon juice
Blend until smooth, then add:
¼ cup dark brown sugar
Stir constantly and simmer for 10 minutes, being careful not to boil. Set aside.

## STEW

Melt ¼ pound butter in a two-gallon pot, then add:
3 cups diced small potatoes
1 cup diced small onion
2 14½-ounce cans chicken broth
1 pound baked chicken
8-10 ounces smoked pork
Bring to a boil, stirring until potatoes are nearly done, then add:
1 8½-ounce can early peas
2 14½-ounce cans stewed tomatoes
1 16-ounce can baby lima beans
¼ cup Liquid Smoke
1 14½-ounce can creamed corn
Stir in sauce. Simmer slowly for two hours. Makes one gallon of Brunswick stew.

the large Mariana Mahlaney Room way up in the restored attic. Another good B&B is the **Brunswick Manor** (825 Egmont St., 912/265-6889, www.brunswickmanor.com, $130), offering four suites in a classic Victorian and a tasty meal each day.

The most unique lodging in the area is the ★ **Hostel in the Forest** (Hwy. 82, 912/264-9738, www.foresthostel.com, $25, cash only). Formed more than 30 years ago as an International Youth Hostel, the place initially gives off a hippie vibe, with an evening communal meal (included in the rates) and a near-total ban on cell phones. But don't expect a wild time: No pets are allowed, the hostel discourages young children, and quiet time is strictly enforced beginning at 11pm. To reach the hostel, take I-95 exit 29 and go west for two miles. Make a U-turn at the intersection at mile marker 11. Continue east on Highway 82 for 0.5 miles. Look for a dirt road on the right with a gate and signage. This is now a "membership" organization, so you'll need to join before booking.



### TRANSPORTATION AND SERVICES

Brunswick is directly off I-95. Take exit 38 to the Golden Isles Parkway, and take a right on U.S. 17. The quickest way to the historic district is to make a right onto Gloucester Street. Plans and funding for a citywide public transit system are pending, but currently Brunswick has no public transportation.

A downtown **information station** (912/262-6934, Tues.-Fri. 9am-5pm, Sat. 10am-2pm) is in the Ritz Theatre (1530 Newcastle St.).

The newspaper of record in town is the ***Brunswick News*** (www.thebrunswicknews.com). The main **post office** (805 Gloucester St., 912/280-1250) is downtown.

## Jekyll Island

Few places in the United States have as paradoxical a story as Jekyll Island (www.jekyllisland.com). Once the playground of the world's richest people—whose indulgence allowed the island to escape the overdevelopment that plagues nearby St. Simons—Jekyll then became a dedicated vacation area for Georgians of modest means, by order of the state legislature. Today, it's somewhere in the middle—a great place for a relaxing nature-oriented vacation that retains some of the perks of luxury of its Gilded Age pedigree.

After securing safe access to the island from the Creek people in 1733, Georgia's founder, General James Oglethorpe, gave the island its modern name, after his friend Sir Joseph Jekyll. In 1858, Jekyll Island was the final port of entry for the infamous voyage of *The Wanderer,* the last American slave ship. After intercepting the ship and its contraband manifest of 409 enslaved Africans—the importation of enslaved people having been banned in 1808—its owners and crew were put on trial and acquitted in Savannah.

As a home away from home for the country's richest industrialists—including J. P. Morgan, William Rockefeller, and William Vanderbilt—in the late 1800s and early 1900s, Jekyll Island was the unlikely seat of some of the most crucial events in modern American history. It was at the Jekyll Island Club in 1910 that the Federal Reserve banking system was set up, the result of a secret convocation of investors and tycoons. Five years later on the grounds of the club, AT&T president Theodore Vail would listen in on the first transcontinental phone call.

### ORIENTATION

You'll have to stop at the entrance gate and pay a $6 "parking fee" to gain daily access to this state-owned island; a weeklong pass is $28. (Bicyclists and pedestrians don't need to pay.) Debit and credit cards are accepted.

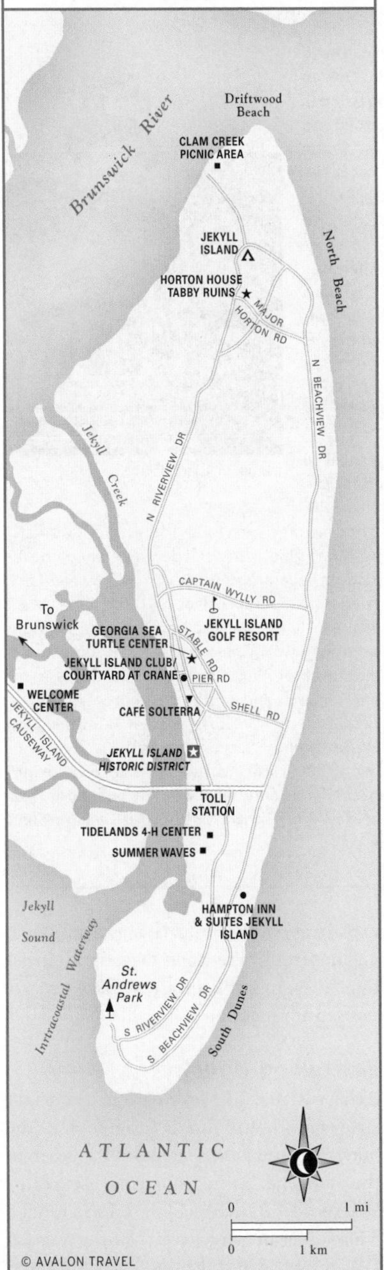


As the smallest of Georgia's barrier islands, Jekyll is very easy to get around on. North and South Beachview Roads essentially circle the perimeter of the island, with dedicated, separate bike paths more or less paralleling that route.

## SIGHTS

### ★ Jekyll Island Historic District

A living link to one of the most glamorous eras of American history, the **Jekyll Island Historic District** is also one of the largest ongoing restoration projects in the southeastern United States. A visit to this 240-acre riverfront area is like stepping back in time to the Gilded Age, with croquet grounds, manicured gardens, and even ferry boats with names like the *Rockefeller* and the *J. P. Morgan*. The historic district essentially comprises the buildings and grounds of the old **Jekyll Island Club,** not only a full-service resort complex—consisting of the main building and several amazing "cottages" that are mansions themselves—but a sort of living-history exhibit chronicling that time when Jekyll was a gathering place for the world's richest and most influential people.

The Queen Anne-style main clubhouse, with its iconic turret, dates from 1886. Within a couple of years the club had already outgrown it, and the millionaires began building the ornate cottages on the grounds surrounding it. In 2000 renovations were done on the most magnificent outbuilding, the 24-bedroom Crane Cottage, a Mediterranean villa that also hosts a fine restaurant. Other historic outbuildings are used as charming little shops.

### Georgia Sea Turtle Center

Within the historic district in a whimsically renovated 1903 building is the **Georgia Sea Turtle Center** (214 Stable Rd., 912/635-4444, www.georgiaseaturtlecenter.org, daily 9am-5pm, $8 adults, $6 children), which features interactive exhibits on these important marine creatures, for whom Jekyll Island is a major nesting ground. Don't miss the attached

## Jekyll Island's Millionaires' Club

the Jekyll Island Club

After the Civil War, as the Industrial Revolution gathered momentum seemingly everywhere but Georgia's Golden Isles, a couple of men decided to do something to break the foggy miasma of Reconstruction that had settled into the area and make some money in the process. In the late 1870s, John Eugene DuBignon and his brother-in-law Newton Finney came up with a plan to combine DuBignon's long family ties to Jekyll with Finney's extensive Wall Street connections in order to turn Jekyll into an exclusive winter hunting club. Their targeted clientele was a no-brainer: the newly minted American mega-tycoons of the Industrial Age. Finney found 53 such elite millionaires willing to pony up to become charter members of the venture, dubbed the Jekyll Island Club. Among them were William Vanderbilt, J. P. Morgan, and Joseph Pulitzer. As part of the original business model, in 1886 Finney purchased the island from DuBignon for $125,000.

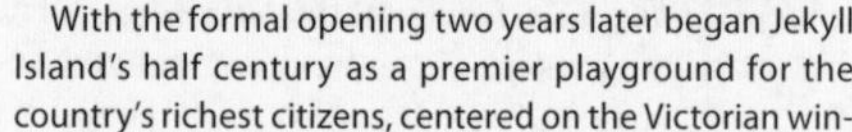

With the formal opening two years later began Jekyll Island's half century as a premier playground for the country's richest citizens, centered on the Victorian winter homes, called "cottages," built by each member and preserved today in the historic district.

In 1910, secret meetings of the so-called "First Name Club" led to the development of the Aldrich Plan, which laid the groundwork for the modern Federal Reserve System. A few years later, AT&T president Theodore Vail, nursing a broken leg at his Mound Cottage on Jekyll, participated in the first transcontinental telephone call on January 25, 1915, among New York City, San Francisco, and the special line strung down the coast from New York and across Jekyll Sound to the club grounds. Also on the line were the telephone's inventor, Alexander Graham Bell, his assistant Thomas Watson, the mayors of New York and San Francisco, and President Woodrow Wilson.

The millionaires continued to frolic on Jekyll through the Great Depression, but worsening international economic conditions reduced the club's numbers, even though the cost of membership was lowered in 1933. The outbreak of World War II and the resulting drain of labor into the armed forces put a further cramp in the club's workings, and it finally closed for good in 1942. The state would acquire the island after the war in 1947, turning the once-exclusive playground of millionaires into a playground for all the people.

rehabilitation building, where you can see the center's turtles in various states of treatment and rehabilitation before they are released into the wild. Children and adults alike will enjoy this unique opportunity to see these creatures up close and learn about the latest efforts to protect them.

In an effort to raise awareness about the need to protect the nesting areas of the big loggerheads that lay eggs on Jekyll each summer, the Sea Turtle Center also guides **nighttime tours** (early June-Aug. daily 8:30pm and 9:30pm) on the beach in order to explain about the animals and their habitat and hopefully to see some loggerheads in action. These tours fill up fast, so make reservations in advance.

### Driftwood Beach

Barrier islands like Jekyll are in a constant state of southward flux as currents erode the north end and push sand down the beach to the south end. This phenomenon has created **Driftwood Beach,** as the soil has eroded from under the large trees, causing them to fall and settle into the sand. In addition to being a naturalist's wonderland, it's also a starkly beautiful and strangely romantic spot. Drive north on Beachview Drive until you see a pullover on your right immediately after the Villas by the Sea (there's no signage). Park and take the short trail through the maritime forest, and you'll find yourself right there among the fallen trees and sand. Dogs are allowed on Driftwood Beach, off-leash as long as they are under voice control.

### Horton House Tabby Ruins

Round the curve and go south on Riverview Drive, and you'll see the large frame of a two-story house on the left (east) side of the road. That is the magnificent tabby ruins of the old **Horton House,** built by Jekyll's original English-speaking settler, William Horton. The house has survived two wars, a couple of hurricanes, and a clumsy restoration in 1898. Its current state of preservation is thanks to the Jekyll Island Authority and various federal, state, and local partners.

Frenchman Christophe Poulain du Bignon would live in the Horton House for a while after purchasing the island in the 1790s. Across the street from the house is the poignant little **Du Bignon Cemetery,** around which winds a nicely done pedestrian and bike path overlooking one of the most beautiful areas of marsh you'll see in all the Golden Isles.

## ENTERTAINMENT AND NIGHTLIFE

There's not much nightlife on Jekyll, it being intended for quiet, affordable daytime relaxation. The focus instead is on several annual events held at the **Jekyll Island Convention Center** (1 N. Beachview Dr., 912/635-3400), which has undergone a massive restoration to bring it in line with modern convention standards. The convention center itself is part of a dramatic new reinvestment called the Jekyll Island Beach Village, which comprises the convention center, a retail area, and the new Westin hotel.

At the beginning of the New Year comes one of the area's most beloved and well-attended events, the **Jekyll Island Bluegrass Festival** (www.adamsbluegrass.com). Many of the genre's biggest traditional names come to play at this casual multiday gathering. The focus here is on the music, not the trappings, so come prepared to enjoy wall-to-wall bluegrass played by the best in the business.

In September as the harvest comes in off the boats, the **Wild Georgia Shrimp and**



Driftwood Beach

**Grits Festival** (www.jekyllisland.com, free admission) promotes the value of the Georgia shrimping industry by focusing on how good the little critters taste in various regional recipes.

## SHOPS

The best bet for unique shopping opportunities on Jekyll is in the Historic District near the Jekyll Island Club, in the collection of venues called the Pier Road Shops. These are in various cute historic outbuildings. Highlights include the tiny but fun Goodyear Shop, featuring arts and crafts from Jekyll Island Art Association members, and Gypsea Glass, for individually handblown art glass items.

The new Beach Village shops, in the area of the Convention Center and the new Westin, include Kennedy Outfitters (31 Main St., 912/319-2079) for your outdoorsy needs, and Whittle's Gift Shop (31 Main St., 912/635-2552) for trinkets and fun stuff.



## SPORTS AND ACTIVITIES

### Hiking and Biking

Quite simply, Jekyll Island is a paradise for bicyclists and walkers, with a well-developed and very safe system of paths totaling about 20 miles and running the circumference of the island. The paths go by all major sights, including the Jekyll Island Club in the historic district. In addition, walkers and bicyclists can enjoy much of the seven miles of beachfront at low tide.

### Golf and Tennis

True to Jekyll Island's intended role as a playground for Georgians of low to medium income, its golf and tennis facilities—all centrally located at the middle of the island—are quite reasonably priced. The **Jekyll Island Golf Resort** (322 Captain Wylly Rd., 912/635-2368, www.jekyllisland.com, greens fees $40-60) is the largest public golf resort in Georgia. A total of 63 holes on four courses—Pine Lakes, Indian Mound, Oleander, and Ocean Dunes (nine holes)—await. Check the resort's website for "golf passport" packages that include local lodging.

The adjacent **Jekyll Island Tennis Center** (400 Captain Wylly Rd., 912/635-3154, $25 per hour) boasts 13 courts, 7 of them lighted, as well as a pro shop (daily 9am-6pm). Reservations are required for court time.

**Great Dunes** (100 Great Dune Lane, 912/635-2170, $15-25) offers both a 9-hole course and a cute and well-lit mini-golf course ($6.50 per round).

### Water Parks

**Summer Waves** (210 S. Riverview Dr., 912/635-2074, www.jekyllisland.com, Memorial Day-Labor Day, $20 adults, $16 children under 48 inches tall) is just what the doctor ordered for kids with a surplus of energy. The 11-acre facility has a separate section for toddlers to splash around in, with the requisite more daring rides for hard-charging preteens. Hours vary, so call ahead.

### Horseback Riding and Tours

**Three Oaks Carriage and Trail** (Clam Creek Rd., 912/635-9500, www.threeoaksfarm.org) offers numerous options. Horseback rides include guided beach rides (from $58 pp). These leave from the Clam Creek Picnic Area on the north end of the island, directly across the street from the Jekyll Island Campground. Horse-drawn carriage tours with a guide leave from the river side of the Jekyll Island Club and start at $15pp for daytime tours, with private evening tours at $40 for two people.

The **Tidelands 4-H Center** (912/635-5032) gives 1.5- to 2-hour Marsh Walks (Mon. 9am, $5 adults, $3 children) leaving from Clam Creek Picnic Area, and Beach Walks ($5 adults, $3 children) leaving at 9am Wednesday from the St. Andrews Picnic Area and at 9am Friday from South Dunes Picnic Area.

## RESTAURANTS

Culinary offerings are few and far between on Jekyll. I'd suggest you patronize one of the dining facilities at the **Jekyll Island Club**

the Courtyard at Crane

(371 Riverview Dr.), which are all open to nonguests. They're not only delicious but pretty reasonable as well, considering the swank setting. My favorite is the ★ **Courtyard at Crane** (912/635-2400, lunch Sun.-Fri. 11am-4pm, Sat. 11am-2pm, dinner Sun.-Thurs. 5:30pm-9pm, $27-38). Located in the circa-1917 Crane Cottage, one of the beautifully restored tycoon villas, the Courtyard offers romantic evening dining (call for reservations) as well as tasty and stylish lunch dining in the alfresco courtyard area or inside.

For a real and figurative taste of history, make a reservation at the **Grand Dining Room** (912/635-2400, breakfast Mon.-Sat. 7am-11am, Sun. 7am-10am, lunch Mon.-Sat. 11:30am-2pm, brunch Sun. 10:45am-2pm, dinner daily 6pm-10pm, dinner $26-35), the club's full-service restaurant. Focusing on continental cuisine—ordered either à la carte or as a prix fixe "sunset dinner"—the Dining Room features a pianist each evening and for Sunday brunch. Jackets or collared shirts are required for men.

For a tasty breakfast, lunch, or dinner on the go or at odd hours, check out **Café Solterra** (912/635-2600, daily 7am-10pm, $8-12), great for deli-type food and equipped with Starbucks coffee.

There is a great riverfront dining place within a stone's throw of the Jekyll Island Club: **The Wharf** (371 Riverview Dr., 912/635-3612, www.jekyllwharf.com, Tues.-Sun. 11:30am-9:30pm, $12-25) is an upscale seafood-oriented spot with frequent live music. Go for the chilled seafood platter.

## HOTELS

### Under $150

The **Days Inn** (60 S. Beachview Dr., 912/635-9800, www.daysinnjekyll.com, $100) has undergone remodeling lately and is the best choice if budget is a concern (and you don't want to camp, that is). It has a good location on the south side of the island with nice ocean views.

### $150-300

Any discussion of lodging on Jekyll Island begins with the legendary ★ **Jekyll Island Club** (371 Riverview Dr., 800/535-9547, www.jekyllclub.com, $199-490), which is reasonably priced considering its history, postcard-perfect setting, and delightful guest rooms. Some of its 157 guest rooms in the club and annex areas are available for under $200. There are 60 guest rooms in the main club building, and several outlying cottages, chief among them the Crane, Cherokee, and Sans Souci Cottages, are also available. All rates include use of the big outdoor pool overlooking the river, and a neat amenity is a choice of meal plans for an extra daily fee.

The first hotel built on the island in 35 years, the ★ **Hampton Inn & Suites Jekyll Island** (200 S. Beachview Dr., 912/635-3733, www.hamptoninn.com, $180-210) was constructed according to an exacting set of conservation guidelines, conserving much of the original tree canopy and employing various low-impact design and building techniques.

It's one of the best eco-friendly hotel designs I've experienced.

The **Westin Jekyll Island** (110 Ocean Way, 912/635-4545, www.westinjekyllisland.com, $200) is part of the larger Jekyll Island Beach Village development, essentially one of the first things you encounter when first coming on the island. These rooms are the newest on the island and range from large ocean-view suites to smaller "coastal studio suites."

### Camping

One of the niftiest campgrounds in the area is the **Jekyll Island Campground** (197 Riverview Dr., 912/635-3021, tent sites $26, RV sites $41). It's a friendly place with an excellent location at the north end of the island. There are more than 150 sites, from tent to full-service pull-through RV sites. There's a two-night minimum on weekends and a three-night minimum on holiday and special-event weekends; reservations are recommended.

## TRANSPORTATION AND SERVICES

Jekyll Island is immediately south of Brunswick. You'll have to pay a $6 per vehicle fee to get onto the island. Once on the island, most sites are on the north end (a left as you reach the dead-end at Beachview Dr.). The main circuit route around the island is Beachview Drive, which suitably enough changes into Riverview Drive as it rounds the bend to landward at the north end.

Many visitors choose to bicycle around the island once they're here, which is certainly the best way to experience both the sights and the beach itself at low tide.

The **Jekyll Island Visitor Center** (901 Downing Musgrove Causeway, 912/635-3636, daily 9am-5pm) is on the long causeway along the marsh before you get to the island. Set in a charming little cottage it shares with the Georgia State Patrol, the center has a nice gift shop and loads of brochures on the entire Golden Isles region.



# St. Simons Island

Despite a reputation for aloof affluence, the truth is that St. Simons Island is also very visitor-friendly, and there's more to do here than meets the eye.

Fort Frederica, now a National Monument, was a key base of operations for the British struggle to evict the Spanish from Georgia—which culminated in 1742 in the decisive Battle of Bloody Marsh. In the years after American independence, St. Simons woke up from its slumber as acre after acre of virgin live oak was felled to make the massive timbers of new warships for the U.S. Navy, including the USS *Constitution*. In their place was planted a new crop—cotton. The island's antebellum plantations boomed to world-class heights of profit and prestige when the superior strain of the crop known as Sea Island cotton came in the 1820s.

The next landmark development for St. Simons didn't come until the building of the first causeway in 1924, which led directly to the island's resort development by the mega-rich industrialist Howard Coffin of Hudson Motors fame, who also owned nearby Sapelo Island to the north.

## ORIENTATION

Because it's only a short drive from downtown Brunswick on the Torras Causeway, St. Simons has much less of a remote feel than most other Georgia barrier islands, and it's much more densely populated than any other Georgia island except Tybee. Most visitor-oriented activity on this 12-mile-long, heavily residential island is clustered at the south end, where St. Simons Sound meets the Atlantic.

## Golden Isles on the Page

And now from the Vast of the Lord will the waters of sleep
Roll in on the souls of men,
But who will reveal to our waking ken
The forms that swim and the shapes that creep
Under the waters of sleep?
And I would I could know what swimmeth below when the tide comes in
On the length and the breadth of the marvelous marshes of Glynn.

Sidney Lanier

Many authors have been inspired by their time in the Golden Isles, whether to pen flights of poetic fancy, page-turning novels, or politically oriented chronicles. Here are a few of the most notable names:

- **Sidney Lanier:** Born in Macon, Georgia, Lanier was a renowned linguist, mathematician, and legal scholar. Fighting for the Confederacy during the Civil War, he was captured while commanding a blockade runner and taken to a POW camp in Maryland, where he came down with tuberculosis. After the war, he stayed at his brother-in-law's house in Brunswick to recuperate, and it was during that time that he took up poetry, writing the famous "Marshes of Glynn," quoted above.
- **Eugenia Price:** Although not originally from St. Simons, Price remains the best-known local cultural figure, setting her *St. Simons Trilogy* here. After relocating to the island in 1965, she stayed here until her death in 1996. She's buried in the Christ Church cemetery on Frederica Road.
- **Tina McElroy Ansa:** Probably the most notable literary figure currently living on St. Simons Island is award-winning African American author Tina McElroy Ansa. Few of her books are set in the Golden Isles region, but they all deal with life in the South, and Ansa is an ardent devotee of St. Simons and its relaxed, friendly ways.
- **Fanny Kemble:** In 1834, this renowned English actress married Georgia plantation heir Pierce Butler, who would become one of the largest slave owners in the United States. Horrified by the treatment of the enslaved people at Butler Island, just south of Darien, Georgia, Kemble penned one of the earliest antislavery chronicles, *Journal of a Residence on a Georgian Plantation in 1838-1839*. Kemble's disagreement with her husband over slavery hastened their divorce in 1849.

## SIGHTS

### ★ The Village

Think of **The Village** at the extreme south end of St. Simons as a mix of Tybee's downscale accessibility and Hilton Head's upscale exclusivity. This compact, bustling area only a few blocks long offers not only boutique shops and stylish cafés, but also vintage stores and busking musicians.

On the Village waterfront you'll find the **St. Simons Island Pier,** which, while not extremely long, does offer attractive views of the island. Adjacent to the pier is oak-lined **Neptune Park**, a family-friendly play area. Overlooking Neptune Park is the old **St. Simons Casino Building**, now the home of the theater troupe St. Simons Players, as well as the St. Simons Public Library.

### St. Simons Lighthouse Museum

Unlike many East Coast lighthouses, which tend to be in hard-to-reach places, anyone can walk right up to the **St. Simons Lighthouse Museum** (101 12th St., 912/638-4666, www.coastalgeorgiahistory.org, Mon.-Sat. 10am-5pm, Sun. 1:30pm-5pm, $12 adults, $5 children). Once inside, you can enjoy the museum's exhibit and take the 129 steps up to the top of the 104-foot beacon—which is, unusually, still active—for a gorgeous view of the island and the ocean beyond.

## ★ Fort Frederica National Monument

The expansive and well-researched **Fort Frederica National Monument** (Frederica Rd., 912/638-3639, www.nps.gov/fofr, daily 9am-5pm, free) lies on the landward side of the island. Established by General James Oglethorpe in 1736 to protect Georgia's southern flank from the Spanish, the fort (as well as the village that sprang up around it, in which the Wesley brothers preached for a short time) was named for Frederick Louis, the Prince of Wales. The feminine suffix *-a* was added to distinguish it from the older Fort Frederick in South Carolina.

You don't just get to see a military fort here (actually the remains of the old powder magazine—most of the fort itself eroded into the river long ago); this is an entire colonial town site a mile in circumference, originally modeled after a typical English village. A self-guided walking tour through the beautiful grounds shows foundations of building sites that have been uncovered, including taverns, shops, and the private homes of influential citizens. Closer to the river is the large tabby structure of the garrison barracks.

## Bloody Marsh Battlefield

There's not a lot to see at the site of the **Battle of Bloody Marsh** (Frederica Rd., 912/638-3639, www.nps.gov/fofr, daily 8am-4pm, free). Essentially just a few interpretive signs overlooking a beautiful piece of salt marsh, the site is believed to be near the place where British soldiers from nearby Fort Frederica ambushed a force of Spanish regulars on their way to besiege the fort. The battle wasn't actually that bloody—some accounts say the Spanish lost only seven men—but the stout British presence convinced the Spanish to leave St. Simons a few days later, never again to project their once-potent military power that far north in the New World.

While the Battle of Bloody Marsh site is part of the National Park Service's Fort Frederica unit, it's not at the same location. Get to the battlefield from the fort by taking Frederica Road south, and then a left (east) on Demere Road. The site is on the left as Demere Road veers right, in the 1800 block.



Fort Frederica National Monument

### Christ Church

Just down the road from Fort Frederica is historic **Christ Church** (6329 Frederica Rd., 912/638-8683, www.christchurchfrederica.org, daily 2pm-5pm). The first sanctuary dates from 1820, but the original congregation at the now-defunct town of Frederica held services under the oaks at the site as early as 1736. The founder of Methodism, John Wesley, and his brother Charles both ministered to island residents during 1736-1737.

Christ Church's claim to fame in modern culture is as the setting of local novelist Eugenia Price's *The Beloved Invader*, the first work in her Georgia trilogy. The late Price, who died in 1996, is buried in the church cemetery.

### Tours

**St. Simons Island Trolley Tours** (912/638-8954, www.stsimonstours.com, Sept.-Mar. daily 11am, Apr.-Aug. daily 11am and 1pm, $20 adults, $10 ages 4-12, free under age 4) offers a ride around the island in comparative comfort, departing from the pier.

## ENTERTAINMENT AND NIGHTLIFE

### Nightlife

Unlike some areas this far south on the Georgia coast, there's usually a sizable contingent of young people on St. Simons out looking for a good time. The island's main club for the younger party set is **Rafters** (315½ Mallory St., 912/634-9755, www.raftersblues.com, Mon.-Sat. 4:30pm-2am). For more of a classic friendly dive bar feel, try out **Murphy's** (415 Mallory St., 912/638-8966).

My favorite spot on St. Simons for a drink or an espresso—or a panini, for that matter—is **Palm Coast Coffee, Cafe, and Pub** (316 Mallory St., 912/634-7517, www.palmcoastssi.com, daily 8am-10pm). This handy little spot, combining a hip, relaxing coffeehouse with a hearty menu of brunch items, is in the heart of the Village. The kicker, though, is the cute little bar the size of a large walk-in closet right off the side of the main room—a little bit of Key West on St. Simons.

Inside the Village Inn is the popular nightspot the **Village Pub** (500 Mallory St., 912/634-6056, www.villageinnandpub.com, Mon.-Sat. 5pm-midnight, Sun. 5pm-10pm). Slightly more upscale than most watering holes on the island, this is the best place for a quality martini or other premium cocktail.

## SHOPS

Most visitor-oriented shopping on St. Simons is concentrated in the Village and is a typical beach town mix of hardware and tackle, casual clothing, and souvenir stores. A funky highlight is **Beachview Books** (215 Mallory St., 912/638-7282, Mon.-Sat. 10:30am-5:30pm, Sun. 11:30am-3pm), a rambling used bookstore with lots of regional and local goodies, including books by the late great local author Eugenia Price. Probably the best antiques shop in this part of town is **Village Mews** (504 Beachview Dr., 912/634-1235, Mon.-Sat. 10am-5pm).

The local edition of the **Savannah Bee Company** (315 Mallory St., 912/771-8972, www.savannahbee.com) might be the best in the regional franchise, with a very friendly staff and an immaculate, and very interesting, store with all the honey-based edible and cosmetic products the company offers.

The **Shops at Pier Village Market** is a collection of übercute shops in a cluster of mini-cottages, including Island Pearl Boutique, All Things Princess & Fairy, and the Island Gallery. This is a great place for families to wander and browse. The shops keep varying hours, both daily and seasonally.

## SPORTS AND ACTIVITIES

### Beaches

Keep going from the pier past the lighthouse to find **Massengale Park** (daily dawn-dusk), with a playground, picnic tables, and restrooms right off the beach on the Atlantic side. The beach itself on St. Simons is underwhelming compared to some in these parts, but it's easily accessible from the pier area and good for a romantic stroll if it's not high tide. There's a great playground, Neptune Park, right next to the pier overlooking the waterfront.

## Kayaking and Boating

With its relatively sheltered landward side nestled in the marsh and an abundance of wildlife, St. Simons Island is an outstanding kayaking site, attracting connoisseurs from all over. A good spot to put in on the Frederica River is the **Golden Isles Marina** (206 Marina Dr., 912/634-1128, www.gimarina.com), which is actually on little Lanier Island on the Torras Causeway right before you enter St. Simons proper. For a real adventure, put in at the ramp at the end of South Harrington Street off Frederica Road, which will take you out Village Creek on the seaward side of the island.

Undoubtedly the best kayaking outfitter and tour operator in this part of the Golden Isles is **SouthEast Adventure Outfitters** (313 Mallory St., 912/638-6732, www.southeastadventure.com, daily 10am-6pm), which also has a location in nearby Brunswick.

## Biking

The best place to rent bikes is **Monkey Wrench Bicycles** (1700 Frederica Rd., 912/634-5551). You can rent another kind of pedal-power at **Wheel Fun Rentals** (532 Ocean Blvd., 912/634-0606), which deals in four-seat pedaled carts with steering wheels.

## Golf and Tennis

A popular place for both sports is the **Sea Palms Golf and Tennis Resort** (5445 Frederica Rd., 800/841-6268, www.seapalms.com, greens fees $70-80) in the middle of the island, with three 9-hole public courses and three clay courts. The **Sea Island Golf Club** (100 Retreat Rd., 800/732-4752, www.seaisland.com, greens fees $185-260) on the old Retreat Plantation as you first come onto the island has two award-winning 18-hole courses, the Seaside and the Plantation. Another public course is the 18-hole **Hampton Club** (100 Tabbystone Rd., 912/634-0255, www.hamptonclub.com, greens fees $95) on the north side of the island, part of the King and Prince Beach and Golf Resort.

# RESTAURANTS

While the ambience at St. Simons has an upscale feel, don't feel like you have to dress up to get a bite to eat—the emphasis is on relaxation and having a good time.

The Village on St. Simons Island

## Breakfast and Brunch

★ **Palmer's Village Cafe** (223 Mallory St., 912/634-5515, www.palmersvillagecafe.com, Tues.-Sun. 7:30am-2pm, $10-15), formerly called Dressner's, is right in the middle of the Village's bustle. It's one of the island's most popular places but still has enough seats that you usually don't have to wait. Sandwiches and burgers are great, but breakfast all day is the real attraction and includes lovingly crafted omelets, hearty pancakes, and a "build your own biscuit" menu.

## Seafood

A popular seafood place right in the action in the Village is **Barbara Jean's** (214 Mallory St., 912/634-6500, www.barbarajeans.com, Sun.-Thurs. 11am-9pm, Fri.-Sat. 11am-10pm, $7-20), which also has a variety of imaginative veggie dishes to go along with its formidable seafood menu, including some excellent she-crab soup and crab cakes. They also have plenty of good landlubber treats.

## Fine Dining

★ **Nancy** (26 Market St., 912/634-0885, www.nancyssi.com, lunch Tues.-Sat. 11:30am-2pm, dinner Thurs.-Sat. 6pm-10pm, $30) is an interesting concept: an upscale fine-dining spot with an affiliated women's clothing boutique. Nancy Herdlinger and chef Abney Harper run this enterprise in a newer area a short drive outside the Village. It's one of the premier fine-dining spots on the Georgia coast south of Savannah. Any seafood dish is great, but I suggest the short ribs if they're on the tightly curated menu.

Inside the King and Prince Resort, you'll find the old-school glory of the **Blue Dolphin** (201 Arnold Rd., 800/342-0212, lunch daily 11am-4pm, dinner daily 5pm-10pm, $15-30), redolent of the *Great Gatsby* era. The Blue Dolphin claims to be the only oceanfront dining on the island, and the views are certainly magnificent.

# HOTELS

## Under $150

A charming and reasonable place a stone's throw from the Village is **Queens Court** (437 Kings Way, 912/638-8459, $85-135), a traditional roadside motel from the late 1940s, with modern upgrades that include a nice outdoor pool in the central courtyard area. Despite its convenient location, you'll feel fairly secluded.

You couldn't ask for a better location than that of the **St. Simons' Inn by the Lighthouse** (609 Beachview Dr., 912/638-1101, www.saintsimonsinn.com, $120-300), which is indeed in the shadow of the historic lighthouse and right next to the hopping Village area. A so-called "condo-hotel," each of the standard and deluxe suites at the inn are individually owned by off-site owners—however, each gets full maid service and complimentary breakfast.

## $150-300

The best-known lodging on St. Simons Island is the ★ **King and Prince Beach and Golf Resort** (201 Arnold Rd., 800/342-0212, $249-320). Originally opened as a dance club in 1935, the King and Prince brings a swank old-school glamour similar to the Jekyll Island Club (though less imposing). And like the Jekyll Island Club, the King and Prince is also designated as one of the Historic Hotels of America. Its nearly 200 guest rooms are spread over a complex that includes several buildings, including the historic main building, beach villas, and freestanding guesthouses. Some standard rooms can go for under $200 even in the spring high season. Winter rates for all guest rooms are appreciably lower and represent a great bargain. For a dining spot overlooking the sea, try the **Blue Dolphin** (lunch daily 11am-4pm, dinner daily 5pm-10pm, $15-30). The resort's Hampton Club provides golf for guests and the public.

An interesting B&B on the island that's also within walking distance of most of the action on the south end is the 28-room **Village Inn & Pub** (500 Mallory St., 912/634-6056, www.

villageinnandpub.com, $160-245), nestled among shady palm trees and live oaks. The pub, a popular local hangout in a renovated 1930 cottage, is a nice plus.

### Over $300

Affiliated with the Sea Island Resort, the **Lodge at Sea Island** (100 Retreat Ave., 912/638-3611, $650-2,500) is actually on the south end of St. Simons Island on the old Retreat Plantation. Its 40 grand guest rooms and suites all have great views of the Atlantic Ocean, the associated Plantation Course links, or both. Full butler service makes this an especially pampered and aristocratic stay.



## TRANSPORTATION AND SERVICES

Get to St. Simons through the gateway city of Brunswick. Take I-95 exit 38 for Golden Isles, which will take you to the Golden Isles Parkway. Take a right onto U.S. 17 and look for the intersection with the Torras Causeway, a toll-free road that takes you the short distance onto St. Simons.

The **St. Simons Visitors Center** (530-B Beachview Dr., 912/638-9014, www.bgivb.com, daily 9am-5pm) is across the street from the old Casino Building near Neptune Park and the Village. The main newspaper in St. Simons is the ***Brunswick News*** (www.thebrunswicknews.com). The **U.S. Postal Service** (800/275-8777) has an office at 620 Beachview Drive.

## LITTLE ST. SIMONS ISLAND

This 10,000-acre privately owned island, accessible only by water, is almost totally undeveloped—thanks to its salt-stressed trees, which discouraged timbering—and boasts seven miles of beautiful beaches. All activity centers on the circa-1917 ★ **Lodge on Little St. Simons Island** (1000 Hampton Point Dr., 888/733-5774, www.littlestsimonsisland.com, from $625), named one of the top five U.S. resorts by *Condé Nast Traveler* in 2016. Within it lies the famed Hunting Lodge, where meals and cocktails are served. With 15 ultra-plush guest rooms and suites in an assortment of historic buildings, all set amid gorgeous natural beauty—there are five full-time naturalists on staff—the lodge is a reminder of what St. Simons used to look like. The guest count is limited to 30 people.

### Transportation

Unless you enlist the aid of a local kayaking charter company, you have to be a guest of the lodge to have access to Little St. Simons. The ferry, a 15-minute ride, leaves from a landing at the northern end of St. Simons at the end of Lawrence Road. Guests have full use of bicycles once on the island and can also request shuttle transportation just about anywhere.

## SEA ISLAND

The only way to enjoy Sea Island—basically a tiny appendage of St. Simons facing the Atlantic Ocean—is to be a guest at ★ **The Sea Island Resort** (888/732-4752, www.seaisland.com, from $700). The legendary facility, which underwent extensive renovations in 2008, is routinely ranked as one of the best resorts in the United States. The rooms at the resort's premier lodging institution, **The Cloister,** nearly defy description—enveloped in Old World luxury, they also boast 21st-century technology.

### Transportation

Get to Sea Island by taking Torras Causeway onto the island and then making a left onto Sea Island Causeway, which takes you all the way to the gate marking the only land entrance to the island.

# Darien and McIntosh County

The small fishing and shrimping village of Darien in McIntosh County has an interesting and historic pedigree of its own. It is centrally located near some of the best treasures the Georgia coast has to offer, including the Harris Neck National Wildlife Refuge, the beautiful Altamaha River, and the sea island of Sapelo, and it also boasts what many believe to be the best traditional seafood restaurants in the state.

Unlike Anglophilic Savannah to the north, the Darien area has had a distinctly Scottish flavor from the beginning. In 1736, Scottish Highlanders established a settlement at the mouth of the Altamaha River at the bequest of General James Oglethorpe, who wanted the tough Scots protecting his southern border from the Spanish.

Darien's heyday was in that antebellum period, when for a brief time the town was the world's largest exporter of cotton, floated down the Altamaha on barges and shipped out through the town's port. The Bank of Darien was the largest bank south of Philadelphia in the early 1800s. Almost nothing from this period remains, however, because on June 11, 1863, a force of mostly African American Union troops burned Darien's homes and warehouses to the ground (the incident was portrayed in the movie *Glory*).

In the pre-interstate highway days, U.S. 17 was the main route south to booming Florida. McIntosh County got a bad reputation for "clip joints," which would fleece gullible travelers with a variety of illegal schemes. This period is recounted in the best-seller *Praying for Sheetrock* by Melissa Fay Greene.



## SIGHTS

### Smallest Church in North America

While several other churches claim that title, fans of the devout and of roadside kitsch alike will enjoy the tiny and charming little **Memory Park Christ Chapel** (U.S. 17, daily 24 hours). The original 12-seat chapel was built in 1949 by local grocer Agnes Harper, when the church was intended as a round-the-clock travelers' sanctuary on what was then the main coastal road, U.S. 17. Upon

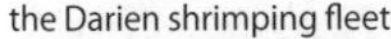
the Darien shrimping fleet

her death, Harper simply willed the church to Jesus Christ. Sadly, in 2015 an arsonist burned Mrs. Harper's church to the ground. A community effort, however, rebuilt it as closely as possible. Get there by taking I-95 exit 67 and going south a short way on U.S. 17; the church is on the east side of the road.

## ★ Harris Neck National Wildlife Refuge

Literally a stone's throw from the "Smallest Church" is the turnoff onto the seven-mile Harris Neck Road leading east to the **Harris Neck National Wildlife Refuge** (912/832-4608, www.fws.gov/harrisneck, daily dawn-dusk, free). In addition to being one of the single best sites in the South from which to view wading birds and waterfowl in their natural habitat, Harris Neck also has something of a poignant backstory. For generations after the Civil War, an African American community descended from the area's original enslaved population quietly struggled to eke out a living here by fishing and farming.

The settlers' land was taken by the federal government during World War II to build a U.S. Army Air Force base. Now a nearly 3,000-acre nationally protected refuge, Harris Neck gets about 50,000 visitors a year to experience its mix of marsh, woods, and grassland ecosystems and for its nearly matchless bird-watching. Most visitors use the four-mile "wildlife drive" to travel through the refuge, stopping occasionally for hiking or bird-watching.

Kayaks and canoes can put in at the public boat ramp on the Barbour River. Near the landing is the **Gould Cemetery,** an old African American cemetery that is publicly accessible. Charming handmade tombstones evoke the post-Civil War era of Harris Neck before the displacement of local citizens to build the airfield.

To get here, take I-95 exit 67 and go south on U.S. 17 about one mile, then east on Harris Neck Road (Hwy. 131) for seven miles to the entrance gate on the left.

## Shellman Bluff

Just northeast of Darien is the old oystering community of **Shellman Bluff.** It's notable not only for the stunning views from the high bluff, but also for fresh seafood. Go to **Shellman's Fish Camp** (1058 River Rd., 912/832-4331, call ahead) to put in for a kayak or canoe ride. Save room for a meal; there are some great seafood places here.

## Fort King George State Historic Site

The oldest English settlement in what would become Georgia, **Fort King George State Historic Site** (1600 Wayne St., 912/437-4770, www.gastateparks.org/fortkinggeorge, Tues.-Sun. 9am-5pm, $7.50 adults, $4.50 children) for a short time protected the Carolinas from attack, from its establishment in 1721 to its abandonment in 1727. Walking onto the site, with its restored 40-foot-tall cypress blockhouse fort, instantly reveals why this place was so important: It guards a key bend in the wide Altamaha River, vital to any attempt to establish transportation and trade in the area.

## Tours

**Altamaha Coastal Tours** (229 Ft. King George Rd., 912/437-6010, www.altamaha.com) is your best bet for taking a guided kayak tour (from $50) or renting a kayak (from $20 per day) to explore the beautiful Altamaha River.

Hunters Café at Shellman Bluff



## RESTAURANTS

McIntosh County is a powerhouse in the food department, and as you might expect, fresh and delicious seafood in a casual atmosphere is the order of the day here.

**The Old School Diner** (1080 Jesse Grant Rd. NE, Townsend, 912/832-2136, http://oldschooldiner.com, Wed.-Fri. 5:30pm-9:30pm, Sat.-Sun. noon-9:30pm, $15-30, cash only) is located in a whimsical semirural compound seven miles off U.S. 17, just off Harris Neck Road on the way to the wildlife refuge. The draw here is succulent fresh seafood in the coastal Georgia tradition. Old School's prices aren't so old school, but keep in mind that the portions are huge, rich, and filling.

Even farther off the main roads than the Old School Diner, the community of Shellman Bluff is well worth the drive. Find ★ **Hunters Café** (Shellman Bluff, 912/832-5771, lunch Mon.-Fri. 11am-2pm, dinner Mon.-Fri. 5pm-10pm, Sat.-Sun. 7am-10pm, $10-20) and get anything that floats your boat—it's all fresh and local. Wild Georgia shrimp are a particular specialty, as is the hearty cream-based crab stew. Take a right off Shellman Bluff Road onto Sutherland Bluff Drive, then a left onto New Shellman Road. Take a right onto the unpaved River Road and you can't miss it.

Another Shellman Bluff favorite is ★ **Speed's Kitchen** (Shellman Bluff, 912/832-4763, Thurs.-Sat. 5pm-close, Sun. noon-close, $10-20), where people move anything but fast, and the fried fish and crab-stuffed flounder are out of this world. Take a right off Shellman Bluff Road onto Sutherland Bluff Drive. Take a right onto Speed's Kitchen Road.

## HOTELS

If you want to stay in McIntosh County, I recommend booking one of the five charming guest rooms at ★ **Open Gates Bed and Breakfast** (301 Franklin St., Darien, 912/437-6985, www.opengatesbnb.com, $110-150). This lovingly restored and reasonably priced historic inn, circa 1876, overlooks relaxing Vernon Square in downtown Darien.

## SAPELO ISLAND

One of those amazing, undeveloped Georgia barrier islands that can only be reached by boat, Sapelo also shares with some of those islands a link to the Gilded Age.

### History

The Spanish established a Franciscan mission on the north end of the island in the 1500s. Sapelo didn't become fully integrated into the Lowcountry plantation culture until its purchase by Thomas Spalding in the early 1800s. After the Civil War, many of the nearly 500 formerly enslaved people on the island remained, with a partnership of freedmen buying land as early as 1871.

Hudson Motors mogul Howard Coffin bought all of Sapelo, except for the African American communities, in 1912, building a palatial home and introducing modern infrastructure. Coffin hit hard times in the Great Depression and in 1934 sold Sapelo to tobacco heir R. J. Reynolds, who consolidated the island's African Americans into the single Hog Hammock community. By the mid-1970s the Reynolds family had sold the island to the state, again with the exception of the 430 acres of Hog Hammock, which at the time had slightly more than 100 residents. Today most of the island is administered for marine research purposes under the designation of **Sapelo Island National Estuarine Research Reserve** (www.sapelonerr.org).



## Sapelo Island

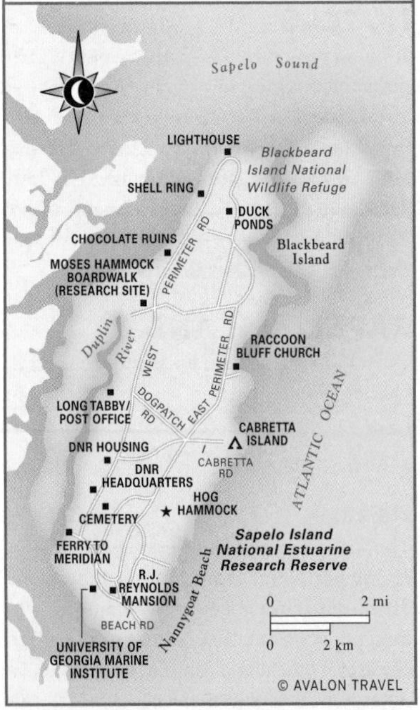

Sapelo Sound
LIGHTHOUSE
Blackbeard Island National Wildlife Refuge
SHELL RING
DUCK PONDS
CHOCOLATE RUINS
PERIMETER RD
Blackbeard Island
MOSES HAMMOCK BOARDWALK (RESEARCH SITE)
Duplin River
WEST PERIMETER RD
RACCOON BLUFF CHURCH
EAST PERIMETER RD
LONG TABBY/ POST OFFICE
DOGPATCH RD
ATLANTIC OCEAN
CABRETTA ISLAND
DNR HOUSING
CABRETTA RD
DNR HEADQUARTERS
HOG HAMMOCK
CEMETERY
FERRY TO MERIDIAN
Sapelo Island National Estuarine Research Reserve
R.J. REYNOLDS MANSION
Nannygoat Beach
BEACH RD
0 2 mi
0 2 km
UNIVERSITY OF GEORGIA MARINE INSTITUTE



### Sights

Once on the island, you can take guided tours under the auspices of the Georgia Department of Natural Resources. A tour of the island (Wed. 8:30am-12:30pm) includes the **R. J. Reynolds Mansion** (www.reynoldsonsapelo.com) on the south end as well as Hog Hammock and the Long Tabby ruins. A tour covers the historic **Sapelo Lighthouse** on the north end along with the rest of the island (Sat. 9am-1pm). June-Labor Day there's an extra lighthouse and island tour Friday 8:30am-12:30pm. March-October on the last Tuesday of the month they do an extra-long day trip, 8:30am-3pm. Tours cost $10 adults, $6 children, free under age 6. Call 912/437-3224 for reservations. You can also arrange private tours.

Another key sight on Sapelo is a 4,500-year-old **Native American shell ring** on the north end, one of the oldest and best preserved anywhere. Beach lovers will especially enjoy the unspoiled strands on Sapelo, including the famous **Nannygoat Beach.**

### Hotels

While it's theoretically possible to stay overnight at the **R. J. Reynolds Mansion** (www.reynoldsonsapelo.com), it is limited to groups of at least 16 people. Realistically, to stay overnight on Sapelo you need a reservation with one of the locally owned guesthouses. One recommendation is Cornelia Bailey's six-room **The Wallow** (912/485-2206, call for rates) in historic Hog Hammock. The Baileys also run a small campground, **Comyam's Campground** (912/485-2206, $10 pp). Another option is **The Weekender** (912/485-2277, call for rates).

### Transportation and Services

Visitors to Sapelo must embark on the ferry at the **Sapelo Island Visitors Center** (912/437-3224, www.sapelonerr.org, $15 adults, $10 ages 6-18) in little Meridian, Georgia, on Highway 99 north of Darien. The ferry runs three times a day Monday-Saturday, twice on Sunday. The website keeps an up-to-date schedule.

The visitors center actually has a nice nature hike of its own as well as an auditorium where you can see an informative video. From here it's a half-hour trip to Sapelo over the Doboy Sound. Keep in mind you must call in advance for reservations before showing up at the visitors center. April-October it's recommended to call at least a week in advance.

# Cumberland Island and St. Marys

Actually two islands—Great Cumberland and Little Cumberland—Cumberland Island National Seashore is the largest and one of the oldest of Georgia's barrier islands, and also one of its most remote and least developed. Currently administered by the National Park Service, it's accessible only by ferry or private boat. Most visitors to Cumberland get here from the gateway town of St. Marys, Georgia, a nifty little fishing village.

## ST. MARYS

Much like Brunswick to the north, the fishing town of St. Marys plays mostly a gateway role, in this case to the Cumberland Island National Seashore. During the colonial period, St. Marys was the southernmost U.S. city. In 1812 a British force took over Cumberland Island and St. Marys, with a contingent embarking up the St. Marys River to track down the customs collector.

Unlike towns such as Darien, which was put to the torch by Union troops, St. Marys was saved from destruction in the Civil War. A hotel was built in 1916 (and hosted Marjorie Kinnan Rawlings, author of *The Yearling*), but tourists didn't discover the area until the 1970s. It was also then that the U.S. Navy built the huge nuclear submarine base at Kings Bay, currently the area's largest employer with almost 10,000 workers.

### Orientation

Most activity in downtown St. Marys happens up and down Osborne Street, which perhaps not coincidentally is also how you get to the **Cumberland Island Visitor Center** (113 St. Marys St., 912/882-4335, daily 8am-4:30pm) and from there board the *Cumberland Queen* for the trip to the island. The Cumberland Island Visitor Center and the Cumberland Island Museum are in two different places, about a block apart.

### Sights and Events

Tying the past to the present, it's only fitting that the home of the Kings Bay Submarine Base (not open to the public) has a museum dedicated to the "Silent Service." The **St. Marys Submarine Museum** (102 St. Marys St., 912/882-2782, www.stmaryswelcome.com, Tues.-Sat. 10am-5pm, Sun. 1pm-5pm, $5 adults, $3 children) on the riverfront has a variety of exhibits honoring the contribution of American submariners, including a bunch of cool models. There's a neat interactive exhibit where you can look through the genuine sub periscope that sticks out of the roof of the museum.

A block down Osborne Street from the waterfront—and not at the actual Cumberland Island Visitor Center or the actual ferry dock—is the handsome little **Cumberland Island National Seashore Museum** (129 Osborne St., 912/882-4336, www.stmaryswelcome.com, Wed.-Sun. 1pm-4pm, free). It has several very informative exhibits on the natural and human history of Cumberland, as well as a room devoted to the short but fascinating role the island played in the War of 1812.

The most notable historic home in St. Marys is the **Orange Hall House Museum** (311 Osborne St., 912/576-3644, http://orangehallstmarys.org, Mon.-Fri. 11am-3pm, Sat. 10am-3pm, Sun. 1pm-4pm, $5 adults). This beautiful Greek Revival home, circa 1830, survived the Civil War and was the center of town social life during the Roaring '20s.

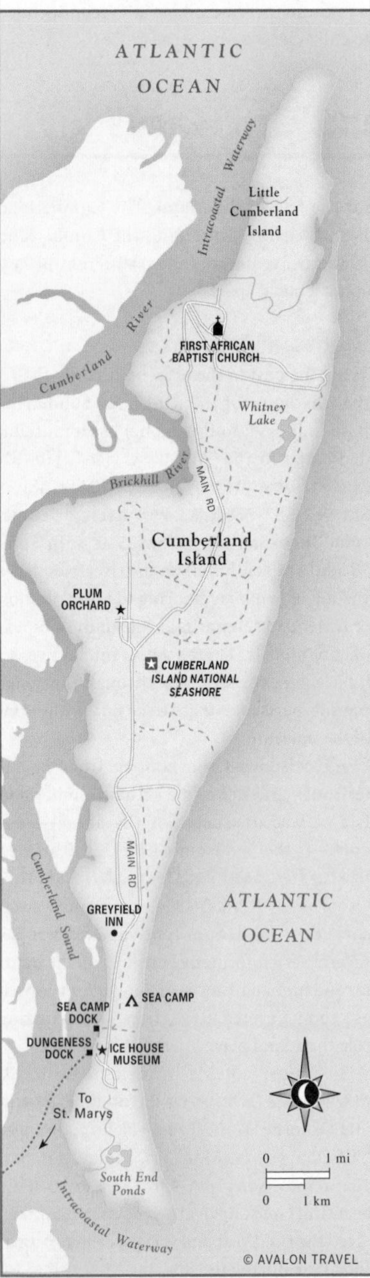


## Restaurants

St. Marys cannot compete in culinary sophistication with Charleston or Savannah, but it does have some of the freshest seafood around. One of the best places to eat seafood on the waterfront in St. Marys is at **Lang's Marina Restaurant** (307 W. St. Marys St., 912/882-4432, lunch Tues.-Fri. 11am-2pm, dinner Wed.-Sat. 5pm-9pm, $15-20). Another pair of good waterfront spots, right next to each other, are **The Shark Bite** (104 W. St. Marys St., 912/576-6993, Tues.-Sat. 11am-9pm, $12-20), which has great burgers and live music, and **Riverside Café** (106 W. St. Marys St., 912/882-3466, Tues.-Sat. 11am-9pm, $15-20), which specializes in Greek favorites.

## Hotels

The most notable lodging for historical as well as economic value is the 18-room **Riverview Hotel** (105 Osborne St., 912/882-3242, www.riverviewhotelstmarys.com, under $100). It was built in the 1920s and has hosted such notables as author Marjorie Rawlings, John Rockefeller, poet Sidney Lanier, and Andrew Carnegie. ★ **Emma's Bed and Breakfast** (300 W. Conyers St., 912/882-4199, www.emmasbedandbreakfast.com, under $200) is situated on four beautiful acres in downtown St. Marys in a grand Southern-style mansion with all the trappings and hospitality you'd expect.

More outdoorsy visitors can stay at cottage, tent, or RV sites at **Crooked River State Park** (6222 Charlie Smith Sr. Hwy., 912/882-5256, www.gastateparks.org). There are 62 tent and RV sites (about $22) and 11 cottages ($85-110) as well as primitive camping ($25).

## Transportation and Services

Take I-95 exit 3 for Kingsland-St. Marys Road (Hwy. 40). This becomes Osborne Road, the main drag of St. Marys, as it gets closer to town. The road by the waterfront is St. Marys Street.

The **St. Marys Convention and Visitors Bureau** (406 Osborne St., 912/882-4000, www.stmaryswelcome.com) is a good source of information not only for the town but for Cumberland Island, but keep in mind that this is not actually where you catch the ferry to the island.

## ★ CUMBERLAND ISLAND NATIONAL SEASHORE

Not only one of the richest estuarine and maritime forest environments in the world, **Cumberland Island National Seashore** (912/882-4335, reservations 877/860-6787, www.nps.gov/cuis) is one of the most beautiful places on the planet, as everyone learned when the "it" couple of their day, John F. Kennedy Jr. and Carolyn Bessette, were wed on the island in 1996. With more than 16 miles of gorgeous beach and an area of over 17,000 acres, there's no shortage of scenery.

Cumberland is far from pristine: It has been used for timbering and cotton, is dotted with evocative abandoned ruins, and hosts a band of beautiful but voracious wild horses. But it is still a remarkable island paradise in a world where those kinds of locations are getting harder and harder to find.

There are two ways to enjoy Cumberland: day trip or overnight stay. An early arrival and departure on the late ferry, combined with bike rental and a tour, still leaves plenty of time for day-trippers to relax. Camping overnight on Cumberland is quite enjoyable, but it's a bit rustic and isn't for novices.

Important note: Distances on the map can be deceiving. Cumberland is very narrow but also very long—about 18 miles tip to tip. You can walk the width of the island in minutes, but you will not be able to hike its length even in a day.

You can have a perfectly enjoyable time on Cumberland just hanging out on the more populated south end, but those who want to explore the island fully should consider renting a bike or booking seats on the new National Park Service van tour around the island.

### History

The indigenous Timucuan people revered this site, visiting it often for shellfish and for sassafras, a medicinal herb common on the island. Cumberland's size and great natural harbor made it a perfect base for Spanish friars, who established the first mission on the island, San Pedro Mocama, in 1587. The first Christian martyr in Georgia was Father Pedro Martinez, killed by indigenous people.

As part of his effort to push the Spanish back into Florida, General James Oglethorpe

maritime forest on Cumberland Island

## Wild Horses of Cumberland

wild horses near the Dungeness Ruins

Contrary to popular opinion, Cumberland Island's famous wild horses are not direct descendants of the first horses brought to the island by Spanish and English settlers, although feral horses have certainly ranged the island for most of recorded history. The current population of about 140 or so is actually descended from horses brought to the island by the Carnegie family in the 1920s. Responding to overwhelming public opinion, the National Park Service leaves the herd virtually untended and unsupervised. The horses eat, live, fight, grow up, give birth, and die largely without human influence, other than euthanizing animals who are clearly suffering and have no hope of recovery.

You're not guaranteed to see wild horses on Cumberland, but the odds are heavily in your favor. They often congregate to graze around the Dungeness ruins, and indeed any open space. Over the years they've made trails through the forest and sand dunes, and can often be seen cavorting on the windy beach in the late afternoon and early evening.

Each stallion usually acquires a "harem" of dependent mares, and occasionally you might even witness spirited competition between stallions for mares or territory.

Gorgeous and evocative though these magnificent animals are, they have a big appetite for vegetation and frankly are not the best thing for this sensitive barrier island ecosystem. But their beauty and visceral impact on the visitor is undeniable, which means the horses are likely to stay as long as nature will have them.

And yes, these really are *wild* horses, meaning you should never try to feed or pet them, and you certainly won't be riding them.

established Fort William at the south end of Cumberland—the remains of which are now underwater—as well as a hunting lodge named Dungeness, an island place-name that persists today.

Inevitably, the Lowcountry planters' culture made its way down to Cumberland, which was soon the site of 15 thriving plantations and small farms. After the Civil War, Cumberland was set aside as a home for freed African Americans—part of the famous and ill-fated "40 acres and a mule" proposal—but politics intervened: Most of Cumberland's enslaved people were rounded up and taken to Amelia Island, Florida, although some remained and settled at Cumberland's north end (the "Settlement" area today).

As elsewhere on the Georgia coast, the Industrial Revolution came to Cumberland in the form of a vacation getaway for a mega-tycoon, in this case Thomas Carnegie, industrialist and brother of the better-known Andrew Carnegie of Carnegie Library fame. Carnegie built a new, even grander Dungeness, which suffered the same fate as its predecessor in a 1959 fire.

Cumberland Island narrowly avoided becoming the next Hilton Head—literally—in 1969, when Hilton Head developer Charles Fraser bought the northern tip of the island and began bulldozing a runway. The dwindling but still influential Carnegies joined with the Georgia Conservancy to broker an agreement that resulted in dubbing Cumberland a National Seashore in 1972, saving it from further development. A $7.5 million gift from the Mellon Foundation enabled the purchase of Fraser's tract and the eventual incorporation of the island within the national park system.

To learn more about Cumberland's fascinating history, visit the **Cumberland Island National Seashore Museum** (129 Osborne St., 912/882-4336, www.stmaryswelcome.com, Wed.-Sun. 1pm-4pm, free) while you're in St. Marys, a block away from the actual ferry docks.

## Sights

The ferry typically stops at two docks a short distance from each other, the Sea Camp dock and the Dungeness dock. At 4pm, rangers offer a "dockside" interpretive program at the Sea Camp. A short way farther north at the Dungeness Dock, rangers lead a highly recommended "Dungeness Footsteps Tour" at 10am and 12:45pm, concentrating on the historic sites at the southern end of the island. Also at the Dungeness dock is the little **Ice House Museum** (912/882-4336, daily 9am-5pm, free), containing a range of exhibits on the island's history from Native American times to the present day.

Down near the docks are also where you'll find the stirring, almost spooky **Dungeness Ruins** and the nearby grave marker of Light-Horse Harry Lee. (You're very likely to see some wild horses around this area too.) The cause of the 1866 fire that destroyed the old Dungeness home is still unknown. Another even grander home was built on the same site during the Victorian era, but also fell victim to fire in the 1950s. It's these Victorian ruins you see today.

A very nice addition to the National Park Service offerings is a daily "Lands and Legacies" van tour (reservations 877/860-6787, $15 adults, $12 seniors and children) that takes you all around the island, eliminating the need for lengthy hikes. It's ideal for day-trippers—if a bit long, at six hours—but anyone can take the ride. It leaves from the Sea Camp Ranger Station soon after the first morning ferry arrives. Reservations are strongly advised.

Moving north on the Main Road (Grand Ave.)—a dirt path and the only route for motor vehicles—you come to the **Greyfield Inn** (904/261-6408, www.greyfieldinn.com). Because it is a privately owned hotel, don't trespass through the grounds. A good way farther north, just off the main road, you'll find the restored, rambling 20-room mansion **Plum Orchard** (912/882-4335), another Carnegie legacy. Guided tours (2nd and 4th Sun. of the month, $6 plus ferry fare) of Plum Orchard are available; call to reserve a space.

At the very north end of the island, accessible only by foot or by bicycle, is the former freedmen's community simply known as **The Settlement,** featuring a small cemetery and the now-famous **First African Baptist Church** (daily dawn-dusk)—a 1937 version of the 1893 original—a humble and rustic one-room church made of whitewashed logs and in which the 1996 Kennedy-Bessette wedding took place.

## Sports and Activities

There are more than 50 miles of hiking trails all over Cumberland, about 15 miles of nearly isolated beach to comb, and acres of maritime forest to explore—the latter an artifact of Cumberland's unusually old age for a barrier island. Upon arrival, you might want to rent a bicycle at the **Sea Camp dock** (no reservations, arrange rentals on the ferry, adult bikes $16 per day, youth bikes $10, overnight $20). The only catch with the bikes is that you shouldn't plan on taking them to the upcountry campsites.

Shell and sharks' teeth collectors might want to explore south of Dungeness Beach as well as between the docks. Unlike some parks, you are allowed to take shells and fossils off the island. Wildlife enthusiasts will be in heaven. More than 300 species of birds have been recorded on the island, which is also a favorite nesting ground for female loggerhead turtles in late summer. Of course, the most iconic image of Cumberland Island is its famous **wild horses,** a free-roaming band of feral equines who traverse the island year-round, grazing as they please.

Cumberland Island is home to some creepy-crawlies, including mosquitoes, gnats, and, yes, ticks, which are especially prevalent throughout the maritime forest as you work your way north. Bring high-strength insect repellent with you, or buy some at the camp store. Rangers recommend you do a frequent "tick check" on yourself and your companions.

## Hotels

The only "civilized" lodging on Cumberland is the 13-room ★ **Greyfield Inn** (Grand Ave., 904/261-6408, www.greyfieldinn.com, $475), ranked by the American Inn Association as one of the country's "Ten Most Romantic Inns." Opened in 1962 as a hotel, the Greyfield was built in 1900 as the home of the Carnegies. The room rates include meals, transportation, tours, and bicycle usage.

Many visitors opt to camp on Cumberland (reservations 877/860-6787, limit of 7 nights, $4) in one of three basic ways: at the **Sea Camp,** which has restrooms and shower facilities and allows fires; the remote but pleasant **Stafford Beach,** a vigorous three-mile hike from the docks and with a basic restroom and shower; and pure wilderness camping farther north at **Hickory Hill, Yankee Paradise,** and **Brickman Bluff,** all of which are a several-mile hike away, do not permit fires, and have no facilities of any kind. Reservations are required for camping. All trash must be packed out on departure, as there are no refuse facilities on the island. Responsible alcohol consumption is limited to those 21 and over. Insect life is abundant: Bring heavy-duty repellent or purchase some at the camp store.

## Transportation and Services

The most vital information about Cumberland is how to get ashore in the first place. Most visitors do this by purchasing a ticket on the *Cumberland Queen* at the **Cumberland Island Visitor Center** (113 St. Marys St., St. Marys, 877/860-6787, daily 8am-4:30pm, $20 adults, $18 seniors, $12 under age 13) on the waterfront in St. Marys. I strongly suggest calling ahead. Be aware that there are often long hold times by phone.

The ferry ride is 45 minutes each way. You can call for reservations Monday-Friday 10am-4pm. The ferry does not transport pets, bicycles, kayaks, or cars. However, you can rent bicycles at the Sea Camp dock once you're there. Every visitor to Cumberland over age 16 must pay a $4 entry fee, including campers.

March 1 to November 30, the ferry leaves St. Marys daily at 9am and 11:45am, returning from Cumberland at 10:15am and 4:45pm. March 1 to September 30 Wednesday-Saturday, there's an additional 2:45pm departure from Cumberland back to St. Marys. December 1 to February 28, the ferry operates only Thursday-Monday. Make sure you arrive and check in at least 30 minutes before your ferry leaves.

One of the quirks of Cumberland, resulting from the unusual way in which it passed into federal hands, is the existence of some private property on which you mustn't trespass, except where trails specifically allow it. Also, unlike the general public, these private landowners are allowed to use vehicles. For these reasons, it's best to make sure you have a map of the island, which you can get before you board the ferry at St. Marys or at the ranger station at the Sea Camp dock.

There are no real stores and very few facilities on Cumberland. *Bring whatever you think you'll need,* whether it be food, water, medicine, suntan lotion, insect repellent, toilet paper, or otherwise.

# The Okefenokee Swamp

Scientists often refer to Okefenokee as an "analogue," an accurate representation of a totally different epoch in the earth's history. In this case it's the Carboniferous Period, about 350 million years ago, when the living plants were lush and green and the dead plants simmered in a slow-decaying peat that would one day end up as the oil that powers our civilization.

But for the casual visitor, Okefenokee might also be simply a wonderful place to get almost completely away from human influence and witness firsthand some of the country's most interesting wildlife in its natural habitat. Despite the enormous wildfires of spring 2007 and summer 2011—some of the largest the Southeast has seen in half a century, so large they were visible from space—the swamp has bounced back, for the most part, and is once again hosting visitors who wish to experience its timeless beauty.

## ★ OKEFENOKEE NATIONAL WILDLIFE REFUGE

It's nearly the size of Rhode Island and just a short drive off I-95, but the massive and endlessly fascinating **Okefenokee National Wildlife Refuge** (912/496-7836, www.fws.gov/okefenokee, Mar.-Oct. daily dawn-7:30pm, Nov.-Feb. daily dawn-5:30pm, $5 per vehicle) is one of the lesser-visited national public lands. Is it that very name "swamp" that keeps people away, with its connotations of fetid misery and lurking danger? Or simply its location, out of sight and out of mind in south Georgia?

In any case, while it long ago entered the collective subconscious as a metaphor for the most untamed, darkly dangerous aspects of the American South—as well as the place where Pogo the Possum lived—the Okefenokee remains one of the most intriguing natural areas on the planet.

The Okefenokee Swamp was created by an accident of geology. About 250,000 years ago, the Atlantic Ocean washed ashore about 70 miles farther inland from where it does today. Over time, a massive barrier island formed off this primeval Georgia coastline, running from what is now Jesup, Georgia, south to Starke, Florida. When the ocean level dropped during the Pleistocene Era, this sandy island became a topographical feature known today as the Trail Ridge, its height effectively creating a basin to its west. Approximately 90 percent of the Okefenokee's water comes from rainfall into that basin, which drains slowly via the Suwannee and St. Marys Rivers.

Native Americans used the swamp as a hunting ground and gave us its current name, which means "Land of the Trembling Earth," a reference to the floating peat islands, called "houses," that dominate the landscape.

It's a common mistake to call the Okefenokee "pristine," because like much of the heavily timbered and farmed southeastern coast, it is anything but. The swamp's ancient cypress stands and primordial longleaf pine forests were heavily harvested in the early 20th century. About 200 miles of old rail bed through the swamp remain as a silent testament to the scope of that logging operation. In 1937, President Franklin Roosevelt brought the area within the federal wildlife refuge system.

The state has also opened the **Suwannee**

## The Okefenokee Swamp

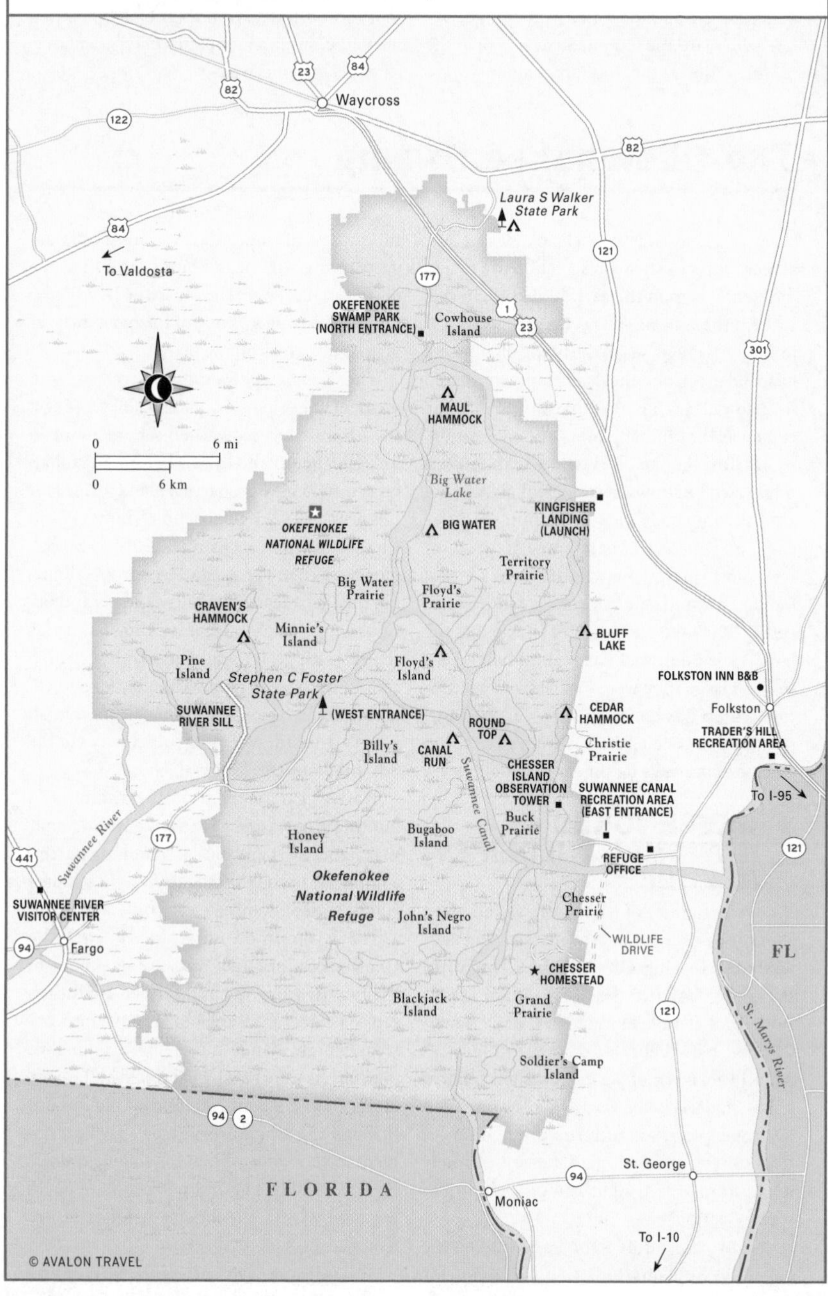

**River Visitor Center** (912/637-5274, www.gastateparks.org, Wed.-Sun. 9am-5pm), a "green" building featuring an orientation video and exhibits.

## Sights

The Okefenokee features a wide variety of ecosystems, including peat bogs, sand hills, and black gum and bay forests. Perhaps most surprising are the wide-open vistas of the swamp's many prairies or extended grasslands, 22 in all. And as you kayak or canoe on one of the water trails or on the old **Suwannee Canal** (a relic of the logging era), you'll notice the water is all very dark. This blackwater is not due to dirt or silt but to natural tannic acid released into the water from the decaying vegetation that gave the swamp its name.

As you'd expect in a national wildlife refuge, the Okefenokee hosts a huge variety of animal life—more than 400 species of vertebrates, including over 200 varieties of birds and more than 60 types of reptiles. Birders get a special treat in late November-early December when sandhill cranes come south to winter in the swamp.

A great way to see the sandhill cranes and other birds of the Okefenokee is to hike the 0.75-mile boardwalk out to the 50-foot **Chesser Island Observation Tower** on the eastern end of the swamp. This boardwalk was built after the huge 2011 fire; you can see the charred piers of the old boardwalk as you stroll.

You can get to the tower by driving or biking the eight-mile round-trip **Wildlife Drive,** which also takes you by the old **Chesser Homestead,** the remnants of one of the oldest settlements in the swamp.

## Touring the Refuge

For most visitors, the best way to enjoy the Okefenokee is to book a guided tour through **Okefenokee Adventures** (866/843-7926, www.okefenokeeadventures.com), the designated concessionaire of the refuge. They offer a 90-minute guided boat tour ($18.50 adults, $11.25 children) that leaves each hour, and a 2.5-hour reservation-only sunset tour ($25 adults, $17 children) that takes you to see the gorgeous sunset over Chesser Prairie. Extended or custom tours, including multiday wilderness excursions, are also available. They also rent bikes, canoes, and camping gear, and even run a decent little café where you can either sit down and have a meal or take it to go out on the trail.

You never know when you'll come across an alligator in the Okefenokee.

Privately owned canoes and boats with motors under 10 hp may put in with no launch fee, but you must sign in and out. No ATVs are allowed on the refuge, and bicycles are allowed only on designated bike trails. Keep in mind that some hunting goes on in the refuge at designated times. Pets must be leashed at all times.

## Camping

If fire and water levels permit, it's possible to stay the night in the swamp, canoeing to one of the primitive camping "islands" in the middle of the refuge. You need to make reservations up to two months in advance, however, by calling **U.S. Fish and Wildlife** (912/496-3331, Mon.-Fri. 7am-10am). A nonrefundable fee of $10 pp (which also covers your entrance fee) must be received 16 days before you arrive (mailing address: Okefenokee National Wildlife Refuge, Route 2, Box 3330, Folkston, GA 31537). Campfires are allowed only at Canal Run and Floyds Island. A camp stove is required for cooking at all other shelters. Keep in mind that in times of extreme drought or fire threat, boat trips may not be allowed. Always check the website for the latest announcements.

At **Stephen Foster State Park** (17515 Hwy. 177, 912/637-5274, fall-winter daily 7am-7pm, spring-summer daily 6:30am-8:30pm), a.k.a. the **West Entrance,** near Fargo, Georgia, there are 66 tent sites ($24) and nine cottages ($100). This part of the Okefenokee is widely considered the best way to get that "true swamp" experience.

## Transportation and Services

For anyone using this guide as a travel resource, the best way to access the Okefenokee—and the one I recommend—is the **East Entrance** (912/496-7836, www.fws.gov/okefenokee, Mar.-Oct. daily dawn-7:30pm, Nov.-Feb. daily dawn-5:30pm, $5 per vehicle), otherwise known as the **Suwannee Canal Recreation Area.** This is the main U.S. Fish and Wildlife Service entrance and the most convenient way to hike, rent boating and camping gear, and observe nature. The **Richard S. Bolt Visitor Center** (912/496-7836) has some cool nature exhibits and a surround-sound orientation video. Get to the East Entrance by taking I-95 exit 3 for Kingsland onto Highway 40 west. Go through Kingsland and into Folkston until Highway 40 dead-ends. Take a right, and then an immediate left onto Main Street. At the third light, make a left onto Okefenokee Drive (Hwy. 121) south.

Families with kids may want to hit the **North Entrance** at the privately run **Okefenokee Swamp Park** (U.S. 1, 912/283-0583, www.okeswamp.com, daily 9am-5:30pm, $12 adults, $11 ages 3-11) near Waycross, Georgia. (Fans of the old *Pogo* will recall Waycross from the comic strip, and yes, there's a real "Fort Mudge" nearby.) Here you will find a more touristy vibe, with a reconstructed pioneer village, a serpentarium, and animals in captivity. From here you can take various guided tours for an additional fee.

There's camping at the nearby but unaffiliated **Laura S. Walker State Park** (5653 Laura Walker Rd., 800/864-7275, www.gastateparks.org). Be aware the state park is not in the swamp and isn't very swampy, but it does have a nice man-made lake where you can rent canoes. Get to the North Entrance by taking I-95 exit 29 and going west on U.S. 82 about 45 miles to Highway 177 (Laura Walker Rd.). Go south through Laura S. Walker State Park; the Swamp Park is several miles farther.

If you really want that cypress-festooned classic swamp look, take the long way around the Okefenokee to **Stephen Foster State Park** (17515 Hwy. 177, 912/637-5274, fall-winter daily 7am-7pm, spring-summer daily 6:30am-8:30pm), a.k.a. the **West Entrance,** near Fargo, Georgia. Guided tours are available. Get to Stephen Foster State Park by taking I-95 exit 3 and following the signs to Folkston. Get on Highway 121 south to St. George, and then go west on Highway 94.

# FOLKSTON

The chief attraction in Folkston and its main claim to fame is the viewing depot for the **Folkston Funnel** (912/496-2536, www.folkston.com), a veritable train-watcher's paradise. This is the spot where the big CSX double-track rail line—following the top of the ancient Trail Ridge—hosts 60 or more trains a day. They say 90 percent of all freight trains to and from Florida use this track.

Railroad buffs from all over the South congregate here, anticipating the next train by listening to their scanners. The first Saturday each April brings buffs together for the all-day Folkston RailWatch.

The old Atlantic Coast Line depot across the track from the viewing platform has been converted into the very interesting **Folkston Railroad Transportation Museum** (3795 Main St., 912/496-2536, www.charltoncountyga.us, Mon.-Fri. 9am-5pm, Sat. 10am-3pm, free), with lots of history, maps, and technical stuff for the hard-core rail buff and novice alike.

## Restaurants

To fuel up in Folkston for your trek in the swamp, go no farther than the friendly ★ **Okefenokee Restaurant** (1507 Third St., 912/496-3263, daily 11am-8pm, $10-20), across from the handsome county courthouse. Their huge buffet is a steal at under $10; come on Friday nights for a massive seafood buffet (mostly fried) for under $20 pp. In any case don't miss the fried catfish, featured at both buffets. It's some of the best I've had anywhere in the South.

## Hotels

For a bit of luxury in town, right outside the refuge's East Entrance is the excellent ★ **Inn at Folkston Bed and Breakfast** (509 W. Main St., 888/509-6246, www.innatfolkston.com, $120-170). There is nothing like coming back to its cozy Victorian charms after a long day out in the swamp. The four-room inn boasts an absolutely outstanding breakfast, an extensive reading library, and a whirlpool tub.



the Folkston Railroad Transportation Museum

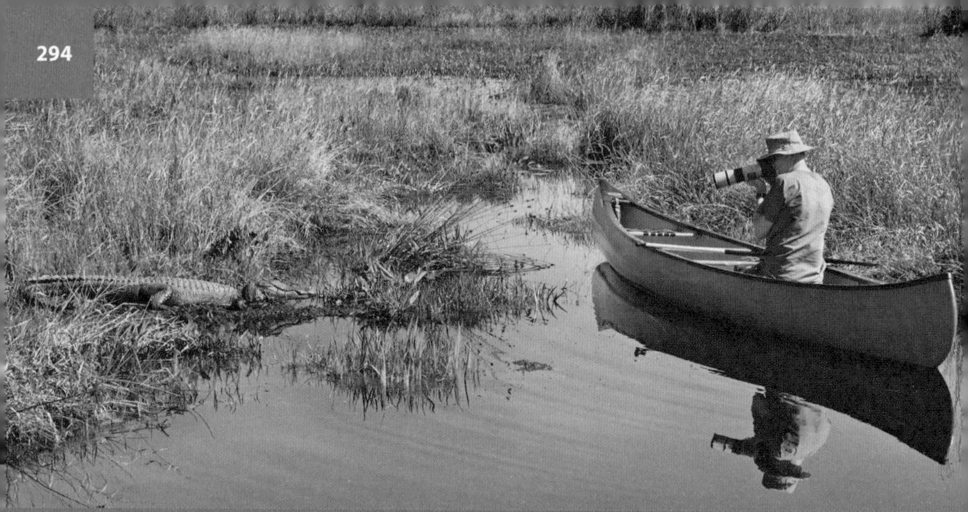

# Background

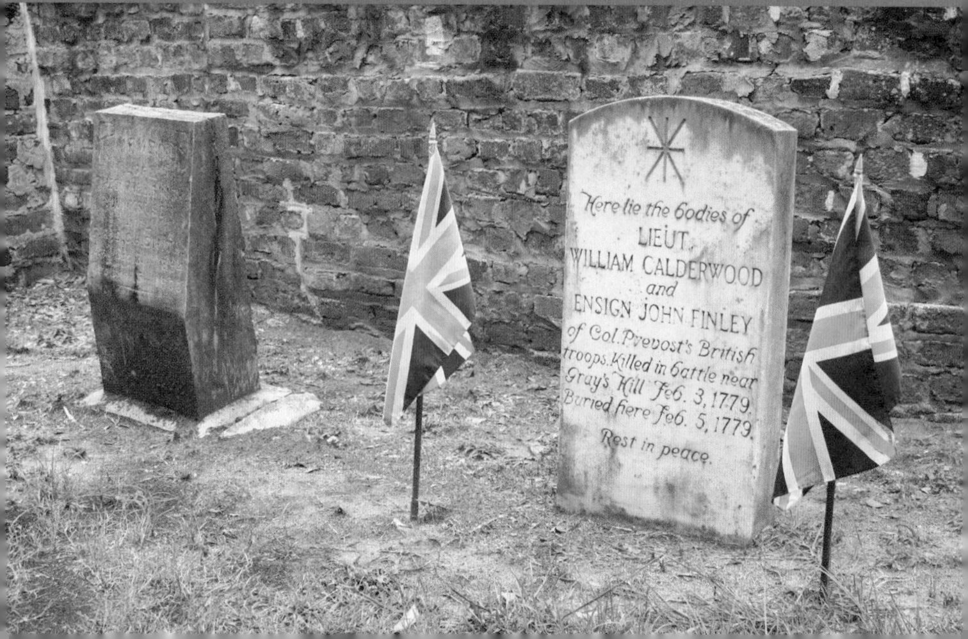

# The Landscape

## GEOGRAPHY

The area covered by this guide falls within the **Coastal Plain** region of the southeastern United States, which contains some of the most unique ecosystems in North America. It's a place where water is never far away and features large in the daily lives, economy, and folkways of the region's people.

Although it's hundreds of miles away, the Appalachian mountain chain has a major influence on the southeastern coast. It's in Appalachia where so much of the coast's freshwater—in the form of rain—comes together and flows southeast—in the form of rivers—to the Atlantic Ocean. Moving east, the next level down from the Appalachians is the hilly **Piedmont** region, the eroded remains of an ancient mountain chain.

At the Piedmont's eastern edge is the **fall line,** so named because it's where rivers make a drop toward the sea, generally becoming navigable. Around the fall line zone in the **Upper Coastal Plain** you can sometimes spot **sand hills,** usually only a few feet in elevation, generally thought to be the vestigial remains of primordial sand dunes and offshore sandbars. Well beyond the fall line and the sometimes nearly invisible sand hills lies the **Lower Coastal Plain,** gradually built up over a 150-million-year span by sedimentary runoff from the Appalachian Mountains, which at that time were as high or even higher than the modern-day Himalayas.

The Coastal Plain was sea bottom for much of the earth's history, and in some eroded areas you can see dramatic proof of this in the form of prehistoric shells, shark's teeth, and fossilized whale bones and oyster beds, often many miles inland. Sea level has fluctuated wildly with climate and geological changes through the eons. At various times over the last 50 million years, the Coastal Plain has submerged, surfaced, and submerged again. At the height of the last major ice age, when global sea levels were very low, the east coast of North America extended out nearly 100 miles farther than the present shoreline. (We now call this former coastal region the **continental shelf.**) The Coastal Plain has been roughly in its current form for about the last 15,000 years.

### Rivers

Visitors from drier climates are sometimes shocked to see how huge the rivers can get in coastal Georgia and South Carolina. Wide and voluminous as they saunter to the sea, their seemingly slow speed belies the massive power they contain. Georgia and South Carolina's big **alluvial,** or sediment-bearing, rivers originate in the region of the Appalachian mountain chain.

The headwaters of the Savannah River, for example, are near Tallulah Gorge in extreme north Georgia. Some rivers form out of the confluence of smaller rivers, such as Georgia's mighty Altamaha River, actually the child of the Ocmulgee and Oconee Rivers in the middle of the state. Others, like the Ashley and Cooper Rivers in South Carolina, originate much closer to the coast in the Piedmont.

The **blackwater river** is a particularly interesting Southern phenomenon, duplicated only in South America and in one example each in New York and Michigan. While alluvial rivers generally originate in highlands and carry with them a large amount of sediment, blackwater rivers originate in low-lying areas and move slowly toward the sea, carrying with them very little sediment. Rather,

**Previous:** a canoeist photographing an American alligator in the Okefenokee Swamp; graves at St. Helena's Church in Beaufort.

their dark tea color comes from the tannic acid of decaying vegetation all along their banks, washed out by the slow, inexorable movement of the river toward the sea.

Blackwater courses featured prominently in this guide are the Edisto River (the longest blackwater river in the world), Ebenezer Creek near Savannah, and Georgia's Suwannee River, which originates in the Okefenokee Swamp and empties into the Gulf of Mexico. Georgia's Altamaha River is a hybrid of sorts because it is partially fed by the blackwater Ohoopee River.

## The Intracoastal Waterway

You'll often see its acronym, ICW, on signs—and sadly you'll probably hear the locals mispronounce it "intercoastal"—but the casual visitor might actually find the Intracoastal Waterway difficult to spot. Relying on a natural network of interconnected estuaries and channels, combined with artificial **cuts,** the ICW often blends in rather subtly with the region's already extensive network of creeks and rivers.

Mandated by Congress in 1919 and maintained by the U.S. Army Corps of Engineers, the Atlantic portion of the ICW runs from Key West, Florida, to Boston and carries recreational and barge traffic away from the perils of offshore currents and weather. Even if they don't use it specifically, kayakers and boaters often find themselves on it at some point during their nautical adventures.

## Estuaries

Most biologists will tell you that the Coastal Plain is where things get interesting. The place where a river interfaces with the ocean is called an estuary, and it's perhaps the most interesting place of all. Estuaries are heavily tidal in nature (indeed, the word derives from *aestus,* Latin for "tide"), and feature brackish water and heavy silt content. This portion of the U.S. coast typically has about a six- to eight-foot tidal range, and the coastal ecosystem depends on this steady ebb and flow for life. At high tide, shellfish open and feed. At low tide, they literally clam up, keeping saltwater inside their shells until the next tide comes. Waterbirds and small mammals feed on shellfish and other animals at low tide, when their prey is exposed. High tide brings an influx of fish and nutrients from the sea, in turn drawing predators like dolphins, who often come into tidal creeks to feed. In the region covered by this guide, key estuaries from north to south are Cape Romain, Charleston Harbor, the ACE (Ashepoo, Combahee, Edisto) Basin, Beaufort River, May River, Calibogue Sound, Savannah River, Wilmington River, Midway River, Altamaha River, and the Brunswick River.

## Salt Marshes

All this water action in both directions—freshwater coming from inland, saltwater encroaching from the Atlantic—results in the phenomenon of the salt marsh, the single most recognizable and iconic geographic feature of the Georgia and South Carolina coast, also known simply as "wetlands." (Freshwater marshes are rarer, Florida's Everglades being perhaps the premier example.) Far more than just a transitional zone between land and water, marshes are also nature's nursery. Plant and animal life in marshes tends not only to be diverse, but to encompass multitudes as well.

You may not see its denizens easily, but on close inspection you'll find a marsh absolutely teeming with creatures. Visually, the main identifying feature of a salt marsh is its distinctive, reedlike marsh grasses, adapted to survive in brackish water. Like estuaries, marshes and all life in them are heavily influenced by the tides, which bring in nutrients.

The marsh has also played a key role in human history, for it was here that the massive rice and indigo plantations grew their signature crops, aided by the natural ebb and flow of the tides. While most marshes you see will look quite undisturbed, very little of them could be called pristine. In the heyday of the rice plantations, much of the coastal salt marsh was crisscrossed by the canal-and-dike system of the paddy fields.

You can still see evidence almost everywhere in this area if you look hard enough (the best time to look is right after takeoff or before landing in an airplane, since many approaches to regional airports take you over wetlands). Anytime you see a low, straight ridge running through a marsh, that's likely the eroded, overgrown remnant of an old paddy field dike. Kayakers occasionally find old wooden sluice gates on their paddles.

In the Lowcountry, you'll often hear the term **pluff mud.** This refers to the area's distinctive variety of soft, dark mud in the salt marsh, which often has an equally distinctive odor that locals love but some visitors have a hard time getting used to. Extraordinarily rich in nutrients, pluff mud helped make rice such a successful crop in the marshes of the Lowcountry.

In addition to their vital role as wildlife incubators and sanctuaries, wetlands are also one of the most important natural protectors of the health of the coastal region. They serve as natural filters, cleansing runoff from the land of toxins and pollutants before it hits the ocean. They also help humans by serving as natural hurricane barriers, their porous nature helping to ease the brunt of the damaging storm surge.

### Beaches and Barrier Islands

The beautiful broad beaches of Georgia and South Carolina are almost all situated on barrier islands, long islands parallel to the shoreline and separated from the mainland by a sheltered body of water. Because they're formed from the deposit of sediment by offshore currents, they change shape over the years, with the general pattern of deposit going from north to south (meaning the northern end will begin eroding first). Most of the barrier islands are geologically quite young, only having formed within the last 25,000 years or so. Natural erosion by currents and by storms, combined with the accelerating effects of dredging for local port activity, has quickened the decline of many barrier islands. Many beaches in the area are subject to a mitigation of erosion called **beach renourishment,** which generally involves redistributing dredged material closely offshore so that it will wash up on and around the beach.

As the name indicates, barrier islands are another of nature's safeguards against hurricane damage. Historically, the barrier islands have borne the vast bulk of the damage done by hurricanes in the region. Tybee Island near Savannah was completely under water in the hurricane of 1898, and parts of it were again submerged due to 2017's Hurricane Irma. More recently, Sullivan's Island near Charleston was submerged by 1989's Hurricane Hugo. Like the marshes, barrier islands also help protect the mainland by absorbing the brunt of the storm's wind and surging water.

Though barrier islands are ephemeral by nature, they have played an important role in the area's geography from the beginning of time. In fact, nearly every major settlement on the Georgia coast today—including Savannah, Darien, and Brunswick—is built on the vestiges of massive barrier islands that once guarded a primordial shoreline many miles inland from the present one. By far the largest of these ancient barrier islands, now on dry land, is the fabled **Trail Ridge,** which runs from Jesup, Georgia, to Starke, Florida. The Trail Ridge's height all along its distance made it a favorite route first for Native Americans and then for railroads, which still run along its crest today. The Trail Ridge is such a dominant geographical feature even today that it's actually responsible for the formation of the Okefenokee Swamp. The ridge effectively acts as a levee on the swamp's eastern side, preventing its drainage to the sea.

## CLIMATE

One word comes to mind when one thinks about Southern climate: *hot.* That's the first word that occurs to Southerners as well, but virtually every survey of why residents are attracted to the area puts the climate at the top of the list. Go figure. How hot is hot? The average high for July, the region's hottest month, in Savannah is about 92°F, in Charleston about 89°F. While that's nothing compared to Tucson or Death Valley, when coupled with the region's notoriously high **humidity** it can have an altogether miserable effect.

Heat aside, there's no doubt that one of the most difficult things for an outsider to adjust to in the South is the humidity. The average annual humidity in Charleston and Savannah is about 55 percent in the afternoons and a whopping 85 percent in the mornings. The most humid months are August and September. There is no real antidote to humidity—other than air conditioning, that is—although many film crews and other outside workers swear by the use of Sea Breeze astringent. If you and your traveling companions can deal with the strong minty odor, dampen a hand towel with the astringent, drape it across the back of your neck, and go about your business.

Don't assume that because it's humid you shouldn't drink fluids. Just as in any hot climate, you should drink lots of water if you're going to be out in the Southern heat.

August and September are by far the wettest months in terms of rainfall, with averages well over six inches for each of those months. July is also quite wet, coming in at over five inches on average.

Winters here are pretty mild but can seem much colder than they actually are because of the dampness in the air. The coldest month is January, with a high of about 58°F for the month and 42°F the average low. You're highly unlikely to encounter snow in the area, but if you do, it will likely be only skimpy flurries that a resident of the Great Lakes region wouldn't even notice as snow. But don't let this lull you into a false sense of security.

If such a tiny flurry were to hit, be aware that most people down here have no clue how to drive in rough weather and will not be prepared for even such a small amount of snowfall. Visitors from snow country are often surprised, sometimes bordering on shocked, by how completely a Southern city will shut down when that once-in-a-decade few tenths of an inch of snow finally hits.

## Hurricanes

The major weather phenomenon of concern for residents and visitors alike is the mighty hurricane. These massive storms, with counterclockwise-rotating bands of clouds and winds that can push 200 mph, are an ever-present danger to the southeast coast June-November each year.

As most everyone is aware of now from the horrific, well-documented damage from such killer storms as Hugo, Andrew, Katrina, Harvey, Maria, and many more, hurricanes are not to be trifled with. Old-fashioned drunken "hurricane parties" are a thing of the past for the most part, the images of cataclysmic destruction everyone has seen on TV having long since eliminated any lingering romanticism about riding out the storm.

**Tornadoes**—especially those that come in the "back door" through the Gulf of Mexico and overland to the Georgia or Carolina coast—are a very present danger with hurricanes. As hurricanes die out over land, they can spawn dozens of tornadoes, which in many cases prove more destructive than the hurricanes that produced them.

Local TV, websites, and print media can be counted on to give more than ample warning in the event a hurricane is approaching the area during your visit. Whatever you do, do not discount the warnings; it's not worth it. If the locals are preparing to leave, you should too. Typically when a storm is likely to hit the area, there will first be a suggested evacuation. But if authorities determine there's an overwhelming likelihood of imminent hurricane damage, they will issue a **mandatory evacuation order.** What this means in practice is that if you do choose to stay behind, you cannot count on any type of emergency services or help whatsoever.

Generally speaking, the most lethal element of a hurricane is not the wind but the

**storm surge,** the wall of ocean water that the winds drive before them onto the coast. During 1989's Hurricane Hugo, Charleston's Battery was inundated with a storm surge of over 12 feet, with an amazing 20 feet reported farther north at Cape Romain.

In the wake of such devastation, local governments have dramatically improved their once tepid disaster-response plans. For example, the large red traffic barriers you see stowed in their ready positions at many exits along I-16 in Georgia are a direct result of the chaos of the botched evacuation during Hurricane Floyd in 1999. Learning from that lesson, Georgia officials decided to make all four lanes of I-16 westbound in the event of a major evacuation, and those red barriers are there today to reroute traffic should they ever be needed.

## ENVIRONMENTAL ISSUES

The coast of Georgia and South Carolina is currently experiencing a double whammy, environmentally speaking: Not only are its distinctive wetlands extraordinarily sensitive to human interference, this is one of the most rapidly developing parts of the country. New and often poorly planned subdivisions and resort communities are popping up all over the place. Vastly increased port activity is also taking a devastating toll on the salt marsh and surrounding barrier islands. Combine all that with the South's often skeptical attitude toward environmental activism and you have a recipe for potential ecological disaster.

Thankfully, there are some bright spots. More and more communities are seeing the value of responsible planning and not greenlighting every new development sight unseen. Land trusts and other conservation organizations are growing in size, number, funding, and influence. The large number of marine biologists in these areas at various research and educational institutions means there's a wealth of education and talent available to advise local governments and citizens on how best to conserve the area's natural beauty.

Here's a closer look at some of the most urgent environmental issues facing the region today:

### Marsh Dieback

The dominant species of marsh grass, *Spartina alterniflora* (pronounced spar-TINE-uh) and *Juncus roemerianus,* thrive in the typically brackish water of the coastal marsh estuaries, their structural presence helping to stem erosion of banks and dunes. While drought and blight have taken their toll on the grass, increased coastal development and continued channel deepening have also led to a steady creep of ocean saltwater farther and farther into remaining marsh stands.

### Effects of Dredging

When Oglethorpe first sailed up the Savannah River, it was less than 20 feet deep. Today the Savannah River has been dredged to an average depth of 42 feet—and another deepening is planned, to nearly 50 feet.

Port activity is economically vital—and becoming more so—to the coastal cities of Charleston, Savannah, and Brunswick. The downside of such large-scale industrial dredging is threefold:

- The deeper the channel, the farther upstream salty ocean water is able to infiltrate. This destroys freshwater and brackish habitats such as the salt marsh.
- Deepening the channel increases both the volume and the velocity of the river, quickening erosion of the riverbanks.
- Too much dredging risks the intrusion of ocean saltwater into underground freshwater aquifers that provide drinking water to millions of people in the area.

Currently the debate over harbor deepening has hit home in both Charleston and Savannah, two of the country's busiest ports. The states of South Carolina and Georgia are both pursuing deepening at each city's port, much to the consternation of local environmentalists.

## The Paper Industry

Early in the 20th century, the Southeast's abundance of cheap undeveloped land and plentiful free water led to the establishment of massive pine tree farms to feed coastal pulp and paper mills. Chances are, if you used a paper grocery bag recently, it was made in a paper mill in the South.

But in addition to making a whole lot of paper bags and providing lots of employment for residents through the decades, the paper industry also gave the area lots of air and water pollution, stressed local rivers (it takes a lot of freshwater to make paper from trees), and took away natural species diversity from the area by devoting so much acreage to a single crop, pine trees.

When driving near rivers in this region, anytime you see a large industrial facility on the riverside, it's probably a paper mill. The rotten egg smell that comes next is from the sulfurous discharge from its smokestacks.

## Aquifers

Unlike parts of the western United States, where individuals can enforce private property rights to water, the South has generally held that the region's water is a publicly held resource. The upside of this is that everybody has equal claim to drinking water without regard to status or income or how long they've lived here. The downside is that industry also has the same free claim to the water that citizens do—and they use a heck of a lot more of it.

Currently much of the Georgia and South Carolina coasts get their water from aquifers, which are basically huge underground caverns made of limestone. Receiving **groundwater** drip by drip, century after century, from rainfall farther inland, the aquifers essentially act as massive sterile warehouses for freshwater, accessible through wells.

The aquifers have human benefit only if their water remains fresh. Once saltwater from the ocean begins intruding into an aquifer, it doesn't take much to render all of it unfit for human consumption—forever. What keeps that freshwater fresh is natural water pressure, keeping the ocean at bay.

But nearly a century ago, paper mills began pumping millions and millions of gallons of water out of coastal aquifers. Combined with the dramatic rise in coastal residential development and a continuing push to deepen existing shipping channels, the natural water pressure of the aquifers has decreased, leading to measurable saltwater intrusion at several points under the coast.

Currently, local and state governments in both states are increasing their reliance on **surface water** (treated water from rivers and creeks) to relieve the strain on the underground aquifer system. But it's too soon to tell if that has contained the threat from saltwater intrusion.

## Air Pollution

Despite growing awareness of the issue, air pollution is still a big problem in the coastal region. Paper mills still operate, putting out their distinctive rotten-eggs odor, and auto emissions standards are notoriously lax in both Georgia and South Carolina. The biggest culprits, though, are coal-powered electric plants, which are the norm throughout the region and which continue to pour large amounts of toxins into the atmosphere.

# Plants and Animals



## PLANTS

Probably the most iconic plant life of the coastal region is the **Southern live oak** (*Quercus virginiana*), the official state tree of Georgia. Named because of its evergreen nature, a live oak is technically any of a number of evergreens in the *Quercus* genus, many of which reside on the Georgia and South Carolina coast, but in local practice almost always refers to the Southern live oak.

Capable of living over 1,000 years and possessing wood of legendary resilience, the Southern live oak is one of nature's most magnificent creations. The timber value of live oaks has been well known since the earliest days of the American shipbuilding industry—when the oak dominated the entire coast inland of the marsh—but their value as a canopy tree has finally been widely recognized.

However, much of the current canopy in the coastal region was deliberately planted in the late Victorian era, and many of the specimens are nearing the end of their natural lifespans. In most situations, they aren't being replanted at an equivalent rate.

Fittingly, the other iconic plant life of the coastal region grows on the branches of the live oak. Contrary to popular opinion, **Spanish moss** (*Tillandsia usneoides*) is neither Spanish nor moss. It's an air plant, a wholly indigenous cousin to the pineapple. Also contrary to folklore, Spanish moss is not a parasite nor does it harbor parasites while living on an oak tree—although it can after it has already fallen to the ground.

Also growing on the bark of a live oak, especially right after a rain shower, is the **resurrection fern** (*Polypodium polypodioides*), which can stay dormant for amazingly long periods of time, only to spring back to life with the introduction of a little water. You can find live oak, Spanish moss, and resurrection fern anywhere in the **maritime forest** ecosystem of coastal Georgia and South Carolina, a zone generally behind the **interdune meadows,** which is right behind the beach zone.

The oak may be Georgia's state tree, but far and away its most important commercial tree is the pine, used for paper, lumber,

the iconic live oak entrance at Wormsloe State Historic Site

and turpentine. Rarely seen in the wild today due to tree farming, which has covered most of southern Georgia, the dominant species is now the **slash pine** (*Pinus elliottii*), often seen in long rows on either side of rural highways. Before the introduction of large-scale monoculture tree farming, however, a rich variety of native pines flourished in the **upland forest** inland from the maritime forest, including **longleaf** (*Pinus palustris*) and **loblolly** (*Pinus taeda*) pines.

Right up there with live oaks and Spanish moss in terms of instant recognition would have to be the colorful, ubiquitous **azalea,** a flowering shrub of the *Rhododendron* genus. Over 10,000 varieties have been cultivated through the centuries, with quite a wide range of them on display during blooming season, March-April, on the Georgia and South Carolina coast (slightly earlier farther south, slightly later farther north).

The area's other great floral display comes from the **camellia** (*Camellia japonica*), a large, cold-hardy evergreen shrub that generally blooms in late winter (Jan.-Mar.). An import from Asia, the southeastern coast's camellias are close cousins to *Camellia sinensis,* also an import and the plant from which tea is made.

Other colorful ornamentals of the area include the ancient and beautiful **Southern magnolia** (*Magnolia grandiflora*), a native plant with distinctive large white flowers that evolved before the advent of bees; and the **flowering dogwood** (*Cornus florida*), which, despite its very hard wood—great for daggers, hence its original name "dagwood"—is actually quite fragile. An ornamental imported from Asia that has now become quite obnoxious in its aggressive invasiveness is the **mimosa** (*Albizia julibrissin*), which blooms March-August.

Moving into watery areas, you'll find the remarkable **bald cypress** (*Taxodium distichum*), a flood-resistant conifer recognizable by its tufted top, its great height (up to 130 feet), and its distinctive "knees," parts of the root that project above the waterline and which are believed to help stabilize the tree in lowland areas. Much prized for its beautiful pest-resistant wood, great stands of ancient cypress once dominated the marsh along the coast; sadly, overharvesting and destruction of wetlands has made the magnificent sight of this ancient, dignified species much less common. The acres of **smooth cordgrass** for which the Golden Isles are named are plants of the *Spartina alterniflora* species. (A cultivated cousin, *Spartina anglica,* is considered invasive.) Besides its simple natural beauty, *Spartina* is also a key food source for marsh denizens. Playing a key environmental role on the coast are **sea oats** (*Uniola paniculata*). This wispy, fast-growing perennial grass anchors sand dunes and hence is a protected species on the Georgia coast (it's a misdemeanor to pick them).

South Carolina isn't called the "Palmetto State" for nothing. Palm varieties are not as common up here as in Florida, but you'll definitely encounter several types along the Georgia and South Carolina coast. The **cabbage palm** (*Sabal palmetto*), for which South Carolina is nicknamed, is the largest variety, up to 50-60 feet tall. Its "heart of palm" is an edible delicacy, which coastal Native Americans boiled in bear fat to make porridge. In dunes and sand hills you'll find clumps of the low-lying **saw palmetto** (*Serenoa repens*). The **bush palmetto** (*Sabal minor*) has distinctive fan-shaped branches. The common **Spanish bayonet** (*Yucca aloifolia*) looks like a palm, but it's actually a member of the agave family.

## ANIMALS

### On the Land

Perhaps the most iconic land animal—or semi-land animal, anyway—of the Georgia and South Carolina coast is the legendary **American alligator** (*Alligator mississippiensis*), the only species of crocodilian native to the area. Contrary to their fierce reputation, locals know these massive reptiles, 6 to 12 feet long as adults, to be quite shy. If you come in the colder months, you won't see them at all,

a river otter in the Suwannee River

since alligators require an outdoor temperature over 70°F to become active and feed (indeed, the appearance of alligators was once a well-known symbol of spring in the area).

Often all you'll see is a couple of eyebrow ridges sticking out of the water, and a gator lying still in a shallow creek can easily be mistaken for a floating log. But should you see one or more gators basking in the sun—a favorite activity on warm days for these cold-blooded creatures—it's best to admire them from afar. A mother alligator, in particular, will destroy anything that comes near her nest. Despite the alligator's short, stubby legs, it can run amazingly fast on land—faster than you, in fact.

If you're driving on a country road at night, be on the lookout for **white-tailed deer** (*Odocoileus virginianus*), which, besides being quite beautiful, also pose a serious road hazard. Because coastal development has dramatically reduced the habitat—and therefore the numbers—of their natural predators, deer are very plentiful throughout the area, and as you read this they are hard at work devouring vast tracts of valuable vegetation. No one wants to hurt poor little Bambi, but the truth is that area hunters perform a valuable service by culling the local deer population, which is in no danger of extinction anytime soon.

The coast hosts fairly large populations of playful **river otters** (*Lontra canadensis*). Not to be confused with the larger sea otters of the West Coast, these fast-swimming members of the weasel family inhabit inland waterways and marshy areas, with dominant males sometimes ranging as much as 50 miles within a single waterway. While you're unlikely to encounter an otter, if you're camping, you might easily run into the **raccoon** (*Procyon lotor*), an exceedingly intelligent and crafty relative of the bear, sharing that larger animal's resourcefulness in stealing your food. Though nocturnal, raccoons will feed whenever food is available. Rabies is prevalent in the raccoon population, and you should always, always keep your distance.

Another common campsite nuisance, the **opossum** (*Didelphis virginiana*) is a shy, primitive creature that is much more easily discouraged. North America's only marsupial, an opossum's usual "defense" against predators is to play dead. That said, however, they have an immunity to snake venom and often feed on the reptiles, even the most poisonous ones.

While you're unlikely to actually see a **red fox** (*Vulpes vulpes*), you might very well see their distinctive footprints in the mud of a marsh at low tide. These nocturnal hunters, a nonnative species introduced by European settlers, range the coast seeking mice, squirrels, and rabbits.

Once fairly common in Georgia and South Carolina, the **black bear** (*Ursus americanus*) has suffered from hunting and habitat destruction. Of the regions in this guide, the Okefenokee Swamp area is the only place in which you'll be close to one.

## In the Water

Without a doubt the most magnificent denizen—if only part-time—of the southeastern coast is the **North Atlantic right whale** (*Eubalaena glacialis*), which can approach 60 feet in length. Each year December-March the mothers give birth to their calves and nurse them in the warm waters off the Georgia coast in an eons-old ritual. (In the summers they like to hang around the rich fishing grounds off the New England coast, although biologists still can't account for their whereabouts at other times of the year.) Their numbers were so abundant in past centuries that the Spanish name for Jekyll Island, Georgia, was Isla de las Ballenas (Island of the Whales). Whaling and encounters with ship propellers have taken their toll, and numbers of this endangered species are dwindling fast now, with fewer than 500 estimated left in the world.

Another of humankind's aquatic cousins, the **bottlenose dolphin** (*Tursiops truncatus*) is a well-known and frequent visitor to the coast, coming far upstream into creeks and rivers to feed. Children, adults, and experienced sailors alike all delight in encounters with the mammals, sociable creatures who travel in family units. They will gather near boats, surfacing often with the distinctive chuffing sound of air coming from their blowholes. Occasionally they'll even lift their heads out of the water to have a look at you; consider yourself lucky indeed to have such a close encounter. Don't be fooled by their cuteness, however. Dolphins live life with gusto and aren't scared of much. They're voracious eaters of fish, energetic lovers, and will take on an encroaching shark in a heartbeat.

Another beloved part-time marine creature of the barrier islands of the Georgia and South Carolina coast is the **loggerhead turtle** (*Caretta caretta*). Though the species prefers to stay well offshore most of the year, females weighing up to 300 pounds come out of the sea each May-July to dig a shallow hole in the dunes and lay over 100 leathery eggs, returning to the ocean and leaving the eggs to hatch on their own after two months.

Interestingly, the mothers prefer to nest at the same spot on the same island year after year. After hatching, the baby turtles then make a dramatic, extremely dangerous (and extremely slow) trek to the safety of the waves, at the mercy of various predators. A series of dedicated research and conservation efforts, like the Caretta Project based on Wassaw Island, Georgia, are working hard to protect the loggerheads' traditional nursery grounds to ensure survival of this fascinating, loveable, and threatened species.

Of course, the coastal waters and rivers are chockablock with fish. The most abundant and sought-after recreational species in the area is the **spotted sea trout** (*Cynoscion nebulosus*), followed by the **red drum** (*Sciaenops ocellatus*). Local anglers also pursue many varieties of **bass, bream, sheepshead,** and **crappie.** It may sound strange to some accustomed to considering it a "trash" fish, but many types of **catfish** are not only plentiful here but are a common and well-regarded food source. Many species of **flounder** inhabit the silty bottoms of estuaries all along the coast. Farther offshore are game and sport fish like **marlin, swordfish, shark, grouper,** and **tuna.**

Each March, anglers jockey for position on coastal rivers for the yearly running of the **American shad** (*Alosa sapidissima*) upstream to spawn. This large (up to eight pounds) catfish-like species is a regional delicacy as a seasonal entrée as well as for its tasty roe. There's a catch limit of eight shad per person per season. One of the more interesting fish species in the area is the endangered **shortnose sturgeon** (*Acipenser brevirostrum*). A fantastically ancient species that has evolved little in hundreds of millions of years, this small freshwater fish is known to exist in the Altamaha, Savannah, and Ogeechee Rivers of Georgia and the estuaries of the ACE Basin in South Carolina. Traveling upriver to spawn in the winter, the sturgeons remain around the mouths of waterways the rest of the year, venturing near the ocean only sparingly.

Crustaceans and shellfish have been a key food staple in the area for thousands of years, with the massive shell middens of the coast being testament to Native Americans' healthy appetite for them. The beds of the local variant, the **eastern oyster** (*Crassostrea virginica*), aren't what they used to be due to overharvesting, water pollution, and disruption of habitat. In truth, these days most local restaurants import the little filter feeders from the Gulf of Mexico. Oysters spawn May-August, hence the old folk wisdom about eating oysters only in months with the letter *r* so as not to disrupt the breeding cycle.

Each year April-January, shrimp boats up and down the southeastern coast trawl for **shrimp,** most commercially viable in two local species, the white shrimp (*Litopenaeus setiferus*) and the brown shrimp (*Farfantepenaeus aztecus*). Shrimp are the most popular seafood item in the United States and account for bringing hundreds of millions of dollars in revenue into the coastal economy. While consumption won't slow down anytime soon, the Georgia and South Carolina shrimping industries are facing serious threats, both from species decline due to pollution and overfishing as well as from competition from shrimp farms and the Asian shrimp industry.

Another important commercial crop is the **blue crab** (*Callinectes sapidus*), the species used in such Lowcountry delicacies as crab cakes. You'll often see floating markers bobbing up and down in rivers throughout the region. These signal the presence directly below of a crab trap, often of an amateur crabber.

A true living link to primordial times, the alien-looking **horseshoe crab** (*Limulus polyphemus*) is frequently found on beaches of the coast during the spring mating season (it lives in deeper water the rest of the year). More closely related to scorpions and spiders than crabs, the horseshoe has evolved hardly a lick in hundreds of millions of years.

Any trip to a local salt marsh at low tide will likely uncover hundreds of **fiddler crabs** (*Uca pugilator* and *Uca pugnax*), so-named for the way the males wave their single enlarged claw in the air to attract mates. (Their other, smaller claw is the one they actually eat with.) The fiddlers make distinctive burrows in the pluff mud for sanctuary during high tide, recognizable by the little balls of sediment at the entrances (the crabs spit out the balls after sifting through the sand for food).

One charming beach inhabitant, the **sand dollar** (*Mellita quinquiesperforata*), has seen its numbers decline drastically due to being entirely too charming for its own good. Beachcombers are now asked to enjoy these flat little cousins to the sea urchin in their natural habitat and to refrain from taking them home. Besides, they start to smell bad when they dry out.

The **sea nettle** (*Chrysaora quinquecirrha*), a less-than-charming beach inhabitant, is a jellyfish that stings thousands of people on the coast each year (although only for those with severe allergies are the stings potentially life threatening). Stinging their prey before transporting it into their waiting mouths, the jellyfish also sting when disturbed or frightened. Most often, people are stung by stepping on the bodies of jellyfish washed up on the sand. If you're stung by a jellyfish, don't panic. You'll probably experience a stinging rash for about half an hour. Locals say applying a little baking soda or vinegar helps cut the sting. (Some also swear fresh urine will do the trick, and I pass that tip along to you purely in the interest of thoroughness.)

### In the Air

When enjoying the marshlands of the coast, consider yourself fortunate to see a **wood stork** (*Mycteria americana*), very recently taken off the endangered species list. The only storks to breed in North America, these graceful long-lived birds (routinely living over 10 years) are usually seen on a low flight path across the marsh, although at some birding spots beginning in late summer you can find them at a **roost,** sometimes numbering over 100 birds. Resting at high tide, they fan out over the marsh to feed at low tide on foot. Old-timers sometimes call them "Spanish buzzards" or simply "the preacher."

Often confused with the wood stork is

the gorgeous **white ibis** (*Eudocimus albus*), distinguishable by its orange bill and black wingtips. Like the wood stork, the ibis is a communal bird that roosts in colonies.

Other similar-looking coastal denizens are the white-feathered **great egret** (*Ardea alba*) and **snowy egret** (*Egretta thula*), the former distinguishable by its yellow bill and the latter by its black bill and the tuft of plumes on the back of its head. Egrets are in the same family as herons.

The most magnificent in that family is the **great blue heron** (*Ardea herodias*). Despite their imposing height—up to four feet tall—these waders are shy. Often you hear them rather than see them, a loud shriek of alarm that echoes over the marsh.

So how to tell the difference between all these wading birds at a glance? It's actually easiest when they're in flight. Egrets and herons fly with their necks tucked in, while storks and ibis fly with their necks extended.

Dozens of species of shorebirds comb the beaches, including **sandpipers, plovers,** and the wonderful and rare **American oystercatcher** (*Haematopus palliatus*), instantly recognizable for its prancing walk, dark-brown back, stark white underside, and long bright-orange bill. **Gulls** and **terns** also hang out wherever there's water. They can frequently be seen swarming around incoming shrimp boats, attracted by the catch of little crustaceans.

The chief raptor of the salt marsh is the fish-eating **osprey** (*Pandion haliaetus*). These large grayish birds of prey are similar to eagles but are adapted to a maritime environment, with a reversible outer toe on each talon (the better for catching wriggly fish) and closable nostrils so they can dive into the water after prey. Very common all along the coast, they like to build big nests on top of buoys and channel markers in addition to trees.

The **bald eagle** (*Haliaeetus leucocephalus*) is making a comeback in the area thanks to increased federal regulation and better education of trigger-happy locals. Apparently not as all-American as their bumper stickers might sometimes indicate, local farmers would often regard the national symbol as more of a nuisance and fire away anytime they saw one. Of course, as we all should have learned in school, the bald eagle is not actually bald but has a head adorned with white feathers. Like the osprey, bald eagles prefer fish, but unlike the osprey will settle for rodents and rabbits.

Inland among the pines you'll find the most common area woodpecker, the huge **pileated woodpecker** (*Dryocopus pileatus*) with its large crest. Less common is the smaller, more subtly marked **red-cockaded woodpecker** (*Picoides borealis*). Once common in the vast primordial pine forests of the Southeast, the species is now endangered, its last real refuge being the big tracts of relatively undisturbed land on military bases.

## Insects

Down here they say that God invented bugs to keep the Yankees from completely taking over the South. And insects are probably the most unpleasant fact of life in the southeastern coastal region. The list of annoying indigenous insects must begin with the infamous **sand gnat** (*Culicoides furens*). This tiny and persistent nuisance, a member of the midge family, lacks the precision of the mosquito with its long proboscis. No, the sand gnat is more torture master than surgeon, brutally gouging and digging away its victim's skin until it hits a source of blood. Most prevalent in the spring and fall, the sand gnat is drawn to its prey by the carbon dioxide trail of its breath. While long sleeves and long pants are one way to keep gnats at bay, the only real antidote to the sand gnat's assault—other than never breathing—is the Avon skin-care product Skin So Soft, which has taken on a new and wholly unplanned life as the South's favorite anti-gnat lotion. In calmer moments, grow to appreciate the great contribution sand gnats make to the salt marsh ecosystem—as food for birds and bats.

Running a close second to the sand gnat are the over three dozen species of highly aggressive **mosquito,** which breeds anywhere a few drops of water lie stagnant. Not surprisingly, massive populations blossom in the rainiest months, in late spring and late summer, feeding in the morning and late afternoon. Like the gnat, the mosquito—the biters are always female—homes in on its victim by trailing the plume of carbon dioxide exhaled in the breath. More than just a biting nuisance, mosquitoes are now carrying West Nile disease to the Lowcountry and Georgia coast, signaling a possibly dire threat to public health. Alas, Skin So Soft has little effect on the mosquito. Try over-the-counter sprays, anything smelling of citronella, and wearing long sleeves and long pants when weather permits.

But undoubtedly the most viscerally loathed of all pests on the Lowcountry and Georgia coasts is the so-called "palmetto bug," or **American cockroach** (*Periplaneta americana*). These black, shiny, and sometimes grotesquely massive insects—up to two inches long—are living fossils, virtually unchanged over hundreds of millions of years. And perfectly adapted as they are to life in and among wet, decaying vegetation, they're unlikely to change a bit in 100 million more years. While they spend most of their time crawling around, usually under rotting leaves and tree bark, American cockroaches can indeed fly—sort of. There are few more hilarious sights than a room full of people frantically trying to dodge a palmetto bug that has just clumsily launched itself off a high point on the wall. Because the cockroach doesn't know any better than you do where it's going, it can be a particularly bracing event—though the insect does not bite and poses few real health hazards.

Popular regional use of the term *palmetto bug* undoubtedly has its roots in a desire for polite Southern society to avoid using the ugly word *roach* and its connotations of filth and unclean environments. But the colloquialism actually has a basis in reality. Contrary to what anyone tells you, the natural habitat of the American cockroach—unlike its kitchen-dwelling, much-smaller cousin the German cockroach—is outdoors, often up in trees. They only come inside human dwellings when it's especially hot, especially cold, or especially dry outside. Like you, the palmetto bug is easily driven indoors by extreme temperatures and by thirst.

Other than visiting the Southeast during the winter, when the roaches go dormant, there's no convenient antidote for their presence. The best way to keep them out of your life is to stay away from decaying vegetation and keep doors and windows closed on especially hot nights.

# History

## BEFORE THE EUROPEANS

Based on artifacts found throughout the state, anthropologists know the first humans arrived on the coasts of South Carolina and Georgia at least 13,000 years ago, at the tail end of the last ice age. During this **Paleo-Indian Period,** sea levels were over 200 feet lower than present levels, and large mammals such as woolly mammoths, horses, and camels were hunted for food and skins. However, rapidly increasing temperatures, rising sea levels, and efficient hunting techniques combined to quickly kill off these large mammals, relics of the Pleistocene Era, ushering in the **Archaic Period.** Still hunter-gatherers, Archaic Period people began turning to small game such as deer, bears, and turkeys, supplemented with fruit and nuts. The latter part of the Archaic era saw more habitation on the coasts, with an increasing reliance on fish and shellfish. It's to this time that the great **shell middens** of the Georgia and South Carolina coasts trace their origins. Basically serving as trash heaps for discarded oyster shells, as the middens grew in size they also took on a ceremonial status, often being used as sites for important rituals and meetings. Such sites are often called **shell rings,** and the largest yet found was over nine feet high and 300 feet in diameter.

The introduction of agriculture and improved pottery techniques about 3,000 years ago led to the **Woodland Period** of Native American settlement. Extended clan groups were much less migratory, establishing year-round communities of up to 50 people, who began the practice of clearing land to grow crops. The ancient shell middens of their ancestors were not abandoned, however, and were continually added onto. Native Americans had been cremating or burying their dead for years, a practice that eventually gave rise to the construction of the first **mounds** during the Woodland Period. Essentially built-up earthworks sometimes marked with spiritual symbols, often in the form of animal shapes, mounds not only contained the remains of the deceased but items like pottery to accompany the deceased into the afterlife.

Increased agriculture led to increased population, and with that population growth came competition over resources and a more formal notion of warfare. This period, about AD 800-1600, is termed the **Mississippian Period.** It was the Mississippians who would be the first Native Americans in what's now the continental United States to encounter European explorers and settlers after Columbus. The Native Americans who would later be called **Creek Indians** were the direct descendants of the Mississippians in lineage, language, and lifestyle. Native American social structure north of Mexico reached its apex with the Mississippians, who were not only prodigious mound builders but constructed elaborate wooden villages and evolved a top-down class system. The defensive palisades surrounding some of the villages attest to the increasingly martial nature of the groups and their chieftains, or *micos*.

Described by later European accounts as a tall, proud people, the Mississippians often wore elaborate body art and, like the indigenous inhabitants of Central and South America, used the practice of **head shaping,** whereby an infant's skull was deliberately deformed into an elongated shape by tying the baby's head to a board for about a year.

## THE SPANISH ARRIVE

The first known contact by Europeans on the southeastern coast came in 1521, roughly concurrent with Cortés's conquest of Mexico. A party of Spanish slavers ventured into what's now Port Royal Sound, South Carolina, from Santo Domingo in the Caribbean. Naming the area Santa Elena, they kidnapped a few Native American people and left, ranging as far north as the Cape Fear River in present-day North Carolina.

The first serious exploration of the coast came in 1526, when Lucas Vázquez de Ayllón and about 600 colonists made landfall at Winyah Bay in South Carolina, near present-day Georgetown. They didn't stay long, however, immediately moving down the coast and trying to set down roots in the St. Catherine's Sound area of modern-day Liberty County, Georgia.

That colony—called San Miguel de Gualdape—was the first European settlement in North America since the Vikings (the continent's oldest continuously occupied settlement, St. Augustine, Florida, wasn't founded until 1565). The colony also brought with it the seed of a future nation's dissolution: enslaved people from Africa. While San Miguel lasted only six weeks due to political tension and a slave uprising, artifacts from its brief life have been discovered in the area.

Hernando de Soto's ill-fated trek of 1539-1543 from Florida through Georgia to Alabama (where De Soto died of a fever) did not find the gold he anticipated, nor did it enter the coastal region covered in this guide. But De Soto's legacy was indeed soon felt there and throughout the Southeast in the form of various diseases for which the Mississippian people had no immunity whatsoever: smallpox, typhus, influenza, measles, yellow fever, whooping cough, diphtheria, tuberculosis, and bubonic plague.

While the cruelties of the Spanish certainly took their toll, these deadly diseases were far more damaging to a population totally unprepared for them. Within a few years, the Mississippian people—already in a state of internal decline—were losing huge percentages of their population to disease, echoing what had already happened on a massive scale to the indigenous people of the Caribbean after Christopher Columbus's expeditions. As the viruses they introduced ran rampant, the Europeans themselves stayed away for a couple of decades after the ignominious end of De Soto's fruitless quest.

During that quarter-century, the once-proud Mississippian culture continued to disintegrate, dwindling into a shadow of its former greatness. In all, disease would claim the lives of at least 80 percent of all indigenous inhabitants of the Western Hemisphere.

## THE FRENCH MISADVENTURE

The next European presence on the Georgia and South Carolina coast was another ill-fated attempt, the establishment of Charlesfort in 1562 by French Huguenots under Jean Ribault on present-day Parris Island, South Carolina. Part of a covert effort by the Protestant French admiral Gaspard II de Coligny to send Huguenot colonists around the globe, Ribault's crew of 150 first explored the mouth of the St. Johns River near present-day Jacksonville, Florida, before heading north.

After establishing Charlesfort, Ribault returned to France for supplies. In his absence, religious war had broken out in his home country. Ribault sought sanctuary in England but was clapped in irons anyway. Meanwhile, most of Charlesfort's colonists grew so demoralized they joined another French expedition led by René Laudonnière at Fort Caroline on the St. Johns River. The remaining 27 built a ship to sail from Charlesfort back to France; 20 of them survived the journey, which was cut short in the English Channel when they had to be rescued.

Ribault himself was dispatched to reinforce Fort Caroline, but was headed off by a contingent from the new Spanish settlement at St. Augustine. The fate of the French presence on the southeast coast was sealed when not only did the Spanish take Fort Caroline but a storm destroyed Ribault's reinforcing fleet; Ribault and all survivors were killed as soon as they came ashore. To keep the French away for good and cement Spain's hold on this northernmost part of their province of La Florida, the Spanish built the fort of Santa Elena directly on top of Charlesfort. Both layers are currently being excavated and studied.

## THE MISSION ERA

With Spanish dominance of the region ensured for the near future, the lengthy mission era began. It's rarely mentioned as a key part of U.S. history, but the Spanish missionary presence on the Georgia coast was longer and more comprehensive than its much more widely known counterpart in California. St. Augustine's governor Pedro Menéndez de Avilés—sharing "biscuits with honey" on the beach at St. Catherine's Island with a local *mico*—negotiated for the right to establish a system of Jesuit missions in two coastal chiefdoms: the Mocama on and around Cumberland Island, and the Guale (pronounced "wallie") to the north. Those early missions, the first north of Mexico, were largely unsuccessful. But a renewed, organized effort by the Franciscan Order came to fruition during the 1580s. Starting with Santa Catalina de Guale on St. Catherine's Island, missions were established all along the Georgia coast.

The looming invasion threat to St. Augustine from English adventurer and privateer Sir Francis Drake was a harbinger of trouble to come, as was a Guale uprising in 1597. The Spanish consolidated their positions near St. Augustine, and Santa Elena was abandoned. As Spanish power waned, in 1629 Charles I of England laid formal claim to what is now the Carolinas, Georgia, and much of Florida, but made no effort to colonize the area. Largely left to their own devices and facing an indigenous population dying from disease, the missions in the Georgia interior nonetheless carried on. A devastating raid by indigenous people in 1661 on a mission at the mouth of the Altamaha River, possibly aided by the English, persuaded the Spanish to pull the mission effort to the barrier islands. But even as late as 1667, right before the founding of Charles Towne far to the north, there were 70 missions still extant in the old Guale kingdom.

Pirate raids and uprisings by enslaved people finished off the Georgia missions for good by 1684. By 1706 the Spanish mission effort in the Southeast had fully retreated to St. Augustine. In an interesting postscript, 89 Native Americans—the only surviving descendants of Spain's Georgia missions—evacuated to Cuba with the final Spanish exodus from Florida in 1763.

## ENTER THE ENGLISH

With indigenous populations in steep decline due to disease and a wholesale retrenchment by European powers, a sort of vacuum came to the southeastern coast. Into the vacuum came the first English-speaking settlers of South Carolina. The first attempt was an expedition by a Barbadian colonist, William Hilton, in 1663. While he didn't establish a new colony, he did leave his name on the most notable geographic feature he saw—Hilton Head Island.

In 1665 King Charles II gave a charter to eight **Lords Proprietors** to establish a colony, generously to be named Carolina after the monarch himself. (One of the Proprietors, Lord Ashley Cooper, would see not one but both rivers in the Charleston area named after him.) Remarkably, none of the Proprietors ever set foot in the colony they established for their own profit. Before their colony was even set up, the Proprietors themselves set the stage for the vast human disaster that would eventually befall it. They encouraged slavery by promising that each colonist would receive 20 acres of land for every enslaved black man and 10 acres for every enslaved black woman brought to the colony within the first year.

In 1666 explorer Robert Sandford officially claimed Carolina for the king. The Proprietors then sent out a fleet of three ships from England, only one of which, the *Carolina,* would make it the whole way. After stops in the thriving English colonies of Barbados and Bermuda, the ship landed in Port Royal. The settlers were greeted without violence, but the fact that the local indigenous people spoke Spanish led the colonists to conclude that perhaps the site was too close for comfort to Spain's sphere of influence.

A Kiawah chief, eager for allies against the fierce slave-trading Westo people, invited the colonists north to settle instead. So the colonists—148 of them, including three enslaved Africans—moved 80 miles up the coast and in 1670 pitched camp on the Ashley River at a place they dubbed Albemarle Point after one of their lost ships. Living within the palisades of the camp—you can visit it today at the Charles Towne Landing State Historic Site just outside Charleston—the colonists farmed 10-acre plots outside the walls.

A few years later some colonists from Barbados, which was beginning to suffer the effects of overpopulation, joined the Carolinians. The Barbadian influence, with an emphasis on large-scale slave labor and a caste system, would have an indelible imprint on the colony. Indeed, within a generation a majority of settlers in the new colony would be enslaved Africans.

By 1680, however, Albemarle Point was feeling growing pains as well, and the Proprietors ordered the site moved to Oyster Point at the confluence of the Ashley and Cooper Rivers (the present-day Battery). Within a year Albemarle Point was abandoned, and the walls of Charles Towne were built a few hundred yards up from Oyster Point on the banks of the Cooper River.

The original Anglican settlers were quickly joined by various **Dissenters,** among them French Huguenots, Quakers, Congregationalists, and Jews. A group of Scottish Presbyterians established the short-lived Stuart Town near Port Royal in 1684.

## Henry Woodward, Colonial Indiana Jones

He's virtually unsung in the history books, and there are no movies made about him, but Dr. Henry Woodward, the first English settler in South Carolina, lived a life that is the stuff of novels and screenplays. Educated in medicine in London, Woodward first tried his hand in the colony of Barbados. But Barbados, crowded and run by the elite planters, was no place for a young man with a sense of adventure but no contacts in the sugar industry. Still in his teens, Woodward left Barbados in Captain Robert Sandford's 1664 expedition to Carolina. Landing in the Cape Fear region, Sandford's cohort made its way down to Port Royal Sound to contact the Cusabo people. In 1666, in what is perhaps the New World's first "cultural exchange program," Woodward volunteered to stay behind while the rest of the expedition returned to England with a Native American man named Shadoo.

Woodward learned the local language and established political relations with surrounding Native American communities, actions for which the Lords Proprietors granted him temporary "formall possession of the whole Country to hold as Tennant att Will." The Spanish had different plans, however. They came and kidnapped the young Englishman, taking him to what turned out to be a very permissive state of house arrest at the Spanish stronghold of St. Augustine in Florida. Surprising the Spanish with his request—in Latin, no less—to convert to Catholicism, Woodward was popular and treated well. An excellent student of the Catechism, Woodward became a favorite of the Spanish governor and was even promoted to official surgeon. During that time, he studied Spanish government, commerce, and culture, with the same diligence with which he had studied the indigenous people a year earlier. In 1668, Woodward was "rescued" by English privateers—pirates, really—under the command of Robert Searle, who'd come to sack St. Augustine. Woodward's sojourn with the pirates would last two years, during which he was kept on board as ship's surgeon. Was the pirate raid a coincidence? Or, as some scholars suggest, was Woodward really one of history's greatest spies? We will probably never know.

Incredibly, the plot thickens. In another coincidence, in 1670 Woodward was rescued when the pirates shipwrecked on the Caribbean island of Nevis. His rescuers were none other than the settlers on their way to found Charles Towne. Upon landfall, Woodward asserted his previous experience in the area to direct the colonists away from Port Royal to an area of less Spanish influence. That same year he began a series of expeditions to contact Native Americans in the Carolina interior—the first non-Spanish European to set foot in the area. Using economic espionage gained from the Spanish, Woodward's goal was to jump-start the trade in deerskins that would be the bulwark of the Charles Towne colony. Woodward's unlikely 1674 alliance with the aggressive Westo people was instrumental in this burgeoning trade. As if all this weren't enough, in 1680 Woodward, now with property of his own on Johns Island, would introduce local farmers to a certain strange crop recently imported from Madagascar: rice.

Woodward made enemies, however, of settlers who were envious of his growing affluence and suspicious of his friendship with the Westo. His outspoken disgust with the growing practice of enslaving indigenous people brought a charge against him of undermining the interests of the crown. But Woodward, by now a celebrity of sorts, returned to England to plead his case directly to the Lords Proprietors. They not only pardoned him but made him their official agent in trading with indigenous people—with a 20 percent share of the profits. Woodward would never again see the land of his birth. He returned to the American colonies to trek inland, making alliances with groups of Creek people in Spanish-held territory. Hounded by Spanish troops, Woodward fell ill of a fever somewhere in the Savannah River valley. He made it to Charleston and safety but never fully recovered and died around 1690—after living the kind of life you usually only see in the movies.

Recognizing this diversity, the colony in 1697 granted religious liberty to all "except Papists," meaning Roman Catholics. The Anglicans attempted a crackdown on Dissenters in 1704, but two years later Queen Anne stepped in and ensured religious freedom for all Carolinians (again with the exception of Catholics, who wouldn't be a factor in the colony until after the American Revolution).

## THE YAMASEE WAR

Within 20 years the English presence had expanded throughout the Lowcountry to include Port Royal and Beaufort. Charles Towne became a thriving commercial center, dealing in deerskins with traders in the interior and with foreign concerns from England to South America. Its success was not without a backlash, as the local **Yamasee** people became increasingly disgruntled at the settlers' growing monopolies on deerskin and the trade in enslaved Native Americans.

As rumors of war spread, on Good Friday, 1715, a delegation of six Carolinians went to the Yamasee village of Pocataligo to address some of the Yamasee grievances in the hopes of forestalling violence. Their effort was in vain, however, as warriors murdered four of them in their sleep, the remaining two escaping to sound the alarm.

The attack signaled the beginning of the two-year Yamasee War, which would claim the lives of nearly 10 percent of the colony's population and an unknown number of Native Americans—making it one of the bloodiest conflicts fought on American soil.

Energized and ready for war, the Yamasee attacked Charles Towne itself and killed almost all the white traders in the interior, effectively ending commerce in the area. As Charles Towne began to swell with refugees from the hinterland, water and supplies ran low, and the colony's very existence was in peril.

After an initially poor performance by the Carolina militia, a professional army—including armed enslaved Africans—was raised. Well trained and well led, the new army more than held its own despite being outnumbered. A key alliance with local Cherokee people was all the advantage the colonists needed to turn the tide. While the Cherokee never received the overt military backing from the settlers that they sought, they did garner enough supplies and influence to convince their Creek rivals, the Yamasee, to begin the peace process. The war-weary settlers, eager to get back to life and to business, were eager to negotiate with them, offering goods as a sign of their earnest intent. By 1717 the Yamasee threat had subsided and trade in the region began flourishing anew.

No sooner had the Yamasee War ended, however, that a new threat emerged: the dreaded pirate Edward Teach, a.k.a. Blackbeard. Entering Charleston harbor in May 1718 with his flagship *Queen Anne's Revenge* and three other vessels, he promptly plundered five ships and began a full-scale blockade of the entire settlement. He took a number of prominent citizens hostage before finally departing northward.

## SLAVERY

For the colonists, the Blackbeard episode was the final straw. Already disgusted by the lack of support from the Lords Proprietors during the Yamasee War, the humiliation of the pirate blockade was too much to take. To almost universal agreement in the colony, the settlers threw off the rule of the Proprietors and lobbied in 1719 to become a crown colony, an effort that came to final fruition in 1729.

While this outward-looking and energetic Charleston was originally built on the backs of merchants, with the introduction of the rice and indigo crops in the early 1700s it would increasingly be built on the backs of enslaved people. For all the wealth gained through the planting of rice and cotton seeds, another seed was sown by the Lowcountry plantation culture. The area's total dependence on slave labor would ultimately lead to a disastrous war, a conflict signaled for decades to those smart enough to read the signs.

## Pirates of the Atlantic

Pirates, along with their close cousins, slavers, were among the earliest explorers of the Atlantic seaboard of North America, and other than Native American chiefs, were the only real authority in the area for decades. The creeks and barrier islands of the Georgia and Carolina coast provided important hard-to-find sanctuaries away from the regular pirate circuit in the booty-laden Spanish Caribbean.

For most of us, pirate stories and movies are a form of escapism, in which the most unlikely scenarios happen with ease. But a real-life pirate story from the earliest days of the Charleston seems almost too unbelievable, even for Hollywood. The encounter was at the hands of the infamous Edward Teach, a.k.a. Blackbeard. A tall, terrifying bully of a man, the legendary pirate also had a flair for the dramatic, as all proper pirates should. Given to twisting flaming wads of cloth into his beard when he attacked his prey, Blackbeard was also quite eccentric, as his Charleston escapade shows. In May 1718, Blackbeard, driven north from his usual hunting grounds in the Bahamas by a concerted effort of the British Navy, approached Charleston Harbor in his flagship *Queen Anne's Revenge,* accompanied by three smaller vessels. He immediately seized several ships and kidnapped several leading citizens, including Councilman Samuel Wragg and his four-year-old son. He sent one captive ashore with the message that unless his demand was met, the heads of Wragg and son would soon be delivered to the colonial governor's doorstep. Blackbeard's demand? A chest of medicine. For what purpose, we still aren't sure, but apparently it really was all he wanted. The medicines were delivered in short order, and Blackbeard released his hostages and sailed north to Ocracoke Island, North Carolina, to enjoy a royal pardon he'd just received.

One of the pirates serving under Blackbeard during the Charleston escapade was Stede Bonnet, quite a contrasting figure in his debonair nature and posh finery. When Charleston's Colonel William Rhett—his house at 54 Hasell Street, the city's oldest, is still standing—got wind that Bonnet and crew were still a-pirating off Cape Fear, North Carolina, he set out with a fleet to bring him to justice. And that he did, bringing pirate and crew back to Charleston for a trial that almost didn't happen after Bonnet escaped from custody dressed as a woman (he was captured on Sullivan's Island). The dashing Bonnet actually garnered quite a bit of public sympathy—especially when he begged not to be hanged—but it wasn't enough to forestall the grim fate of the pirate and his crew: public execution at White Point, the bodies left to dangle as a warning to other buccaneers. Another coastal menace, Richard Worley, was also hanged in Charleston. He was supposedly buried in a marshy creek downtown, where Meeting and Water Streets intersect today.

Though Savannah is home to the famous Pirate's House restaurant and got a major shout-out in Robert Louis Stevenson's *Treasure Island,* actual pirate history there is hard to nail down. There seems little doubt that a host of ne'er-do-wells made their way onto the rowdy Savannah waterfront, but the port's location nearly 20 miles upriver would have made it less-than-ideal territory for a true buccaneer, who always needed a fast getaway handy.

As for Blackbeard, his retirement plans were interrupted by a contingent of Virginians who tracked him down and killed him near Ocracoke. However, his legend lives to this day on Blackbeard Island, Georgia, a gorgeous, undeveloped barrier island that has changed little since the days when Teach himself allegedly stopped over between pirate raids. The legends even say he left some treasure there, but don't try to look for it—Blackbeard Island is now a National Wildlife Refuge.

By the early 18th century Charleston and Savannah were firmly established as the key American ports for the importation of enslaved Africans, with about 40 percent of the trade centered in Charleston alone. As a result, the black population of the coast outnumbered the white population by more than three to one, and much more than that in some areas. The fear of violent slave uprisings had great influence over not only politics but day-to-day affairs.

These fears were eventually realized in the **Stono Rebellion** on September 9, 1739. Twenty African American slaves led by an

Angolan known only as Jemmy met near the Stono River near Charleston. Marching with a banner that read "Liberty," they seized guns with the plan of marching all the way to Spanish Florida and finding sanctuary in the wilderness. On the way they burned seven plantations and killed 20 more whites. A militia eventually caught up with them, killing 44 of the rebels while losing 20 of their own. The prisoners were decapitated and had their heads spiked on every milepost between the spot of that final battle and Charleston. Inspired by the rebellion, at least two other uprisings would take place over the next two years in South Carolina and Georgia.

## OGLETHORPE'S VISION

In 1729, Carolina was divided into north and south. In 1731, a colony to be known as Georgia, after the new English king, was carved out of the southern part of the Carolina land grant. A young general, aristocrat, and humanitarian named James Edward Oglethorpe gathered together a group of Trustees—similar to Carolina's Lords Proprietors—to take advantage.

While Oglethorpe would go on to found Georgia, his wasn't the first English presence in the area. A garrison built Fort King George in modern-day Darien, Georgia, in 1721, which you can visit today. A cypress blockhouse surrounded by palisaded earthworks, the fort defended the southern reaches of England's claim for seven years before being abandoned in 1728.

On February 12, 1733, after stops in Beaufort and Charleston, the ship *Anne* with its 114 passengers made its way to the highest bluff on the Savannah River. The area was controlled by the peaceful Yamacraw people, who had been encouraged by the powers-that-be in Charleston to settle on this vacant land 12 miles up the Savannah River to serve as a buffer for the Spanish. Led by an elderly chief, or *mico,* named Tomochichi, the Yamacraw enjoyed the area's natural bounty of shellfish, fruit, nuts, and small game.

A deft politician, Oglethorpe struck up a treaty and eventually a genuine friendship with Tomochichi. To the Yamacraw, Oglethorpe was a rare bird—a white man who behaved with honor and was true to his word. The Native Americans reciprocated by helping the settlers and pledging fealty to the crown. Oglethorpe reported to the Trustees that Tomochichi personally requested "that we would Love and Protect their little Families."

In negotiations with local indigenous communities using Mary Musgrove, a Creek-English settler in the area, as translator, the persuasive Oglethorpe convinced the coastal Creek to cede to the crown all Georgia land to the Altamaha River. Oglethorpe's impact was soon felt farther down the Georgia coast, as St. Simons Island, Jekyll Island, Darien, and Brunswick were settled in rapid succession and with them the entrenchment of the plantation system and slave labor.

While the Trustees' utopian vision was largely economic in nature, like Carolina the Georgia colony also emphasized religious freedom. While to modern ears Charleston's antipathy toward "papists" and Oglethorpe's original ban of Roman Catholics from Georgia might seem incompatible with this goal, the reason was a coldly pragmatic one for the time: England's two main global rivals, France and Spain, were both staunchly Catholic countries.

## SPAIN VANQUISHED

Things heated up on the coast in 1739 with the so-called **War of Jenkins' Ear,** which despite its seemingly trivial beginnings over the humiliation of a British captain by Spanish privateers was actually a proxy struggle emblematic of changes in the European balance of power. A year later Oglethorpe cobbled together a force of settlers, Native American allies, and Carolinians to reduce the Spanish fortress at St. Augustine, Florida. The siege failed, and Oglethorpe retreated to St. Simons Island to await the inevitable counterattack. In 1742, a Spanish force invaded the island but was eventually turned back for good at the **Battle of Bloody Marsh.** That clash marked the end of Spanish overtures on England's colonies in what is now the United States.

Though Oglethorpe returned to England a national hero, things fell apart in Savannah. The settlers became envious of the success of Charleston's slave-based rice economy and began wondering aloud why they couldn't also make use of free labor. With Oglethorpe otherwise occupied in England, the Trustees of Georgia—distant in more ways than just geographically from the new colony—bowed to public pressure and relaxed the restrictions on slavery and rum. By 1753 the Trustees voted to return their charter to the crown, officially making Georgia the 13th and final colony of England in America. With first the French and then the Spanish effectively shut off from the American East Coast, the stage was set for an internal battle between England and its burgeoning colonies across the Atlantic.

## REVOLUTION AND INDEPENDENCE

The population of the colonies swelled in the mid-1700s, not only from an influx of enslaved Africans, but also from a corresponding flood of European immigrants. The interior began filling up with Germans, Swiss, Scottish, and Irish settlers. Their subsequent demands for political representation led to tension between them and the coastal inhabitants, typically depicted through the years as an Upcountry versus Lowcountry competition. It is a persistent but inaccurate myth that the affluent elite on the southeastern coast were reluctant to break ties with England. While the Lowcountry's cultural and economic ties to England were certainly strong, the **Stamp Act** and the **Townshend Acts** combined to turn public sentiment against the mother country here as elsewhere in the colonies.

South Carolinian planters like Christopher Gadsden, Henry Laurens, John Rutledge, and Arthur Middleton were early leaders in the movement for independence. Planters in what would be called Liberty County, Georgia, also strongly agitated for the cause. War broke out between the colonists and the British in New England, and soon made its way southward. The British failed to take Charleston—the fourth-largest city in the colonies—in June 1776, an episode that gave South Carolina its "Palmetto State" moniker when redcoat cannonballs bounced off the palm tree-lined walls of Fort Moultrie. The British under General Sir Henry Clinton successfully took the city in 1780, however, occupying it until 1782.

The British, under General Archibald Campbell, took Savannah in 1778. Royal Governor Sir James Wright returned from exile to Georgia to reclaim it for the crown, the only one of the colonies to be subsumed again into the British Empire. A polyglot force of colonists, Haitians, and Hessians attacked the British fortifications on the west side of Savannah in 1779 but were repulsed with heavy losses. Although the area's two major cities had fallen to the British, the war raged on throughout the surrounding area.

Indeed, throughout the Lowcountry, fighting was as vicious as anything yet seen on the North American continent. With over 130 known military engagements occurring here, South Carolina sacrificed more men during the war than any other colony—including Massachusetts, the "Cradle of the Revolution."

The struggle became a guerrilla war of colonists versus the British as well as a civil war between patriots and loyalists, or **Tories.** Committing what would today undoubtedly be called war crimes, the British routinely burned homes, churches, and fields and massacred civilians. Using Daufuskie Island as a base, British soldiers staged raids on Hilton Head plantations.

In response, patriots of the Lowcountry bred a group of deadly guerrilla soldiers under legendary leaders such as Francis Marion, "the Swamp Fox," and Thomas Sumter, "the Gamecock," who attacked the British in daring hit-and-run raids staged from swamps and marshes. A covert group of patriots called the **Sons of Liberty** met clandestinely throughout the Lowcountry, plotting revolution over pints of ale. Sometimes their efforts transcended talk, however, and atrocities were committed against area loyalists.

In all, four South Carolinians signed the Declaration of Independence (Thomas Heyward Jr., Thomas Lynch Jr., Arthur Middleton, and Edward Rutledge), as did three Georgians (Button Gwinnett, Lyman Hall, and George Walton).

## HIGH COTTON

True to form, the new nation wasted no time in asserting its economic strength. Rice planters from Georgetown north of Charleston on down to the Altamaha River in Georgia built on their already impressive wealth, becoming the new nation's richest men by far—with fortunes built on the backs of the enslaved people working in their fields.

In 1786, a new crop was introduced that would only enhance the financial clout of the coastal region: cotton. A former loyalist colonel, Roger Kelsal, sent some seed from the West Indies to his friend James Spaulding, owner of a plantation on St. Simons Island, Georgia. This crop, soon to be known as **Sea Island cotton** and considered the best in the world, would supplant rice as the crop of choice for coastal plantations. At the height of the Southern cotton boom in the early 1800s, a single Sea Island cotton harvest on a single plantation might go for $100,000—in 1820 dollars. While Charleston was still by far the largest, most powerful, and most influential city on the southeastern coast of the United States, at the peak of the cotton craze Savannah was actually doing more business—a fact that grated to no end on the Holy City's elite. Unlike Charleston, where the planters themselves dominated city life, in Savannah it was cotton brokers called **factors** who were the city's leading class. During this time most of the grand homes of downtown Savannah's historic district were built. This boom period, fueled largely by cotton exports, was perhaps most iconically represented by the historic sailing of the SS *Savannah* from Savannah to Liverpool in 29 days, the first transatlantic voyage by a steamship.

During the prosperous antebellum period, the economy of Charleston, Savannah, and surrounding areas was completely dependent on slave labor, but the cities themselves boasted large numbers of African Americans who were active in business and agriculture. For example, the vending stalls at the City Markets of both Charleston and Savannah were predominantly staffed by African American workers, some of them free.

## SECESSION

Much of the lead-in to the Civil War focused on whether slavery would be allowed in the newest U.S. territories in the West, but there's no doubt that all figurative roads eventually led to South Carolina. During Andrew Jackson's presidency in the 1820s, his vice president, South Carolina's John C. Calhoun, became a thorn in Jackson's side with his aggressive advocacy for **nullification.** In a nutshell, Calhoun said that if a state decided the federal government wasn't treating it fairly—in this case with regard to tariffs that were hurting the cotton trade in the Palmetto State—it could simply nullify the federal law, superseding it with law of its own.

As the abolition movement gained steam and tensions over slavery rose, South Carolina congressman Preston Brooks took things to the next level. On May 22, 1856, he beat fellow senator Charles Sumner of Massachusetts nearly to death with his walking cane on the Senate floor. Sumner had just given a speech criticizing pro-slavery forces—including a relative of Brooks—and called slavery "a harlot." (In a show of support, South Carolinians sent Brooks dozens of new canes to replace the one he broke over Sumner's head.)

In 1860, the national convention of the Democratic Party, then the dominant force in U.S. politics, was held in—where else?—Charleston. Rancor over slavery and state's rights was so high that they couldn't agree on a single candidate to run to replace President James Buchanan. Reconvening in Maryland, the party split along sectional lines, with the Northern wing backing Stephen A. Douglas.

## Nathanael Greene and Mulberry Grove

Like John Wesley, Nathanael Greene's time in Savannah was short and mostly unfortunate. Unlike Wesley, however, Greene never got a chance to leave and start anew. One of the American Revolution's greatest heroes, Greene rose from the rank of private in the Continental Army to become George Washington's right-hand man. Ironically, this skillful soldier was born into a family of pacifist Quakers in Rhode Island in 1742. As a brigadier general in the Rhode Island militia, Greene's innate military prowess caught Washington's eye during the siege of Boston, whereupon the future president gave Greene command of the entire Southern theater of the fight for independence. While Greene never attempted the suicidal aim of taking on Lord Cornwallis's large and well-trained Southern contingent of British veterans, his guerrilla tactics did force the English contingent to divide and hence weaken itself. It was Greene who sent General "Mad Anthony" Wayne in 1782 to finally free Savannah from the British, who had resisted an earlier attempt to retake the city in 1779. Perhaps in a nod to his Quaker roots, Greene insisted that no revenge be taken on Savannah's loyalists, instead welcoming them into the new nation as partners. As a reward for his service, Washington granted Greene a large estate on the banks of the Savannah River known as Mulberry Grove, primarily known to history as the place where Eli Whitney would later invent the cotton gin while serving as tutor to the Greene children. (Wayne was awarded nearby Richmond Plantation.)

Mulberry Grove was less productive for Greene himself, however, who as a lifelong abolitionist refused to use slave labor on the plantation, and hence paid a steep financial price. The 44-year-old Greene spent less than a year at Mulberry Grove, mostly worrying about finances, when he suffered sunstroke on a particularly brutal June day in 1786 and died shortly thereafter.

And there's where the real mystery begins. At some point Greene's remains were said to have been lost after a family vault in Colonial Cemetery was vandalized by Union troops. Almost a century passed until in 1900 the Society of the Cincinnati of Rhode Island appointed a search committee to find and properly inter the general's long-lost remains. The remains were indeed found—right in the vault in Colonial Cemetery where they were supposed to have been, which you can see to this day. However, they were underneath someone else: After removing the coffin of one Robert Scott, excavators found "a mass of rotten wood and human bones mixed with sand," along with a rusty coffin plate reading:

Nathanael Greene,
Obit June 19, 1786
Age, 41 Years

So it was that in 1902, Greene's remains were finally put to rest under his monument in Johnson Square—dedicated to him by the Marquis de Lafayette 76 years earlier in 1825.

Sadly, all buildings at Mulberry Grove were razed by Sherman's troops in 1864, with only a few brick stairs and portions of foundation remaining. The area—visited not once but twice by George Washington after his friend's untimely death—entered industrial use in 1975 and is currently occupied by the Georgia Ports Authority. No full-scale archaeological dig has ever been done at the site, although the nonprofit Mulberry Grove Foundation (www.mulberrygrove.org) is working toward that as well as a plan to make part of the 2,200-acre parcel a wildlife preserve.

Greene's widow, Catherine, would go on to remarry and build another mostly vanished plantation, the famed Dungeness on Cumberland Island.

---

The Southern wing, fervently desiring secession, deliberately chose its own candidate, John Breckinridge, in order to split the Democratic vote and throw the election to Republican Abraham Lincoln, an outspoken opponent of the expansion of slavery. During that so-called **Secession Winter** before Lincoln took office, seven states seceded from the union, first among them the Palmetto State, followed by Mississippi, Florida, Alabama, Georgia, Louisiana, and Texas.

## CIVIL WAR

Five days after South Carolina's secession on December 21, 1860, U.S. Army major Robert Anderson moved his garrison from Fort Moultrie on Sullivan's Island to nearby Fort Sumter in Charleston Harbor. Over the next few months and into the spring, Anderson would ignore many calls to surrender, and Confederate forces would prevent any Union resupply or reinforcement. The stalemate was broken and the Confederates finally got their *casus belli* when a Union supply ship successfully ran the blockade and docked at Fort Sumter. Shortly before dawn on April 12, 1861, Confederate batteries around Charleston—ironically none of which were at the famous Battery itself—opened fire on Fort Sumter for 34 straight hours, until Anderson surrendered on April 13.

In a classic example of why you should always be careful what you wish for, the secessionists had been too clever by half in pushing for Lincoln. Far from prodding the North to sue for peace, the fall of Fort Sumter instead caused the remaining states in the Union to rally around the previously unpopular tall man from Illinois. Lincoln's skillful management of the Fort Sumter standoff meant that from then on, the South would bear history's blame for initiating the conflict that would claim over half a million American lives.

After Fort Sumter, four more Southern states—Virginia, Arkansas, North Carolina, and Tennessee—seceded to join the Confederacy. The Old Dominion was the real prize for the secessionists, as Virginia had the South's only ironworks and by far the largest manufacturing base.

In November 1861, a massive Union invasion armada landed in Port Royal Sound in South Carolina, effectively taking the entire Lowcountry out of the war. Hilton Head was a Union encampment, and Beaufort became a major hospital center for the U.S. Army. The coast of Georgia was also blockaded, with Union forces using new rifled cannons in 1862 to quickly reduce Fort Pulaski at the mouth of the Savannah River. Charleston, however, did host two battles in the conflict. The **Battle of Secessionville** came in June 1862, when a Union force attempting to take Charleston was repulsed on James Island with heavy casualties.

The next battle, an unsuccessful Union landing on Morris Island in July 1863, was immortalized by the movie *Glory*. The 54th Massachusetts Regiment, an African American unit with white commanders, performed so gallantly in its failed assault on the Confederate **Battery Wagner** that it inspired the North and was cited by abolitionists as further proof that African Americans should be given freedom and full citizenship rights. Another invasion attempt on Charleston would not come, but the city was besieged and bombarded for nearly two more years (devastation made even worse by a massive fire, unrelated to the shelling, that destroyed much of the city in 1861).

Otherwise, the coast grew quiet. From Charleston to Brunswick, white Southerners evacuated the coastal cities and plantations for the hinterland, leaving behind only enslaved people to fend for themselves. In many coastal areas, African Americans and Union garrison troops settled into an awkward but peaceful coexistence. Many islands under Union control, such as Cockspur Island, where Fort Pulaski sat, became endpoints in the Underground Railroad.

In Savannah, General William Sherman concluded his **March to the Sea** in Savannah in 1864, famously giving the city to Lincoln as a Christmas present. While staunch Confederates, city fathers were wise enough to know what would happen to their accumulated wealth and fine homes should they be foolhardy enough to resist Sherman's army of war-hardened veterans.

The only military uncertainty left was in how badly Charleston, the "cradle of secession," would suffer for its sins. Historians and local wags have long debated why Sherman spared Charleston, the hated epicenter of the Civil War. Did he fall in love with the city

## Civil War Historic Sites

Fort Pulaski National Monument

Throughout the region there are plenty of military history sights that highlight the Civil War era.

- In Charleston, take the ferry out to **Fort Sumter,** where the Civil War began. There is also **Fort Moultrie,** which hosted a young Edgar Allan Poe in the years prior to the war.
- See the raised **CSS *Hunley*** at the decommissioned Navy Yard (only open Fri.-Sat.).
- Visit historic **Drayton Hall,** the country's oldest standing plantation home, saved from the torch only because Union troops thought it might have been used to quarantine smallpox victims.
- Beaufort served as a medical center for Union occupation troops, who even used **St. Helena's Episcopal Church** as a hospital.
- In Savannah, stop at the **Green-Meldrim House** where General Sherman made his headquarters.
- Visit **Fort Pulaski,** which a young Lieutenant Robert E. Lee helped build. It was later defeated by the first use of rifled artillery in warfare.
- In Richmond Hill, stop by **Fort McAllister,** overrun by Union troops in 1864.

during his brief posting there as a young lieutenant? Did he literally fall in love there, with one of the city's legendarily beautiful and delicate local belles? We may never know for sure, but it's likely that the Lowcountry's marshy, mucky terrain simply made it too difficult to move large numbers of men and supplies. So Sherman turned his army inland toward the state capital, Columbia, which would not be so lucky.

For the African American population of Charleston and Savannah, however, it was not a time of sadness but the great Day of Jubilee. Soon after the Confederate surrender, black Charlestonians held one of the largest parades the city has ever seen, with one of the floats being a coffin bearing the sign "Slavery is dead."

As for the place where it all began, a plucky Confederate garrison remained underground

## In the Footsteps of Bartram

The West has its stirring tale of Lewis and Clark, but the Southeast has its own fascinating—if somewhat less dramatic—tale of discovery, in the odyssey of William Bartram. In March 1773, the 33-year-old Bartram—son of royal botanist John Bartram and definitely a chip off the old block—arrived in Savannah to begin what would become a four-year journey through eight colonies. As Lewis and Clark would do in the following century, Bartram not only exhaustively documented his encounters with nature and with Native Americans, he also made discoveries whose impact has stayed with us to this day.

Young "Willie," born near Philadelphia in 1739, had a talent for drawing and for plants. A failure at business, Bartram was happy to settle on a traveling lifestyle that mixed both his loves. After accompanying his father on several early trips, Bartram set out on his own at the request of an old friend of his father's in England, Dr. John Fothergill, who paid Bartram 50 pounds per year plus expenses to send back specimens and drawings.

Though Bartram's quest would eventually move farther inland and encompass much of the modern American South, most of its first year was spent in coastal Georgia. After arriving in Savannah he moved southward, roughly paralleling modern U.S. 17, to the now-dead town of Sunbury, through Midway, and on to Darien, where he stayed at the plantation of Lachlan McIntosh on the great Altamaha River, which inspired Bartram to pen some of his most beautiful writing. Bartram also journeyed to Sapelo Island, Brunswick, St. Marys, and even into the great Okefenokee Swamp. Using Savannah and Charleston as bases, Bartram mostly traveled alone, either by horse, by boat, or on foot. Word of his trip preceded him, and he was usually greeted warmly by local traders and indigenous chiefs (except for one encounter with a hostile Native American near the St. Marys River). In many places, he was the first European seen since De Soto and the Spanish. His epic journey ended in late 1776, when Bartram gazed on his beloved Altamaha for the last time. Heading north and crossing the Savannah River south of Ebenezer, he proceeded to Charleston and from there to his hometown of Philadelphia—where he would remain for the rest of his days.

At its publication, his 1791 chronicle, *Travels through North and South Carolina, Georgia, East and West Florida,* was hailed as "the most astounding verbal artifact of the early republic." In that unassuming yet timeless work, Bartram cemented his reputation as the country's first native-born naturalist and practically invented the modern travelogue. Thanks to the establishment of the William Bartram Trail in 1976, you can walk in his footsteps—or close to them, anyway, since historians are not sure of his route. The trail uses a rather liberal interpretation, including memorials, trails, and gardens, but many specific "heritage sites" in coastal Georgia have their own markers, as follows:

- River and Barnard Streets in Savannah to mark the beginning of Bartram's trek
- LeConte-Woodmanston Plantation in Liberty County (Barrington Ferry Rd. south of Sandy Run Rd. near Riceboro)
- 1.5 miles south of the South Newport River off U.S. 17
- St. Simon's Island on Frederica Road near the Fort Frederica entrance
- Off Highway 275 at Old Ebenezer Cemetery in Effingham County

Among the indigenous species Bartram was the first to record are the Fraser magnolia, gopher tortoise, Florida sandhill crane, flame azalea, and oakleaf hydrangea.

at Fort Sumter throughout the war, as the walls above them were literally pounded into dust by the long Union siege. The garrison quietly left the fort under cover of night on February 17, 1865. Major Robert Anderson, who surrendered the fort at war's beginning, returned to Sumter in April 1865 to raise the same flag he'd lowered exactly four years earlier. Three thousand African Americans attended the ceremonies. Later that same night, Abraham Lincoln was assassinated in Washington DC.

## RECONSTRUCTION

A case could be made that slavery need not have led the United States into Civil War. The U.S. government had banned the importation of enslaved people long before, in 1808. The great powers of Europe would soon ban slavery altogether (Spain in 1811, France in 1826, and Britain in 1833). Visiting foreign dignitaries in the mid-1800s were often shocked to find the practice in full swing in the American South. Even Brazil, the world center of slavery, where 4 out of every 10 enslaved people taken from Africa were brought (less than 5 percent came to the United States), would ban slavery in 1888, suggesting that slavery in the United States would have died a natural death. Still, the die was cast, the war was fought, and everyone had to deal with the aftermath.

For a brief time, Sherman's benevolent dictatorship on the coast held promise for an orderly postwar future. In 1865 he issued his sweeping "40 acres and a mule" order seeking dramatic economic restitution for coastal Georgia's free blacks. Politics reared its ugly head in the wake of Lincoln's assassination, however, and the order was rescinded, ushering in the chaotic Reconstruction era, echoes of which linger to this day.

Even as the trade in cotton and naval stores resumed to even greater heights than before, urban life and racial tension became more and more problematic. Urban populations swelled as freed blacks from all over the depressed countryside rushed into the cities. As one of them, his name lost to history, famously said: "Freedom was freer in Charleston."

## RECONCILIATION

The opening of the exclusive Jekyll Island Club in 1886 marked the coming of the effects of the Industrial Revolution to the Deep South and the rejuvenation of regional economies. In Savannah, the Telfair Academy of Arts and Sciences, the South's first art museum, opened that same year. The cotton trade built back up to antebellum levels, and the South was on the long road to recovery.

The Spanish-American War of 1898 was a major turning point for the South, the first time since the Civil War that Americans were joined in patriotic unity. The southeastern coast felt this in particular, as it was a staging area for the invasion of Cuba. President William McKinley addressed the troops bivouacked in Savannah's Daffin Park, and Charlestonians cheered the exploits of their namesake heavy cruiser the USS *Charleston,* which played a key role in forcing the Spanish surrender of Guam.

Charleston would elect its first Irish American mayor, John Grace, in 1911, who would serve until 1923 (with a break 1915-1919). Although it wouldn't open until 1929, the first Cooper River Bridge joining Charleston with Mount Pleasant was the child of the Grace administration, credited today for modernizing the Holy City's infrastructure.

The arrival of the tiny but devastating boll weevil all but wiped out the cotton trade on the coast after the turn of the century, forcing the economy to diversify. Naval stores and lumbering were the order of the day at the advent of World War I, the combined patriotic effort for which did wonders in repairing the wounds of the Civil War, still vivid in many local memories. A major legacy of World War I that still greatly influences life in the Lowcountry is the Marine Corps Recruit Depot Parris Island, which began life as a small Marine camp in 1919.

## RENAISSANCE AND DEPRESSION

In the Roaring '20s, that boom period following World War I, both Charleston and Savannah entered the world stage and made some of their most significant cultural contributions to American life. It was also the era of Prohibition. Savannah became notorious as a major import center for illegal rum from the Bahamas.

As elsewhere in the country, Prohibition

ironically brought out a new appreciation for the arts and just plain having fun. The "Charleston" dance, originated on the streets of the Holy City and popularized in New York, would sweep the world. The Jenkins Orphanage Band, credited with the dance, traveled the world, even playing at President William Howard Taft's inauguration.

In the visual arts, the "Charleston Renaissance" took off, specifically intended to introduce the Holy City to a wider audience. Key work included the Asian-influenced art of self-taught painter Alice Ravenel Huger Smith and the etchings of Elizabeth O'Neill Verner. Edward Hopper was a visitor to Charleston during that time and produced several noted watercolors. The Gibbes Art Gallery, now the Gibbes Museum of Art, opened in 1905. Recognizing the cultural importance of the city and its history, in 1920 socialite Susan Pringle Frost and other concerned Charlestonians formed the Preservation Society of Charleston, the oldest community-based historic preservation organization in the country.

In 1924, lauded Charleston author DuBose Heyward wrote the locally set novel *Porgy.* With Heyward's cooperation, the book would soon be turned into the first American opera, *Porgy and Bess,* by George Gershwin, who labored over the composition in a cottage on Folly Beach. Ironically, *Porgy and Bess,* which premiered with an African American cast in New York in 1935, wouldn't be performed in its actual setting until 1970 because of segregation laws.

In Savannah, the Roaring '20s coincided with the rise of Johnny Mercer, who began his theater career locally in the Town Theater Group. In 1925, Flannery O'Connor was born in Savannah, and the quirky, Gothic nature of the city would mark her later writing indelibly.

The Depression hit the South hard, but since wages and industry were already behind the national average, the economic damage wasn't as bad as elsewhere in the country. As elsewhere in the South, the public works programs of President Franklin D. Roosevelt's New Deal helped not only to keep locals employed but contributed greatly to the cultural and archaeological record of the region. The Civilian Conservation Corps built much of the modern state park system in the area.

## WORLD WAR II AND THE POSTWAR BOOM

With the attack on Pearl Harbor and the coming of World War II, life on the Georgia and South Carolina coast would never be the same. Military funding and facilities swarmed into the area, and populations and long-depressed living standards rose as a result. In many outlying Sea Islands of Georgia and South Carolina, electricity came for the first time.

The Charleston Navy Yard became the city's largest employer, and the city's population soared as workers swarmed in. The "Mighty Eighth" Air Force was founded and based in Savannah, and Camp Stewart, later Fort Stewart, was built in nearby Hinesville. In shipyards in Savannah and Brunswick, hundreds of Liberty ships were built to transport cargo to the citizens and allied armies of Europe.

The postwar U.S. infatuation with the automobile—and its troublesome child, the suburb—brought exponential growth to the great cities of the coast. The first bridge to Hilton Head Island was built in 1956, leading to the first of many resort developments, Sea Pines, in 1961. With rising coastal populations came pressure to demolish more and more fine old buildings to put parking lots and high-rises in their place. A backlash grew among the cities' elites, aghast at the destruction of so much history.

The immediate postwar era brought about the formation of both the Historic Charleston Foundation and the Historic Savannah Foundation, which began the financially and politically difficult work of protecting historic districts from the wrecking ball. They weren't always successful, but the work of these organizations—mostly older women from the upper crust—laid the foundation for the successful coastal tourist industry to come, as well as preserved important American history for the ages.

## CIVIL RIGHTS

The ugly racial violence that plagued much of the country during the civil rights era rarely visited the Georgia and South Carolina coast. Whether due to the laid-back ambience or the fact that African Americans were simply too numerous there to be denied, cities like Charleston and Savannah experienced little real unrest during that time.

Contrary to popular opinion, the civil rights era wasn't just a blip in the 1960s. The gains of that decade were the fruits of efforts begun decades earlier. Many of the exertions involved efforts to expand black suffrage. Though African Americans had secured the nominal right to vote years before, primary contests were not under the jurisdiction of federal law. As a result, Democratic Party primary elections—the de facto general elections because of that party's total dominance in the South at the time—were effectively closed to African American voters.

Savannah was at the forefront of expanding black suffrage, and Ralph Mark Gilbert, pastor of the historic First African Baptist Church, launched one of the first black voter registration drives in the South. In Charleston, the Democratic primary was opened to African Americans for the first time in 1947. In 1955, a successful black realtor, J. Arthur Brown, became head of the Charleston chapter of the NAACP and membership soared, bringing an increase in activism. In 1960, the Charleston Municipal Golf Course voluntarily integrated to avoid a court battle.

Martin Luther King Jr. visited South Carolina in the late 1960s, speaking in Charleston in 1967 and helping reestablish the Penn Center on St. Helena Island as not only a cultural center but a center of political activism as well. The hundred-day strike of hospital workers at the Medical University of South Carolina in 1969—right after King's assassination—got national attention and was the culmination of Charleston's struggle for civil rights. By the end of the 1960s, the city councils of Charleston and Savannah had elected their first black aldermen, and the next phase in local history began.

## A COAST REBORN

The decade of the 1970s brought the seeds of the future success of the South Carolina and Georgia coasts. In Charleston, the historic tenure of Mayor Joe Riley began, and in Savannah came the election of a similarly influential and long-serving mayor, John P. Rousakis. The Irish American and the Greek American would break precedents and forge key alliances in both municipalities, reviving local economies.

In the years 1970-1976, tourism in Charleston would increase by 60 percent. The resort industry, already established on Hilton Head, would hit Kiawah Island, Seabrook Island, and Isle of Palms with a vengeance. In Savannah, Rousakis renovated the then-seedy riverfront district, making it the centerpiece of the city's burgeoning tourist trade. The Savannah College of Art and Design (SCAD) opened in 1979 and began the process of renovating dozens of the city's historic buildings, a process that continues today.

The coast's combination of beautiful scenery and cheap labor proved irresistible to the movie and TV industry, which would begin filming many series and films in the area in the 1970s and continuing to this day. Beaufort, South Carolina, in particular would emerge from its stately slumber as the star of several popular films, including *The Great Santini* and *The Big Chill.*

Charleston received its first major challenge since the Civil War in 1989 when Hurricane Hugo—originally headed directly for Savannah—changed course at the last minute and slammed into the South Carolina coast just north of Charleston. The Holy City, including many of its most historic locations, was massively damaged, with hardly a tree left standing. In a testament to the toughness just beneath Charleston's genteel veneer, the city not only rebounded but came back stronger. In more recent years, Hurricanes Matthew and Irma caused extensive damage, though not catastrophic.

The economic boom of the 1990s was particularly good to Charleston and Savannah, whose ports saw a huge dividend from increasing globalization. Also in the 1990s came the *Midnight in the Garden of Good and Evil* phenomenon, which would put Savannah—already on the upswing—on the tourist map for good. Although not a Savannah native, the iconic Paula Deen brought a new national focus on the city through her long presence on the Food Network and through her local restaurant, The Lady and Sons, which continues to pack in visitors despite recent controversies.

Today Savannah's tourism business is healthier than ever, and Charleston is perennially ranked as one of the top U.S. cities for visitors as well as for residents. Attracted by the coastal region, artists, writers, and entrepreneurs continue to flock, increasing the economic and social diversity of the area and taking it to new heights of livability.

With that has come the usual struggles with growth vs. quality of life, as both Charleston and Savannah are coping with an influx of Airbnb-style short-term vacation rentals in their historic districts.



# Government and Economy

## GOVERNMENT

Charleston is run by the **strong mayor** form of municipal government, which means that the elected mayor has extensive powers, including the ability to veto a measure approved by the city council. In practice this means that a mayor, for better or worse, is able to stamp the city with his or her own vision. Former Mayor Joe Riley's influence can be seen in everything from the chichi Charleston Place to new low-income housing developments.

Savannah, however, is run by the **council-manager** form of municipal government, in which the mayor is but one vote of many on the city council. Day-to-day operations are in the hands of an appointed city manager who answers to the council. In practice this means a generally more professional and objective approach to the nuts-and-bolts of government but an often-frustrating lack of accountability at the top.

Because of both states' strong rural roots, county governments are also very important, but becoming less so as urbanization continues and more areas consider city and county consolidation. In particular, county governments in Georgia hold great sway, in large part because there are so many of them. Visitors to the Peach State are often amazed by how small the counties are, and how many there are—159 in total. In practice this means that county governments hold a greater proportion of political power than in states where the counties are much larger in land area, like South Carolina.

### Political Parties

For many decades, the South was dominated by the Democratic Party. Originally the party of slavery, segregation, and Jim Crow, the Democratic Party began attracting Southern African American voters in the 1930s with the election of Franklin D. Roosevelt. The allegiance of black voters was further cemented in the Truman, Kennedy, and Johnson administrations. The region would remain solidly Democratic until a backlash against the civil rights movement of the 1960s drove many white Southerners, ironically enough, into the party of Lincoln. This added racial element, so confounding to Americans from other parts of the country, remains just as potent today. The default mode in the South is that white voters are massively Republican, and black voters massively Democratic. Since South Carolina is 69 percent white and Georgia 67 percent white, doing the math translates to an overwhelming Republican dominance.

However, the coastal areas covered in this guide, with their large, predominantly Democratic African American populations, function somewhat separately from this realignment. But don't make the mistake of assuming that local African Americans are particularly liberal because of their voting habits. Deeply religious and traditional in background and upbringing, African Americans in the area covered by this guide are among the most socially conservative people in the region, even if their choice of political party does not always reflect that.

### Intrastate Relations

A few years back a sociologist proposed, partially tongue-in-cheek, that since the coastal regions of the Southeast have more in common with each other than with residents of other parts of their own states, the borders should be realigned to reflect this demographic, cultural, and historic affiliation. Anyone who has spent time in the inland areas of South Carolina and Georgia will immediately recognize the basic truth in this proposal, however unlikely it is to actually happen.

The simple, easily observable fact is that Charleston, Beaufort, Savannah, and Brunswick have far more in common with each other than Charleston has with, say, Spartanburg, South Carolina, or Savannah has with Macon, Georgia. I don't know what you would name the state that resulted from the union of the coastal cities and towns, but I do know that the food would be awesome.

Georgia's largest city and capital is Atlanta, which is even farther removed—both physically and metaphysically—from Savannah than Columbia is from Charleston. Indeed, Savannah and Chatham County are considered so different from the rest of Georgia that old-timers still call Savannah the capital of the "State of Chatham."

## ECONOMY

The coastal areas of South Carolina and Georgia are currently experiencing profound changes in economy and business. The rice crop moved offshore in the late 1800s, and the center of the cotton trade moved to the Gulf States in the early 1900s. That left timber as the main cash crop all up and down the coast, specifically huge pine tree farms to

Savannah's shipping industry is vital to the local economy.

feed the pulp and paper business. For most of the 20th century, the largest employers along the coast were massive, sulfur-smelling paper mills, which had as big an effect on the local environment as on its economy. But even that is changing as Asian competition is driving paper companies to sell off their tracts for real estate development—not necessarily a more welcome scenario.

Since World War II, the U.S. Department of Defense has been a major employer and economic driver in the entire South, and the Georgia and South Carolina coast is no exception. Of the services, the U.S. Navy (which includes the Marines) is the dominant military presence in coastal South Carolina, employing over 16,000 military and civilian workers. Coastal Georgia tends to be more Army-dominated. Despite the closing of the Charleston Naval Yard in the mid-1990s, the grounds now host the East Coast headquarters of the Space and Naval Warfare Systems Center (SPAWAR), which provides high-tech engineering solutions for the Navy. Charleston also retains a large military presence in the Charleston Air Force Base near North Charleston, which hosts two airlift wings and employs about 6,000. Farther down the coast, Beaufort is home to the Naval Hospital Beaufort and the Marine Corps Air Station Beaufort and its six squadrons of FA-18 Hornets. On nearby Parris Island is the legendary Marine Corps Recruit Depot Parris Island, which puts all new Marine recruits from east of the Mississippi River through rigorous basic training.

In the middle of south-side Savannah sits Hunter Army Airfield, host to a battalion of U.S. Army Rangers. In nearby and largely rural Liberty County, Georgia, is the sprawling Fort Stewart, home base of the 3rd Infantry Division. Near the Florida border in St. Marys is the Naval Submarine Base Kings Bay, home port of eight Trident subs.

Of course, tourism is also an important factor in the local economies of the area. The Holy City in particular has a well-honed tourist infrastructure, bringing at least $5 billion a year into the local economy. Savannah's tourism industry, though growing very rapidly, is still behind Charleston's at about $2.5 billion a year.

But, despite all other trends, manufacturing and industry remain the largest sectors of the economy in both Charleston and Savannah—due in no small part to the fact that both South Carolina and Georgia are "right to work" states with exceedingly low unionization rates. Increasingly, however, higher education is more and more important to local economies and will only continue to be so.

# People and Culture

Contrary to how the region is portrayed in the media, the coast from Charleston down to the Georgia-Florida border is hardly exclusive to natives with thick, flowery accents who still obsess over the Civil War and eat grits three meals a day. As you will quickly discover, the entire coastal area is heavily populated with transplants from other parts of the country, and in some areas you can actually go quite a long time without hearing even one of those Scarlett O'Hara accents. Some of this is due to the region's increasing attractiveness to professionals and artists, drawn by the temperate climate, natural beauty, and business-friendly environment. Part of it is due to its increasing attractiveness to retirees, most of them from the frigid Northeast. Indeed, in some places, chief among them Hilton Head, the most common accent is a New York or New Jersey one, and a Southern accent is rare.

In any case, don't make the common mistake of assuming you're coming to a place where footwear is optional and electricity is a recent development (though it's true that many of the islands didn't get electricity until the 1950s and 1960s). Because so much new

## Voodoo and Hoodoo

The spiritual system we know as voodoo—the word is a corruption of various West African spellings—came to the western hemisphere with the importation of enslaved people. Contrary to popular belief, voodoo isn't a mere collection of primitive superstitions but is a clearly defined religion in its own right and is still the dominant religion of millions of West Africans.

Like many ancient belief systems, voodoo is based on the veneration of ancestors and the possibility of continued communication with them, and it's perhaps this characteristic that is responsible for so much misunderstanding. For example, up until fairly recently the African American Gullah and Geechee populations of the South Carolina and Georgia Sea Islands still had a common belief that the older enslaved people who were born in Africa could actually fly in spirit form back to the continent of their birth and back again.

While voodoo has always been unfairly sensationalized—the most notable recent example being the "voodoo priestess" Minerva in *Midnight in the Garden of Good and Evil*—it's not necessarily as malevolent in actual practice as in the overactive imaginations of writers and directors. For example, the stereotypical practice of sticking pins in dolls to bring pain to a living person actually has its roots in European and Native American folklore. But sensationalism sells, so you'll sometimes find such items being hawked to the gullible as "voodoo dolls."

Much of what the layperson thinks is voodoo is actually hoodoo, a body of folklore—not a religion—indigenous to the American South. Hoodoo combines elements of voodoo (communicating with the dead) and fundamentalist Christianity (extensive scriptural references). In the United States, most African American voodoo tradition was long ago subsumed within Protestant Christianity, but the Gullah populations of the Sea Islands of South Carolina and Georgia still keep alive the old ways. In the Gullah and Geechee areas of the Georgia and Carolina Sea Islands, the word *conjure* is generally the preferred terminology for this hybrid belief system, which has good sides and bad sides and borrows liberally from African lore and Christian folkways.

The old Southern practice of painting shutters and doors blue to ward off evil comes from hoodoo, where the belief in ghosts, or "haints," is largely a byproduct of poorly understood Christianity (Mediterranean countries also use blue to keep evil at bay, and the word *haint* is of Scots-Irish origin). If you keep your eyes attuned, you can still see this particular shade of "haint blue" on rural and vernacular structures throughout the Lowcountry. (Were you to enter one of these homes, you would almost certainly find a horseshoe tacked over the front door as well.)

Another element of hoodoo that you can still encounter today is the role of the "root doctor," an expert at folk remedies who blends various indigenous herbs and plants in order to produce a desired effect or result. In *Midnight in the Garden of Good and Evil,* this role belongs to the fabled Dr. Buzzard, who teaches Minerva everything she knows about "conjure work." However, a root doctor is not to be confused with a "gifted reader," a fortune-teller born with the talent to tell the future. From the no-doubt embellished account in John Berendt's *Midnight,* scholars would put the late Minerva squarely into the category of root doctor or "conjurer" rather than the undeniably more compelling "voodoo priestess."

construction has gone on in the South in the last quarter-century or so, you might find some aspects of the infrastructure—specifically the roads and the electrical utilities—actually superior to where you came from.

## POPULATION

For demographic purposes, Charleston is part of the Charleston-North Charleston Metropolitan Statistical Area (MSA), which includes Berkeley, Dorchester, and Charleston Counties. In the 2010 census, it comprised about 664,000 people. The city of Charleston proper has a population of about 120,000. The Hilton Head-Beaufort MSA includes Beaufort and Jasper Counties and comprised about 180,000 people in the 2010 census. The town of Hilton Head had about 37,000 residents in 2010, and Beaufort had about 13,000. The Savannah MSA, which includes Chatham,

## Sephardic Jews in the South

Visitors are sometimes surprised to discover that two of the oldest cities in the Anglo-Saxon Protestant South have rich and early histories of an active Jewish presence—specifically, **Sephardic Jews** (those with a Spanish or Portuguese background). Contrary to modern trends, Jews and Muslims on the Iberian Peninsula got along quite well while the Islamic Moors of North Africa dominated the area. But after Ferdinand and Isabella's completion of the Reconquista in that pivotal year of 1492—also the date of Columbus's famous voyage—the Jews of Spain went from being respected citizens to persecuted pariahs nearly overnight. Five years later, Portugal followed suit, expelling all Jews on pain of death unless they became "New Christians," or *conversos*. A sizeable proportion of *conversos*, however, were actually so-called crypto-Jews, who publicly practiced Roman Catholicism while secretly remaining devout Jews. Many synagogues of Sephardic origin today have their floors covered in sand to remember that dark time when Jewish congregations practiced their faith in basements covered with sand to muffle the sounds of their feet.

The diaspora of the Sephardic Jews, ironically, contributed greatly to the health of the global Jewish community, as skilled tradesmen, doctors, and men of letters spread out to Spanish, Portuguese, English, and Dutch colonies where the Inquisition had little sway. It was primarily from the ranks of this Sephardic diaspora that the Jewish settlers of the Lowcountry and Georgia coast came.

The first Jewish presence in Charleston was recorded in 1695, with Jews voting in local elections as early as 1702. Stimulated by the busy port, the Charleston Jewish community quickly grew with the addition of **Ashkenazi,** or Eastern European, Jews in the late 1700s. By 1820, Charleston boasted the biggest Jewish population in the United States. Savannah wasn't the first colonial town to host Jewish settlers, but the group of 42 Sephardic Jews that arrived five months after Oglethorpe's landing in 1733 was by far the largest contingent to travel to North America up to that time. All but eight of this core group were Spanish and Portuguese Jews who immigrated

Bryan, and Effingham Counties, numbered about 347,000 people in the 2010 census. The city of Savannah itself has a population of about 136,000. The Brunswick MSA includes Brantley, Glynn, and McIntosh Counties and has about 100,000 people.

### Racial Makeup

Its legacy as the center of the U.S. slave trade and plantation culture means that the Charleston-Savannah region has a large African American population. The Charleston MSA is about 31 percent African American, and the Savannah MSA about 35 percent. In the cities proper, the black population is higher, about 35 percent in Charleston's case and nearly 60 percent in Savannah's.

The Hispanic population, as elsewhere in the United States, is growing rapidly, but statistics can be misleading. Though Hispanic numbers are growing at a triple-digit clip in the region, they still remain less than 3 percent of each state's population. Bilingual signage is becoming more common but is still quite rare.

## RELIGION

The area from Charleston to Savannah is unusual in the Deep South for its wide variety of religious faiths. While South Carolina and Georgia remain overwhelmingly Protestant—at least three-quarters of all Christians in both states are members of some Protestant denomination, chief among them Southern Baptist and Methodist—Charleston and Savannah's cosmopolitan, polyglot histories have made them real melting pots of faith.

Both cities were originally dominated by the Episcopal Church (known as the Anglican Church in other countries), but from early on they were also havens for those of other faiths. Various types of Protestant offshoots to London after spending years as crypto-Jews in their home countries. Accepted without question by Oglethorpe, the Jews of Savannah quickly rose in power and influence. In fact, the first nonindigenous male child born in Georgia was a Jewish boy, Philip "Uri" Minis.

In one of the great tales of the American melting pot, the assimilation of the Jews into Southern society was so complete that the Secretary of State of the Confederate States of America, Judah Benjamin, was a practicing Jew of Sephardic origin. This assimilation also had a flip side, however, in that the Sephardic Jews were generally just as enthusiastic about owning enslaved people as any other white citizens of the area. In 1830 about 83 percent of Jewish households in Charleston had slaves, compared to an almost-identical percentage of 87 percent of white Christian Charlestonians.

Temple Mickve Israel in Savannah

The center of Jewish culture in Charleston is **Kahal Kadosh Beth Elohim Reform Temple** (90 Hasell St., 843/723-1090, www.kkbe.org, service Sat. 11am, tours Mon.-Fri. 10am-noon, Sun. 10am-4pm), birthplace of Reform Judaism in the United States and the oldest continuously active synagogue in the nation. In Savannah, the key Judaic attraction is **Temple Mickve Israel** (20 E. Gordon St., 912/233-1547, www.mickveisrael.org, 30-minute tours Mon.-Fri. 10am-12:30pm and 2pm-3:30pm, $6 donation), the only Gothic synagogue in the country and the third-oldest Jewish congregation in North America.

soon arrived, including the French Huguenots and Congregationalists in Charleston and the Scottish Presbyterians and German Salzburger Lutherans in the Savannah area. The seeds of Methodism and the "Great Awakening" were planted along the coast from Savannah up to Charleston.

Owing to vestigial prejudice from the European realpolitik of the founding era, the Roman Catholic presence on the coast was late in arriving, but once it came it was there to stay. Savannah, in particular, has quite a large Roman Catholic population by Southern standards, mostly due to the influx of Irish in the mid-1800s.

But most unusually of all for the Deep South, Charleston and Savannah not only have large Jewish populations but ones that have been key participants in the cities from the very first days of settlement. Sephardic Jews of primarily Portuguese descent were among the first settlers of both Charleston and Savannah, and they kept up an energetic trade between the two cities for centuries afterward, continuing to the present day.

## MANNERS

The prevalence and importance of good manners is the main thing to keep in mind about the South. While it's tempting for folks from more outwardly assertive parts of the world to take this as a sign of weakness, that would be a major mistake. Southerners use manners, courtesy, and chivalry as a system of social interaction with one goal above all: to maintain the established order during times of stress. A relic from a time of extreme class stratification, etiquette and chivalry are ways to make sure that the elites are never threatened—and, on the other hand, that even those on the lowest rungs of society are afforded at least a basic amount of dignity. But as a practical matter, it's also true that Southerners of all classes, races, and backgrounds rely on the observation of manners as a way to sum up people quickly. To any Southerner, regardless of class or race, your use or neglect of basic manners and proper respect indicates how seriously they should take you—not in a socioeconomic sense, but in the big picture overall.

The typical Southern sense of humor—equal parts irony, self-deprecation, and good-natured teasing—is part of the code. Southerners are loath to criticize another individual directly, so often they'll instead take the opportunity to make an ironic joke. Self-deprecating humor is also much more common in the South than in other areas of the country. Because of this, conversely you're also expected to be able to take a joke yourself without being too sensitive.

Another key element in Southern manners is the discussion of money—or rather, the nondiscussion. Unlike some parts of the United States, in the South it's considered the height of rudeness to ask someone what their salary is or how much they paid for their house. Not that the subject is entirely taboo—far from it; you just have to know the code. For example, rather than brag about how much or how little they paid for their home, a Southern head of household will instead take you on a guided tour of the grounds. Along the way they'll make sure to detail: (a) all the work that was done; (b) how grueling and unexpected it all was; and (c) how hard it was to get the contractors to show up.

Depending on the circumstances, in the first segment, (a) you were just told either that the head of the house is made of money and has a lot more of it to spend on renovating than you do, or that they are a brilliant negotiator who got the house for a song. In part (b) you were told that you are not messing around with a lazy deadbeat here, but with someone who knows how to take care of themselves and can handle adversity with aplomb. And with part (c) you were told that the head of the house knows the best contractors in town and can pay enough for them to actually show up, and if you play your cards right, they might pass on their phone numbers to you with a personal recommendation. See? Breaking the code is easy once you get the hang of it.

## Etiquette

As we've seen, it's rude here to inquire about personal finances, along with the usual no-go areas of religion and politics. Here are some other specific etiquette tips:

- **Basics:** Be liberal with "please" and "thank you," or conversely, "no thank you" if you want to decline a request or offering.
- **Eye contact:** With the exception of very elderly African Americans, eye contact is not only accepted in the South, it's encouraged. In fact, to avoid eye contact in the South means you're likely a shady character.
- **Handshake:** Men should always shake hands with a *very* firm, confident grip and appropriate eye contact. It's OK for women to offer a handshake in professional circles, but otherwise not required.
- **Chivalry:** When men open doors for women here—and they will—it is not thought of as a patronizing gesture but as a sign of respect. Accept graciously and walk through the door.
- **The elderly:** Senior citizens—or really anyone obviously older than you—should be called "sir" or "ma'am." Again, this is not a patronizing gesture in the South but is considered a sign of respect. Also, in any situation where you're dealing with someone in the service industry, addressing them as "sir" or "ma'am" regardless of their age will get you far.
- **Bodily contact:** Interestingly, though public displays of affection by romantic couples are generally frowned upon here, Southerners are otherwise pretty touchy-feely once they get to know you. Southerners who are well acquainted often say hello or good-bye with a hug.
- **Driving:** With the exception of the interstate perimeter highways around the larger

## Walter Edgar's Journal

He's originally from Alabama, but you could call University of South Carolina (USC) professor Walter Edgar the modern voice of the Palmetto State. From the rich diversity of barbecue to the inner workings of the poultry business and the charms of beach music, Edgar covers the gamut of South Carolina culture and experience on his popular weekly radio show *Walter Edgar's Journal,* airing on South Carolina public radio stations throughout the state.

Currently director of the USC Institute of Southern Studies, the Vietnam vet and certified barbecue contest judge explains the show like this: "On the *Journal* we look at current events in a broader perspective, trying to provide context that is often missing in the mainstream media." More specifically, Edgar devotes each one-hour show to a single guest, usually a South Carolinian—by birth or by choice—with a unique perspective on some aspect of state culture, business, arts, or folkways. By the time the interview ends, you not only have a much deeper understanding of the topic of the show but of the interviewee as well. And because of Edgar's unique way of tying strands of his own vast knowledge and experience into every interview, you also leave with a deeper understanding of South Carolina itself.

In these days of media saturation, a public radio show might sound like a rather insignificant perch from which to influence an entire state. But remember that South Carolina is a small close-knit place, a state of Main Street towns rather than impersonal metro areas. During any given show, many listeners in Edgar's audience will know his guests on a personal basis. And by the end of the show, the rest of the listeners will feel as if they do.

Listen to "Walter Edgar's Journal" each Friday at noon on South Carolina public radio, with a repeat each Sunday at 4pm. Hear podcasts of previous editions at www.scetv.org.

cities, drivers in the South are generally less aggressive than in other regions. Cutting sharply in front of someone in traffic is taken as a personal offense. If you need to cut in front of someone, poke the nose of your car a little bit in that direction and wait for a car to slow down and wave you in front. Don't forget to wave back as a thank-you. Similarly, using a car horn can also be taken as a personal affront, so use your horn sparingly, if at all. In rural areas, don't be surprised to see the driver of an oncoming car offer a little wave. This is an old custom, sadly dying out. Just give a little wave back; they're trying to be friendly.

## THE GUN CULTURE

One of the most misunderstood aspects of the South is the value the region places on the personal possession of firearms. No doubt, the 2nd Amendment to the U.S. Constitution ("A well-regulated Militia, being necessary to the security of a free State, the right of the people to keep and bear Arms, shall not be infringed") is well known here and fiercely protected, at the governmental and at the grassroots levels.

State laws do tend to be significantly more accommodating of gun owners here than in much of the rest of the country. It is legal to carry a concealed handgun in South Carolina and Georgia with the proper permit, and you need no permit at all to possess a weapon in your house or car for self-defense.

Both states now have so-called (and controversial) "stand your ground" laws, whereby if you're in imminent lethal danger, you do not have to first try to run away before resorting to deadly force to defend yourself.

In 2014, Georgia passed what is widely considered to be the most permissive new gun law in the country, allowing those with the proper license to carry an open or concealed handgun into a bar (though if you do, you're not supposed to drink alcohol).

# Essentials

# Transportation

## AIR

The most centrally located airport for the region covered in this guide is **Savannah/ Hilton Head International Airport** (SAV, 400 Airways Ave., 912/964-0514, www.savannahairport.com), directly off I-95 at exit 104, about 20 minutes from downtown Savannah, 45 minutes from Hilton Head Island, and less than two hours from Charleston. Airlines with routes to SAV include American (www.aa.com), Air Canada (aircanada.com), Allegiant (www.allegiant.com), Delta (www.delta.com), JetBlue (www.jetblue.com), Sun Country (www.suncountry.com), and United (www.ual.com).

A bit less convenient to the rest of the region because of its location well north of town is **Charleston International Airport** (CHS, 5500 International Blvd., 843/767-1100, www.chs-airport.com), served by American (www.aa.com), Alaska (alaskaair.com), Delta (www.delta.com), JetBlue (www.jetblue.com), and Southwest (www.southwest.com).

Many travelers to the region are using **Jacksonville International Airport** (JAX, 2400 Yankee Clipper Dr., 904/741-4902, www.jia.com), about 20 miles north of Jacksonville, Florida. While it's a two-hour drive from Savannah, this airport's proximity to the attractions south of Savannah makes it attractive for some visitors, who can often find a good deal on airfare that makes it worth their while to make the drive.

## CAR

The main interstate highway arteries into the region are the heavily traveled north-south I-95, the east-west I-26 to Charleston from Columbia, South Carolina, and the east-west I-16 to Savannah from Macon, Georgia. A common landmark road through the entire area covered by this guide is U.S. 17, which used to be known as the Coastal Highway and which currently goes by a number of local incarnations as it winds its way down the coast, roughly paralleling I-95. Charleston has a "perimeter" interstate, I-526 (the Mark Clark Expressway), while Savannah has a much smaller version, I-516 (Lynes Parkway).

### Rental Car

You don't have to have a car to enjoy Charleston and Savannah, but to really explore the areas surrounding those cities you'll need your own vehicle. Renting a car is easy and fairly inexpensive, as long as you play by the rules, which are simple. You need either a valid U.S. driver's license from any state or a valid International Driving Permit from your home country, and you must be at least 25 years old.

If you do not either purchase insurance coverage from the rental company or already have insurance coverage through the credit card you rent the car with, you will be 100 percent responsible for any damage caused to the car during your rental period. While purchasing insurance at the time of rental is by no means mandatory, it might be worth the extra expense just to have that peace of mind.

Some rental car locations are in the cities, but the vast majority of outlets are in airports, so plan accordingly. The airport locations have the bonus of generally holding longer hours than their in-town counterparts.

## TRAIN

Passenger rail service in the car-dominated United States is far behind other developed nations, both in quantity and quality.



**Previous:** Charleston's cityscape; a Savannah Belles ferry.

Charleston and Savannah are both served by the New York-Miami *Silver Service* route of the national rail system, **Amtrak** (www.amtrak.com), which is pretty good, if erratic at times—although it certainly pales in comparison with European rail transit. Both cities' Amtrak stations are in light industrial parts of town, nowhere near the major tourist centers. Charleston's station is at 4565 Gaynor Street (843/744-8263), while Savannah's is at 2611 Seaboard Coastline Drive (912/234-2611).

## BOAT

One of the coolest things about the Charleston and Savannah area is the presence of the Intracoastal Waterway, a combined artificial and natural sheltered seaway from Miami to Maine. Many boaters enjoy touring the coast by simply meandering up or down the Intracoastal, putting in at marinas along the way.

# Recreation

## BEACHES

Some of the best beaches in the United States are in the region covered by this guide. While the upscale amenities aren't always there and they aren't very surfer friendly, the area's beaches are outstanding for anyone looking for a relaxing, scenic getaway.

By law, beaches in the United States are fully accessible to the public up to the high-tide mark during daylight hours, even if the beach fronts private property and even if the only means of public access is by boat. While certain seaside resorts have over the years attempted to make the dunes in front of their properties exclusive to guests, this is actually illegal, although it can be hard to enforce. On federally run National Wildlife Refuges, access is limited to daytime hours, sunrise to sunset.

It is a misdemeanor to disturb the **sea oats,** those wispy, waving, wheat-like plants among the dunes. Their root system is vital to keeping the beach intact. Also, never disturb a turtle nesting area, whether it is marked or not.

### South Carolina

The barrier islands of the Palmetto State have seen more private development than their Georgia counterparts. Some Carolina islands, like Kiawah, Fripp, and Seabrook, are not even accessible unless you are a guest at their affiliated resorts, which, of course, means that the only way to visit the beaches there if you're not a guest is by boat, which I really don't advise. Charleston-area beaches include **Folly Beach, Sullivan's Island,** and **Isle of Palms.** Folly Beach has a county recreation area with parking at **Folly Beach County Park.** Isle of Palms has a county recreation area with parking at **Isle of Palms County Park.**

Moving down the coast, some delightful beaches are at **Edisto Island** and **Hunting Island,** which both feature state parks with campgrounds. **Hilton Head Island** has about 12 miles of beautiful family-friendly beaches, and while most of the island is devoted to private golf resorts, the beaches remain accessible to the general public at four convenient points with parking: **Driessen Beach Park, Coligny Beach Park, Alder Lane Beach Access,** and **Burkes Beach Road.**

### Georgia

The main beach in Georgia is outside Savannah at **Tybee Island,** with full accessibility from end to end. The beach on the north end is smaller and quieter, while the south end is wider, windier, and more populated. There are public parking lots, but you can park at metered spots near the beach as well.

Farther south, a very good beach is at **Jekyll Island,** a largely undeveloped barrier island owned by the state. There are three picnic areas with parking: **Clam Creek, South Dunes,** and **St. Andrew.** Nearby **St. Simons Island** does have a beach area, but it is comparatively narrow and small. Adjacent **Sea Island** is accessible only if you're a guest of the Sea Island Club.

The rest of Georgia's barrier islands are only accessible by ferry, charter, or private boat. Many outfitters will take you on a tour to barrier islands such as Wassaw or Sapelo; don't be shy about inquiring. The most gorgeous beach of all is at **Cumberland Island National Seashore.**

### Surfing

By far the most popular surfing area in the region is the **Washout** at Charleston's Folly Beach. The key surf shop on Folly is **McKevlin's.** For Folly surf conditions, go to www.mckevlins.com or www.surfline.com. The only other surfing of note in the area is on the south end of **Tybee Island** near the Pier and Pavilion. The key surf shop on Tybee is **High Tide Surf Shop.** For a surf report, go to www.hightidesurfshop.com.

## ON WATER

### Kayaking and Canoeing

Some key kayaking and canoeing areas in the Charleston area are **Cape Romain National Wildlife Refuge, Shem Creek, Isle of Palms,** and the **Charleston Harbor.** The best outfitter and tour operator in the area is **Coastal Expeditions.** Farther south in the Lowcountry are the Ashepoo, Combahee, and Edisto blackwater rivers, which combine to form the **ACE Basin.** Next is **Port Royal Sound** near Beaufort; a good outfitter and tour operator in this area is **Carolina Heritage Outfitters.** The Hilton Head/Bluffton area has good kayaking opportunities at Hilton Head's **Calibogue Creek** and Bluffton's **May River.** The best outfitter and tour operator here is **Outside Hilton Head.**

The Savannah area has rich kayaking and canoeing at **Tybee Island, Skidaway Island,** and the blackwater **Ebenezer Creek.** The best local outfitter and tour operator in this area is **Savannah Canoe and Kayak.** Farther south, down the Georgia coast, the richest kayaking and canoeing area is in the **Altamaha River** estuary, a hybrid blackwater-alluvial river. Good kayaking can be found in the **St. Simons Island** area. The best outfitter and tour operator in the area is **SouthEast Adventures.** Kayaking to **Cumberland Island** is a special experience; contact **Up the Creek Xpeditions** in St. Marys.

### Fishing and Boating

Because of the large number of islands and wide area of salt marsh, life on the water is largely inseparable from life on the land in the Lowcountry and Georgia coast. Fishing and boating are very common pursuits here, with species of fish including spotted sea trout, channel bass, flounder, grouper, mackerel, sailfish, whiting, shark, amberjack, and tarpon. Farther inshore you'll find largemouth bass, bream, catfish, and crappie, among many more. While entire books can be and are devoted to the area's fishing opportunities, here is an overview.

It's easy to fish on piers, lakes, and streams, but if you're over age 16, you have to get a nonresident fishing license from the state. These are inexpensive and available in hardware stores, marinas, and tackle shops anywhere. In Georgia, a regular license is $9, a one-day license $3.50. A separate license is required for trout fishing. Go to http://georgiawildlife.dnr.state.ga.us for more information or to purchase a license online. In South Carolina, a nonresident seven-day license is $11. Go to www.dnr.sc.gov for more information or to purchase a license online.

The most popular places for casual anglers are the various public piers throughout the area. There are public fishing piers at **Folly Beach, Hunting Island, Tybee Island, St. Simons Island,** and **Jekyll Island.** Two nice little public docks are at the **North Charleston Riverfront Park** on the grounds of the old Charleston Navy Yard, and the

**Bluffton public landing** on the May River. Many anglers cast from abandoned bridges, unless signage dictates otherwise. Fishing charters and marinas are ample throughout the region, for both inshore and offshore trips.

## ON LAND

### Golf and Tennis

The first golf club in the country was formed in Charleston, and that area has more than its share of fine courses. As far as quality is concerned, the consensus pick for best course in South Carolina is definitely the Pete Dye-designed Ocean Course at the **Kiawah Island Golf Resort,** which is open to guests of the club. Coming in second would almost certainly be **Harbour Town** on Sea Pines Plantation in Hilton Head. Not coincidentally, both courses host PGA events.

In Georgia, the Ocean Forest Course at the **Sea Island Club** on Sea Island is a gem—though you must be a guest at the club to play—as is the affiliated Seaside Course. For value, go in the off-season, in the colder months, when prices are lowest. Not all courses close, and most are in great shape because of the reduced traffic.

The premier tennis facility in the Charleston area is the new **Family Circle Cup Tennis Center** on Daniel Island, home of the eponymous women's event and some great public courts. Other key tennis facilities are at the **King and Prince** on St. Simons and **Jekyll Island Tennis Center.**

### Hiking and Biking

Due to the flat nature of the Lowcountry and Georgia coast, hiking and biking here are not very strenuous. However, the great natural beauty and prevalence of a rich range of plant and animal life make hiking and biking very rewarding experiences. Probably the best trails can be found at state parks in the region, such as **Edisto Island State Park, Hunting Island State Park,** and **Skidaway Island State Park.** Many national wildlife refuges (NWRs) in the area also feature excellent trails, such as **Pinckney Island NWR, Harris Neck NWR,** and **Cape Romain NWR.**

There are a couple of "rails to trails" projects that might appeal: the **James Island Trail** outside Charleston and the **McQueen Island Trail** on the way to Tybee Island outside Savannah. Some areas are almost defined by the plethora of bike and pedestrian trails running nearly their entire length and breadth, such as Jekyll Island and Hilton Head Island.

Bicycling on the beach is always a fun option.

Wide beaches, very conducive to biking on the sand, are one of the great pleasures of this area. Most bikes you rent in the area will have fat enough tires to do the job correctly. The best beach rides are on **Sullivan's Island, Hilton Head Island, Jekyll Island, St. Simons Island, Cumberland Island,** and **Tybee Island.**



# Travel Tips

## TRAVELING WITH CHILDREN

The Lowcountry and Georgia coast are very kid-friendly, with the possible exception of some B&Bs that are clearly not designed for younger children. If you have any doubts about this, feel free to inquire. Otherwise, there are no special precautions unique to this area. There are no zoos per se in the region, but animal lovers of all ages will enjoy **Charles Towne Landing** in Charleston and **Oatland Island Wildlife Center** in Savannah. Better still, take the kids on nature outings to the amazing national wildlife refuges in the area.

## ACCESS FOR TRAVELERS WITH DISABILITIES

While the vast majority of attractions and accommodations make every effort to comply with federal law regarding those with disabilities, as they're obliged to do, the very historic nature of this region means that some structures simply cannot be retrofitted for maximum accessibility. This is something you'll need to find out on a case-by-case basis, so call ahead. The sites administered by the National Park Service in this guide (Charles Pinckney National Historic Site, Fort Sumter, Fort Moultrie, Fort Pulaski, Fort Frederica, and Cumberland Island National Seashore) are as wheelchair-accessible as possible.

Some special shuttles are available. In Charleston, call the **"Tel-A-Ride"** service (843/724-7420). A couple of cab companies in town to check out are **Express Cab Company** (843/577-8816) and **Flag A Cab** (842/554-1231). In Savannah, Chatham Area Transit (www.catchacat.org) runs a **Teleride** service (912/354-6900). For the visually impaired, in Charleston there's the **Association for the Blind** (1071 Morrison Dr., 843/723-6915, www.afb.org) and in Savannah the **Savannah Association for the Blind** (214 Drayton St., 912/236-4473). Hearing-disadvantaged individuals can get assistance in Charleston at the **Charleston Speech and Hearing Center** (843/552-1212).

## ALTERNATIVE LODGING

The sharing economy is in full swing in both Charleston and Savannah, with Airbnb and various Vacation Rental by Owner facilities available online. Both cities are currently embroiled in an ongoing effort to determine, whether politically or through the courts, how much if any regulation they can assert over Airbnb operations.

As of this writing, Airbnbs are widely available in the Savannah Historic District and most areas north of Victory Drive. This area includes most tourist-frequented areas covered in this book. In other parts of town, however, it is currently illegal by city ordinance.

Charleston is also in the midst of a regulatory battle over Airbnb properties. Currently they are legal in an area of the Historic District roughly bound by Meeting Street on the east, Mary Street on the south, Spring and Line Streets to the north, and President Street to the west, though as of this writing there was a move by the city to loosen restrictions.

In Beaufort, South Carolina, short term vacation rentals are legal and prevalent with the exception of "The Point" neighborhood between Carteret Street and the Beaufort River.

## RIDE SHARING

Uber and Lyft are widely available in both Charleston and Savannah and will serve you well in either location at just about any time of day or night. The other areas covered in this book have significantly less population density, so don't depend on these services there.

## LGBTQ TRAVELERS

The metropolitan areas of Charleston, Beaufort, and Savannah are tolerant, and LGBTQ travelers shouldn't expect anything untoward to happen. Outside the metro areas, locals are perhaps a bit less welcoming, although overt hostility is rare. The best approach is to simply observe dominant Southern mores for anyone, gay or straight. In a nutshell, that means keep public displays of affection and politics to a minimum. Southerners in general have a low opinion of anyone who flagrantly espouses a viewpoint too obviously or loudly.

## SENIOR TRAVELERS

Both because of the large proportion of retirees in the region and because of Southerners' traditional respect for the elderly, the area is quite friendly to senior citizens. Many accommodations and attractions offer a slight senior discount, which can add up over the course of a trip. Always inquire about such discounts before making a reservation, however, as checkout time is too late to do so.

## TRAVELING WITH PETS

While the United States is very pet friendly, that friendliness rarely extends to restaurants and other indoor locations. More and more accommodations are allowing pet owners to bring pets, often for an added fee, but inquire before you arrive. In any case, keep your dog on a leash at all times. Some beaches in the area permit dog walking at certain times of the year, but as a general rule, keep dogs off of beaches unless you see signage saying otherwise.

# Health and Safety

## CRIME

While crime rates are indeed above national averages in many of the areas covered in this guide, especially in inner-city areas, incidents of crime in the more heavily trafficked tourist areas are no more common than anywhere else. In fact, these areas might be safer because of the amount of foot traffic and police attention.

By far the most common crime against visitors here is simple theft, primarily from cars. (Pickpocketing, thankfully, is rare in the United States.) Always lock your car doors. Conversely, only leave them unlocked if you're absolutely comfortable living without whatever's inside at the time. As a general rule, I try to lock valuables—such as CDs, a recent purchase, or my wife's purse—in the trunk. (Just make sure the "valet" button, allowing the trunk to be opened from the driver's area, is disabled.)

Should someone corner you and demand your wallet or purse, just give it to them. Unfortunately, the old advice to scream as loud as you can is no longer the deterrent it once was, and in fact may hasten aggressive action by the robber. If you are the victim of a crime, *always call the police.* Law enforcement wants more information, not less, and at very least you'll have an incident report in case you need to make an insurance claim for lost or stolen property.

Remember that in the United States, as elsewhere, no good can come from a heated argument with a police officer. The place to prove a police officer wrong is in a court of law, perhaps with an attorney by your side, not at the scene.

For emergencies, always call 911.

## AUTO ACCIDENTS

If you're in an auto accident where there's injury or damage to one or both cars, you must at minimum exchange insurance information with the other driver. It's always prudent to wait for police. Unless there is personal injury involved, you should move your car just enough to clear the way for other traffic if able to do so.

Since it's illegal to drive in these states without auto insurance, I'll assume you have some. And because you're insured, the best course of action in a minor accident, where injuries are unlikely, is to patiently wait for the police and give them your side of the story. In my experience, police react negatively to people who are too quick to start making accusations against other people. After that, let the insurance companies deal with it; that's what they're there for. If you suspect any injuries, call 911 immediately.

## ILLEGAL DRUGS

Marijuana, heroin, methamphetamine, and cocaine and all its derivatives are illegal in the United States with only a very few exceptions, none of which apply to the areas covered by this guide. The use of ecstasy and similar mood-elevators is also illegal. The penalties for illegal drug possession and use in South Carolina and Georgia are quite severe.

## ALCOHOL

The drinking age in the United States is 21. Most restaurants that serve alcoholic beverages allow those under 21 inside. Generally speaking, if only those over 21 are allowed inside, you will be greeted at the door by someone asking to see identification. These people are often poorly trained and anything other than a state driver's license may confuse them, so be forewarned.

Drunk driving is a problem on the highways of the United States, and South Carolina and Georgia are no exceptions. Always drive defensively, especially late at night, and obey all posted speed limits and road signs—and never assume the other driver will do the same. You may never drive with an open alcoholic beverage in the car, even if it belongs to a passenger.

As far as retail purchase goes, in South Carolina you may only buy beer and wine, not hard liquor, on Sunday. In most parts of Georgia, no alcoholic beverages are sold at the retail level on Sunday, other than in restaurants that also sell food.

## MEDICAL SERVICES

Unlike most developed nations, the United States has no comprehensive national health care system. Visitors from other countries who need nonemergency medical attention are best served by going to freestanding medical clinics. The level of care is typically very good, but unfortunately you'll be paying out of pocket for the service. For emergencies, however, do not hesitate to go to the closest hospital emergency room, where the level of care is generally also quite good, especially for trauma. Worry about payment later; emergency rooms in the United States are required to take true emergency cases whether or not the patient can pay for services. Call 911 for ambulance service.

### Pharmaceuticals

Unlike many other nations, antibiotics are available in the United States only on a prescription basis and are not available over the counter. Most cold, flu, and allergy remedies are available over the counter, though some require you to provide ID in order to purchase to thwart purchases for illegal drug manufacture. While homeopathic remedies are gaining popularity in the United States, they are nowhere near as prevalent as in Europe.

Drugs with the active ingredient ephedrine are available in the United States without a prescription, but their purchase is tightly regulated to cut down on the use of these products to make the illegal drug methamphetamine.

# STAYING HEALTHY

## Vaccinations

As of this writing, there are no vaccination requirements to enter the United States. Contact your embassy before coming to confirm this before arrival, however. In the autumn, at the beginning of flu season, preventive influenza vaccinations, simply called "flu shots," often become available at easily accessible locations like clinics, health departments, and even supermarkets.

## Humidity, Heat, and Sun

There is only one way to fight the South's high heat and humidity, and that's to drink lots of fluids. A surprising number of people each year refuse to take this advice and find themselves in various states of dehydration, some of which can land you in a hospital. Remember: If you're thirsty, you're already suffering from dehydration. The thing to do is keep drinking fluids *before* you're thirsty as a preventative action rather than a reaction.

Always use sunscreen, even on a cloudy day. If you do get a sunburn, get a pain-relief product with aloe vera as an active ingredient. On extraordinarily sunny and hot summer days, don't even go outside between the hours of 10am and 2pm.

# HAZARDS

## Insects

Because of the recent increase in the mosquito-borne West Nile virus, the most important step to take in staying healthy in the Lowcountry and Georgia coast—especially if you have small children—is to keep **mosquito bites** to a minimum. Do this with a combination of mosquito repellent and long sleeves and long pants, if possible. Not every mosquito bite will give you the virus; in fact, chances are quite slim that one will. But don't take the chance if you don't have to.

The second major step in avoiding insect nastiness is to steer clear of **fire ants,** whose large gray or brown dirt nests are quite common in this area. They attack instantly and in great numbers, with little or no provocation. They don't just bite; they inject you with poison from their stingers. In short, fire ants are not to be trifled with. While the only real remedy is the preventative one of never coming in contact with them, should you find yourself being bitten by fire ants, the first thing to do is to stay calm. Take off your shoes and socks and get as many of the ants off you as you can. Unless you've had a truly large number of bites—in which case you should seek medical help immediately—the best thing to do next is wash the area to get any venom off, and then disinfect with alcohol if you have any handy. Then a topical treatment such as calamine lotion or hydrocortisone is advised. A fire ant bite will leave a red pustule that lasts about a week. Try your best not to scratch it so that it won't get infected.

Outdoor activity, especially in woodsy, undeveloped areas, may bring you in contact with another unpleasant indigenous creature, the tiny but obnoxious **chigger,** sometimes called the redbug. The bite of a chigger can't be felt, but the enzymes it leaves behind can lead to a very itchy little red spot. Contrary to folklore, putting fingernail polish on the itchy bite will not "suffocate" the chigger, because by this point the chigger itself is long gone. All you can do is get some topical itch or pain relief and go on with your life. The itching will eventually subside.

## Threats in the Water

While enjoying area beaches, a lot of visitors become inordinately worried about **shark attacks.** Every couple of summers there's a lot of hysteria about this, but the truth is that you're much more likely to slip and fall in a bathroom than you are to even come close to being bitten by a shark in these shallow Atlantic waters.

A far more common fate for area swimmers is to get stung by a **jellyfish,** or sea nettle. They can sting you in the water, but most often beachcombers are stung by stepping on beached jellyfish stranded on the sand by the tide. If you get stung, don't panic; wash the area with saltwater, not freshwater, and apply

lightning near Tybee Island Light Station

vinegar or baking soda. A product called Jellyfish Squish is also available and seems to work well.

### Lightning

The southeastern United States is home to vicious fast-moving thunderstorms, often with an amazing amount of electrical activity. Death by lightning strike occurs often in this region and is something that should be taken quite seriously. The general rule of thumb is that if you're in the water, whether at the beach or in a swimming pool, and hear thunder, get out of the water immediately until the storm passes. If you're on dry land and see lightning flash a distance away, that's your cue to seek safety indoors. Whatever you do, do not play sports outside when lightning threatens.

# Information and Services

## VISITOR INFORMATION

### Charleston

The main visitors center is the **Charleston Visitor Reception and Transportation Center** (375 Meeting St., 800/774-0006, www.charlestoncvb.com, Mon.-Fri. 8:30am-5pm). Outlying visitors centers are the **Mt. Pleasant-Isle of Palms Visitor Center** (99 Harry M. Hallman Jr Blvd., 800/774-0006, daily 9am-5pm) and the **North Charleston Visitor Center** (4975-B Centre Pointe Dr., 843/853-8000, Mon.-Sat. 10am-5pm).

### Beaufort and the Lowcountry

The Beaufort **Visitors Information Center** is within the Beaufort Arsenal building (713 Craven St., 843/986-5400, www.beaufortsc.org, daily 9am-5:30pm). In Hilton Head, get information, book a room, or secure a tee time just as you come onto the island at the **Hilton Head Island Chamber of Commerce Welcome Center** (100 William Hilton Pkwy., 843/785-3673, www.hiltonheadisland.org, daily 9am-6pm), in the same building as the Coastal Discovery Museum. You'll find Bluffton's visitors center in the **Heyward House Historic Center** (70 Boundary St., 843/757-6293, www.heywardhouse.org, Mon.-Fri. 10am-3pm, Sat. 11am-2pm).

### Savannah

The main place for visitor information in Savannah is the downtown **Savannah Visitors Center** (301 MLK Jr. Blvd., 912/944-0455, Mon.-Fri. 8:30am-5pm, Sat.-Sun. and holidays 9am-5pm). The **Savannah Convention and Visitors Bureau** (101 E. Bay St., 877/728-2662, www.savcvb.com, Mon.-Fri. 8:30am-5pm) keeps an up-to-date list of lodgings at its website. Other visitors centers in the area include the **River Street Hospitality Center** (1 River St., 912/651-6662, daily 10am-10pm), the **Tybee Island Visitor Center** (S. Campbell Ave. and U.S. 80, 912/786-5444, daily 9am-5:30pm) and the **Savannah Airport Visitor Center** (464 Airways Ave., 912/964-1109, daily 10am-6pm).

### The Golden Isles

The **Brunswick-Golden Isles Visitor Center** (2000 Glynn Ave., 912/264-5337, daily 9am-5pm) is at the intersection of U.S. 17 and the Torras Causeway to St. Simons Island. A downtown information station is in **Old City Hall**, at the corner of Mansfield and Newcastle Streets (912/262-6934, daily 8am-5pm).

The **Jekyll Island Visitor Center** (901 Downing Musgrove Causeway, 912/635-3636, daily 9am-5pm) is before you get to the island, on the long causeway along the marsh. The **St. Simons Visitor Center** (530-B Beachview Dr., 912/638-9014, www.bgivb.com, daily 9am-5pm) is in the St. Simons Casino building near Neptune Park and the Village.

The **Darien Welcome Center** is at the corner of U.S. 17 and Fort King George Drive (912/437-6684, Mon.-Sat. 9am-5pm). The **Sapelo Island Visitors Center** (912/437-3224, www.sapelonerr.org, Tues.-Fri. 7:30am-5:30pm, Sat. 8am-5:30pm, Sun. 1:30pm-5pm) is actually not on Sapelo but at the dock where you take the ferry, in Meridian, Georgia, on Highway 99 from Darien.

The **St. Marys Visitor Center** is located at 406 Osborne Street (912/882-4000, www.stmaryswelcome.com, Mon.-Sat. 9am-5pm, Sun. noon-5pm). The **Cumberland Island Visitors Center** is at 113 St. Marys Street (912/882-4336, daily 8am-6pm).

There are several entrances to the Okefenokee Swamp, with the closest thing to a visitors center being the U.S. Fish and Wildlife Service's **Richard S. Bolt Visitor Center** (912/496-7836, daily 9am-5pm) at the eastern entrance near Folkston, Georgia.

## MONEY

Automated teller machines (ATMs) are available in all urban areas covered in this guide. Be aware that if the ATM is not owned by your bank, not only will that ATM likely charge you a service fee, but your bank may charge you one as well. While ATMs have made traveler's checks less essential, traveler's checks do have the important advantage of accessibility, as some rural and less-developed areas covered in this guide have few or no ATMs. You can purchase traveler's checks at just about any bank.

Establishments in the United States only accept the national currency, the U.S. dollar. To exchange foreign money, go to any bank.

Generally, establishments that accept credit cards will feature stickers on the front entrance with the logo of the particular cards they accept, although this is not a legal requirement. The use of debit cards has dramatically increased in the United States. Most retail establishments and many fast-food chains are now accepting them. Make sure you get a receipt whenever you use a credit card or a debit card.

## MEDIA AND COMMUNICATIONS

### Newspapers

The closest thing to a national newspaper in the United States is *USA Today,* which you will find at diverse locations from airports to gas stations. The national paper of record is the *New York Times,* which is available in larger urban areas but only rarely in outlying areas.

In Charleston, the paper of record is the *Post and Courier* (www.charleston.net). Its entertainment insert, "Preview," comes out on Thursday. The free alternative weekly is the *Charleston City Paper* (www.charlestoncitypaper.com), which comes out on Wednesday and is the best place to find local music and arts listings. A particularly well-done and lively metro glossy is *Charleston* magazine (www.charlestonmag.com), which comes out once a month.

In Beaufort, the daily newspaper of record is the *Beaufort Gazette* (www.beaufortgazette.com). An alternative weekly focusing mostly on the arts is *Lowcountry Home* (www.lcweekly.com). Hilton Head's paper of record is the *Island Packet* (www.islandpacket.com). A good Bluffton publication is *Bluffton Today* (www.blufftontoday.com).

In Savannah, the daily newspaper of record is the *Savannah Morning News* (www.savannahnow.com). It puts out an entertainment insert on Thursday called "Do." The independent free weekly newspaper in town is *Connect Savannah* (www.connectsavannah.com), hitting stands each Wednesday.

The main paper in the much more sparsely populated Golden Isles region is the *Brunswick News* (www.thebrunswicknews.com), but many people read the newspaper of record of nearby Jacksonville, Florida, the *Florida Times-Union* (www.jacksonville.com).

## Internet Access

Visitors from Europe and Asia are likely to be disappointed at the quality of Internet access in the United States, particularly the area covered in this guide. Fiber-optic lines are still a rarity, and while many hotels and B&Bs now offer in-room Internet access—some charge, some don't, so make sure to ask ahead—the quality and speed of the connection might prove poor. Wireless (Wi-Fi) networks are also less than impressive, but that situation continues to improve on a daily basis in coffeehouses, hotels, and airports. Unfortunately, many hotspots in private establishments charge fees. Charleston does have a municipal free Wi-Fi network, however.

## Phones

Generally speaking, the United States is behind Europe and much of Asia in terms of cell phone technology. Unlike Europe, where "pay as you go" refills are easy to find, most American cell phone users pay for monthly plans through a handful of providers. Still, you should have no problem with cell phone coverage in urban areas. Where it gets much less dependable is in rural areas and on beaches. Bottom line: Don't depend on having cell service everywhere you go.

As with a regular landline, any time you face an emergency, call 911 on your cell phone.

All phone numbers in the United States are seven digits preceded by a three-digit area code. You may have to dial "1" before a phone number if it's a long-distance call, even within the same area code. The area code for the part of South Carolina covered in this guide is 843. The area code for the part of Georgia covered in this guide is 912.

# Resources

## Suggested Reading

### NONFICTION

#### Georgia

Calonius, Erik. *The Wanderer: The Last American Slave Ship and the Conspiracy That Set Its Sails.* New York: St. Martin's Press, 2006. A page-turning tale of the last illegal slave shipment to land in the United States, on Jekyll Island, Georgia.

Fraser, Walter J. Jr. *Savannah in the Old South.* Athens, GA: University of Georgia Press, 2005. An insightful and balanced history of Georgia's first city, from founding through Reconstruction.

Georgia Writers Project. *Drums and Shadows: Survival Studies among the Georgia Coastal Negroes.* Athens, GA: University of Georgia Press, 1986. Arising from a government-funded research project during the Depression, this still ranks as one of the best oral histories ever assembled, using firsthand accounts from African American residents of Georgia's Sea Islands to paint a picture of a lifestyle gone by.

Greene, Melissa Fay. *Praying for Sheetrock.* New York: Ballantine, 1992. In this modern classic, Greene explores the racism and corruption endemic in McIntosh County, Georgia, during the era of the civil rights movement.

Kemble, Fanny. *Journal of a Residence on a Georgian Plantation in 1838-1839.* Athens, GA: University of Georgia Press, 1984. A famed English actress's groundbreaking antislavery account of her stay on a rice plantation in McIntosh County, Georgia.

Morgan, Philip, ed. *African American Life in the Georgia Lowcountry: The Atlantic World and the Gullah Geechee.* Athens, GA: University of Georgia Press, 2010. The best book I've come by on the history and folkways of Georgia's Gullah or Geechee people. Balanced, scholarly, yet still readable in the extreme.

Seabrook, Charles. *Cumberland Island: Strong Women, Wild Horses.* Winston-Salem, NC: John F. Blair, 2002. An even-handed, journalistic look inside the tension between environmentalists and the residents of Cumberland Island.

Williams, Robin B. *Buildings of Savannah.* Charlottesville, VA: University of Virginia Press, 2016. The best and most practical single source for personally exploring the wide variety of architectural styles in Savannah, from colonial times through the Victorian streetcar era to Modernist examples.

Wood, Betty, ed. *Mary Telfair to Mary Few: Selected Letters, 1802-1844.* Athens, GA: University of Georgia Press, 2007. The revealing, chatty letters of a great arts patron and member of a major Savannah slave-owning family, to her best friend who left the city and moved north because of her abolitionist leanings. We know that Mary Few replied, but her letters remain undiscovered.

## South Carolina

Fraser, Walter J. Jr. *Charleston! Charleston! The History of a Southern City.* Columbia, SC: University of South Carolina Press, 1991. Another typically well-written and balanced tome by this important regional historian.

Gessler, Diana Hollingsworth. *Very Charleston: A Celebration of History, Culture, and Lowcountry Charm.* Chapel Hill, NC: Algonquin Books, 2003. A quick, visually appealing insider's perspective with some wonderfully whimsical cartoon-style illustrations.

Klein, Maury. *Days of Defiance: Sumter, Secession, and the Coming of the Civil War.* New York: Vintage, 1999. A gripping and vivid account of the lead-up to war, with Charleston as the focal point.

Rogers, George C. Jr. *Charleston in the Age of the Pinckneys.* Columbia, SC: University of South Carolina Press, 1980. This 1969 history is a classic of the genre.

Rosen, Robert. *A Short History of Charleston.* Columbia, SC: University of South Carolina Press, 1997. Quite simply the most concise, readable, and entertaining history of the Holy City I've found.

Woodward, C. Vann, ed. *Mary Chesnut's Civil War.* New Haven, CT: Yale University Press, 1981. The Pulitzer Prize-winning classic compilation of the sardonic and quietly heartbreaking letters of Charleston's Mary Chesnut during the Civil War.

## General Background

Aberjhani and Sandra West. *Encyclopedia of the Harlem Renaissance.* New York: Checkmark Books, 2003. A brilliantly researched account of the great African American diaspora out of the South that eventually gave birth to the Charleston dance craze of the 1920s.

Lewis, Lloyd. *Sherman: Fighting Prophet.* Lincoln, NE: University of Nebraska Press, 1993. Though first published in 1932, this remains the most thorough, insightful, and well-written biography of General William Sherman in existence.

Robinson, Sally Ann. *Gullah Home Cooking the Daufuskie Island Way.* Chapel Hill, NC: University of North Carolina Press, 2007. Subtitled "Smokin' Joe Butter Beans, Ol' 'Fuskie Fried Crab Rice, Sticky-Bush Blackberry Dumpling, and Other Sea Island Favorites," this cookbook by a native Daufuskie Islander features a foreword by Pat Conroy.

Stehling, Robert. *Hominy Grill Recipes.* Charleston, SC: Big Cartel, 2009. This humble, hand-illustrated, self-published little tome features 23 great recipes from one of Charleston's most respected Southern cooking joints, Hominy Grill on Rutledge Avenue. At only $12.95, one of the best cookbooks for the money you'll find.

# FICTION

Berendt, John. *Midnight in the Garden of Good and Evil.* New York: Vintage, 1999. Well, not exactly fiction, but far from completely true, nonetheless this modern classic definitely reads like a novel while remaining one of the unique and readable travelogues of recent times.

Caskey, James. *Haunted Savannah: The Official Guidebook to Savannah Haunted History Tour.* Savannah: Bonaventture Books, 2012. The author may quibble with this being in the "fiction" section, but this is an entertaining and also quite educating look at Savannah's various paranormal tales.

Conroy, Pat. *The Lords of Discipline.* New York: Bantam, 1985. For all practical purposes set at the Citadel, this novel takes you behind the scenes of the notoriously insular Charleston military college.

Conroy, Pat. *The Water Is Wide*. New York: Bantam, 1987. Immortal account of Conroy's time teaching African American children in a one-room schoolhouse on "Yamacraw" (actually Daufuskie) Island.

Hervey, Harry. *The Damned Don't Cry*. Marietta, GA: Cherokee Publishing, 2003. The original *Midnight*, this bawdy 1939 potboiler takes you into the streets, shanties, drawing rooms, and boudoirs of real Savannahians during the Depression.

O'Connor, Flannery. *Flannery O'Connor: Collected Works*. New York: Library of America, 1988. For a look into Savannah's conflicted, paradoxical soul, read anything by this native-born writer, so grounded in tradition yet so ahead of her time even to this day. This volume includes selected letters, an especially valuable (and entertaining) insight.

# Internet Resources

## RECREATION

**South Carolina Department of Natural Resources**
**www.dnr.sc.gov**
More than just a compendium of license and fee information—though there's certainly plenty of that—this site features a lot of practical advice on how best to enjoy South Carolina's great outdoors, whether you're an angler, a kayaker, a bird-watcher, a hiker, or a biker.

**Georgia Department of Natural Resources**
**www.gadnr.org**
Ditto for this site, which has lots of great information on the wildlife and geology of Georgia's beautiful and largely undeveloped barrier islands.

**Savannah Bicycle Campaign**
**www.bicyclecampaign.org**
The clearinghouse for routes and rides by Savannah's most dedicated cyclists.

**Georgia State Parks**
**www.gastateparks.org**
Vital historical and visitor information for Georgia's underrated network of historical state park sites along the coast, including camping reservations.

**South Carolina State Parks**
**www.southcarolinaparks.com**
Ditto for this site all about South Carolina's state parks.

## NATURE AND ENVIRONMENT

**Ocean Science**
**http://www.skio.uga.edu/category/blog**
A blog by the staff of Savannah's Skidaway Institute of Oceanography, focusing on barrier island ecology and the maritime environment.

## CUISINE AND ENTERTAINMENT

**A Common Connoisseur**
**www.acommonconnoisseur.com**
An insider's look at the Savannah restaurant scene, with an emphasis on new spots.

**Charleston City Paper Foodie blogs**
**www.charlestoncitypaper.com/blogs/eat**
The collected staff blogs of the Charleston City Paper, dealing with the latest foodie news in town and entertainment options.

**Holy Sinner**
**www.holycitysinner.com**
A popular Web-only magazine focusing on Charleston lifestyle, eats, and the bar scene.

## HISTORY AND BACKGROUND

**South Carolina Information Highway**
**www.sciway.net**
An eclectic cornucopia of interesting South Carolina history and assorted background facts, which makes for an interesting Internet portal into all things Palmetto State.

**New Georgia Encyclopedia**
**www.georgiaencyclopedia.org**
A mother lode of concise, neutral, and well-written information on the natural and human history of Georgia from prehistory to the present.

## TOURISM INFORMATION

**Charleston Convention and Visitors Bureau**
**www.charlestoncvb.com**
This very professional and user-friendly tourism site is perhaps the best and most practical Internet portal for visitors to Charleston.

**Visit Savannah**
**www.visitsavannah.com**
Savannah's Convention & Visitors Bureau is particularly adept at social media.

# Index

## H



## I



## J

## KL



## M



## N



## O

## T

## U



## VWXYZ

# List of Maps

# Photo Credits

Title page photo: © Jim Morekis

page 4 © Sean Pavone | Dreamstime.com; page 5 © Jim Morekis; page 6 (top left) © Jim Morekis, (top right) © Jim Morekis, (bottom) © Jim Morekis; page 7 (top) © Jim Morekis, (bottom left) © Jim Morekis, (bottom right) © Jim Morekis; page 8 © Jim Morekis; page 9 (top) © Jim Morekis, (bottom left) © John Wollwerth | Dreamstime.com, (bottom right) © Jim Morekis; page 10 © Maomatou| Dreasmstime.com; page 12 (top) © Alexander Mychko | Dreamstime.com, (bottom) © Jim Morekis; page 14 © Paul Morgan | Dreamstime.com; page 15 (top) © Visions of America LLC | Dreamstime.com, (bottom) © Howard Nevitt, Jr. | Dreamstime.com; page 16 (top) © F11photo | Dreamstime.com, (bottom) © Scott Hippemsteel | Dreamstime.com; page 17 © Jim Morekis; page 18 © William Manning | Dreamstime.com; page 20 © Jim Morekis; page 21 © Rolf52 | Dreamstime.com; page 22 © Ekaterina Hashbarger | Dreamstime.com; page 33 (top) © Sean Pavone | Dreamstime.com, (bottom) © Sean Pavone | Dreamstime.com; page 50 © Jim Morekis; page 55 © Jim Morekis; page 57 © Jim Morekis; page 58 © Jim Morekis; page 60 © Mfschramm | Dreamstime.com; page 63 © Jim Morekis; page 64 © Jim Morekis; page 65 © Jim Morekis; page 67 © Jim Morekis; page 69 © Jim Morekis; page 76 © Jim Morekis; page 81 © Jim Morekis; page 88 © Jim Morekis; page 89 © Jim Morekis; page 92 © Jim Morekis; page 102 © Jim Morekis; page 105 © Jim Morekis; page 107 © Jim Morekis; page 113 © Jim Morekis; page 114 © Jim Morekis; page 119 (top) © Jim Morekis, (bottom) © Jim Morekis; page 121 © © Cvandyke | Dreamstime.com; page 125 © Jim Morekis; page 132 © Jim Morekis; page 133 © Jim Morekis; page 135 © Jim Morekis; page 136 © Jim Morekis; page 137 © John Wollwerth | Dreamstime.com; page 139 © Jim Morekis; page 145 © Jim Morekis; page 147 © Jim Morekis; page 150 © Jim Morekis; page 155 © Jim Morekis; page 157 © Jim Morekis; page 161 © Jim Morekis; page 164 (top) © Irkin09 | Dreamstime.com, (bottom) © F11photo| Dreamstime.com; page 165 © Jim Morekis; page 181 © Fotoluminate | Dreamstime.com; page 183 © Jim Morekis; page 186 © Jim Morekis; page 192 © Jim Morekis; page 194 © Jim Morekis; page 197 © Jim Morekis; page 200 © Jim Morekis; page 204 © Jim Morekis; page 210 © Jim Morekis; page 212 © Jim Morekis; page 213 © Jim Morekis; page 219 © Jim Morekis; page 226 © Jim Morekis; page 228 © Jim Morekis; page 229 © Jim Morekis; page 230 © Jim Morekis; page 240 © Jim Morekis; page 244 © Jim Morekis; page 247 © Jim Morekis; page 250 © Jim Morekis; page 281 © Jim Morekis; page 256 (top) © Jim Morekis, (bottom) © Justin Rumao | Dreamstime.com; page 257 © Jim Morekis; page 261 © Jim Morekis; page 268 © Jim Morekis; page 269 © Jim Morekis; page 271 © Jim Morekis; page 274 © Jim Morekis; page 276 © Jim Morekis; page 279 © Jim Morekis; page 285 © Jim Morekis; page 286 © Jim Morekis; page 291 © Jim Morekis; page 294 (top) © Brian Lasenby | Dreamstime.com, (bottom) © Jim Morekis; page 301 © Serge Skiba | Dreamstime.com; page 303 © Gonepaddling | Dreamstime.com; page 319 © Jim Morekis; page 325 © Jim Morekis; page 329 © Jim Morekis; page 332 © Sean Pavone | Dreamstime.com; page 336 © Jim Morekis; page 341 © Alex Grichenko | Dreamstime.com

# MAP SYMBOLS

| | | | |
|---|---|---|---|
| Expressway | City/Town | Airport | Golf Course |
| Primary Road | State Capital | Airfield | Parking Area |
| Secondary Road | National Capital | Mountain | Archaeological Site |
| Unpaved Road | Point of Interest | Unique Natural Feature | Church |
| Feature Trail | Accommodation | Waterfall | Gas Station |
| Other Trail | Restaurant/Bar | Park | Glacier |
| Ferry | Other Location | Trailhead | Mangrove |
| Pedestrian Walkway | Campground | Skiing Area | Reef |
| Stairs | | | Swamp |

# CONVERSION TABLES

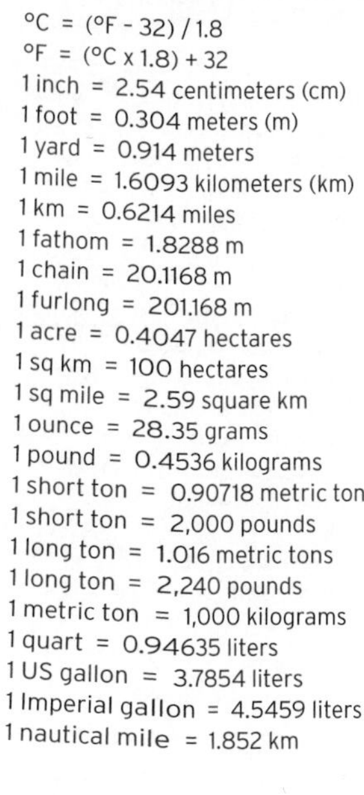

°C = (°F - 32) / 1.8
°F = (°C x 1.8) + 32
1 inch = 2.54 centimeters (cm)
1 foot = 0.304 meters (m)
1 yard = 0.914 meters
1 mile = 1.6093 kilometers (km)
1 km = 0.6214 miles
1 fathom = 1.8288 m
1 chain = 20.1168 m
1 furlong = 201.168 m
1 acre = 0.4047 hectares
1 sq km = 100 hectares
1 sq mile = 2.59 square km
1 ounce = 28.35 grams
1 pound = 0.4536 kilograms
1 short ton = 0.90718 metric ton
1 short ton = 2,000 pounds
1 long ton = 1.016 metric tons
1 long ton = 2,240 pounds
1 metric ton = 1,000 kilograms
1 quart = 0.94635 liters
1 US gallon = 3.7854 liters
1 Imperial gallon = 4.5459 liters
1 nautical mile = 1.852 km

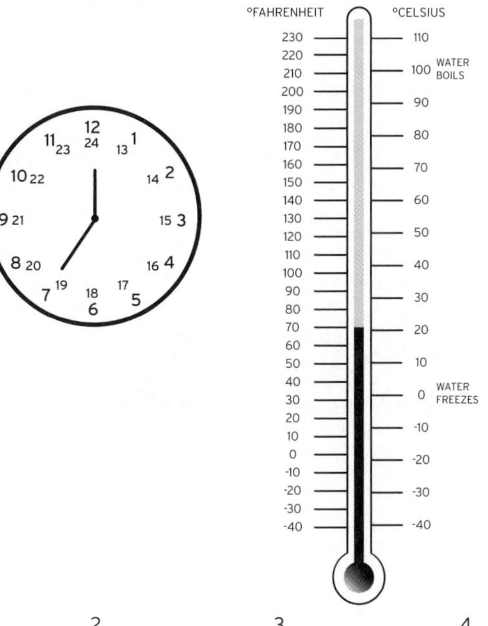


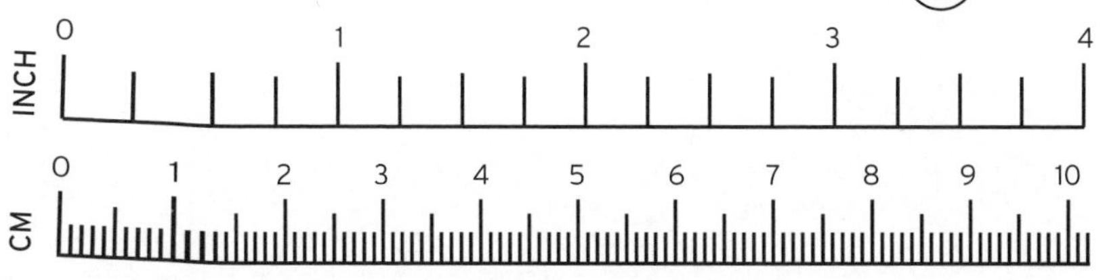

**MOON CHARLESTON & SAVANNAH**
Avalon Travel
Hachette Book Group
1700 Fourth Street
Berkeley, CA 94710, USA
www.moon.com

Editor: Rachel Feldman
Series Manager: Kathryn Ettinger
Copy Editor: Christopher Church
Production and Graphics Coordinator: Suzanne Albertson
Cover Design: Faceout Studios, Charles Brock
Interior Design: Domini Dragoone
Moon Logo: Tim McGrath
Map Editor: Kat Bennett
Cartographer: Stephanie Poulain
Indexer: Greg Jewett

ISBN-13: 978-1-64049-308-7

Printing History
1st Edition — 2002
8th Edition — October 2018
5 4 3 2 1



Front cover photo: cherub fountain with lilacs in the background in Charleston © Phyllis Peterson | Alamy Stock Photo

Back cover photo: bars and restaurants on River Street in Savannah © Sean Pavone | Dreamstime.com

Printed in China by RR Donnelley